IET PROFESSIONAL APPLICATIONS OF COMPUTING SERIES 35

Big Data Recommender Systems

IET Book Series on Big Data – Call for Authors

Editor-in-Chief: Professor Albert Y. Zomaya, University of Sydney, Australia

The topic of Big Data has emerged as a revolutionary theme that cuts across many technologies and application domains. This new book series brings together topics within the myriad research activities in many areas that analyse, compute, store, manage and transport massive amount of data, such as algorithm design, data mining and search, processor architectures, databases, infrastructure development, service and data discovery, networking and mobile computing, cloud computing, high-performance computing, privacy and security, storage and visualization.

Topics considered include (but not restricted to) IoT and Internet computing; cloud computing; peer-to-peer computing; autonomic computing; data centre computing; multi-core and many core computing; parallel, distributed and high-performance computing; scalable databases; mobile computing and sensor networking; green computing; service computing; networking infrastructures; cyberinfrastructures; e-Science; smart cities; analytics and data mining; Big Data applications and more.

Proposals for coherently integrated International co-edited or co-authored handbooks and research monographs will be considered for this book series. Each proposal will be reviewed by the editor-in-chief and some board members, with additional external reviews from independent reviewers. Please email your book proposal for the IET Book Series on Big Data to: Professor Albert Y. Zomaya at albert.zomaya@sydney.edu.au or to the IET at author_support@theiet.org.

Other volumes in this series:

Volume 1 **Knowledge Discovery and Data Mining** M.A. Bramer (Editor)
Volume 3 **Troubled IT Projects: Prevention and turnaround** J.M. Smith
Volume 4 **UML for Systems Engineering: Watching the wheels, 2nd Edition** J. Holt
Volume 5 **Intelligent Distributed Video Surveillance Systems** S.A. Velastin and
         P. Remagnino (Editors)
Volume 6 **Trusted Computing** C. Mitchell (Editor)
Volume 7 **SysML for Systems Engineering** J. Holt and S. Perry
Volume 8 **Modelling Enterprise Architectures** J. Holt and S. Perry
Volume 9 **Model-based Requirements Engineering** J. Holt, S. Perry and M. Bownsword
Volume 13 **Trusted Platform Modules: Why, when and how to use them** Ariel Segall
Volume 14 **Foundations for Model-based Systems Engineering: From patterns to models**
          J. Holt, S. Perry and M. Bownsword
Volume 15 **Big Data and Software Defined Networks** J. Taheri (Editor)
Volume 18 **Modeling and Simulation of Complex Communication** M.A. Niazi (Editor)
Volume 20 **SysML for Systems Engineering: A model-based approach, 3rd Edition** J. Holt
          and S. Perry
Volume 23 **Data as Infrastructure for Smart Cities** L. Suzuki and A. Finkelstein
Volume 24 **Ultrascale Computing Systems** J. Carretero, E. Jeannot and A. Zomaya

Big Data Recommender Systems

Volume 2: Application Paradigms

Edited by
Osman Khalid, Samee U. Khan and Albert Y. Zomaya

The Institution of Engineering and Technology

Published by The Institution of Engineering and Technology, London, United Kingdom

The Institution of Engineering and Technology is registered as a Charity in England & Wales (no. 211014) and Scotland (no. SC038698).

© The Institution of Engineering and Technology 2019

First published 2019

The Institution of Engineering and Technology
Michael Faraday House
Six Hills Way, Stevenage
Herts, SG1 2AY, United Kingdom

www.theiet.org

British Library Cataloguing in Publication Data
A catalogue record for this product is available from the British Library

ISBN 978-1-78561-977-9 (hardback Volume 2)
ISBN: 978-1-78561-975-5 (hardback Volume 1)
ISBN 978-1-78561-976-2 (PDF Volume 1)
ISBN: 978-1-78561-979-3 (hardback 2 volume set)
ISBN 978-1-78561-978-6 (PDF Volume 2)

Typeset in India by MPS Limited
Printed in the UK by CPI Group (UK) Ltd, Croydon

Contents

Foreword   xix

1 Introduction to big data recommender systems—volume 2   1
Osman Khalid, Samee U. Khan, and Albert Y. Zomaya

   1.1 Background   1
   1.2 About the book   3
   Acknowledgments   6
   References   7

2 Deep neural networks meet recommender systems   9
Shuai Zhang, Lina Yao, Aixin Sun, Guibing Guo, Xiwei Xu,
and Liming Zhu

   2.1 Preliminary   10
      2.1.1 Introduction to recommender systems   10
      2.1.2 Introduction to deep neural networks 10
   2.2 Introducing nonlinearity to recommender systems   12
      2.2.1 Deep neural generalization of collaborative filtering 13
      2.2.2 Deep neural generalization of factorization machine 16
   2.3 Representation learning for recommender systems   17
      2.3.1 Representation learning with multilayer perceptron 17
      2.3.2 Representation learning with autoencoder 18
      2.3.3 Representation learning with convolutional
            neural network   18
      2.3.4 Representation learning with Word2Vec 20
   2.4 Sequence modelling for recommender systems   21
      2.4.1 Session-based recommendations   21
      2.4.2 Sequence-aware recommender systems   23
   2.5 Deep hybrid models for recommender systems   24
   2.6 Advanced topics   25
      2.6.1 Metric learning   25
      2.6.2 Generative adversarial networks   26
      2.6.3 Neural autoregressive distribution estimator 27
   2.7 Future challenges and conclusion   27
   References   28

3 Cold-start solutions for recommendation systems   **35**
Farshad Bakhshandegan Moghaddam and Mehdi Elahi

3.1 Introduction   35
     3.1.1 Recommendation approaches   36
3.2 Collaborative filtering   37
3.3 Active learning in recommender systems   38
3.4 Semantic-based recommender systems   40
3.5 Recommendation based on visual features   42
3.6 Personality-based recommender systems   43
3.7 Cross-domain recommender systems   45
3.8 Conclusion   46
References   47

4 Performance metrics for traditional and context-aware big data recommender systems   **57**
Rab Nawaz Jadoon, Wu Yang, and Osman Khalid

4.1 Introduction   58
4.2 CARS—a brief overview   59
4.3 Evaluation of RSs   59
     4.3.1 Evaluation metrics   60
4.4 Diversity and accuracy metrics used in CARS   66
     4.4.1 How recommendation accuracy is measured in CARS?   66
     4.4.2 Diversity measurement in CARS   66
4.5 How to choose an appropriate evaluation metrics?   67
4.6 Conclusion   68
Acknowledgments   68
References   68

5 Mining urban lifestyles: urban computing, human behavior and recommender systems   **71**
Sharon Xu, Riccardo Di Clemente, and Marta C. González

5.1 Mining shopping and mobility patterns   72
     5.1.1 Prediction of shopping behavior with data sparsity   72
     5.1.2 Adding contextual information to location data   72
     5.1.3 Multi-perspective lifestyles   73
5.2 Data   73
5.3 Discovering shopping patterns   74
5.4 Mobility pattern extraction   75
     5.4.1 Extracting cellular tower location types   75
     5.4.2 Baseline methods   77
     5.4.3 Characterizing mobility patterns   77
5.5 Predicting shopping behavior   77
     5.5.1 Collective matrix factorization   77

5.6	Results	78
	5.6.1 Prediction	78
	5.6.2 Dual lifestyles	78
5.7	Discussion	79
	Acknowledgments	79
	References	79

6 Embedding principal component analysis inference in expert sensors for big data applications **83**
Rodrigo Marino, Jose M. Lanza-Gutierrez, and Teresa Riesgo

6.1	Introduction	83
6.2	Related work	86
6.3	Principal component analysis: problem formulation	87
6.4	Workflow description	88
6.5	Embedded architecture	89
	6.5.1 System-level architecture	89
	6.5.2 PCA inference IP description	91
6.6	Experimental methodology	93
6.7	Experimental results	94
	6.7.1 8- vs. 16-bit architectures	95
	6.7.2 Hardware architecture vs. multicore approach	100
6.8	Conclusions	102
	Acknowledgments	102
	References	102

7 Decision support system to detect hidden pathologies of stroke: the CIPHER project **107**
José González Enríquez, Leticia Morales Trujillo,
Sara Moreno Leonardo, Francisco José Domínguez Mayo,
Julián Alberto García García, and Manuel Mejías Risoto

7.1	Introduction	107
7.2	Context: the CIPHER project	109
7.3	Decision support system	112
7.4	Validation	114
	7.4.1 Data processing	114
	7.4.2 Algorithm selection	118
	7.4.3 First results	119
7.5	Conclusions and future works	121
	Acknowledgments	122
	References	122

8 Big data analytics for smart grids **125**
Panagiotis D. Diamantoulakis and George K. Karagiannidis

8.1	Introduction	125

	8.2	Dynamic energy management	127
		8.2.1 Demand side management	128
		8.2.2 Data-driven DEM	128
	8.3	Failure protection	129
	8.4	Load and price forecasting	129
		8.4.1 Load classification	130
		8.4.2 Short-term load forecasting	130
		8.4.3 Renewable generation forecasting	131
		8.4.4 Price forecasting	131
		8.4.5 Predictive control for electric vehicles power demand	131
	8.5	Efficient processing of extreme size of data	132
		8.5.1 Avoidance of redundancies	132
		8.5.2 Dimensionality reduction	133
		8.5.3 Data summarization	133
		8.5.4 MapReduce parallel processing	134
		8.5.5 Distributed data mining	134
		8.5.6 Efficient computing	134
		8.5.7 Testbeds and platforms	135
	8.6	Security and privacy issues in the smart grid	135
		8.6.1 Privacy	135
		8.6.2 Security	136
	8.7	Conclusions	137
	References	137

9   Internet of Things and big data recommender systems to support Smart Grid   145
Mirjana Maksimović and Miodrag Forcan

	9.1	Introduction	145
	9.2	IoT-supported SG—a communication perspective	147
	9.3	Big data in SG	151
	9.4	Making recommendations in SG	156
		9.4.1 Load forecasting	158
		9.4.2 Renewable energy forecasting	159
		9.4.3 DR and energy management program	160
		9.4.4 SG state estimation	162
	9.5	Conclusion	166
	References	167

10   Recommendation techniques and their applications to the delivery of an online bibliotherapy   173
Yunxing Xin and Ling Feng

| | 10.1 | What is bibliotherapy? | 173 |
| | 10.2 | Review of recommendation techniques | 174 |

10.2.1	Stereotyping approach	175
10.2.2	Content-based filtering approach	175
10.2.3	Collaborative filtering approach	176
10.2.4	Co-occurrence recommendation approach	176
10.2.5	Graph-based approach	176
10.2.6	Global relevance approach	176
10.2.7	Hybrid approach	177
10.3	Reading recommendation in bibliotherapy	177
10.3.1	Categories of adolescent stress and reading articles	177
10.3.2	Unifying stress easing and reading interests for articles recommendation	177
10.3.3	Recommending procedure	178
10.4	System implementation	179
10.4.1	The framework	179
10.4.2	System interfaces	179
10.5	Conclusion	183
References		184

11 Stream processing in Big Data for e-health care — **187**
Tariq Lambachri, Amir Hajjam El Hassani,
Abderrahim Sekkaki, and Emmanuel Andres

11.1	Introduction	187
11.2	Stream processing for low-latency analytics	188
11.2.1	Batch processing vs. stream processing	188
11.2.2	Challenges of stream processing	189
11.3	Real-time processors	190
11.3.1	Storm platform	190
11.3.2	Samza platform	192
11.3.3	Spark platform	195
11.4	Stream processing in e-health care	201
11.5	Conclusion	202
References		202

12 How Hadoop and Spark benchmarking algorithms can improve remote health monitoring and data management platforms? — **205**
Anna Karen Garate Escamilla, Amir Hajjam El Hassani,
Emmanuel Andres, and Mohamed Hajjam

12.1	Introduction	205
12.2	E-care platform	206
12.2.1	Security and privacy challenges for healthcare applications	209
12.2.2	Problematic of E-care	210
12.3	Big data	211
12.4	Hadoop ecosystem	212

12.4.1	MapReduce	213
12.4.2	Spark	213
12.4.3	Other tools	214
12.5	Computational techniques	215
12.5.1	Machine learning techniques in medical field	215
12.5.2	Spark with machine learning techniques in medical field	216
12.6	Benchmarking	217
12.6.1	Benchmarking and big data	218
12.6.2	Types of benchmarking	219
12.7	Benchmarks in Hadoop and Spark	220
12.7.1	Amp Lab Benchmark	220
12.7.2	BigBench	220
12.7.3	BigDataBench	220
12.7.4	BigFrame	220
12.7.5	GridMix	221
12.7.6	HiBench	222
12.7.7	PigMix	224
12.7.8	SparkBench	224
12.7.9	Statistical Workload Injector for MapReduce	225
12.8	Benchmark comparison	225
12.9	Proposal	227
12.10	Conclusion	228
	References	228

13 Extracting and understanding user sentiments for big data analytics in big business brands   **235**
Jaiteg Singh, Rupali Gill, and Gaurav Goyal

13.1	Introduction	235
13.2	Consumer behavior for understanding consumer sentiments	236
13.3	User sentiments	236
13.4	What is consumer sentiment?	237
13.4.1	Why sentiment analysis is required?	237
13.4.2	Need for neuromarketing based on psychology principles	238
13.4.3	How sentiment analysis can be correlated to consumer behavior?	238
13.5	The concept of neuromarketing	238
13.5.1	Neuromarketing techniques	240
13.5.2	How it works?	241
13.6	Big data analytics	248
13.6.1	Why big data for understanding of consumer behavior?	249
13.6.2	Big data analytics—next big thing	250
13.6.3	HADOOP	251

	13.6.4	Master/Slave architecture of Hadoop	253
	13.6.5	What is MapReduce?	253
	13.7	Conclusion	253
	References		254
	Bibliography		254

14 A recommendation system for allocating video resources in multiple partitions   **259**
Kostas Kolomvatsos, Maria G. Koziri, and Thanasis Loukopoulos

14.1	Introduction	259
14.2	Related work	261
14.3	Problem description	263
14.4	The proposed approach	264
14.5	Experimental evaluation	267
14.6	Conclusions and future work	272
References		273

15 A mood-sensitive recommendation system in social sensing   **277**
Dong Wang

15.1	Introduction		277
15.2	Related work		278
15.3	Problem formulation and terminology definition		279
15.4	Mood sensitive truth discovery		281
15.5	Evaluation		283
	15.5.1	Datasets and preprocessing	283
	15.5.2	Performance evaluation of MS-EM	284
15.6	Conclusion		288
Acknowledgments			288
References			288

16 The paradox of opinion leadership and recommendation culture in Chinese online movie reviews   **293**
Jie Yang and Brian Yecies

16.1	Introduction		293
16.2	Related work on online leadership and recommendation		295
	16.2.1	The rise of China	295
	16.2.2	Opinion leadership	296
	16.2.3	Recommendation system	298
	16.2.4	Leadership for recommendations among social networks	299
16.3	Methodology		299
	16.3.1	Data collection	301
	16.3.2	Feature builder	302

	16.3.3	Rule-mining functionality	303
	16.3.4	Methodology outline	304
16.4	Leadership and recommendation analytics	305
	16.4.1	Experimental setup	305
	16.4.2	Feature statistics	306
	16.4.3	Discovering leadership patterns	310
	16.4.4	Discussion	312
16.5	Conclusion	313
	References	313

17 Real-time optimal route recommendations using MapReduce   **317**
Majid Khalilian, Lida Farajpour, and Maryam Fathi Ahmadsaraei

17.1	Introduction	317
17.2	An overview of RRSs	317
	17.2.1	Recommendation Systems	318
	17.2.2	Route Recommendation Systems	318
	17.2.3	Classification of RRSs	319
17.3	The requirements for RRS	326
	17.3.1	Data requirements	326
	17.3.2	Big or small Data?	327
	17.3.3	Real-time issue	328
	17.3.4	An architecture	329
	17.3.5	The categories of requirements from another perspective	334
17.4	Summary	335
	References	335

18 Investigation of relationships between high-level user contexts and mobile application usage   **339**
Takahiro Hara and Jun Osawa

18.1	Introduction	339
18.2	Related work	341
	18.2.1	Investigation of mobile user's behavior	341
	18.2.2	Collecting application usage logs	341
	18.2.3	Collecting context information	342
18.3	Log-collection system	342
	18.3.1	Initialization of the system	342
	18.3.2	Questions about contexts	343
	18.3.3	Collection of application usage logs	343
	18.3.4	Game-based approach	345
18.4	Collected logs	345
	18.4.1	High-level contexts	346
	18.4.2	Application usage frequency	346
	18.4.3	Tendency of application usage by time	349

18.5 Relationships between applications and contexts 350
    18.5.1 Characteristic rules 352
    18.5.2 Effect of single context 353
    18.5.3 Effect of combination of contexts 355
18.6 Discussion 356
    18.6.1 Impacts of collecting high-level contexts 356
    18.6.2 Possible applications of high-level contexts 357
18.7 Conclusion 357
References 358

19 Machine learning and stock recommendation **361**
Chulwoo Han and Zhaodong He

19.1 Introduction 361
19.2 Momentum and stock-return predictability 363
    19.2.1 Momentum effects 363
    19.2.2 Jegadeesh–Titman (JT) momentum strategy 364
    19.2.3 52-Week high (52WH) momentum strategy 365
19.3 Machine-learning-based momentum strategy 365
    19.3.1 Feature engineering 365
    19.3.2 Labelling 367
    19.3.3 Training and testing 367
    19.3.4 Portfolio formation 368
19.4 Empirical results 369
    19.4.1 Classification accuracy 369
    19.4.2 Portfolio performance 371
19.5 Machine-learning-based stock recommendation 374
    19.5.1 Design of the model 376
    19.5.2 Empirical results 377
19.6 Conclusion 379
References 381

20 The role of smartphone in recommender systems: opportunities and challenges **385**
Peifeng Yin

20.1 Introduction 385
20.2 Silence is also evidence: interpret dwell time 389
    20.2.1 Modeling the silence behavior 389
    20.2.2 Modeling the dwell time 390
    20.2.3 Model inference and application 391
20.3 App recommendation: contest between temptation and satisfaction 392
    20.3.1 Failure of recommendation 392
    20.3.2 Modeling the contest—actual-tempting model 393
    20.3.3 Insights of the model 395

20.4   POI recommendation: geographical, social and temporal   396
    20.4.1   Geographical influence   396
    20.4.2   Social influence   398
    20.4.3   Temporal influence   400
20.5   Conclusion   402
References   402

**21   Graph-based recommendations: from data representation to
feature extraction and application   407**
*Amit Tiroshi, Tsvi Kuflik, Shlomo Berkovsky, and
Mohamed Ali (Dali) Kaafar*

21.1   Introduction   407
21.2   Background and related work   409
    21.2.1   Graph-based recommender systems   409
    21.2.2   Feature engineering for recommendations   413
21.3   Graph-based data modeling for recommendation systems   414
    21.3.1   The structure of a recommender system dataset   415
    21.3.2   Transforming tabular into graph-based representation   417
    21.3.3   Distilling graph features   421
21.4   Experimental setting and datasets   426
    21.4.1   Dataset I—Last.fm   426
    21.4.2   Dataset II—Yelp (from RecSys-2013)   428
    21.4.3   Dataset III—Yelp II (with social links)   430
    21.4.4   Dataset IV—Movielens   432
    21.4.5   Summary of the datasets, features, and metrics   432
21.5   Results and analysis   433
    21.5.1   Case study I: overall contribution of the
         graph-based approach   433
    21.5.2   Case study II: different graph schemes and their impact
         on recommendations   441
21.6   Discussion and conclusions   446
    21.6.1   Discussion   446
    21.6.2   Conclusions and future work   448
References   449

**22   AmritaDGA: a comprehensive data set for domain generation
algorithms (DGAs) based domain name detection systems and
application of deep learning   455**
*R. Vinayakumar, K.P. Soman, Prabaharan Poornachandran,
Mamoun Alazab, and Sabu M. Thampi*

22.1   Introduction   455
22.2   Related methods toward deep learning-based DGA detection and
    categorization   457
22.3   Summary of submitted systems of DMD 2018 shared task   459

22.4   Domain name system (DNS)   460
22.5   Domain fluxing   463
22.6   Scalable framework   463
22.7   Real-time DNS data collection in an Ethernet LAN   463
22.8   Description of data set   465
22.9   Deep learning   475
    22.9.1   Recurrent structures   475
    22.9.2   Convolutional neural network   475
22.10 AmritaDGANet   476
22.11 AmritaDGA data analysis, results and observations   477
22.12 Conclusion and future work   478
Acknowledgments   483
References   483

Index   **487**

Foreword

The increase in the volumes of data creates new challenges that require novel and more efficient solutions to handle big data and scalability issues. Today we are witnessing advances in many areas that are dependent on recommender systems such as social networks, e-commerce websites, search engines, blogs, and sensor networks. Many of these advances are due to the many developments in algorithmics and analytics, wireless networking, Internet of things, high performance computing, and more.

Big Data Recommender Systems, 2 Volume Set, is an exciting and comprehensive reference that deals with a wide range of topical themes in the field. It is composed of two volumes that showcase the state of the art in recommender systems. Volume 1, *Big Data Recommender Systems: Algorithms, Architectures, Big Data, Security and Trust*, covers aspects related to recommender systems preliminaries, algorithms, and architectures; recommendation approaches for big data; and trust and security measures for recommender systems. Volume 2, *Big Data Recommender Systems: Application Paradigms*, presents a good overview of the many applications that show the richness of this field and its great potential.

This two-volume work will serve as a source of up-to-date and innovative research in this continuously evolving area. The books will provide an opportunity for researchers to explore the use of recommender system technologies and their impact on enhancing our capabilities to conduct more sophisticated studies. It will also be an ideal reference for graduate classes focusing on big data and recommender systems.

I believe that this book set is a great addition to the literature on the topic and should be well received by the research and development community.

Albert Y. Zomaya
Editor-in-Chief
The IET Book Series on Big Data

Chapter 1

Introduction to big data recommender systems—volume 2

Osman Khalid[1], Samee U. Khan[2], and Albert Y. Zomaya[3]

1.1 Background

The rapid development of e-commerce websites and social networking applications has drastically increased the volumes of online generated data, leading to the term *big data*. With the rise in Internet population to 3.2 billion worldwide, on the average, 2.5 quintillion bytes of data is generated on daily basis [1]. Such greater volumes of data introduced information overload problem, when it is difficult to find the most relevant information from numerous diverse sources, e.g., websites, blogs, e-commerce, and social networking applications. The growing size of data has forced the research community to think beyond the simple search problem to the next level of filtering of pertinent information [2]. Past few years have seen significant progress in the development of powerful and intelligent tools to process and analyze the complex patterns in big data to extract the knowledge that is more meaningful for users. The potential ability to create intelligence from the analysis of raw data has been successfully applied to diverse areas, such as business, industry, sciences, social media, and e-commerce, to name a few. The ever-growing volume, complexity, and dynamicity of online information have necessitated the use of recommender systems as an appropriate tool for facilitating and accelerating the process of information engineering. The recommender systems apply numerous knowledge discovery techniques on users' historical and contextual data (e.g., location, time, preference, weather, device, and mood) to suggest information, products, and services that best match the user's preferences [3].

The recommender systems have been implemented in various application domains, including e-commerce, e-health, e-learning, tourism, and knowledge management [4]. Well-known examples include Amazon web store where users are suggested with various products of their choice based on their past purchase history [5]. Similarly, FourSquare has an integrated recommender system to suggest highly

[1]Department of Computer Science, COMSATS University Islamabad, Abbottabad Campus, Pakistan
[2]Department of Electrical and Computer Engineering, North Dakota State University, USA
[3]School of Information Technologies, University of Sydney, Australia

rated venues, Netflix has built-in movie recommender system [6], and YouTube has a video recommender system integrated [7]. Traditional recommender systems perform data processing to compute a list of top K items that satisfy a specific preference criteria identified for a user, and the items in the list are ranked based on the closeness to the user's preferences [8]. A user's context information, such as location, time, and conditions have been increasingly integrated in the recommender systems to provide more accurate or personalized recommendation information, compared to the simple approaches [9]. Most conventional recommender systems are based on collaborative filtering (CF) algorithms, content-based recommender systems, and hybrid recommender systems [3]. The CF utilizes the ratings from multiple users in a collaborative way to predict the missing ratings. The CF-based recommender systems are further subdivided into memory-based and model-based recommender systems. The memory-based approaches can be further subdivided into user-based CF and item-based CF. The user-based approaches compute similarity among users based on the ratings given to the items by the users [5]. A target user is recommended with items that are also rated by other users whose similarity is at its maximum with the target user. In contrast, the item-based CF first computes a set S of items rated by a user u that are most similar to the target item I. The ratings of items in S are used to predict rating of the target item I for the given user u.

The model-based CF makes use of data mining and machine learning (ML) algorithms to establish models based on training data to predict rating for a user for unrated items. There are many techniques of model-based CF, including, Bayesian networks, clustering models, and latent semantic models such as singular value decomposition, probabilistic latent semantic analysis, multiple multiplicative factor, latent Dirichlet allocation, and Markov decision process-based models [10]. The content-based recommender systems maintain a user profile of items rated by the user. The new items are recommended to the user based on their similarity to the items present in the user's profile. Finally, the hybrid approaches combine different approaches based on content-based or CF-based models to develop hybrid recommender systems. Several studies have indicated that hybrid approaches produce more accurate recommendations compared to purely content-based or CF-based techniques [3]. These methods can also be used to overcome some of the common problems in recommender systems such as cold start and the sparsity problem.

Despite significant development, the recommender systems still face numerous challenges, such as data sparsity, cold start, and scalability, to name a few [2]. The data sparsity occurs if there are insufficient ratings against items and the target user has rated only a few items. In this case, the precision of the recommendation system will decrease significantly due to large number of zero similarity values. The cold start issue occurs if a user is new to the system and does not have enough preferences' data stored in the system due to which the system is unable to match the user's preferences with existing users to compute recommendations. A major issue faced by the traditional recommender systems is scalability. With the explosive growth of the information on the Internet, the similarity computations on large size user–item rating matrix have almost become impractical and pose similar challenges to the modern recommender system. Moreover, obtaining a user's real-time contextual information and effectively utilizing it for timely recommendation is also a big challenge as the context information is time varying, and a user's privacy setting may not allow the system to collect such information. In past few years, numerous recommendation approaches have been developed to address various aspects of recommender systems. However, there are still many open issues and challenges that require novel and more efficient recommendation solutions to handle big data.

1.2   About the book

The book *Big Data Recommender Systems* consists of two comprehensive volumes. Each volume consists of good quality chapters contributed by world renowned researchers and domain experts.

Volume 2 of *Big Data Recommender Systems* is in the continuation of Volume 1. The content presented in Volume 1 is aimed to cover the recent advances, issues, novel solutions, and theoretical foundations on big data recommender systems. Volume 1 encompasses original scientific contributions in the form of comparative analysis, surveys, case studies, techniques, and tools for recommender systems. The topics covered in Volume 1 include benchmarking of recommendation algorithms using MapReduce, social recommendations, hybrid approaches, deep learning-based techniques, unstructured big data recommendations, ML-based models, and geo-social recommendations. A special section is included to cover the security and privacy concerns, cyberattacks on recommender systems, and their defensive measures.

The current Volume 2 of *Big Data Recommender Systems* is the collection of chapters written by world-leading researchers and scholars with a specific focus on *application domains* of recommender systems. A specific focus is given to emerging trends and the industry needs associated with utilizing recommender systems. We envisage the book to serve as a professional reference for researchers, research students, and practitioners in the field of data mining and knowledge discovery and also for undergraduate- and graduate-level courses in a wide range of disciplines including computer science, healthcare, automotive, and engineering. The book is also of interest to researchers and industrial practitioners in areas such as knowledge engineering, human–computer interaction, artificial intelligence, intelligent information processing, decision support systems (DSSs), and knowledge management. Volume 2 will help computer scientists to develop new concepts and methodologies for complex, scientific, industrial, and business applications. As there have been numerous developments and advancements in the aforementioned research fields, Volume 2 intends to conclude the quality research in a book and identify future directions. Volume 2 is organized into 23 chapters. A brief summary of the chapters is presented in the following.

Chapter 2: This chapter provides a comprehensive introduction to deep neural network-based recommendation models. The authors discuss in detail several deep neural networks with a discussion on applications areas and the state-of-the-art solutions for deep learning-based recommender systems.

Chapter 3: The chapter describes the cold start problem in recommendation systems. The authors mainly focus on CF systems being the most popular approaches to build recommender systems. Moreover, the authors discuss multiple scenarios where the cold start issues may happen and explain different solutions for them.

Chapter 4: The chapter focuses on the performance metrics identified for both the traditional recommender systems and context-aware recommender systems (CARS). In addition to all the possible performance metrics used in those systems, the authors have discussed various issues affecting the performance of CARS.

Chapter 5: The chapter models the lifestyles of individuals that according to authors become a more challenging problem with higher variability when compared to the aggregated behavior of city regions. Using collective matrix factorization, the authors propose a unified dual view of lifestyles. The application of the proposed solution ranges from the targeted advertisements and promotions to the diffusion of digital financial services among low-income groups.

Chapter 6: This chapter proposes to embed the principal component analysis (PCA) inference stage in a low-cost Field-Programmable System on Chip (FPSoC) while performing a design space exploration for a general PCA inference problem. To this end, the authors analyze metrics, such as latency, scalability, and usage of hardware resources. The resulting architectures are compared to a multi-core OpenMP approach to be executed in an Advanced RISC Machines (ARM) processor to analyze the advantages of using the FPSoC implementation.

Chapter 7: This chapter aims to explain the Cipher project, which is a DSS based on ML and big data technologies, and is capable of alerting a clinician when a situation of risk is detected in a patient suffering from a certain pathology so that the system is able to carry out the appropriate measures.

Chapter 8: In this chapter, it is highlighted that big data analytics (BDA) can provide efficient solutions in specific problems related to data processing in smart grids (SGs). The chapter summarizes the state of the art in specific problems of SGs that can be resolved using data analytics processing and exploitation. The chapter recognizes that data analytics can offer a feasible solution to efficient dynamic energy management, failure detection, estimation of load, and price forecasting. It is reported that in order to deal with the extreme size of data, the smart grid requires the adoption of advanced data analytics, big data management, and powerful monitoring techniques.

Chapter 9: The chapter examines the importance of the Internet of things (IoT) and big data in the development of recommender systems for SGs. It is shown that the involvement of novel technologies contributes to improvements in load forecasting, renewable energy forecasting, demand response and energy management programs as well as SG state estimation. The general aim of this chapter is to provide an overview of the ongoing scientific research, recent technological innovations and breakthroughs, and BDA role in designing recommendation systems that will facilitate the development and evolution of future global energy systems.

Chapter 10: The chapter addresses the problem of traditional bibliotherapy in coping with pressures of adolescents and proposes an online reading recommendation system as a new exploration of bibliotherapy. The chapter first provides a brief review of bibliotherapy and recommendation techniques in the literature. Then, the chapter reports the design and implementation of proposed reading recommendation system for easing teens' psychological stress. Finally some application interfaces are provided to demonstrate the usage of the system.

Chapter 11: The chapter discusses various techniques for big data stream processing for e-healthcare. Moreover, the authors conduct a qualitative comparison of the most popular data processing systems, namely Storm and Spark Streaming. The authors describe their respective underlying bases and the functionalities they provide, and discuss how they can be introduced into e-healthcare analysis programs.

Chapter 12: The chapter presents a discussion about how Hadoop and Spark benchmarking algorithms can improve remote health monitoring and data management. The chapter introduces the characteristics of e-care platform and the concept of ontology to help the reader understand the system that implements big data tools for its migration. Moreover, most popular systems in the Hadoop Ecosystem are illustrated with an emphasis on MapReduce and Spark. A survey on applications using ML techniques in the medical field is presented, with examples for Apache Spark. Finally, a benchmarking comparison of MapReduce, Spark, and Flink is provided.

Chapter 13: The chapter performs data analytics of the sample data using Hadoop framework based on crucial metrics related to consumer behaviors such as (a) customer acquisition cost, (b) customer retention cost, (c) lifetime value, (d) customer satisfaction and happiness, and (e) average purchase amount and behavior. The chapter provides the conclusion of video image based sentiments extraction using neuromarketing techniques.

Chapter 14: The chapter presents a recommendation system for allocating video resources in multiple partitions. The recommendation system is responsible to allocate the data to the most appropriate partition according to their current contents. A decision-making scheme combined with a Naïve Bayesian classifier is developed for deriving the appropriate partition. The focus is on the management of streams of video files. The proposed system derives the appropriate partition for each incoming video file based on a set of characteristics.

Chapter 15: The chapter presents a mood-sensitive recommendation system that incorporates the mood-sensitivity feature into the truth discovery solution. The reviewed recommendation system estimates (i) the correctness and mood neutrality of claims and (ii) the reliability and mood sensitivity of sources. The model is compared with existing truth discovery solutions using four real-world datasets

Chapter 16: The chapter focuses on the methods that seek to address new challenges raised by discovering key opinion leadership behavioral patterns for one of the most popular Chinese social media platforms. A big data analytic framework is proposed by implementing the Hadoop-based cloud-computing platform, which is used as the fundamental tool for storing and processing massive datasets. Accordingly, raw data samples are collected, processed, and categorized to cover details such as film data, textual content, and user profiles. In addition, a parallel rule mining algorithm is employed to discover leadership patterns.

Chapter 17: The chapter presents an overview of route recommendation systems. A classification of route recommendation systems is provided on the basis of services they provide. Besides, a layered architecture of route recommendation systems is discussed to deal with big data and to serve optimal real-time recommendations.

Chapter 18: The chapter investigates the relationships between high-level user contexts and application usage by analyzing a large amount of application usage log. The chapter reports the findings of the experiments that conducted association rule mining on the collected logs. The presented study provides a guideline on how to collect big data on user's high-level contexts and how to utilize it for important context-aware applications such as application recommendation.

Chapter 19: The chapter develops a neural network model for stock classification using input features derived from widely known momentum factors and apply it to two problems: long-short strategy construction and stock recommendation. Empirical findings suggest that the model can create a long-short portfolio generating a significant profit and high Sharpe ratio. It can also be effective in making buy/hold/sell recommendation, although the evidence is less strong.

Chapter 20: The authors discuss new opportunities and challenges brought by smart phones to recommender system. Specifically, three recommendation scenarios are covered: common recommendation, app recommendation, and point of interest (POI) recommendation. Moreover, a probabilistic model is introduced that can learn from the temporal sequence of user–app interactions. Finally, a model of geographical, social, and temporal influence in POI on location-based recommender system is introduced.

Chapter 21: In this chapter, a generic approach for uncovering latent preference patterns from user data is proposed and evaluated. The approach relies on representing the data using graphs and then systematically extracting graph-based features and using them to enrich the original user models. The extracted features encapsulate complex relationships between users, items, and metadata. The enhanced user models can then serve as an input to any recommendation algorithm.

Chapter 22: This chapter presents a fully labeled domain name dataset AmritaDGA, using domain generating algorithm (DGA). The generated data can be used for research in the field of detecting malicious domain names. Additionally, the performances of various deep learning architectures are evaluated on AmritaDGA to detect and categorize malicious domain names to corresponding DGA family.

Chapter 23: This work proposes Deep-Segregation of Plastic architecture which sorts waste materials into plastic and non-plastic using deep learning technique and convolutional neural network. The developed framework is highly scalable and capable of collecting data from different sensors, and preprocessing and analyzing data using distributed algorithms. The framework is specifically developed for plastic segregation. Moreover, the framework can be easily extended to handle large volumes of other waste categories by adding additional resources.

Acknowledgments

We would like to express our sincere thanks to the authors of the chapters for reporting their thoughts and experiences related to their research and also for patiently addressing reviewers' comments and diligently adhering to the hectic deadlines to have the book sent to the publisher in a timely manner. We are indebted to the reviewers for providing insightful and thoughtful comments on the chapters which tremendously improved the quality of the chapters included in this book.

Our thanks are due to IET for publishing this book and for accommodating us at various stages of the publication process. We believe that this book is an important contribution to the community in assembling research work on big data recommender systems from various domains.

References

[1]   "Data Never Sleeps 6.0," [Online]. Available: https://www.domo.com/blog/data-never-sleeps-6/ [accessed 15 October 2018].

[2]   U. Sivarajah, M.M. Kamal and Z. Irani, "Critical Analysis of Big Data Challenges and Analytical Methods," *Journal of Business Research*, vol. 70, pp. 263–286, 2017.

[3]   J. Bobadilla, F. Ortega, A. Hernando and A. GutiéRrez, "Recommender systems survey," *Knowledge-Based Systems*, vol. 46, pp. 109–132, 2013.

[4]   L. Chen and P. Pu, "Critiquing-based Recommenders: Survey and Emerging Trends," *User Modeling and User-Adapted Interaction*, vol. 22, no. 1, pp. 125–150, 2012.

[5]   B. Smith and G. Linden, "Two Decades of Recommender Systems at Amazon.com," *IEEE Internet Computing*, vol. 21, no. 3, 2017.

[6]   C.A. Gomez-Uribe and N. Hunt, "The Netflix Recommender System: Algorithms, Business Value, and Innovation," *ACM Transactions on Management Information Systems*, vol. 6, no. 4, pp. 1–19, 2016.

[7]   J. Davidson, B. Liebald, J. Liu, *et al.*, "The YouTube Video Recommendation System," in *Proceedings of the Fourth ACM Conference on Recommender Systems*, Barcelona, Spain, 2010.

[8]   O. Khalid, M.U.S. Khan, S.U. Khan and A.Y. Zomaya, "OmniSuggest: A Ubiquitous Cloud-based Context-aware Recommendation System for Mobile Social Networks," *IEEE Transactions on Services Computing*, vol. 7, no. 3, pp. 401–414, 2014.

[9]   R. Irfan, O. Khalid, M U.S. Khan, *et al.*, "MobiContext: A Context-aware Cloud-based Recommendation Framework," *IEEE Transactions on Cloud Computing*, vol. 5, no. 4, pp. 712–724, 2017.

[10] X. Su and . T. Khoshgoftaar, "A Survey of Collaborative Filtering Techniques," *Advances in Artificial Intelligence*, vol. 2009, pp. 1–19, 2009.

Chapter 2

Deep neural networks meet recommender systems

Shuai Zhang[1], Lina Yao[1], Aixin Sun[2], Guibing Guo[3],
Xiwei Xu[4], and Liming Zhu[4]

Deep learning has been widely used in many software disciplines in both academia and industry including computer vision, speech recognition and translation, natural languages processing, search engine, bioinformatics, sensor data processing, finance, etc., due to its scalability in big data environments and accuracy at higher level than ever before. Especially, deep neural networks can utilize the parallel computational power of GPU to accelerate the learning process and ensure higher efficiency for big data problems.

Recently, deep learning has been successfully applied to recommender systems and became the primary fuel for driving the progress in many recommendation fields [1] such as e-commerce, image, music, video, article, mobile and desktop applications. There are several advantages of deep neural network based recommendation models: (1) with deep neural networks, we can introduce non-linearity to recommendation models and capture the intricate user–item interaction patterns, (2) deep neural network is powerful in representation learning which makes it an ideal tool to process the abundant side information of users and items, (3) deep neural networks can be used to model the sequential patterns in historical interactions and perform sequential recommendations, (4) the flexibility of deep neural networks makes it possible to combine different neural network models to capture more complex relationships and characteristics of heterogeneous data sources.

In this chapter, we will give a comprehensive introduction to deep neural network based recommendation models. We begin with a brief introduction to several deep neural networks. The following four sections are organized based on the aforementioned four advantages. We detail several representative works in each part and summarize them in at a high level. Section 2.6 introduces several related advanced and promising research topics. Section 2.7 discusses possible challenges and concludes this chapter.

[1] School of Computer Science and Engineering, University of New South Wales, Australia
[2] School of Computer Science and Engineering, Nanyang Technological University, Singapore
[3] Software College, Northeastern University, China
[4] Data61, The Commonwealth Scientific and Industrial Research Organization, Australia

2.1   Preliminary

Before diving into the details of deep neural network based recommendation model, we would like to give a brief introduction to recommender systems and deep neural networks.

2.1.1   Introduction to recommender systems

In a standard setting of recommender system, we have a list of M users and a list of N items. The preferences of users to items will form an $M \times N$ matrix, and we denote it as $X \in \mathbf{R}^{M \times N}$. Let X_{u*} denote the uth row of the interaction matrix X, and X_{*i} denote the ith column. The value of X_{ui} can either be explicit ratings (e.g., 1–5) or binary implicit feedback ([0, 1]). The binary implicit feedback can represent a broad range of interactions such as clicks, buy, watch, like/dislike. To make recommendations, we need to generate a list of items ranked based on the predicted preference scores. In addition, we can also take user or item side information, such as age, gender, used languages, item description, appearance, images, prices, into consideration. In some cases, context information like time, location, weather and mood can also be utilized.

2.1.2   Introduction to deep neural networks

A standard deep neural network consists of multiple connected hidden layers between the input and output layer, with each hidden layer having a number of neurons. It has demonstrated the revolutionizing performance on applications such as image and speech recognition, language translation, question answering, self-driving, image generating [2]. For a clear presentation, we would like to briefly introduce four basic neural networks: multilayer perceptron (MLP), autoencoder, convolutional neural network and recurrent neural network (RNN).

2.1.2.1   Multilayer perceptron

MLP consists of three or more fully connected layers (input layer, output layer and one or more hidden layers) with nonlinear transformations. It is learned in a supervised manner and can be applied to both regression and classification tasks. In formal, an MLP is defined as follows:

$$h_1(x) = a_1(W_1 x + b_1)$$
$$h_2(x) = a_2(W_2 h_1 + b_2)$$
$$\cdots$$
$$f_{MLP}(x) = o(W_L h_{L-1} + b_L)$$

where W_* and b_* are the weights and biases. a_* is the nonlinear hidden activation function which can be hyperbolic tangent (tanh): $g(x) = (e^x - e^{-x})/(e^x + e^{-x})$, sigmoid: $g(x) = 1/(1 + e^{-x})$ or rectifier (ReLU): $g(x) = \max(0, x)$. $o(x)$ is the output activation which is adjusted based on the tasks. For example, we usually use linear activation for regression task and sigmoid (binary classification) or softmax (multi-label classification) for classification problem.

2.1.2.2 Autoencoder

Autoencoder is an unsupervised neural network. It is primarily used for dimensionality reduction. A typical autoencoder consists of three layers. The input and output have the same dimensionality and the size of hidden layer is usually smaller. The process from input to hidden layer is referred as encoder and that from hidden layer to output layer is called decoder. Suppose the input x is a d dimensional vector, we have:

$$z = a_1(W_1 x + b_1)$$
$$x' = a_2(W_2 z + b_2)$$

where $z \in \mathbf{R}^k$ is the low-dimensional representation and x' is the reconstruction of input. Autoencoder learns its parameters by minimizing the reconstruction error:

$$\mathscr{L}(x, x') = \| x - x' \|^2$$

We can stack several autoencoders to formulate a deep neural network. There are many variants of autoencoder such as variational autoencoder [3], contractive autoencoder [4] and marginalized autoencoder [5]. Denoising technique (reconstructing the corrupted inputs) could be applied to prevent the autoencoder from learning the identity function [2].

2.1.2.3 Convolutional neural network

Convolution neural network (CNN) has achieved tremendous success in dealing with grid-like data such as images. The success mainly ascribes to the two key operations: convolution and pooling.

Convolutional layer is the building block of CNN. In many real world data, such as images, the original pixel representations are very huge and there exist some spatial relations between pixels. MLP will encounter scalability problem and miss some key relationships when processing these data. The basic idea of CNN is using some predefined small filter matrices to scan the original inputs grid-by-grid and project the big inputs into small ones while preserving the spatial relationships between pixels. With different filters, we can detect various small or meaningful features like edges.

Pooling is mainly used for dimensionality reduction and makes the model more invariant to small translations of input. For example, if our task is to detect cats on an image, we need to focus on whether there is a cat rather than where the cat is. Pooling can help the model to reduce the side effects of position translations. In practice, max pooling, average pooling and sum pooling are usually adopted.

There are many standard CNN architectures such as LeNet, AlexNet, VGG, GoogleNet, ResNet and DenseNet [6].

2.1.2.4 Recurrent neural network

In the abovementioned models, all inputs are assumed to be independent of each other, which means that they cannot capture the dependencies patterns of sequential information. RNNs are proposed to solve such problems. RNN allows operation on sequential and time-series data to model their temporal dependencies. Figure 2.1

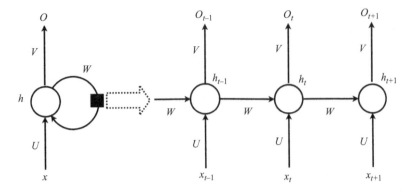

Figure 2.1   The structure of basic RNNs and its unrolled version

shows a basic RNN and the unfolded full network. Mathematically, RNN can be expressed as

$$h_t = a_h(Ux_t + Wh_{t-1} + b_h)$$
$$o_t = a_y(Vh_t + b_y)$$

where x_t is the input at time step t. h_t is the hidden state and o_t is the output. W, U, V and $b*$ are model weight matrices and biases. a_* is the activation function.

The major problem of RNN is the gradient vanishing problem that the gradient tends to vanish when being passed back through many time steps. This problem prevents RNN from modelling long-term dependencies. Two popular variants of RNN were proposed to tackle this issue: long short-term memory and gated recurrent unit (GRU) [2]. Both of these two variants adopt the gate mechanisms to control the previous memory and current inputs. GRU is more popular in recent years due to its lower computational cost and complexity. Readers are referred to [2] for more details on these two variants.

2.2   Introducing nonlinearity to recommender systems

Most notable recommendation models such as matrix factorization and factorization machine (FM) are essentially linear methods, for example, matrix factorization models user–item interaction patterns with inner product and can be deemed as a linear model of latent factors; FM also models the feature relationships in a linear manner. This makes it difficult to capture the non-linear and intricate inherent structures of real-world big data. One feasible solution is to introduce nonlinearity to these models with nonlinear activation functions such as sigmoid, tanh and ReLU. Several recent work achieved this by generalizing these methods with deep neural networks, such as neural matrix factorization [7,8], deep FM [9].

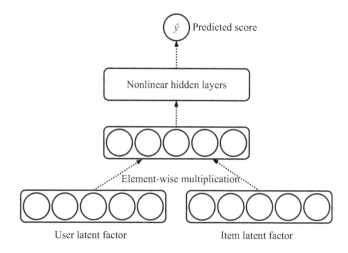

Figure 2.2 Basic component of neural matrix factorization

2.2.1 Deep neural generalization of collaborative filtering

2.2.1.1 Neural matrix factorization

Figure 2.2 shows the basic component of neural matrix factorization. The basic idea of neural matrix factorization is to add some nonlinear layers over the results of element-wise multiplication between user and item vectors.

$$\hat{y}_{ui} = f_{MLP}(P_u \odot Q_i)$$

where $P \in \mathbf{R}^{M \times k}$ and $Q \in \mathbf{R}^{N \times k}$ are user and item latent factors. $\odot$ is element-wise multiplication. Traditional matrix factorization scores each user–item pair with dot product which is the sum of the products of the corresponding entries of user and item latent factors, while neural matrix factorization replaces the simple addition with a neural network. It not only allows varying the importance of each latent factor but also makes it possible to integrate nonlinear transformations for matrix factorization. If we enforce f_{MLP} to be a one-layer network with uniform weights of 1, the above scoring function will be boiled down to traditional matrix factorization. This structure can be applied to both rating prediction and item-ranking tasks. Here, we introduce two representative works: neural network matrix factorization (NNMF) [7] and neural collaborative filtering (NeuMF) [8].

NNMF is designed for rating prediction. This model has four latent matrices: $P \in \mathbf{R}^{M \times k}$, $Q \in \mathbf{R}^{N \times k}$, $P' \in \mathbf{R}^{M \times d}$ and $Q' \in \mathbf{R}^{M \times d}$. The former two vectors are the user and item latent factors, while the last two vectors can be viewed as the user and item biases. The input of NNMF is the concatenation vector $[P_u \odot Q_i, P'_u, Q'_i]$. The ratings are predicted with an MLP and the objective function is defined as

$$\mathcal{L} = \sum_{(u,i) \in \mathcal{O}} (X_{ui} - f_{MLP}([P_u \odot Q_i, P'_u, Q'_i]))^2 + \lambda \Omega(\Theta)$$

where $\Theta = \{W, b, P, Q, P', Q'\}$ is the model parameters; W and b denote the weights and biases of neural network; λ is a regularization rate; Ω is Frobenius norm regularization; $\mathcal{O}$ denotes the observed ratings set. Optimization is done with gradient descent and RMSProp is used to adjust the learning rate.

Another similar model is neural collaborative filtering (NeuMF) which is designed for top-N recommendation. NeuMF consists of two components, a generalized matrix factorization (GMF) and an MLP, and models the interactions in dual embedding space (thus, we reuse the notations P_u, Q_i, P'_u, Q'_i). NeuMF allows GMF and MLP to learn separate embeddings.

$$\phi^{GML} = P_u \odot Q_i, \tag{2.1}$$

$$\phi^{MLP} = f_{MLP}([P'_u, Q'_i]), \tag{2.2}$$

$$\hat{y}_{ui} = \sigma(h^T[\phi^{GML}, \phi^{MLP}]) \tag{2.3}$$

where $\sigma(\cdot)$ is the sigmoid function. The GMF does not have any nonlinear transformation. The combination of GMF and MLP enables NeuMF to capture both the linear and nonlinear relationships. With this neural framework, the two components can mutually enhance each other to learn more effective user and item embeddings.

To learn the model parameters, NeuMF treats the ranking problem as a classification task by minimizing the binary cross-entropy loss.

$$\mathcal{L} = - \sum_{(u,i) \in \mathcal{O} \cup \mathcal{O}^-} y_{ui} \log \hat{y}_{ui} + (1 - y_{ui}) \log(1 - \hat{y}_{ui})$$

where $\mathcal{O}^-$ is the negative sample set. We uniformly sample them from unobserved interactions in each iteration with controlled sampling ratio. To avoid getting stuck in local-minimum, pretraining is usually adopted to train GMF and MLP separately first and then use their model parameters to initialize the corresponding parts of NeuMF. The pretraining step is done with Adam algorithm and the final model is trained with vanilla SGD.

Both NNMF and NeuMF are based on matrix factorization. NeuRec [10] provides another idea to introduce nonlinearity to recommendation model. NeuRec is built upon sparse linear method (SLIM) [11]. It aims to replace the linear projection of SLIM with nonlinear projection and shows promising performance on personalized ranking task. NeuRec has two variants user-based NeuRec (U-NeuRec) and item-based NeuRec (I-NeuRec). Both of them consist of two components: an MLP with user historical interactions (or item historical interactions) as input and item embeddings (or user embeddings). U-NeuRec learns user latent factors from user consumption records while I-NeuRec learns item latent factors from item click-through data.

2.2.1.2 Autoencoder-based collaborative filtering

Autoencoder can be structured to model the collaborative effects for users and items. Instead of focusing on the bottleneck layer like traditional autoencoder, it usually relies on the reconstruction of autoencoder. As shown in Figure 2.3, the inputs are the columns or rows of the interaction matrix X, and the outputs are the reconstructed columns or rows. The inputs are partially observed, autoencoder reconstructs

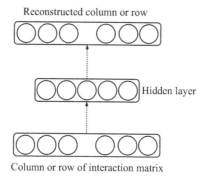

Figure 2.3　Autoencoder based collaborative filtering

the partially observed columns/rows and attempts to anticipate a value for missing observation. It is suitable for both rating prediction and item-ranking tasks as well.

AutoRec [12] is an autoencoder-based rating prediction model. It has two variants: I-AutoRec and U-AutoRec. The inputs of I-AutoRec are the columns of interaction matrix, while that of U-AutoRec are the rows. Basic AutoRec corresponds to a single hidden layer autoencoder. Formally, I-AutoRec solves the following objective:

$$\mathscr{L} = \sum_{i=1}^{N} \|X_{*i} - a(W \cdot g(VX_{*i} + \mu) + b)\|_{\mathcal{O}}^2 + \lambda(\|W\|_F^2 + \|V\|_F^2)$$

where $\| \cdot \|_{\mathcal{O}}^2$ means that it only considers the observed ratings during training. $W \in \mathbf{R}^{M \times k}$ and $V \in \mathbf{R}^{k \times M}$ are weight matrices (k is the dimension of hidden layer). $\mu \in \mathbf{R}^k$ and $b \in \mathbf{R}^M$ are the biases. $a(\cdot)$ and $g(\cdot)$ are activation functions. U-AutoRec can be easily derived from the above equation. A deep version of AutoRec can be built by adding more hidden layers. Dropout technique can be adopted to prevent overfitting [13].

CDAE [14] is a ranking extension of U-AutoRec. Nonetheless, it only works on implicit feedback and takes binary user preferences as inputs. CDAE projects the corrupted inputs to a low-dimensional hidden layer and then mapped it back to the original input space and get the predicted ranking score. The scoring function is formulated as follows:

$$\hat{y}_{u*} = a(W' \cdot g(W\tilde{X}_{u*} + V_u + \mu) + b)$$

where V_u is the user-specific bias. $\tilde{X}_{u*}$ is the corrupted version of X_{u*}. The elements of input X_{u*} are corrupted and set to 0 with a probability of q which is also known as corruption level. The objective function is defined as

$$\mathscr{L} = \frac{1}{M} \sum_{u=1}^{M} \ell(X_{u*}, \hat{y}_{u*}) + \lambda(\|W'\|_2^2 + \|W\|_2^2 + \|V\|_2^2 + \|b\|_2^2 + \|\mu\|_2^2)$$

where the loss ℓ could be squared loss or logistic loss similar to NeuMF. To accelerate the training process, negative sampling strategy is usually employed and the overall complexity is linear to the size of observed instances. This model can be optimized in pairwise or pointwise manner. Empirical study suggests that pointwise approach performs much better. The parameters are learned with AdaGrad which can adapt the step size and save the trouble for learning rate tuning. CDAE can also be viewed as a generalization of latent factor models and latent factorized similarity model.

2.2.2   Deep neural generalization of factorization machine

FM is a generic approach that combines the generality of feature engineering with the superiority of factorization models. It is very effective for sparse and feature-rich datasets and can be applied to a variety of tasks such as regression, classification and ranking. Recent studies show that FM is essentially a linear approach and may not be expressive enough to capture the complex and nonlinear structures of real-world datasets [9]. Here, we will introduce two approaches that incorporate deep nonlinear transformations to FM.

The first approach is neural FM (NFM) [9], NFM proposed adding nonlinear layers to the core component (order-2 interaction part) of FM. NFM achieves this goal via a Bi-interaction layer. Formally, let $x \in \mathbf{R}^n$ denote the real-valued feature vector, and $v_i \in \mathbf{R}^k$ denote the embedding representation of the ith feature. The bi-interaction layer is defined as

$$f_{BI} = \sum_{i=1}^{n} \sum_{j=i+1}^{n} x_i v_i \odot x_j v_j$$

here the output of this operation is a k dimensional vector, which makes is easy to add nonlinear transformation layers over the output like GMF. Finally, the scoring formulation of NFM is given as

$$\hat{y}(x) = w_0 + \sum_{i=1}^{n} w_i x_i + h^T f_{MLP}(f_{BI})$$

where h^T is the neuron weight for scaling the output of MLP. Similar to FM, the first term is the global bias and the second term is a linear transformation. NMF replaces the final term with a neural network. It is proved that FM is a special case of NMF with no hidden layers. To further improve the performances, dropout regularization can be adopted to prevent overfitting, and batch normalization could be applied for faster convergence.

Another model is called DeepFM [15]. Instead of adding nonlinear transformation to the third term of FM, this model consists of an FM component and a deep component (MLP). These two components have different model parameters but shared inputs. The FM component is used to model the low-order feature interactions, while the deep component is used to model the higher order interaction patterns. The prediction rule of this joint model is as follows:

$$\hat{y} = \sigma(y_{FM}(x) + y_{MLP}(x))$$

where y_{FM} is the result of the FM component while y_{MLP} is the result of MLP. The two components are learned together by minimizing the cross-entropy loss.

2.3   Representation learning for recommender systems

Deep neural network, to some extent, is a representation methodology as it learns multilevel of representations from original inputs [16]. Abundant auxiliary information, such as abstract of article, plot and posters of movies, music audio signals, of items and users is usually available. Incorporating these descriptive data sources will usually enhance the performances of recommender systems. With deep neural networks, we could process this auxiliary information more effectively and get a deep understanding about the items and users. Moreover, learning user and item embedding representations from interaction history (watches, clicks, searches, etc.) with deep neural networks is also viable.

2.3.1   Representation learning with multilayer perceptron

MLP is a basic yet powerful supervised feedforward neural networks. It cannot only be used to incorporate nonlinearity as introduced in the former section, it is also possible to be applied on feature representation learning [17–21]. Due to its effectiveness and scalability, it is widely employed in many real-world applications to feature representations of users and items, such as video recommendation in YouTube [17], Android application recommendation in Google play store [18], App, TV recommendation in Microsoft [19,20].

For instance, the recommendation in YouTube [17] is divided into two separate tasks. The first task is candidate generation which aims to select hundreds of candidates from a very large corpus. In this step, to ensure the personalization, users' video watches, search tokens, location and gender are embedded in the input layer, and the user embeddings are learned via several fully connected nonlinear layers. The video age is also considered during this stage to capture viral effects. The second task refines the ranks of the picked candidates with another MLP. More features like the impression video ID, watched video ID, user language, time since last watch are coded in this step. At last, the ranks are generated based on the predicted watch time with weighted logistic regression.

Another MLP based industry-level recommendation model is named Wide and Deep [18], which is employed in the Google Play store. It consists of two parts: the wide part and the deep part. The wide part is a generalized linear model while the deep part is a fully connected neural network. The motivation of this combination is to reach some degree of balance between generalization and memorization, because the deep part does well in generalization and the wide part can memorize some important features. This model is formulated as

$$\hat{y} = \sigma(W_{wide}[x, \phi(x)] + W_{deep}f_{MLP}(x) + b)$$

Note that $\phi(x)$ is the cross-product transformation. Usually, this transformation is applied to a small number of selected features.

In addition, a semantic matching approach based on MLP called deep semantic similarity model (DSSM) can also be applied to make recommendations. DSSM has a query network and a candidate network. In recommendation task, the query is replaced by a users' profiles, and the candidates are made up of items the user has not seen. High-level semantic user and item representations can be obtained with DSSM.

From the above models, we observe that feature engineering such as feature transformation, crossing, rescaling, normalization is a critical step for industrial recommender systems; abundant side information of usage history and item properties are usually available in the systems; scalability is one of the most important considerations for quick response to online users.

2.3.2   *Representation learning with autoencoder*

We have discussed the use of autoencoder for nonlinearity modelling where the reconstruction layer is the main focus. The encoder and decoder structure of autoencoder is initially proposed for dimensionality reduction. Thus, it is also suitable for feature representation learning in recommender systems.

To utilize the representation learning capability of autoencoder, one feasible solution is to integrate it into traditional recommendation models. Wang *et al.* (collaborative deep learning (CDL)) [22] proposed integrating autoencoder to probabilistic matrix factorization by constructing the autoencoder from a Bayesian perspective. Autoencoder is used to learn low-dimensional feature embedding vectors from item side information. Li *et al.* (collaborative variational autoencoder (CVAE)) [23] suggested replacing the traditional autoencoder of CDL with variational autoencoder. Li *et al.* [24] proposed utilizing marginalized autoencoder to extract features from both user and item side information and feed them into latent factor models. Zhang *et al.* (AutoSVD++) [25] proposed combining contractive autoencoder with SVD++ to model item content information as well as implicit feedback. These works are very close and can be included in a generic framework: deep collaborative filtering [24]. Let S_{user} and S_{item} denote the side information of users and items, respectively. The generic framework is formulated as

$$\mathscr{L} = \ell(X, P, Q) + \beta(\|P\|_F^2 + \|Q\|_F^2) + \gamma L(S_{user}, P) + \delta L(S_{item}, Q)$$

where β, γ and δ are trade-off parameters. $L(S_{user}, P)$ and $L(S_{item}, Q)$ act as link functions that connect autoencoder with the latent factor model.

Figure 2.4 illustrates the architecture of the deep collaborative filtering. By specializing the variants of autoencoder and used side information, we can get many variants. It is obvious that CDL, CVAE and AutoSVD++ are special cases of this framework.

Another feature representation learning approach is based on the model AutoRec. AutoRec uses the rows or columns of the rating matrix as inputs. We can easily extend the inputs to incorporate side information [26,27] and further enhance the performances.

2.3.3   *Representation learning with convolutional neural network*

CNN is capable of extracting the local and global feature representations from heterogeneous data sources. The convolution and pooling operation make it more effective

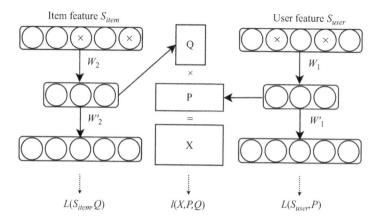

Figure 2.4   Architecture of deep collaborative filtering

to process textual, visual, audio and even video information. In many real-life applications, there are many texts, visual and multimedia sources about items such as plots, posters, screen-shots, movie (film) trailer available. Here, we introduce several works using CNN for text, image and audio representation learning.

CNN for text representation learning. Zheng *et al.* [28] presented a deep cooperative neural network (DeepCoNN) for rating prediction by jointly modelling both user and item reviews. It couples two CNNs together and maps users and items review texts into a common feature space. However, this model assumes that the review texts (of test set) are known when performing rating prediction, which limits its practical use [29]. To solve this problem, Catherine *et al.* [30] extended the DeepCoNN by adding an additional layer to represent the target user–item pair. Shen *et al.* [31] proposed using CNN to learn latent representations from text information of learning resources. Kim *et al.* [32] proposed using CNN to learn representations from documents. They advised that CNN is very suitable for document modelling as it considers the contextual information like surroundings words in articles.

CNN for image representation learning. CNN has achieved tremendous success on image analysing tasks. Recent works show that it can also be applied to image processing in recommendation scenarios. He *et al.* [33] presented an image ranking algorithm, visual Bayesian personalized ranking (VBPR), under the Bayesian pairwise scheme. VBPR adopts CNN to extract visual features from products and then integrates them into Bayesian personalized ranking (BPR)–based matrix factorization model. The predictor of VBPR takes the form

$$\hat{y}_{ui} = \mu + b_u + b_i + P_u^T Q_i + \theta_u^T(\mathbf{E}f_i) + b'^T f_i$$

here μ, b_u, b_i are global bias, user bias and item bias. P_u and Q_i are user and item latent factors. f_i is the visual features obtained with pretrained deep CNN. $\mathbf{E}$ is a transformation matrix. θ_u is the user visual factor. b' is a visual bias term used to model user's overall preferences on the visual appearance of given items.

He *et al.* [34] extended VBPR by incorporating fashion awareness but still adopted CNN to extract product images representations. Niu *et al.* [35] proposed a pairwise image recommendation model NPR with abundant contextual information. In this model, CNN is also utilized to derive visual features. Wang *et al.* [36] explored the effectiveness of using CNN to extract features from images for point-of-interest recommendation. Here, VGG16 is adopted for visual feature extraction. Chu *et al.* [37] presented a restaurants recommender system by modelling user preferences from restaurants images with CNN.

CNN for audio-representation learning. One of the most seen audio-based recommendation tasks is music recommendation. Music plays a very important role in our daily life, and personalized music recommendation services also play a key role in music vendors. Van den Oord *et al.* [38] proposed using CNN to predict latent factors from music audio as CNN allows intermediate feature sharing and operations on multiple timescales of music audio signals.

2.3.4   Representation learning with Word2Vec

The former three subsections mainly focus on feature representation learning. Most of these models are built in the same way of traditional recommendation algorithm (latent factor model). However, with the increase of users and items, it will become highly expensive to compute. Especially, in some real-world applications, the number of users (millions/billions of) is far more than the quantity of items, which will result in high sparsity to user–item matrix. Moreover, user and item interactions are not always available in some cases, for example, a portion of online shopping transactions are done without user identifications. To solve these problem, it is more feasible to learn item and user embeddings separately.

Word2Vec is a two-layer neural network that is used to generate low-dimensional word embeddings. It captures the relationship between words and their surroundings. In general, the continuous skip-gram architecture is adopted to predict the surrounding context words given the current word. Word2Vec train the neural network and consider the weight matrix as word representations.

Inspired by this word embedding model, Barkan *et al.* [20] proposed an Item2Vec approach to learn item embeddings and model the item–item relations; it treats the set of items as the sentences in word2Vec. These sets or sequences of items are generated from interaction logs such as "shopping baskets," "Click sequences." The user identification is not compulsory for constructing these sets. Afterwards, item2Vec adopts the same idea of skip-gram algorithm and learns a k dimensional dense embedding for each item (Figure 2.5). Formally, item2vec aims to maximize the following objective:

$$\frac{1}{K}\sum_{i=1}^{K}\sum_{j\neq i}^{K}\log p(item_j|item_i)$$

where K is the size of the item sets. This model does not consider the spatial/time information and do not use the window size of Word2Vec. Similar to Word2Vec, a negative sampling strategy is used to reduce the computational complexity of calculating

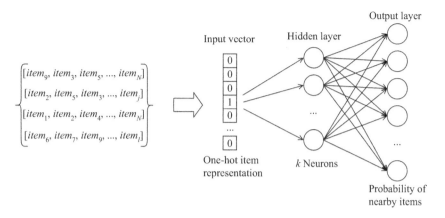

Figure 2.5   Architecture of the neural item embedding technique Item2Vec

the Softmax probability in the output layer. After training, we can get the item embeddings from weight matrix (the input-hidden weight matrix or the hidden-output weight matrix, or their combination). Afterwards, we can calculate the affinity between items from the embeddings with cosine similarity and make recommendations with item–item collaborative filtering approach.

2.4   Sequence modelling for recommender systems

In many recommendation models, the temporal dynamics are usually ignored, which means that these models cannot model the sequential patterns of user activities. Nevertheless, the time information will also reflect the change of user interests somehow. Figure 2.6 illustrates a high-level overview of sequential recommender systems [39]. Note that the user can be identifiable or anonymous; we categorize the sequential modelling recommender systems into session-based recommender system, where interactions are presented session-by-session, and sequence-aware recommender systems.

2.4.1   Session-based recommendations

Let us first consider an unappreciated problem: session-based recommender system where user identifications are not present. Here, recommendations are usually made based on the most recent interactions. The system need to predict the next action based on time-ordered logs of historical actions. Just like session in web browser, each session records an action sequence (e.g., click[$item_3, item_7, item_1, \ldots, item_9$], means that one clicked $item_3$, then $item_7$, then $item_1$,...) during that session. The sequential pattern theoretically favours sequence modelling techniques such as RNN.

GRU4REC [40] is the first session-based recommendation model using RNN. In formal, assume we have T sessions $s_m \in [s_1, s_2, \ldots, s_T]$. Each session is made up of a sequence of items $s_m = [i_{m,1}, i_{m,2}, \ldots, i_{m,n}, \ldots, i_{m,|s_m|}]$. During the training stage,

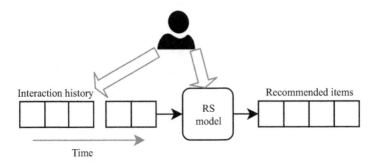

Figure 2.6   Sequential modelling for recommender systems

it takes the current item in the session as input. The output is the probability of being the next item in this session for all items.

$$h_{m,n} = GRU(i_{m,n}, h_{m,n-1}), n = 1, \ldots, |s_m|$$

where m denotes the session s_m, $i_{m,n}$ is the one-hot representation of the current item n. $h_{m,n}$ is the hidden state at step n (it iterates over all items one-by-one in the session). The output is formulated as

$$\hat{y}_{m,n} = g(h_{m,n}), n = 1, \ldots, |s_m|$$

where g is a nonlinear activation function. The output indicates the likelihood being the next item for all items. However, computing scores for all items is very computationally expensive and will lead to unstable results when the number of items is large. Thus, pairwise loss such as BPR or TOP1 is usually adopted. The BPR loss is defined as

$$\mathcal{L} = -\frac{1}{N_S} \sum_{j=1}^{N_S} \log\left(\sigma\left(\hat{y}_{m,i} - \hat{y}_{m,j}\right)\right)$$

where N_S denotes the number of negative samples sampled for each positive item (i is the next item since we know the next item in the training stage). The authors also devised an improved pairwise loss TOP1 which is formulated as

$$\mathcal{L} = \frac{1}{N_S} \sum_{j=1}^{N_S} (\hat{y}_{m,j} - \hat{y}_{m,i}) + \sigma(\hat{y}_{m,j}^2)$$

TOP1 has a regularization term $\sigma(\hat{y}_{m,j}^2)$ to force the scores of negative items to zero. Figure 2.7 gives the general structure of the GRU4REC model. In the original paper, the authors found that using one-hot encoding of the preceding item (instead of all previous items) as input and single hidden GRU layer will lead to the best performance.

There are many follow-up works which attempt to improve the performance of GRU4REC. Hidasi *et al.* [41] proposed a parallel RNN to incorporate the rich side information of items for session-based recommendation. It uses two parallel GRU to process item ID and features (e.g., images or text). The authors also explored four

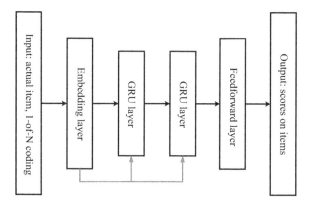

Figure 2.7   General architecture of the GRU4REC

training strategies to train the two sub-nets: simultaneous, alternating, residual and interleaving. Twardowski *et al.* [42] suggested that incorporating the contextual information will also enhance the performance. Jannach *et al.* [43] found that combining the recommendation lists of session-based neighbourhood approach with GRU4REC will lead to superior performances. Tan *et al.* [44] proposed improving the GRU4REC model with data augmentation, model pretraining and distillation of privileged information with a teacher model. Li *et al.* [45] presented a neural attentive model to further increase the accuracy by capturing user's main purpose in the session with attention mechanism. Bogina *et al.* [46] proposed considering the dwell time (the time spent on an item) and showed a huge improvement over basic GRU4REC. In some session-based recommendation scenarios, the user identification can be available, which makes it possible to generate personalized recommendations for each user and consider the user's interests and intents in the specific session [47,48].

2.4.2   *Sequence-aware recommender systems*

In sequence-aware recommender systems, both user identifications and timestamp of interactions are present and utilized. There are no sessions in this task and the datasets are usually in the form of four-tuple $\langle item, user, interaction, time \rangle$. As we mentioned in the preliminary section, we still have a user set with M users: $U = \{u_1, \ldots, u_M\}$ and an item set with N items: $I = \{i_1, \ldots, i_N\}$. In the sequence-aware recommender systems, we also have a user historical interaction sequence for each user u derived from the timestamp: $S^u = \{S_1^u, \ldots, S_t^u, \ldots, S_{|S^u|}^u\}$, where $S^u \in I$ (the exact time does not necessarily need to be taken into account). The goal of sequence-aware recommender system is to predict a list of items that the user will interact (e.g., watch, buy, click) in the near future given the historical interaction S^u. Compared with traditional collaborative filtering problem, there are mainly two differences: (1) the historical interactions are organized as sequences based on the timestamp instead of set without chronological order. (2) Train and test sets are strictly partitioned with time, so there will be no leakage of future information, while in one-class collaborative filtering, train and test sets are selected based on random split with ignoring the time information.

Similar to session-based recommender systems, RNN is the most widely investigated approach among all the deep neural network techniques for sequence-aware recommender systems. Donker *et al.* [49] proposed revising the GRU cells of RNN to incorporate the user specific vectors. They designed three variants: linear user-based GRU, rectified linear GRU and attentional user based GRU. Cui *et al.* [50] proposed a hierarchical GRU to explore the contextual information (historical interactions) for sequential recommendation. The hierarchical GRU consists of two hierarchical attention layers. The first attention layer is used to catch the user short-term interests, while the second attention layer is used to model the long-term dependencies. Liu *et al.* [51] also used the RNN to incorporate the different types of context information including external contexts (e.g., location, time, weather) and transition contexts (the sequences of historical interactions) for sequential recommendation. It is worth pointing out that attention mechanism can also be coupled with other deep neural networks such as MLP or CNN for other recommendation tasks [52,53].

Other nonrecurrent models are also viable for modelling the sequential information. Chen *et al.* [54] designed a user memory-augmented network which makes use of memory network to model user's embeddings. Tang *et al.* [55] proposed solving the sequential recommendation problem with the convolutional sequence embedding approach via modelling the user consumption history with horizontal and vertical convolutional layers.

Next basket recommendation can be considered as a special case of sequence-aware recommender system. The only difference is that the historical interactions S^u are organized in baskets. One basket consists of several items that are bought at the same time. Deep neural networks can also be applied to solve this task. For example, Yu *et al.* [56] proposed a dynamic RNN model for next basket recommendation. It tries to simultaneously integrate dynamic representations and global sequential behaviours. Wan *et al.* [57] proposed using MLP to model the interactions between users and their bought baskets.

Sequence modelling in recommendation has attracted much attention specially in recent years when deep neural networks become the jack of all trades. Nevertheless, most research works are scattered, and there is no common understanding and well-established evaluation strategies. More works are expected to well shape this research area.

2.5   Deep hybrid models for recommender systems

We have introduced recommendation models based on several different neural networks. These techniques have different advantages and limitations. For example, CNN performs well in image processing; RNN is good at capturing the sequential patterns of time series data. Naturally, we could integrate these techniques to form a combined model which enjoys all the advantages. Luckily, the flexible structure of deep neural networks makes it easy to integrate several techniques together to better model the complex relations and characteristics of real-world datasets. Here, we briefly reviewed

Table 2.1 Deep hybrid models with different deep neural networks. ✓ Means that the network is present in the corresponding

Models	MLP	Autoencoder	ConvolutionalNN	RecurrentNN
Zhang *et al.* [58]		✓	✓	
Li *et al.* [59]	✓			✓
Ni *et al.* [60]	✓			✓
Lei *et al.* [61]	✓	✓		
Zhang *et al.* [62]			✓	✓
Wang *et al.* [63]		✓		✓
Rawat *et al.* [64]	✓		✓	
Lee *et al.* [65]			✓	✓
Zhang *et al.* [66]	✓		✓	

some representative works. Table 2.1 illustrates several research studies who exploit the combinations of deep neural networks for recommendation.

With these combinations, the model can usually achieve some goals that a single model cannot achieve. For example, Zhang *et al.* [58] adopted the stacked convolutional autoencoders (combination of autoencoder and CNN) to extract feature representations from images and feed them into the collaborative filtering framework. Li *et al.* [59] adopted MLP to model the user–item interaction and RNN to generate reviews to explain the recommendations. Similar idea can also be found from a simultaneous work [60]. Lei *et al.* [61] proposed an image recommendation model by using CNN to learn image representations and MLP to learn user embeddings. Wang *et al.* [63] designed a recurrent autoencoder to learn the sequential patterns from item side information. Rawat *et al.* [64] proposed an image tag recommendation system by utilizing CNN to learn image representations and MLP to model user context information. Lee *et al.* [65] combined RNN with CNN for quote recommendations where CNN is used to learn high-level representations from sentences, and RNN is used to model the sequential information of dialogues. Zhang *et al.* [66] proposed a joint representation learning approach using CNN to learn representations from images and MLP to learn embeddings from rating data. Many combinations could be inverted for various application fields. There is no standard rule for how to combine them, but each neural network is integrated for specific purpose.

2.6 Advanced topics

In this section, we will introduce several advanced recommendation techniques based on deep neural networks.

2.6.1 Metric learning

Recently, metric learning has been successfully applied to recommendation task [67–69]. Metric learning models the user–item closeness with Euclidean distance

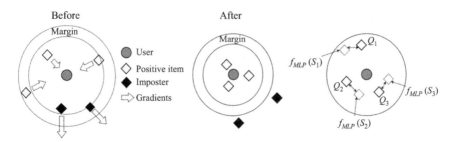

Figure 2.8   Architecture of collaborative metric learning

instead of dot product. The dot product does not satisfy the triangle inequality, which might greatly limit its expressiveness and feasibility. Hsieh *et al.* [67] first introduced the idea of large margin nearest neighbour to collaborative filtering task and designed the collaborative metric learning (Figure 2.8). This model is trained with weighted approximate-rank pairwise loss (WARP) by pushing the items that the user dislikes away from items that she likes. The authors further improved this model by incorporating item side information with MLP. The incorporation approach is similar to the idea of deep collaborative framework. The complete objective function is defined as follows:

$$\mathscr{L} = \sum_{(u,i)\in\mathscr{O}} \sum_{(u,k)\in\mathscr{O}^-} w_{ij}[m + d(u,i)^2 - d(u,k)^2]_+ + \lambda_f \sum_{j\in I} \| f_{MLP}(s_j) - v_j \|^2$$

where w_{ij} is precomputed weight of WARP loss (the interested readers are referred [70]). d is the Euclidean distance. The second term is used to make the learned embeddings for items close to its feature representation extracted with MLP. λ_f is used to control the weight of feature loss.

Tay *et al.* [71] argued that the distance function of CML is an ill-posed algebraic system when there are a large number of interactions. To better model the distances, they proposed incorporating the relation vectors into the distance function.

$$d(u,i) = \|P_u + r - Q_i\|_2$$

The relation vector r is learned via the neural attentive memory module from the user and item embeddings. This model can also be optimized with hinge loss.

2.6.2   Generative adversarial networks

Generative adversary network (GAN) [72] is a generative model which has been successfully applied to image generation and text generation. GAN is made up of two components: discriminator and generator. The generator generates new data instances, while the discriminator evaluates the data authenticity. The whole network is trained by playing a minmax game between discriminator and generator.

Recent work IRGAN [73] proposed applying the idea of GAN to the information retrieval tasks including web search, question answering and recommendation. In information retrieval, there are two schools of thinking: generative retrieval and discriminative retrieval. They happen to correspond to the generator and discriminator of GAN. Thus, we could let the generative retrieval model and discriminative retrieval model to compete with each other and finally find an equilibrium. The performance will also be enhanced via the minmax game.

2.6.3   Neural autoregressive distribution estimator

Neural autoregressive distribution estimator (NADE) is a tractable distribution and density estimator. Recently, NADE has been successfully applied to recommendation tasks. For example, Zheng *et al.* [74] proposed using NADE to model the distribution of user ratings for rating prediction. In the follow-up work [75], they extended it to top-N recommendations on implicit feedback. These models usually have a user-based and an item-based variants, which means that each variant can only capture either the user–user or item–item correlations. To exploit both correlations, Du *et al.* [76] proposed a user–item co-autoregressive recommendation model to make use of the two aspects of information for further improvement.

2.7   Future challenges and conclusion

In this book chapter, we introduced the deep neural networks based recommender systems in details. As seen from aforementioned works, the collisions between deep neural networks and recommender systems have sparked many new ideas for solving the recommendation problems in various domains.

Despite the effectiveness and popularity of deep neural network based recommendation models, there are still many open-research issues that remain to be solved. Moreover, the incorporation of deep neural networks and the emergence of big data also pose some interesting new challenges for this research area.

- Hyper-parameters study. Neural network heavily relies on hyper-parameter tuning, such as number of hidden layers, activation functions, number of neurons of each layers. The increase of hyper-parameters has aggravated the difficulty of parameter-selection process and makes it harder to find the optimal solutions. What's worse, the hyper-parameters settings of deep neural networks are usually not transferable, that is, a set of hyper-parameters which work well on one datasets might not lead to satisfying results on other datasets.
- Data volume and model complexity. In the big data era, the increase number of users and items has hindered the use of many models proposed in the academia. In many real world applications, millions and even billions of users and items are available, which makes it very hard to employ those proposed models. Especially, the number of users is usually very large, which greatly makes personalized recommendation become a tough task. The introduced work item2vec has shed some light for embedding learning on big data.
- Modelling multimedia data-sources. Deep neural networks have achieved tremendous success on multimedia data-sources such as images, audio and video. However, a vast majority of deep learning based recommendation model still

focus upon images related recommendations. Few works attempt to model the audio and video signals directly. Recommender systems might get a better understanding of the content from the video frames instead of mining the textual or visual descriptors.

There are many novel neural networks proposed each year, and some of them might be suitable for solving some specific recommendation problems. Deep neural networks bring many opportunities for recommender systems as well as some challenges. Some of the recommendation tasks are still in their early stage, and more advanced models are expected.

References

[1]   Zhang S, Yao L, Sun A. Deep Learning Based Recommender System: A Survey and New Perspectives. arXiv preprint arXiv:1707.07435. 2017.

[2]   Goodfellow I, Bengio Y, Courville A, *et al.* Deep learning. vol. 1. Cambridge: MIT Press; 2016.

[3]   Doersch C. Tutorial on Variational Autoencoders. arXiv preprint arXiv: 1606.05908. 2016.

[4]   Rifai S, Vincent P, Muller X, *et al.* Contractive auto-encoders: Explicit invariance during feature extraction. In: Proceedings of the 28th International Conference on International Conference on Machine Learning. Omnipress; 2011. p. 833–840.

[5]   Chen M, Xu Z, Weinberger KQ, *et al.* Marginalized denoising autoencoders for domain adaptation. In: Proceedings of the 29th International Conference on International Conference on Machine Learning. ICML'12. USA: Omnipress; 2012. p. 1627–1634. Available from: http://dl.acm.org/citation. cfm?id=3042573.3042781.

[6]   Alom MZ, Taha TM, Yakopcic C, *et al.* The History Began from AlexNet: A Comprehensive Survey on Deep Learning Approaches. arXiv preprint arXiv:1803.01164. 2018.

[7]   Dziugaite GK, Roy DM. Neural Network Matrix Factorization. arXiv preprint arXiv:1511.06443. 2015.

[8]   He X, Liao L, Zhang H, *et al.* Neural collaborative filtering. In: Proceedings of the 26th International Conference on World Wide Web. International World Wide Web Conferences Steering Committee; 2017. p. 173–182.

[9]   He X, Chua TS. Neural factorization machines for sparse predictive analytics. In: Proceedings of the 40th International ACM SIGIR Conference on Research and Development in Information Retrieval. ACM; 2017. p. 355–364.

[10] Zhang S, Yao L, Sun A, *et al.* NeuRec: On Nonlinear Transformation for Personalized Ranking. In: Proceedings of the 27th International Joint Conference on Artificial Intelligence. AAAI Press; 2018. p. 3669–3675.

[11] Ning X, Karypis G. SLIM: Sparse linear methods for top-n recommender systems. In: 2011 11th IEEE International Conference on Data Mining. IEEE; 2011. p. 497–506.

[12] Sedhain S, Menon AK, Sanner S, *et al*. AutoRec: Autoencoders meet collaborative filtering. In: Proceedings of the 24th International Conference on World Wide Web. ACM; 2015. p. 111–112.

[13] Kuchaiev O, Ginsburg B. Training Deep AutoEncoders for Collaborative Filtering. arXiv preprint arXiv:1708.01715. 2017.

[14] Wu Y, DuBois C, Zheng AX, *et al*. Collaborative denoising auto-encoders for top-n recommender systems. In: Proceedings of the Ninth ACM International Conference on Web Search and Data Mining. ACM; 2016. p. 153–162.

[15] Guo H, Tang R, Ye Y, *et al*. DeepFM: A factorization-machine based neural network for CTR prediction. In: Proceedings of the 26th International Joint Conference on Artificial Intelligence. IJCAI'17. AAAI Press; 2017. p. 1725–1731. Available from: http://dl.acm.org/citation.cfm?id=3172077.3172127.

[16] LeCun Y, Bengio Y, Hinton G. Deep learning. Nature. 2015;521(7553):436.

[17] Covington P, Adams J, Sargin E. Deep neural networks for YouTube recommendations. In: Proceedings of the 10th ACM Conference on Recommender Systems. ACM; 2016. p. 191–198.

[18] Cheng HT, Koc L, Harmsen J, *et al*. Wide & deep learning for recommender systems. In: Proceedings of the 1st Workshop on Deep Learning for Recommender Systems. ACM; 2016. p. 7–10.

[19] Elkahky AM, Song Y, He X. A multi-view deep learning approach for cross domain user modeling in recommendation systems. In: Proceedings of the 24th International Conference on World Wide Web. International World Wide Web Conferences Steering Committee; 2015. p. 278–288.

[20] Barkan O, Koenigstein N. Item2vec: Neural item embedding for collaborative filtering. In: Machine Learning for Signal Processing (MLSP), 2016 IEEE 26th International Workshop on. IEEE; 2016. p. 1–6.

[21] Zhang S, Yao L, Ning X, *et al*. Coupled linear and deep nonlinear method for Meetup service recommendation. In: International Conference on Web Services. Springer; 2018. p. 246–260.

[22] Wang H, Wang N, Yeung DY. Collaborative deep learning for recommender systems. In: Proceedings of the 21th ACM SIGKDD International Conference on Knowledge Discovery and Data Mining. ACM; 2015. p. 1235–1244.

[23] Li X, She J. Collaborative variational autoencoder for recommender systems. In: Proceedings of the 23rd ACM SIGKDD International Conference on Knowledge Discovery and Data Mining. ACM; 2017. p. 305–314.

[24] Li S, Kawale J, Fu Y. Deep collaborative filtering via marginalized denoising auto-encoder. In: Proceedings of the 24th ACM International on Conference on Information and Knowledge Management. ACM; 2015. p. 811–820.

[25] Zhang S, Yao L, Xu X. AutoSVD++: An efficient hybrid collaborative filtering model via contractive auto-encoders. In: Proceedings of the 40th International ACM SIGIR Conference on Research and Development in Information Retrieval. SIGIR'17. New York, NY, USA: ACM; 2017. p. 957–960. Available from: http://doi.acm.org/10.1145/3077136.3080689.

[26] Strub F, Gaudel R, Mary J. Hybrid recommender system based on autoencoders. In: Proccedings of the 1st Workshop on Deep Learning for

Recommender Systems. DLRS 2016. New York, NY, USA: ACM; 2016. p. 11–16. Available from: http://doi.acm.org/10.1145/2988450.2988456.

[27]   Zhang S, Yao L, Xu X, *et al.* Hybrid collaborative recommendation via semi-AutoEncoder. In: Liu D, Xie S, Li Y, *et al.*, editors. Neural information processing. Cham: Springer International Publishing; 2017. p. 185–193.

[28]   Zheng L, Noroozi V, Yu PS. Joint deep modeling of users and items using reviews for recommendation. In: Proceedings of the Tenth ACM International Conference on Web Search and Data Mining. ACM; 2017. p. 425–434.

[29]   Catherine R, Cohen W. TransNets: Learning to transform for recommendation. In: Proceedings of the Eleventh ACM Conference on Recommender Systems. ACM; 2017. p. 288–296.

[30]   Catherine R, Cohen W. TransNets: Learning to transform for recommendation. In: Proceedings of the Eleventh ACM Conference on Recommender Systems. RecSys'17. New York, NY, USA: ACM; 2017. p. 288–296. Available from: http://doi.acm.org/10.1145/3109859.3109878.

[31]   Shen X, Yi B, Zhang Z, *et al.* Automatic recommendation technology for learning resources with convolutional neural network. In: Educational Technology (ISET), 2016 International Symposium on. IEEE; 2016. p. 30–34.

[32]   Kim D, Park C, Oh J, *et al.* Convolutional matrix factorization for document context-aware recommendation. In: Proceedings of the 10th ACM Conference on Recommender Systems. ACM; 2016. p. 233–240.

[33]   He R, McAuley J. VBPR: Visual Bayesian Personalized Ranking from implicit feedback. In: Proceedings of the Thirtieth AAAI Conference on Artificial Intelligence. AAAI'16. AAAI Press; 2016. p. 144–150. Available from: http://dl.acm.org/citation.cfm?id=3015812.3015834.

[34]   He R, McAuley J. Ups and downs: Modeling the visual evolution of fashion trends with one-class collaborative filtering. In: Proceedings of the 25th International Conference on World Wide Web. WWW'16. Republic and Canton of Geneva, Switzerland: International World Wide Web Conferences Steering Committee; 2016. p. 507–517. Available from: https://doi.org/10.1145/2872427.2883037.

[35]   Niu W, Caverlee J, Lu H. Neural personalized ranking for image recommendation. In: Proceedings of the Eleventh ACM International Conference on Web Search and Data Mining. WSDM'18. New York, NY, USA: ACM; 2018. p. 423–431. Available from: http://doi.acm.org/10.1145/3159652.3159728.

[36]   Wang S, Wang Y, Tang J, *et al.* What your images reveal: Exploiting visual contents for point-of-interest recommendation. In: Proceedings of the 26th International Conference on World Wide Web. International World Wide Web Conferences Steering Committee; 2017. p. 391–400.

[37]   Chu WT, Tsai YL. A hybrid recommendation system considering visual information for predicting favorite restaurants. World Wide Web. 2017;20(6):1313–1331. Available from: https://doi.org/10.1007/s11280-017-0437-1.

[38]   Van den Oord A, Dieleman S, Schrauwen B. Deep content-based music recommendation. In: Advances in Neural Information Processing Systems; 2013. p. 2643–2651.

[39] Quadrana M, Cremonesi P, Jannach D. Sequence-Aware Recommender Systems. ACM Computing Surveys. vol. 51; 2018. p. 66:1–66:36. Available from: http://doi.acm.org/10.1145/3190616.

[40] Hidasi B, Karatzoglou A, Baltrunas L, *et al.* Session-based Recommendations with Recurrent Neural Networks. arXiv preprint arXiv:1511.06939. 2015.

[41] Hidasi B, Quadrana M, Karatzoglou A, *et al.* Parallel recurrent neural network architectures for feature-rich session-based recommendations. In: Proceedings of the 10th ACM Conference on Recommender Systems. RecSys'16. New York, NY, USA: ACM; 2016. p. 241–248. Available from: http://doi.acm.org/10.1145/2959100.2959167.

[42] Twardowski B. Modelling contextual information in session-aware recommender systems with neural networks. In: Proceedings of the 10th ACM Conference on Recommender Systems. ACM; 2016. p. 273–276.

[43] Jannach D, Ludewig M. When recurrent neural networks meet the neighborhood for session-based recommendation. In: Proceedings of the Eleventh ACM Conference on Recommender Systems. RecSys'17. New York, NY, USA: ACM; 2017. p. 306–310. Available from: http://doi.acm.org/10.1145/3109859.3109872.

[44] Tan YK, Xu X, Liu Y. Improved recurrent neural networks for session-based recommendations. In: Proceedings of the 1st Workshop on Deep Learning for Recommender Systems. ACM; 2016. p. 17–22.

[45] Li J, Ren P, Chen Z, *et al.* Neural attentive session-based recommendation. In: Proceedings of the 2017 ACM on Conference on Information and Knowledge Management. ACM; 2017. p. 1419–1428.

[46] Bogina V, Kuflik T. Incorporating dwell time in session-based recommendations with recurrent neural networks. In: CEUR Workshop Proceedings. vol. 1922; 2017. p. 57–59.

[47] Quadrana M, Karatzoglou A, Hidasi B, *et al.* Personalizing session-based recommendations with hierarchical recurrent neural networks. In: Proceedings of the Eleventh ACM Conference on Recommender Systems. ACM; 2017. p. 130–137.

[48] Ruocco M, Skrede OSL, Langseth H. Inter-session modeling for session-based recommendation. In: Proceedings of the 2nd Workshop on Deep Learning for Recommender Systems. DLRS 2017. New York, NY, USA: ACM; 2017. p. 24–31. Available from: http://doi.acm.org/10.1145/3125486.3125491.

[49] Donkers T, Loepp B, Ziegler J. Sequential user-based recurrent neural network recommendations. In: Proceedings of the Eleventh ACM Conference on Recommender Systems. RecSys'17. New York, NY, USA: ACM; 2017. p. 152–160. Available from: http://doi.acm.org/10.1145/3109859.3109877.

[50] Cui Q, Wu S, Huang Y, *et al.* A Hierarchical Contextual Attention-based GRU Network for Sequential Recommendation. arXiv preprint arXiv:1711.05114. 2017.

[51] Liu Q, Wu S, Wang D, *et al.* Context-aware sequential recommendation. In: Data Mining (ICDM), 2016 IEEE 16th International Conference on. IEEE; 2016. p. 1053–1058.

[52]   Tay Y, Tuan LA, Hui SC. Multi-Pointer Co-Attention Networks for Recommendation. In: Proceedings of the 24th ACM SIGKDD International Conference on Knowledge Discovery & Data Mining. ACM; 2018. p. 2309–2318.

[53]   Tay Y, Tuan LA, Hui SC. CoupleNet: Paying Attention to Couples with Coupled Attention for Relationship Recommendation. In: Twelfth International AAAI Conference on Web and Social Media; 2018.

[54]   Chen X, Xu H, Zhang Y, *et al.* Sequential recommendation with user memory networks. In: Proceedings of the Eleventh ACM International Conference on Web Search and Data Mining. ACM; 2018. p. 108–116.

[55]   Tang J, Wang K. Personalized top-N sequential recommendation via convolutional sequence embedding. In: Proceedings of the Eleventh ACM International Conference on Web Search and Data Mining. WSDM'18. New York, NY, USA: ACM; 2018. p. 565–573. Available from: http://doi.acm.org/10.1145/3159652.3159656.

[56]   Yu F, Liu Q, Wu S, *et al.* A dynamic recurrent model for next basket recommendation. In: Proceedings of the 39th International ACM SIGIR Conference on Research and Development in Information Retrieval. ACM; 2016. p. 729–732.

[57]   Wan S, Lan Y, Wang P, *et al.* Next basket recommendation with neural networks. In: RecSys Posters; 2015.

[58]   Zhang F, Yuan NJ, Lian D, *et al.* Collaborative knowledge base embedding for recommender systems. In: Proceedings of the 22nd ACM SIGKDD International Conference on Knowledge Discovery and Data Mining. ACM; 2016. p. 353–362.

[59]   Li P, Wang Z, Ren Z, *et al.* Neural rating regression with abstractive tips generation for recommendation. In: Proceedings of the 40th International ACM SIGIR Conference on Research and Development in Information Retrieval. ACM; 2017. p. 345–354.

[60]   Ni J, Lipton ZC, Vikram S, *et al.* Estimating reactions and recommending products with generative models of reviews. In: Proceedings of the Eighth International Joint Conference on Natural Language Processing (Volume 1: Long Papers). vol. 1; 2017. p. 783–791.

[61]   Lei C, Liu D, Li W, *et al.* Comparative deep learning of hybrid representations for image recommendations. In: Proceedings of the IEEE Conference on Computer Vision and Pattern Recognition; 2016. p. 2545–2553.

[62]   Zhang Q, Huang H, Huang X, Gong Y, Wang J. Hashtag recommendation for multimodal microblog using co-attention network. In: Proceedings of the Twenty-Sixth International Joint Conference on Artificial. AAAI Press; 2017. p. 3420–3426. Available from: https://doi.org/10.24963/ijcai.2017/478.

[63]   Wang H, Xingjian S, Yeung DY. Collaborative recurrent autoencoder: Recommend while learning to fill in the blanks. In: Advances in Neural Information Processing Systems; 2016. p. 415–423.

[64]   Rawat YS, Kankanhalli MS. ConTagNet: Exploiting user context for image tag recommendation. In: Proceedings of the 2016 ACM on Multimedia

Conference. MM'16. New York, NY, USA: ACM; 2016. p. 1102–1106. Available from: http://doi.acm.org/10.1145/2964284.2984068.

[65] Lee H, Ahn Y, Lee H, *et al.* Quote recommendation in dialogue using deep neural network. In: Proceedings of the 39th International ACM SIGIR Conference on Research and Development in Information Retrieval. ACM; 2016. p. 957–960.

[66] Zhang Y, Ai Q, Chen X, *et al.* Joint representation learning for top-N recommendation with heterogeneous information sources. In: Proceedings of the 2017 ACM on Conference on Information and Knowledge Management. CIKM'17. New York, NY, USA: ACM; 2017. p. 1449–1458. Available from: http://doi.acm.org/10.1145/3132847.3132892.

[67] Hsieh CK, Yang L, Cui Y, *et al.* Collaborative metric learning. In: Proceedings of the 26th International Conference on World Wide Web. International World Wide Web Conferences Steering Committee; 2017. p. 193–201.

[68] Tay Y, Luu AT, Hui SC. Latent relational metric learning via memory-based attention for collaborative ranking. In: Proceedings of the 2018 World Wide Web Conference on World Wide Web. International World Wide Web Conferences Steering Committee; 2018. p. 729–739.

[69] Zhang S, Yao L, Tay Y, *et al.* Metric Factorization: Recommendation beyond Matrix Factorization. arXiv preprint arXiv:1802.04606. 2018.

[70] Weston J, Bengio S, Usunier N. WSABIE: Scaling up to large vocabulary image annotation. In: IJCAI. vol. 11; 2011. p. 2764–2770.

[71] Tay Y, Anh Tuan L, Hui SC. Latent relational metric learning via memory-based attention for collaborative ranking. In: Proceedings of the 2018 World Wide Web Conference on World Wide Web. WWW'18. Republic and Canton of Geneva, Switzerland: International World Wide Web Conferences Steering Committee; 2018. p. 729–739. Available from: https://doi.org/10.1145/3178876.3186154.

[72] Goodfellow I, Pouget-Abadie J, Mirza M, *et al.* Generative adversarial nets. In: Advances in Neural Information Processing Systems; 2014. p. 2672–2680.

[73] Wang J, Yu L, Zhang W, *et al.* IRGAN: A minimax game for unifying generative and discriminative information retrieval models. In: Proceedings of the 40th International ACM SIGIR Conference on Research and Development in Information Retrieval. SIGIR'17. New York, NY, USA: ACM; 2017. p. 515–524. Available from: http://doi.acm.org/10.1145/3077136.3080786.

[74] Zheng Y, Tang B, Ding W, *et al.* A Neural Autoregressive Approach to Collaborative Filtering. In: Proceedings of the 33rd International Conference on International Conference on Machine Learning. vol. 48; 2016. p. 764–773.

[75] Zheng Y, Liu C, Tang B, *et al.* Neural autoregressive collaborative filtering for implicit feedback. In: Proceedings of the 1st Workshop on Deep Learning for Recommender Systems. DLRS 2016. New York, NY, USA: ACM; 2016. p. 2–6. Available from: http://doi.acm.org/10.1145/2988450.2988453.

[76] Du C, Li C, Zheng Y, *et al.* Collaborative Filtering with User–Item Co-Autoregressive Models. In: Thirty-Second AAAI Conference on Artificial Intelligence; 2018.

Chapter 3

Cold-start solutions for recommendation systems

Farshad Bakhshandegan Moghaddam[1] and Mehdi Elahi[2]

Recommendation systems are essential tools to overcome the choice overload problem by suggesting items of interest to users. However, they suffer from a major challenge which is the so-called cold-start problem. The cold-start problem typically happens when the system does not have any form of data on new users and on new items. In this chapter, we describe the cold-start problem in recommendation systems. We mainly focus on collaborative filtering systems which are the most popular approaches to build recommender systems and have been successfully employed in many real-world applications. Moreover, we discuss multiple scenarios that cold start may happen in these systems and explain different solutions for them.

3.1 Introduction

One of the challenges in everyday life is to make the right decision when purchasing a product. This challenge has been worsen due to the growing *volume, variety* and *velocity* of data associated with products.[1] Although the massive increase in the number of choices has been an opportunity for consumers to choose the most interesting products, however, this has led to the problem of *choice overload*, i.e., the problem of having unlimited number of choices, especially when they do not differ significantly from each other [1,2].

Recommender systems (RSs) can mitigate this problem by choosing and suggesting a short list of items for users, based on their personal needs and constraints [3–6]. These systems, that have been primarily developed and integrated into the eCommerce websites, have shown to be effective in supporting users when making decision. However, their application has gone far beyond that as now they have been extensively exploited almost anywhere, from social networks to intelligent personal assistants. Their effectiveness has been proved whenever an enhanced decision support is required in assisting users during their interaction with a system. Such an enhanced support enables the users to expand their experience, e.g., by receiving

---

[1] Institute AIFB, Karlsruhe Institute of Technology, Germany
[2] Faculty of Computer Science, Free University of Bozen-Bolzano, Italy
[1] https://www.zdnet.com/article/volume-velocity-and-variety-understanding-the-three-vs-of-big-data/

serendipitous suggestions from a less-explored part of item catalog and allowing the users to experience surprising items that might not be known to them.

For that aim, RSs carefully observe the users' behaviors and collect different forms of user preferences, in order to understand the personal tastes of users [7–9]. These systems then attempt to filter a long list of items and choose a shortlist of suggestions. This capability has made them to become an essential component of any type of commercial information systems that needs to deal with a large catalog of items [10].

3.1.1 Recommendation approaches

From the mid-1990s when early works on RSs [4,11] have been emerged, till now, variety of recommendation approaches have been proposed. These various approaches still share commonalities, based on their underlying algorithms, that makes it possible to classify them into a number of classes [9,10,12,13]. We can briefly describe each of these classes based on the definitions in the literature.

One of the most popular class of RSs is **collaborative filtering (CF)** [14,15] which analyzes a set of known ratings and predicts the unknown ratings, expected to be given to the items by the users. A CF system, then, recommends to a user the items with the highest predicted ratings. **Content-based (CB)** [16,17] class of RSs analyze the content of the items and recommends items based on their associated content attributes (features). **Utility-based** [18,19] class of RSs predicts the utility scores of users corresponding to the different items (as choice options). This is done by taking into account the needs and constrains of each user when computing the utility scores. The items with the highest predicted utility scores are recommended to the users. **Demographic** [20,21] class of RSs considers the demographic data associated with the users and builds recommendations by taking into account the particular demographic group a user may belong to. **Knowledge-based** [22,23] class of RSs adopts a specific reasoning process which begins by formulating the users' needs and preferences and ends with identifying whether or not an item matches the specific criteria for a target user. **Hybrid** [24,25] class of RSs combines a number of different approaches from a single or multiple class(es) of RSs in order to cope with the limitations of each single approach.

Regardless of the class of the implemented recommendation approach, a prerequisite to any RS is the availability of the data that may indicate the needs and preferences of the users. Indeed, in spite of the fact that the algorithm performance plays an important role, however, the quality of recommendations based on any class of RSs may become poor if no or low quality data has been provided by users [26,27]. This is a situation known as *cold-start* problem, which typically happens when a new user registers to the system and no preference data is available for that user. This is a major problem in RSs specially with large number of users.

In this chapter, we address the cold-start problem in RS. We mainly focus on CF systems as they are very popular type of the real-world RSs. We describe different scenarios that cold start may happen in these systems and survey the solutions for the problem that have been proposed by the literature.

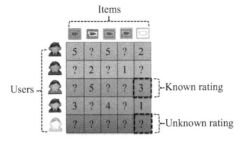

Figure 3.1   Rating matrix: rows represent users and columns represent items. The entries of the matrix contain the "known" ratings, users have provided to items. The "unknown" ratings are represented with question marks

3.2   Collaborative filtering

CF-based RSs exploit a dataset of user feedbacks, mainly in the form of *ratings*, that have been provided by a network of users to a catalog of items. The dataset is typically represented as matrix where rows represent users and columns represent items (see Figure 3.1). CF systems then use this dataset and predict which items could be interesting to a target user [14,15]. For that, these systems mine patterns of relationships and similarities among the users and use them to learn predictive models that can generate recommendations.

Such predictions are computed for every unknown rating for a pair of user–item within the rating matrix. This results in a rank list of items, computed for a target user, where items are sorted accordingly to their predicted ratings. CF system selects a short list of items with the highest predicted ratings and recommends it to the target user.

While RSs based on CF approach have presented promising performance; however, they can largely suffer from cold-start problem due to the lack of data for certain users or certain items [12,28]. The main form of cold-start problem is the *new user* problem which occurs when a new user registers to the system and requests to receive recommendations before she has provided any rating to any item (see Figure 3.2). Another type of cold start is the *new item* problem which occurs when a new item is added to the item catalog, and none of the users has yet rated that new item (see Figure 3.2). The *sparsity* of the data can be also considered as relevant issue to the cold-start problem. In severe cases of data sparsity, the performance of the CF systems can be seriously damaged leading to a very poor quality of recommendation. This is a situation where the number of *known* ratings is extremely smaller than the number of *unknown* ratings, and the system has to compute predictions for the unknown ratings [12,29].

The remaining sections discuss a set of solutions that have been proposed by the literature, in addressing the cold-start problem.

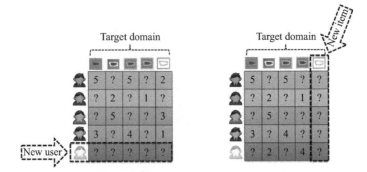

Figure 3.2   Illustration of cold-start problem in recommender systems: new user problem (left) and new item problem (right)

3.3   Active learning in recommender systems

One of the main solutions to the cold-start problem in RSs is *active learning*. Generally, active learning is part of a broader research topic of *machine learning*, a well-known research area which focuses on design and development of novel algorithms in solving a large variety of tasks such as regression and classification tasks [30–33]. These algorithms typically need big datasets to learn patterns behind data and build models that can be used to predict unprecedented data [34]. This is a form of learning process that is called *passive learning* [35]. However, the availability of such big data cannot be always presumed as there are realistic cases where the data is (e.g.) partially available. In such cases, the system may not be able to achieve a certain level of accuracy unless more data is collected. While this could be beneficial, however, collecting more data can be an expensive process and may require extensive human involvement. Therefore, the system has to focus on collecting only high-quality data by carefully controlling the data collection process. This will help the system to minimize the cost of data collection while maximizing the expected benefit. This form of learning process is called *active learning* [27,35,36].

In comparison to the passive learning, there can be two big advantageous, brought by the active learning. The first advantage is that, in active learning, the system does not need to have access to the entire data and instead, it can iteratively obtain further data. The second advantage is that, active learning allows the system to carefully analyze the available data and decide which data to be collected. This process will disallow the noisy data to be collected and may improve the quality of the input data.

In the context of RSs, active learning can bring similar advantageous, and hence, it can be a natural solution to the cold-start problem. This can be the reason why the initial interaction of new users with RSs begins with active learning where the system requests the new users to provide ratings for a set of *selected* items [37]. This allows the system to obtain a minimum amount of data that can describe the preference of a new user (see Figure 3.3). Hence, an active learner follows a set of defined rules that is used to automatically regulate the *item selection* process. By applying these rules,

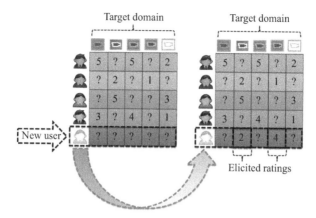

Figure 3.3   *Active learning in recommender systems: a new user registers to the system, where active learner proposes her to rate a selection of items, and elicits the ratings*

the system *elicits* ratings from the (new) users and use them to build or update their profiles. The very precise definition for selecting items to propose to a user to rate is called active learning *strategy* [8,27,38,39].

While there has been a broad range of active learning strategies, proposed in the literature, however, according to [27,37], these strategies can be classified into few classes, listed below:

- **Uncertainty reduction** [8,38] strategies try to select items with more diverse ratings as the system is less certain about them. Suppose that a lot of users have given high ratings to an item, while many users have given low ratings to the same item. In such a case, it will be difficult for the system to predict whether or not to recommend that item. Conversely, an item that has received low ratings from nearly all users can be easily excluded from the recommendation. Hence, collecting the ratings of items with diverse ratings may be very informative and may decrease the uncertainty of the system when computing predictions [8,38].
- **Error reduction** [27,39] strategies attempt to select items that collecting their ratings may directly reduce the prediction error. This is due to the fact that there are items with highly diverse ratings where the ratings are poorly correlated with the ratings of the other items (e.g., *Napoleon Dynamite* movie in *Netflix* dataset) [39]. While selection of such items for active learning may not contribute to the predictive power of the system, still uncertainty reduction strategies may select them for active learning. Instead, error reduction strategies may ignore these items and focus more on items with ratings that can positively improve the prediction accuracy [27].
- **User adaptation** [38,40] strategies try to personalize the active learning process to the particular characteristics of the users by selecting and proposing different items for different users to rate. This is due to the fact that different users may have different knowledge, familiarity and preferences toward different category

of items, and hence, it is not very convenient to select a similar set of items for these different types of users. Accordingly, taking into account such differences among users in active learning process could lead to collecting higher quality and quantity of ratings.

- **Acquisition probability** [27,41] strategies try to maximize the chance that a user can rate an item and hence they select items that are more likely to be known by a user. Suppose that a user has not been in a restaurant while the system requests her to rate that restaurant. The rating of that user may not be so informative and instead may increase the level of noise within the data. Hence, it is crucial for the active learner to take into account the likelihood that a user is familiar with an item when requesting her to rate the same.

- **Decision-tree-based** [38,42] strategies adopt decision tree algorithms in order to identify informative items to be selected for active learning. Each node of such decision tree contains a candidate item to be proposed to a new user to rate. Therefore, the node somehow represents a group of like-minded users who has rated that candidate item similarly. Accordingly, each node splits the users into three groups, i.e., those who have given that candidate item (i) high rating, (ii) low ratings or (iii) no rating. The active learner builds this decision tree based on an optimization term that leads to the reduction of the prediction error. Once the decision tree is built, the system can use it to iteratively select items to propose to a new user, hence traversing from root node of the tree to the leaf nodes, depending on the ratings provided by the user.

- **Prediction-based** [36,43] strategies build prediction models that are used to decide which items to be selected for active learning. The prediction-based strategies rank items according to the predicted ratings and select the top items with highest predicted ratings. The adopted predictive models may vary from *probabilistic* models [27,40,44] to *matrix factorization* models [45,46]. An advantageous of these strategies is that they select items that are likely to be interesting for users, and hence, the users are not bothered during the active learning process. Indeed, the users may even enjoy checking and rating the selected items. It is also highly probable that the proposed items are familiar to the users, and hence, the chance to actually obtain the ratings by these strategies is high.

- **Hybrid** [47,48] strategies combine a number of individual strategies in order to take advantages of multiple ones. This may allow the hybrid strategies to simultaneously optimize different metrics, such as *accuracy*, *diversity* and *user satisfaction*. Moreover, there are situations that an individual strategy may fail to properly select items to propose to a target user to rate. However, in such particular situations, hybridizing the individual strategies can tackle the problem and lead to improving the performance of the individual strategies.

3.4   Semantic-based recommender systems

The traditional solutions for the cold-start problem are based on the popular CB filtering approaches. These approaches build user profiles by associating their preferences

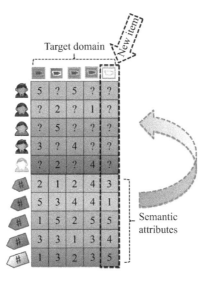

*Figure 3.4   Recommendation based on semantic attributes, in addressing the new
item problem as part of cold-start problem*

with the semantic attributes of the item content [6,49–53]. Exploiting the content of
the items has been used to address the new item problem. When a new item is added
to the catalog, the item profile is built by various types of semantic attributes (see
Figure 3.4). The recommender can use such profiles to compute similarity or built
machine-learning models to generate relevant recommendations.

In early RSs, semantic attributes were based on less-structured form of semantic
content such as item category or item description. These attributes are exploited by
the RSs to establish *vector space model* [17], where, each item is represented by a
multidimensional vector of content attributes [54].

More novel class RSs has been emerged after the famous article of Berners-Lee[2]
(as known as the father of the Semantic Web) [55]. He proposed to formulate a set
of rules to create the Web of Data, known as *linked data* principles [56]. In order to
better understand linked data, the following brief description of content architecture
in Web could be beneficial.

Current Web, as known as *Web of Document*, contains billions of documents
which are related to each other by *hyperlinks*. This architecture makes it possible for
users to traverse the Web by visiting hyperlinks. While the content of the Web is human
readable, however, it still suffers from massive ambiguity originated from the lack of
a proper structure with respect to the *representation* of information. This ambiguity

---

[2]https://en.wikipedia.org/wiki/Tim_Berners-Lee

in information consequently makes it incapable for machines to understand the provided information. Linked data principles [56] are indeed proposed in addressing this problem.

According to the noted proposal, the knowledge is modeled by *Resource Description Framework (RDF)* which provides a generic graph-based data model for describing *resources*, including their relationships with other resources [57]. By interlinking some publicly available linked data dataset such as DBpedia[3] and Wikidata,[4] *Linked Open Data* has been emerged as a network of interconnected datasets, accessible via endpoints. It is possible to query Linked Open Data by query languages such as *RDF query language* [58].

Such database has been used by novel class of RSs that are relied on the new form of semantic data that can better represent the *knowledge* of human. These novel semantic RSs focused on exploiting the *semantic* content information rather than the *raw* content data based on the *Web of Data* [59]. This has brought variety of advantages to RSs, such as, mitigating the new item cold-start problem, as well as, empowering RSs to provide semantic-aware explanations for recommendations.

3.5   Recommendation based on visual features

Another group of recommendation approaches, that can address the cold-start problem, implements the idea of enriching the item profiles with additional source of data. The enriching mechanism allows them to be capable of coping with the *new item* problem. A representative technique within this group of RSs is proposed by [60] where the authors exploited a set of visual features in a multimedia RS (see Figure 3.5). The proposed features are called *Mise-en-scene* features, and they are based on variation of colors, camera and object motions, and lighting within the multimedia items. The results of the experiments have shown that these automatically extracted features can solve the new item cold-start problem [60–62]. The same authors have extended that work and proposed another recommendation technique based on exploiting *MPEG7* and *deep learning* visual features [63]. Again, the results have shown the substantial power of visual features in solving the new item problem in RSs. There have been many recent related works that have used visual features in RSs but mainly focused on deep learning features [64–67].

There have been also earlier works that have studied the potential of building *style-aware* RSs based on visual features [68–73]. As an example, the authors of [71] introduced *VideoReach* which is an RS that can extend the semantic item profile with visual features. The results of their experiments have shown that this extension has positively affected the click-through-rate. The work in [72] presented an algorithm that can integrate different ranking lists, generated based on visual features and nonevisual attributes. The results have shown improvement.

---

[3]https://wiki.dbpedia.org/
[4]https://www.wikidata.org/wiki/Wikidata:Main_Page

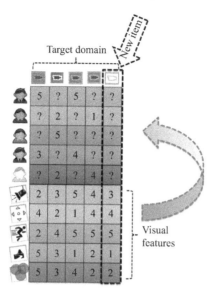

Figure 3.5 *Recommendation based on visual features, in addressing the new item problem as part of cold-start problem*

A limitation of these works is that they have typically assumed that there are already a set of semantic attributes collected and the visual features are used in combination with these semantic attributes. Therefore, further studies are needed in investigating the actual power of visual features, mainly when traditional semantic attributes are not available.

3.6 Personality-based recommender systems

One of natural solutions to tackle with the cold-start problem is to use additional user attributes (as known as *side information*), in order to build the initial profile of a new user [74,75]. There have been already different types of such attributes, proposed in the literature. However, one of the most representative forms of attributes is the psychological ones related to the *personality traits* of users. These personal traits are based on predictable and stable characteristics of users, and they describe the "consistent behavior pattern and interpersonal processes originating within the individuals" [76]. Personality traits can portray the differences of users in terms of *emotional, interpersonal, experiential, attitudinal* and *motivational* aspects [77].

Psychology literature is already mature in the personality field and various psychological models are available on how to represent the personality aspects of an individual person. One of the most well-known models is the *Five Factor Model* [78], which is commonly adopted in different research disciplines [79]. This model describes the personality of a person with respect to five dimensions as known as *big five* traits: *openness, conscientiousness, extroversion, agreeableness* and *neuroticism* (as known as *OCEAN*).

It has been shown that users with different personality traits express differences in their decision-making process [80,81]. Accordingly, users with similar personality traits are more likely to share similar preferences [82]. Authors of [83] have studied the correlation of personality traits with musical preferences and showed that users with high openness trait typically share similar preferences for jazz, blues and classical musical genres, and users with high extroversion and agreeableness traits are likely to enjoy rap, hip-hop, funk and electronic musical genres. The authors of [84] have conducted an experiment that showed a strong relation between the preferences of users for certain web applications and their particular personality traits. In [85], the relation of personality traits and emotional expressions have been investigated for users who were watching movies in different social contexts. The results have showed that different patterns of emotional expressions can be observed for different users with their unique personality traits.

The promising results of the above-described works, showing the correlation of personality and preferences of users, has motivated further studies on the idea of exploiting personality in RSs, e.g., in addressing the cold-start scenario [29,43,81, 82,86]. Hence, when a new user enters the system and has not provided any data associated with her preferences, personality traits can be used to profile her and generate personalized recommendation (see Figure 3.6). Hence, the personality can be used either to compute the similarity among users for *similarity*-based RSs, or as additional user attributes, in *model*-based RSs.

As an example of works within this area, the authors of [87] adopted different recommendation approaches and showed that incorporation of personality may lead to a

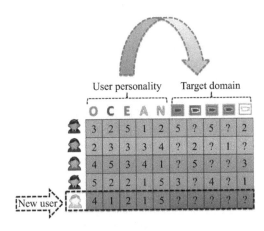

Figure 3.6   Personality-based recommender systems, in addressing the new user problem as part of cold-start problem

better recommendation quality in cold-start scenario. Reference [88] has investigated the potential of using personality and showed that personality characteristics can lead to improvement in the performance of RSs. In [79,89], the relation of personality of musical tastes is exploited in order to generate relevant recommendation for users. Finally, [90] has developed an RS that uses personality profiles of users to generate recommendations for them. This is done by first analyzing the hotel reviews written by users. Then using the correlations among the reviews and the personality traits, the system extracts the personality profiles of the users and compute similarities among the users in order to build similarity-based recommendations.

A limitation of personality-based approaches is that, before the personality data is used, the users should complete a personality questionnaire, which can be a time-consuming process. This is why there are recent machine-learning techniques that are built to extract the personality traits from other sources such as social network profiles of the users.

3.7 Cross-domain recommender systems

Another solution for the cold-start problem in RSs is based on exploitation of axillary domains in order to generate recommendations in a target domain. This is called *cross-domain recommendation* and it is one of the research topics that have been well-studied in the community of RSs. The reason can be due to the fact that current e-commerce web applications typically operate in multiple domains, and they use mechanisms to aggregate multiple types of data from multiple domains. Availability of such data can bring benefits to an RS and enables it to perform, e.g., *cross-selling* or coping with the cold-start problem in its target domain.

There have been various algorithms developed for cross-domain recommendation [91–93]. While these algorithms may implement different mechanisms for the cross-domain recommendation, they share commonalities which enables us to classify them into two major classes, i.e., *knowledge aggregation* approaches [94–97] and *knowledge transfer* approaches [98–101].

The former approach aims to *aggregate* the knowledge from different auxiliary domains in order to generate recommendations in the target domain (Figure 3.7). The latter approach is based on the idea of eliciting the user ratings from auxiliary domains and *transfer* this knowledge to the target domain. In this sense, the latter approach attempts to *link* different domain knowledge in order to support the recommendation for the target domain [98].

An example of former approach can be the work in [102], that proposed various knowledge aggregation mechanisms that have proved to be effective in improving the accuracy of target domain recommendations in cold start. An example of the latter approach is presented in [103] where the authors propose leveraging the preference knowledge transfer from an auxiliary domain to the target domain. The results of evaluation have shown that the proposed recommendation method overtakes the classical recommendation methods.

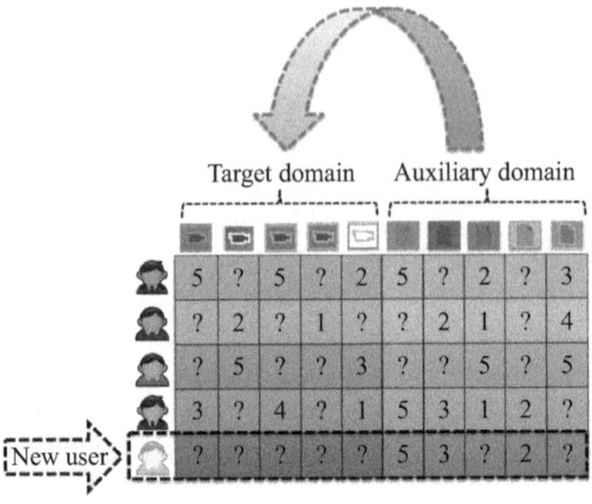

Target domain   Auxiliary domain

5	?	5	?	2	5	?	2	?	3
?	2	?	1	?	?	2	1	?	4
?	5	?	?	3	?	?	5	?	5
3	?	4	?	1	5	3	1	2	?
?	?	?	?	?	5	3	?	2	?

New user

Figure 3.7   Cross-domain recommender systems, in addressing the new user problem as part of cold-start problem

A limitation of the cross-domain recommendation is that, there has to be a considerable overlap among the adopted datasets in different domains. Hence, without having the axillary domain and the target domain overlap, it would be not feasible to apply the techniques described in this section.

3.8   Conclusion

In this book chapter, we addressed the cold-start problem in RSs. This problem happens when the system is not able to recommend relevant items to a *new user* or to recommend a *new item* to the existing users.

We discussed various solutions that have been proposed in the literature. These solutions are summarized in Table 3.1. These solutions can be classified into five classes, i.e., *active learning, semantic attributes, visual features, personality traits* and *cross-domain recommendation.* Although all of these solutions have been successfully applied and evaluated in prior works, however, none of these solutions can be seen as a conclusive remedy to the cold start as a generic problem. Indeed, each of these solutions can be effective in a particular situation of cold start. Some of these solutions (semantic attributes and visual features) can address the new item problem while some others (personality traits and cross domain) can address the new user problem. Active-learning techniques can address both of these problems.

It is worth noting that, the cold-start research area in RSs is a multidisciplinary field of research and involves disciplines of machine learning, psychology and human–computer interaction. For instance, each of the cold-start solutions need proper adoption of the interface design patterns [117] when obtaining user preferences or presenting a recommended item. Therefore, collaboration among researchers

Table 3.1   Summary of the solutions for the cold-start problem

Solution	Cold start		Methods
	New user	New item	
Active learning	✓	✓	• Uncertainty reduction [8,38,104] • Error reduction [39,105] • User adaptation [8,39,106] • Acquisition probability [107–109] • Decision tree based [38,42,46] • Prediction based [36,40,45] • Hybrid [36,47,110]
Semantic attributes		✓	• Graph-based [111,112] • Machine learning [113–115]
Personality traits	✓		• Similarity based on personality [102] • Personality traits in the model [103]
Visual features		✓	• Mise-en-scene features [60,61,116] • MPEG7 features [62] • Deep learning features [65–67]
Cross domain	✓		• Knowledge aggregation [102] • Knowledge transfer [103]

within these disciplines can surely be useful in improving the quality of the current state-of-the-art approaches.

In conclusion, this chapter shall hopefully provide an overall overview of the research on cold-start and can be a useful source of guidelines for researchers in the academia and practitioners in the industry. It can hopefully advance the knowledge in this area, as well as the related areas.

References

[1]   Bollen D, Knijnenburg BP, Willemsen MC, *et al.* Understanding choice overload in recommender systems. In: Proceedings of the Fourth ACM Conference on Recommender Systems. ACM; 2010. p. 63–70.

[2]   Anderson C. The Long Tail. Random House Business; 2006.

[3]   Resnick P, Varian HR. Recommender systems. Communications of the ACM. 1997;40(3):56–58.

[4]   Shardanand U, Maes P. Social information filtering: Algorithms for automating "word of mouth". In: Proceedings of the SIGCHI Conference on Human Factors in Computing Systems. CHI'95. New York, NY, USA: ACM Press/Addison-Wesley Publishing Co.; 1995. p. 210–217. Available from: http://dx.doi.org/10.1145/223904.223931.

[5]   Ricci F, Rokach L, Shapira B, *et al*. Recommender Systems Handbook. Springer; 2011.

[6]   Jannach D, Zanker M, Felfernig A, *et al*. Recommender Systems: An Introduction. Cambridge University Press; 2010.

[7]   Rubens N, Kaplan D, Sugiyama M. Active Learning in Recommender Systems. In: Ricci F, Rokach L, Shapira B, *et al*., editors. Recommender Systems Handbook. Springer Verlag; 2011. p. 735–767.

[8]   Rashid AM, Albert I, Cosley D, *et al*. Getting to know you: Learning new user preferences in recommender systems. In: Proceedings of the 2002 International Conference on Intelligent User Interfaces, IUI 2002. ACM Press; 2002. p. 127–134.

[9]   Su X, Khoshgoftaar TM. A survey of collaborative filtering techniques. Advances in Artificial Intelligence. 2009;2009:421425:1–421425:19. Available from: http://dx.doi.org/10.1155/2009/421425.

[10]   Burke R. Hybrid recommender systems: Survey and experiments. User Modeling and User-Adapted Interaction. 2002;12(4):331–370. Available from: ./papers/burke-umuai-ip-2002.pdf.

[11]   Resnick P, Iacovou N, Suchak M, *et al*. GroupLens: An open architecture for collaborative filtering of netnews. In: Proceedings of the 1994 ACM Conference on Computer Supported Cooperative Work. CSCW'94. New York, NY, USA: ACM; 1994. p. 175–186. Available from: http://doi.acm.org/10.1145/192844.192905.

[12]   Adomavicius G, Tuzhilin A. Toward the next generation of recommender systems: a survey of the state-of-the-art and possible extensions. IEEE Transactions on Knowledge and Data Engineering. 2005;17(6):734–749.

[13]   Ricci F, Rokach L, Shapira B. Introduction to Recommender Systems Handbook. In: Ricci F, Rokach L, Shapira B, *et al*., editors. Recommender Systems Handbook. Springer Verlag; 2011. p. 1–35.

[14]   Koren Y, Bell R. Advances in Collaborative Filtering. In: Ricci F, Rokach L, Shapira B, *et al*., editors. Recommender Systems Handbook. Springer Verlag; 2011. p. 145–186.

[15]   Desrosiers C, Karypis G. A Comprehensive Survey of Neighborhood-based Recommendation Methods. In: Ricci F, Rokach L, Shapira B, *et al*., editors. Recommender Systems Handbook. Springer; 2011. p. 107–144.

[16]   Balabanović M, Shoham Y. Fab: Content-based, collaborative recommendation. Communications of the ACM. 1997;40(3):66–72. Available from: http://doi.acm.org/10.1145/245108.245124.

[17]   Pazzani MJ, Billsus D. The Adaptive Web. Berlin, Heidelberg: Springer-Verlag; 2007. p. 325–341. Available from: http://dl.acm.org/citation.cfm?id=1768197.1768209.

[18]   Guttman RH, Moukas AG, Maes P. Agent-mediated electronic commerce: A survey. The Knowledge Engineering Review. 1998;13(2):147–159. Available from: http://dx.doi.org/10.1017/S0269888998002082.

[19]   Huang SL. Designing utility-based recommender systems for e-Commerce: evaluation of preference-elicitation methods. Electronic

Commerce Research and Applications. 2011;10(4):398–407. Available from: http://dx.doi.org/10.1016/j.elerap.2010.11.003.

[20] Pazzani MJ. A framework for collaborative, content-based and demographic filtering. Artificial Intelligence Review. 1999;13(5-6):393–408. Available from: http://dx.doi.org/10.1023/A:1006544522159.

[21] Wang Y, Chan SCF, Ngai G. Applicability of demographic recommender system to tourist attractions: A case study on trip advisor. In: Proceedings of the 2012 IEEE/WIC/ACM International Joint Conferences on Web Intelligence and Intelligent Agent Technology – Volume 03. WI-IAT'12. Washington, DC, USA: IEEE Computer Society; 2012. p. 97–101. Available from: http://dx.doi.org/10.1109/WI-IAT.2012.133.

[22] Burke R. Knowledge-Based Recommender Systems. CRC Press; 2000.

[23] Felfernig A, Burke R. Constraint-based recommender systems: Technologies and research issues. In: Proceedings of the 10th International Conference on Electronic Commerce. ICEC'08. New York, NY, USA: ACM; 2008. p. 3:1–3:10. Available from: http://doi.acm.org/10.1145/1409540.1409544.

[24] Claypool M, Gokhale A, Miranda T, *et al.* Combining content-based and collaborative filters in an online newspaper. In: Proceedings of the ACM SIGIR'99 Workshop on Recommender Systems: Algorithms and Evaluation. Berkeley, California: ACM; 1999.

[25] Li Q, Kim BM. An approach for combining content-based and collaborative filters. In: Proceedings of the Sixth International Workshop on Information Retrieval with Asian Languages – Volume 11. AsianIR'03. Stroudsburg, PA, USA: Association for Computational Linguistics; 2003. p. 17–24. Available from: http://dx.doi.org/10.3115/1118935.1118938.

[26] Elahi M, Ricci F, Rubens N. A survey of active learning in collaborative filtering recommender systems. Computer Science Review. 2016;20(C):29–50. Available from: http://dx.doi.org/10.1016/j.cosrev.2016.05.002.

[27] Rubens N, Elahi M, Sugiyama M, *et al.* Active Learning in Recommender Systems. In: Recommender Systems Handbook – Chapter 24: Recommending Active Learning. US: Springer; 2015. p. 809–846.

[28] Schein AI, Popescul A, Ungar LH, *et al.* Methods and metrics for cold-start recommendations. In: SIGIR'02: Proceedings of the 25th Annual International ACM SIGIR Conference on Research and Development in Information Retrieval. New York, NY, USA: ACM; 2002. p. 253–260.

[29] Braunhofer M, Elahi M, Ricci F. Techniques for cold-starting context-aware mobile recommender systems for tourism. Intelligenza Artificiale. 2014;8(2):129–143.

[30] Sipser M. Introduction to the Theory of Computation. 1st ed. International Thomson Publishing; 1996.

[31] Alpaydin E. Introduction to Machine Learning. 2nd ed. The MIT Press; 2010.

[32] Abu-Mostafa YS, Magdon-Ismail M, Lin HT. Learning From Data. AML-Book; 2012.

[33] Flach P. Machine Learning: The Art and Science of Algorithms That Make Sense of Data. New York, NY, USA: Cambridge University Press; 2012.

[34]   Ge M, Helfert M. A Review of Information Quality Research – Develop a Research Agenda. In: ICIQ; 2007. p. 76–91.

[35]   Tong S. Active Learning: Theory and Applications. The Department of Computer Science. Stanford University; 2001.

[36]   Elahi M, Ricci F, Rubens N. Active learning strategies for rating elicitation in collaborative filtering: A system-wide perspective. ACM Transactions on Intelligent Systems and Technology. 2014;5(1):13:1–13:33.

[37]   Elahi M, Ricci F, Rubens N. Active learning in collaborative filtering recommender systems. In: E-Commerce and Web Technologies. Springer; 2014. p. 113–124.

[38]   Rashid AM, Karypis G, Riedl J. Learning preferences of new users in recommender systems: an information theoretic approach. SIGKDD Explorations Newsletter. 2008;10:90–100. Available from: http://doi.acm.org/10.1145/1540276.1540302.

[39]   Golbandi N, Koren Y, Lempel R. On bootstrapping recommender systems. In: Proceedings of the 19th ACM International Conference on Information and Knowledge Management. CIKM'10. New York, NY, USA: ACM; 2010. p. 1805–1808. Available from: http://doi.acm.org/10.1145/1871437.1871734.

[40]   Harpale AS, Yang Y. Personalized active learning for collaborative filtering. In: SIGIR'08: Proceedings of the 31st Annual International ACM SIGIR Conference on Research and Development in Information Retrieval. New York, NY, USA: ACM; 2008. p. 91–98.

[41]   He L, Liu NN, Yang Q. Active dual collaborative filtering with both item and attribute feedback. In: AAAI; 2011.

[42]   Golbandi N, Koren Y, Lempel R. Adaptive bootstrapping of recommender systems using decision trees. In: Proceedings of the Fourth ACM International Conference on Web Search and Data Mining. WSDM'11. New York, NY, USA: ACM; 2011. p. 595–604. Available from: http://doi.acm.org/10.1145/1935826.1935910.

[43]   Elahi M, Braunhofer M, Ricci F, *et al.* Personality-Based Active Learning for Collaborative Filtering Recommender Systems. In: Baldoni M, Baroglio C, Boella G, *et al.*, editors. AI*IA. vol. 8249 of Lecture Notes in Computer Science. Springer; 2013. p. 360–371. Available from: http://dblp.uni-trier.de/db/conf/aiia/aiia2013.html#ElahiBRT13.

[44]   Jin R, Si L. A Bayesian approach toward active learning for collaborative filtering. In: UAI'04, Proceedings of the 20th Conference in Uncertainty in Artificial Intelligence, July 7–11, 2004, Banff, Canada; 2004. p. 278–285.

[45]   Karimi R, Freudenthaler C, Nanopoulos A, *et al.* Non-myopic active learning for recommender systems based on matrix factorization. In: IRI. IEEE Systems, Man, and Cybernetics Society; 2011. p. 299–303.

[46]   Karimi R, Freudenthaler C, Nanopoulos A, *et al.* Active learning for aspect model in recommender systems. In: CIDM. IEEE; 2011. p. 162–167.

[47]   Rubens N, Sugiyama M. Influence-based collaborative active learning. In: Proceedings of the 2007 ACM Conference on Recommender Systems.

RecSys'07. New York, NY, USA: ACM; 2007. p. 145–148. Available from: http://doi.acm.org/10.1145/1297231.1297257.

[48] Elahi M, Ricci F, Rubens N. Adapting to natural rating acquisition with combined active learning strategies. In: ISMIS'12: Proceedings of the 20th International Conference on Foundations of Intelligent Systems. Berlin, Heidelberg: Springer-Verlag; 2012. p. 254–263.

[49] Degemmis M, Lops P, Semeraro G. A content-collaborative recommender that exploits WordNet-based user profiles for neighborhood formation. User Modeling and User-Adapted Interaction. 2007;17(3):217–255.

[50] Eirinaki M, Vazirgiannis M, Varlamis I. SEWeP: Using site semantics and a taxonomy to enhance the Web personalization process. In: Proceedings of the ninth ACM SIGKDD International Conference on Knowledge Discovery and Data Mining. ACM; 2003. p. 99–108.

[51] Magnini B, Strapparava C. Improving User Modelling with Content-based Techniques. In: User Modeling 2001. Sonthofen, Germany; Springer; 2001. p. 74–83.

[52] García-Crespo A, Chamizo J, Rivera I, *et al.* SPETA: Social pervasive e-Tourism advisor. Telematics and Informatics. 2009;26(3):306–315. Available from: http://dblp.uni-trier.de/db/journals/tele/tele26.html#Garcia-CrespoCRMPB09.

[53] Towle B, Quinn C. Knowledge based recommender systems using explicit user models. In: Papers from the AAAI Workshop, AAAI Technical Report WS-00-04. Menlo Park, CA: AAAI Press; 2000. p. 74–77.

[54] Lops P, De Gemmis M, Semeraro G. Content-Based Recommender Systems: State of the Art and Trends. In: Recommender Systems Handbook. Springer; 2011. p. 73–105.

[55] Berners-Lee T, Hendler J, Lassila O. The Semantic Web. Scientific American. 2001 May;284(5):34–43. Available from: http://www.sciam.com/article.cfm?articleID=00048144-10D2-1C70-84A9809EC588EF21.

[56] Berners-Lee T. Linked-Data Design Issues; 2009. W3C design issue document. Available from: http://www.w3.org/DesignIssues/LinkedData.html.

[57] Hitzler P, Krötzsch M, Rudolph S. Foundations of Semantic Web Technologies. CRC Press; 2010.

[58] Krummenacher R, Norton B, Marte A. Towards linked open services and processes. In: Berre AJ, Gómez-Pérez A, Tutschku K, *et al.*, editors. Future Internet – FIS 2010 – Proceedings of the Third Future Internet Symposium, Berlin, Germany, September 20–22, 2010. vol. 6369 of Lecture Notes in Computer Science. Springer; 2010. p. 68–77. Available from: http://dx.doi.org/10.1007/978-3-642-15877-3_8.

[59] Damljanovic D, Stankovic M, Laublet P. Linked Data-Based Concept Recommendation: Comparison of Different Methods in Open Innovation Scenario. In: Simperl E, Cimiano P, Polleres A, *et al.*, editors. ESWC. vol. 7295 of Lecture Notes in Computer Science. Springer; 2012. p. 24–38. Available from: http://dblp.uni-trier.de/db/conf/esws/eswc2012.html#DamljanovicSL12.

[60] Deldjoo Y, Elahi M, Cremonesi P, *et al.* Content-based video recommendation system based on stylistic visual features. Journal on Data Semantics. 2016;5:1–15.

[61] Elahi M, Deldjoo Y, Bakhshandegan Moghaddam F, *et al.* Exploring the semantic gap for movie recommendations. In: Proceedings of the Eleventh ACM Conference on Recommender Systems. ACM; 2017. p. 326–330.

[62] Deldjoo Y, Quadrana M, Elahi M, Cremonesi P. Using Mise-En-Scène Visual Features based on MPEG-7 and Deep Learning for Movie Recommendation. arXiv preprint arXiv:170406109. 2017. Available from: https://dblp.org/rec/bib/journals/corr/DeldjooQEC17.

[63] Deldjoo Y, Elahi M, Quadrana M, *et al.* Using visual features based on MPEG-7 and deep learning for movie recommendation. International Journal of Multimedia Information Retrieval. 2018;7.

[64] Lin K, Yang HF, Liu KH, *et al.* Rapid clothing retrieval via deep learning of binary codes and hierarchical search. In: Proceedings of the 5th ACM on International Conference on Multimedia Retrieval. ACM; 2015. p. 499–502.

[65] Bracher C, Heinz S, Vollgraf R. Fashion DNA: Merging Content and Sales Data for Recommendation and Article Mapping. arXiv preprint arXiv:160902489. 2016. Available from: https://dblp.org/rec/bib/journals/corr/BracherHV16.

[66] McAuley J, Targett C, Shi Q, *et al.* Image-based recommendations on styles and substitutes. In: Proceedings of the 38th International ACM SIGIR Conference on Research and Development in Information Retrieval. ACM; 2015. p. 43–52.

[67] Messina P, Dominquez V, Parra D, *et al.* Exploring Content-based Artwork Recommendation with Metadata and Visual Features. arXiv preprint arXiv:170605786. 2017. Available from: https://dblp.org/rec/bib/journals/corr/MessinaDPTS17.

[68] Deldjoo Y, Elahi M, Cremonesi P, *et al.* Recommending movies based on Mise-en-scene design. In: Proceedings of the 2016 CHI Conference Extended Abstracts on Human Factors in Computing Systems. ACM; 2016. p. 1540–1547.

[69] Deldjoo Y, Elahi M, Quadrana M, *et al.* Toward effective movie recommendations based on Mise-en-Scène film styles. In: Proceedings of the 11th Biannual Conference on Italian SIGCHI Chapter. ACM; 2015. p. 162–165.

[70] Lehinevych T, Kokkinis-Ntrenis N, Siantikos G, *et al.* Discovering similarities for content-based recommendation and browsing in multimedia collections. In: Signal-Image Technology and Internet-Based Systems (SITIS), 2014 Tenth International Conference on. IEEE; 2014. p. 237–243.

[71] Yang B, Mei T, Hua XS, *et al.* Online video recommendation based on multimodal fusion and relevance feedback. In: Proceedings of the 6th ACM International Conference on Image and Video Retrieval. ACM; 2007. p. 73–80.

[72] Zhao X, Li G, Wang M, *et al.* Integrating rich information for video recommendation with multi-task rank aggregation. In: Proceedings of the 19th ACM International Conference on Multimedia. ACM; 2011. p. 1521–1524.

[73] Canini L, Benini S, Leonardi R. Affective recommendation of movies based on selected connotative features. IEEE Transactions on Circuits and Systems for Video Technology. 2013;23(4):636–647.

[74] Braunhofer M, Elahi M, Ricci F. User Personality and the New User Problem in a Context-Aware Point of Interest Recommender System. In: Information and Communication Technologies in Tourism 2015. Lugano, Switzerland; Springer; 2015. p. 537–549.

[75] Nasery M, Elahi M, Cremonesi P. PoliMovie: A feature-based dataset for recommender systems. In: ACM RecSys Workshop on Crowdsourcing and Human Computation for Recommender Systems (CrawdRec). vol. 3; 2015. p. 25–30.

[76] Burger JM. Personality. Belmont, CA., USA: Wadsworth Publishing; 2010.

[77] John OP, Srivastava S. The Big Five Trait Taxonomy: History, Measurement, and Theoretical Perspectives. In: Handbook of Personality: Theory and Research. Vol. 2; 1999. University of California. pp. 102–138.

[78] Costa PT, McCrae RR. Revised NEO Personality Inventory (NEO PI-R) and NEO Five-Factor Inventory (NEO FFI): Professional Manual. Psychological Assessment Resources; 1992.

[79] Hu R, Pu P. Enhancing collaborative filtering systems with personality information. In: Proceedings of the Fifth ACM Conference on Recommender Systems. RecSys'11. New York, NY, USA: ACM; 2011. p. 197–204. Available from: http://doi.acm.org/10.1145/2043932.2043969.

[80] Nunes MASN, Hu R. Personality-based recommender systems: An overview. In: Proceedings of the 6th ACM Conference on Recommender Systems; 2012. p. 5–6.

[81] Fernández-Tobías I, Braunhofer M, Elahi M, *et al.* Alleviating the new user problem in collaborative filtering by exploiting personality information. User Modeling and User-Adapted Interaction. 2016;26(2-3):221–255.

[82] Schedl M, Zamani H, Chen CW, *et al.* Current challenges and visions in music recommender systems research. International Journal of Multimedia Information Retrieval. 2018;7(2):95–116.

[83] Rentfrow PJ, Gosling SD. The do re mi's of everyday life: The structure and personality correlates of music preferences. Journal of Personality and Social Psychology. 2003;84(6):1236–1256.

[84] Kosinski M, Stillwell D, Kohli P, *et al.* Personality and website choice. In: Proceedings of the 3rd Annual ACM Web Science Conference. ACM; 2012.

[85] Odic A, Tkalcic M, Tasic JF, *et al.* Personality and social context: Impact on emotion induction from movies. In: UMAP'13 Workshops; 2013.

[86] Braunhofer M, Elahi M, Ge M, *et al.* Context dependent preference acquisition with personality-based active learning in mobile recommender systems. In: International Conference, HCI International 2014 (HCII'14). Springer; 2014.

[87] Tkalcic M, Kunaver M, Košir A, *et al.* Addressing the new user problem with a personality based user similarity measure. In: Proceedings of the

1st International Workshop on Decision Making and Recommendation Acceptance Issues in Recommender Systems; 2011. p. 106.

[88]   Nunes MASN. Recommender Systems based on Personality Traits: Could Human Psychological Aspects Influence the Computer Decision-Making Process?. VDM Verlag; 2009.

[89]   Hu R, Pu P. A comparative user study on rating vs. personality quiz based preference elicitation methods. In: Proceedings of the 14th International Conference on Intelligent User Interfaces. IUI'09. New York, NY, USA: ACM; 2009. p. 367–372. Available from: http://doi.acm.org/10.1145/1502650.1502702.

[90]   Roshchina A. TWIN Personality-based Recommender System. Dublin: Institute of Technology Tallaght; 2012.

[91]   Fernández-Tobías I, Cantador I, Kaminskas M, *et al.* Cross-domain recommender systems: A survey of the state of the art. In: Proceedings of the 2nd Spanish Conference on Information Retrieval; 2012. p. 187–198.

[92]   Winoto P, Tang TY. If you like the Devil Wears Prada the book, will you also enjoy the Devil Wears Prada the movie? A study of cross-domain recommendations. New Generation Computing. 2008;26(3):209–225. Available from: http://dx.doi.org/10.1007/s00354-008-0041-0.

[93]   Pagano R, Quadrana M, Elahi M, *et al.* Toward Active Learning in Cross-domain Recommender Systems. arXiv preprint arXiv:170102021. 2017.

[94]   Abel F, Herder E, Houben GJ, *et al.* Cross-system user modeling and personalization on the Social Web. User Modeling and User-Adapted Interaction. 2013;23(2–3):169–209. Available from: http://dx.doi.org/10.1007/s11257-012-9131-2.

[95]   Berkovsky S, Kuflik T, Ricci F. Mediation of user models for enhanced personalization in recommender systems. User Modeling and User-Adapted Interaction. 2008;18(3):245–286. Available from: http://dx.doi.org/10.1007/s11257-007-9042-9.

[96]   Shapira B, Rokach L, Freilikhman S. Facebook single and cross domain data for recommendation systems. User Modeling and User-Adapted Interaction. 2013;23(2–3):211–247. Available from: http://dx.doi.org/10.1007/s11257-012-9128-x.

[97]   Cantador I, Tobías IF, Berkovsky S, *et al.* Cross-domain recommender systems. In: Recommender Systems Handbook. 2nd ed. Springer; 2015. p. 919–959.

[98]   Cremonesi P, Tripodi A, Turrin R. Cross-domain recommender systems. In: Proceedings of the 11th International Conference on Data Mining Workshops; 2011. p. 496–503.

[99]   Tiroshi A, Berkovsky S, Kâafar MA, *et al.* Cross social networks interests predictions based on graph features. In: Proceedings of the 7th ACM Conference on Recommender Systems; 2013. p. 319–322.

[100] Gao S, Luo H, Chen D, *et al.* Cross-domain recommendation via cluster-level latent factor model. In: Proceedings of the 2013 European Conference on Machine Learning and Knowledge Discovery in Databases; 2013. p. 161–176.

[101] Li B, Yang Q, Xue X. Can movies and books collaborate? cross-domain collaborative filtering for sparsity reduction. In: Proceedings of the 21st International Joint Conference on Artificial Intelligence; 2009. p. 2052–2057.

[102] Berkovsky S, Kuflik T, Ricci F. Distributed collaborative filtering with domain specialization. In: Proceedings of the 2007 ACM Conference on Recommender Systems. ACM; 2007. p. 33–40.

[103] Enrich M, Braunhofer M, Ricci F. Cold-start management with cross-domain collaborative filtering and tags. In: Proceedings of the 14th International Conference E-Commerce and Web Technologies; 2013. p. 101–112.

[104] Kohrs A, Merialdo B. Improving Collaborative Filtering For New-Users By Smart Object Selection; Sophia-Antipolis, France: Institut EURECOMŁ, Department of Multimedia Communications; 2001.

[105] Liu NN, Meng X, Liu C, *et al.* Wisdom of the better few: Cold start recommendation via representative based rating elicitation. In: Proceedings of the Fifth ACM Conference on Recommender Systems. ACM; 2011. p. 37–44.

[106] Teixeira IR, de Carvalho FAT, Ramalho G, *et al.* ActiveCP: A method for speeding up user preferences acquisition in collaborative filtering systems. In: Proceedings of the 16th Brazilian Symposium on Artificial Intelligence: Advances in Artificial Intelligence. SBIA'02. London, UK: Springer-Verlag; 2002. p. 237–247. Available from: http://dl.acm.org/citation.cfm?id=645853.669613.

[107] Rashid AM, Albert I, Cosley D, *et al.* Getting to know you: learning new user preferences in recommender systems. In: Proceedings of the 7th International Conference on Intelligent User Interfaces. ACM; 2002. p. 127–134.

[108] Elahi M, Repsys V, Ricci F. Rating Elicitation Strategies for Collaborative Filtering. In: Huemer C, Setzer T, editors. EC-Web. vol. 85 of Lecture Notes in Business Information Processing. Toulouse, France: Springer; 2011. p. 160–171.

[109] Elahi M, Braunhofer M, Ricci F, *et al.* Personality-based active learning for collaborative filtering recommender systems. In: Proceedings of the 13th International Conference of the Italian Association for Artificial Intelligence. Springer; 2013. p. 360–371.

[110] Zhou K, Yang SH, Zha H. Functional matrix factorizations for cold-start recommendation. In: Proceedings of the 34th International ACM SIGIR Conference on Research and Development in Information Retrieval. SIGIR'11. New York, NY, USA: ACM; 2011. p. 315–324. Available from: http://doi.acm.org/10.1145/2009916.2009961.

[111] Kaminskas M, Fernández-Tobías I, Ricci F, *et al.* Knowledge-based music retrieval for places of interest. In: Liem CCS, Müller M, Tjoa SK, *et al.*, editors. MIRUM; 2012. p. 19–24. Available from: http://dblp.uni-trier.de/db/conf/mm/mirum2012.html#KaminskasFRC12.

[112] Passant A. dbrec – Music recommendations using DBpedia. In: Proceedings of the 9th International Semantic Web Conference (ISWC 2010). Springer; 2010. p. 209–224.

[113]   Ristoski P, Mencía EL, Paulheim H. A Hybrid Multi-strategy Recommender System Using Linked Open Data. In: Presutti V, Stankovic M, Cambria E, *et al.*, editors. SemWebEval@ESWC. vol. 475 of Communications in Computer and Information Science. Springer; 2014. p. 150–156. Available from: http://dblp.uni-trier.de/db/conf/esws/ semwebeval2014.html#RistoskiMP14.

[114]   Ostuni VC, Noia TD, Sciascio ED, *et al.* Top-N recommendations from implicit feedback leveraging linked open data. In: Yang Q, King I, Li Q, *et al.*, editors. RecSys. ACM; 2013. p. 85–92. Available from: http://dblp. uni-trier.de/db/conf/recsys/recsys2013.html#OstuniNSM13.

[115]   Zhang Y, Wu H, Sorathia VS, *et al.* Event recommendation in social networks with linked data enablement. In: Hammoudi S, Maciaszek LA, Cordeiro J, *et al.*, editors. ICEIS (2). SciTePress; 2013. p. 371–379. Available from: http://dblp.uni-trier.de/db/conf/iceis/iceis2013-2.html#ZhangWSP13.

[116]   Deldjoo Y, Elahi M, Cremonesi P, *et al.* How to combine visual features with tags to improve movie recommendation accuracy?. In: International Conference on Electronic Commerce and Web Technologies. Springer; 2016. p. 34–45.

[117]   Cremonesi P, Elahi M, Garzotto F. Interaction design patterns in recommender systems. In: Proceedings of the 11th Biannual Conference on Italian SIGCHI Chapter. ACM; 2015. p. 66–73.

Chapter 4

Performance metrics for traditional and context-aware big data recommender systems

Rab Nawaz Jadoon[1,2], Wu Yang[1], and Osman Khalid[2]

Recommender System (RS) concept was coined in the mid-1990s, when researchers took interest in recommendation problems that primarily used the concept of ratings to obtain the user preferences for different items. A lot of work has been exercised and investigated in this area for recommending the most relevant information and contents to users without taking the contextual information, such as date, time, location and event. In the last few years, context-aware recommender systems (CARS) have made tremendous contributions in all domains of life and improved the recommendation process based on the contextual information along with the traditional approaches. The effectiveness of an algorithm can be measured in the sense that how efficiently it returns the recommendation to users/customers with respect to context or occasion. To assess the effectiveness and performance of any recommender algorithms completely, some common metrics are defined to assess the performance of the recommender algorithm beforehand.

There are numerous performance metrics that can be used to efficiently evaluate any recommender algorithm, but the root-mean-squared error (RMSE) is the most important and commonly used to appraise a recommender algorithm. Normally, RMSE is used to measure the difference between the predicted preferences and actual/true preferences over items, while the Recall method is used to compute the favored items that are recommended. Other variants include the mean square error (MSE), mean average error (MAE), and normalized MAE (NMAE). *NMAE basically normalizes MAE by the range of the ratings for ease of comparing errors across domains. RMSE is very suitable for the prediction task, because it measures the inaccuracies on all the ratings, whether negative or positive.* Predicted ratings are assessed based on the accuracy of these predictions. Usually, it is done through regression analysis and classification algorithms in the machine learning domain. In CARS, accuracy and diversity are major performance metrics for measuring the effectiveness of the real-time context-aware recommender algorithms.

[1]School of Information Science and Technology, University of Science and Technology of China, China
[2]Department of Computer Science, COMSATS University Islamabad, Pakistan

In this chapter, we primarily focus on the performance metrics identified for both the traditional RSs and CARS. In addition to all the possible performance metrics used in those systems, we have discussed various issues affecting the performance of CARS. These performance metrics are used to measure the accuracy and to categorize/grade the recommender algorithms. Some of these measure the similar features, while the others measure significantly different quantities. Moreover, we have also presented the common criteria for evaluating the metric selection for any recommender algorithm in order to measure its performance.

4.1   Introduction

Recommender Systems (RSs) are primarily used for providing recommendation to users or customers in diverse online social and commercial services. These algorithms are popular among both the researchers as well as the commercial community [1]. These systems have different nature with respect to various computational domains and applications. It is quite important to know beforehand the nature and application area of interest of an algorithm to be developed.

Many evaluation metrics have been suggested for comparing recommender algorithms with respect to different usage environment. The selection of the proper evaluation metric for any recommender algorithm is often very difficult because each metric may be used in an algorithm based on some specific scenario [2].

In many modern online social and commercial applications, the RS provided the user a diverse set of recommended items. Such systems assist the customers to select the appropriate items of his/her choice of interest. For example, Netflix[1] recommender engine publishes the predicted ratings for every released movie in order to assist the users to select an appropriate movie of their choice. Amazon[2] (the online book retailer) displays the average user ratings for the published books along with a list of other similar books which are bought by other users [2]. Microsoft provides many free software downloads such as bug fixers, antiviruses, and many other products and plug-ins. When a user downloads something, the system presents an additional list of the similar items that can be downloaded together. Such systems provide diverse services and works as an intermediate agent for providing a win-win situation for both the parties (seller and buyer) [3].

In the recent past, a lot of new efficient algorithms for recommendation tasks have been proposed. An application designer can add the most appropriate recommendation system from the list to his/her application. Normally, such selection is made by comparing the performance of several algorithms of the same type of category over the real data. The developer then selects the best algorithm that has the possible structural constraints as per the application requirements. Furthermore, most of the researchers have compared the performance of their proposed algorithm to a set

[1]www.netflix.com
[2]www.amazon.com

of existing approaches. Such comparisons are typically exercised by defining some evaluation metrics for ranking/grading the algorithm.

Several performance metrics are exercised in the literature to measure and rank/grade/categorize the recommendation algorithms. Among those, some are used for computing the same features, while the others are used for measuring the different quantities. For instance, root-mean-squared error (RMSE) computes the distance between the actual and predicted preferences against the items, and recall is used to measure the favored items that can be or recommended already.

More specifically, it is unlikely that a single algorithm would outperform all the others against all possible methods. Therefore, we have a number of options to select the most appropriate metrics for ranking the recommender algorithm.

This chapter is an attempt to briefly discuss the different performance evaluation metrics that are used to evaluate the RS algorithms specifically in big data environment. In Section 4.2, we briefly discuss the context-aware recommender systems (CARS). How the recommender algorithms are evaluated and what are the basic metrics used to evaluate the recommender algorithms are discussed in Section 4.3. Section 4.4 discusses the diversity and accuracy measurement in the CARS. The criteria of choosing an appropriate performance metric for the recommendation algorithm with respect to the application domain area are presented in Section 4.5. Finally, Section 4.6 concludes the chapter.

4.2 CARS—a brief overview

Majority of the recommender algorithms may not consider the contextual information (i.e., time, location, event, people, etc.) while recommending the items or information to the user [4]. The conventional algorithms depend only on two entities, i.e., users and items, and do not consider any real-time information while providing the recommendation. In our daily life, we encounter such scenarios where we could not rely merely on the user and items, but we need to use the real-time data while recommending something to users [5]. To elaborate this concept further, consider a vocational package in which only the personalized contents are not sufficient, but we need to know and embed the contextual information into the recommender process.

For instance, the recommendation of the travel RS that uses the temporal context would be quite different in the winter and summer. Similarly, in case of personalized content delivery on a website, it is important to determine what content is recommended to a user and when [3]. More specifically, on weekdays a user might prefer to read world news and check the stock market report in the evening, and read movie reviews and do other things.

4.3 Evaluation of RSs

Before going into the details, we first need to highlight the most common scenario, where an RS can be used.

The most common tasks for an RS are prediction, ranking, and classification. The ratings against unread items are predicted in the prediction tasks. For example, a movie rental website might publish the predicted ratings in order to aid the users for easy decision-making.

Recommender algorithm used ranking to generate a top k list of items. This can be commonly seen in e-commerce applications, where a top k items are shown in a sidebar or on a dedicated page. However, the web news portals, contents, and other information providers make heavy use of such top k lists.

In classification, the algorithm finds a set of limited number of recommended items having no order among them; e.g., the items of interest to a user are predicted and then highlighted explicitly on the page. After that, a top k list of recommended items is generated as a classification task, especially if the number of items is less and the order is less dominant; e.g., recommended items are presented in the form of a grid or in a circular fashion on the webpage (Amazon.com).

4.3.1 Evaluation metrics

Generally the evaluation metrics for an RS can be categorized into the following three classes [2]:

1. Prediction accuracy metrics
2. Classification accuracy metrics
3. Rank accuracy metrics.

4.3.1.1 Prediction accuracy metrics

Prediction accuracy is the most popular and commonly discussed metric in the RS literature. Almost all the RSs have the prediction engine which predicts the user opinions over items or the usage probability.

Accuracy measurement for rating predictions
In some applications, rating is predicted normally through 5-star rating heuristics. In such applications, it is very important to calculate the accuracy against the predicted ratings. Some commonly used methods are as follows:

1. **Root-mean-squared error**
   Generally, this method is used to calculate the accuracy of the predicted ratings. The algorithm makes the predicted ratings Pr against the test set T having user–item pairs (u, i) for which the true ratings Tr are known. Normally, true ratings are known as these are hidden in the offline processing. The RMSE between the predicted and actual ratings is given in the following equation:

$$RMSE = \sqrt{\frac{1}{|T|} \sum_{(u,i) \in T} (Pr - Tr)^2} \qquad (4.1)$$

2. **Mean absolute error**

   Mean average error (MAE) is the most popular and commonly used substitute of the RMSE and is generally represented by the following equation:

$$MAE = \frac{1}{|T|} \sum_{(u,i) \in T} |Pr - Tr| \tag{4.2}$$

   Unlike MAE, RMSE excessively castigates large errors. For a test set containing four hidden items, RMSE generates an error of 2 on 3 ratings and 0 on the 4th to one that makes an error of 3 on 1 rating and 0 on all others 3, while MAE would favor the 2nd system.

3. **Normalized RMSE and normalized MAE**

   Normalized RMSE and normalized MAE are the versions of the RMSE and MAE used primarily for normalizing the range of the ratings (i.e., $r_{max} - r_{min}$).

4. **Average RMSE and average MAE**

   These metrics are used where the dataset is uneven. For example, for a dataset having unbalanced entries/items, the RMSE or MAE has high chances of producing error on a few very frequent items. If we are interested to calculate the prediction error of any item, it is better to calculate MAE or RMSE separately against each item and later take the average.

   RMSE and MAE are used for measuring the errors. In some applications, the prediction error does not depend on its magnitude. In such cases, one may need to calculate the proper distortion measure $d(Pr, Tr)$, and then square the difference. For example, a system having 3-star rating in which 1 is used for "disliked," 2 for "neutral," and 3 for "liked." One of the main conditions in the algorithm is to recommend an item that user dislikes is worse against not recommending an item to a user that he or she likes. The distortion measures against different predicted and true ratings with following pairs are reasonable.

$$d(3, 1) = 5, d(2, 1) = 3, d(3, 2) = 3, d(1, 2) = 1, d(2, 3) = 1, \text{and } d(1, 3) = 2.$$

4.3.1.2 Usage prediction measurement/classifying accuracy metrics

A user preference for items is not predicted by the RS in many applications, but RS still recommends items that may favor users. For example, when movies are queued, Netflix recommend movies that may also have an interesting factor. In this case, we are highly interested that the algorithm correctly predicts that those movies would be queued by the user.

In offline processing, we are interested in a dataset comprising items that are used by the user. In this way, we randomly select a user, hide some of its information, and then ask the RS to predict a set of items that the user might be interested in. We then have four ultimate possibilities against the recommended and unrecommended items, as shown in Figure 4.1.

Sometimes a user may not be interested in an item due to its unavailability, but once the RS exposed that item, then a user may aware of it and can select it. In this case, the numbers of false positives are overestimated.

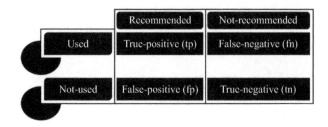

Figure 4.1   Possible outcomes of recommending an item to a user

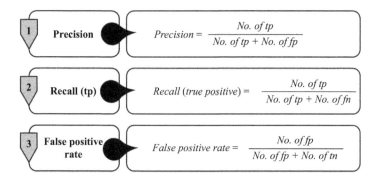

Figure 4.2   Precision, recall, and false positive rate computation

All possible scenarios fall into each cell of the table and computed against the following quantities presented in Figure 4.2.

In some cases, the recommendations are predetermined to the user. In such cases, the most powerful measure is the "Precision."

In some cases when we have the recommendations that are not determined beforehand, then it is better to run algorithms over a range of recommendation list's length. And after this, it is important to compute the true positive rate to false positive rate. The former types of curves are known as precision–recall curves, while the later referred as Receiver Operating Characteristic[3] or ROC curves.

As both the curves are used to measure the recommended preferred items, precision–recall curves highlight the fraction of the recommended items that are ideal while ROC curves highlight the fraction of items that are not ideal, but end up being recommended to the user.

The appropriate selection between the ROC and precision recall is based on the application domain area; e.g., an online video rental service recommends movies to the users. The precision metric checks the recommendations that are according to the user choice. The irrelevant recommendations represent a small/large proportion of the unsuitable movies that could have been recommended, but may not be relevant

[3]A reference to their origins in signal detection theory.

to the fraction of the similar items that the system recommends to the user. So a precision–recall curve best answers this situation. On the opposite side, taking an example of marketing system, in which an item is marketed through an e-mail aid to a customer who may ignore it if the items are in lack of interest. In this case, we are actually interested to increase the sale, while minimizing the marketing cost. ROC curves outperform precision–recall curves.

4.3.1.3 Rank accuracy metrics

In many cases, a list of recommendations is presented to the user by an application, normally displayed in vertical or horizontal order that shows a standard browsing heuristic. For example, in Netflix, the "movies you'll love" tab has subcategories, and each predicts a list of movies that the users like. As these lists have a lot of data spans across the multiple pages, so a user may visit all the pages till reaching the end. In such systems, predicting an explicit rating is not an ultimate goal, but items are arranged and presented as per user's likings. Normally, this is done through rankings. Such situations are handled through two methods that measure the accuracy against the ranking. The correct order can be determined for each user and found how a system is near optimum to this corrected order or an attempt is made to calculate the system's ranking to a user against the utility. These methods are described first for offline measurements, and then its applicability to user studies and online assessments.

Reference ranking
In order to evaluate a ranking algorithm with respect to reference ranking, it is necessary to first have such reference. In some cases, an item rating by the users is explicitly available, which is ranked in descending order. For example, Netflix DVDs are ranked in descending order, with 5-star movies tied, followed by the others and so on (like 4-star and 3-star). In case of usage data, it can be suitable to build a reference ranking in which used items are ranked on top of the unused items. However, this is only valid once the user is aware of the unused items, so it can easily infer that the used items are favored over the unused items by the user. The best-suited example of an online music application (Pandora[4]) uses reference ranking, where the listened tracks are ranked on top of the skipped ones.

In both the types discussed above, two items are tied together when we have no idea about the user's relative ranking. However, an RS is responsible for ranking items having no ties. In reference ranking, a system might not be punished for ranking one item over another as they have strong coupling.

Normalized distance-based performance measure
The normalized distance-based performance measure (NDMP) is best suitable for the above cases. If we have reference rankings RR_{ui} and system rankings SR_{ui} of N_u items i for user u, we can define the ranking as follows:

$$T^+ = \sum_{ij} sgn(RR_{ui} - RR_{uj})sgn(SR_{ui} - SR_{uj}) \tag{4.3}$$

---

[4]www.pandora.com

$$T^- = \sum_{ij} sgn(RR_{ui} - RR_{uj})sgn(SR_{uj} - SR_{ui}) \tag{4.4}$$

$$T^u = \sum_{ij} sgn^2(RR_{ui} - RR_{uj}) \tag{4.5}$$

$$T^s = \sum_{ij} sgn^2(SR_{ui} - SR_{uj}) \tag{4.6}$$

$$T^{u0} = T^u - (T^+ + T^-) \tag{4.7}$$

where the sums ranges over the $\frac{1}{2}n_u(n_u - 1)$ pairs of items. Thus, T^u is the number of item pairs for which the reference ranking is ordered. The system ranking does the correct and incorrect order of these pairs, and it is presented by T^+ and T, respectively. T^{u0} is the number of pairs where the system ranking has strong coupling, but the reference ranking does not have such provision. The NDPM is calculated in the following equation:

$$NDPM = \frac{T^- + \frac{1}{2}(T^{u0})}{T^u} \tag{4.8}$$

The above equation returns 0 to the system upon correctly predicting all the preferred relations stated by the reference. If 1 is returned to the system, this means that every reference preferred relation is contradicted.

A system is said to be perfect that might not rank one item higher than the other. In such cases, Spearman's ρ is used as a rank correlation measure or measure of rank correlation [6] and handling ties in ranking [7] can be used. These are highly correlated in practice [8]. Kendall's τ is calculated in the following equation:

$$\tau = \frac{T^+ - T^-}{\sqrt{T^u}\sqrt{T^s}} \tag{4.9}$$

Equation (4.10) shows the Spearman's ρ:

$$\rho = \frac{1}{n_u} \frac{\sum_i (RR_{i,u} - RR^/)(SR_{i,u} - SR^/)}{\sigma(RR)\sigma(SR)} \tag{4.10}$$

where τ and σ are mean and standard deviation respectively.

Utility-based ranking

As the reference ranking is based on correlation with some "true" ranking, there exists another criterion that is used for ordering a list of items. One popular alternative assumption is that the utility of a list of recommendations is additive by taking the summation of utilities of the individual recommendations. The utility of each recommendation is the utility of the recommended item that is discounted by a factor that primarily depends on its position.

Normally, the recommendation list is traversed from the start to end with an assumption that the utility of the recommendations are tailored toward the end of the list. The outcome of this analysis is to observe a particular position in the list not the item that is recommended.

In many applications, a very small set of items is used by the users. In such cases, the recommendation engine is not used as a browser. The users may predict only a few items located at top of the list. The R-Score metric [9] returns the following score for each user u in the ranked list, where the value is declined exponentially in the list.

$$R_u = \sum_j \frac{\max{(R_{u,i_j} - d, 0)}}{2^{\frac{j-1}{\alpha-1}}}$$

(4.11)

Variables	Description
i_jm	i_jm (Jth location)
$R_{u,i}$	User u's rating for item i
d	Task-dependent rating (also called do not care rating as well.)
a	Half-life parameter

In case of ratings prediction tasks, each item is rated by $R_{u,i}$ (e.g., 4 stars), and d is the task-dependent neutral rating (e.g., 3 stars). Items with higher ranking (e.g., 4, 5 star) are get credited by the algorithms. In case of the usage prediction, $R_{u,i}$ would be 1 if the user u selects an item i and 0 otherwise, while d is 0.

Using,

$$R_{u,i} = -\log(popularity(item\ i))$$

(4.12)

If i is used and having value 0 otherwise, we can get the recommended information [10]. Per-user scores are accumulated by the following equation:

$$R = 100\frac{\sum_u R_u}{\sum_u \hat{R}_u}$$

(4.13)

where $\hat{R}_u$ represents the score of ranking for user u.

Online evaluation of ranking

This is evaluated by knowing the interaction of users with the system. User may select items from the presented list following an assumption that a user has scanned the list deeply at least once.

That is, if item number 1, 3, and 10 are selected by the user, this means the user has seen all the items from 1 to 10. Another assumption that can be made is the user has found items 1, 3, and 10 of his utmost interest, and all the others are of his no interest. In certain cases, we have some extra information to check whether more items are observed by the user or not? Let's take a simple scenario, if the list is too long and spans across several pages and each page has 20 results, and the user visits the second page and has seen results from 11 to 20 and finds nothing as per his/her choice. In this case, the results of this session are divided into three parts—first, the items of interest (1, 3, 10 in the scenario stated above), the least interested items (items from 1 to 20), and the unfamiliar items (starting from 21 till the end). Then, to score the original list, reference ranking metric is used. There are two methods to do the measurements. First, all the interested and desired items are located at the top of the reference list, unfamiliar located at the middle, and the undesired items are at the end of the list. Through this reference list, a user may choose only few interesting items, and unfamiliar list may have high number of probability of having more interesting items.

Second, the interesting items are located at the top of the reference list, after that the undesired items, while the rest are ignored. This is somehow handier, especially when some unknown items are favored to the undesired items. In either case, the main crux of the reference ranking is quite different from the offline measurements. In offline experiments, we assumed that the single reference ranking is acceptable in all respect, and we calculate the RS result deviation from the correct rankings. In case of online evaluation, the user is assumed to be preferred by the recommender's ranking. In simple words, this can be concluded as there is only one correct ranking in the offline evaluation, but multiple correct rankings are assumed in the online evaluation.

4.4   Diversity and accuracy metrics used in CARS

Accuracy and diversity measures are taken into consideration when we are interested to compare the performance of pre-filtering, post-filtering, and contextual modeling techniques that are the main techniques used in CARS.

4.4.1   How recommendation accuracy is measured in CARS?

The recommendation accuracy is measured only through simple Precision, Recall and F-measure methods [11].

The Precision and Recall methods are calculated as follows: against the "find all relevant items" strategy, the threshold between relevant and irrelevant items is set to 1, so we assume that if a user chose an item more than once, it is relevant ("good") for that client and we recommend it; otherwise, it is not recommended. Then, check the selected items are validated or not? If yes, it seems a "good" recommendation, otherwise it's treated as a "bad" one. To "recommend top k items," we determine the top k items as "good" items to be presented as a good recommendation to a user. For Precision and Recall measurements, the actual items selected by the user are compared with the predicted ones. Finally, each dataset is partitioned into two parts normally referred as the training and validation sets, where the training and validation set should be 2/3 and 1/3 of the whole dataset, respectively.

4.4.2   Diversity measurement in CARS

The recommendation diversity is measured in CARS are classified into three divers metrics [12]:

1. Probability-based
2. Logarithm-based
3. Rank-based.

Simpson's diversity index, the Shannon's entropy, and the Tidemann & Hall's index [12] are the popular measurement techniques against the above stated categories.

1. **The normalized Simpson's diversity**
    The normalized Simpsons's diversity index (D) is calculated as follows:

    $$Diversity\ Index\ (D) = \frac{1 - \sum_i \rho_i^2}{1 - \frac{1}{n}} \qquad (4.14)$$

    where ρ_i the proportion of recommended items in the ith category and n is the number of categories. The denominator of the formula is a normalization factor.

2. **The normalized Shannon's diversity index (E)**

   It is calculate as:

$$Shannon's\ Diversity\ Index\ (E) = -\sum_i \rho_i\ log_n\ \rho_i \tag{4.15}$$

   where p_i is the amount of recommended items in the ith category and n is the total number of categories. In this case, the normalization factor is treated as the base of the logarithm, which is equal to the number of categories, i.e., k.

3. **The Tidemann & Hall's diversity index (TH)**

   Its general form is as follows:

$$Tidemann\ \&\ Hall's\ Diversity\ Index\ (TH) = 1 - \frac{1}{(2\sum_i r\rho_i) - 1} \tag{4.16}$$

   In the above equation, r is the rank for the ith category. In TH, there is no need to normalize the index because its value always tends to 1 (1 mean, the maximum value). Second, 1 shows the increase in the number of items.

4.5 How to choose an appropriate evaluation metrics?

It is quite important to select which evaluation metric is the most appropriate for the given recommender algorithm. The appropriate category can be selected from Figure 4.3 with respect to an application domain area [13].

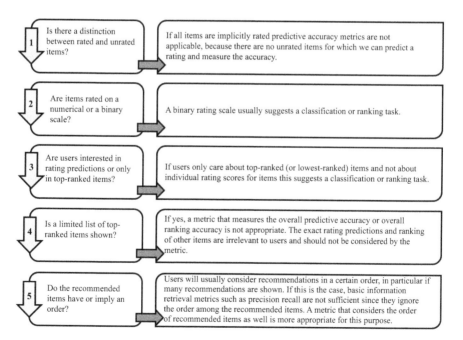

Figure 4.3   Criteria for selecting an appropriate evaluation metric for recommender algorithm

4.6   Conclusion

In this chapter, we have primarily focused on the performance metrics used in traditional systems as well as the CARS. Along with all the possible performance metrics used in those systems, we have discussed different methods to measure the accuracy and the ranking of the recommender algorithms. Moreover, we have also presented the common criteria for selecting an appropriate metric for any recommender algorithm in order to measure its performance.

Acknowledgments

We acknowledge the Chinese Academy of Science (CAS) and Third World Academy of Science (TWAS) for supporting this work (TWAS 2016-045). Moreover this work is financially supported by National Natural Science Foundation of China (NSFC) (Grant no. 61461136002).

References

[1]   Bobadilla, J., Ortega, F., Hernando, A., and Gutiérrez, A. "Recommender systems survey." Knowledge-Based Systems 46:109–132, 2013.

[2]   Shani, G., and A. Gunawardana. "Evaluating recommendation systems." Recommender Systems Handbook. Springer, Boston, MA, 2011. pp. 257–297.

[3]   Collins, A., and G.B. Daniel, eds. Representation and Understanding: Studies in Cognitive Science. Department of Anthropology University of California Berkeley, USA. Elsevier, 2017.

[4]   Bao, J., Zheng, Y., Wilkie, D., and Mokbel, M. "Recommendations in location-based social networks: a survey." GeoInformatica 19(3):525–565, 2015.

[5]   Adomavicius, G., and A. Tuzhilin. "Context-aware recommender systems." Recommender Systems Handbook. Springer, Boston, MA, 2015. pp. 191–226.

[6]   Kendall, M.G. "A new measure of rank correlation." Biometrika 30(1–2): 81–93, 1938.

[7]   Kendall, M.G. "The treatment of ties in ranking problems." Biometrika 33(3):239–251, 1945.

[8]   Fredricks, G.A., and R.B. Nelsen. "On the relationship between Spearman's rho and Kendall's tau for pairs of continuous random variables." Journal of Statistical Planning and Inference 137(7):2143–2150, 2007.

[9]   Breese, J.S., D. Heckerman, and C.M. Kadie. "Empirical analysis of predictive algorithms for collaborative filtering." In Proceedings of the Fourteenth Conference on Uncertainty in Artificial Intelligence (UAI1998). Morgan Kaufmann Publishers Inc., San Francisco, CA, 1998. pp. 43–52.

[10]   Shani, G., D. Heckerman, and R.I. Brafman. "An MDP-based recommender system." Journal of Machine Learning Research, 6:1265–1295, 2005.

[11]   Herlocker, J.L., J.A. Konstan, L.G. Terveen, and J.T. Riedl. "Evaluating collaborative filtering recommender systems." ACM Trans. Inf. Syst. 22(1):5–53, 2004.

[12]   McDonald, D., and J. Dimmick. "The conceptualization and measurement of diversity." Commun. Res. 30(1):60–79, 2003.

[13]   Schröder, G., M. Thiele, and W. Lehner. "Setting goals and choosing metrics for recommender system evaluations." UCERSTI2 Workshop at the 5th ACM Conference on Recommender Systems, Chicago, USA. Vol. 23, 2011.

Chapter 5

Mining urban lifestyles: urban computing, human behavior and recommender systems

Sharon Xu[1], Riccardo Di Clemente[2], and Marta C. González[3]

In the last decade, the digital age has sharply redefined the way we study human behavior. With the advancement of data storage and sensing technologies, electronic records now encompass a diverse spectrum of human activity, ranging from location data [1,2], phone [3,4], and email communication [5] to Twitter activity [6] and open-source contributions on Wikipedia and OpenStreetMap [7,8]. In particular, the study of the shopping and mobility patterns of individual consumers has the potential to give deeper insight into the lifestyles and infrastructure of the region. Credit card records (CCRs) provide detailed insight into purchase behavior and have been found to have inherent regularity in consumer shopping patterns [9]; call detail records (CDRs) present new opportunities to understand human mobility [10], analyze wealth [11], and model social network dynamics [12].

Regarding the analysis of CDR data, there exists a wide body of work characterizing human mobility patterns. As a notable example, [10] describes the temporal and spatial regularity of human trajectories, showing that each individual can be described by a time-independent travel distance and a high probability of returning to a small number of locations. Further, the authors are able to model individual travel patterns using a single spatial probability distribution. There has also been work at the intersection of similar datasets, such as the inference of friendships from mobile phone data [13], or the analysis such data in relation to metrics on spending behavior such as diversity, engagement, and loyalty [14]. Recent work [15] uses the Jaccard distance as a similarity measure on motifs among spending categories and then applies community-detection algorithms to find clusters of users. These studies propose models for either mobility or spending behavior, but not in conjunction.

The only known paper that incorporates both aspects [16] frames its analysis only on an aggregate scale of city regions. However, the coupled collaborative filtering methods (also known as collective matrix factorization) used in [16] have been successfully applied in a variety of urban computing applications for data fusion and

[1]Operations Research, Massachusetts Institute of Technology, United States
[2]Centre for Advance Spatial Analysis, University College London, United Kingdom
[3]City and Regional Planning Department, University of California, Berkeley, United States

prediction [17–19], from location-based activity recommendations [20,21] to travel speed estimation on road segments [22]. Recent work includes methods that use Laplacian regularization [23] to leverage social network information and use geometric deep learning matrix completion methods to model nonlinearities [24].

In this chapter, we jointly model the lifestyles of individuals, a more challenging problem with higher variability when compared to the aggregated behavior of city regions. Using collective matrix factorization, we propose a unified dual view of lifestyles. Understanding these lifestyles will not only inform commercial opportunities but also help policymakers and nonprofit organizations understand the characteristics and needs of the entire region, as well as of the individuals within that region. The applications of this range from targeted advertisements and promotions to the diffusion of digital financial services among low-income groups.

5.1   Mining shopping and mobility patterns

Location and transactional data offer valuable perspectives on the lifestyles of each user. For example, we may expect the shopping purchases of middle-aged parents to include groceries and fuel, while their mobility patterns may center around localities near home and work locations, in addition to points of interest such as supermarket and laundry. We use mobility information to aid in the prediction of shopping behavior, connecting the two views using collective matrix factorization [25]. In this way, we discover representative patterns relating shopping and mobility, characterizing behavior for a richer understanding into urban lifestyles and improved prediction of behavior.

The high granularity of such digital records allows modeling at the level of the individual, providing a new framework in which to relate movement and spending. However, in using CDR data for data on individuals, we must deal with issues of sparsity and lack of contextual information on the user's activities. In proposing this dual view of lifestyles, our contributions can be summarized as follows.

5.1.1   Prediction of shopping behavior with data sparsity

There are many individuals for which we have no CDR data. To deal with this data sparsity issue, we construct a framework that uses mobility patterns as supplementary information in the prediction of shopping behavior. We connect the two perspectives on lifestyles using collective matrix factorization (collective matrix factorization). In comparison to modeling only shopping behavior, we find that incorporating mobility information in the prediction of shopping lifestyles leads to a significant reduction in root mean square error (RMSE).

5.1.2   Adding contextual information to location data

We transform mobility data using external data sources to better relate CCR to CDR data. Although CCRs provide high granularity at the level of the individual user, spatial granularity can range from a radius of 200–1,000 m, and there is no contextual

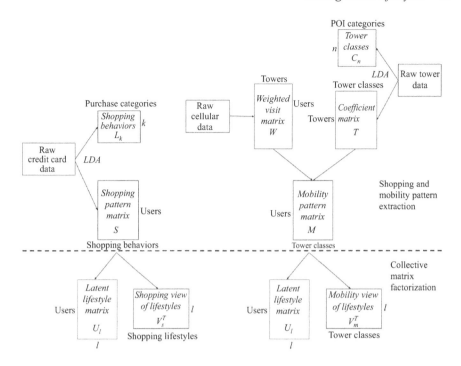

Figure 5.1   Our framework

information for the user's activities within that region. Thus, there has been little previous work leveraging CCR data for prediction with CDR data.

5.1.3   *Multi-perspective lifestyles*

We describe the mappings between shopping and mobility patterns, connecting the two views to provide a novel understanding of consumer behavior in urban regions (Figure 5.1).

5.2   Data

The primary datasets used in this chapter consist of two sets of anonymized data for residents in Mexico throughout five months in 2015:

- CDRs. CDRs are produced with each telephone exchange. These location records give the nearest cellular tower at the time of a placed call. There are 1192 cell towers throughout Mexico City—as users tend to visit a small subset of these towers, this mobility data is extremely sparse. In a count matrix denoting user visits to towers, 98% of entries indicate zero visits.

- CCRs. CCRs are recorded with each purchase and denote the purchase category, or Merchant Category Code (MCC), of the transaction as well as the amount spent. Each month, we have on the order of 10 million financial transactions and 200 million location records.

5.3   Discovering shopping patterns

Our spending habits reflect our lifestyles, capturing an essential aspect of our behavior. Within the computational social science community, the question remains whether pervasive trends exist among disparate groups at urban scale [15]. In this chapter, we use latent Dirichlet allocation (LDA) [26] to identify topics (behavioral patterns) among individuals, representing each individual's spending lifestyle as a finite mixture of an underlying set of behaviors. Each behavioral pattern, in turn, is modeled as a mixture of a set of words (MCCs). These topics are determined by co-occurrences of words within a document. For example, in an article database, we may uncover a topic containing the words "data," "processing," "computer," and so on because these words frequently appear in an article together.

By putting a Dirichlet prior on the per-user behavior distribution and per-behavior MCC distribution, LDA controls the sparsity of the number of topics per document (the number of behaviors per individual), as well as the number of words per topic (the number of MCCs per behavioral pattern). In this way, each individual is represented by a small number of behaviors, and each behavior involves making a small set of purchase categories with high frequency.

As a generative model, LDA allows us to calculate the probabilities (assignments to shopping behaviors) of previously unseen users. We train the model on 40% of the users and generate the matrix S for the remaining 60%. In so doing, we set up the prediction of lifestyles for unseen users, assessing the LDA model itself in addition to the relation of shopping with mobility patterns. We experiment with the choice of number of behaviors to learn, as well as adding a categorical variable describing amount spent to each MCC. To maximize interpretability, we choose five topics while using MCCs as input only.

In Figure 5.2, we plot the 20 most highly weighted MCCs of the five shopping behaviors. The first shopping behavior describes credit card usage that is centered on food-related purchases such as grocery stores, misc. food stores and restaurants. The second shopping behavior seems to be associated primarily with business purchases, with spending within MCCs such as fax services and financial institutions. The third shopping behavior is dominated by relative "luxuries" such as purchases in the cable and department store categories and is characterized by a relatively high proportion of air travel and hotel lodging MCCs. The fourth shopping behavior contains primarily purchases in computer network services and service stations (gas stations). The third and fourth shopping behavior describe a slightly wealthier portion of the population, as only 35% of Mexicans owned a computer in 2010 [27], and only 44.2% own a car [28]. Lastly, the fifth shopping behavior captures purchase primarily for toll fees and subscription services.

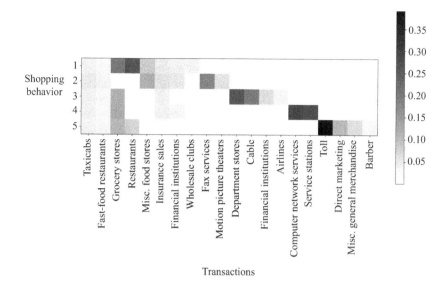

Figure 5.2   The top weighted purchase categories of the five shopping behaviors learned from LDA

5.4   Mobility pattern extraction

5.4.1   Extracting cellular tower location types

Within the CDR data, each tower is the site for a corresponding cell within the Voronoi diagram, i.e., it is the closest tower to any point within this cell. We define a "visit" to a cellular tower as a call placed within its corresponding cell. In order to relate cellular towers to spending behavior, for each tower, we crawl Google's API for points of interest within a certain radius. To determine this radius, we use Delaunay triangulation, a widely used method in computational geometry. Delaunay triangulation gives the dual graph to the Voronoi diagram, maximizing the minimum angle among all the triangles within the triangulation and connecting the sites in a nearest neighbor fashion [29]. For each tower, we set the crawling radius to be half the average distance from the site to its neighbors.

Treating each of the Voronoi cells as a document and the POI categories as words, we use LDA to discover underlying tower "classes" that will be more informative of shopping behavior. We remove from the vocabulary any POI categories that occur with over 25% frequency. These removed categories are uninformative classifications such as "point of interest" and "establishment." For purposes of interpretability, we learn the LDA model with 20 classes on the 1,192 towers.

In Figure 5.3, we show a subset of tower classes highly weighted within our final lifestyles (see Section 5.6), and the corresponding points of interest with the

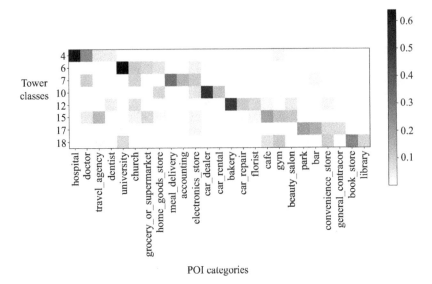

Figure 5.3   The top weighted POI categories of a subset of tower classes learned from LDA

```
0.617"hospital" + 0.264"doctor"
+ 0.041"travel_agency"
+ 0.038"dentist" + 0.023"gym"

0.569"clothing_store"
+ 0.090"department_store"
+ 0.048"shopping_mall"

0.765"lodging" + 0.059"bar"
+ 0.052"museum" + 0.018"travel_agency"

0.247"atm" + 0.176"bank" + 0.118"police"
+ 0.088"post_office" + 0.079"city_hall"
 + 0.071"local_government_office"
```

Figure 5.4   Sample topics from learned from LDA, treating each tower as a document and each POI as a word

highest probabilities. From the sample topics in Figure 5.4, we see each tower class puts specific emphasis on related points of interest, such as "hospital" and "doctor," "car rental" and "car repair," or "book store" and "library." In this way, we cluster the towers in terms of nearby POI categories, obtaining contextual information more directly related to shopping.

5.4.2 Baseline methods

Before introducing our model, we present the results of several baseline methods, illustrating the challenges of incorporating CDR data into the prediction of shopping patterns.

5.4.2.1 Regression on average amount spent

Using the columns of the per tower count matrix W directly as features, we use regression with L1 regularization to predict the average amount spent by the user per week. As we increase regularization, we increase the test R-squared, but due to a combination of sparsity and lack of signal, we achieve a maximum test R-squared of 0 as the coefficients shrink to 0.

5.4.2.2 Classification of primary shopping behavior

For each user, we take as our outcome the highest weighted shopping behavior from the topic proportions learned from LDA. This is the user's primary behavior. Again using the columns of W as our features, we employ a range of classifiers including SVM and AdaBoost to predict primary behavior. We find that the best classifier achieves only 21.6% accuracy, when already 21.9% of users fall into a single class.

5.4.3 Characterizing mobility patterns

From the Voronoi diagram of the p cell tower locations, we construct a matrix $W \in \mathbb{R}^{nxp}$ where each entry w_{ij} is the number of days individual i visited tower j throughout five months. We weight these counts using TF-IDF, a common method for text representation [30]. Using TF-IDF, we offset the tower counts by the frequency of the tower in the data, so that a user's visit to an uncommonly visited tower is assigned a higher weight. We now have a matrix $W \in \mathbb{R}^{nxp}$ that characterizes users in terms of tower visits, and a matrix $C_m \in \mathbb{R}^{pxd}$, where d is the chosen number of tower classes. We define our mobility pattern matrix as $M = WT$, achieving a significant dimensionality reduction with $M \in \mathbb{R}^{nxd}$. In this manner, we obtain a representation of mobility more closely related to shopping behavior, as users are now characterized by their visits to tower classes defined by POI categories.

5.5 Predicting shopping behavior

For many users, we have access to data on mobility patterns (M) but not shopping patterns (S). In this section, we describe our methodology for incorporating mobility information in addition to shopping information for the matrix completion problem of predicting the shopping behavior of unseen users.

5.5.1 Collective matrix factorization

We denote S as the matrix of behavior proportions obtained from LDA, and M as the matrix of weighted visit frequencies to the different tower classes. Modeling each user's shopping and mobility behavior as two views of the same lifestyle, we assume that S and M are generated from a matrix U_l containing the latent lifestyle information of each user.

$$S \approx U_l V_s^T$$

$$M \approx U_l V_m^T$$

Traditionally, the objective function under this model is represented as

$$\mathcal{L}(U_l, V_s, V_m) = ||S - U_l V_s^T||^2 + ||M - U_l V_m^T||^2 + \lambda_1 ||U_l||^2$$
$$+ \lambda_2 ||V_s||^2 + \lambda_3 ||V_m||^2$$

In this chapter, we use group-wise sparse collective matrix factorization [31], which puts group-sparse priors following $\mathcal{N}(0, \sigma_k^2)$ on the columns of matrices V_s and V_m, where the columns are the groups indexed by k and σ_k^2 is small. This allows the matrix to learn private factors for the relation between latent lifestyles (U_l) and the shopping aspect (V_s), and correspondingly between latent lifestyles (U_l) and the mobility aspect (V_m). More specifically, if the kth column of V_m is null, the kth factor impacts only the shopping pattern matrix S.

5.6   Results

5.6.1   Prediction

In our problem, credit card data is unknown for many users, but we would like to use mobility information to predict their shopping behavior, i.e., S contains many empty rows. Thus, to test the performance within this setting, we remove rows from the shopping behavior S to predict the shopping behavior of users for which we have no credit card information. We use 10-fold cross validation and compare our collective matrix factorization predictions with the actual values. We use the popular metric RMSE to evaluate our model.

$$\text{RMSE} = \sqrt{\frac{1}{T} \sum_{i,j} (S_{i,j} - \hat{S}_{i,j})^2}$$

Using cross-validation to determine the rank (number of lifestyles), we find that the inclusion of mobility data leads to a 1.3% decrease in RMSE and obtain a test error of 21.6%.

5.6.2   Dual lifestyles

Using collective matrix factorization, we also obtain both the dual shopping and mobility views of these latent lifestyles, in V_s and V_m, respectively.

Lifestyle 1 is connected with wealthier shopping behavior typical common to urban white collars. The top weighted shopping patterns indicate spending on cable, air travel, hotels, and at department stores as well as gas stations and computer network services (Figure 5.2: behaviors 3 and 4, respectively). This suggests that people who can afford to spend on relative luxuries tend to have vehicles and thus higher mobility, visiting a wider range of tower classes. The mobility patterns of this lifestyle focus on areas with points of interest such as universities, accounting, electronics, bakeries, and car repair (Figure 5.3: tower classes 6, 7, 12, 17, and 20).

Lifestyle 2 is extremely food oriented, with high weight on shopping behavior 1. Mobility patterns suggest visits to cafes, gyms, and convenience stores.

Lifestyle 3 primarily captures the transportation aspect of lifestyles. Top-weighted mobility patterns indicate visits to areas with car rental and car repair (tower classes 10 and 12), while shopping patterns include gas stations in behavior 4 and food in behavior 1.

5.7   Discussion

In this study, we relate the shopping and mobility patterns of consumers on an individual level for the first time. Viewing these as aspects of the same underlying lifestyle, we set up a framework to incorporate CDR data in the prediction of shopping patterns for unseen users. We achieve a significant increase in prediction and recover interesting relationships between shopping and mobility.

There are many directions for future work. In terms of modeling formulation, it would be interesting to introduce a temporal dimension into the task of shopping prediction, as human behavior and needs vary over time. There is also the opportunity to include social regularization in the collective matrix factorization formulation, constraining each user to be similar to his or her neighborhood. In addition, stronger prediction methods may be achieved by modeling nonlinear relationships using geometric deep learning methods described by [24].

Acknowledgments

We thank Grandata for supplying the data. (For contractual and privacy reasons, the raw data cannot be provided.)

References

[1]   Song C, Qu Z, Blumm N, *et al.* Limits of predictability in human mobility. Science. 2010;327(5968):1018–1021.

[2]   Hasan S, Schneider CM, Ukkusuri SV, *et al.* Spatiotemporal patterns of urban human mobility. Journal of Statistical Physics. 2013;151(1–2):304–318.

[3]   Jo HH, Karsai M, Kertész J, *et al.* Circadian pattern and burstiness in mobile phone communication. New Journal of Physics. 2012;14(1):013055.

[4]   Aledavood T, López E, Roberts SG, *et al.* Daily rhythms in mobile telephone communication. PLoS One. 2015;10(9):e0138098.

[5]   Malmgren RD, Stouffer DB, Motter AE, *et al.* A Poissonian explanation for heavy tails in e-mail communication. Proceedings of the National Academy of Sciences of the United States of America. 2008;105(47):18153–18158.

[6]   Ten Thij M, Bhulai S, Kampstra P. Circadian patterns in twitter. Data Analytics. 2014:12–17.

[7]   Yasseri T, Sumi R, Kertész J. Circadian patterns of Wikipedia editorial activity: A demographic analysis. PLoS One. 2012;7(1):e30091.

[8]   Yasseri T, Quattrone G, Mashhadi A. Temporal analysis of activity patterns of editors in collaborative mapping project of OpenStreetMap. In: Proceedings of the 9th International Symposium on Open Collaboration. ACM; 2013. p. 13.

[9]   Krumme C, Llorente A, Cebrian M, *et al.* The predictability of consumer visitation patterns. Scientific Reports. 2013;3:1645..

[10] Gonzalez MC, Hidalgo CA, Barabasi AL. Understanding individual human mobility patterns. Nature. 2008;453(7196):779–782. Available from: http://dx.doi.org/10.1038/nature06958.

[11] Blumenstock J, Cadamuro G, On R. Predicting poverty and wealth from mobile phone metadata. Science. 2015;350(6264):1073–1076.

[12] Morse S, González MC, Markuzon N. Persistent cascades: Measuring fundamental communication structure in social networks. 2016 IEEE International Conference on Big Data (Big Data). IEEE; 2016. p. 969–975.

[13] Eagle N, Pentland AS, Lazer D. Inferring friendship network structure by using mobile phone data. Proceedings of the National Academy of Sciences of the United States of America. 2009;106(36):15274–15278. Available from: http://dx.doi.org/10.1073/pnas.0900282106.

[14] Singh VK, Freeman L, Lepri B, *et al.* Predicting spending behavior using socio-mobile features. In: Proceedings of the 2013 International Conference on Social Computing. SOCIALCOM'13. Washington, DC, USA: IEEE Computer Society; 2013. p. 174–179. Available from: http://dx.doi.org/10.1109/SocialCom.2013.33.

[15] Di Clemente R, Luengo-Oroz M, Travizano M, *et al.* Sequence of purchases in credit card data reveal life styles in urban populations. Nature Communications. 2017;9.

[16] Hu T, Song R, Wang Y, *et al.* Mining shopping patterns for divergent urban regions by incorporating mobility data. In: Proceedings of the 25th ACM International on Conference on Information and Knowledge Management. ACM; 2016. p. 569–578.

[17] Zheng Y. Methodologies for cross-domain data fusion: An overview. IEEE Transactions on Big Data. 2015;1(1):16–34.

[18] Zheng Y, Capra L, Wolfson O, *et al.* Urban computing: Concepts, methodologies, and applications. ACM Transactions on Intelligent Systems and Technology (TIST). 2014;5(3):38.

[19] Zheng Y. Trajectory data mining: An overview. ACM Transactions on Intelligent Systems and Technology (TIST). 2015;6(3):29.

[20]   Zheng VW, Zheng Y, Xie X, *et al.* Collaborative location and activity recommendations with GPS history data. In: Proceedings of the 19th international conference on World wide web. ACM; 2010. p. 1029–1038.

[21]   Zheng VW, Cao B, Zheng Y, *et al.* Collaborative filtering meets mobile recommendation: A user-centered approach. In: AAAI. vol. 10; 2010. p. 236–241.

[22]   Shang J, Zheng Y, Tong W, *et al.* Inferring gas consumption and pollution emission of vehicles throughout a city. In: Proceedings of the 20th ACM SIGKDD International Conference on Knowledge Discovery and Data Mining. ACM; 2014. p. 1027–1036.

[23]   Cai D, He X, Han J, *et al.* Graph regularized nonnegative matrix factorization for data representation. IEEE Transactions on Pattern Analysis and Machine Intelligence. 2011;33(8):1548–1560.

[24]   Bronstein MM, Bruna J, LeCun Y, *et al.* Geometric deep learning: Going beyond Euclidean data. IEEE Signal Processing Magazine. 2017;34(4):18–42.

[25]   Singh AP, Gordon GJ. Relational learning via collective matrix factorization. In: Proceedings of the 14th ACM SIGKDD International Conference on Knowledge Discovery and Data Mining. KDD'08. New York, NY, USA: ACM; 2008. p. 650–658. Available from: http://doi.acm.org/10.1145/1401890.1401969.

[26]   Blei DM, Ng AY, Jordan MI. Latent Dirichlet allocation. Journal of Machine Learning Research. 2003;3:993–1022. Available from: http://dl.acm.org/citation.cfm?id=944919.944937.

[27]   Villagram L. For most Mexicans, the digital age is still out of reach; 2012.

[28]   Censo de Población y Vivienda. INEGI; 2010.

[29]   Aurenhammer F. Voronoi diagrams—A survey of a fundamental geometric data structure. ACM Computing Surveys. 1991;23(3):345–405. Available from: http://doi.acm.org/10.1145/116873.116880.

[30]   Zhang W, Yoshida T, Tang X. A comparative study of TF* IDF, LSI and multi-words for text classification. Expert Systems with Applications. 2011;38(3):2758–2765.

[31]   Klami A, Bouchard G, Tripathi A. Group-sparse embeddings in collective matrix factorization. International Conference on Learning Representations. 2013.

Chapter 6

Embedding principal component analysis inference in expert sensors for big data applications

Rodrigo Marino[1], Jose M. Lanza-Gutierrez[1], and Teresa Riesgo[1]

The increasing relevance of big data applications in fields as the Internet of Things (IoT) and Industry 4.0 implies that sensors are requested to be secure and accurate. In the last years, sensors are evolving toward complex monitoring functionalities, increasing the complexity of data, meaning that the analysis stage is usually performed away from the sensor layer, i.e., the fog or the cloud. This separation entails issues for response time and security. As a possible way to address this data analysis closer to the edge, embedded machine-learning (ML) techniques have shown to be a good solution, leading to *expert* sensors. Feature extraction tools, as principal component (PC) analysis (PCA), might offer a solution to reduce the amount of data transmitted through the network, adding additional security because information is not transmitted as raw data. However, PCA is time-consuming and therefore, it should be carefully optimized according to the hardware used in the sensor device. This chapter proposes to embed the PCA inference stage in a low-cost field-programmable system on chip (SoC) (FPSoC) while performing a design space exploration for a general PCA inference problem. To this end, the authors analyze metrics, such as latency, scalability, and usage of hardware resources. The resulting architectures are compared to a multicore OpenMP approach to be executed in an ARM processor, analyzing the advantages of using the FPSoC implementation in speedup.

6.1 Introduction

As is well known, big data solutions try to enhance productivity and system capabilities by identifying trends of interest in large-volume of sophisticated datasets, which usually come from multiple distributed sources, leading to a collaborative

[1]Centro de Electrónica Industrial, Escuela Técnica Superior de Ingenieros Industriales, Universidad Politécnica de Madrid, Spain

complex environment [1]. During the last years, big data approaches are gaining special attention in fields as physics, finance, industry, social media, and healthcare due to the interesting results offered by this data-analytic technology [2,3].

A general big data application usually considers four main stages: data generation, data acquisition, data storage, and data analysis [4]. Data generation focuses on defining the type and amount of data which the system needs to manage. Data acquisition focuses on acquiring the data previously defined in the data generation stage, considering different technologies as sensors and actuators. Data storage includes the tools needed for managing huge amounts of data as specialized databases. Data analysis focuses on developing techniques to extract information and trends of interest from all the data in the system.

Big data approaches usually combine technologies capable of generating huge amounts of data to detect trends of interests. A technology of distinctive relevance today fulfilling this premise is the IoT. As is well known, IoT consists of the interconnection of many tiny computing devices embedded in everyday objects, transmitting, storing, and processing data all over the world via the Internet [5]. From a computing capacity point of view, IoT is divided into three layers: cloud, fog, and edge. The cloud layer takes place in large computing centers far away from end users, handling the highest computing intensity stages of the systems, including for example ML and deep-learning algorithms. The fog layer has a medium computing capacity and takes place in switches and routers, which are relatively close to end users [6,7]. The need of highly processing-demanding IoT applications leads to the creation of this layer, in which the cloud layer cannot manage certain constraints related to the distance from the place where the action is taking place. Some examples of such constraints are the real-time response and the sending of confidential data via the Internet. The edge layer takes place in the "things," i.e., the everyday objects interacting with the environment and end users. This layer has the most limiting constraints related to computing capacity and energy consumption. Therefore, it is usually composed of low-power low-cost devices as field-programmable gate arrays (FPGAs), small microprocessors and microcontrollers, and SoC as FPSoCs[1] [8].

Along with this chapter, the authors address the issue of improving both data acquisition and data-analysis stages of big data applications. To this end, they focus on how to enhance the edge layer, bringing the computation closer to end users. For instance, implementing some intelligence in the edge nodes instead of being simple sensing devices, which send data to be processed in upper layers. This is the transformation known as from "smart sensors" to "expert sensors" [5]. Specifically, the proposal in this chapter is motivated by the following facts: (i) sensing systems are becoming more sophisticated, and then the data generated increment in size and complexity, meaning a high cost in data transmission through upper layers; (ii) more and more applications require near instant response time close to end devices, which leads to reducing the data traffic going toward upper layers; (iii) sending data as captured toward upper layers could mean a security risk for many applications [9].

---

[1]An heterogeneous system, including a hard processor and an FPGA in the same chip.

Thus, the goal of this chapter is to embed ML algorithms in edge devices as a quick response mechanism for end users, but taking into account the hardware limitations in this layer. Of course, under certain situations, an edge device could ask for a more accurate prediction to upper layers, which implement more complex intelligent algorithms because of the higher computing capacity. As the first step in this task, we propose to study how to embed one of the most hardware-demanding steps in ML, the feature extraction stage. Note that feature extraction is also considered as a compression step because it is possible to transmit a reduced set of features extracted instead of all the data, which leads to improving security, energy cost, and response time. Specifically, we propose to study how to embed in edge nodes the feature extraction tool known as PCA [10]. This tool has been applied intensely during the last decades in a wide range of applications, such as natural disaster prevention [11], spectrum sensing [12], arrhythmia detection [13], tumor margin diagnosis [14], seizure detection [15], intelligent video surveillance [16], and triggering control for the Large Hadron Collider [17].

PCA is a multivariate statistical technique, which applies an orthogonal transformation to convert a set of high-dimensional correlated variables (a problem with many attributes) to a set of linearly uncorrelated ones called PCs. The PCA method consists of two stages: training and inference. During the inference stage, the PCs for new data projections are calculated based on coefficients previously obtained during the training stage. As PCA is a demanding task, there are specialized implementations for platforms as graphics processing units [18,19] and massively parallel processor arrays [14,20], which could be considered in powerful devices in both fog and cloud layers.

Based on this knowledge, this chapter provides a design space study for implementing a general PCA inference stage taking into account the hardware limitations in the edge layer. Thus, the authors compare different architectures under a low-cost state-of-the-art FPSoC,[2] analyzing features as scalability (number of PCs and attributes), latency, hardware parameters (pipelining and unrolling), and FPGA resources used, i.e., digital signal processors (DSPs), flip-flops (FF), and lookup tables (LUTs). The hardware implementations presented in this chapter are based on both 8- and 16-bit architectures because most analog–digital converters, used in embedded systems for the data acquisition, usually move in a precision range from 8 to 16 bits. The resulting architectures are compared to a multicore PCA implementation executed under an ARM processor usually found in embedded devices. Note that the architectures proposed in this chapter could be implemented under a traditional FPGA with similar resources. The reason for selecting an FPSoC is because of the flexibility offered by the platform for future implementation of the ML system.

The remainder of this chapter is structured as follows. Section 6.2 includes the related work on PCA inference implementations within both FPGAs and FPSoCs. Section 6.3 includes the PCA mathematical formulation focusing on the inference stage. Section 6.4 discusses the workflow followed to embed the PCA inference in

---

[2]An FPSoC with a trade-off between performance and cost, which allows doing massive deployments in IoT applications.

the edge layer. Section 6.5 describes embedded architectures proposed. Section 6.6 discusses the experimental methodology followed. Section 6.7 includes the experimental results obtained applying the PCA inference in the 8- and 16-bit architectures, as well as the multicore approach. Section 6.8 concludes the paper with some final remarks and future directions of research.

6.2   Related work

This section gives a brief overview of PCA inference implementation within FPGAs and FPSoCs. The works discussed below are grouped by the word size of the architecture.

Starting with 32-bit architectures, the authors in [11,21,22] proposed an implementation under a high-cost Virtex-7 FPGA by Xilinx. To this end, they used a soft processor inside the FPGA to deploy some parts in software instead of implementing the whole PCA in hardware. This fact causes a system latency issue because of a communication bottleneck and a loss of parallelism, which the authors tried to mitigate using a direct memory access module. In [9], the authors considered a high-cost Arria 10 FPSoC by Intel, where they implemented a PCA inference for 32 PCs using 1,518 DSPs, a number exceeding, by far, the typical values in low-cost FPGAs. In [16], the authors used a high-cost Virtex-6 FPGA by Xilinx, designing an architecture which takes advantage of the Peripheral Component Interconnect express (PCIe) communication, meaning that the system is intended to be used with a high-performance system, such a computer, instead of an edge device. In [12], the authors considered a low-cost Cyclone II FPGA by Xilinx. However, the system was not fully deployed in the FPGA because of the high-resource utilization, so implementing part of the system in a computer.

Following with 16-bit architectures, the authors in [23] considered a low-cost Zynq-7020 FPSoC by Xilinx, for a problem with 23 attributes and a floating-point data type. In [17], the authors proposed to consider the DSP logic block inside a high-cost Kintex 7 FPGA by Xilinx.

Finishing with 8-bit architectures, the authors in [24] considered a low-cost Spartan-6 FPGA by Xilinx, using a soft processor inside the FPGA. This fact causes the same communication problem discussed before for [11,21,22]. In [25], the authors considered a low-cost Zynq-7010 FPSoC by Xilinx. However, in this proposal, the architecture is designed to be controlled externally using a computer, and then it is not intended to be used within an edge device. Moreover, the design presented used an external random access memory (RAM), reducing the performance when running in parallel. The authors in [26] designed a PCA inference architecture using a high-cost Virtex-7 FPGA by Xilinx. As a result, the proposal utilizes up to 99% of DSPs, meaning that it is not suitable to deploy the architecture in a low-cost device with a reduced number of DSP. In [27], the authors deployed a CORDIC soft processor inside a Virtex 7 FPGA. This implementation might increase latency as discussed before for [11,21,22,24].

In addition to the traditional 32/16/8 bit architectures, there are also custom designs for specific applications. In [28], the authors developed a 64-bit floating-point architecture, under an Arria 5 FPSoC by Intel, to detect different carrier signals in telecommunication applications. In [29], the authors considered an 18-bit architecture, under an Arria 5 FPSoC, including a CORDIC soft processor with the same limitation as before.

From the previous literature, we have found that there are a large number of architectures proposed to solve the PCA inference for specific applications, most of them using high-cost FPGAs and FPSoCs. However, as far as we know, there is no study, which performs a design space exploration for a general PCA inference problem. Thus, the study in this chapter could be particularly interesting for system designers, facilitating decision-making when selecting the hardware needed to build an expert sensor. This is the reason why the authors of this chapter, according to the edge layer constraints, focus on using low-cost hardware devices.

The proposal in this document is based on a preliminary work [30], where the authors performed a design space exploration for a specific problem with 3,648 attributes and two PCs under a 32-bit architecture, studying number of block RAMs (BRAMs), pipelining usage, latency, data type, number of unrolls, and FPGA resources (DSPs, FF, and LUTs). As will be discussed in Section 6.5, some details of the embedded architecture proposed are supported by the main conclusions in this preliminary work.

6.3 Principal component analysis: problem formulation

Let n be the number of attributes of the problem. Let k be the number of observations for the training stage. Let X be a matrix of initial observations for the training stage with as many columns as attributes and as many rows as observations. The PCA training stage provides two sets of data, which will be used before during the inference stage:

- The sample mean vector $\overline{X}$, which contains the average of the observations for each attribute during the training stage, that is,

$$\overline{X} = [\overline{x}_1, \overline{x}_2, \ldots, \overline{x}_n]^T, \tag{6.1}$$

where $\overline{x}_j \in \overline{X}$ is the average value of the jth attribute for the k observation, with $j \in 1, \ldots, n$, that is,

$$\overline{x}_j = \frac{1}{k} \sum_{i=1}^{k} x_{ij}, \tag{6.2}$$

where $x_{ij} \in X$ is the value of the jth attribute of the ith observation, with $i \in 1, \ldots, k$.

- The matrix of eigenvectors W obtained based on X, that is,

$$W = [w_1, w_2, \ldots, w_m]^T, \tag{6.3}$$

where $w_z \in W$ is the zth n-dimensional eigenvector, with $z \in 1, \ldots, m$. m is the maximum number of PCs, with $m \ll n$. Based on that, an eigenvalue shows how much variance there is in the data in that direction, the eigenvector with the highest eigenvalue is the PC (w_1). The eigenvector with the second highest eigenvalue is the second PC (w_2), and so on. Additional information about eigenvector calculation is in [10].

Once PCA training is performed, PCA inference transforms new input samples $B \in \mathbb{R}^n$ according to the reference space defined by the PCs. To this end, the usual criterion is to consider a reduced number of PCs m' instead of using the previously obtained value m, with $m' \leq m$. The idea is to use the minimum number of PCs to reach at least 95% of variance explained according to eigenvalues. Thus, a new sample is transformed as given by

$$Y = W'(B - \overline{X}), \tag{6.4}$$

where $Y \in \mathbb{R}^{m'}$ and

$$W' = [w_1, w_2, \ldots, w_{m'}]^T. \tag{6.5}$$

6.4 Workflow description

This section describes the workflow considered to embed the PCA inference in the edge device, which comprises online and offline tasks to be done. Generally speaking, offline tasks refer to processes whose performance does not require to satisfy time, resource, or energy constraints. On the contrary, online tasks should satisfy specific requirements as the ones introduced before. A two-stage workflow as the one considered in this chapter allows system engineers to only perform online tasks under the constrained edge devices while demanding offline tasks are performed in powerful devices. Thus, PCA training is performed offline, i.e., at a conventional device, such as a computer, and PCA inference is performed online, i.e., at the edge device.

PCA training is fully performed in software using third-party tools as the ones provided by MATLAB in the Statistics and Machine Learning Toolbox. As usual, the data used to train the system should be revised through data-cleansing methods as outlier study. Data usually come within a table with as many columns as attributes the problem has and as many rows as observations. Note that the data type used during the training should be converted to the same data type considered in the architecture of the embedded device, then reducing the precision error during the inference stage.

PCA inference is fully performed in the embedded device according to the sample mean vector and the matrix of eigenvectors obtained during the training stage, as discussed before in Section 6.3. This stage is implemented using high-level synthesis (HLS) tools, specifically Vivado HLS by Xilinx, transforming C/C++ code into a hardware description language as VHDL. Moreover, Vivado by Xilinx is considered to design the whole architecture and Xilinx software development kit (SDK) by Xilinx is used for programming the processor and running/debugging the whole system.

Based on this workflow, Figure 6.1 shows the methodology considered for debugging the embedded PCA inference implementation. Thus, after performing the training stage, as usual, PCA inference is performed in both hardware and software

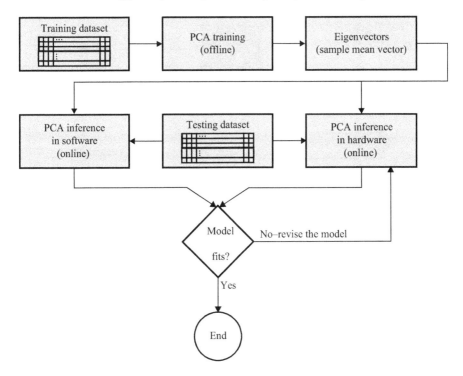

Figure 6.1   Methodology for debugging the PCA inference implementation

with the goal of checking whether the hardware implementation coincides with the software one. Otherwise, the hardware implementation is revised and verified again.

6.5   Embedded architecture

This section presents the embedded architecture proposed for PCA inference calculation while considering a top-down methodology. Thus, we first describe the system-level-architecture, including the main types of hardware blocks, as memories and intellectual property (IP) blocks. Next, we provide specific details for the PCA inference IP proposed, going from a simplistic to a generalist design.

6.5.1   System-level architecture

This section describes the PCA inference implementation from a system-level point of view. As Figure 6.2 shows, the architecture proposed has two main high-level elements according to the FPSoC concept: ARM processor and FPGA.

The ARM processor deals with controlling the FPGA and proving connectivity with the physical world. Both ARM processor and FPGA are connected through a communication bus, which not only handles data transmission but also controls the IP blocks implemented inside the FPGA.

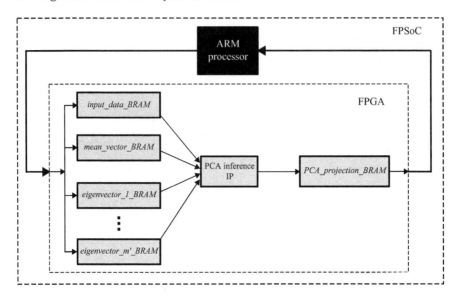

Figure 6.2   System-level design architecture of the embedded system

The architecture includes two main types of blocks focusing on the FPGA: memories and an IP for PCA inference calculation. The memory blocks considered are as follows:

- An *input_data BRAM* saving the data to be transformed through PCA inference, i.e., B in (6.4). This BRAM has as many storage units as attributes that the problem has. Without loss of generality, we assume that a storage unit is equivalent to the word size of the architecture considered. This BRAM is updated by the ARM processor each time a PCA inference must be calculated.
- m' BRAMs saving the eigenvectors obtained during the training stage, denoted as *eigenvector*$_1$ *BRAM* to *eigenvector*$_{m'}$ *BRAM*. Each of these BRAMs has as many storage units as attributes the problem has (see W' definition in (6.5)). The m' BRAMs are initialized by the ARM processor with the values obtained during the PCA training stage after starting the system.
- A *mean_vector BRAM* saving the sample mean vector obtained during the training (see $\overline{X}$ in (6.1)). This BRAM has as many storage units as attributes the problem has and is initialized by the ARM processor with the values obtained during PCA training after starting the system.
- A *PCA_projection_BRAM* saving the output of the PCA inference stage (see Y in (6.4)). This BRAM has as many storage units as the number of PCs (m') was defined during the training. This memory is updated each time the PCA inference IP is executed.

The fact that each eigenvector is in a different BRAM instead of having the m' eigenvectors in the same BRAM provides benefits in terms of parallelism as the authors shown in [30]. Thus, PCA inference IP applies the same mathematical operation using data from different eigenvectors in parallel by following a single instruction multiple data (SIMD) approach. Otherwise, the information from different eigenvectors should be sequentially obtained.

6.5.2 PCA inference IP description

Let z be the word size of the architecture considered in bits. Let a be the memory alignment[3] value in bits. Let $k = a/z$ be the parallelism factor based on the relation between the memory alignment and the word size of the architecture. For the case in this chapter, $a = 32$, $z \in \{8, 16\}$, and then, $k \in \{2, 4\}$. Note that memories are aligned on 32 bits because BRAM access from/to ARM processor is restricted to this value when using the platform considered in this work. As will be discussed below, the architecture presented here takes advantage of this limitation in memory alignment to reduce the system latency by performing some operations in parallel.

Figure 6.3 shows a simplification of the PCA inference IP for a PC depending on k. This IP has three input memory words with a width of a bits, where the words come from a reading in *input_data_BRAM*, *eigenvector_1_BRAM*, and *mean_vector_BRAM*. A *splitter* block divides the memory word into k sub-words according to the architecture considered, providing parallelism with factor k when applying subtraction and multiplication operations according to (6.4). The k values obtained after this step are summed and accumulated in the same addition block, resulting in a word of a bits. After n/k iterations of this process, i.e., from reading the memory blocks to accumulating the k values, the PC value is fully calculated and then it is written in *PCA_projection_BRAM*. The ARM processor manages how this accumulation process is initialized and finished.

Based on Figure 6.3, Figure 6.4 shows a generalization of the PCA inference IP for z PCs depending on k. This IP has $2 + m'$ input words with a width of a bits, where the words come from a reading task in *input_data_BRAM*, *mean_vector_BRAM*, and *eigenvector_1_BRAM* to *eigenvector_m'_BRAM*. The procedure for the first

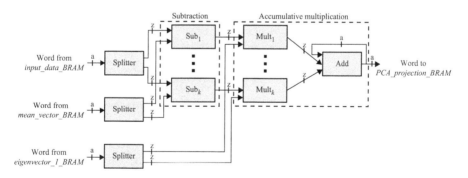

Figure 6.3 Simplification of the PCA inference IP for a PC according to k

---

[3]It refers to the way in which data is arranged and accessed in memory.

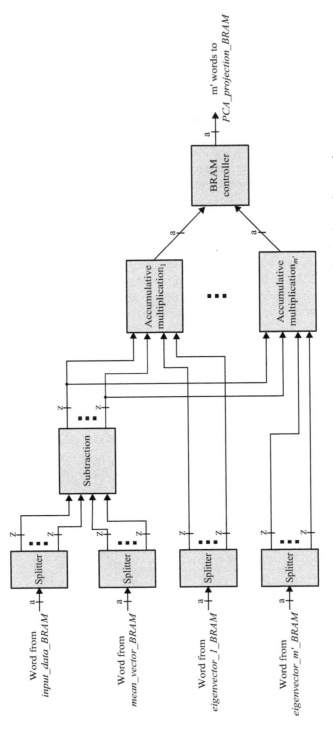

Figure 6.4 Generalization of the PCA inference IP for m' PCs depending on k

PC is the same as for Figure 6.3. For the remaining PCs, input words from *eigenvector_2_BRAM* to *eigenvector_m'_BRAM*, the procedure is similar, but taking the values directly from the subtraction block, saving resources. As before, n/k iterations are needed to fully calculate the m' PCs, then the values are written in *PCA_projection_BRAM*, in this case through a BRAM controller, which manages how to write the m' values in memory.

The architecture proposed in this chapter could be affected by a critical path risk, causing that the design is not synthesizable. This risk comes from the accumulative multiplication block in Figure 6.3. This situation is due to the synthesizer is trying to execute multiplication and addition operations in the same clock cycle. However, the resulting latency executing this block surpasses the time for a clock circle. As a solution, the summing step is forced to use DSPs of 32 bits instead of 8 or 16 bits, having a greater latency. Thus, the synthesizer is forced to execute the two operations independently.

6.6 Experimental methodology

This section describes the experimental methodology followed to perform the experimentation, in which the hardware architecture proposed is studied based on several problem and hardware parameters to analyze some metrics of interests, as latency and FPGA resources used (see Table 6.1). Moreover, it describes how the hardware architecture is compared to the multicore equivalent.

The main problem parameters are the number of PCs and attributes, both related to how the architecture scales with the problem size. For the number of PCs, we consider a range which goes from 1 to 10 PCs. This range is adequate for most applications in the literature [31–34]. For the number of attributes, there is no clear trend in the literature with applications which move from a few attributes [23] to a great deal of them [11]. Thus, we consider a wide range of values from 100 to 5,000 attributes to represent most applications.

The main parameters related to hardware are the data type, word size of the architecture, and the usage of unrolling and pipelining optimizations during hardware synthesis. For data type, fixed-point architectures perform better in terms of latency if compared to traditional floating-point ones, as the authors shown in [30] for a PCA inference use case. For word size of the architecture, we consider 8 and 16-bit architectures as we justified before. For unrolling, this optimization increases the parallelism (concurrency) by replicating hardware elements following a SIMD approach but also consumes FPGA resources. Thus, we consider several unroll values to study how different degrees of parallelism affect performance and the use of resources, specifically we consider 2, 4, 8, and 16 unrolls. In the architecture in this chapter, the unroll parameter affects the way in which subtraction and multiplication blocks are implemented. For pipelining, this optimization is considered because pipelining provides better performance in terms of latency, as the authors shown in [30] for a PCA inference use case.

Table 6.1　Details of the experimental methodology

Problem parameters	
Number of attributes:	100, 500, 1,000, 2,500, 5,000, 7,500, 10,000, 25,000, 50,000
Number of PCs:	[1,10]

Hardware parameters	
Data type:	Fixed point
Word size of the architecture:	8, 16
Number of unrolls:	2, 4, 8, 16
Pipelining:	Yes

Platform	
Device:	Zynq-XC7020400CLG-1
Vendor:	Xilinx
Software:	Vivado 2017.2, Vivado HLS 2017.2, Vivado SDK 2017.2

Metrics to analyze	
Latency, DSP usage, FF usage, LUT usage	

For each combination of both problem and hardware parameters, a hardware design is synthesized. Each design is used for executing the PCA inference stage a number of 30 independent runs for getting statistical conclusions measuring latency. Note that W', B, and $\overline{X}$ were synthetically generated because it is not necessary to consider real data to perform the study in this work. Each hardware design is compared to the multicore equivalent by using the same problem parameters. Algorithm 1 shows the implementation considered using OpenMP directives for C/C++. This implementation will be run using as many threads as the number of cores the ARM processor has. The notation in Algorithm 1 is inspired by the one used in Section 6.3, where $b_j \in B$ is the value of the jth attribute of B, y_d is the value of the dth PC, and w'_{dj} is the value of the jth position of the dth eigenvector, with $j \in 1, \ldots, n$ and $d \in 1, \ldots, m'$.

All hardware experiments are performed using the low-cost Zynq XC7Z020400-CLG-1 FPSoC by Xilinx with a frequency of 125 MHz within a bare-mental approach. The multicore experiments are performed using the ARM Cortex-A9 dual-core processor inside the FPSoC within a Linux operating system.

6.7　Experimental results

This section first discusses the experimental results obtained in terms of latency and FPGA resources for the 8- and 16-bit architectures proposed for PCA inference calculation. To this end, the authors study several problem and hardware parameters.

Second, the results obtained using both architectures are compared to an OpenMP multicore implementation, using to this end latency and speedup metrics.

Algorithm 1: Multicore PCA inference code based on OpenMP for C/C++.

```
#pragma omp parallel
    #pragma omp for
    for j = 1 to n step 1  do
        bx_j ← b_j − x̄_j
    end for
    #pragma omp for
    for d = 1 to m' step 1  do
        for j = 1 to n step 1  do
            y_d ← y_d + w'_cj bx_j
        end for
    end for
```

$$bx_j \leftarrow b_j - \overline{x}_j$$

$$y_d \leftarrow y_d + w'_{cj}\, bx_j$$

6.7.1   8- vs. 16-bit architectures

Table 6.2 shows the latency metric in μs for the configurations synthesized using the 8-bit architecture while studying the number of unrolls, attributes, and PCs. In this table, we check that latency is increased with the number of attributes, as expected. This fact is because the number of iterations needed to calculate the PCs directly depends on n, as discussed in Section 6.5.2. The increment observed in latency is almost linear with the number of attributes and, therefore, the proposed architecture properly scales with the problem size as Figure 6.5 shows. Focusing on the number of unrolls, it is expected that a greater value of this parameter provides a higher level of parallelism, reducing latency. However, latency remains constant independently of the number of unrolls for the same number of attributes. This fact is due to a limitation in the parallelism, which causes that pipeline is stalled waiting for the completion of the addition block in Figure 6.3. Thus, it makes sense that increasing the number of unrolls, and therefore the number of resources, does not reduce latency. Focusing on the number of PCs, latency follows the same trend as for unrolls due to the same reason as before, and then increasing the number of PCs does not modify latency. From this analysis, we conclude that the architecture properly scales with the number of attributes and that the number of unrolls and PCs do not affect latency because of a limitation in the parallelism caused by the accumulative multiplication.

Table 6.3 shows the FPGA resources used for the configurations synthesized using the 8-bit architecture while studying the number of unrolls and PCs. The number of attributes does not affect the resources used because it only affects the number of iterations needed for calculating the PCs. In this table, the number of DSPs is increased with the number of PCs because the number of multiplications and additions is also increased. However, the number of DSPs remains constant independently of the number of unrolls. This fact is due to the HLS synthesizer detects a limitation in parallelism caused by the addition block and decides not to implement more DSPs.

Table 6.2   Latency (in (μs) for the configurations synthesized using the 8-bit architecture, while studying the number of unrolls, attributes, and PCs

		Number of attributes								
PCs	**Unrolls**	**100**	**500**	**1,000**	**2,500**	**5,000**	**7,500**	**10,000**	**25,000**	**50,000**
1	1	1.0	4.2	8.2	20.2	40.2	60.2	80.2	200.2	400.2
1	2	1.0	4.2	8.2	20.2	40.2	60.2	80.2	200.2	400.2
1	4	1.0	4.2	8.2	20.2	40.2	60.2	80.2	200.2	400.2
2	1	1.0	4.2	8.2	20.2	40.2	60.2	80.2	200.2	400.2
2	2	1.0	4.2	8.2	20.2	40.2	60.2	80.2	200.2	400.2
2	4	1.0	4.2	8.2	20.2	40.2	60.2	80.2	200.2	400.2
3	1	1.0	4.2	8.2	20.2	40.2	60.2	80.2	200.2	400.2
3	2	1.0	4.2	8.2	20.2	40.2	60.2	80.2	200.2	400.2
4	1	1.0	4.2	8.2	20.2	40.2	60.2	80.2	200.2	400.2
4	2	1.0	4.2	8.2	20.2	40.2	60.2	80.2	200.2	400.2
5	1	1.0	4.2	8.2	20.2	40.2	60.2	80.2	200.2	400.2
6	1	1.0	4.2	8.2	20.2	40.2	60.2	80.2	200.2	400.2

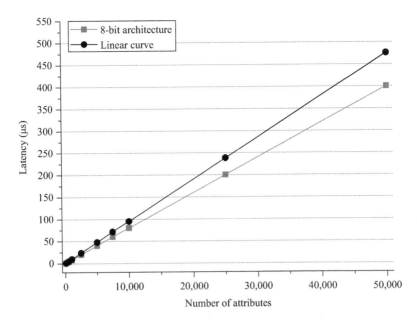

Figure 6.5   Comparing latency to the number of attributes for a general 8-bit architecture vs. the linear case

Table 6.3   *FPGA resources used for the configurations synthesized using the 8-bit*
             architecture while studying the number of unrolls and PCs

| | DSP usage (%) | | | | | | | FF usage (%) | | | | | |
| | PCs | | | | | | | PCs | | | | | |
Unrolls	1	2	3	4	5	6		1	2	3	4	5	6
1	12	18	23	29	34	40		14	20	26	32	38	44
2	12	18	23	29	–	–		20	29	38	47	–	–
4	12	18	–	–	–	–		35	50	–	–	–	–

| | LUT usage (%) | | | | | |
| | PCs | | | | | |
Unrolls	1	2	3	4	5	6
1	28	41	54	66	79	92
2	39	56	73	91	–	–
4	60	87	–	–	–	–

Focusing on FF usage, the number of FFs is increased with both the number of PCs
and unrolls because the usage of registers is also increased. Focusing on LUT usage,
we check that this is the most limiting resource because of the combinatorial logic
needed, increasing LUT usage up to 10% for each PC in the system. Thus, Tables 6.2
and 6.3 only show architectures using resources below the maximum allowed. This is
the reason why no configuration with PCs between 7 and 10 nor unrolls greater than
4 are shown. Note that entries with a dash in Table 6.3 also refer to this problem of
resource usage exceeding the limit.

Table 6.4 shows the latency metric in μs for the configurations synthesized using
the 16-bit architecture while studying the number of unrolls, attributes, and PCs.
Comparing Tables 6.4 to 6.2 for the 8-bit architecture, we check that latency values
are almost identical in both tables. This fact is due to a limitation in the parallelism,
where the pipeline is stalled waiting for the addition block in Figure 6.3. From this
analysis, we conclude that both 8- and 16-bit architectures provide a similar latency,
and then, the conclusions reached for the 8-bit architecture are also valid, i.e., the
16-bit architecture properly scales with the number of attributes and the number of
unrolls, and PCs do affect latency in most cases.

Table 6.5 shows the FPGA resources used for the 16-bit architectures synthesized
while studying the number of unrolls and PCs. As before, the number of attributes does
not affect the resources used because it only affects the number of iterations needed
for calculating the PCs. In this table, the number of DSPs is increased with the number
of PCs and unrolls. Focusing on FF usage, the number of FFs is increased with both
the number of PCs and unrolls because it increments the data stored between blocks,

Table 6.4 Latency (in μs) for 16-bit architectures, while studying the number of unrolls, attributes, and PCs

		Number of attributes								
PCs	**Unrolls**	**100**	**500**	**1,000**	**2,500**	**5,000**	**7,500**	**10,000**	**25,000**	**50,000**
1	1	1.0	4.2	8.2	20.2	40.2	60.2	80.2	200.2	400.2
1	2	1.0	4.2	8.2	20.2	40.2	60.2	80.2	200.2	400.2
1	4	1.0	4.2	8.2	20.2	40.2	60.2	80.2	200.2	400.2
1	8	1.0	4.2	8.2	20.2	40.2	60.2	80.2	200.2	400.2
1	16	1.1	4.3	8.3	20.3	40.3	60.3	80.2	200.3	400.2
2	1	1.0	4.2	8.2	20.2	40.2	60.2	80.2	200.2	400.2
2	2	1.0	4.2	8.2	20.2	40.2	60.2	80.2	200.2	400.2
2	4	1.0	4.2	8.2	20.2	40.2	60.2	80.2	200.2	400.2
2	8	1.0	4.2	8.2	20.2	40.2	60.2	80.2	200.2	400.2
2	16	1.1	4.3	8.3	20.3	40.3	60.3	80.2	200.3	400.2
3	1	1.0	4.2	8.2	20.2	40.2	60.2	80.2	200.2	400.2
3	2	1.0	4.2	8.2	20.2	40.2	60.2	80.2	200.2	400.2
3	4	1.0	4.2	8.2	20.2	40.2	60.2	80.2	200.2	400.2
3	8	1.0	4.2	8.2	20.2	40.2	60.2	80.2	200.2	400.2
3	16	1.1	4.3	8.3	20.3	40.3	60.3	80.2	200.3	400.2
4	1	1.0	4.2	8.2	20.2	40.2	60.2	80.2	200.2	400.2
4	2	1.0	4.2	8.2	20.2	40.2	60.2	80.2	200.2	400.2
4	4	1.0	4.2	8.2	20.2	40.2	60.2	80.2	200.2	400.2
4	8	1.0	4.2	8.2	20.2	40.2	60.2	80.2	200.2	400.2
5	1	1.0	4.2	8.2	20.2	40.2	60.2	80.2	200.2	400.2
5	2	1.0	4.2	8.2	20.2	40.2	60.2	80.2	200.2	400.2
5	4	1.0	4.2	8.2	20.2	40.2	60.2	80.2	200.2	400.2
5	8	1.1	4.3	8.2	20.3	40.2	60.3	80.2	200.2	400.2
6	1	1.0	4.2	8.2	20.2	40.2	60.2	80.2	200.2	400.2
6	2	1.0	4.2	8.2	20.2	40.2	60.2	80.2	200.2	400.2
6	4	1.0	4.2	8.2	20.2	40.2	60.2	80.2	200.2	400.2
6	8	1.1	4.3	8.2	20.3	40.2	60.3	80.2	200.2	400.2
7	1	1.0	4.2	8.2	20.2	40.2	60.2	80.2	200.2	400.2
7	2	1.0	4.2	8.2	20.2	40.2	60.2	80.2	200.2	400.2
7	4	1.0	4.2	8.2	20.2	40.2	60.2	80.2	200.2	400.2
7	8	1.1	4.3	8.2	20.3	40.2	60.3	80.2	200.2	400.2
8	1	1.0	4.2	8.2	20.2	40.2	60.2	80.2	200.2	400.2
8	2	1.0	4.2	8.2	20.2	40.2	60.2	80.2	200.2	400.2
8	4	1.0	4.2	8.2	20.2	40.2	60.2	80.2	200.2	400.2
9	1	1.0	4.2	8.2	20.2	40.2	60.2	80.2	200.2	400.2
9	2	1.0	4.2	8.2	20.2	40.2	60.2	80.2	200.2	400.2
9	4	1.0	4.2	8.2	20.2	40.2	60.2	80.2	200.2	400.2
10	1	1.0	4.2	8.2	20.2	40.2	60.2	80.2	200.2	400.2
10	2	1.0	4.2	8.2	20.2	40.2	60.2	80.2	200.2	400.2
10	4	1.0	4.2	8.2	20.2	40.2	60.2	80.2	200.2	400.2

Table 6.5 *FPGA resources used for 16-bit architectures, while studying the number of unrolls and PCs*

| | DSP usage (%) | | | | | | | | | |
| | PCs | | | | | | | | | |
Unrolls	1	2	3	4	5	6	7	8	9	10
1	3	5	7	9	10	12	14	16	18	20
2	4	6	8	10	13	15	17	20	22	24
4	5	8	11	14	17	20	24	27	30	33
8	6	11	16	21	26	31	36	–	–	–
16	10	19	27	–	–	–	–	–	–	–

| | FF usage (%) | | | | | | | | | |
| | PCs | | | | | | | | | |
Unrolls	1	2	3	4	5	6	7	8	9	10
1	3	5	7	8	10	12	13	15	17	18
2	5	8	10	12	15	17	20	22	25	27
4	9	13	17	22	26	30	35	39	43	47
8	15	23	31	39	46	54	62	–	–	–
16	29	45	59	–	–	–	–	–	–	–

| | LUT usage (%) | | | | | | | | | |
| | PCs | | | | | | | | | |
Unrolls	1	2	3	4	5	6	7	8	9	10
1	7	10	13	16	19	22	26	29	32	35
2	9	13	18	22	26	31	35	39	44	48
4	14	21	27	34	41	47	54	61	68	74
8	23	35	46	58	69	80	92	–	–	–
16	43	63	84	–	–	–	–	–	–	–

thus, the usage of registers increases. Focusing on LUT usage, we check that this is the most limiting resource because of the combinatorial logic needed, increasing LUT usage up to 5% for each PC in the system. Thus, Tables 6.4 and 6.5 only show architectures using resources below the maximum allowed. Note that entries with a dash in Table 6.5 also refer to this problem of resource usage.

Comparing Tables 6.5 to 6.3 for the 8-bit architecture, we check that the 16-bit architecture requires less resources than the 8-bit ones. This fact is due to the 8-bit architecture that implements a higher level of parallelism (see k definition in Section 6.5.2), and then it consumes more resources for the same problem configuration. This situation causes that there are more synthesizable configurations for the 16-bit architecture than for the 8-bit one. As a result, we conclude that the 16-bit architecture is more appropriate for implementing the PCA inference than the 8-bit one because it consumes fewer resources and provides the same latency.

6.7.2   Hardware architecture vs. multicore approach

Table 6.6 shows the latency metric in μs for the multicore approach based on Algorithm 1, while studying number of attributes and PCs. In this table, latency is increased with the number of attributes and PCs. According to that, the 16-bit architecture outperforms the 8-bit one as concluded in Section 6.7.1, Table 6.7 compares the latency metric for the 16-bit architecture in Table 6.4 to the multicore approach in Table 6.6. To this end, the speedup metric in latency from Amdahl's law is considered, which is given by

$$S_{\text{latency}} = \frac{l_1}{l_2}, \tag{6.6}$$

where l_1 and l_2 are the latency of the multicore approach and the hardware architecture, respectively.

Analyzing Table 6.7, we reach that considering the hardware implementation is advantageous in latency with speedups up to 27.5 for ten PCs. Moreover, we check that the speedup metric is higher than 1.0 for all the cases, specifically the minimum speedup is 1.9, and then the hardware implementation provides a lower latency for all the cases. This behavior is shown in Figure 6.6, evidencing how scales in latency with the number of attributes the multicore approach, the hardware implementation (either 8- or 16-bit architectures), and the linear curve (generated based on the latency for 100

Table 6.6   *Latency (in μs) for the multicore approach, while studying the number of attributes and PCs*

	Number of attributes								
PCs	**100**	**500**	**1,000**	**2,500**	**5,000**	**7,500**	**10,000**	**25,000**	**50,000**
1	15.7	13.1	24.3	37.67	86.8	170.3	345.38	877.1	1,762.8
2	18.6	16.3	26.8	48.8	114.6	227.8	464	1,170.4	2,422.9
3	21.8	19.2	32.7	60.6	144	290.2	592.1	1,486	3,134.3
4	20.3	21.9	38.2	71.3	172.6	347	703.4	1,772.1	3,808.1
5	21.23	24.8	44.3	83.6	205.1	412.2	833.34	2,115.8	4,566.9
6	23.5	27.9	49.9	94.5	233.7	472.4	947.6	2,400.7	5,269.1
7	24.6	30.6	55.6	106.1	263.3	532.2	1,069.2	2,803.7	6,125.7
8	25.1	33.2	60.6	126.8	291.2	591.3	1,200.6	3,120.9	6,675
9	27	36.8	67.8	132.6	326.2	656.6	1,317.2	3,510	7,470.4
10	28.2	38.8	71.7	140.4	346.8	703.6	1,403.3	3,776.6	8,030.3

Table 6.7   Speedup metric comparing the 16-bit architecture to the multicore implementation, while studying the number of attributes and PCs

PCs	Number of attributes								
	100	500	1,000	2,500	5,000	7,500	10,000	25,000	50,000
1	16.5	3.2	3.0	1.9	2.2	2.8	4.3	4.4	4.4
2	19.4	3.9	3.3	2.4	2.9	3.8	5.8	5.8	6.1
3	22.5	4.6	4.0	3.0	3.6	4.8	7.4	7.4	7.8
4	20.8	5.2	4.7	3.5	4.3	5.8	8.8	8.9	9.5
5	21.6	5.9	5.4	4.1	5.1	6.8	10.4	10.6	11.4
6	23.7	6.7	6.1	4.7	5.8	7.8	11.8	12.0	13.2
7	24.6	7.3	6.8	5.3	6.5	8.8	13.3	14.0	15.3
8	24.9	7.9	7.4	6.3	7.2	9.8	15.0	15.6	16.7
9	26.6	8.7	8.3	6.6	8.1	10.9	16.4	17.5	18.7
10	27.5	9.2	8.7	6.9	8.6	11.7	17.5	18.9	20.1

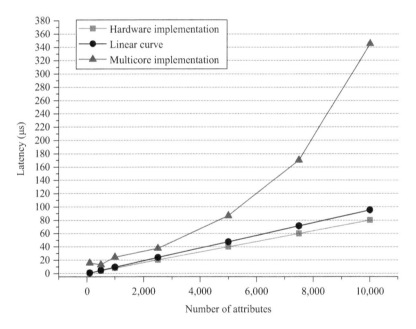

Figure 6.6   Evolution of latency with the number of attributes for the multicore approach, the hardware implementation, and the linear curve

attributes using the hardware implementation). In this figure, we opted for showing the best case (the lowest latency) for the multicore approach, where the number of PCs equals one. Note that for the hardware implementation, latency remains constant interdependently of the number of PCs.

6.8　Conclusions

This chapter addressed the issue of improving both data acquisition and data analysis stages in big data applications. To this end, the authors focused on improving the edge layer in IoT as a quick response mechanism for end users. As the first step in this task, the authors proposed to study how to embed one of the most hardware-demanding steps in ML, the feature stage. Specifically, they proposed to embed the PCA inference stage in a low-cost FPSoC, while performing a design space exploration for a general PCA inference problem.

Thus, the authors proposed two hardware architectures for solving the PCA inference stage using a word size of 8 and 16 bits. The two architectures were compared analyzing features as scalability (number of PCs and attributes), latency, hardware parameters (pipelining and unrolling optimizations), and FPGA resources.

As a result of this comparison, the authors reached that both 8- and 16-bit architectures provided a similar latency, which scaled linearly with the number of attributes, and that the number of unrolls and PCs do not affect latency because of a limitation in the parallelism. Focusing on FPGA resources, the authors reached that the 16-bit architecture consumes fewer resources than the 8-bit one, implying that there are more synthesizable configurations for the 16-bit architecture than for the 8-bit one. As a result, the authors concluded that the 16-bit architecture is more appropriate for implementing the PCA inference than the 8-bit one.

Based on the previous conclusion, the 16-bit architecture was compared to a multicore OpenMP approach to be executed in the dual-core ARM processor inside the FPSoC. As a result, the authors concluded that the hardware implementation was beneficial in latency, with speedups up to 27.5. Moreover, they reached that the hardware implementation provided a lower latency for all the cases.

As future lines of research, it could be interesting to include a power consumption analysis in the design space exploration, as well as to analyze different data sizes in fixed-point architectures.

Acknowledgments

This work has been partially funded by the Spanish R&D project PLATINO (Ref. TEC2017-86722-C4-2-R). Rodrigo Marino holds a predoctoral contract under RD99/2011 by Universidad Politécnica de Madrid.

References

[1]　Wu X, Zhu X, Wu GQ, *et al.* Data mining with big data. IEEE Transactions on Knowledge and Data Engineering. 2014;26(1):97–107.

[2]　Yin S, Kaynak O. Big data for modern industry: challenges and trends [point of view]. Proceedings of the IEEE. 2015;103(2):143–146.

[3] Zhang Y, Qiu M, Tsai CW, *et al.* Health-CPS: Healthcare cyber-physical system assisted by cloud and big data. IEEE Systems Journal. 2017;11(1):88–95.

[4] Chen M, Mao S, Liu Y. Big data: a survey. Mobile Networks and Applications. 2014;19(2):171–209.

[5] Xia F, Yang LT, Wang L, *et al.* Internet of Things. International Journal of Communication Systems. 2012;25(9):1101.

[6] Al-Fuqaha A, Guizani M, Mohammadi M, *et al.* Internet of Things: a survey on enabling technologies, protocols, and applications. IEEE Communications Surveys & Tutorials. 2015;17(4):2347–2376.

[7] Mohan N, Kangasharju J. Edge-Fog cloud: a distributed cloud for Internet of Things computations. In: Cloudification of the Internet of Things (CIoT). IEEE; 2016. p. 1–6.

[8] García GJ, Jara CA, Pomares J, *et al.* A survey on FPGA-based sensor systems: towards intelligent and reconfigurable low-power sensors for computer vision, control and signal processing. Sensors. 2014;14(4):6247–6278.

[9] Nazemi M, Eshratifar AE, Pedram M. A Hardware-Friendly Algorithm for Scalable Training and Deployment of Dimensionality Reduction Models on FPGA. In: 2018 19th International Symposium on Quality Electronic Design (ISQED). IEEE; 2018, p. 395–400.

[10] Abdi H, Williams LJ. Principal component analysis. Wiley Interdisciplinary Reviews: Computational Statistics. 2010;2(4):433–459.

[11] Fernandez D, Gonzalez C, Mozos D, *et al.* FPGA implementation of the principal component analysis algorithm for dimensionality reduction of hyperspectral images. Journal of Real-Time Image Processing. 2016:1–12.

[12] Elrharras A, El Moukhlis S, Saadane R, *et al.* FPGA-based fully parallel PCA-ANN for spectrum sensing. Computer and Information Science. 2015;8(1):108.

[13] Wess M, Manoj PS, Jantsch A. Neural network based ECG anomaly detection on FPGA and trade-off analysis. In: Circuits and Systems (ISCAS), 2017 IEEE International Symposium on. IEEE; 2017. p. 1–4.

[14] Lazcano R, Madroñal D, Salvador R, *et al.* Porting a PCA-based hyperspectral image dimensionality reduction algorithm for brain cancer detection on a manycore architecture. Journal of Systems Architecture. 2017;77: 101–111.

[15] Tamilarasi S, Sundararajan J. FPGA based seizure detection and control for brain computer interface. Cluster Computing. 2018:1–8.

[16] Rouhani BD, Mirhoseini A, Koushanfar F. RISE: an automated framework for real-time intelligent video surveillance on FPGA. ACM Transactions on Embedded Computing Systems (TECS). 2017;16(5s):158.

[17] Magalotti D, Alunni L, Biesuz N, *et al.* A pattern recognition mezzanine based on associative memory and FPGA technology for Level 1 track triggers for the HL-LHC upgrade. Journal of Instrumentation. 2016;11(02):C02063.

[18] Giordano R, Guccione P. ROI-based on-board compression for hyperspectral remote sensing images on GPU. Sensors. 2017;17(5):1160.

[19]   Cao Q, Li B, Fan L. Medical image fusion based on GPU accelerated nonsub-sampled shearlet transform and 2D principal component analysis. In: Signal and Image Processing (ICSIP), 2017 IEEE 2nd International Conference on. IEEE; 2017. p. 203–207.

[20]   Lazcano R, Madroñal D, Fabelo H, *et al.* Parallel implementation of an iterative PCA algorithm for hyperspectral images on a manycore platform. In: Design and Architectures for Signal and Image Processing (DASIP), 2017 Conference on. IEEE; 2017. p. 1–6.

[21]   Fenzández D, González C, Mozos D. Dimensionality reduction of hyperspectral images using reconfigurable hardware. In: Field Programmable Logic and Applications (FPL), 2016 26th International Conference on. IEEE; 2016. p. 1–2.

[22]   Gonzalez C, Lopez S, Mozos D, *et al.* FPGA implementation of the HySime algorithm for the determination of the number of endmembers in hyperspectral data. IEEE Journal of Selected Topics in Applied Earth Observations and Remote Sensing. 2015;8(6):2870–2883.

[23]   Akbar MA, Ali AAS, Amira A, *et al.* An empirical study for PCA-and LDA-based feature reduction for gas identification. IEEE Sensors Journal. 2016;16(14):5734–5746.

[24]   Schellhorn M, Fütterer R, Rosenberger M, *et al.* Smart parallel spectral imager based on heterogeneous FPGA system on chip. In: Engineering for a Changing World: Proceedings; 59th IWK, Ilmenau Scientific Colloquium, Technische Universität Ilmenau, September 11–15, 2017. vol. 59; 2017.

[25]   Schaffer L, Kincses Z, Pletl S. FPGA-based low-cost real-time face recognition. In: Intelligent Systems and Informatics (SISY), 2017 IEEE 15th International Symposium on. IEEE; 2017. p. 000035–000038.

[26]   Zhou Y, Wang W, Huang X. FPGA design for PCANet deep learning network. In: Field-Programmable Custom Computing Machines (FCCM), 2015 IEEE 23rd Annual International Symposium on. IEEE; 2015. p. 232–232.

[27]   Smitha KG, Vinod AP. Facial emotion recognition system for autistic children: a feasible study based on FPGA implementation. Medical & Biological Engineering & Computing. 2015;53(11):1221–1229.

[28]   Jaruat P, Tripathi GC, Rawat M, *et al.* Independent component analysis for multi-carrier transmission for 4G/5G power amplifiers. In: Microwave Measurement Conference (ARFTG), 2017 89th ARFTG. IEEE; 2017. p. 1–4.

[29]   He C, Hou B, Wang L, *et al.* A novel hardware Trojan detection method based on side-channel analysis and PCA algorithm. In: Reliability, Maintainability and Safety (ICRMS), 2014 International Conference on. IEEE; 2014. p. 1043–1046.

[30]   Marino R, Lanza-Gutierrez JM, Riesgo T, *et al.* Design space exploration for PCA implementation of embedded learning in FPGAs. In: Circuits and Systems (ISCAS), 2018 IEEE International Symposium on. IEEE; 2018. p. 1–4.

[31]   Kume A, Kawai S, Kato R, *et al.* Exploring high-affinity binding properties of octamer peptides by principal component analysis of tetramer peptides. Journal of Bioscience and Bioengineering. 2017;123(2):230–238.

[32]   Pizzi A, Toscano G, Pedretti EF, *et al.* Energy characteristics assessment of olive pomace by means of FT-NIR spectroscopy. Energy. 2018;147:51–58.

[33]   Lin QB, Song XC, Fang H, *et al.* Migration of styrene and ethylbenzene from virgin and recycled expanded polystyrene containers and discrimination of these two kinds of polystyrene by principal component analysis. Food Additives & Contaminants: Part A. 2017;34(1):126–132.

[34]   Kallio M, Guillaume JH, Kummu M, *et al.* Spatial variation in seasonal water poverty index for Laos: an application of geographically weighted principal component analysis. Social Indicators Research. 2017;140:1131–1157.

Chapter 7

Decision support system to detect hidden pathologies of stroke: the CIPHER project

José González Enríquez[1], Leticia Morales Trujillo[1], Sara Moreno Leonardo[1], Francisco José Domínguez Mayo[1], Julián Alberto García García[1], and Manuel Mejías Risoto[1]

Currently, it is difficult to find platforms connected to health systems that exploit data in a coherent way and that allow, on the one hand, to send sanitary warnings and on the other, to validate the performance of medical specialists according to the models set by the best practices of the specialty.

This chapter aims to explain the CIPHER project, a decision support system (DSS), based on machine-learning (ML) and big data technologies, capable of alerting a clinician when a situation of risk is detected in a patient suffering from a certain pathology, so that could be able to carry out the appropriate measures.

CIPHER, is a project born from scratch. For its development, different methodologies, such as design sprint (for product prototyping), navigational development techniques (for product analysis and testing) or SCRUM (for product development), have been applied. In addition, this product has been defined in direct contact with medical specialists and under the umbrella of international standards and models such as ISO 13606, SNOMED, REGICOR or CHADS2.

As a result of the development of this product, we have obtained a DSS, which offers health professionals the possibility of receiving alerts from patients who may be at risk of suffering from a specific pathology, based on a series of criteria defined by international standards. Moreover, health professionals would be able to find hidden symptomatology of the pathology mentioned above, which, a priori, are not known.

7.1 Introduction

The technological development achieved at present, has allowed any health entity to be able to store all the data generated by its activity. This facility to generate and store information has fostered in recent years the development and improvement of

---

[1] Department of Computer Languages and Systems, University of Seville, Spain

data mining and ML techniques for the extraction of knowledge from large data sets (knowledge discovery in databases) and the development of DSS. A DSS [1] has inference mechanisms (rules and ways of interpreting the problems) and a knowledge base drawn from experts in the field, which evaluate different alternatives and allow to warn the decision maker about the risks and benefits of the decision that is going to take. In the health context, the union of Information Technology and new technologies in the field of biomedicine has given rise to a new scientific area known as "Bioinformatics" [2], which has not been developed in our country (Spain) due to the lack of clear objectives and a strategic approach to global issue.

Currently, it is difficult to find platforms connected to health systems that exploit data in a coherent way and that allow, on the one hand, to send sanitary warnings and on the other, to validate the performance of medical specialists according to the models set by the best practices of the specialty. In this context, the CIPHER project emerges, whose main objective, creating a platform on the vertical health and using the specific case of brain strokes as use case for validation.

Brain stroke is a sudden disorder of cerebral blood flow that transiently or permanently alters the function of a certain region of the brain [3]. Today, according to data from the World Health Organization [4], it represents the second cause of death, after heart diseases. In the comparison with the national of Spain, it is observed that, although this pathology occurs less frequently in Andalusia, the mortality rate is higher there than in the whole of Spain. For this reason, its study to identify possible symptoms for early detection, as well as the identification and assimilation of possible risk factors, is essential to reduce the impact that it may have on an aging population.

There is a scientific consensus to define a temporal period, which is known as a "therapeutic window" [5], during which it is still possible to reverse or reduce the effects of cerebrally with the appropriate treatment. But that requires having a well-thought and coordinated care system that ensures fast and efficient patient care. In this sense, CIPHER intends to be a platform that, through an expert system, analysis algorithms and big data technologies, acts within such "therapeutic window."

In addition, it is essential to corroborate that the action protocols, diagnostic tests and prescriptions (pharmacological or not) have the expected effect. In this sense, several research [6–8] have been carried out to corroborate the existence of micro-strokes in a population at risk but apparently healthy that are not diagnosed and that entail a significant cognitive deterioration and a high risk of definitive strokes. This lack of capacity for symptomatic analysis is a habitual pattern in other very diverse pathologies.

At present, thanks to the advancement of information systems, there are sufficient tools to maintain a digitized information on the clinical history of patients. This is known as electronic health record (EHR) [9]. However, the analytical exploitation of this information and its predictive capacity is very poorly developed. There is a great research potential in the EHR that, together with the synergy produced by the joint work of health professionals and technological professionals and specialized in the treatment of information, can generate great scientific contributions.

The remainder of this chapter is organized as follows: after this introduction, Section 7.2 explains in detail the CIPHER project based on its objectives; in

Section 7.3, the standards used and the models that have been defined and implemented during the development of the project are described. Section 7.4 details a real-world case study on which the solution obtained has been applied and its threats to validity. Finally, Section 7.5 states our ongoing work and conclusions.

7.2   Context: the CIPHER project

The general objective of the CIPHER project is the creation of an expert system based on ML algorithms and big data technologies, capable of discovering characteristic symptomatology of the pathology studied in EHR that are not considered or adequately valued today. This detection must serve to feed a DSS that alerts the clinician at the moment in which a situation of risk is detected so that it is possible to begin the appropriate measures for the treatment of the patient. In addition, the development of the project must be carried out thinking about its reuse for any kind of pathology, although, at this moment, the case study will be focused on brain strokes.

As a secondary objective, but not less important, it is proposed that the procedures of the expert system mentioned above facilitates the monitoring of compliance with the guidelines and good clinical practices associated with the pathologies treated by the medical specialists.

As a result of the objectives described, the following specific objectives have been defined for the CIPHER project:

- Definition and implementation of loading, normalization and temporal referencing processes of EHR for its semantic exploitation.
- Definition and implementation of assisted learning processes based on associated ontologies. Typification of results in the identification of underlying pathological variables.
- Obtaining software solutions that allow, over the results obtained in the previous phases, alerts to the medical specialists through integration with the corresponding EHR repositories and clinical stations.
- Obtaining quantitative and qualitative simulation software solutions based on the impact of the variation in diagnostic and therapeutic techniques, as well as decision support tools based on the application of the developed procedures.

In order to give a solution to the objectives proposed above, the following conceptual model (Figure 7.1) was proposed. As illustrated in Figure 7.1, CIPHER will be a system based on three main pillars: (i) hospital extension, (ii) pathologies and (iii) big data storage an processing.

- **Hospital extension:** Its main objective is the analysis and normalization of EHR on the CIPHER system.
- **Pathologies (for this particular case, brain stroke):**
  - **Pathology analysis:** Its main objective is to incorporate the intelligence for the early detection of the pathology based on the analysis of the EHR of the users.

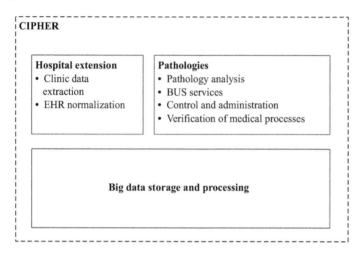

Figure 7.1   Conceptual model of CIPHER

- **BUS services:** Its main objective is the integration of all elements involved in the CIPHER architecture through services, in such a way that all internal accesses be crosscutting to all parties involved.
- **Control and administration:** Its main objective is the management and control of the interfaces of the CIPHER system aimed at users with different profiles.
- **Verification of medical processes:** Its main objective is the verification of medical processes according to the data that the application contains and on which it has been learning throughout the analysis of them.
- **Big data storage and processing:** Elements that make up the unit large volumes of data and where the analysis tasks will be carried out and processing them by the detection and learning algorithms.

As possible to see in Figure 7.2, to land this model, a technological architecture was defined. The design of this architecture contemplates a series of subsystems and elements in each of them. Going into the detail of the purpose of each of them, we found the following:

- **Big data storage and processing subsystem:** It is the subsystem that contains the capacity to store the data, be cataloged as large data volumes or not, and process them in large quantities by running of simple or recurring algorithms.
  - **Node X:** Under large storage and processing capacity data volumes, more than one element of this type shapes the cluster designed to offer the said capacity within the system. Initially, consider that the cluster consists of two nodes that, according to the need to be more real, they can be extended to form a cluster with the nodes needed according to the demand.
  - **DBMS SQL:** As a complement to the storage and processing of large data volumes (Not Only Structured Query Language (NoSQL)), the system must be

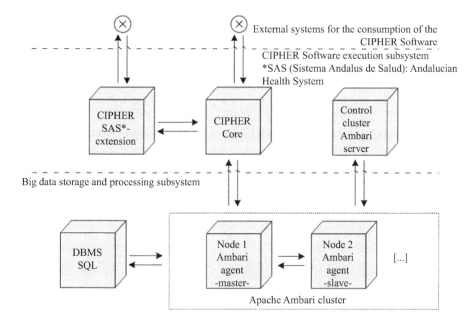

Figure 7.2   Technological architecture of CIPHER

prepared for the management of other elements such as relational configuration data sets, users or metrics. To satisfy this requirement, this element is included within the subsystem, which offers this capability through a relational database management system (SQL).

- **CIPHER Software execution subsystem:** In this case, it is the element destined to offer the necessary infrastructure for the correct execution of services functions of the CIPHER Software. The existing elements in this subsystem have all in common the ability to communicate with the elements external to the project CIPHER, process the operations accessing the data and respond with the results of the same.
    - **CIPHER core:** Element on which all the functionality of the CORE is executed of CIPHER, where the user interfaces for management are included, standardized communication interfaces and procedures on pathology of brain stroke. It can be said that all the properties of this element are abstracts to third systems, everything being encapsulated characteristics of CIPHER, its model and its interfaces.
    - **CIPHER Sistema Andaluz de Salud (SAS, Andalucian Health System in English)–extension:** Element on which all the functionality is executed specific to the SAS, which provides the necessary transformations for the use of the functionality deployed on the CIPHER Core element by the SAS. Unlike the previous element, it can be said that the properties of this element are specific to the SAS systems to which it offers support standardization and checking of EHR.

       –   **Cluster control:** Element that contains all the functionalities of the control and management of the large storage and the cluster data volumes processing. This element is not part of the remit of this characteristic, but it provides the necessary functionality to perform the monitoring operations of the cluster at a general level and of each node at a particular.

•   **External systems for the consumption of the CIPHER Software:** Although this section of the diagram does not belong to the CIPHER project, it has been embodied in the design of the technological environment to inform that CIPHER is ready to be consumed by external systems. In this context, at the level of the network and interconnection diagram, user interfaces and web services may have been published.

7.3 Decision support system

Currently, health professionals use risk classification tables to identify patients who are candidates of suffering a brain stroke. There are a set of classification tables of cardiovascular risk and identification of patients candidates for lipid-lowering or anti-hypertensive treatment such as REGICOR [10], SCORE [11], CHADs2, CHADs2d2 and ATRIA [12], which have the function of stratification of the risk of suffering from diseases, relating values of defined factors of influence on stroke (age, smoker, cholesterol, etc.) with estimated percentages of presenting the mentioned disorder.

    Thanks to the CIPHER platform, an automation of this process of diagnosis of brain stroke is achieved, changing the manual analysis of the classification tables performed by medical specialists, by an expert system that, considering the clinical data of the patients and the predefined rules extracted from the tables, shows as result the percentage of stroke disease calculated from the combination of patient factors.

    This automation makes up what is known in CIPHER as "decision model" (DM) module. This module is one of the main pillars of the CIPHER core component. Figure 7.3 shows a state machine where the behavior of this module is described.

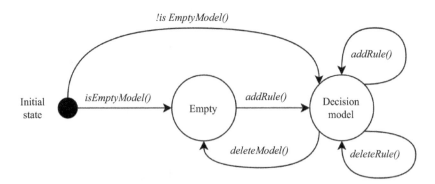

Figure 7.3   Decision model

As illustrated in Figure 7.3, the first function that the DM state machine performs is to check if the model is empty. If there is no model, the first state of the machine will be "empty" and the navigation to the next state, called "decision model," will be once the function "addRule()" had been executed. This function consists of adding a new rule to the DS. It is possible to go back to the "empty" state by executing the "delete-Model()" function, which consists of deleting the all DM. When the machine is in the "decision model" state, there are two available functions: (i) "addRule()" that consists of adding a new rule to the DM and (ii) "deleteRule()" that consists of removing a rule of the defined DM. Finally, it is possible to go directly to the "decision model" state if at the beginning of the process the model is already created and it is not empty.

Considering what was mentioned in the context section, the CIPHER project do not only aim to help the medical specialists to make decisions based on an automatized version of the known standards but also it tries to discover new hidden symptomologies, so that the treatment of this type of disease is more effective. In this sense, a new module called "predictive model" was defined for the CIPHER Core component. This module is another one of the main pillars of the CIPHER Core. Figure 7.4 shows a state machine where the behavior of this module is described.

This module considers all patient parameters that a group of medical specialists, experts in this disease, have considered relevant to consider (the decision model only takes the parameters collected in the standards) when making a forecast. This model must be trained in advance with information regarding to the patients who have experienced strokes and with patients that, in principle, do not show signs of being possible candidates to suffer it. With this information, underlying relationships between the registered factors are created, and subsequently, the prediction of a diagnosis of a new patient may be obtained.

Predictive model (Figure 7.4) starts as well as decision model, from an empty state that is completed as patient parameters are inserted. This model is fed periodically with patient information, although it can be also done manually if it is considered necessary by the medical specialist.

By means of the comparison between the decision model and the predictive model, CIPHER aims to discover new rules for the detection of stroke that can be incorporated into the decision model. To do this, the results obtained for a patient

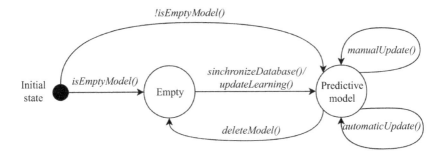

Figure 7.4   Predictive model

Table 7.1 Comparative models

Decision model	Predictive model	Result
Greater than percentage	Yes	Patient presents risk of stroke
Less than percentage	No	Patient does not present risk of stroke
Greater than percentage	Yes	The predictive model requires more training data
Less than percentage	No	There is a possibility of existence of hidden symptomatology detected

The percentage of column "decision model" must be defined by a medical specialist in the CIPHER management module. This percentage is not always the same, and it depends on the hospital in which the patient is being treated; therefore, it is a parameter that is left open for modification.

after applying the algorithms are compared in each case through both models. In this sense, as showed in Table 7.1, it is possible to obtain the following interpretations.

Both the input data of the predictive model and that of the decision model is obtained from the analytics of the patients, being this direct obtaining; since numerical values do not need to be normalized, the problem lies in the information that is necessary to extract from clinical reports.

In the clinical reports, the information is structured in several sections of which in this case, the background, clinical judgment and treatments are selected. The information contained in each of these sections is plain text so that the knowledge they contain must be extracted and normalized before entering it in the database. For them, information extraction algorithms have been used, algorithms that process in natural language and obtain the information that is indicated to be relevant.

All patient information is stored in the CIPHER database in a way that complies with the CEN/ISO EN13606 [13] standard, designed to achieve semantic interoperability in the EHR communication of a single patient.

7.4 Validation

7.4.1 Data processing

To provide data to the decision model and train and validate the predictive model, it was necessary to retrieve information of patients that have suffered a brain stroke. This was one of the main problems of the project. Due to bureaucratic issues with the protection of the data, we are still waiting to receive this data. For this reason, it was decided to carry out a generation of a sample as close as possible to the hospital reality to execute the performance tests of the algorithms.

The collaboration with the Instituto de Biomedicina de Sevilla (Institute of Biomedicine of Seville in English) research group and some studies that they have developed [14–18], an initial sample of 400 patients were taken as reference to generate the missing characteristics according to the CIPHER data model and complete the sample that the algorithms should query.

As mentioned before, this project has been developed under the umbrella of the CEN/ISO EN13606 standard [13]. Following the recommendations of that standard, the data model defined for CIPHER (Figure 7.5) contains the following storage requirements (SR):

- **SR-01. Patient**: Sick person who is attended by a health professional.
- **SR-02. General analysis**: Clinical analysis to know the health status of a patient or establish a diagnosis.
- **SR-03. Prescription**: Document by means of which the legally trained doctors prescribe the medication to the patient for its dispensation by the pharmacist.
- **SR-04. Clinical report**: Document that certifies the findings obtained by the medical evaluation of a patient; it is issued by the attending physician.
- **SR-05. Anamnesis**: Set of data that are collected in the clinical history of a patient with a diagnostic objective.
- **SR-06. Discharged clinical report**: Document issued by a responsible doctor about the care of a patient and that refers to an episode of hospitalization.
- **SR-07. EHR**: Mechanized registry of the social, preventive and medical data of the patient.
- **SR-08. Clinical data**: Information that the doctor gathers through the patient's interview, physical exams or complementary explorations.
- **SR-09. Analysis**: Clinical analysis or group of them to know the state of health of a patient or establish a diagnosis.
- **SR-10. Medication**: Set of medicines and means used to cure or prevent a disease.
- **SR-11. Antecedent**: Conditions that a certain patient experiences.
- **SR-12. Consequent**: Results obtained according to certain conditions.
- **SR-13. Alarm**: Alarms that specify the percentage with which a patient has to be referred to primary care or specialist.
- **SR-14. Role**: Roles of users that interact with the system.
- **SR-15. User**: User that operates with the different functionalities offered by the system, both in the administration and management roles.
- **SR-16. Rule**: Rules that are predefined for a particular result.
- **SR-17. Category**: Categories associated with the users that interact in the system.
- **SR-18. Alarm manager**: Set of alarms to be managed.
- **SR-19. Medical group**: It will collect the information of the percentage of alarm and the medical group to which the patients will derive.
- **SR-20. Medical groups**: Contains the collection of media groups that have been defined.
- **SR-21. Model**: Model that includes both the predictive model and the decision model.
- **SR-22. Preprocessing**: The standardization manager will have the EHR as entered and will return the clinical history in a standardized manner.
- **SR-23. Decision model**: Model that contemplates learning through rules.
- **SR-24. Predictive model**: Model that contemplates predictive learning.
- **SR-25. Input data**: Data entry for the algorithms.

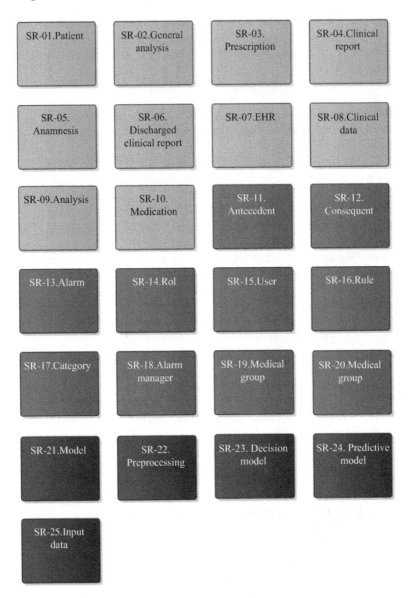

Figure 7.5   Storage requirements diagram

A set of interesting parameters, such as smoking, alcoholism or brain strokes in family history, are stored in the clinical reports of the patients as clinical narratives that describe the medical reasoning behind the prescription [19]. Medical specialists consider that this kind of information will take a very important value when analyzing data of the sample. In this sense, these clinical narratives must be processed to obtain the knowledge it contains.

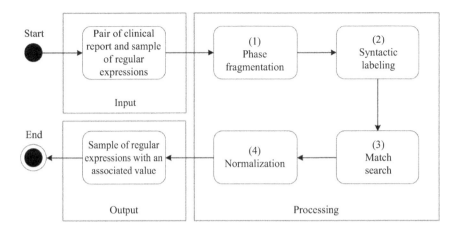

Figure 7.6 Activity diagram of clinical narratives processing algorithm

An information extraction algorithm has been defined to process the information mentioned above. Figure 7.6 shows the activity diagram, divided in three blocks (input, processing, output), that makes up the algorithm as well as the sequence of logical and ordered steps with which the problem is solved.

The purpose of this algorithm is to obtain, from a clinical report and a set of regular expressions (input), another sample of regular expressions, with associated values (output).

Next, each step of the processing block (from second to fifth activity of Figure 7.6) of the process followed to deal with the information of the input is detailed.

1. First, the sentences were fragmented. The heterogeneous formats of the clinical reports include several headings, sections and footnotes. Thanks to a rigorous study of the sample, it was noticed that most of the sections begin with a new line, capitalized and end with a dot. Therefore, a regular expression and an algorithm was used to extract each section. Within the clinical reports, three sections were identified as relevant. These are as follows:

     i. **Family history:** It is unique for each person. The key factors in the family history are the diseases that have occurred at a younger age than usual, those that appear in more than one close family member, those that usually do not affect one of the sexes in particular and certain combinations of diseases within a family.

     ii. **Personal history:** Collection of information about a person's health which allows them to manage and follow-up on their own health information.

     iii. **Clinical judgment:** It consists of the evaluation of the set of symptoms and signs of a patient, together with the data provided by the complementary tests, to make an estimate on the diagnosis of the same, the state of the patient and the most appropriate treatment

     iv. **Treatment:** It is the set of means whose purpose is the healing or relief (palliation) of diseases or symptoms. It is a type of clinical judgment.

2. Once the sentences are extracted, we proceed to syntactic labeling (third activity), so that each of the words are labeled according to nouns, adjectives, adverbs, etc. For this labeling, the Stanford CoreNLP [20] library has been used. Only the words labeled as nouns and adjectives preceded by nouns are selected from the classification that is generated.
3. Fourth activity deals with a search for matches between the different regular expressions obtained from syntactic labeling and the regular expressions that the algorithm receives as input. In addition, each of the regular expressions received as input in the algorithm has a list of associated synonyms that are also compared. The list of synonyms forms what is known as an ontology, in this case written in OWL (Ontology Web Language) [21] format, a language designed to formalize ontologies. OWL's expressive resources include union, intersection, complement and equivalence of concepts, functional roles, inverse roles, existential and universal quantification of roles and numerical restrictions.
4. It is common to find words (regular expressions) that differ morphologically (for example, "diabetes" and "diabetic") or have spelling errors because medical specialists usually write the reports during the medical consultation. For this reason, for each comparative regular expression, a normalization process is carried out in the fifth activity. To eliminate these differences, an algorithm that calculates the percentage of proximity that exists between two strings of characters (words) making use of the distance of Levenshtein [22], which calculates the minimum number of operations required to transform one character string into another, has been used. Therefore, two strings of characters are considered equal if they exceed a certain percentage of proximity.

Finally, a sample of regular expressions with an associated value is returned based on whether matches have been found or not with the regular expressions extracted from the clinical reports.

7.4.2 Algorithm selection

To make sure that the choice of algorithms that was going to be used was the optimal one, a comparative study was made of the most used tools on the market that solve this type of problem. To achieve this goal, it created a classification framework based on different characteristics. These are as follows:

- **License:** Type of license (free or not).
- **API:** The solution offers an application programming interface.
- **Language:** Type of language programming of the algorithms.
- **Input/Output**
  - **ARFF:** The input or the output is given in Attribute-Relation File Format.
  - **Other formats:** The input or the output is given in other formats.
  - **Database connection:** The solution offers connection to one or more databases.

- **Preprocessing**
  - **Discretization:** The solution offers discretization of parameters.
  - **Parameters selection:** The solution offers parameters selection.
  - **Instances selection:** The solution offers instances selection.
  - **Lost values imputation:** The solution offers lost values imputation.
- **Learning**
  - **Classification:** The solution offers classification algorithms.
  - **Regression:** The solution offers regression algorithms.
  - **Clustering:** The solution offers clustering algorithms.
  - **Association rules:** The solution offers association rules algorithms.
- **Execution**
  - **Online start:** The solution offers the possibility of online start.
  - **Offline start:** The solution offers the possibility of offline start.
- **Advanced characteristics**
  - **Post-processing:** The solution offers post-processing algorithms.
  - **Meta-learning:** The solution offers meta-learning.
  - **Statistic test:** The solution offers statistic tests.
  - **EAs:** The solution offers evolutionary algorithms.

Once the classification framework was created, twelve frameworks, applications or tools were selected to be analyzed. In addition, it set the values that each of the characteristics could take. These were as follows:

- **B**: The solution offers basic support of the characteristic.
- **M**: The solution offers medium support of the characteristic.
- **A**: The solution offers advanced support of the characteristic.
- **Y**: Yes, the solution presents the characteristic.
- **N**: No, the solution does not present the characteristic.
- **N/S**: Not stipulated or unknown.

Figure 7.7 represents the results obtained from the study. Finally Apache Spark [23] was chosen by three reasons: (i) it offers a large number of programming languages; therefore, the migration from one language to another would be less expensive than using other alternatives, (ii) it is 100% compatible with the framework chosen for the processing of big data and (iii) most of the qualifications obtained in most of the characteristics are A or Y (the highest ones).

7.4.3 First results

Once the algorithms for generating the sample were developed and the algorithms applying the ML were implemented according to the data model defined for CIPHER, the first results were obtained.

Different tests were executed to select the best algorithms that Apache Spark offers, being selected the "DecissionTree" [24] because of its highest accuracy. Figure 7.8 shows the preliminary results of the execution of the "DecissionTree" algorithm for the sample described before of 400 EHRs.

Software	Licence	API	Language
RapidMiner	N/S	Y	Java
Weka	Free	Y	Java
Orange	Free	Y	C++
KNIME	Free	Y	Java
R	Free	Y	R
ADaM	Free	Y	Java
Apache SINGA	Free	Y	C++
Deeplearning4j	Free	Y	Java/JVM
Dlib	Free	Y	C++
TensorFlow	Free	Y	C++,Python
MS Cognitive Toolkit	Free	Y	C++
Apache Spark	Free	Y	Scala,Python, R, Java

Software	Input/Output				Preprocessing		
	ARFF format	Other formats	Database connection	Discretization	Parameters selection	Instances selection	Lost values imputation
RapidMiner	Y	Y	M	A	B	B	A
Weka	Y	Y	Y	M	A	B	B
Orange	N	Y	N	A	M	B	B
KNIME	Y	Y	Y	M	A	B	B
R	Y	Y	Y	B	B	B	B
ADaM	Y	N	N	N	A	B	N
Apache SINGA	N	Y	Y	N	A	B	N
Deeplearning4j	Y	Y	Y	M	A	N	N
Dlib	N	Y	Y	N	B	B	N
TensorFlow	N	Y	Y	M	A	B	N
MS Cognitive Toolkit	N	Y	Y	N	A	A	N
Apache Spark	N	Y	Y	A	A	A	B

Software	Learning				Execution	
	Classification	Regression	Clustering	Association rules	Online Start	Offline Start
RapidMiner	A	A	A	A	Y	N
Weka	A	A	A	A	Y	N
Orange	M	N	M	M	N	Y
KNIME	A	A	A	A	Y	N
R	A	M	A	B	N	N
ADaM	M	N	A	B	Y	N
Apache SINGA	A	M	A	N	N	Y
Deeplearning4j	A	M	A	N	Y	Y
Dlib	A	A	A	M	Y	Y
TensorFlow	A	A	A	M	Y	Y
MS Cognitive Toolkit	A	A	A	A	Y	Y
Apache Spark	A	A	A	A	Y	Y

Software	Advanced characteristics			
	Postprocessing	Meta learning	Statistic test	EAs
RapidMiner	N	A	B	M
Weka	N	M	N	B
Orange	N	N	N	N/S
KNIME	N	N	M	B
R	Y	B	M	B
ADaM	N	N	N	B
Apache SINGA	Y	N	B	N/S
Deeplearning4j	Y	B	N	N/S
Dlib	A	A	A	N/S
TensorFlow	Y	M	A	N/S
MS Cognitive Toolkit	N	N	B	N/S
Apache Spark	Y	M	A	N/S

Figure 7.7   Comparative study of algorithms

```
Accuracy = 99.1402125207%
Error = 0.859787479264%
CORRECT: PID 7432 process (PID 2452 secondary process) has been finished
CORRECT: PID 2452 process (PID 7208 secondary process) has been finished
CORRECT: PID 7208 process (PID 7356 secondary process) has been finished
```

Figure 7.8   Accuracy of tests

```
Time to execute Predictive --> 47450.708669 ms
```

Figure 7.9   Performance test of predictive model

```
Time to execute Atria --> 95197.625179 ms
Time to execute Chads2Ds2 --> 65241.902264 ms
Time to execute Chads2Ds2Vas --> 39599.256579 ms
Time to execute Regicor --> 146276.055527 ms
Time to execute Score --> 119960.205471 ms
```

Figure 7.10   Performance test of decision model

Next, some performance tests were executed to check how fast the algorithm runs in the architecture defined based on a large workload. Figure 7.9 shows the preliminary results of the execution of the predictive model for 4,000 EHRs.

Finally, Figure 7.10 shows the preliminary results of the execution of the decision model for the same number of EHRs (considering the time showed in the figure, the time of analysis for each EHR).

7.5   Conclusions and future works

This chapter has presented the CIPHER project, the main objective of which is to create an expert system software, based on big data and ML algorithms able to discover hidden symptomatology characteristic of the studied pathology. In addition, this detection must serve to feed a DSS that alerts the medical specialists at the moment in which a situation of risk is detected so that they will be able to carry out the appropriate measures.

The definition of the DSS system has been based on two main pillars: (i) a decision model and (ii) a predictive model.

The decision model is an implementation of the known standards that are applied in the brain strokes context (case of study of the validation). These standards are REGICOR [10], SCORE [11], CHADs2, CHADs2d2 and ATRIA [12].

The predictive model is an implementation of decision tree algorithms of Apache Spark [23]. The configuration that have been set for this algorithm takes 70% of the data to perform the training and for the remaining 30%. The algorithm eliminates parameter result of the CIPHER data model and applies the model generated by the training to calculate the result of whether the patient is susceptible to suffer a brain stroke.

The DSS system takes the output from both, decision and predictive models, and shows a final result based on the study of the results. This final result depends on three factors: (i) the percentage defined by the medical specialist of having a high risk of suffering a brain stroke, (ii) the percentage of suffering a brain stroke obtained from the decision model and (iii) a Boolean parameter that indicates if the patient has risk of suffering a brain stroke based on the knowledge generated by the ML algorithms and the training of the sample. With all this, the medical specialist obtains one of the following results: the patient presents risk of stroke, the patient does not present risk of stroke, the predictive model requires more data training and there is a possibility of existence of hidden symptomatology detected.

One of the main problems that have been encountered in the development of the project has been obtaining real data due to bureaucratic problems. Due to this problem and with the objective of testing and validating the system in an environment as close to reality as possible, different algorithms were designed to generate data, based on an anonymized sample resulting from previous studies. The model of data generated was based on the recommendations of the international standard of clinical history CEN/ISO EN13606 [13].

Preliminary results show that the selection of "DecisionTree" has been a very good option, obtaining an accuracy very close to the 100% considering a sample of 400 EHRs. In addition, the design of the data model of CIPHER and the algorithms for processing the information and the ML modeling, also works great, obtaining, in the worst case, an execution time of less than 2 min for a sample of 4,000 EHRs.

As far as what future work is concerned, the main and most ambitious one is to overcome the bureaucratic obstacles found and to be able to put CIPHER to work in a real environment with real data. On the other hand, a very interesting work in which many efforts are being made is in the automation of the detection of hidden symptoms without the medical specialist having to do complementary studies to the results obtained. Finally, and once validated for the case study of cerebral infarcts, it will be very interesting to create a new data model of a different pathology and check the behavior of the system as well as the results obtained.

Acknowledgments

This research has been supported both by the Pololas project (TIN2016-76956-C3-2-R) of the Spanish Ministry of Economy and Competitiveness, the CIPHER project (P113-16/E09) and by the Fifth Internal Research Plan (VPPI) of the University of Seville.

References

[1]   Power DJ. Decision support systems: concepts and resources for managers. Greenwood Publishing Group, London; 2002.

[2] Saeys Y, Inza I, Larrañaga P. A review of feature selection techniques in bioinformatics. Bioinformatics. 2007;23(19):2507–2517.

[3] Ropper AH, Samuels MA. Adams and Victor's principles of neurology. vol. 179. McGraw-Hill Medical Pub. Division, New York, NY; 2005.

[4] World Health Organization [homepage on the Internet]. WHO; [cited 2018 Jul 15]. Available from: http://www.who.int/home.

[5] Novak BV. Rang & Dale's pharmacology flash cards. MA Healthcare, London; 2011.

[6] Álvarez-Sabín J, Molina C, Montaner J, *et al.* Beneficios clínicos de la implantación de un sistema de atención especializada y urgente del ictus. Medicina clínica. 2004;122(14):528–531.

[7] Chauhan G, Arnold CR, Chu AY, *et al.* Identification of additional risk loci for stroke and small vessel disease: a meta-analysis of genome-wide association studies. The Lancet Neurology. 2016;15(7):695–707.

[8] Kilarski LL, Achterberg S, Devan WJ, *et al.* Meta-analysis in more than 17,900 cases of ischemic stroke reveals a novel association at 12q24.12. Neurology. 2014;83(8):678–685.

[9] Bevilacqua V, Cassano F, Dimauro G, *et al.* A Dynamic Approach to Medical Data Visualization and Interaction. In: VVH@ AVI; 2016. p. 7–12.

[10] Velescu A, Clara A, Peñafiel J, *et al.* Adding low ankle brachial index to classical risk factors improves the prediction of major cardiovascular events. The REGICOR study. Atherosclerosis. 2015;241(2):357–363.

[11] López-González Á, García-Agudo S, Tomás-Salvá M, *et al.* FINDRISC Test: relationship between cardiovascular risk parameters and scales in Spanish Mediterranean population. Revista Médica del Instituto Mexicano del Seguro Social. 2017;55(3):309.

[12] Aspberg S, Chang Y, Atterman A, *et al.* Comparison of the ATRIA, CHADS2, and CHA2DS2-VASc stroke risk scores in predicting ischaemic stroke in a large Swedish cohort of patients with atrial fibrillation. European Heart Journal. 2016;37(42):3203–3210.

[13] Muñoz P, Trigo JD, Martínez I, *et al.* The ISO/EN 13606 standard for the interoperable exchange of electronic health records. Journal of Healthcare Engineering. 2011;2(1):1–24.

[14] Moniche F, Escudero I, Zapata-Arriaza E, *et al.* Intra-arterial bone marrow mononuclear cells (BM-MNCs) transplantation in acute ischemic stroke (IBIS trial): protocol of a phase II, randomized, dose-finding, controlled multicenter trial. International Journal of Stroke. 2015;10(7):1149–1152.

[15] Delgado P, Riba-Llena I, Tovar JL, *et al.* Prevalence and associated factors of silent brain infarcts in a Mediterranean cohort of hypertensives. Hypertension. 2014;64(3):658–663.

[16] Riba-Llena I, Penalba A, Pelegrí D, *et al.* Role of lipoprotein-associated phospholipase A2 activity for the prediction of silent brain infarcts in women. Atherosclerosis. 2014;237(2):811–815.

[17] Vilar-Bergua A, Riba-Llena I, Penalba A, *et al.* N-terminal pro-brain natriuretic peptide and subclinical brain small vessel disease. Neurology. 2016;87(24):2533–2539.

[18] Vilar-Bergua A, Riba-Llena I, Ramos N, *et al.* Microalbuminuria and the combination of MRI markers of cerebral small vessel disease. Cerebrovascular Diseases. 2016;42(1–2):66–72.

[19] Sociedad Española de Ingeniería de la Salud [homepage on the Internet]. SEIS; [cited 2018 Jul 15]. Available from: http://seis.es/.

[20] Manning C, Surdeanu M, Bauer J, *et al.* The Stanford CoreNLP Natural Language Processing Toolkit. In: Proceedings of 52nd Annual Meeting of the Association for Computational Linguistics: System Demonstrations; 2014. p. 55–60.

[21] McGuinness DL, Van Harmelen F, *et al.* OWL web ontology language overview. W3C Recommendation. 2004;10(10):2004.

[22] Yujian L, Bo L. A normalized Levenshtein distance metric. IEEE Transactions on Pattern Analysis and Machine Intelligence. 2007;29(6):1091–1095.

[23] Meng X, Bradley J, Yavuz B, *et al.* MLlib: machine learning in Apache Spark. The Journal of Machine Learning Research. 2016;17(1):1235–1241.

[24] Salloum S, Dautov R, Chen X, *et al.* Big data analytics on Apache Spark. International Journal of Data Science and Analytics. 2016;1(3–4):145–164.

Chapter 8

Big data analytics for smart grids

Panagiotis D. Diamantoulakis[1] and
George K. Karagiannidis[1]

The Internet of Things (IoT) has recently emerged as an enabling technology for the next-generation electricity grid, namely, smart grid (SG). The efficient operation of the smart electricity grid depends on the efficient acquiring, analyzing, and processing of a large volume of data generated by the utilized smart sensors, individual smart meters, energy-consumption schedulers, aggregators, solar radiation sensors, wind-speed meters, and relays. In order to deal with the extreme size of data, the adoption of advanced data analytics, big data management, and powerful monitoring techniques is required. This approach creates huge opportunities and challenges, especially considering the real-time monitoring, load, renewable energy, and prices forecasting, identification and prediction of faults, and integration of electric vehicles, functioning in a mobile SG environment. Among others, intelligent algorithms, robust data analytics, high performance computing (HPC), efficient data network management, and cloud computing (CC) techniques are critical toward the optimized operation of SG. This chapter presents the big data issues faced by SG networks and the corresponding solutions.

8.1 Introduction

The development of new applications and requirements, such as the integration of millions of alternative distributed systems, the electric vehicles, the two-way flow of power, etc., places tremendous pressure on the existing power electricity grids, which need to be rapidly evolved [1–3]. The IoT is one of the major driving forces behind the next-generation power electricity grids, termed as SGs. The IoT refers to the use of advanced digital information technologies, such as sensing, data communications, and actuation [4], which are coordinated and controlled in a completely automatic manner, without any human intervention, by an end-to-end platform. The integration of this platform with the power electricity grid generates many new opportunities, such as the ability to manage electricity demand in a sustainable, reliable, and economic

---

[1]Electrical and Computer Engineering, Aristotle University of Thessaloniki, Greece

manner. More specifically, SGs, by properly exploiting the new capabilities provided by the IoT, are envisioned to achieve

- steady availability of power,
- energy sustainability,
- environmental protection,
- prevention of failures, as well as optimized operational expenses of power production and distribution, and
- reduced future capital expenses for thermal generators and transmission networks [1].

For this purpose, each consumption/production location, as well as several components of the transmission and distribution network, such as relays, switches, transformers, and substations, has to be equipped with a smart meter for monitoring and measuring the bidirectional flow of power and data. Also, supervisory control and data acquisition (SCADA) systems are needed to control the grid operation [5–10]. Data mining is the standard process to harvest useful information from a stream of data, such as users' electricity demand, renewable power generation, and state of battery of electric vehicles (EVs), and transform it into an understandable structure for further use. The data-mining process is based on the utilization of algorithms for discovering patterns among the data [11]. Efficient and effective data mining is crucial toward the optimized operation of the SG, since it strongly affects the related costs, the reliability of the grid and the service interruptions, the provided level of security, and the self-organization capability. Indeed, most of the research related to data mining in SGs deal with predictive analytics and load classification (LC), which are necessary for the load forecasting, bad data correction, anomaly detection, determination of the optimal energy resources scheduling, and setting of the power prices [12,13].

In order to deal with the stochastic nature of the SG, the data volume, variety, and velocity, as well as and the requirement for real-time learning/decision-making and collective awareness, the SG demands advanced data analytic techniques, big data management, and powerful monitoring techniques [14–16]. Various techniques such as artificial intelligence, distributed and HPC, simulation and modeling, data network management, database management, and data warehousing are to be used to guarantee smooth running of SGs. The main challenges of efficient data processing in SGs is the selection, deployment, monitoring, and analysis of aggregated data in real-time [17]. The efficient processing of the produced vast amount of data requires increased data storage and computing resources, which create the need for cloud and HPC techniques.

In this chapter, it is highlighted that big data analytics (BDA) can provide efficient solutions in specific problems related to data processing in SGs, which are described in the next sections. Section 8.2 focuses on the application of big data processing techniques for dynamic energy management (DEM) in SGs. Section 8.3 presents the main challenges in failure detection using data analytics. Load, price, and renewable generation forecasting is discussed in Section 8.4. Section 8.5 focuses on efficient smart meter data stream mining and presents the most commonly used methods in

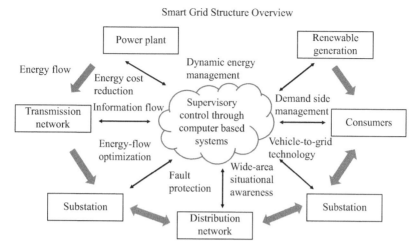

Figure 8.1   The integration of electrical and communication network in smart grid

the available literature. Section 8.6 is dedicated to privacy and security challenges, while Section 8.7 concludes the chapter.

8.2   Dynamic energy management

DEM requires system monitoring, power and data flow optimization, real-time operation, and plannings of productions [18]. DEM is a complicated procedure in SG, because SG has enabled an interconnected network of power distribution through two-way flow of data and power, as shown in Figure 8.1. In contrast, in a traditional power grid, the electricity is generated centrally and distributed to consumers. As a consequence to bidirectional flow of power and information, the grids are more adaptive to distributed energy sources. This encourages the participation of users in cooperative energy saving through demand-side management (DSM) mechanism [13,19,20]. For example, traditionally passive consumers, such as households and small businesses, are being empowered to be outfitted with generation capacity, such as roof-mounted solar photovoltaic (PV) panels; hence, they can take a more active role in the system. SG could potentially produce millions of alternate microenergy sources (solar, wind, etc.). The locational, and sometimes intermittent, character of distributed generation will emphasize local energy management and require higher stakeholder engagement, such as through the creation of cooperatives, or "energy communities" [21], and local electricity markets [22]. One of the main goals is to reduce the power peak load and to balance between the power supply and demand [23].

Although DEM in conventional electricity grids is a well-investigated topic, the corresponding algorithms cannot be directly applied to SGs. The latter is far more complicated, mainly due to the complex decision-making processes that are required by the control centers [24,25]. Energy-management systems (EMSs) in SGs include

- through advanced monitoring and metering systems, wide-area, real-time situational awareness of SG status;
- participation of consumers through DSM algorithms, EMSs, and vehicle-to-grid technology; and
- computer-based system supervisory control [26].

8.2.1   Demand side management

DSM can be applied to industrial and domestic loads (e.g., heating, cooling, charging). DSM constitutes of [27] (a) demand-wise shifting of energy production/consumption to periods of low/high demand, (b) reduction in energy consumption, and (c) storage systems' efficient utilization [28]. Taking into account for the careful scheduling of charging/discharging processes has benefits, however, with the increased complexity of DEM algorithms, as new parameters are added [29]. Therefore, it is critical to manage the demand response (DR) in SGs to reduce electricity load at peak times, thereby making efficient use of renewable energy and storage systems. The effectivity of DR algorithm depends on various parameters, such as demand, load, price, forecasting ability of renewal energy that mandates the requirements for sophisticated signal processing techniques [30].

DSM can be realized in three ways, namely, direct load control (DLC) [31], autonomous DR [20], and/or dynamic pricing [32]. Due to users' demand for privacy, DLC, which is a completely centralized approach, is not appropriate for residential electrical load control. On the other hand, autonomous DR is a very important mechanism for the future SGs, since it enables the automatic scheduling of the energy consumption. Also, if autonomous DR is combined with an incentive-based consumption scheduling scheme, it leads to promising results on reducing the energy costs and the peak to average power ratio. Similarly to autonomous DR, dynamic pricing does not require users to allow direct access of the operator to their electrical appliances. Also, it does not require users to declare their usage hours before turning on the switch. However, one major problem in dynamic power pricing is load synchronization, especially when there are limitations on the exchanged information. Since the power provider sets the power price selfishly without a proper contract on time-of-use and prices between operator and users, it is difficult for the operator to accurately predict and set an appropriate power price.

8.2.2   Data-driven DEM

There are several factors that affect the demand and production of SG environment, such as microclimatic variations, weather conditions, random disturbances, time of day, DSM profiles, electricity prices, micro-grids, storage cells, and the manufacturing of EVs [33–36]. To increase the reliability and reduction in operation cost, the accurate forecasting helps in appropriate generation and transmission planning of power plants that which of those should operate and how much power they generate at a specific time period [37]. This also helps in accurate estimation of electricity cost and setting up of prices, and also finding the dependencies among demand and prices [38]. For instance, the load synchronization is one such example of interdependency where a load is shifted from high-price to low-price hours without effecting the peak-to-average ratio [33].

DEM depends highly on quality of data collected and its reliability. To effectively manage and utilize the sensor data, the data-mining tools for predictive analytics become essential [39], as DEM depends on short-time power price forecasting, power supply, and consumption [40]. Moreover, the important correlations, patterns, and trends exist in sensor data that need to be exploited for optimized energy consumption [24].

8.3 Failure protection

Insufficient monitoring and control of the power flow can increase the possibility of failure (e.g., due to load synchronization, overloading, congestion). The power grid, which consists of multiple components such as relays, switches, transformers, and substations, must be carefully monitored. Lack of robustness of the power grid is well known; the grid is running to capacity and has become prone to failures caused by overloads, human errors, and natural disasters. Therefore, the SG requires intelligent real-time monitoring techniques in order to be capable of detecting abnormal events, finding their location and causes, and most importantly predicting and eliminating faults before they happen. This self-healing behavior renders the power grid a real 'immune system', which is one of the most important characteristics of an SG framework [41,42]. One major problem of self-healing control is the 'uninterrupted power supply problem', that is, real-time monitoring of network operation, prediction of the state power grid, timely detection, rapid diagnosis and elimination of hidden faults, without human intervention or only in a few cases. With self-healing capacity, the SG can also monitor a variety of disturbances, compensate for reactive power, redistribute the trend, and avoid expansion of accidents.

Critical events in SGs usually have temporal–spatial properties, which calls for temporal–spatial analysis [43]. A promising approach of BDA for fault detection, identification, and causal impact analysis has been proposed in [44], which manages to keep comprehensive information from synchrophasor measurements in spatial and temporal domains, while substantially reducing data volume. The derived scheme manages to achieve a high level of situational awareness, which is investigated based on hidden Markov model. Interestingly, the proposed scheme has been tested on IEEE 39-bus and IEEE 118-bus systems. Also, five representative fault types are employed for evaluating the proposed characterization approach, i.e., generator grounding, load loss, generator outage, single transmission line outage, and three-phase transmission line outage.

8.4 Load and price forecasting

The load data in SG environment is massive, dynamic, high-dimensional, and heterogeneous [12]. Thus, in order to build an accurate real-time monitoring and forecasting system, two novel concepts have to be taken into account in the system design. First, all available information from different sources, such as individual smart meters, energy consumption schedulers, aggregators, solar radiation sensors, wind-speed meters and relays, has to be integrated, while a communication point has to be designed where multiple artificial experts can interact and make decisions on data. The factors that affect the load forecasting can be separated in two categories: (a) the traditional factors and (b) the SG factors [37]. The traditional factors include the weather conditions, time of the day, season of the year, and random events and disturbances. On the other hand, the SG factors include the electricity prices, DSM, distributed energy sources, storage cells, and electric vehicles.

The timeliness and accuracy of the load forecasting have significant effects on power system operations and production costs. The importance of these factors is predominant in the SG environment as the spot-market prices and electricity demand are interdependent [37]. If the forecasted demand by utility is less compared to the actual value, it may end up buying the deficit power at higher prices than the market prices. On the other hand, if the forecasted demand is high compared to the actual value, utilities end up starting too many units resulting in high operating costs.

8.4.1   Load classification

The classification tries to predict the class label for a given test item through a classifier trained on a training data set [13]. LC is based on the unsupervised method of clustering to identify groups in the data provided. For LC in SGs, the artificial neural networks (ANNs) are used that are computational models to predict approximate functions against large number of inputs and are used when no accurate mathematical model is available to describe the phenomenon [45]. The ANNs have been used for consumer load curves classification to generate consumption patterns and facilitate selection of appropriate DSM technique [46]. The authors in [12,47] utilized self-organizing mapping for LC. The other classification approaches proposed in the literature are K-means, fuzzy c-means, hierarchical clustering, and so on [12]. In [48], a scalable online clustering method is proposed by improving the eXtended classifier system for clustering that suits well to dynamical nature of SGs, and it outperforms the off-line schemes in the performance of storage system [49].

8.4.2   Short-term load forecasting

The various models of short-term forecasting are developed, such as linear time-series based, regression models, nonlinear time-series based, state-space models [50]. Little progress has been made in load forecasting in SGs, in terms of very-short-term (VST), and ultra-short-term, which is also necessary for self-recovery of SG [50–52]. For load forecasting in micro-grids, the authors in [53] propose a short-term load forecasting method based on extended Kalman filter, empirical mode decomposition, and extreme learning with Kernel. In the area of STLF, the Kernel methods have been frequently utilized in research [54,55] as they increase the energy efficiency of computing [56–59]. The user convenience has also been taken into account for effective price forecasting, which is performed using supervised learning algorithms [60].

Online learning is an effective way of dealing with prediction and load monitoring in SGs, as the online learning algorithm observes a stream of examples and performs prediction for each stream element [61]. The statistical machine-learning (ML) properties of a target variable may change with time in the load forecasting in SGs. This makes the predictions less accurate as the time passes. The authors in [62] discuss solutions based on online learning to mitigate the aforementioned problem.

8.4.3 Renewable generation forecasting

For VST wind-power-generation forecast, there are myriad of approaches, which can be divided into two big categories: (a) forecasting the wind and direction for a specific windmill farm and (b) forecasting the generated power in a single step [63]. More interesting details on this issue can be found in [63]. Finally, short-term PV power prediction is mainly based on the past power output [64].

8.4.4 Price forecasting

The accurate point forecasting is essential for most DEM concepts [23] and directly affects the decision-making process of both the industries and the customers [23]. In contrast to accurate price forecasting, electricity price classification requires lower accuracy, while it might be sufficient, in order to set the user-defined thresholds, which determine if the load will be turned on or off [65].

The most common approaches used for electricity price forecasting are ML and time-series [23]. Neural networks have been used by [66] and [67,68] to provide per day and per hour electricity forecasting, respectively. On the other hand, electricity prices forecasting using time series has been investigated by [69] and [70], where an ARIMA based and a seasonal autoregressive moving average Hilbertian model is proposed, respectively. A different approach is proposed in [23], which integrates three modules, i.e., a hybrid feature selector based on gray correlation analysis (GCA) that helps to avoid redundancy, a combination of Kernel function and principle component analysis for feature extraction, and a differential evolution-based support vector machine classifier for the price classification forecasting [23].

8.4.5 Predictive control for electric vehicles power demand

Plug-in electric vehicles (PEVs) can substantially reduce the greenhouse gas emissions, due to their lower dependency on fossil fuel [71]. Also, PEVs can substantially reduce the corresponding expenses, which also depend on efficient battery charging. PEVs power demand is fundamentally different to other types of power demand, i.e., residence, since it is only known after random PEVs arrivals [72].

To this end, a novel method has been proposed in [73], in order to accurately estimate charging load using a fuzzy logic method, that accounts for random driver behaviors and statistical distribution of different vehicle types. Also, a practical scenario is investigated in [72], where unlike in related works, no assumptions are made about the probability distribution of PEVs. More specifically, joint PEV charging

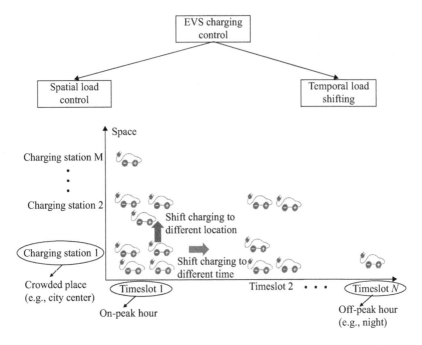

Figure 8.2   Charging load shifting using two dimensions, space and time

scheduling and power control is issued by the development of a novel model predictive control-based computational algorithm that can achieve a globally optimal solution.

In general, accurate PEV's power demand estimation depends on many parameters, such as speed information, roads congestion, the level of charge in each PEV, the PEV's location, historical data, tire pressure. Also, different use-case scenarios have to be considered, such as plug-in hybrid electric vehicles, i.e., vehicles that use a mix of electric motor and combustion engine and self-driven PEVs. For example, joint optimization of route planning and charging planning of PEVs is a challenging problem [71], while temporal and spatial load shifting options, illustrated in Figure 8.2, have to be jointly considered. Consequently, exploitation of BDA for accurate predicting of the charging loads is a promising direction that needs to be further investigated.

8.5   Efficient processing of extreme size of data

8.5.1   Avoidance of redundancies

Due to large volumes of data from the sensors installed around SG being collected, the features extracted in this phase also need to be refined as there is noise and redundancy in the features. For example, the weather condition that may affect both the generation of solar and wind energy will be reflected in the redundancy among weather, solar, and wind. If the input features contain redundant information (e.g., highly correlated features), ML algorithms in general perform poorly because of numerical instabilities. Some regularization techniques can be imposed to solve such problems. The techniques that can be used to build an optimal subset for the load or price predicting problem in SG are greedy hill climbing [74], minimum-redundancy-maximum-relevance [75], regularized trees [76], random multinomial logit [77], GCA [23], etc.

8.5.2   Dimensionality reduction

Smart meters generate large volume of data, and thus acquiring and processing all of them is inefficient—if not prohibitive—in terms of communication cost, computing complexity, and data storage resources utilization. For this purpose, dimensionality reduction has been applied in [78], in order to provide a reduced version (sketch) of meters' original data via random projection (RP). It is shown that processing the produced summarized version of data instead of the original stream of data leads to an acceptable relative error. The main advantage of RP is scalability, complexity reduction, and execution speed increase.

Dimensionality reduction has mainly been explored in the area of synchrophasor data. More specifically, online dimensionality reduction has been proposed in [79], in order to extract correlations between synchrophasor measurements, such as voltage, current and frequency. The proposed method can be utilized as a preprocessing method in data analysis and storage, when solely an approximation of the initial data is needed. Online dimensionality reduction has also been successfully used in for early event detection in [80], where an early event detection algorithm is proposed.

8.5.3   Data summarization

As it is pointed out in [81], summarization can significantly improve the scalability and efficiency of various SG data analytic tasks including transactional database mining and data streams mining, intrusions and anomalies detection, network monitoring, point of sales data mining, and information retrieval. Summarization is a perfect fit for the explosive volume of SG data, in order to extract useful and actionable intelligence. For this reason, a summarization paradigm has been developed in [81], which facilitates the utility company to accurately infer various energy consumption patterns in real-time by automatic monitoring of SG data, reducing using substantially the corresponding complexity. Moreover, the proposed paradigm takes into account spatiotemporal properties of the data, i.e., both the period of time and graphical locations. Note that the consideration of spatiotemporal is extremely important in many SG operations, such as faults detection and DEM. Also, it is highlighted that such composite analysis of SG data cannot be supported by most of existing management systems, due to the lack of support for arbitrary hierarchical and temporal analysis of data [81].

8.5.4   *MapReduce parallel processing*

It has been recognized that MapReduce deployment is suitable for SG data processing [61]. MapReduce is a programming model for processing large data sets with a
parallel, distributed algorithm on a computing cluster of low-cost commodity computers. A MapReduce application typically consists of two phases (or operations);
map and *reduce* with many tasks in each phase [82]. A map/reduce task deals with a
chunk of data independently and thus, tasks in a given phase can be easily parallelized
and effectively processed in a large-scale computing platform. In order to improve
the system's efficiency, two main mechanisms have to be taken into account, namely:

• the data locality-aware scheduling algorithm, and
• the application-specific resource allocation mechanisms.

Specifically, tasks requiring common data sets are dispatched to computers (compute
nodes) with close proximity to those data sets. For the majority of SG data processing
applications, storage capacity, such as disk and memory, is more important than
computing power.

8.5.5   *Distributed data mining*

The traditional centralized frameworks for acquiring, analyzing, and processing data,
require huge exchange of information among the remote sensors (e.g., the smart
meters and the centralized processor), which is inefficient in terms of telecommunication resources management and economic cost. To this end, the authors in [24]
present several distributed data analysis techniques that can be successively used
for energy demand prediction. The provided analysis emphasizes on the problem of
multivariate regression and rank ordering in a distributed scenario that is based on
polynomially bounded computations per node. Decentralized data-mining algorithms
have the advantage of scalability, while they are less affected by peer failures and they
need little computing and communication resources [83].

8.5.6   *Efficient computing*

Real-time monitoring, DEM, and power flow optimization are all based on fast data
processing and BDA, which need high-computing power. Efficient data-mining algorithms based on task parallelism, using multi-core, cluster, and grid computing, can
reduce the computational time [84]. However, covering the increased data storage and
computing resources needs is still a big economic challenge, mainly for the operators
of the electricity grids. Therefore, distributed computing seems to be a promising
perspective [85].

In order to enhance the existing computational capabilities and increase efficiency, a dedicated grid-computing-based framework is proposed in [86]. In more
detail, an architecture of three layers is proposed, namely, (a) the resource layer,
which consists of the hardware part of the computing grid, (b) the grid middleware,
which provides access of grid resources to the grid services, and (c) the application

layer, which consists of the services. It is shown that this computational grid can provide HPC by combining the processing power, memory, and storage of the available computers.

The CC model meets the requirements of data and computing intensive SG applications [87,88]. The main advantages of CC over traditional models are energy saving, cost saving, agility, scalability, and flexibility, since computational resources are used on demand [89]. Many approaches have been developed so far to further increase the energy efficiency of HPC data centers, such as energy conscious scheduling in [90], the cooperation with the SG in [91], and thermal-aware task scheduling in [53]. In [87], a model for SG data management is presented, taking advantage of the main characteristics of CC computing, such as distributed data management, parallelization, fast retrieval of information, accessibility, interoperability, and extensibility. Most of SG applications, such as advanced metering infrastructure, SCADA, and energy management, can be facilitated by the available cloud service models, namely, software as a service, platform as a service, and infrastructure as a service [92]. For the selection of the most appropriate cloud models, the recovery of data in the case of a possible failure of the cloud service needs is highly prioritized [92].

8.5.7   Testbeds and platforms

The majority of the available power grid testbeds focus on modeling of traditional network components, i.e., the generation systems, loads, and transmission network. A different approach is followed in [93], where a distribution grid testbed has been proposed, which can be used to test the designs of integrated information management systems. The purpose of this testbed is to successfully represent the correlation and interdependency among data sets, aiming to efficiently monitor the status of the SG and detect abnormalities.

Storing and processing the large SG's data sets generated by the smart meters, require improved platforms and appropriate for BDA, such as Hadoop, Cassandra and Hive [94]. Hadoop is a collection of open-source tools and includes the concept of MapReduce. Cassandra database, which supports the cloud infrastructure, can be used in order to store the large data sets which are needed for the effective DEM. Moreover, Hive data warehouse software utilizes a simple Structured Query Language (SQL) like language and be used to query data sets which are stored in a distributed environment.

8.6   Security and privacy issues in the smart grid

Security, privacy, and confidentiality are major challenges for the application of BDA on SG data processing [95,96].

8.6.1   Privacy

In order to ensure privacy, there are two different approaches, i.e.,

* Approach 1: data processing before sending it to the utility provider.
* Approach 2: modifying the actual user demand.

According to the first approach, which is the most common in the available literature, privacy of end users can be guaranteed by data aggregation, data anonymization, and data obfuscation, which is used in most SG architectures. Data aggregation is based on aggregating power measurements over a group of households so that the provider cannot have knowledge of individual consumption [97]. In data anonymization, pseudonyms are used instead of the real identities [98]. The aggregation can be performed by a trusted third party, when necessary. Data obfuscation refers to the perturbation of metering data by adding noise [99]. Note that the designed data architectures must be multi-tenant, following one of the three different approaches for such architectures, namely, the separate databases, separate schemas, or shared schemas [87]. Although the first approach is quite practical, its main disadvantage is that it still suffers from a privacy risk, since the operator is able to install a sensor for directly monitoring a residence or a business. Even worse, extra sensors can be placed by intelligent agencies or thieves. Also, data obfuscation method may provoke a mismatch between the real energy consumption and the reported values.

The second approach is investigated in [100–103], among others. In this approach, privacy is measured by the information leakage rate [103], which denotes the average mutual information between the user's real energy consumption and the energy requested from the grid, which the smart meter reads and reports to the utility provider. The minimum information leakage rate is a computable information theoretic single-letter expression, when the battery capacity is infinite or zero. It is noted that by using this approach, an interesting trade-off between privacy and cost is created [101]. This is because higher privacy can be achieved by modifying the smart meters readings, which, however, might have a negative impact on energy cost. Furthermore, when renewable energy sources are available, they directly affect the level of privacy that can be achieved [103]. More specifically, although the information leakage rate decreases with the renewable energy increase, larger storage capacity is required to take full advantage of the available energy to improve the privacy.

8.6.2 Security

Security is a challenging problem from both consumers' and electrical companies' perspective, since the hackers of systems located in the cloud cannot be easily traced. Also, data injection attacks, which aim to corrupt the estimate that the operator obtains, are among the most important concerns. Authentication, encryption, trust management, and intrusion and attack detection are important security mechanisms that can prevent, detect, and mitigate such network attacks [26,104].

The cybersecurity threats to which the SG is exposed requires a multidisciplinary approach, combining cryptography-advanced ML and information theoretic security [105]. Using ML, the measurements are classified either as secure or attacked [106]. Although cryptography and ML are well-known concepts, information theoretic security in SGs is a relatively new approach, which aims to quantify the information loss sue to the attack, as well as the probability of attack detection.

8.7 Conclusions

In this chapter, we have summarized the state-of-the-art in specific problems of SGs that can be resolved using data analytics processing and exploitation, as well as the proposed solutions, approaches, and concepts. More specifically, it has been recognized that data analytics can offer a feasible solution to efficient dynamic energy management, failure detection, estimation of load, and price forecasting. It has been highlighted that, in order to deal with the extreme size of data, the SG requires the adoption of advanced data analytics, big data management, and powerful monitoring techniques. We also presented a brief survey on the works that investigate efficient smart meter data processing, such as avoidance of redundancies, dimensionality reduction, data summarization distributed and parallel processing, cloud-based computing, and HPC. Finally, we have elaborated on challenging issues that are related to privacy and security, which call for a multidisciplinary approach, combining cryptography, advanced ML, and information theoretic security.

References

[1]   Bush SF, Goel S, Simard G. IEEE Vision for Smart Grid Communications: 2030 and Beyond Roadmap. IEEE Std Association. 2013 Sep; p. 1–19.

[2]   Goncalves Da Silva P, Ilic D, Karnouskos S. The Impact of Smart Grid Prosumer Grouping on Forecasting Accuracy and Its Benefits for Local Electricity Market Trading. IEEE Trans Smart Grid. 2014;5(1):402–410.

[3]   Lopez MA, de la Torre S, Martin S, *et al.* Demand-side management in smart grid operation considering electric vehicles load shifting and vehicle-to-grid support. Int J Electr Power Energy Syst. 2015;64(0):689–698.

[4]   Gore R, Valsan SP. Big data challenges in smart Grid IoT (WAMS) deployment. In: Proc. 2016 8th International Conference on Communication Systems and Networks (COMSNETS); 2016. p. 1–6.

[5]   Ukil A, Zivanovic R. Automated analysis of power systems disturbance records: Smart Grid big data perspective. In: Proc. IEEE Innovative Smart Grid Technologies – Asia (ISGT Asia); 2014. p. 126–131.

[6]   Simmhan Y, Aman S, Kumbhare A, *et al.* Cloud-based software platform for big data analytics in smart grids. Comput Sci Eng. 2013;15(4):38–47.

[7]   Leeds DJ. The Soft Grid 2013-2020: Big Data & Utility Analytics for Smart Grid. Tech. Rep. GTM Research; 2012. Available from: http://www.greentechmedia.com/research/report/the-soft-grid-2013.

[8]   Stimmel CL. Big Data Analytics Strategies for the Smart Grid. Boca Raton, FL: CRC Press; 2014.

[9]   Nguyen T, Nunavath V, Prinz A. Big data metadata management in smart grids. In: Big Data and Internet of Things: A Roadmap for Smart Environments. vol. 546 of Studies in Computational Intelligence. Springer International Publishing; 2014. p. 189–214.

[10]　Group IS. Managing Big Data for Smart Grids and Smart Meters. Whitepaper; 2012.

[11]　Chicco G, Napoli R, Postolache P, *et al.* Customer Characterization Options for Improving the Tariff Offer. IEEE Trans Power Syst. 2003;18(1): 381–387.

[12]　le Zhou K, lin Yang S, Shen C. A Review of Electric Load Classification in Smart Grid Environment. Renewable Sustainable Energy Rev. 2013;24(0):103–110.

[13]　Vale Z, Morais H, Ramos S, *et al.* Using data mining techniques to support DR programs definition in smart grids. In: Proc. IEEE Power and Energy Society General Meeting; 2011. p. 1–8.

[14]　Diamantoulakis PD, Kapinas VM, Karagiannidis GK. Big Data Analytics for Dynamic Energy Management in Smart Grids. Big Data Res. 2015;2(3): 94–101. Big Data, Analytics, and High-Performance Computing. Available from: http://www.sciencedirect.com/science/article/pii/S2214579615 000283.

[15]　Aung Z, Toukhy M, Williams J, *et al.* Towards accurate electricity load forecasting in smart grids. In: Proc. 4th International Conference on Advances in Databases, Knowledge, and Data Applications (DBKDA); 2012. p. 51–57.

[16]　Mack P. Chapter 35 – Big Data, Data Mining, and Predictive Analytics and High Performance Computing. In: Jones LE, editor. Renewable Energy Integration. Boston: Academic Press; 2014. p. 439–454.

[17]　Baek J, Vu Q, Liu J, *et al.* A Secure Cloud Computing based Framework for Big Data Information Management of Smart Grid. IEEE Trans Cloud Comput. 2014; 3:233–244.

[18]　Manfren M. Multi-Commodity Network Flow Models for Dynamic Energy Management-Mathematical Formulation. Energy Procedia. 2012;14(0):1380–1385.

[19]　Samadi P, Mohsenian-Rad H, Wong VWS, *et al.* Real-Time Pricing for Demand Response Based on Stochastic Approximation. IEEE Trans Smart Grid. 2014;5(2):789–798.

[20]　Mohsenian-Rad AH, Wong VWS, Jatskevich J, *et al.* Autonomous Demand-Side Management Based on Game-Theoretic Energy Consumption Scheduling for the Future Smart Grid. IEEE Trans Smart Grid. 2010;1(3): 320–331.

[21]　Julian C, Dobson J. Re-energising our communities: Transforming the energy market through local energy production. In: ResPublica Green Paper; 2012.

[22]　Hvelplund F. Renewable Energy and the Need for Local Energy Markets. Energy. 2006;31(13):2293–2302.

[23]　Wang K, Xu C, Zhang Y, *et al.* Robust Big Data Analytics for Electricity Price Forecasting in the Smart Grid. IEEE Trans Big Data. 2017;5:34–35.

[24]　Mallik R, Sarda N, Kargupta H, *et al.* Distributed data mining for sustainable smart grids. In: Proc. of ACM SustKDD'11; 2011. p. 1–6.

[25]　Balac N. "Green Machine" Intelligence: Greening and Sustaining Smart Grids. IEEE Intell Syst. 2013;28(5):50–55.

[26] Ancillotti E, Bruno R, Conti M. The Role of Communication Systems in Smart Grids: Architectures, Technical Solutions and Research Challenges. Comput Commun. 2013;36(17–18):1665–1697.

[27] Hardin D. Smart Grid and Dynamic Power Management. In: Kini PG, editor. Energy Management Systems. Rijeka: InTech; 2011. Available from: http://dx.doi.org/10.5772/20368.

[28] Siano P. Demand Response and Smart Grids–A Survey. Renewable Sustainable Energy Rev. 2014;30(0):461–478.

[29] Xiaojun W, Wenqi T, Jinghan H, *et al.* The application of electric vehicles as mobile distributed energy storage units in smart grid. In: Proc. Power and Energy Engineering Conference (APPEEC'11), 2011 Asia-Pacific; 2011. p. 1–5.

[30] Chan SC, Tsui KM, Wu HC, *et al.* Load/Price Forecasting and Managing Demand Response for Smart Grids: Methodologies and Challenges. IEEE Signal Process Mag. 2012;29(5):68–85.

[31] Ramanathan B, Vittal V. A Framework for Evaluation of Advanced Direct Load Control with Minimum Disruption. IEEE Trans Power Syst. 2008;23(4):1681–1688.

[32] Wang Q, Liu M, Jain R. Dynamic pricing of power in smart-grid networks. In: Proc. IEEE 51st IEEE Conference on Decision and Control (CDC); 2012. p. 1099–1104.

[33] Mohsenian-Rad AH, Leon-Garcia A. Optimal Residential Load Control with Price Prediction in Real-Time Electricity Pricing Environments. IEEE Trans Smart Grid. 2010;1(2):120–133.

[34] Carpinelli G, Celli G, Mocci S, *et al.* Optimal Integration of Distributed Energy Storage Devices in Smart Grids. IEEE Trans Smart Grid. 2013;4(2):985–995.

[35] Saber AY, Venayagamoorthy GK. Resource Scheduling Under Uncertainty in a Smart Grid with Renewables and Plug-in Vehicles. IEEE Syst J. 2012;6(1):103–109.

[36] Avila F, Saez D, Jimenez-Estevez G, *et al.* Fuzzy demand forecasting in a predictive control strategy for a renewable-energy based microgrid. In: Proc. European Control Conference (ECC); 2013. p. 2020–2025.

[37] Balantrapu S. Load Forecasting in Smart Grid. 2013. http://www.energy central.com/enduse/demandresponse/articles/2760.

[38] Motamedi A, Zareipour H, Rosehart WD. Electricity Price and Demand Forecasting in Smart Grids. IEEE Trans Smart Grid. 2012;3(2):664–674.

[39] Fan Z, Chen Q, Kalogridis G, *et al.* The power of data: Data analytics for M2M and smart grid. In: Proc. 3rd IEEE PES International Conference and Exhibition on Innovative Smart Grid Technologies (ISGT Europe); 2012. p. 1–8.

[40] Mirowski P, Chen S, Ho TK, *et al.* Demand Forecasting in Smart Grids. Bell Labs Tech J. 2014;18(4):135–158.

[41] Pitt J, Bourazeri A, Nowak A, *et al.* Transforming Big Data into Collective Awareness. Computer. 2013;46(6):40–45.

[42] DongLi J, Xiaoli M, Xiaohui S. Study on technology system of self-healing control in smart distribution grid. In: Proc. International Conference on Advanced Power System Automation and Protection (APAP). vol. 1; 2011. p. 26–30.

[43] Fu Z, Almgren M, Landsiedel O, *et al.* Online temporal-spatial analysis for detection of critical events in cyber-physical systems. In: 2014 IEEE International Conference on Big Data (Big Data); 2014. p. 129–134.

[44] Jiang H, Dai X, Gao DW, *et al.* Spatial-Temporal Synchrophasor Data Characterization and Analytics in Smart Grid Fault Detection, Identification, and Impact Causal Analysis. IEEE Trans Smart Grid. 2016;7(5):2525–2536.

[45] Taheri J, Zomaya AY. Artificial Neural Networks. In: Handbook of Nature-Inspired and Innovative Computing. Integrating Classical Models with Emerging Technologies. New York: Springer; 2006. p. 147–185.

[46] Macedo MNQ, Galo JJM, de Almeida LAL, *et al.* Demand Side Management Using Artificial Neural Networks in a Smart Grid Environment. Renewable Sustainable Energy Rev. 2015;41(0):128–133.

[47] Verdu SV, Garcia MO, Franco FJG, *et al.* Characterization and identification of electrical customers through the use of self-organizing maps and daily load parameters. In: IEEE Power Systems Conference and Exposition (PES). vol. 2; 2004. p. 899–906.

[48] Monti A, Ponci F. Power grids of the future: Why smart means complex. In: Proc. IEEE Complexity in Engineering (COMPENG'10); 2010. p. 7–11.

[49] Sancho-Asensio A, Navarro J, Arrieta-Salinas I, *et al.* Improving Data Partition Schemes in Smart Grids via Clustering Data Streams. Expert Syst Appl. 2014;41(13):5832–5842.

[50] Kyriakides E, Polycarpou M. Short Term Electric Load Forecasting: A Tutorial. In: Chen K, Wang L, editors. Trends in Neural Computation. vol. 35 of Studies in Computational Intelligence. Berlin, Heidelberg: Springer; 2007. p. 391–418.

[51] Guan C, Luh PB, Michel LD, *et al.* Very Short-Term Load Forecasting: Wavelet Neural Networks with Data Pre-Filtering. IEEE Trans Power Syst. 2013;28(1):30–41.

[52] Han XS, Han L, Gooi HB, *et al.* Ultra-Short-Term Multi-node Load Forecasting—A Composite Approach. IET Gener, Transm Distrib. 2012;6(5): 436–444.

[53] Tang Q, Gupta SKS, Varsamopoulos G. Energy-Efficient Thermal-Aware Task Scheduling for Homogeneous High-Performance Computing Data Centers: A Cyber-Physical Approach. IEEE Trans Parallel Distrib Syst. 2008;19(11):1458–1472.

[54] Mori H, Kurata E. An efficient kernel machine technique for short-term load forecasting under smart grid environment. In: Proc. IEEE Power and Energy Society General Meeting; 2012. p. 1–4.

[55] Kramer O, Gieseke F. Analysis of wind energy time series with kernel methods and neural networks. In: Proc. 7th International Conference on Natural Computation (ICNC). vol. 4; 2011. p. 2381–2385.

[56] Yoo PD, Zomaya AY. Combining analytic kernel models for energy-efficient data modeling and classification. J Supercomput. 2013;63(3): 790–799.

[57] Yoo PD, Ng JWP, Zomaya AY. An energy-efficient kernel framework for large-scale data modeling and classification. In: Proc. IEEE International Symposium on Parallel and Distributed Processing Workshops and PhD Forum (IPDPSW); 2011. p. 404–408.

[58] Yoo PD, Zhou BB, Zomaya AY. A Modular Kernel Approach for Integrative Analysis of Protein Domain Boundaries. BMC Genomics. 2009;10(Suppl 3):S21.

[59] Yoo PD, Ho YS, Zhou BB, *et al.* Adaptive locality-effective kernel machine for protein phosphorylation site prediction. In: Proc. IEEE International Symposium on Parallel and Distributed Processing (IPDPS); 2008. p. 1–8.

[60] Li B, Gangadhar S, Cheng S, *et al.* Predicting user comfort level using machine learning for Smart Grid environments. In: Proc. IEEE PES Innovative Smart Grid Technologies (ISGT); 2011. p. 1–6.

[61] Wang B, Huang S, Qiu J, *et al.* Parallel online sequential extreme learning machine based on MapReduce. Neurocomputing. 2015;149, Part A(0): 224–232.

[62] Anderson T. The Theory and Practice of Online Learning. Edmonton, Canada: Athabasca University Press; 2008.

[63] Couceiro M, Ferrando R, Manzano D, *et al.* Stream analytics for utilities. Predicting power supply and demand in a smart grid. In: Proc. International Workshop on Cognitive Information Processing (CIP); 2012. p. 1–6.

[64] Murakami Y, Takabayashi Y, Noro Y. Photovoltaic power prediction and its application to smart grid. In: Proc. IEEE Innovative Smart Grid Technologies-Asia (ISGT Asia); 2014. p. 47–50.

[65] Diamantoulakis PD, Pappi KN, Kong PY, *et al.* Game theoretic approach to demand side management in smart grid with user-dependent acceptance prices. In: Proc. 2016 IEEE 84th Vehicular Technology Conference (VTC-Fall); 2016. p. 1–5.

[66] Varshney H, Sharma A, Kumar R. A hybrid approach to price forecasting incorporating exogenous variables for a day ahead electricity market. In: Proc. IEEE 1st International Conference on Power Electronics, Intelligent Control and Energy Systems (ICPEICES); 2016. p. 1–6.

[67] Rafiei M, Niknam T, Khooban MH. Probabilistic Forecasting of Hourly Electricity Price by Generalization of ELM for Usage in Improved Wavelet Neural Network. IEEE Trans Ind Inf. 2017;13(1):71–79.

[68] Mosbah H, El-hawary M. Hourly Electricity Price Forecasting for the Next Month Using Multilayer Neural Network. Can J Electr Comput Eng. 2016;39(4):283–291.

[69] Ozozen A, Kayakutlu G, Ketterer M, *et al.* A combined seasonal ARIMA and ANN model for improved results in electricity spot price forecasting: Case study in Turkey. In: Proc. Portland International Conference on Management of Engineering and Technology (PICMET); 2016. p. 2681–2690.

[70]   Portela J, Munoz A, Alonso E. Forecasting Functional Time Series with a New Hilbertian ARMAX Model: Application to Electricity Price Forecasting. IEEE Trans Power Syst. 2017;33:545–556.

[71]   Kong PY, Karagiannidis GK. Charging Schemes for Plug-In Hybrid Electric Vehicles in Smart Grid: A Survey. IEEE Access. 2016;4:6846–6875.

[72]   Shi Y, Tuan H, Savkin A, Duong TQ, Poor HV. Model Predictive Control for Smart Grids with Multiple Electric-Vehicle Charging Stations. IEEE Trans Smart Grid. 2019;10(2):2127–2136.

[73]   Tan J, Wang L. Integration of Plug-in Hybrid Electric Vehicles into Residential Distribution Grid Based on Two-Layer Intelligent Optimization. IEEE Trans Smart Grid. 2014;5(4):1774–1784.

[74]   Alajmi BN, Ahmed KH, Finney SJ, *et al.* Fuzzy-Logic-Control Approach of a Modified Hill-Climbing Method for Maximum Power Point in Microgrid Standalone Photovoltaic System. IEEE Trans Power Electron. 2011;26(4):1022–1030.

[75]   Peng H, Long F, Ding C. Feature Selection based on Mutual Information Criteria of Max-Dependency, Max-Relevance, and Min-redundancy. IEEE Trans Pattern Anal Mach Intell. 2005;27(8):1226–1238.

[76]   Deng H, Runger G. Feature selection via regularized trees. In: Proc. 12th IEEE International Joint Conference on Neural Networks (IJCNN); 2012. p. 1–8.

[77]   Prinzie A, den Poel DV. Random Forests for Multiclass Classification: Random MultiNomial Logit. Expert Syst Appl. 2008;34(3):1721–1732.

[78]   Dieb Martins A, Gurjao EC. Processing of smart meters data based on random projections. In: Proc. IEEE PES Conference On Innovative Smart Grid Technologies Latin America (ISGT LA), 2013; 2013. p. 1–4.

[79]   Dahal N, King RL, Madani V. Online dimension reduction of synchrophasor data. In: Proc. IEEE PES Transmission and Distribution Conference and Exposition (T&D); 2012. p. 1–7.

[80]   Xie L, Chen Y, Kumar PR. Dimensionality Reduction of Synchrophasor Data for Early Event Detection: Linearized Analysis. IEEE Trans Power Syst. 2014;29(6):2784–2794.

[81]   Shah Z, Anwar A, Mahmood AN, *et al.* A Spatio-Temporal Data Summarization Paradigm for Real-Time Operation of Smart Grid. IEEE Trans Big Data. 2017;PP(99):1.

[82]   Rizvandi NB, Taheri J, Moraveji R, *et al.* A Study on Using Uncertain Time Series Matching Algorithms for MapReduce Applications. Concurr Comput: Pract Exp. 2013;25(12):1699–1718.

[83]   Bhaduri K, Kargupta H. An efficient local algorithm for distributed multivariate regression in peer-to-peer networks. In: SIAM Conference on Data Mining (SDM); 2008. p. 153–164.

[84]   Green RC, Wang L, Alam M. Applications and Trends of High Performance Computing for Electric Power Systems: Focusing on Smart Grid. IEEE Trans Smart Grid. 2013;4(2):922–931.

[85]   Zomaya AY, Lee YC. Energy Efficient Distributed Computing Systems. Hoboken, NJ: Wiley-IEEE Computer Society Press; 2012.

[86] Ali M, Dong ZY, Li X, *et al.* RSA-grid: A grid computing based frame-work for power system reliability and security analysis. In: IEEE Power Engineering Society General Meeting; 2006. p. 1–7.

[87] Rusitschka S, Eger K, Gerdes C. Smart grid data cloud: A model for utilizing cloud computing in the smart grid domain. In: Proc. IEEE International Conference on Smart Grid Communications (SmartGridComm'10); 2010. p. 483–488.

[88] Bera S, Misra S, Rodrigues JJPC. Cloud Computing Applications for Smart Grid: A Survey. IEEE Trans Parallel Distrib Syst. 2014;26:1477–1494.

[89] Hayes B. Cloud Computing. Commun. ACM. 2008 11;51(7):9–11.

[90] Lee YC, Zomaya AY. Energy Conscious Scheduling for Distributed Computing Systems under Different Operating Conditions. IEEE Trans Parallel Distrib Syst. 2011;22(8):1374–1381.

[91] Ghamkhari M, Mohsenian-Rad AH. Energy and Performance Management of Green Data Centers: A Profit Maximization Approach. IEEE Trans Smart Grid. 2013;4(2):1017–1025.

[92] Markovic DS, Zivkovic D, Branovic I, *et al.* Smart Power Grid and Cloud Computing. Renewable Sustainable Energy Rev. 2013;24(0):566–577.

[93] Lu N, Du P, Paulson P, *et al.* The development of a smart distribution grid testbed for integrated information management systems. In: Proc. IEEE Power and Energy Society General Meeting; 2011. p. 1–8.

[94] Mayilvaganan M, Sabitha M. A cloud-based architecture for Big-Data analytics in smart grid: A proposal. In: Proc. IEEE International Conference on Computational Intelligence and Computing Research (ICCIC); 2013. p. 1–4.

[95] Yigit M, Gungor VC, Baktir S. Cloud Computing for Smart Grid applications. Comput Networks. 2014;70(0):312–329.

[96] Kasper A. Legal Aspects of CyberSecurity in Emerging Technologies: Smart Grids and Big Data. In: Kerikmäe T, editor. Regulating eTechnologies in the European Union. Basel, Switzerland: Springer International Publishing; 2014. p. 189–216.

[97] Li F, Luo B, Liu P. Secure and Privacy-Preserving Information Aggregation for Smart Grids. Int J Secur Netw. 2011;6(1):28–39.

[98] Efthymiou C, Kalogridis G. Smart grid privacy via anonymization of smart metering data. In: Smart Grid Communications (SmartGridComm), 2010 First IEEE International Conference on. IEEE; 2010. p. 238–243.

[99] Kim Y, Ngai ECH, Srivastava MB. Cooperative state estimation for preserving privacy of user behaviors in smart grid. In: Proc. IEEE International Conference on Smart Grid Communications (SmartGridComm); 2011. p. 178–183.

[100] Tan O, Gunduz D, Poor HV. Increasing Smart Meter Privacy Through Energy Harvesting and Storage Devices. IEEE J Sel Areas Commun. 2013;31(7):1331–1341.

[101] Tan O, Gomez-Vilardebo J, Gunduz D. Privacy-Cost Trade-offs in Demand-Side Management with Storage. IEEE Trans Inf Forensics Secur. 2017;12(6):1458–1469.

[102]   Li S, Khisti A, Mahajan A. Privacy-optimal strategies for smart metering systems with a rechargeable battery. In: 2016 American Control Conference (ACC); 2016. p. 2080–2085.

[103]   Giaconi G, Gunduz D, Poor HV. Smart Meter Privacy with Renewable Energy and an Energy Storage Device. IEEE Trans Inf Forensics Secur. 2017;13: 129–142.

[104]   Ericsson GN. Cyber Security and Power System Communication-Essential Parts of a Smart Grid Infrastructure. IEEE Trans Power Delivery. 2010;25(3):1501–1507.

[105]   Sun K, Esnaola I, Perlaza SM, Poor HV. Information-Theoretic Attacks in the Smart Grid. In: Proc. IEEE International Conference on Smart Grid Communications (SmartGridComm); 2017. p. 455–460.

[106]   Ozay M, Esnaola I, Vural FTY, *et al.* Machine Learning Methods for Attack Detection in the Smart Grid. IEEE Trans Neural Networks Learn Syst. 2016;27(8):1773–1786.

Chapter 9

Internet of Things and big data recommender systems to support Smart Grid

Mirjana Maksimović[1] and Miodrag Forcan[1]

Since its appearance, the Internet of Things (IoT) has completely revolutionized almost all aspects of our lives. Among present and potential numerous and diverse applications of IoT, its utilization in the energy sector is of particular interest. The IoT inclusion in the power industry and Smart Grid (SG) evolution opens a whole world of high-potential opportunities to optimize the grid operation. The realization of SGs utilizing smart metering technology or advanced metering infrastructure with bidirectional IoT-based communication between demand and utility could improve existing energy balancing procedures. Keeping energy consumption and supply in balance with minimal operating costs and optimal grid conditions is not an easy task, especially in presence of renewable energy sources. As the IoT is established on the utilization of a large number of smart things/devices that generate a prodigious amount of data on a daily basis, successfully managing big data represents a key issue. In order to obtain valuable insights and knowledge from data gathered, the appliance of big data analytics is demanded. Hence, effective analysis and utilization of a massive amount of diversity of data that arrive at high speed and can be of uncertain provenance are mandatory in the process of obtaining valuable insights and enable the creation of knowledge-based recommender systems. Big data analytics applied to data gathered from smart meters could be used to make valuable recommendations regarding consumption prediction, demand response and management programs, voltage and frequency control, state estimation, and power quality. The overall operation of SG could be certainly optimized in various aspects by using large-scale near real-time measurements. The general aim of this chapter is to provide an overview of ongoing scientific research, recent technological innovations and breakthroughs, and big data analytics role in making recommendation systems that will facilitate the development and evolution of future global energy systems.

9.1 Introduction

The IoT paradigm is based on the Internet working "things" that are able to sense the environment and collect, process, and analyze large quantities of data in order to

---

[1]Faculty of Electrical Engineering, University of East Sarajevo, Bosnia and Herzegovina

perform actions of interest. It is a ubiquitous network which can connect anyone and anything, anytime, at any place, ideally using any path and any service. Therefore, IoT progress can be looked as a technological revolution which holds the potential to dramatically reshape and transform almost all the aspects of our lives. The IoT evolution is accompanied by the rapidly increasing number of a wide range of smart interconnected devices and systems. According to Cisco estimations, 50 billion diverse devices will be connected to the Internet by 2020 [1]. Present Internet-aware devices already produce huge amounts of a variety of data on a daily basis. Some predictions highlight that the volume of data produced by IoT devices will be 507.5 ZB (1 zettabyte = 1 trillion gigabytes) of data per year or 42.3 ZB per month by 2019 [2]. An analysis of large volumes of fast generating diverse IoT data is essential for achieving useful insights and knowledge on which basis appropriate decision can be made and actions performed.

Just like numerous application areas, IoT implementation has also improved the energy sector. A better balance between energy demand and energy supply can be achieved by using energy network integrated with a large network of Information and Communication Technology (ICT) which automatically monitors energy flows and adjusts it to change. This network of billions of smart objects (smart appliances, smart meters, actuators, sensors, etc.) is known as the Smart Grid (SG) [3,4]. It is forecasted that SG in the future will be composed of micro-grid networks, connected to each other via the Cloud, and be able to monitor, run, or disconnect themselves and heal based on the data collected with smart metering devices [4,5]. It is anticipated that by the end of the decade, the expected number of installed smart meters will reach 250 million in Europe, 150 million in the United States of America and Canada, and 400 million in China [6]. The increasing number of smart meters and other smart devices in large SGs will create an enormous quantity of data and its management poses several challenges such as reliability, security, and scalability.

Traditionally, processing, analyzing, and storing data from large-scale distributed system, such as SG, are handled by the Cloud architecture [7]. However, transmitting a large volume of complex data sets generated in SG to the Cloud causes problems with the bandwidth demands, latency issues, and the amount of time. Data processing, storage, and networking services at the edge of the Cloud, instead of routing it over Cloud channels and enabling real-time decision without transmitting an amount of data to the Cloud, are known as Fog computing [8]. Fog layer is a middle layer between end devices and Cloud which collects data, stores and processes it locally, and then transmits the outcome to the Cloud in order to store or perform in-depth data analysis. With the assistance of accurate prediction algorithms, both better renewable energy integration to the system and reduction of the amount of energy wasted, can be achieved [9]. Hence, Fog infrastructure implementation in SG makes data processing faster, reduces latency and the need for bandwidth, improves security and quality of services (QoS), and provides reliability and location awareness in SG. Still, there are numerous challenges for Fog computing implementation. They are mainly related to the load balancing between edge devices and Cloud. The potential solution for overcoming this problem is seen in Osmotic computing [10–12]. Osmotic computing is a paradigm that enables decision where analytic tasks will be performed, with

Cloud- or edge-based resource, and in such way balances load of resources, minimizes latency, and maximizes throughput.

Irrespective of infrastructure implemented in SG vision, the constant analysis of continually arriving data from smart meters and other smart devices in SG is mandatory. Historical analysis, real-time analysis, and predictive analytics naturally lead to the development of recommender systems that, based on the performed analysis and obtained knowledge and insights, make recommendations which appliance in particular cases significantly contribute to optimized SG work and its reliability. In other words, the massive volumes of heterogeneous data collected in SG and its effective, on-time, and precise analysis hold the potential to dramatically transform the energy sector.

Therefore, this paper is an attempt to briefly present the inclusion of novel technologies, IoT and big data, particularly in the power sector. The second section is devoted to the communication principles in IoT-supported SG while the power of collection, analysis, and decision-making based on big data is discussed in Section 9.3. The attention of Section 9.4 is given to the development of recommender systems in SG vision, with the emphasis on their potential utilization in load forecasting (LF), renewable energy forecasting (REF), demand response (DR) and energy management programs, and SG state estimation. The last section contains concluding remarks, and directions of future work.

9.2   IoT-supported SG—a communication perspective

The technology development consequently leads to the modernization of the power grid, at both the transmission levels and distribution levels, in order to provide a reliable and sustainable supply of electricity but at the same time makes it affordable [13]. The inclusion of smart devices, intelligent sensing, control, and communication results in the realization of SG vision (Figure 9.1), which poses significant differences compared to existing grid [14] (Figure 9.2).

The main building blocks of an SG infrastructure shown in Figure 9.1 can be classified into three categories:

- Smart energy system—power grid, transmission grid, distribution grid, and micro-grid;
- Smart information system—smart sensors, smart meters, phasor measurement units (PMUs), and information metering and measurement;
- Smart communication system—communication networks (HAN, home area network; LAN, local area network; BAN, business area network; NAN, neighborhood area network; WAN, wide area network), and communication technologies (wired and wireless).

A number of sensors and control devices, supported by dedicated communication infrastructure, are used in smart meters that play an important role in SG vision [15]. Basic innovative features of these advanced energy meters are real-time measurements, bidirectional communication with utility and house appliances,

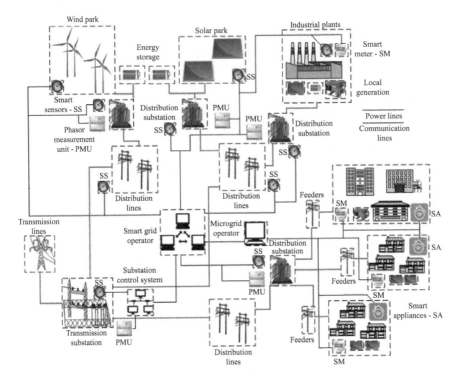

Figure 9.1   SG vision

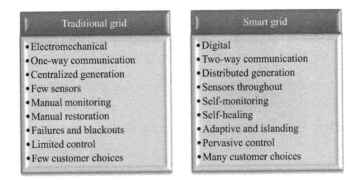

Figure 9.2   Comparison between the existing grid and the SG

remote service disconnects, power outage notification, and power quality monitoring. Besides conventional energy measurements, smart meters are capable of recording and periodically transferring various electric variables such as frequency and harmonic distortion. The smart meters offer several benefits to a customer, such as the ability to estimate bills and hence manage their energy consumptions based on the gathered data. The collected information from SGs helps companies to realize real-time pricing and optimize the power flows as well as limit the maximum electricity consumption, with appropriate mechanisms remotely [15].

As SG is composed of smart meters, HANs, LANs, BANs, NANs, WANs, data centers, and substation automation integration systems [7,16], it must be supported by an integrated communications network and well-defined communications protocols. Deployment of IoT technology in SG results in an immense smart network composed of people and equipment that collaborate with the existing technologies and enable dynamic and optimized monitoring and control based on fast and accurate information exchange of the following [17,18]:

- temperature, humidity, air pressure, and other parameters of the electrical equipment in power system;
- electrical parameters that monitor all network nodes in the power system;
- health state in power system;
- management information of technical personnel; and
- service condition of environmental protection equipment.

For the communication and exchange of such information, wired and wireless technologies can be utilized, depending on various factors [18]. This communication is commonly split into two types of information flows: between smart meters and IoT devices, sensors and home appliances, and between smart meters and utility control centers [19]. Hence, communication depends on different types of networks. In a case of access networks, a sensing information about the power grid device states can be transmitted using short-range communication technologies (e.g. WiFi, Bluetooth, or ZigBee), while in area networks are usually implemented machine to machine (M2M), Cellular networks (2G, 3G, 4G), Ethernet, IP/MPLS (Internet Protocol/Multiprotocol Label Switching) approach is implemented in the core network, while the backbone network includes both wired and wireless point-to-point and point-to-multipoint broadband systems, fiber and microwave systems [20,21]. In other words, wide area communication technologies that can be implemented in IoT-supported SG vision are IP-based Internet, power line carrier (PLC), optical fiber composite low-voltage cable (OPLC), power information wireless network, public 2G/3G/4G mobile communication network, Time-Division Long-Term Evolution (TD-LTE) 4G network, and satellite communication network [22]. In the case of Fog-assisted SG, it is important to keep in mind that implementation of Fog computing means that most of the functions of data processing are executed out from the Cloud. Therefore, a reliable and efficient communication system is mandatory in order to get a robust, affordable, and secure power supply through SG. Fog infrastructure in SG supports real-time two-way communication flows between utilities and consumers, enabling at the same time customers access to their own applications at any time, through a device connected to the edge of the network [8]. Authors of [7] proposed a model that follows a three-tier architecture, i.e. smart meters, Fog servers, and the traditional Cloud (Figure 9.3), while four types of communication are performed among tiers, i.e. smart device to smart device, smart device to Fog server, Fog server to Fog server, and Fog server to Cloud server. For instance, the

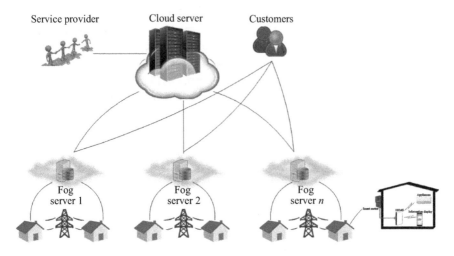

Figure 9.3   Fog infrastructure implementation in SG

smart device can communicate with each other using ZigBee, USB, or Bluetooth, while smart device and Fog server can communicate through Ethernet. Furthermore, connecting Fog server to the Internet, through WiFi or General Packet Radio Service (GPRS), enables the user to perform monitoring and controlling actions locally or remotely through the Internet [23].

During literature research, we have not found papers that implement Osmotic computing paradigm in SG. However, we believe that the inclusion of Osmotic computing and IoT symbiosis in SG holds the potential to completely revolutionize energy sector. The idea of Osmotic computing is established on the well-known principle of osmosis [11]. For instance, the implementation of Osmotic computing at the Fog servers as shown in Figure 9.3 makes this Fog layer a place where decisions when, where (to a Cloud data center or Edge resource), and how to move micro-services across different computing infrastructures are being made. In other words, displacement of services is performed within Cloud data centers and Edge resources in such way that lightweight micro-services are deployed at the Edge devices while more complex micro-services are deployed at the Cloud data centers. This leads to balancing a load and resource utilization, what is of immense importance.

Reduction of both energy consumption and CO_2 emissions in SG can be also achieved through the implementation of green technologies. Green SG (G-SG) is a new vision that includes green communication and green computing technologies implementations in SG alongside green power resources integration into the energy distribution system, control power usage, and balance energy load [7]. The next-generation SG will be highly automated and IoT based, allowing variable and decentralized energy generation, storage, and distribution, as well as facilitating distributed and renewable energy sources [5]. ICT-enabled solutions are able to better incorporate green and renewable energy sources into the grid, making G-SG vision more present. Self-healing and autonomous system, environmental protection, high reliability and quality, security, and optimized asset utilization and minimized cost are the fundamental characteristic of G-SG [24,25]. Having in mind that the most energy is spent during communication and that IoT devices, including smart meters, are energy-limited, the deployment of green communication and the system model in IoT has been a core challenging issue [26]. Consequently, the realization of G-SG vision requires the utilization of green communication techniques. Fog infrastructure significantly contributes to the realization of green communication principles in G-IoT-supported SG. The primary focus on green communication technology is in decreasing energy consumption and CO_2 transmission in communication and networking device. Evolving communications architectures, green wireless communication, energy-efficient routing, relay selection strategies for green communication, energy efficient packet forwarding, and networking games are the main research points of interest in green communication technology. The utilization of G-SG communications leads to decreased energy use and reduced emission in SG products and services, and consequently reduced carbon footprint in other industries, such as networks powered by the SG. More efficient energy usage and better integration of alternative energy sources into the power grid consequently lead to economic growth without damaging the environment.

9.3   Big data in SG

The realization of IoT-supported SG is based on the utilization of a large number of smart metering devices and various sensors that produce a great quantity of high-dimensional, dynamic, and heterogeneous data. These data must be treated in an appropriate manner in order to gain benefits of IoT-supported SG systems, which implies the requirement for a successful data management. In order to obtain valuable insights and knowledge, the data have to be collected, processed, and analyzed, which makes dealing with the complex nature of the data (usually described with 5 Vs—volume, velocity, variety, value, and veracity), significant storage capacity, and utilization of advanced data analytics main demands for an effective data management system [21]. In the modern approaches, the solution can be found in the big data techniques that enable advanced and efficient management of large amounts of diverse types of data that need more real-time analysis. The successful SG data management contributes to better understanding the numerous aspects of SG and whole energy sector through the information regarding energy conservation, consumption and demand, power failures, customer behavior, etc. In other words, based on the knowledge and insights gained from collected, processed, and analyzed data, the big data recommender systems for providing relevant and effective recommendations can be developed followed by certain decision-making and action execution. In this way, IoT and big data enable the modernization of the traditional power grid enabling feedback data about the energy demanded, consumed and delivered, recommendations regarding most suitable tariffs for customers, the adjusting electricity needs in a facility on a daily basis, and at the end leading to general optimizations over how the energy is managed and consumed.

Before computing recommendation models, there are certain steps that have to be performed and include five phases of big data life cycle: data sources, data integration, data storage, data analysis, and data visualization.

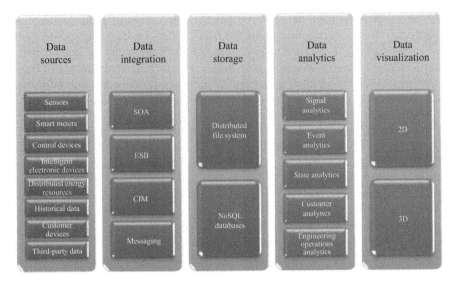

Figure 9.4   Big data architecture for SG

The precondition for efficient data management is the quality and reliability of the data collected from various sources, such as smart meters, sensory devices, substations, mobile data terminals, distributed energy resources (DERs), customer devices, and historical data (Figure 9.4) [21]. These various sources, according to [21], generate distinct data classes, such as operational data (e.g. the data regarding real and reactive power flows, DR capacity, and voltage), nonoperational data (e.g. data related to power quality and reliability), meter usage data (e.g. data associated to power usage), event message data (e.g. voltage loss/restoration data and fault detection event data), and metadata that is used to describe any other kind of data. Hence, the big data in SG is diverse and includes data related to power utilization habits of users, data from PMU for situational awareness, data from energy consumption measured by the widespread smart meters, energy market pricing and bidding data collected by automated revenue metering system, data from management, control, and maintenance of device and equipment in the electric power generation, transmission, and distribution in the grid, and operational data for running utilities, like financial data and large data sets, not directly obtained through the SG measurement, but used in decision-making, like weather data or geographical information system (GIS) data [6,27].

All these data, after collection, have to be integrated, usually implementing some of software architectures (Figure 9.4) such as service-oriented architecture (SOA), which enables data integration and information exchange seamless (essentially used on demand systems) [28–30], Enterprise Service Bus (ESB) for interconnecting devices and systems of very different capabilities alongside reduced cost and time effort associated with an integration [21,30], Common Information Model (CIM) as an integration framework that refers to the integration of applications in an energy management system accompanied with the reduced latency and expenses [31,32], and messaging platforms that represent communication systems based on exchanging messages (data and other information from different applications managed by messaging server) [21,33].

Another step is data storage that is of crucial interest since SG is a source of complex data, generated in massive amounts and high velocity and quite often with the demand for fast responses. The data have to be systematically stored and be available for retrieving, processing, and analysis either immediately or later. The detailed analysis of database systems, modern database management technologies, and their applications in SG is presented in [34]. Among various types of big data databases, such as in-memory or main memory databases, object-oriented database management systems, time-series database servers, and spatial and GIS-based databases [35], it is important to highlight the following two storage mechanisms, mostly applied to SG applications:

1. Distributed File System that allows multiple users and applications to share data and storage, enabling every user to get a local copy of the stored data on their own computer [21,36].
2. Not Only Structured Query Language (NoSQL) databases, relying on a key-value store approach to data storage and lookup, are useful when working with a huge quantity of data and when the data's nature does not require a relational model [34,37,38]. Some of the most known NoSQL database types are the Key Value Pairs, Column-based, Document-based, and Graph-based databases [39].

Regarding big data processing, it can be performed in several ways: batch processing, which is performed in a period of time and suitable for static and non-real-time applications of IoT-supported SG systems (e.g. weather forecasting), stream processing used for real-time applications (e.g. online monitoring, self-healing, and fraud detection), and hybrid processing that can handle both batch and real-time processing [19,21].

Having in mind that latency requirements are an important aspect of energy management system [32] (Table 9.1), sending and storing all data on the Cloud does not seem as the most adequate solution.

Posting data on the Cloud and transmitting response data back requires a larger bandwidth and a considerable amount of time, can suffer from latency issues, and is not tolerable in cases when there is a need for fast reactions. Instead, carrying out miniature data analysis centers closer to the place where data are being produced reduces greatly the quantity of data being transmitted to and from Cloud, and seems a far better approach, especially for large-scale distributed control systems such as SG, where on-time information can improve the efficiency, reliability, and security of energy management. This approach is known as Fog computing and supports decentralized and intelligent processing, and posts only obtained results to the Cloud for further analysis and storage (Figure 9.3) [43]. In this way, Fog computing has successfully dealt with congestion and latency issues, enabling real-time and online analytic even in the event of loss of connectivity or poor connection with the Cloud. Hence, even Cloud computing solves many problems related to big data management

Table 9.1   Requirements of SG applications [40–42]

Application	Security	Bandwidth	Reliability	Latency
Substation automation	High	9.6–56 kbps	99.0–99.99%	15–200 ms
Overhead transmission line monitoring	High	9.6–56 kbps	99.0–99.99%	15–200 ms
Home energy management (HEM)	High	9.6–56 kbps	99.0–99.99%	300–2,000 ms
Advanced metering infrastructure (AMI)	High	10–100 kbps per node, 500 kbps for backhaul	99.0–99.99%	2,000 ms
Wide-area situational awareness (WASA) systems	High	600–1,500 kbps	99.0–99.99%	15–200 ms
DR management	High	14–100 kbps per node	99.0%	500 ms-several min
Outage management	High	56 kbps	99.0%	2,000 ms
Distribution automation	High	9.6–56 kbps	99.0–99.99%	20–200 ms
Distribution management	High	9.6–100 kbps	99.0–99.99%	100 ms to 2 s
Asset management	High	56 kbps	99.0%	2,000 ms
Meter data management	High	56 kbps	99.0%	2,000 ms
DERs and storage	High	9.6–56 kbps	99.0–99.99%	300 ms to 2 s
Vehicle-to-Grid (V2G) technology	High	9.6–56 kbps	99.0–99.99%	2 s to 5 min
Electrical vehicles charging	High	9.6–56 kbps	99.0–99.99%	2 s to 5 min

for SG [18], the Fog computing poses numerous advantages compared to traditional Cloud computing utilization in SG [7]:

- The Fog layer splits big data to sub-data that is easier to handle, and hence it simplifies extracting key data when handling with big data.
- Scalable real-time services enable customers to monitor electricity usage information in almost real time. SG empowered with the Fog infrastructure offers detailed information to its customers with a low latency while reducing the amount of the data. Clients can supervise and analyze their daily/weekly/monthly electric use.
- The faster reaction time and less congestion possibility and fewer problems with connectivity loss are a few advantages.
- Fault-tolerant and consistent services are an advantage.
- It provides enhanced data privacy through separating the public and private data.
- Geographically distributed Fog services in the SG enhance locality awareness and reduce response time issues.
- It's supported with a large number of nodes, heterogeneity and mobility support, and wireless access.

Authors of [8] have classified Fog-based SG issues able to handle with large quantities of data into three classes: energy management, information management, and security.

Implementation of Osmotic computing paradigm at the Fog layer will undoubtedly lead to improved outcomes. Osmotic computing enables distribution, management, and execution of data tasks across any available Cloud data center and Edge devices and therefore contributes to faster and nonredundant computation and load balancing.

In order to perform the environmentally aware utilization of ICT equipment and related resources in SG, it is necessary to implement green computing principles. As a highly virtualized platform accompanied with storage consolidations, Fog computing can be considered as a green computing paradigm to support IoT applications [44], thereby presenting a great potential in realizing the G-SG vision.

To make grids smart, efficient, and gainful, collected and stored data must be processed so that certain insights and knowledge can be obtained. There are various kinds of analytics in SGs, such as signal analytics (e.g. sensor signals, substation, and line sensor waveforms), event analytics (e.g. detection, classification, filtering, and correlation), state analytics (e.g. system identification, grid topology, and electrical state in real time), engineering operations analytics (e.g. system performance, operational effectiveness, load trends, and forecasts), and customer analytics (e.g. customer segmentation, demand profiles and responses, and diversion analytics) (Figure 9.4) [21]. Data analytics holds a potential to contribute to improved efficiency and reliability of power grids, increased consumer satisfaction, better capital spend, and reduced cost.

Several models, such as descriptive, diagnostic, predictive, and prescriptive models describe an operational side of the grid and can combine the various kinds of the previous analytics classes, depending on the business goals. While descriptive models describe customers' behaviors that can be performed using a variety of data mining techniques (e.g. frequent pattern mining, classification, clustering, association rule mining, regression, and outlier detection), diagnostic models help to understand customers' behaviors and to analyze their decisions [21]. Before applying some of the traditional data mining techniques or new distributed data mining, data stream mining, or time-series data mining that are most relevant to the SG, it is compulsory to perform cleanup, integration, and reduction of the data alongside data transformation and discretization. Literature reviews show a number of data mining applications for power generation, transmission, distribution, and utilization [34]. These activities are a precondition for making predictive models of customers' decisions in the future with the help of statistical models or forecast techniques. A prescriptive model, implementing machine learning, business rules, or computational modeling procedures, affects marketing, engagement strategies, and the decisions to make [21,35].

Data visualization is of immense importance as it improves the assessment of SG through the visualization of historical information, geographical visualization, or a sort of visualization techniques that enable the 2D and the 3D visualization that can be utilized for the SG purposes. The visualization technologies can be used for real-time monitoring of power system status and intuitively and accurately present a clear picture of the current status of the SG, identifying potential relationships and patterns in SG [13,27].

All the five discussed phases of big data life cycle are affected by data transmission. Hence, a key requirement of SG is to enable high performance and advanced communication capabilities for bidirectional data flows (e.g., high bandwidth capacity and rate, high-level of security and privacy) [33].

9.4 Making recommendations in SG

The lack of efficient monitoring, fault diagnostic, and automation techniques are the main causes of unreliability in the traditional power grids. Compared to these grids, where dynamic energy management is being employed, energy management systems in SGs involve real-time wide-area situational awareness (WASA) of grid status with the help of advanced metering and monitoring systems, consumers' participation through HEMs, DR algorithms, Vehicle-to-Grid (V2G) technology, and supervisory control through computer-based systems [45]. The evolution of SG technology contributes to more secure, reliable, efficient, flexible, and sustainable power systems. This is achieved by developing and integrating intelligent algorithms for information collection and processing, which enables automated control over the power grid. In the case when natural accidents or catastrophes occur, it is of essential interest to realize a reliable and real-time monitoring and ensure real-time responses, so that power disturbance and outage can be prevented [46]. This implies the necessity of building a recommender system that uses different sources of data and is capable of dealing with the continuously arriving newest data in order to enable the recommendations to the user very fast. With the technology advancements, the accuracy of predictions and recommendations of such system have raised. However, they try to balance among accuracy, novelty, dispersity, and stability in the recommendations [47]. The most common methods used in recommender systems are based on filtering techniques such as collaborative filtering that enable the creation of recommendations based on experience and existing knowledge, content-based filtering (making recommendations based on context analysis), and hybrid filtering (recommendations are made through different known technologies) (Figure 9.5) [47,48].

The increasing use of mobile devices and the development of IoT lead to the evolution of location-aware collaboration filtering and location-aware recommender systems. However, the choice of recommender system type depends on numerous factors: the type of data stored in a database, the implemented filter algorithm, the chosen model (memory based or model based), the used techniques (e.g. probabilistic approaches, fuzzy networks, Bayesian networks, nearest-neighbors algorithm, neural networks, and singular-value decomposition techniques), scalability, system performance, the desired QoS, and demanded objectives. The evaluation of recommender systems can be executed through prediction metrics such as accuracy and coverage (e.g., mean absolute error (MAE), root of mean square error (RMSE), normalized MAE (NMAE)), recommendation metrics (e.g. Precision, Recall, and Receiver Operating Characteristic), rank recommendation metrics (e.g. the half-life and the discounted cumulative gain), and diversity metrics (e.g. the diversity and the novelty of the recommended items) [47,48].

In order to improve the quality of recommender systems' predictions and recommendations, current and future research is focused on a proper combination of

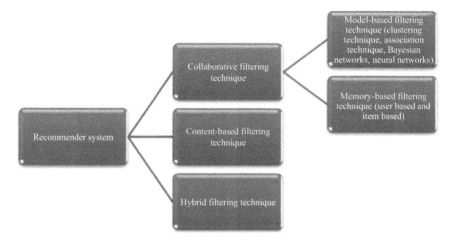

Figure 9.5   Recommendation techniques

existing recommendation methods that use various types of data, together with the development of novel data mining techniques and evaluation measures and flexible frameworks for automated analysis of diverse data. In addition, the evolution of new recommender systems involves the maximum use of smart IoT devices and sensors potential, enabling security and privacy as well as current trends related to the customers' habits [47].

Efficient data analysis, using a variety of algorithms and data mining techniques, has a tremendous influence on decision-making processes (e.g. determination of the optimal energy resources scheduling, setting of the power prices) and hence is of essential interest for the optimized SG work and its reliability. As an important part of recommender systems for SG, predictive analytics and load classification are crucial in order to predict load and hence give some recommendations regarding the energy consumption, optimal energy resources scheduling, energy production level adjustments, and setting of the power prices and maximizing return on investment for SG infrastructure. Several factors such as weather, time of the day, electricity prices, GIS data, sources of renewable energy, DRs, and storage cells affect the electricity demand and renewable production in the SG [45]. The aim of the forecast analytics and recommender system in SG is to save energy and money through the predictions of power demands and costs. This is of particular interest in the case when there is available a small quantity of historical data or when some rapid and dramatic changes can happen when prediction and prevention of future incidents are immensely important [35]. There is a wide scope of electricity forecasting methods, with different complexity and estimation procedures. However, every forecasting method should pose next several performances: objectivity, validity, reliability, accuracy, confidence, and sensitivity. Some of forecasting methods used in electricity demand forecasting are fuzzy logic, neural networks, multiple regression, and knowledge-based expert systems [49]. Evidently, a large amount of reliable and quality data contributes to better short- to long-term predictions and more accurate recommendations. The most important aspects of SG where forecasting and making recommendations are of immense importance are presented in the rest of the paper.

9.4.1   Load forecasting

The most important activity in the planning of power production is short-term LF (STLF)—demand prediction for the next few hours up to one week. Based on STLF, several important power system operations are performed: generating unit commitment, load shedding, spinning reserve scheduling, determination of transfer capability and stability margins, etc. [50]. Conventional STLF methods use mathematical and statistical load models (parametric methods), load historical data (nonparametric methods) and artificial neural networks (ANNs) load models (ANN methods) [51]. Forecasters mainly use historical load (hourly averaged), weather, and time data to establish load models and predict future variations. In deregulated power systems, very STLF (VSTLF)—demand prediction for the next few minutes—enables load-frequency control and economic dispatching functions [52]. Forecasters perform extrapolation of recently measured data to the nearest future.

According to [53], a load can be classified as deterministic, weather-independent, weather-dependent, and remaining (error component). VSTLF of weather-dependent load component can be very challenging due to an uncertainty of input data. Input data certainty can be improved by using real-time and more accurate measurements of load and weather variables. The ultimate goal is to achieve reliable real-time LF (RTLF) in modern SG. Powerful sensor networks are required for fast and reliable measurements of power demand and weather variables in real time [54].

Unlike conventional supervisory control and data acquisition system (SCADA), limited with the number of installed remote terminal units (RTUs) and communication latency, smart metering architecture with IoT communication technology seems to be promising for future SG. The application of IoT would lead to more precise and reliable RTLF. A simple diagram of IoT-based RTLF in future SG is presented in Figure 9.6.

Reliability of RTLF also depends on a number of significant input variables. Weather-dependent load variations are affected by air temperature, precipitation, wind speed and direction, humidity, pressure, etc. A larger number of significant input variables provide more accurate RTLF, but also require a large number of sensors, huge communication traffic support, complex computing ability and training of the ANN, expensive physical and cyber security systems, huge data analytics, etc. RTLF based on IoT would require reliable, fast computation and small communication latency. The implementation of Fog computing principles in SG holds a potential to contribute to solving latency-related issues. The big data recommender system can be used for processing of huge data related to load and weather variables. In the absence of a cluster or super computers, the time complexity problem can be solved by using parallel processing based on particle swarm optimization algorithm and/or designing small ANNs [51].

There are relatively new interesting papers dealing with IoT applications for LF. In [51], authors introduce IoT-based LF, where weather data at a given location is

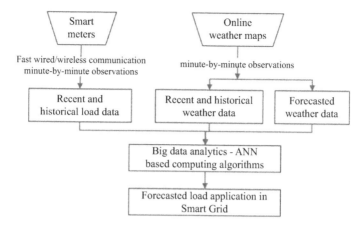

Figure 9.6 IoT-based RTLF in future SG

collected from Internet. An IoT-based deep learning system to automatically extract features from the captured data and, ultimately, give an accurate estimation of future load is recommended in [55]. The proposed method is compared to some existing approaches, and significant advantages are illustrated.

9.4.2 Renewable energy forecasting

Future SG concept includes real-time REF (RTREF) beside RTLF in order to achieve optimal economic dispatching functions. Both solar and wind plants require backup ancillary power generation for periods with highly variable weather conditions (sudden wind power deficit and fast movement of Clouds covering the sun represent the most critical conditions for dispatching). A special analysis is required to determine the impact and cost benefits of energy storage systems in economic dispatching. With the aim to efficiently reduce backup operational costs fast, precise and reliable RTREF methods are necessary. Modern telecommunication networks with low latency need to provide qualitative data transfer from remote sensors to control centers in SG.

Nonlinear and chaotic effect of Cloud motion on solar irradiance at the ground level represents the key issue for real-time solar energy forecasting (RTSEF) [56]. The intermittent nature of wind makes forecasting of its speed and power very challenging [57]. All methods for REF are based either on deterministic or statistical approach. For real-time applications, statistical methods using historical data and based on artificial intelligence are preferred. To achieve precise prediction in a variation of variables such as solar irradiation, ambient temperature, wind speed and power, etc., in the nearest future (few minutes up to an hour), high-speed sensors for intra-minute dispatching of data to high-performance computers are required. A typical example is intra-minute solar irradiance forecasting using wireless sensor networks (WSNs) proposed in [58]. WSNs and IoT communication technology have the potential to enable the development of the new, intra-minute, low-cost, and very accurate methods for RTREF. RTREF approaches based on ANN algorithms using readings of significant

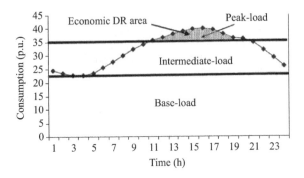

Figure 9.7   Typical daily consumption diagram in power system

weather variables from recent past would be of great benefit to economic dispatching in the modern deregulated market.

Currently, there is no scientific information publicly available about IoT-based REF systems, but it is known that companies such as Hitachi use IoT, big data analytics, and machine learning to make it more predictable and secure to forecast energy generation and delivery [59].

9.4.3   DR and energy management program

DR implies manipulation of end-use customers' power consumption with the main goal to reduce operating costs and optimize network conditions. Meeting of standard peaks and occasional spikes in consumption are the main tasks of utility. By utilizing DR strategy instead of adding extra generation capabilities, significant cost reductions could be achieved. DR could be classified into three types according to application purpose: emergency DR, economic DR, and ancillary services DR. Emergency DR is mainly used to improve system reliability in the case of generating unit failures. Economic DR often implies the introduction of the near real-time pricing system to motivate dynamic consumption changes convenient for reducing peak power demand, as shown in Figure 9.7. Ancillary services DR is defined as the employment of variable consumption for implementation of special power system services, such as reactive power and voltage control, frequency control, and system protection.

Residential, commercial, and industrial customers all could take place in DR strategy through bidirectional communication with utility enabled by smart metering technology. A number of customers with local energy production from renewable sources and storage capabilities are increasing every day. It is a very complicated task for customers to alternately use energy from the network and renewable sources to achieve efficiency and simultaneously participate in DR programs. As a part of demand side management (DSM) programs, complex algorithms must be created for efficient control of modern consumption. DR and energy management program based on smart metering technology in future SG is illustrated in Figure 9.8. The program is designed to utilize wireless local and wide area communication networks to establish IoT concept.

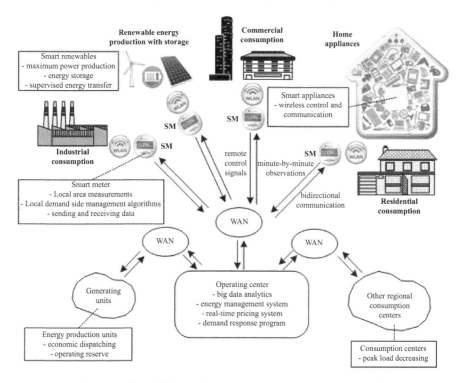

Figure 9.8 IoT-based DR and energy management program in future SG

According to IoT-based program in Figure 9.8, network operator would be able to remotely decrease consumption in the period of peak demand by sending determined pricing information to customers or even to directly manipulate consumption to the level of even individual house appliances. Additionally, available renewable energy can be stored in the period of low demand and again used in the period of peak demand by the remote instructions from a network operator. In order to support such sophisticated control, high-speed IoT communication network is required along with fast and efficient algorithms containing multiple tariff schemes. Powerful computational resources are needed to analyze big data in short-time frames at operating center level.

An interesting algorithm for smart direct load control and load shedding is introduced in [60]. The presented approach relies on IoT to provide real-time load control, based on their demands, comfort, and the forecasted load model. This research can be used as a role model for future in-depth analysis of IoT-based DR.

9.4.3.1 Home demand management

Future smart households will be equipped with a local energy management program integrated into smart meters and designed to control individual appliances and stored energy from local renewables. The household consumption scheduling can be defined as linear optimization problem [61]:

$$\min_{L, x_{a,h} \in R} L \tag{9.1}$$

where L is the peak hourly load and $x_{a,h}$ represents the power demand of appliance a in the particular hour h. The corresponding cost function is to minimize the hourly load L subject to the following constraints:

$$\sum_{a \in A} x_{a,h} \leq L, \forall h \in \mathbf{H} \tag{9.2}$$

$$\mathbf{I}^{\mathrm{T}} \mathbf{x}_a = l_a, \forall a \in \mathbf{A} \tag{9.3}$$

$$x_{a,h} \geq 0 \tag{9.4}$$

where $\mathbf{I} = [1, 1, \ldots, 1]^{\mathrm{T}}$. a is defined as individual appliance in a set of appliances $\mathbf{A}$. $h \in \mathbf{H}$, $\mathbf{H} \in [1, 2, \ldots, 24]$, represents the particular hour of the day. In every hour, load should be greater than or equal to the sum of the scheduled power for all appliances. According to (9.3), daily supply for each appliance has to meet the constraint l_a.

As appliances are classified as power shiftable and non-shiftable, additional constraints are added:

$$x_{a,h} \geq \delta_a, \forall h \in \mathbf{H}_{\mathrm{op}} \tag{9.5}$$

$$\alpha_a \leq x_{a,h} \leq \beta_a, \forall h \in \mathbf{H}_{\mathrm{op}} \tag{9.6}$$

where δ_a is fixed hourly power requirement of power non-shiftable appliances. α_a and β_a are standby power and maximum working power of power shiftable appliances, respectively. $\mathbf{H}_{\mathrm{op}}$ is hourly based operating time. Additional constraints are required to account time-shiftable appliances with specific consumption patterns [61].

In modern future households, local renewable energy production will be an important part of the DSM programs. Previously described household consumption scheduling optimization problem needs to be extended to account renewable energy production and storage. DSM for residential customers with renewables is conceptualized in [62]. High-speed communication networks will allow shorter time frames for home demand management (HDM) (minute-based scheduling). Thousands of local DSM algorithms operated on the users' smart meters will send huge amounts of data every minute to central DR algorithms at the power system level.

9.4.4   SG state estimation

Electrical network state is determined by complex bus voltages' values, from which all complex power flows and injections can be calculated. Power system safe operation depends on the accurate knowledge of the electrical quantities in the grid [63]. State estimation algorithms use network topology data, power system elements data, available measurements, and pseudo-measurements (measurements from the past). Computation is traditionally done by the least square solution to the following equation (more measurements than states):

$$\mathbf{y} = \mathbf{A}\mathbf{x} + \boldsymbol{\varepsilon} \tag{9.7}$$

where $\mathbf{y}$ and $\mathbf{x}$ are vectors of measurements and state, respectively. $\mathbf{A}$ is a matrix with more rows than columns and $\boldsymbol{\varepsilon}$ represents a vector of measurement errors.

The solution of the optimization problem is to find an estimate that minimizes errors:

$$\mathbf{x}_e = (\mathbf{A}^{\mathrm{T}}\mathbf{A})^{-1}\mathbf{A}^{\mathrm{T}}\mathbf{y} \tag{9.8}$$

When more information about the errors $\boldsymbol{\varepsilon}$ is known, weighted least squared method is used. In the case of nonlinear functionality between measurements and states, nonlinear weighted least squared method based on recursive minimization is used.

Nowadays, state estimation is mainly calculated for high-voltage transmission networks by network operators and rarely in distribution networks (DNs) due to lack of measurement units. Observability of transmission networks is significantly higher when compared to DNs. However, modern DN is rapidly evolving because of the growing presence of DERs, including small-scale generators, electric vehicles, and new high efficiency residential and commercial appliances [64]. While the evolutionary process is taking place, significance and observability of the DNs is increasing and state estimation is becoming more important for the concept of SG.

Prior to PMU application, state estimation algorithms relied on unsynchronized data measurements delivered from RTU by utilizing SCADA system. Power system state was considered as static between two successive scans. Modern PMUs have a high reporting rate (RR), and with corresponding communication, infrastructure scans could be performed near real time. PMUs introduce the new idea of the dynamic state estimation capable of tracking even power system transients. PMU measurements are available as often as every cycle or two (20–40 ms) and counting communication delays of a few hundred milliseconds leaves dynamic estimation imaginable in future [65]. Basic communication requirements for power systems related to data transfer delays are presented in Table 9.2.

Table 9.2   Communication requirements for power systems [66]

Performance class	Data transfer time threshold (ms)	Service examples
TT0	>1,000	Files, events, log contents, SCADA
TT1	1,000	Events, alarms
TT2	500	Operator commands
TT3	100	Slow automatic interactions
TT4	20	Fast automatic interactions
TT5	10	Releases, status changes
TT6	3	Trips, blockings

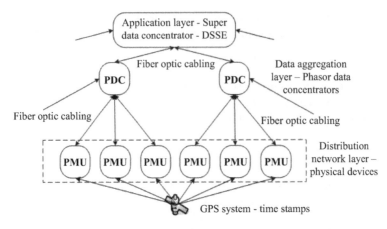

Figure 9.9   Conventional vertical hierarchy type communication architecture for PMU-based WAM system

9.4.4.1   Communication architectures for PMU-based DSSE

In most current applications, phasor data are used remotely, and corresponding communication network is required. Typical and generally accepted communication architecture for wide area measurement (WAM) is of vertical hierarchy type and it is presented in Figure 9.9.

It can be seen in Figure 9.9 that conventional communication architecture for PMU-based WAM system consists of three layers: DN, phasor data concentrator (PDC), and super data concentrator. DN layer represents physical PMU devices connected to current and voltage transformers in substations, measuring phase currents, bus voltage, frequency, rate of change of frequency (ROCOF), etc. PMUs receive the referent time stamp (pulse) signals from Global Positioning System (GPS) satellites every second with coincidence error lower than 1 μs. The next level communication layer consists of regionally placed PDCs. PDCs align received PMU signals in the same time frame with high accuracy. Aggregated and time-tagged data is then sent to the application layer or super data concentrator which is responsible for distribution system state estimation (DSSE). The typical communication medium is fiber optic technology.

Cloud-based IoT communication for DSSE is recently proposed in [67]. Corresponding PMU-based WAM system communication architecture is presented in Figure 9.10. The new concept of WAM is based on virtualization of the PMUs, context-awareness at the PMUs, and Cloud-IoT-based DSSE application [68].

Unlike conventional communication architecture (Figure 9.9), the new one (Figure 9.10) consists of four layers: DN (PMUs), virtual objects (VOs), composite VOs (CVOs), and Cloud-based application. The first layer is the same as in the case of conventional communication architecture. The key point of virtualization layer is the creation of digital counterparts of real PMUs in IoT (VOs), which enables a higher level of an object's context awareness. Instead of PDC technology, CVOs are

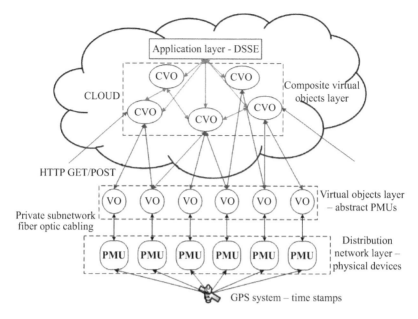

Figure 9.10   Novel communication architecture for PMU-based WAM system

introduced in the third layer to enhance decentralized communication. Unlike PDCs, many CVOs can receive data from the same VOs, and mutual communication is established. DSSE is performed in the Cloud at the top-level application layer. The most common local communication medium between PMUs and corresponding VOs is fiber optic cabling, while CVOs and VOs communicate utilizing HTTP GET/POST commands.

9.4.4.2   Big data of dynamic Cloud-based DSSE

Real-time dynamic DSSE represents the ultimate goal of SG concept. The RR of PMUs can be as fast as 50 f/s (frames per second). In SG normal operating state, typical high-speed PMU RR is second-based, e.g. 1 f/s. With thousands of anticipated PMUs in SG, typical RR would already produce huge amounts of data to be transferred, computed, and stored. In order to capture transient operation in SG, minimum RR needs to be 50 f/s, which is 50 times more data than in the case of the normal state. By utilizing powerful Cloud computational resources, modern high-speed DSSE algorithms can solve (9.7) in less than 10 ms. Cloud technology is also capable of storing thousands of gigabytes of desired DSSE resulting data. The main problem in the handling of dynamic big data is communication network capability—latency and channel bandwidth. These issues can be successfully overcome with the implementation of Fog infrastructure. Authors of [68] and [69] propose the introduction of adaptive DSSE and LAN communication between CVOs and VOs for solving channel bandwidth problem. Due to communication latency, measurements from PMUs will be available for computing with a delay of few hundreds of milliseconds. According to data in Table 9.2, communication requirements for alarms, events reporting, and operator commands would be fulfilled.

9.4.4.3 Application benefits of dynamic DSSE

More precise and efficient DSSE would be achieved by increasing observability of the SG through placing PMUs in almost every network node. Dynamic DSSE based on IoT concept has potential to enable proper operational reactions in case of fast-paced changes in the electric grid. With increasing presence of DERs, SG operation is becoming more dynamic, which requires up-to-date DSSE with a proper RR of PMUs. The power production of DERs could be very variable in time with significant impact on power flows in SG. Capturing of fine-resolution power flow data could reveal near real-time voltage state in SG and enable fast operational action involving voltage regulators. More frequent data related to reactive power flows in SG would lead to more efficient remote control of compensation devices. High-speed power quality estimation in SG relying on voltage, frequency, and ROCOF measurements would enable more efficient reaction.

9.5 Conclusion

The rapid technological advancements in ICTs have the tremendous influence on all aspects of our lives. The power sector, as an important part of socioeconomic development, did not remain immune to innovative technologies. The future of energy and power sector consists in SGs, and evolution depends on the development of well-defined ICT solutions. Novel concepts and approaches, mainly the utilization of smart devices, sensors, and smart meters, IoT vision, and big data, have led to the realization of SGs that compared to the traditional power grids enable dynamic and optimized management and control of the energy demanded, consumed, and delivered. The inclusion of G-IoT concepts and Fog infrastructure in SG vision holds a potential to completely revolutionize the power sector. The main benefits of these approaches are significant energy savings and reduced negative impacts on the environment. As SGs consist of numerous smart devices (sensors and meters), they represent a source of voluminous, heterogeneous, and fast-generated data. The availability and accessibility of such data generated in SGs contribute to more efficient energy management through the use of appropriate recommendation techniques and systems. Hence, with the help of a variety of data mining techniques and artificial intelligence, the data can be processed and analyzed in appropriate manners leading to the extraction of valuable knowledge and insights. On this way, adequate recommender systems that enable consumption predictions, the selection of the most suitable tariffs and adjustment of electricity needs, reduction of outages, etc., can be created. The inclusion of Osmotic computing at the Fog servers will contribute to more optimal load balancing and resource utilization. Depending of application scenario and data tasks that have to be performed, Osmotic computing will enable distribution, management, and execution of those tasks at the edge devices or within Cloud data centers. Hence, the recommendation can be made much faster and certain actions can be performed in real time.

This chapter examines the importance of IoT and big data in the development of recommender systems for SGs. It has been shown that the involvement of novel technologies contributes to improvements in LF, REF, DR, and energy management programs as well as SG state estimation. Smart meters and PMUs have been identified as key elements in the future SG infrastructure. Application of the IoT concept as basic communication technology certainly represents an efficient solution for collecting and managing huge amounts of data necessary for power system operator activities. Further technological advancement related to bandwidth and latency has potential to enable new application areas. As a result of more up-to-date measurements available, advanced algorithms will be based on selected information provided by big data recommender systems. Hence, the development of recommender systems leads to the general optimizations over how the energy is managed and consequently contributes to the immense improvements in the power sector, making it more secure, reliable, efficient, flexible, and sustainable than ever before.

Nevertheless, on the way of most effective use of the IoT (G-IoT), big data techniques, Cloud/Fog/Edge, and Osmotic computing in the energy sector are numerous challenges. Some of them are related to data aggregation and distribution strategies, handling and management of a variety of types and range of services, resource orchestration, data mining techniques, energy conservation, privacy and security issues, QoS demands, etc.

Our future research will address selected issues and limits in existing sensor and communication networks applied in conventional power grids with the aim to highlight practical and economically justified solutions based on IoT. We also plan to propose big data recommender systems specialized for certain sets of algorithms with potential to be used by future SG operators. As Osmotic computing and G-IoT symbiotic approach promises to deal successfully with present challenges related to load balancing, latency, and bandwidth issues, their utilization in SGs will be the direction of our future work.

References

[1] Evans D. *The Internet of Things—How the Next Evolution of the Internet Is Changing Everything*, San Jose, CA: Cisco Internet Business Solutions Group (IBSG), 2011 [online]. Available from https://www.cisco.com/c/dam/en_us/about/ac79/docs/innov/IoT_IBSG_0411FINAL.pdf [Accessed 28 May 2017].

[2] Daecher R., Schmid R. *Internet of Things: From Sensing to Doing,* London: Deloitte University Press, 2016 [online]. Available from http://dupress.com/articles/internet-of-things-iot-applications-sensing-to-doing/ [Accessed 2 June 2017].

[3] European Commission. *Smart Grids and Meters,* 2017 [online]. Available from https://ec.europa.eu/energy/en/topics/markets-and-consumers/smart-grids-and-meters [Accessed 8 June 2017].

[4]   Vijayapriya T., Kothari D.P. "Smart grid: An overview," *Smart Grid and Renewable Energy*, vol. 2, no. 4, pp. 305–311, 2011.

[5]   GeSi. *#SMARTer2030-ICT Solutions for 21st Century Challenges.* Global e-Sustainability Initiative (GeSI), Brussels, Belgium, 2015 [online]. Available from http://smarter2030.gesi.org/downloads/Full_report.pdf [Accessed 13 June 2017].

[6]   Lai C.S., Lai L.L. "Application of big data in smart grid," *IEEE International Conference on Systems, Man, and Cybernetics*, China, 2015

[7]   Okay F.Y., Ozdemir S. "A Fog computing based smart grid model," *International Symposium on Networks, Computers and Communications (ISNCC)*, Tunisia, 2016.

[8]   Vinueza Naranjo P.G., Shojafar M., Vaca-Cardenas L., Canali C., Lancellotti R., Baccarelli E. "Big data over smart grid—A Fog computing perspective," *24th International Conference on Software, Telecommunications and Computer Networks SoftCOM*, Split, Croatia, pp. 1–6, 2016.

[9]   System Energy Efficiency Lab. *Internet of Things with Applications to Smart Grid and Green Energy*, 2015 [online]. Available from http://seelab.ucsd.edu/greenenergy/overview.shtml [Accessed 13 May 2017].

[10] Nardelli M., Nastic S., Dustdar S., Villari M., Ranjan R. "Osmotic flow: Osmotic computing + IoT workflow," *IEEE Cloud Computing*, vol. 4, no. 2, pp. 68–75, March–April 2017. doi: 10.1109/MCC.2017.22

[11] Villari M., Fazio M., Dustdar S., Rana O., Ranjan R. "Osmotic computing: A new paradigm for edge/cloud integration," *IEEE Cloud Computing*, vol. 3, pp. 76–83, 2016.

[12] Villari, M. Celesti A., Fazio M. "Towards Osmotic computing: Looking at basic principles and technologies," In L. Barolli and O. Terzo (eds.), *Complex, Intelligent, and Software Intensive Systems*, Advances in Intelligent Systems and Computing 611, pp. 906–915, Cham: Springer International Publishing AG, 2018.

[13] Jiang Z., Li F., Qiao W., *et al.* "A vision of smart transmission grids," *IEEE Power & Energy Society General Meeting – PES '09*, Canada, 2009.

[14] Xi F., Satyajayant M., Guoliang X., Dejun Y. "Smart grid – The new and improved power grid: A survey," *Communications Surveys & Tutorials,* IEEE, vol. 14, no. 4, pp. 6–9, 2012.

[15] Zheng J., Gao D.W., Lin L. "Smart meters in smart grid: An overview," *IEEE Green Technologies Conference*, USA, 2013.

[16] Klaimi J., Rahim-Amoud R., Merghem-Boulahia L., Jrad A. "Energy management algorithms in smart grids: State of the art and emerging trends," *International Journal of Artificial Intelligence and Applications (IJAIA)*, vol. 7, no. 4, pp. 25–45, 2016.

[17] Xun L., Qing-wu G., Hui Q. "The application of IOT in power systems," *Power System Protection and Control*, vol. 38, no. 22, pp. 232–236, 2010.

[18] Kaur M., Kalra S. "A review on IOT based smart grid," *International Journal of Energy, Information and Communications*, vol. 7, no. 3, pp.11–22, 2016.

[19] Saleem Y., Crespi N., Rehmani M. H., Copeland R. "Internet of Things-aided smart grid: Technologies, architectures, applications, prototypes, and future research directions," 2017 [online]. Available from https://arxiv.org/ftp/arxiv/papers/1704/1704.08977.pdf [Accessed 26 July 2017].

[20] GlobalTech. *Enabling the SmartGrid through Cloud Computing,* 2012 [online]. Available from https://energy.gov/sites/prod/files/Friday_Trinity_Ballroom_3_0855_Primetica_final.pdf [Accessed 26 July 2017].

[21] Daki H., El Hannani A., Aqqal A., Haidine A., Dahbi A. "Big Data management in smart grid: Concepts, requirements and implementation," *Journal of Big Data*, vol. 4, no. 13, pp. 1–19, 2017. doi: 10.1186/s40537-017-0070-y

[22] Ou Q., Zhen Y., Li X., Zhang Y., Zeng L. "Application of Internet of Things in smart grid power transmission," *Third FTRA International Conference on Mobile, Ubiquitous, and Intelligent Computing (MUSIC),* Canada, 2012.

[23] Vatanparvar K., Al Faruque M.A. "Energy management as a service over Fog computing platform," In *Proceedings of the ACM/IEEE Sixth International Conference on Cyber-Physical Systems (ICCPS '15).* ACM, New York, NY, USA, pp. 248–249, 2015.

[24] Brown R.E. "Impact of smart grid on distribution system design," In *IEEE Power and Energy Society General Meeting—Conversion and Delivery of Electrical Energy in the 21st Century*, pp. 1–4, 2008.

[25] Rahimi F., Ipakchi A. "Demand response as a market resource under the smart grid paradigm," *IEEE Transactions on Smart Grid,* vol. 1, no. 1, pp. 82–88, 2010.

[26] Abedin S.F., Alam M.G.R., Haw R., Hong C.S. "A system model for energy efficient green-IoT network," *2015 International Conference on Information Networking (ICOIN),* Cambodia, pp. 177–182, 2015. doi: 10.1109/ICOIN.2015.7057878.

[27] Jiang H., Wang K., Wang Y., Gao M., Zhang Y. "Energy big data: A survey," *IEEE Access, Special Section on Theoretical Foundations for Big Data Applications: Challenges and Opportunities*, vol. 4, pp. 3844–3861, 2016.

[28] Minguez J., Jakob M., Heinkel U. "A SOA-based approach for the integration of a data propagation system," In *Proceedings of the 9th International Conference on Information Reuse and Integration*, Melbourne, pp. 47–52, 2009.

[29] Malarvizhi R., Kalyani S. "SOA-based open data model for information integration in smart grid," *2013 Fifth International Conference on Advanced Computing (ICoAC),* Chennai, pp. 143–148, 2013. doi: 10.1109/ICoAC.2013.6921941.

[30] Martínez J.F., Rodríguez-Molina J., Castillejo P., de Diego R. "Middleware architectures for the smart grid: Survey and challenges in the foreseeable future," *Energies,* vol. 6, pp. 3593–3621, 2013.

[31] Naumann A., Bielchev I., Voropai N., Styczynski Z. "Smart grid automation using IEC 61850 and CIM standards," *Control Engineering Practice*, vol. 25, pp. 102–111, 2014.

[32] Rohr M., Osterloh A., Gründler M., Luhmann T., Stadler M., Vogel N. "Using CIM for smart grid ICT integration," *IBIS—Interoperability in Business Information Systems*, vol. 6, no. 1, pp. 45–61, 2011.

[33] Albano M., Lino Ferreira L., Pinho L.M., Alkhawaja A.R. "Message-oriented middleware for smart grids," *Computer Standards & Interfaces* 38, pp. 133–143, 2015.

[34] Aung Z. *Database Systems for the Smart Grid, in Smart Grids*, New York, NY, USA: Springer, pp. 151–168, 2013.

[35] Stimmel C.L. *Big Data Analytics Strategies for the Smart Grid*, Boca Raton, FL: CRC Press, Taylor & Francis Group, 2015.

[36] Bžoch P., Šafařík J. "Security and reliability of distributed file systems," In *The 6th IEEE International Conference on Intelligent Data Acquisition and Advanced Computing Systems: Technology and Applications*, Prague, Czech Republic, 2011.

[37] Ghavami P.K. *Big Data Governance: Modern Data Management Principles for Hadoop, NoSQL & Big Data Analytics*, Scotts Valley, CA: CreateSpace Independent Publishing, 2015.

[38] Amato A., Venticinque S. "Big data management systems for the exploitation of pervasive environments," In N. Bessis and C. Dobre (eds.), *Big Data and Internet of Things: A Roadmap for Smart Environments*, Studies in Computational Intelligence 546, pp. 67–90, 2014

[39] Stackowiak R., Licht A., Mantha V., Nagode L. *Big Data and The Internet of Things, Enterprise Information Architecture for a New Age,* New York: Apress, 2015.

[40] Washington, DC: Dept. Energy, Communications *Requirements of Smart Grid Technologies*, 2010.

[41] Yan Y., Qian Y., Sharif H., Tipper D. "A survey on smart grid communication infrastructures: Motivations, requirements and challenges," *IEEE Commun. Surveys & Tutorials*, vol. 15, no. 1, pp. 5–20, 2013. doi: 10.1109/SURV.2012.021312.00034.

[42] Cagri Gungor V., Sahin D., Kocak T., *et al.* "A survey on smart grid potential applications and communication requirements," *IEEE Transactions on Industrial Informatics*, vol. 9, no. 1, pp. 28–42, 2013. doi: 10.1109/TII.2012.2218253.

[43] Maksimovic M. "Necessity of the Internet of things and Fog computing integration," *International Scientific Conference on Information Technology and Data Related Research "Sinteza",* Belgrade, Serbia, pp. 176–181, 2017.

[44] Misra S., Sarkar S. "Theoretical modelling of fog computing: A green computing paradigm to support IoT applications," *IET Networks*, vol. 5, no. 2, pp. 23–29, 2016.

[45] Diamantoulakis P.D., Kapinas V.M., Karagiannidis G.K. "Big data analytics for dynamic energy management in smart grids," *Big Data Research*, vol. 2, pp. 94–101, 2015.

[46] Jaradat M., Jarrah M., Bousselham A., Jararweh Y., Al-Ayyoub M. "The Internet of energy: Smart sensor networks and big data management for smart

grid," *The International Workshop on Networking Algorithms and Technologies for IoT (NAT-IoT 2015), Procedia Computer Science*, vol. 56, pp. 592–597, 2015.

[47] Bobadilla J., Ortega F., Hernando A., Gutierrez A. "Recommender systems survey," *Knowledge-Based Systems*, vol. 46, pp. 109–132, 2013.

[48] Isinkaye F.O., Folajimi Y.O., Ojokoh B.A. "Recommendation systems: Principles, methods and evaluation," *Egyptian Informatics Journal*, vol. 16, pp. 261–273, 2015.

[49] Weranga K.S.K, Kumarawadu S., Chandima, D.P. *Smart Metering Design and Applications*, Springer Briefs in Applied Sciences and Technology, Singapore: Springer, 2014.

[50] Tsekouras G.J., Kanellos F.D., Mastorakis N. "Short term load forecasting in electric power systems with artificial neural networks," In N. Mastorakis, A. Bulucea, and G. Tsekouras (eds.), *Computational Problems in Science and Engineering,* Lecture Notes in Electrical Engineering, vol. 343. Cham: Springer, Cham, 2015.

[51] Saber A.Y., Khandelwal T., "IoT based online load forecasting," In *Ninth Annual IEEE Green Technologies Conference (GreenTech),* Denver, CO, pp. 189–194, 2017.

[52] Gross G., Galiana F.D., "Short-term load forecasting," *Proceedings of the IEEE*, vol. 75, no. 12, pp. 1558–1573, 1987.

[53] Fan J.Y., McDonald J.D., "A real-time implementation of short-term load forecasting for distribution power systems," *IEEE Trans. Power Syst.*, vol. 9, no. 2, pp. 988–994, 1994.

[54] Hernandez L., Baladron C., Aguiar J.M., *et al.* "A study of the relationship between weather variables and electric power demand inside a smart grid/smart world framework," *Sensors* (Switzerland), vol. 12, no. 9, pp. 11571–11591, 2012.

[55] Li, L., Ota, K., Dong, M. "When weather matters: IoT-based electrical load forecasting for smart grid," *IEEE Communications Magazine,* vol. 55, no. 10, pp. 46–51, 2017.

[56] Inman R.H., Pedro H.T.C., Coimbra C.F.M., "Solar forecasting methods for renewable energy integration," *Prog. Energy Combust. Sci.,* vol. 39, pp. 535–576, 2013.

[57] Wang X., Guo P., Huang X., "A review of wind power forecasting models," *Energy Procedia*, vol. 12, pp. 770–778, 2011.

[58] Kamthe A., Marquez R., Coimbra C.F.M., Cerpa A. *Sub-Minute Solar Irradiance Forecasting Using Wireless Sensor Network*. Merced: University of California, 2011.

[59] Hitachi. *Wind Turbine Energy Forecast* [online]. Available from http://social-innovation.hitachi/us/solutions/energy/wind-turbine-energy-forecast/index.html [Accessed 31 January 2018].

[60] Mortaji H., Siew Hock O., Moghavvemi M., Almurib H.A.F. "Smart grid demand response management using internet of things for load shedding and smart-direct load control," *IEEE Industry Applications Society Annual Meeting*, pp. 1–7., Portland, OR, 2016.

[61] Zhu Z., Tang J., Lambotharan S., Chin W.H., Fan Z., "An integer linear programming based optimization for home demand-side management in smart grid," *Innov. Smart Grid Technol.* (ISGT), IEEE PES, pp. 1–5, 2012.

[62] Guo Y., Pan M., Fang Y. "Optimal power management of residential customers in the smart grid," *IEEE Trans. Parallel Distrib. Syst.,* vol. 23, no. 9, pp. 1593–1606, 2012.

[63] Celli G., Pegoraro P.A., Pilo F., Pisano G., Sulis S. "DMS cyberphysical simulation for assessing the impact of state estimation and communication media in smart grid operation," *IEEE Trans. Power Syst.,* vol. 29, no. 5, pp. 2436–2446, 2014.

[64] Heydt G., "The next generation of power distribution systems," *IEEE Trans. Smart Grid,* vol. 1, no. 3, pp. 225–235, 2010.

[65] Phadke A.G., Thorp J.S. *Synchronized Phasor Measurements and Their Applications,* New York: Springer, p. 246, 2008.

[66] IEC61850-5 Edition, Communication networks and systems in substations—part 5: Communication requirements for functions and device models. International Electrotechnical Commission, Technical Committee 57, 2013.

[67] Pegoraro P.A., Meloni A., Atzori L., Castello P., Sulis S. "Adaptive PMU-based distribution system state estimation exploiting the Cloud-based IoT paradigm," *Proc. IEEE Int. Instrum. Meas. Technol. Conf. (I2MTC),* pp. 1–6, 2016.

[68] Meloni A., Pegoraro P.A., Atzori L., Castello P., Sulis S. "IoT cloud-based distribution system state estimation: Virtual objects and context-awareness," *IEEE International Conference on Communications (ICC),* Kuala Lumpur, pp. 1–6, 2016.

[69] Meloni A., Pegoraro P.A., Atzori L., Sulis S. "An IoT architecture for wide area measurement systems: A virtualized PMU based approach," In *IEEE International Energy Conference, ENERGYCON,* 2016.

Chapter 10

Recommendation techniques and their applications to the delivery of an online bibliotherapy

Yunxing Xin[1] and Ling Feng[1]

With the rapid progress of economy and society, people have to undertake unprecedented consistent and severe stress. Bibliotherapy is an effective way to help people cope with psychological stress. By selecting and recommending specific reading materials to patients with mental illness or emotional disturbance, it facilitates patients recovery and rehabilitation. Currently existing bibliotherapy requires professional staff with the background of both psychological and library service to give reading recommendation, which is quite labor costly and demanding, and the booklists for variant individuals need to be highly customized by therapists. To address this limitation, this chapter delivers an automatic reading recommendation solution for online bibliotherapy, whose aim is specifically for adolescents to manage their stress coming from study, family, peer relationship, self-cognition, to romantic relationship. The 6-week user study preliminarily demonstrated the effectiveness of the solution, in which the recommended articles hold both high-stress easing effect and good attractiveness.

This chapter first gives a brief review of bibliotherapy and recommendation techniques in the literature. Then reports the design and implementation of our reading recommendation system for easing teens psychological stress. Finally some application interfaces are provided to demonstrate the usage of the system.

10.1 What is bibliotherapy?

Bibliotherapy is recognized as an effective method of psychotherapy [1–5]. There are two interpretations of bibliotherapy according to *Webster's Third New International Dictionary*: (1) the use of selected reading materials as therapeutic adjuvants in medicine and in psychiatry and (2) guidance in the solution of personal problems through directed reading [6].

The first interpretation says bibliotherapy could be used as a treatment of diseases caused by physiology or psychology. The second one explains from a broad

[1]Department of Computer Science and Technology, Centre for Computational Mental Healthcare Research, Institute of Data Science, Tsinghua University, China

perspective that bibliotherapy could deal some personal problems. More specifically, Rongione categorized the applicable scenarios of bibliotherapy into five areas, including physical disability, chronic illness, emotional problems, personality disorders, and socioeconomic issues [7].

Research on bibliotherapy has lasted hundreds of years in the west. In 1848, John M. Galt read the paper in the annual convention of the American Psychological Association about the effects of bibliotherapy and analyzed the classification of patients and corresponding reading measures. This paper is considered to be the first one in bibliotherapy [8]. The formal and systematic research on bibliotherapy began with Samuel McChord Crothers. He published a paper named *A Literary Clinic* at *Atlantic Monthly* and invented the word *bibliotherapy* [9]. After 1930s, bibliotherapy has received more attentions from relevant institutions in Western countries. In 1939, the Hospital Library Branch of American Library Association (ALA) set up a bibliotherapy committee. In 1964, ALA held the first seminar on bibliotherapy. In 1970s, there were more than 4,000 hospitals providing bibliotherapy services in the Soviet Union. Later in 1980s, a new wave of research on bibliotherapy occurred with the rapid rising of people's psychological problems. International Federation of Library Associations and Institutions had affirmed the significance of bibliotherapy in patients' recovery.

The doctors of University of Bristol in England believe that after years of research, reading poetry is more effective in treating anxiety and depression than swallowing pills. After the analysis of the experiment statistics, it was concluded that bibliotherapy is effective, especially in enhancing self-confidence, perfecting behavior, and improving interpersonal relationships [1].

To explain the mechanism of bibliotherapy, Hou took reading as a process that not only includes the recognition of characters, languages, and image symbols but also provides a way in which their inner feelings and emotions are deeply communicating with the works [10]. Yang also argued these good mental stimulations from reading are able to regulate people's immune function [11]. Wang *et al.* further explained the mechanism of bibliotherapy based on physiology and psychology. The reason why a book could cure is that the feelings it conveys to the reader have just weakened or offset the hidden unhealthy emotions. This is helpful in easing and alleviating reader's pathogenetic condition [12].

Nowadays, bibliotherapy has formed a fairly complete theory system and become an important research content in both library science and medical rehabilitation.

With the advent of information age, the notion of computer-based bibliotherapy, coined as e-bibliotherapy [13,14], arises. But until now, there is no effective solution to put it into practice.

10.2   Review of recommendation techniques

This section gives a summary of some widely used recommendation approaches. Recommender systems could automatically provide users with predictions and recommendations based on users' preferences from massive sources of information.

They are getting more essential to people's daily life, especially in the age of big data. There are many recommendation approaches proposed in the last 20 years, which can generally be divided into seven categories, namely, *stereotyping, content-based filtering (CBF), collaborative filtering (CF), co-occurrence, graph-based, global relevance,* and *hybrid* [15].

10.2.1   Stereotyping approach

Stereotyping is one of the earliest recommendation approaches and was first introduced by Rich in his article recommender system *Grundy* [16]. Rich defines stereotype as a collection of characteristics and recommend articles with the maximum matching with the stereotypes. The advantage of stereotyping is that it works effectively even with little computing power and may perform quite well in some specific area, e.g., article recommendation. However, there are two major problems with stereotyping. The first one is its inflexibility. Stereotypes may rigidly pigeonhole people. For instance, many men may have a negative interest in shopping, but it is not true for all men. The second one is its labor cost. Characteristics are manually classified into different stereotypes. This is labor consuming and limits the scale of items.

10.2.2   Content-based filtering approach

CBF is one of the most widely used recommendation approaches [17]. Its basic process is to match up the attributes of users preferences and interests with the attributes of the content object, with an aim to recommend new interesting items to users. Specifically, the CBF recommendation process proceeds in the following three steps:

- Content analyzer. There are many feature-extraction techniques in this component to shift the original content of items (e.g., text, webpages, news) from different sources to the structured representation suitable for further analysis.
- Profile learner. This module collects the representations of items that have been rated by the user to construct the user profile, which contains users interests. Machine-learning techniques are generally used in profile-learner component.
- Filtering component. This module recommends to users the most relevant items by matching the user profile against that of candidate items. The relevance is judged by some similarity metrics, e.g., cosine similarity.

CBF has many advantages. First, CBF is user independent, which means the ratings of candidates is only relevant to the user's own profile and have nothing to do with her/his neighbors. Second, there are good explanations on how CBF works by explicitly listing content features of users and items. This is much better than CF. Third, CBF has no problem of new items, because the new items can also be recommended based on their item profiles. Nevertheless, CBF also has some shortcomings. The most important is the limitation of features for items. Content analyzer can hardly be able to assign complete features to represent items. Take a movie for example, some users want to know its directors, actors and themes, however, some others pay more attention to its box-office and user rating. Another problem of CBF is over-specialization. CBF only recommends items similar to the user profile, while the user profile is generated from what items have been rated. Hence, other items that have not been rated will never be recommended. Lastly, for a new user, there is no recommendations because she/he has no enough ratings for generating a valid user profile.

10.2.3   Collaborative filtering approach

CF was first introduced by Resnick *et al.* [18], whose general idea is that if two users have similar historical ratings, they may like the same items. Compared to CBF, CF has two main advantages. First, CF need not assign features to items and recommend only based on users real ratings. Second, CF could provide serendipitous recommendations, which is rated by the similar users. But CF faces the difficulty of sparse matrix and cold start. Sparse matrix problem refers to the situation where there are masses of users and masses of items, but the ratings of users are not that enough, so most elements in users–items matrix are not defined. Sparse matrix problem poses a challenge on storage and recommendation accuracy. As for cold start, new users without ratings cannot get recommendations.

10.2.4   Co-occurrence recommendation approach

Co-occurrence recommendation was first used in Small's co-citation analysis system [19]. Small proposed that if the two papers are frequently co-cited, they are likely related to each other. Different from CBF and CF, co-occurrence recommendation focus on the relatedness instead of similarity (either feature similarity of CBF or ratings similarity of CF). Similarity is often not ideal because of the limited features or user ratings. In contrast, relatedness only cares about how frequently two items appears. Its complexity is rather low but can provide more serendipitous recommendations. Co-occurrence works quite well, except for the situation where the number of co-occurrence is extremely small, just like arXiv.org [15].

10.2.5   Graph-based approach

Graph-based approach build grapy network based on the inherent connections. These connections could be citations, purchases, authorship, relatedness, co-occurrence, and so on. Once the graph is built, the recommender system will find the closest items using graph metrics.

10.2.6   Global relevance approach

Global relevance is based on a very simple assumption that people like what most others like. So the relevance is not calculated for specific users, e.g., the similarity of items with user profile in CBF, but for overall popularity. Taking the book recommender system as example: the system will recommend to every user the most popular books during the last 1 month.

10.2.7   Hybrid approach

Hybrid approaches combine several recommendation classes to enhance the recommending effect and make up for the shortcomings of one specific method. TechLens is one of the most influential hybrid recommender system, which consists of three CBF variations, two CF variations, and five hybrid approaches [15].

10.3   Reading recommendation in bibliotherapy

Different from the previous work, this chapter aims to facilitate teens to release their psychological stress by reading recommendation. Thus, it shall not only recommend articles with the best easing effect to users, but also recommend attractive articles to users to make them willing to read.

10.3.1   Categories of adolescent stress and reading articles

To unify the two factors (stress easing and reading interest) into recommendation, we categorize users stress and interested readings.

1. Six typical categories of adolescent psychological stress, denoted as $SC_{ategory} = \{$study-life, family-life, peer-relation, self-cognition, romantic-relation, employment$\}$. An user may experience different kinds of stress at the same time period.
2. Over ten categories of articles, denoted as $AC_{ategory} = \{$study-life, family-life, peer-relation, self-cognition, romantic-relation, employment, daily-life, art, humor, book, ...$\}$, where $SC_{ategory} \subset AC_{ategory}$. Due to the diversity and huge volume of reading materials, we further classify reading materials into subcategories, as shown in Table 10.1. We use $AsC_{ategory}$ to denote the set of all subcategories in the whole reading repository.

An article may belong to multiple categories and multiple subcategories. For example, an article entitled "Advice into Society" gives suggestions on job, personnel relation, self-cognition, etc., falling into multiple categories and subcategories.

10.3.2   Unifying stress easing and reading interests for articles recommendation

Given an article a, assume function $AC(a)$ and $AsC(a)$ returns the categories and subcategories which article a belongs to, where $AC(a) \subseteq AC_{ategory}$ and $AsC(a) \subseteq AsC_{ategory}$.

Assume user u bears stress of categories, denoted as $Stress(u) \subseteq SC_{ategory}$. Furthermore, assume an user u has a reading interest set, containing a set of categories and subcategories, returned from function $InterestAC(u) \subseteq AC_{ategory}$ and $InterestAsC(u) \subseteq AsC_{ategory}$, respectively.

Table 10.1   Article categories and article subcategories

No.	Category	Subcategory
1	Study life	University, course, resource, competition, rank, dual-degree, final year project, exempt from postgraduate recommendation, postgraduate entrance exam, study-abroad, etc.
2	Family life	Family member, kinship, blind date, trifles, etc.
3	Peer relation	Peer, roommate, classmate, society, etc.
4	Self cognition	Self-observation, self-evaluation, etc.
5	Romantic relation	Love, gloom, setback, psychology, etc.
6	Employment	Job selection, internship, part-time-job, job-seeking, written-test, interview, hiring, etc.
7	Daily life	Campus life, food, entertainment, sports, outdoors, life experience, encouragement, realization, travel, popular science fiction, etc.
8	Art	Literature, painting, music, dance, movie, drama, building, sculpture, poem, etc.
9	Humor	Joke, anecdote, satire, gossip, etc.
10	Book	History, figure, reading, philosophy, etc.

10.3.3   Recommending procedure

The recommending method adopted by our system is a type of content-based method. Based on the above two steps, the system assign for each article with corresponding stress categories and article (sub-)categories. In the meanwhile, the system maintains for each user with a stress vector $S(u)$ and an interest vector $I(u)$, each element of which indicates the degree of user's stress level or interest level to one category, donated as $S_i(u)$ and $I_i(u)$, where i is one category. Users can explicitly configure their stress and interest vectors at the first use as shown in Figure 10.3. After setting, the system will further tune users' stress and interest based on their reading behavior, e.g., the specific articles they read, the time cost on reading, the supporting, committing and sharing behaviors, and so on. In the phase of recommending, the system computes the score of articles based on their correlation with users' stress vector and interest vector:

$$Score(a, u) = \alpha \cdot Sim(AC(a), S(u)) + (1 - \alpha) \cdot Sim(AsC(a), I(u)) \quad (10.1)$$

$$Sim(AC(a), S(u)) = \sum_{i \in AC(a)} S_i(u) \quad (10.2)$$

$$Sim(AsC(a), I(u)) = \sum_{i \in AsC(a)} I_i(u) \quad (10.3)$$

where α is the coefficient balancing the weight of stress easing effect and reading interest.

The higher $Score(a, u)$ returns, the more likely that article a is recommended to user u.

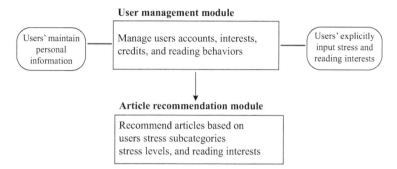

Figure 10.1   Reading recommendation based on users' stress and reading interests in bibliotherapy

10.4   System implementation

10.4.1   The framework

Figure 10.1 briefs our reading recommendation framework, which comprises two major modules:

1. **User-management module.** It is in charge of the following three tasks. (1) Registration and login. The system will check the validity of users' login information. In case a user forgets his/her password, there is also a way to help him/her to reset a password. (2) Update of users reading interests and stress categories. The system maintains users' reading interests and stress categories and allows users' manual modification. (3) Management of users personal information, including user account information, credits, and online reading behaviors such as reading time reading sequence, sharing and commenting actions for future analysis and inference.
2. **Article-recommendation module.** It leverages users stress categories and reading interests to recommend a few articles (which is 4 per week in the study) to the users.

10.4.2   System interfaces

In this section, we show how to use the reading recommendation system. All the figures are screen shots of Safari on a mobile iPhone.

1. Users registration and login (Figure 10.2).
   In registration, new users are requested to input a valid email to receive the verification code. In login, users provide their emails and passwords, and the system provides a way to reset the passwords in case they forget their passwords.
2. Users setting of reading interests and stress categories (Figure 10.3).
3. Weekly recommending a reading theme associated with four articles under each theme (Figures 10.4–10.7).

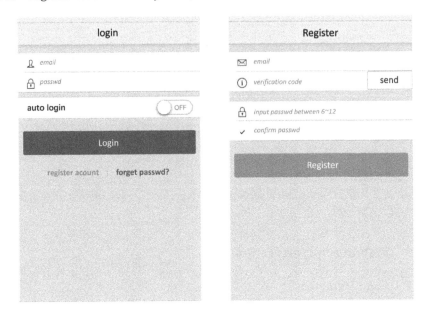

Figure 10.2   Users setting of reading interests and stress categories

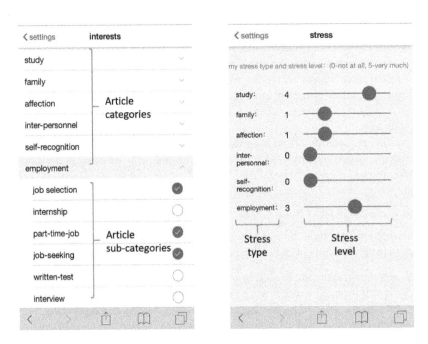

Figure 10.3   Users' setting of reading interests and stress categories

Figure 10.4   Example of reading theme—new life begins

Figure 10.5   Example of reading theme—courses selection

Figure 10.6   Example of reading theme—beauty of sports

Figure 10.7   Example of reading theme—career planning

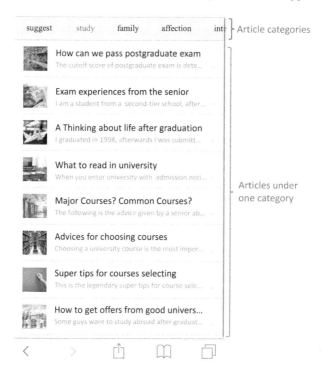

Figure 10.8   Article lists, where the top menu lists article categories, and specific articles are listed under each category

4. Article lists under different categories and subcategories (Figure 10.8).
5. For each recommended article, users commenting, agreeing, and sharing activities are supported in order to get feedbacks and better serve the users' needs (Figure 10.9).

10.5   Conclusion

The chapter addressed the problem of traditional bibliotherapy in coping with pressures of adolescents and proposed an online reading recommendation system as a new exploration of bibliotherapy. Its major advantage is that articles with stress-easing effects as well as much attraction are automatically recommended to users without human intervention. The recommendation process is based on CBF, where user profile is represented as interest vector and stress easing vector, and article features consist of one or more categories and subcategories. Our 6-week user study with 10 stressful college students showed that the recommended articles are thought interesting with 3.22 (the maximal score is 5) and stress easing effect with 2.89 (the maximal score is 5). This preliminary experiment demonstrates the effectiveness of

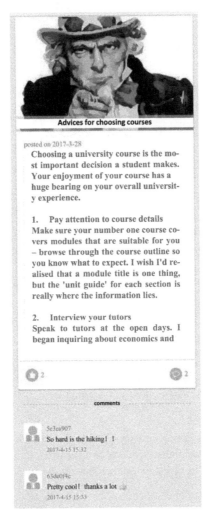

Figure 10.9   Users can comment, agree, and share an article

the online reading recommendation system in dealing with adolescent psychological problems.

Regarding to the dynamic evolution of users' reading interests and stress status, real-time monitoring and automatically adjusting the users profile information are desirable functions worth exploration in the future work.

References

[1]   Doll B, Doll C. Bibliotherapy with young people: librarians and mental health professionals working together. Englewood, CO: Libraries Unlimited; 1997.

[2] Cornett CE, Cornett CF. Bibliotherapy: the right book at the right time. Bloomington, IN: Phi Delta Kappa Intl. Inc.; 1980.

[3] Peske N, West B. Bibliotherapy: the girl's guide to books for every phase of our lives. New York: Dell Inc.; 2001.

[4] Pardeck JT, Pardeck JA. Using books in clinical social work practice: a guide to bibliotherapy. Abingdon-on-Thames: Routledge; 1992.

[5] Karges-Bone L. Bibliotherapy. Dayton, OH: Lorenz Educational Press; 2015.

[6] Webster N. Webster's third new international dictionary of the English language. Springfield, IL: Merriam-Webster; 1993.

[7] Rongione LA. Bibliotherapy: its nature and uses. Phoenix, AZ: Oryx Press; 1978.

[8] Li F, Chen Y, Zhang J. Review of the bibliotherapy study in china. Journal of Modem Information. 2010;30(2):173–177.

[9] Crothers SM. A literary clinic. The Atlantic Monthly. September 1916: 291–300.

[10] Hou Y. Promoting bibliotherapy and building sunshine of soul for college students. Journal of Business, Education, and Economy Research. 2008;1: 9–10.

[11] Yang Z. Bibliotherapy in china: a review. Chinese Journal of Medical Library and Information Science. 2007;16(3):1–4.

[12] Wang B, Fu X. The principle of bibliotherapy. Library. 2003;3:1–12.

[13] Elizabeth PH, Simon Md S, Szilvia Ma B. E-Bibliotherapy, Computer Based Bibliotherapy – Development Perspectives in Relation to The Effectiveness, Reliability and Economy. In: Proc. of 55th ISERD International Conference. Houston, USA; 2016. p. 51–56.

[14] Phornphatcharaphong W. E-bibliotherapy system: book contents for improving quality of youth's life. TEM Journal. 2012;1(3):192–199.

[15] Beel J, Gipp B, Langer S, *et al.* Research paper recommender systems: a literature survey. International Journal on Digital Libraries. 2016;17(4): 305–338.

[16] Rich E. User modeling via stereotypes. Cognitive Science. 1979;3(4):329–354.

[17] Lops P, Gemmis M, Semeraro G. Content-based recommender systems: state of the art and trends. In: Ricci F, Rokach L, Shapira B, *et al.*, editors. Recommender Systems Handbook. Bari: Springer; 2011. p. 73–105.

[18] Resnick P, Iacovou N, Suchak M, *et al.* GroupLens: An Open Architecture for Collaborative Filtering of Netnews. In: Proceedings of the ACM Conference on Computer Supported Cooperative Work; 1994. p. 175–186.

[19] Small H. Co-citation in the scientific literature: a new measure of the relationship between two documents. Journal of the American Society for Information Science. 1973;24:265–269.

Chapter 11

Stream processing in Big Data for e-health care

Tariq Lambachri[1,2], Amir Hajjam El Hassani[1], Abderrahim Sekkaki[3], and Emmanuel Andres[4,5]

11.1 Introduction

For quite some time now, data have become the new oil of the digital industry. The spread and the evolution of information technologies as well as the connectivity between people and devices have enabled a new dimension of Big Data storage and analytics. This can bring massive improvements across many industries, including healthcare.

However, while performance remains mandatory for any software trying to deal with a huge amount of data, only a small part of the today's data potential can be exploited using traditional Big Data systems based on batch-oriented approaches. For the last couple of years, the business needs have driven data processing systems to deviate from the batch-oriented approaches to the processing of data items as they arrive, recognizing by such the importance of the low latency and the velocity in Big Data analytics.

The idea of processing data in motion is not new, and it is used in a lot of fields. Complex event processing (CEP) and stream event processing (SEP), e.g., can provide a low latency, but they are much more complicated to set up and to manage, conversely to new systems presented in the course of this chapter. In fact, the achievement of these new systems is the abstraction from scaling issues which makes development, deployment and maintenance easier.

Throughout this chapter, we will present the stream processing and batch processing. Besides, we will conduct a qualitative comparison of the most popular data processing systems, namely Storm and Spark streaming. We will describe their

[1]Nanomedicine Laboratories, Université de Bourgogne Franche-Comté, UTBM, France
[2]ADBI, Paris, France
[3]Laboratoire de Recherche et Innovation Informatique, Faculté des Sciences Aïn Chock, Université Hassan II Casablanca, Morocco
[4]Service de Médecine Interne, Diabète et Maladies Métaboliques de la Clinique Médicale B, CHRU de Strasbourg, France
[5]Centre de Recherche Pédagogique en Sciences de la Santé, Faculté de Médecine de Strasbourg, Université de Strasbourg, France

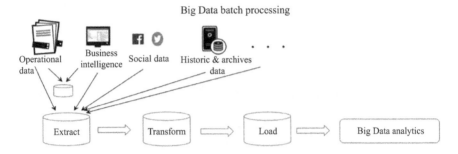

Figure 11.1   Big Data and batch processing

respective underlying bases and the functionalities they provide and discuss how they can be introduced into e-health care analysis programs.

11.2   Stream processing for low-latency analytics

In an increasingly connected world, the volume of available data is growing on a massive scale. The Internet of things (IoT) is generating real-time events that are transforming the way companies engage their customers and deliver their services. Companies such as Amazon, Google and Netflix have already established processes to monitor their users' activity to optimize their recommendation systems. As a result, they become more efficient and react to business conditions in real time. In contrast to traditional approaches that collect and periodically process huge volumes of static data, stream processing acts on data as it becomes available, minimizing the amount of time it takes for a single data item to be processed. In this way, results are available the moment data start entering the system. Thus, we can consider that the purpose of a real-time infrastructure is to have the necessary flexibility to intervene at the right time [1].

11.2.1   Batch processing vs. stream processing

Before introducing the streaming data, it is worthwhile to compare and contrast batch processing and stream processing. Batch processing is an efficient way to process large volumes of data when we have all the data required for our analysis. As illustrated in Figure 11.1, data are first collected, entered and processed, and then the batch results are displayed. Batch processing uses separate algorithms to collect, process and display results.

Real-time data processing is generally associated to a continual input, a processing system and an output of data. Data must be processed in a small time period (or near real time). This manner of processing data allows organizations to react instantaneously upon data entry. The aim of this approach is to obtain the insight required to act carefully at the right time. The main differences between the real-time data processing and the batch processing lie in the fact that real-time data process data in memory, before it hits the disc [2,3]; see Figure 11.2.

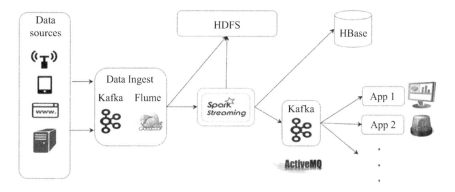

Figure 11.2   Canonical stream processing architecture

A good example of stream processing is when sensors track the behaviour of an object and send data to a streaming application. The goal is to monitor the performance and detect any potential defects prior to equipment downtime.

To sum up, stream processing and batch processing can be regarded as two sides of the same coin. Each of them can be efficient depending on the business objective. Real-time processing is better when time matters. Batch processing is more suitable when all the data required for analysis are available. *So, when and how can one say that stream processing is better than batch processing?*

To answer this question, let's consider the following example: the detection of credit card fraud, which is one of many examples where stream processing approach is used. In order to have a more accurate fraud detection system, banks and financial services use streaming data application to be able to take immediate action without impacting the customer's banking experience. It means that the stream-based archi-tecture is powerful where new and dynamic data are generated on a continual basis. Companies often start with simple applications and evolve to more sophisticated real-time processing software. Initially, companies used to implement applications based on data stream architecture to perform simple actions, such as emitting alarms when a threshold is exceeded. Eventually, these applications perform more sophisti-cated analysis, like extracting deeper insights from the data using machine learning processing algorithms.

11.2.2   Challenges of stream processing

Dealing with streaming data processing requires two layers: a storage layer and a processing layer.

The storage layer has to deal with the heterogeneity of data and the data quality. In fact, the storage layer needs to enable cheap, fast and recurrent reads and writes of large volumes of data. Concerning the processing layer, it constitutes the part of the architecture that consumes data from the storage layer, executes the computation and notifies the storage layer in order to delete data that are no longer needed. Besides, streaming data architecture needs to be scalable and fault tolerant in both layers.

Currently, many platforms have been set up to provide the infrastructure required to build streaming data applications. In the following sections, we will give a qualitative comparison of the most popular contenders, namely Storm, Samza and Spark (Streaming).

11.3   Real-time processors

Once data are collected, they need to be processed. There are a considerable number of streaming platforms that are suitable to a large part of business objectives. The difficulty lies in choosing the solution that is the most suitable to the need. In the following subsections, we will introduce the most famous platforms namely Storm, Samza and Spark.

11.3.1   Storm platform

Apache Storm [4,5] is a free and open source distributed real-time message computation system for processing fast and large streams of data. Storm was born as a project of Back-Type, a marketing intelligence company bought by Twitter in 2011. After being open sourced by Twitter, it moved to the Apache software foundation.

Storm is designed for massive scalability, supports fault tolerance and guarantees that every tuple will be processed. Storm is written in Clojure and made from the three following abstractions:

- **Stream:** It is an uninterrupted flow of a long sequence of tuples.
- **Spout:** It is a source of streams in a computation. Typically, it can read from a broker such as Kafka. It can also read from somewhere else like the Twitter streaming application programming interface (API). Besides, they are considered as one of the strengths of Storm due to their capacity of receiving data from all types of sources.
- **Bolts:** These are the nodes that consume the sequences of tuples emitted by one or more spouts. Their role is to perform different operations (filters, aggregations, joins, read/write to and from a database, etc.) and if necessary to generate a new sequence of tuples.
- **Topology:** It is the cornerstone of Storm. It is a class where we describe how spots and bolts will be connected. A topology is a complex multi-stage stream computation that runs indefinitely when deployed.

Storm is considered as a simple framework where developers can use any programming language to write Storm topologies (see Figure 11.3).

There are six characteristics that make Storm one of the best solutions for real-time data processing. These characteristics could be summarized as follows:

- Storm is *Open source*.
- Fast: Storm processes more than 100 bytes/s.
- Scalable: Storm is a distributed calculating platform that runs across a cluster of machines.

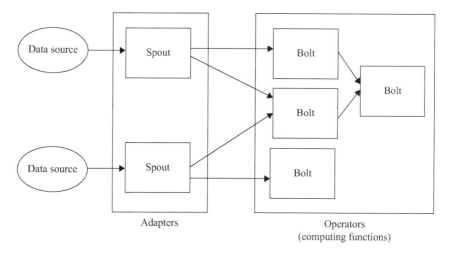

Figure 11.3 Topology concept of Storm

- Fault tolerant: When a worker dies, Storm will automatically restart it. If a node dies, the worker will be restarted on another node. The Storm daemons, Nimbus and Supervisors, are designed to be stateless and fail-fast. If they die, they will restart seamlessly.
- Reliable: Storm guarantees that each tuple will be processed at least once or exactly once. Messages are only replayed when there are failures.
- Easy to operate: Standard configurations are suitable for production from the first day.

For a better understanding of Storm's mechanism, let us consider the below example. The aim of this example is to count the occurrence of words in a text message using Storm. As illustrated in Figure 11.4, the required topology will be constituted of the following:

- **One Spout:** It will split the text into sentences.
- **Three Bolts:** The first one for splitting sentences into words, the second one for counting the word's occurrence and the third one for displaying the result.

In our case, we will have three types of streams (see Figure 11.5):

- **Type 1:** Streams containing sentences. They are created by the spout and used by the blot that splits these sentences into words.
- **Type 2:** Streams containing words. They are created by the bolt of splitting and used by the bolt of counting.
- **Type 3:** Sequence of tuples < word, occurrences > containing the occurrences of each word.

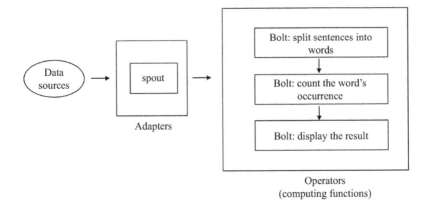

Figure 11.4   Topology used in the example

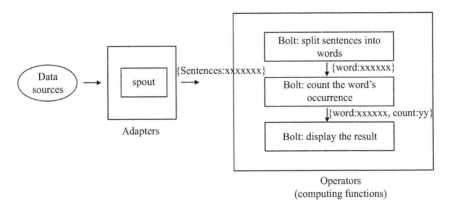

Figure 11.5   Word count topology

11.3.2   Samza platform

Apache Samza [6] is a distributed stream processing framework. It uses Apache Kafka for messaging and Apache Hadoop YARN [7] to provide fault tolerance, processor isolation, security and resource management. Samza was born as a project of LinkedIn, after it was moved to the Apache software foundation.

To understand the idea behind the use of Samza, let us consider the use case of LinkedIn. On this website, you can probably get information such as user's profiles, companies and universities. If recruiters are looking for a developer on LinkedIn, there is a good chance that they would also like the search to display the profiles of 'Rockstar', 'Code artist' and other original names because basically they mean the same thing. On the other hand, the recruiter does not wish that the profiles of 'Rockstar' or developers in real estate to be displayed. LinkedIn has therefore developed a

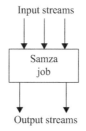

Figure 11.6   Samza process streams [6]

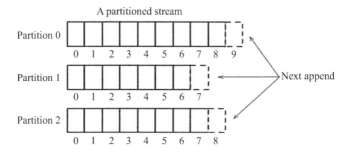

Figure 11.7   Samza partitioned stream [6]

system of standardization for its main information (job titles, company name, etc.) with some constraints:

- When a new data entry is made by a user, the standardization system must be able to quickly retrieve the associated synonyms and update the search index so that members can be retrieved easily.
- When a standardization model is updated, it is necessary to reprocess the existing data so that they take into consideration the model updated instantaneously.

Thus, LinkedIn uses Samza to rework existing data and process new data.
Now, we will focus on the key concepts of Samza:

- **Streams:** They are uninterrupted flows of a long sequence of data (see Figure 11.6).
- **Jobs:** A job is a part of code in charge of making transformations in a stream. It receives one or more streams in the input and generates the transformed data in the output.

To insure performance and efficiency, Samza uses the concept of partitions and tasks:

- **Partitions:** As shown in Figure 11.7, each stream is broken into one or more partitions. Each partition in the stream is a totally ordered sequence of messages. Each message in this sequence has an identifier called the offset, which is unique per

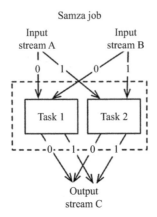

Figure 11.8   Samza job [6]

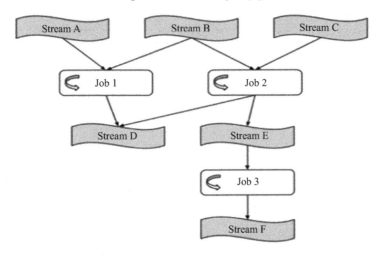

Figure 11.9   Dataflow graph [6]

partition. The offset can be a sequential integer, bytes offset or string depending on the underlying system implementation.

- **Tasks:** A job is split into tasks. Each task consumes data from one partition for each of the job's input stream (see Figure 11.8).
- **Dataflow graph:** A dataflow graph is the combination of multiple jobs. The graphs are made up of streams that have been transformed by jobs (see Figure 11.9).

11.3.2.1   Samza architecture

Samza architecture [8] consists of three components (see Figure 11.10):

- **A streaming Layer:** It provides partitioned streams that are replicated and durable.

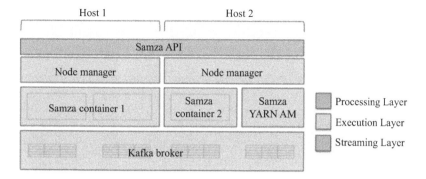

Figure 11.10   Samza architecture [8]

- **An Execution Layer:** It schedules and coordinates tasks across the machines.
- **A processing Layer:** It processes the input stream and applies transformations.

The advantage of this architecture is that we can include any existing implementation. For instance, Kafka or Hadoop [9] can be used as a Streaming Layer. Similarly, solutions like Mesos [10] and Yarn can be plugged-in for job execution systems.

11.3.3   Spark platform

Apache Spark [11, 12, 13] is an open source Big Data processing framework built around speed. It was developed in 2009 in UC Berkeley's AMP Lab., and open sourced in 2010 as an Apache project.

Spark is a fast and general engine for large-scale data processing that has several advantages compared to other Big Data platforms such as Storm and Hadoop. Spark allows rich programming APIs like SQL, machine learning and graph processing to run on clusters of computers to achieve large-scale data processing and analysis. Besides, Spark makes distributed processing easy by providing a distributed and parallel processing framework in addition to scalability, fault tolerance and a programming paradigm that makes it easy to write code in a parallel manner. Moreover, Spark provides API for data munging, ETL (extract, transform, load), machine learning, graph processing, streaming, and interactive and batch processing. It can replace several SQL, streaming and complex analytics systems with one unified environment.

It is also considered as Lightning fast speeds due to in-memory caching and DAG-based processing engine. Spark is considered 100 times faster than Hadoop's MapReduce for in-memory computations and 10 times faster for on disk. [11]

Another particularity of Spark lies on the fact that it is not a data storage system. Indeed, Spark is not a data store, but it is versatile in reading from and writing to a variety of data sources including Hadoop Distributed File System (HDFS), Cassandra, S3 and Hbase. It can also access to traditional BI tools using a server mode that provides a standard Java Database Connectivity (JDBC) and Open DataBase Connectivity (ODBC) connectivity.

11.3.3.1 Spark use cases

In this section, we will present some use cases that require dealing with the velocity, variety and volume of Big Data, for which Spark is also well-suited:

- Fraud detection: Spark streaming and machine learning applied to prevent fraud.
- Network intrusion detection: Machine learning applied to detect cyber hacks.
- Customer segmentation and personalization: Spark SQL and machine learning is applied to maximize customer lifetime value.
- Social media sentiment analysis: Spark streaming, Spark SQL and Stanford's CoreNLP wrapper help achieve sentiment analysis.
- Real-time ad targeting: Spark is used to maximize online ad revenues.
- Predictive healthcare: Spark is used to optimize healthcare costs.

In the following, we describe how companies such as Uber, Netflix and Yahoo use Spark:

- **Spark at Uber**
  - *Business problem*: A simple problem of getting people around a city with an army of more than 100,000 drivers and using data to intelligently size the business in an automated and real-time way.
    - o Accurately paying drivers according to a dataset based on their trips
    - o Maximizing profits by positioning cars optimally
    - o Helping drivers avoid accidents
    - o Computing surge pricing.
  - *Solution*: Use Spark streaming and Spark SQL as the ETL system and Spark MLlib and GraphX for advanced analytics
- **Spark at Netflix**
  - *Business problem*: A video streaming service with emphasis on data quality, agility and availability. Using analytics to help users discover movies and showing them what they like is the key to Netflix's success.
    - o Streaming applications are long-running tasks that need to be resilient in cloud deployments.
    - o Optimize content buying.
    - o Renowned personalization algorithms.
  - *Solution*: Use Spark streaming in AWS cloud and Spark GraphX for recommender system.
- **Spark at Yahoo**
  - *Business problem*: Deep learning is critical for Yahoo's product team to acquire intelligence from huge amounts of online data. Examples are image recognition and speech recognition for improved search on photo sharing service Flickr.
    - o Run deep learning software on existing infrastructure.
    - o Distribute deep learning processes across multiple Big Data clusters.
    - o Handle potential system failures on long running deep learning jobs.
  - *Solution*: Create a way to run deep learning system Caffe on Spark.

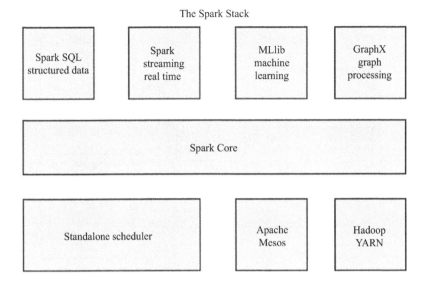

Figure 11.11   Spark ecosystem [13]

Components and architecture of Spark

The Spark Core constitutes the base engine of the framework. It is in charge of the following tasks:

- Workloads distribution
- Applications monitoring across the cluster
- Tasks scheduling
- Memory management
- Fault recovery
- Storage systems interaction
- Housing of API that defines Resilient Distributed Datasets (RDDs).

In addition to Spark Core API, Spark powers additional libraries that are part of the Spark ecosystem and provides additional capabilities in Big Data analytics and machine learning areas (see Figure 11.11).

These libraries include the following:

- **Spark SQL:** Provides structured data processing.
- **Spark streaming:** Enables processing of live streams of data.
- **Spark MLlib:** Contains common machine learning functionalities.
- **GraphX:** Library for manipulating graphs and performing graph parallel computations.
- **SparkR:** R package that provides a lightweight frontend to use Apache Spark from R.

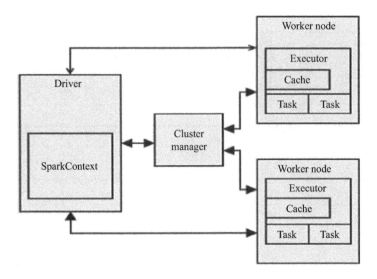

Figure 11.12   Spark runtime architecture [13]

The spark cluster managers are the part of the framework responsible for allocating resources across applications on a cluster. Spark supports the following three cluster managers:

- **Standalone:** A cluster manager included with Spark that makes it easy to set up a cluster.
- **Apache Mesos:** A general cluster manager that can also run Hadoop MapReduce and service applications.
- **Hadoop YARN:** A resource manager in Hadoop 2.

Spark runtime architecture
In this part, we will introduce the Spark runtime architecture. Spark has a master/slave architecture where the master is the driver and the slaves are the executors. Drivers and executors run in their own Java processes (see Figure 11.12).

The Spark runtime architecture is composed of a SparkContext, a driver, a cluster manager and executors. Table 11.1 summarizes the role of each of these elements:

To finish this part, we will summarize the execution flow inside a Spark program.

- **Step 1:** The user submits an application that launches the driver program.
- **Step 2:** The driver calls the main ( ) method specified by the user.
- **Step 3:** The driver asks the cluster manager for resources to launch the executors.
- **Step 4:** The cluster manager launches the executors.
- **Step 5:** The driver divides the user program into tasks and sends them to the executors.
- **Step 6:** The executors run the tasks, compute and save the results, and return results to the driver.
- **Step 7:** When the driver's main () method exits or SparkContext.stop () is called, the executors are terminated and the cluster manager releases the resources.

Table 11.1   Roles of Spark components

Component	Roles
SparkContext	• Main entry point to all Spark's libraries • Defined in the main/driver program • Tells Spark how and where to access a cluster • Connects to cluster managers • Coordinates Spark processes running on different cluster nodes • Used to create RDDs and shared variables on the cluster
Driver	• The process where the main ( ) method of the Spark program runs • Responsible for converting a user program into tasks • Driver schedules the tasks on executors • Results from these tasks are delivered back to the driver
Executors	• Launched at the beginning of the application and typically run for the entire lifetime of an application • Executors register themselves with the driver, thus allowing the driver to schedule tasks on the executors • Worker processes run the individual tasks and return results to the driver • Provide in-memory storage for RDDs, as well as disc storage
Cluster Manager	• A pluggable service for acquiring resources on the cluster

Figure 11.13   Spark streaming [14]

Spark streaming: network word count use case [14]

Before presenting our example, let us introduce the Spark streaming API. Spark streaming uses the scheduling of the Spark Core for streaming analytics on mini batches of data. It permits to ingest data from many sources like Kafka [15], Flume [16], Twitter, ZeroMQ [17], Kinesis [18] or TCP sockets. Data can further be processed using MLlib, Graph processing or high-level functions like map, reduce, join, and window (see Figure 11.13).

As described in Figure 11.14, Spark streaming follows the following steps:

• Spark streaming starts by collecting live input data streams and divides data into batches.
• Batches of data are processed by the Spark engine to produce batches of results.
• High-level API called DStream (Discretized Stream) represents continuous stream of data.
• Internally DStreams is represented as a sequence of RDDs.

Figure 11.14   Steps in Spark streaming [14]

- DStreams can be created either from input data streams from sources such as Kafka, Flume and Kinesis, or by applying high-level operations on other DStreams.
- **Example:** Network word count using Spark streaming:
  - Create a StreamingContext, main entry point to all streaming functionality

```
from pyspark import SparkContext
from pyspark.streaming import StreamingContext
#Create a local StreamingContext with two working thread and batch interval of 1
Second sc =SparkContext("local[2]) ","NetworkWordCount")
scc=StreamingContext(sc,1)
```

  - Create a DStream from a Transmission Control Protocol (TCP) source

```
#Create a DStream that will connect to hostname:port, like localhost:9999
lines =ssc.socketTextStream("localhost",9999)
```

  - Define MapReduce functions to count the number of words from the streaming data

```
#Split each line into words
words= lines.flatMap(lambda line:line.split(" "))
# Count each word in each batch
pairs = words.map(lambda word: (word 1))
wordCounts = pairs.reduceByKey(lambda x,y:x+y)
#Print the first ten elements of each RDD generated in this DStream to the console
wordCounts.pprint()
```

  - Start processing after setting up of all transformations

```
ssc.start()              # Start the computation
ssc.awaitTermination()   # Wait for the computation to terminate
```

  - Start the Netcat server in terminal 1: 'nc–lk 9999'
  - Submit Spark command in terminal 2: ./bin/spark-submit examples/src/main/python/streaming/network_wordcount.py localhost 9999
  - The result is illustrated in Figure 11.15.

Figure 11.15   Results of the example word count using Spark streaming

11.4   Stream processing in e-health care

So far, we have introduced the stream processing and have given an overview of the stream processors for low-latency Big Data analytics. We have also conducted a qualitative comparison between Storm, Spark and Samza. In this section, we will discuss on how this concept can be introduced to the e-health care analysis programs.

Nowadays, the healthcare industry is increasingly moving towards a value-based model. There are more needs on real-time decision-making to personalize patient marketing campaigns, improve patient outcomes and create greater patient engagement.

When everything is connected, from administrative perspective to historical data and output in near real-time data points, health institutions have the opportunity to deepen the patient and physician connections and enhance their experiences. This helps for better understanding of the correlation between genetic and environmental factors and also for the development and the spread of diseases.

Real-time and near-real-time data processing allow healthcare systems to make better decisions based on more robust and better data quality. As a result, they can take immediate actions based on data analysis, which can be significant on the health of a patient as well as their experience with a hospital or a health institution.

Through the following example, we will be able to measure the importance of the introduction of real-time data processing in healthcare.

For the NeoNatal Intensive Care unit at the Hospital for Sick Children (SickKids) in Toronto, Big Data tools have proven valuable. They allow doctors to monitor the vital signs of premature infants around the clock. The introduction of a stream data process has permitted the early identification of newborn babies with an infection called late-onset neonatal sepsis, a blood infection that occurs in children between days 8 and 89.

Doctors get digital reporting that provide real-time data about respiratory rates, heart rates, blood pressure and blood oxygen saturation, and can analyse these data using a platform called Artemis. This platform allows doctors to monitor infants' vital signs in real-time and detect changes in their conditions [19].

Table 11.2   Spark, Storm and Samza in direct comparison

	Storm	**Samza**	**Spark streaming**
Strictest guarantee	At-least-once	At-least-once	Exactly-once
State management	Yes	Yes	Yes
Processing model	One-at-a-time	One-at-a-time	Micro-batch
Backpressure mechanism	Yes	Not required (buffering)	Yes
Ordering guarantees	No	Within stream partitions	Between batches
Elasticity	Yes	No	Yes

11.5   Conclusion

In this chapter, we described some of the aspects that make real-time processors such as Storm, Samza and Spark (Streaming very powerful). Besides, we gave some examples that illustrate how real-time processors could improve human's life especially when applied in e-health domain.

To sum up, Spark streaming is an incremental micro-batching stream processing that uses the scheduling of the Spark Core for streaming analytics on mini batches of data. One of the Streaming distinctions of Spark is its use of DStream (Discretized Stream) that simplifies the work with continuous data streams by using one single RDD at a time.

Apache Storm is a distributed real-time data processing platform focused on complex event processing. Storm is designed to process multiple computations or large amount of data in a fault tolerant and horizontal scalable method. It is generally used to transform real-time data into a desired format.

The main difference between Storm and Spark streaming lies in the fact that Spark performs Data-Parallel computations while Storm performs Task-Parallel computations. Hence, Spark streaming is considered as ten times faster than Storm using the Word Count benchmark.

Concerning Samza, it's claimed to be the most suitable solution to deal with vast amount of states. Samza co-locates storage and processing on the same machines in order to process efficiently the states that won't fit in memory. Besides the framework, it gives the possibility to plug in engines: the storage, execution and messaging engines can each be replaced with many choices of alternatives. Table 11.2 provides a quick comparison on the properties of these systems.

References

[1]   T. Akidau, A. Balikov, K. Bekiroglu, *et al.* Millwheel: Fault-tolerant stream processing at internet scale. In Very Large Data Bases, pp. 734–746, 2013.

[2]   L. Neumeyer, B. Robbins, A. Nair and A. Kesari. S4: Distributed stream computing platform. In ICDMW '10 Proceedings of the 2010 IEEE International Conference on Data Mining Workshop, pp. 170–177, 2010.

[3]   M. Walker. Batch processing vs stream processing [online]. 2013. Available from http://www.datasciencecentral.com/profiles/blogs/batch-vs-real-time-data-processing [Accessed 1 June 2017].

[4]   Apache Storm. http://storm.apache.org [Accessed 1 Jun 2017].

[5]   Z. Ahmed. Streaming data processing – storm vs spark [online]. 2015. Available from: https://zubayr.github.io/storm-vs-spark/ [Accessed 2 June 2017].

[6]   Apache Samza. http://samza.apache.org [Accessed 7 July 2017].

[7]   Apache Yarn. http://hadoop.apache.org/docs/stable/hadoop-yarn/hadoop-yarn-site/YARN.html [Accessed 7 July 2017].

[8]   Samza Architecture. https://samza.apache.org/learn/documentation/0.13/introduction/architecture [Accessed 1 July 2017].

[9]   Hadoop ecosystem. https://hadoopecosystemtable.github.io [Accessed 1 July 2017].

[10]   Apache Mesos. http://mesos.apache.org/ [Accessed 3 July 2017].

[11]   Apache Spark. https://spark.apache.org/docs/1.2.0/streaming-programming-guide.html [Accessed 4 July 2017].

[12]   H. Karau and R. Warren. High Performance Spark: Best Practices for Scaling and Optimizing Apache Spark, Sebastopol, CA: O'Reilly Media, Inc., pp. 17–35, 2016.

[13]   Apache Spark. https://spark.apache.org/docs/1.1.0/cluster-overview.html [Accessed 4 July 2017].

[14]   Spark Streaming. https://www.cloudera.com/documentation/enterprise/5-5-x/topics/spark_streaming.html [Accessed 4 July 2017].

[15]   Apache Kafka. http://kafka.apache.org/ [Accessed 3 June 2017].

[16]   Apache Flume. https://flume.apache.org/ [Accessed 3 June 2017].

[17]   ZeroMq. http://zeromq.org [Accessed 3 June 2017].

[18]   Kinesis. https://aws.amazon.com/fr/kinesis/ [Accessed 20 June 2017].

[19]   B.T. Horowitz. Big Data Help Toronto Hospital Monitor Premature Infants [Online]. 2013. Available from: http://www.eweek.com/enterprise-apps/ibm-infosphere-big-data-help-toronto-hospital-monitor-premature-infants [Accessed 20 June 2017].

Chapter 12

How Hadoop and Spark benchmarking algorithms can improve remote health monitoring and data management platforms?

Anna Karen Garate Escamilla[1], Amir Hajjam El Hassani[1], Emmanuel Andres[2,3], and Mohamed Hajjam[4]

12.1 Introduction

Telemedicine, mobile applications, and electronic health systems have changed the medical rules. Having high quality equipment and facilities is no longer adequate, and now they have to be connected to improve their management and have better results. From a medical standpoint, it is vital to improve medical care with aspects such as the integration of medical records with technology and medical devices interconnected through the Internet. This helps medical staff to collect information and improve the treatments and the attention of the patient. Internet of things (IoT) is the interconnection of devices through the web. The development of this concept is what makes it possible to improve healthcare with the help of telemedicine.

E-care project is an intelligent platform with interest in the health sector. Through telemedicine and tools, it allows the reduction of rehospitalizations, better patients' quality of life, remote health monitoring, and an improvement in management. With the large-scale deployment of the E-care platform within the framework of the PRADO (Programme d'Accompagnement du Retour à Domicile) program of the French healthcare system (CPAM, i.e. Caisse Primaire d'Assurance Maladie), E-care will have a large amount of data from different sources. It is important to keep the patients' information in a low-cost cloud storage that helps the remote monitoring of the information and a better data management. In fact, this is what brings big data to E-care. Big data can handle the volume, variety, and velocity of the information, stored in a distributed, scalable, and resilient database system. Big data most famous analytics tools are the ones inside Hadoop ecosystem, such as MapReduce, Spark,

[1]Nanomedicine Laboratories, Université de Bourgogne Franche-Comte, UTBM, France
[2]Service de Médecine Interne, Diabète et Maladies métaboliques de la Clinique Médicale B, CHRU de Strasbourg, France
[3]Centre de Recherche Pédagogique en Sciences de la Santé, Faculté de Médecine de Strasbourg, Université de Strasbourg, France
[4]PREDIMED Technology, France

Flink, and Storm. One way to judge the performance of E-care, with the analytics tools from Hadoop ecosystem, is using benchmark testing software.

The concept of benchmarking was introduced by Xerox in response to the lack of innovation in its products and the necessity to provide a feedback to its processes. Benchmarks are important tools to evaluate systems through different scenarios to answer important questions of performance, management, and behavior and reveal the weaknesses and strengths of any company. They run with a particular program, kernel, or workload to measure and predict the performance of the system, or make a comparison with another one. They are the most important aspect of IT system evaluation. The benchmarking itself is a complicated process because it is not standardized. As a result, big data benchmarking is even a greater challenge considering that it does not have precise characteristics and it is more complicated than the traditional systems characterized for having a small amount of data.

The remainder of the chapter is organized as follows. Section 12.2 introduces the characteristics of E-care platform and the concept of ontology which helps the reader understand the system that will implement big data tools for its migration. Section 12.3 explores the concept of big data, while Section 12.4 focuses on the most popular systems in the Hadoop ecosystem, emphasizing MapReduce and Spark. Section 12.5 surveys applications using machine learning techniques in the medical field. Examples are given with Apache Spark. Section 12.6 applies the concept of benchmarking in big data. Section 12.7 presents the benchmarking tools in Hadoop and Spark and Section 12.8 provides a benchmarking comparison between MapReduce, Spark, and Flink. Section 12.9 presents the system considered most suitable for E-care platform as well as the best benchmarking tools that align to its purposes. Finally, Section 12.10 concludes the chapter.

12.2   E-care platform

E-care project [1] is an intelligent platform developed by academic laboratories and industries. Its interest is the health sector, more particularly patients with heart failure. Through telemedicine and its tools, the E-care platform reduces rehospitalizations and the days of hospital stay, and ensures a better quality of life for patients with heart failure in Stage III. The New York Heart Association (NYHA) Functional Classification [2] describes Stage III patients as marked with (1) limitation of physical activity; (2) comfort in a resting state; (3) and fatigue, palpitations, and dyspnea caused by common activities. Patients with these characteristics need constant monitoring of their health in order to achieve early detection of dangerous situations.

In 2011, the E-care project was selected among projects under "Health and autonomy at home through digital technology" from the program *Investissements d'Avenir* [3]. This is a French national program with 22 million euros to be spent in higher education and research [4] in e-health. E-care started as a prototype deployed at the Strasbourg CHRU in October 2013 [5]. Clinical experimentation was carried out and the concept was tested with 20 beds inside the internal medicine unit. Since 2015, it has been deployed at homes, where it provides assistance to the medical staff with the help of noninvasive sensors communicating via Bluetooth with tablets applications. E-care processes data from multiple sources, including, weight, blood pressure, pulse oximetry (the monitoring of oxygen saturation), patient ergonomics, and diet; all these are combined with the notes and comments from patients and medical staff, mostly nurses and doctors [3]. The integration and processing of this information allows the platform to generate alerts in case of risky situations related to cardiovascular diseases and their underlying pathologies. It is understood that the concept of underlying pathology refers to the way a disease manifests. For example, a person that bleeds and the subjacent cause is leukemia; or a person that has a yellow skin and the subjacent cause is hepatitis. Also, the alerts are generated by related chronic pathologies like diabetes mellitus, fatigue, renal failure, and respiratory insufficiency. This information reaches an information repository where doctors can access the data at any time; this helps the medical staff to have a better understanding of the clinical picture as it improves the existing ontologies.

The E-care platform uses an ontology that improves the decision support system [6] through data, semantics coupling and an extended vocabulary with diseases, medications, and the symptoms and contraindications that are related to heart failure monitoring. Ontologies provide a common semantics that improves the quality of diagnosis, the decision-making process, the accuracy of information, and the level of daily workflow abstraction [7,8]. For every patient, collected data from the sensors are processed in real time, and then analyzed with the ontologies. This will provide the first learning process by adding new data to the patient's information. Then, E-care consolidates the information and improves the system by looking for similar patterns in critical events [3]. The goal of E-care is the creation of new knowledge by the enrichment of this ontology. This enrichment generates an assessment that will consider quality aspects and consistency validation [5]. The rules are generic and evolve with the patient. If an abnormal condition is detected, the system should send an alert to the medical staff. For example, weight measurements are retrieved from the ontologies. If it increases two or three days in a row, an alert will be sent to medical staff to review its cause. Also, there are cases in which it is important to have all the patient's information connected to make the system reliable; e.g. if the heart rate of 70 beats per minute is not dangerous for a normal patient, it may be dangerous if we know that the patient is alcohol-dependent [7].

Ontology includes the patients' profile and their associated measures, alerts, and data. Also, it describes all the system users (medical doctor, administrator, patient, and nurse), their tasks, and equipment definitions (sensors, tablets, etc.) [7].

The E-care architecture illustrated in Figure 12.1 is based on ontologies for telemonitoring elderly persons suffering from chronic diseases. The architecture is generic and relies on three principal components: (1) physiological, environmental, and behavioral sensors; (2) a medium of communication to transmit the data; and (3) institutional information system where data are stored and processed. It also makes a patient–medical staff interaction through a call center, a tablet, and a website. Some projects have educational tools.

The ontology architecture [7] presented in Figure 12.2 is a patient center. It means that the patient data are collected by a sensor (structured data) and other

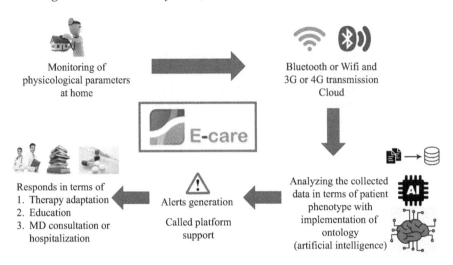

Figure 12.1   E-care architecture

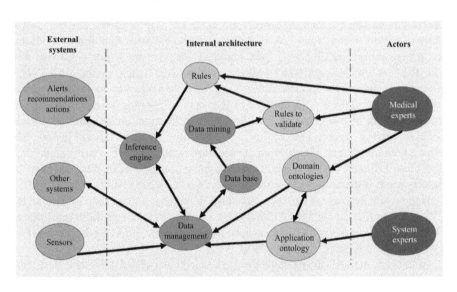

Figure 12.2   E-care ontology architecture

information can be entered by medical staff and the patients themselves (unstructured data). The two principal actors involved are medical experts and system experts. The most important part of the internal architecture is the data management. Its main tasks are the following:

- To receive data from external systems like sensors.
- To communicate with other systems.

- To receive the alert recommendations and the rules provided for the inference engine and the reception of the data.
- To manage the data base and the ontologies. The architecture contains two types of ontologies:
  - **Application ontologies:** They describe the components of the system such as the users, the sensors, the measurements, the input data, and the generated alerts. They also define the tasks of the different system actors.
  - **Domain ontologies:** They provide a controlled vocabulary. These ontologies can provide a language to facilitate data sharing between different system actors, so it can interact easily with other systems. These ontologies are built by medical experts, aided by engineers' knowledge to formalize them. These ontologies can be linked to other elements; e.g. they can link a disease with its symptoms.

12.2.1 Security and privacy challenges for healthcare applications

If there is an area where security in IT is paramount, then it's the healthcare. This is because there is no other information more private than the personal data of the patient. E-care, like any health system, has the obligation to maintain the patient information safely. Patients must be certain that no one will see their information or that it will be used for harmful purposes. This section addresses aspects of security and privacy regulations in electronic healthcare systems.

As information has increased over the past few years in the healthcare setting, the risk associated with a person who has unauthorized access to confidential data has also increased. The literature addresses the challenges of security and privacy in the health community and the regulations that their own systems must have to address the problem of information sensitivity. The study of [9] proposes a software that uses SMS to transfer information using the Health Insurance Portability and Accountability Act (HIPAA) regulations and explains the mechanisms and authentication requirements of the system taking into account that it will be treated with personal health information, the document ends with the comparison between the message with encryption and without encryption, showing improved performance with encryption. In another studies [10], they monitor in real-time health conditions through smartphones and pose the challenges of security and privacy using mobile health networks with the perspective of Quality of Protection (QoP), concluding that without QoP, mobile health networks are still at an immature stage. There are also investigations [11,12] that discuss the security and privacy challenges in wireless body area network (WBAN) which is a tool that monitors and collects the patient's health history through portable sensors.

There are security and privacy policies that health agencies must follow. The National Agency for Shared Health Information Systems, ASIP Santé (Agence des Systèmes d'Information Partagés de Santé), is a digital health agency created to develop shared systems in the field of health. Taking into account the growth of medical data and the need to move to electronic health, the goal of ASIP is to do this in a safe and secure environment. ASIP facilities the development or improvement of e-health projects focused on the actors of the health community, such as health professionals, health institutions, the industrial sector, or the institutional entrepreneur.

ASIP creates a series of documents, the General Security Policy of Health Information Systems (PGSSI-S), [13] to improve the security and privacy of data in the field of health, thus ensuring better protection of patient information through a better approach for IT tools. These documents complete the international e-health safety standards. One of the objectives is the authentication of the health actors, knowing them as an individual or group with interest in patient care. To verify identity, they must choose one or more authentication options (password, ID, smartcard, one-time password (OTP) token, or something the individual is or does). Authentication can be just one factor (simple authentication) or combine multiple factors (strong authentication). In addition, user accounts must be personal unless temporary access is necessary.

Comparable with France, the federal government of the United States launched the HIPAA in 1996 [14] to guarantee people that they have rights to their own information and to ensure that healthcare providers establish a safeguard to protect the patient information.

The important security measures that systems can use are the following:

- Access controls: It include numbers and passwords to restrict access to patient information.
- Encrypting: This means that only authorized parties can access patient information using a key generated by an encryption algorithm.
- Audit trail: It registers who has accessed the patient's information and the changes made to their file.

Although it is a new project, E-care considers that it is essential to take care of the privacy and safety of patients. For security, E-care uses a username and a password. Each patient has a security code generated specifically for a slot and the system gives it to the user; e.g. each patient can only see their own information with the tablet. It is planned in the near future to implement the encryption of the data to reinforce the protection of hacking.

E-care establishes an anonymous relationship between the patient and the data with an algorithm called Anonymization [15]. It is a type of data privacy protection, which attempts to preserve the format of the data without revealing the identity of persons; this could be done removing or encrypting data.

This is a strong method to counteract the problems of security data. Anonymization is used when the data is sensible, there is an increase in employees, it has an external collaboration or a partner, and it wants to comply with all legal requirements. It should be added that for this method to be adequate, it must be supported by laws and policies. Some of the advantages of data anonymization are the following: it reduces the misuse of information, adjusts to privacy laws, and lowers operating costs.

12.2.2 Problematic of E-care

It is expected that E-care will provide a coherent solution in the field of telemedicine. One of its biggest challenges is to achieve an algorithm sequence that can exploit all this amount of data.

All tests are currently in a pilot program with few patients. With the large-scale deployment of the E-care platform within the framework of the PRADO program of the French healthcare system (CPAM), it is expected that in a near future E-care will have thousands of patients and millions of data. For a regular daily use, all patients will use the platform almost at the same time in the morning. This can represent a big challenge for E-care and it must be tested for its capacity of resilience and support.

The necessity of a benchmarking test came as a solution for this problem. It can evaluate the performance of the platform by stressing the system and checking the number of patients that E-care can handle and its response time. Also, the application needs to support streaming data. For the data characteristics, the evaluation of the benchmark will consider the methods, techniques, or algorithms used to test the big data Hadoop and Spark systems. Another thing to consider is the other evaluations that E-care will need to perform in the future, such as a machine learning test.

12.3   Big data

Big data does not have a single definition. Not only is it important for the IT industry, it has also become relevant on different fields such as healthcare, manufacturing, transportation, and the public sector [16]. Big data refers to a large amount of information that flows continuously in the organization, including video, text, sensor, and transactional records [17].

Big data analytics is the process that involves large and different types of information to enable data miners to analyze it with nontraditional tools [18,19]. Big data analysis requires data mining or machine learning algorithms [20]. More often, big data analytics evaluates and processes the information in Hadoop and Spark [21]. Both have advanced algorithms processes to analyze large data sets. Section 4 will discuss the Hadoop ecosystem and the most common analytical tools.

Big data [22] provides valuable information from the analyzed data, which can be transformed into real competitive advantages for the organization. The advantages may include the following [17]:

- Anticipate changes in behavior.
- Evaluate competitive threats.
- Improve marketing campaigns.
- Improve relations with stakeholders.

The first question that organizations ask is why quitting their traditional platforms? Traditional platforms such as relational database (RD) and enterprise data warehouse (EDW) have been used over the past decades by organizations to store and analyze data. The systems are used by most companies and designed to work with structured data. Companies use a traditional ETL (extract, transform, load) process that extracts and analyzes data [17]. The biggest challenge occurs when the data source is large and unstructured.

Most platforms, including E-care, deal with different types of information and the increasing volume of their data. These characteristics make it difficult for companies to continue using traditional platforms: they are complex and expensive and require a long time to operate their system.

In response to the limitations of traditional platforms, big data characteristics, known as the Vs [18,22,23], were introduced by Gartner [24] to describe its elemental features. The three aspects are categorized: (1) volume, (2) variety, and (3) velocity. The definition of the three Vs and their qualities on the healthcare field are the following:

1. Volume: It represents the amount of data such as terabyte or petabyte [25]. The volume is growing considerably in the medical domain. This is because of the great amount of data that are generated by electronic health records, medical imaging (magnetic resonance imaging (MRI), electrocardiography, scan, and XR), sensors, devices, and healthcare applications [19,26].
2. Variety: It denotes the types and sources of data [25]. The information is presented in different ways including structured, semi-structured, and unstructured data [27]. This is a challenge because most of the data came from different sources such as medical notes, images, and sensors [26].
3. Velocity: It is the speed of creating, updating, and processing the data [25]. In many medical areas, such as public health, it is important for researchers and medical staff to have time-saving tools to improve patient's care.

E-care will retrieve the information from structured and unstructured data (sensors and notes from patients and medical staff). Also, the volume will increase exponentially with the integration of real-time data. The system will migrate to a big data platform that supports batch and streaming processes.

12.4   Hadoop ecosystem

Apache Hadoop [28] is an open-source software for reliable, scalable, and distributed computing. It has emerged as the predominant platform for big data and many companies have adopted it: Google, Facebook, IBM, Adobe, EBay, Hulu, LinkedIn, and The New York Times. It is a big data system which includes structured, semi-structured, and unstructured data that allows less storage and processing algorithms [29]. It is ideal for data management of sensors, videos and images, medical records, and geolocation information.

There are multiple advantages of the Hadoop ecosystem; some of them are cost-effective management, massive scalable platform, failure recovery, efficient use of resources, and the fact that it is designed with the assumption that hardware will fail. Hadoop framework is mostly written in Java language and has native C applications. There are four basic components of Hadoop framework [28]:

*   **Hadoop Common:** Common libraries and utilities to support other Hadoop modules.

- **Hadoop Distributed File System (HDFS):** A distributed file system that provides high-throughput access to its application. It is the Hadoop core and supports the framework, storing large files across multiple machines.
- **Hadoop Yet Another Resource Negotiator (YARN):** A framework responsible for computer resource management and job scheduling. It was introduced as a Hadoop 2.0 and born from the need to enable other interaction patterns for data stored in HDFS beyond MapReduce framework.
- **Hadoop MapReduce:** YARN-based system for parallel processing of large data sets that escalates data across different processes.

Hadoop ecosystem arrives as the best solution for big data information processing. Hadoop has different systems to cover different needs. An advantage of a program that will migrate, such as E-care, is that it can analyze the big data architecture and the advantages of Hadoop tools in order to choose the ones that meet their needs and improve their architecture.

There are different tools that are on the top of the Hadoop framework [30]. In their ecosystem, they have a variety of vendor architectures that influence the performance of the systems. All applications evolved to meet the needs of companies (e.g. Google and Facebook). They had to process and collect all their newly generated information. A brief description of the most important tools, namely MapReduce and Spark, will be presented in the following sections.

12.4.1 MapReduce

Apache MapReduce [31] framework is developed by Google. It was designed to process large data sets. It enables computation through two simple functions: Map and Reduce. The operation can be with a parallel and distributed algorithm on a cluster.

The idea is that the job splits data into chunks across all the computer nodes. When the map tasks are over, the framework sorts the output, and the reduced tasks will use the map sorting data as input and perform reduction operations, giving the output of the program.

An example is having a big amount of data that is growing and you will need many hard drives. Probably all the information came from different parts of the Internet and spread out among the hard drives. You need to process the data, but you do not want to spend time and effort making links between them with the imminent probability of ending up with chaotic results. If you need a simple process, then it would be optimal to have a system with a framework like MapReduce that helps organize the spread of data and generate an output.

12.4.2 Spark

Apache Spark [32] was originally developed in the AMPLab at UC Berkeley. Spark emerged as the replacement of MapReduce and solves similar problems. It runs programs 100 times faster than MapReduce in memory and 10 times faster on disk. Spark differs from MapReduce in the implementation of multiple Resilient Distributed Dataset (RDD), a collection of data blocks across a cluster, which makes it fast not only for task computations, but also for store cache. The framework sorts the output, and the reduced tasks will use the map sorting data as input [33]. If necessary, Spark can run without YARN and could run directly on HDFS. It can be integrated with Hadoop and other tools like Shark, Spark Streaming, Cassandra, and HBase.

Spark is a flexible engine for large-scale processing. Most of the functions and workloads are easy to handle. It can manage cyclic data flows, which makes it more efficient in cases like processing machine learning and stream algorithms. Another good thing about Spark is that it can be accessed from Java, Python, Scala, and R. It has important extensions like its exiting libraries that can handle machine learning, streaming applications, Structured Query Language (SQL) applications, graphics, and batch applications.

12.4.3   Other tools

The other tools on top of the Hadoop framework are the following:

- Apache HBase [34] is inspired by Google BigTable. It is a non-relational distributed database and the key component of the Hadoop stack. It can handle massive data tables in real time. HBase goal is to host massive tables with billions of rows and billions of columns. It has the capacity of backing up MapReduce jobs with HBase tables. HBase has a linear and modular scalability, a database shard and an automatic failover support.
- Apache Pig [35] provides an engine to execute data flows in parallel on Hadoop. It is a platform that analyzes a large data set and comprises a series of high-level data operations for MapReduce. Pig includes a language called Pig Latin to express data flows, which has the properties of being easy to program. Pig optimizes its execution automatically and users can create their own functions to do special processing.
- Apache Hive [36] is data warehouse software that facilitates the query and management of large data sets that reside in the storage of distributed files. Its EDW infrastructure was developed by Facebook and employs MapReduce framework. A programmer familiar with SQL language can prefer operations with Hive even if the data are not stored in a traditional RD. It provides an SQL language called HiveQL.
- Apache Storm [37] is a complex event processor and a distributed computation framework. It is distributed in real time for fast processing. Storm consists of a master and working nodes, with the coordination by Zookeeper. It is simple and fast and can be used with any programming language, but it is mostly written in the Clojure programming language. Storm does for stream data what Hadoop MapReduce did for batch processing.
- Apache Flink [38] is a powerful framework for Java and Scala programming and has a high runtime performance. It is listed as a data processing system among MapReduce and Spark. Flink is an alternative of MapReduce and can work separately from the Hadoop ecosystem because it is not built on MapReduce. It can also access HDFS and YARN. Flink has a distributed stream processing that is fault-tolerant and scalable and performs at large scale.

12.5 Computational techniques

The increase in the analysis of medical information has been a relevant issue in recent decades. If the medical staff want to have a good management of the information and improve the health systems, they should look for the adequate tools to make this happen. This section addresses different studies focused on talking about the different techniques of machine learning in the field of health and examples using Apache Spark.

12.5.1 Machine learning techniques in medical field

Machine learning offers many tools that help in the decision process, improves the quality of life of patients, and optimizes costs. Studies that use their tools are present in many areas such as genomics, imaging, preventive medicine, cardiovascular diseases, diabetes, and chronic and epidemiological diseases.

In a recent investigation [39], the authors reviewed the state of the art of different computational intelligence (CI) techniques used for analyze the accuracy, sensitivity, and specificity of single and hybrid (two or more methods) machine learning techniques. For both, they conclude that Support Vector Machine (SVM) is the algorithm with the best results in medical studies. In the case of the hybrid method, it is determined that SVM together with the techniques of artificial immune recognition system (AIRS), genetic algorithm (GA), artificial immune system (AIS), fuzzy logic (FSVM), and extreme learning machine (ELM) has the best results, highlighting the SVM–AIRS method as the remarkable of all. They also conclude that hybrid methods provide better results than the single methods. Analyzing the accuracy, sensitivity, and specificity, the following results were obtained: the most accurate hybrid methods were SVM–AIRS, SVM–GA, AIS–SVM, and FSVM; the most sensitivity hybrid methods were SVM–AIRS, GA and particle swarm optimization (GA-MLP), FSVM, AIS and GA (AIS–GA), and SVM–ELM; and the most specificity hybrid methods were SVM–AIRS, fuzzy logic and GA (FGA), FSVM, AIS-GA, GA-MLP, and wavelet packet transform and ELM (WPT–ELM). Nithya [40] also explores the literature to understand the different processes of machine learning, highlighting the techniques of decision tree, Bayesian methods, artificial neural network, instance-based learning, clustering methods, and regression algorithms. Furthermore, the author mentions the models applied to different areas of health such as cardiovascular diseases, hepatitis disease, and cancer.

In another study [41], the authors used a data set of patients at Boston hospital to predict the rehospitalizations caused by heart diseases. The goal is to avoid a hospitalization before this happens. They check the accuracy with two indicators: the false alarm rate (the false positives) and the detection rate (the true positives). For this, matrix of correlation coefficients is used. They apply five supervised machine learning techniques SVM, AdaBoost using decision tree, logistic regression and naïve Bayes and a similar technique of K-likelihood ratio test. The comparison puts AdaBoost as the method with the best performance and Naïve Bayes with the worst in the experiment. The resulting precision was of 82%. Also, the K-likelihood ratio test helps to know the important characteristics for the doctor's visit.

The present study [42] applies the deep learning model to improve the decision-making process, considering the clinical features of the patients. They use two data sets: the first was the personal records and disease history from an electronic medical record (EMR), and the second data set was retrieved from a hospital information system and was focused on hypertension. For the analysis of unsupervised learning, they employ a version of deep belief network (DBN) and then use the parameters to perform the supervised analysis, using a model with DBN and support vector machines (SVM), a standard SVM, and a decision tree model. The best predictions were with the DBN and SVM model; the author considers that this result is due to the fact that in this model, key features of the problems were used.

Other problems that are solved through machine learning are the detection of diseases centered in the epidemic field, such as influenza, dengue, and hepatitis B, among others. This is explored in this study [43], where the machine learning approach is to predict the outbreak forecasting process, peak time, maximum height, activities per day, and duration of the outbreak and to review the most commonly used techniques, e.g. SVM for text processing, firefly algorithm for optimization, autoregressive moving average, and linear or nonlinear regressions, concluding that the best technique to predict outbreak forecasting is the SVM. Epidemiological problems should be treated as quickly and efficiently as possible, in order to help decision-making.

12.5.2   *Spark with machine learning techniques in medical field*

The use of machine learning in Spark has become popular in the different studies; this is due to the speed of processing that Spark has with the use of RDDs and its capacity for parallelism. Spark has been replacing both traditional systems and Hadoop in the medical area. Its development and integration are considered as a challenge due to the high complexity of biomedical data. That is why the present studies show the way in which Spark's architecture and its models of information analysis have overcome these challenges, becoming the most viable option for its purposes.

In [44], authors used real information of cell phones and sensors to predict the probability of miscarriages using an unsupervised machine learning algorithm called K-means for clustering with Apache Spark Databricks. To create the model, they used a data set that contains 10,000 documents that had factors such as age, body mass index (BMI), the number of previous miscarriages, activity, location, weight, and height. As a result, the authors not only consider that they had a low error rate, but also the time it took to process the information was efficient.

In another research [45], the authors modify the Chemogenomics pipeline of a pharmaceutical that develops drugs to find the molecules of certain proteins, trying to change from a single node to a multiple parallel node with Spark. They use machine learning techniques for making the predictions and discover drugs. They made the comparison with the original pipeline and found that Spark is 8 times faster using 8 nodes and 13 times faster using 16 nodes. They concluded that Spark solved their problem, saving time and network bandwidth and making better predictions for the searching of proteins. This is another study [46] that improved their system taking advantage of Spark's parallelization. They present a monitoring platform for elderly people using Spark to cluster information with the SVM algorithm and process it in real time via Spark Streaming. The authors used the data set of University of California Irvine (UCI) machine learning repository [47] to make a clustering and classification test. For this, they used 2, 4, and 12 cores with the method of K-means clustering analysis. Regardless of the number of cores, Spark always got better results than Hadoop. This will help to make the analysis of the information and the feedback faster.

In another recent investigation [48], the authors propose a mechanism to find the relationship between symptoms and diseases in a more efficient way with the algorithm Faster-interactive and adaptive partitioned incremental (IAPI) that runs in Spark RDD. The data they used to test the model were taken from the UCI machine learning repository and considered the factors of age, sex, chest pain type, resting blood pressure, cholesterol, fasting blood sugar, and resting electrocardiographic results.

This work [49] develops a system that predicts the health status of a person considering attributes in previous tweets. They process the information with a machine learning model and Apache Spark streaming, sending back the results to the user. The information is retrieved from the Heart Disease Data Set of University of California Irvine (UCI) machine learning repository and processed with a decision tree algorithm on real time. Once the prediction has been completed, the user receives a direct message that says "Your health status is OK" or "You are requested to consult a Cardiologist immediately."

Another important use of Spark with machine learning is the improvement of medical ontologies, which is one of the topics addressed by E-care. For example, the techniques by Chen *et al.* [50] propose a Disease Diagnosis and Treatment Recommendation System (DDTRS) to be more accurate in the identification of a disease using a Density-Peaked Clustering Analysis (DPCA). They benefit from Spark's parallelism and data mining techniques using the Apriori algorithm. With this information, the authors construct a medical domain ontology with the association rules for diagnosis and treatment; this is for the knowledge of patients and new doctors. For the experimental part, they are taken into account the accuracy, recommendation quality, and performance of the DDTRS. Then they compare classification algorithms (C4.5 and Random Forest) with clustering algorithm (K-means). For diseases with a few treatment stages, such as influenza and diabetes mellitus, the classification algorithms has higher accuracy than the clustering ones. On the contrary, for diseases with more treatment stages or symptoms, the clustering algorithm has a higher accuracy compared to the classification algorithm.

12.6   Benchmarking

Benchmarking is a tool that seeks to improve competitiveness by comparing the best in the industry and how they do it. Michael Spendolini [51] points out one of the first definitions of benchmarking: "A continuous, systematic process for evaluating the products, services, and work processes of organizations that are recognized as representing best practices for the purpose of organization improvement" (p. 9).

Benchmarking began as a business technique in Xerox [51] as a consequence of a bad run that the company was going through. Xerox had the best machines in the field compared to its competitors; Xerox stopped innovating its products and had bankruptcy threats from the Japanese market that offered more attractive machines. Despite the resistance of the people who could not understand how someone else could do it better than them, Xerox instituted the benchmarking process. When the process started, the company benchmarked each function and task in terms of productivity, cost, time, and quality.

Like Xerox, other companies adopted benchmarking for evaluation. There was no any real standard, and those created were of dubious credibility. The creation of TPC (Transaction Processing Performance Council) came as a solution to this problem in the computing field.

The TPC is a leading benchmarking nonprofit corporation [52]. Two of its major activities are (1) creating good benchmarks (2) and creating a good process for the evaluation of the benchmarks. TPC was created to answer the question: "Who was the best in the competition among computer vendors?" [53].

Even if TPC has been evolving slowly and presents new benchmarks and workloads [54], it recently reinvented itself and introduced a benchmark that standardizes big data systems.

In July 2014, an express benchmark called TPCx-HS was developed. The first TPC standard was designed to benchmark the Hadoop ecosystem [55]. TPCx-HS Version 2 for Apache Spark and Hadoop was announced in May 2017, bringing TPC on the cloud [56].

TPCx-HS provides verifiable measurements of performance, price, availability, and energy consumption. It is also used to stress the Hadoop cluster [57].

TPCx-HS measurements include the following:

- Hadoop runtime
- Hadoop File system
- API compatible systems
- MapReduce layers.

TPCx-HS processing reduces the cost of TPC participation and makes it approachable to more practitioners, including academics, consumers, analysts, and computer manufactures [54].

12.6.1   Benchmarking and big data

Benchmarking is the foundation of any computer system research that provides a real quantitative evaluation [23]. Benchmarks are the most important tools for assessing the performance of the system, and it is vital for them to have transparency and to be able to replicate the evidence [54]. They are designed to predict the performance of systems and reveal their weaknesses and strengths [51]. The accuracy of these predictions is what determines the quality of the benchmarking [58].

Benchmarking is designed for a particular type of systems. It is important to decide the kind of benchmark that will be better for the system. Many benchmarks only evaluate system performance, architecture, and application protocols [58]. The evaluation is difficult, since there is not a single benchmark that can have all the requirements and satisfy all the system's standards [27]; even TPC standards cannot fulfill everything. In addition, it is used to compare the performance of different systems with different architectures.

Now, with the new big data applications, platforms have become more complex, diverse, and difficult to analyze. Big data is constantly changing. It is still considered a new technology not very well understood compared to traditional systems [22]. One of the problems is that currently, the characteristics of big data applications are not completely defined [60].

Without clear standards and characteristics of big data, benchmarking is relevant for the understanding of a platform. It is also used to evaluate the fault tolerance of a big data system [22]. Benchmarking is developed to meet different needs; some are for specific algorithms and others for multiple platforms, where they can stress the system with microbenchmarks or with multiple types of loads.

12.6.2   Types of benchmarking

A classification of benchmarks can be microbenchmarks, macrobenchmarks, program kernels, and application benchmarks programs [58]:

- **Microbenchmarks**
  They measure a specific part of the computer system: CPU speed, memory speed, I/O speed, and network. In general, they are used to characterize the maximum performance that the system could obtain if it was limited by a single component. They tend to be a kernel.
- **Macrobenchmarks**
  They measure the performance of the complete system. These benchmarks do not show if the system performs in a right or wrong way.
- **Program kernel**
  It measures a small program usually extracted from the actual program. It is used to characterize the main part of a specific type of program. Program kernel makes an accurate comparison and prediction of the performance.
- **Application programs**
  They measure a specific application. They are normally described in terms of the functions to be performed and use almost all the resources of the program. These benchmarks are real and complete and give significant results.

A Benchmark can be a real program with a real performance or a synthetic program designed to evaluate specific functions and conditions. In the case of big data benchmark programs, benchmarks use specific workloads for an application [25] that provide an input to the real system under the study used [58]. Workloads are important benchmarking operations that allow some optimal behavior evaluations, leading to competent and cost-effective architectures [58]. They need to be representative, diverse, and focused on a core operation [61] and specific to match the system requirements [17]. Workloads can be real-world data based or synthetics.

Both alternatives work; the choice depends on whether you can get real information (concerning confidentiality issues) and whether its truthfulness is vital to the results, or if synthetic results can emulate real-world scenarios and the results will not be affected.

12.7   Benchmarks in Hadoop and Spark

There are many efforts in the area of big data benchmarking such as PigMix [62], GridMix [63], Big Data Generator Suite (BDGS) [64], BigBench [65], BigDataBench [66], BigFrame [67], HiBench [68], Hive [36], SparkBench [69], and SWIM [70]. These benchmarks are shown with their characteristics or workloads.

12.7.1   Amp Lab Benchmark

The AMPLab [71] at UC Berkeley provides quantitative and qualitative comparisons of five systems: Redshift [72] of Amazon, Hive [36] of Hadoop, Shark [73] (now included in Spark SQL), Impala [74], and Tez [75] of Hadoop too. The SQL workloads that use AMPLab are Scan, Aggregation, Join, and External Script.

12.7.2   BigBench

BigBench [65] is a recent effort to design a benchmark that has elements of existing ones, such as TPC-xHS, GridMix, PigMix, and HiBench. The BigBench has two key components: data and workload specifications. The structured part is adopted from the TPC-DS [76]. Information from stores and web sales distribution channels are used by BigBench.

12.7.3   BigDataBench

BigDataBench [66] is an open-source software under the Apache version 2.0. The current version, BigDataBench 3.2, models five application domains, and includes 14 real-world data sets and 33 big data workloads. Table 12.1 shows the summary of the implemented workloads in BigDataBench 3.2.

Big data systems include Hadoop, Spark, Flink, Hive, and Impala and cover offline batch processing, machine learning, and query processing [77].

12.7.4   BigFrame

BigFrame [67] is a benchmark generator for big data and relies on Hadoop to do parallel data generation. Unlike microbenchmarks or very specific benchmarks, BigFrame generates a specific set of data and workloads. It has two different types of workloads: offline analytics and real-time analytics. The latest version implemented is Business Intelligence which provides relational data, nested text data, and graph data [78].

Table 12.1   Summary of the workloads implemented in BigDataBench 3.2

Applications	Workloads or algorithm	Types
Search Engine	Grep	Offline analytics, streaming
	WordCount	Offline analytics
	Index	Offline analytics
	PageRank	Offline analytics
	Nutch Server	Offline analytics
	Search	Streaming
	Sort	Offline analytics
	Read	Cloud online transaction processing (OLTP)
	Scan	Cloud OLTP
Social Networks	Rolling Top Words	Streaming
	Connected Components (CC)	Graph
	K-means	Streaming, offline analytics
	Label Propagation	Graph
	Triangle Count	Graph
	BFS	Graph
E-commerce	Select Query	EDW
	Aggregation	EDW
	Join Query	EDW
	Collaborative Filtering (CF)	Streaming, offline analytics
	Bayes	Offline analytics
	Project	EDW
	Filter	EDW
	Cross Product	EDW
	Order By	EDW
	Union	EDW
	Difference	EDW
Multimedia Analytics	BasicMPEG	Offline analytics
	Scale-invariant feature transform (SIFT)	Offline analytics
	DBN	Offline analytics
	Speech Recognition	Offline analytics
	Ray Tracing	Offline analytics
	Image Segmentation	Offline analytics
	Face Detection	Offline analytics
Bioinformatics	Scalable Assembly at Notre Dame (SAND)	Offline analytics
	Basic local alignment search tool (BLAST)	Offline analytics

12.7.5   GridMix

GridMix [63] is a benchmark for Hadoop clusters that consists of a combination of synthetic jobs reading in bytes. It evaluates MapReduce and HDFS performance and not the projects on top of them. The benchmark emulates different users of the same cluster and submits different types of job, identifies bottlenecks, and stresses the framework at scale. The following characteristics of job load can be captured in job traces and reproduced in GridMix:

- File system properties: It does not have block sizes matching, namespace hierarchies, or any properties of input. This means that some heavy parts of the system, such as processing and streaming, cannot be tested with the current implementation.
- I/O rates: The rate at which the records are consumed is limited by the speed of the reader/writer.
- Memory profile: The data on the memory usage of the task is not available.
- Job failure: It is assumed that the user code is correct.
- Job Independence: The output of a job does not affect the next one.

12.7.6 HiBench

HiBench [68] is a big data benchmark suit for different big data frameworks (speed, throughput, and resource utilization) and applications (Hadoop MapReduce, Hive, Spark, Storm, and Flink). The versions that HiBench supported are the following:

- Hadoop: Apache Hadoop 2.x, CDH5, Hortonworks Data Platform (HDP)
- Spark: Spark 1.6.x, Spark 2.0.x
- Flink: 1.0.3
- Storm: 1.0.1
- Gearpump: 0.8.1
- Kafka: 0.8.2.2.

Table 12.2 summarizes the six categories and the 19 workloads of HiBench. The benchmark consists of microbenchmarks and real-world applications. These include the following:

- **Microbenchmarks**
  - Sort, WordCount, and Terasort are popular programs representative of MapReduce. Sort and WordCount are generated using RandomTextWriter and TeraSort is generated by Hadoop TeraGen. Sleep will snooze on each task to test the framework. Enhanced DFSIO performs measures on HDFS using MapReduce. This benchmark does not have a Spark implementation. DFSIO processes the average I/O rate of each map task and throughput each map task.
- **Machine learning**
  - Machine learning is another important use of MapReduce. The Bayesian Classification and K-means Clustering are contained in Mahout/Spark-MLLib. Both workloads are part of a classification algorithm for data mining and knowledge discovery. The Bayesian Classification generates documents through Zipfian distribution and K-means through GenKMeansDataset. The inputs of K-means are samples represented by a numerical d-dimensional vector.

*Table 12.2   Summary of the workloads
             implemented in HiBench*

Category	Workloads
Microbenchmarks	Sort WordCount Terasort Sleep Enhanced DFSIO
Machine learning	Bayesian Classification K-means Logistic Regression Alternating Least Squares
SQL	Scan, Join, Aggregate
Websearch benchmarks	PageRank Nutch
Graph benchmark	NWeight
Streaming benchmarks	Identity Repartition Stateful WordCount Fixwindows

- – Logistical Regression and Alternating Least Squares are implemented in Spark-MLLib. The input data by Logistic Regression are generated by LabeledPointDataGenerator and contain three types of data, including categorical data, continuous data, and binary data. The Alternating Least Squares workload is generated by RatingDataGenerator.
- **SQL**
  - – Contains Hive queries performing online analytical processing (OLAP) queries. Its input is generated by Zipfian.
- **Websearch Benchmarks**
  - – PageRank is an algorithm implemented in Spark-MLLib/Hadoop. The data source is also generated from Zipfian distribution. The workload consists of a series of Hadoop jobs and is used in web search engines like Google. The Nutch indexing is a subsystem of Nutch [64], an open-source search engine of Apache. Workloads use automatically generated web data whose hyperlinks and words follow the Zipfian distribution.
- **Graph Benchmark**
  - – NWeight is an iterative graph-parallel algorithm implemented by Spark GraphX. The algorithm computes associations between two vertices that are *n*-hop away.
- **Streaming Benchmarks**
  - – Workloads arrive through Kafka [79]. It is a distributed streaming system of Apache. Identity reads input data from Kafka and writes back the result.

Table 12.3   Summary of the workloads implemented in SparkBench

Category	Workload
Machine learning workloads	Logistic Regression SVM Matrix Factorization
Graph computation workloads	PageRank SVD++ Triangle Count
SQL workloads	Hive RDD Relation
Streaming workloads	Twitter Tag Page View
Other workloads unclassified	K-Means LinearRegression DecisionTree ShortestPaths LabelPropagation ConnectedComponent StronglyConnectedComponent PregelOperation

Repartition reads input data from Kafka and changes the level of parallelism by creating more or fewer partition tests, testing the efficiency of data shuffle in the streaming frameworks. Stateful WordCount counts the words received from Kafka every few seconds. It is used for testing the performance of the operator and the cost of Checkpoint/Acker in the streaming frameworks. Fixwindow performs a window-based aggregation.

12.7.7   PigMix

PigMix [62] is a set of queries used to test Pig performance. PigMix has a set of 12 queries, and PigMix2 includes another 5 additional queries. Some of the queries test some features, such as data loading, scalability, different joins, groups, and unions.

12.7.8   SparkBench

SparkBench [69] is a benchmarking suit specific for Apache Spark developed by IBM. It has four different types of application with multiple workloads. The complete workloads can stress an entire cluster and identify the system resource bottlenecks. It can analyze the workloads with respect to the CPU memory, disk, and network I/O [33]. Table 12.3 summarizes the category and workloads of SparkBench.

12.7.9 Statistical Workload Injector for MapReduce

Statistical Workload Injector for MapReduce (SWIM) [70] is a framework that can run real-life workloads from MapReduce systems. SWIM uses some synthetic workloads with the characteristics of an original workload. It reproduces a mix of job submission [78]. SWIM includes a repository of workloads from MapReduce, synthetic tools, and replay tools.

The system mentioned in this section is used to stress a complete system or its parts. Some use similar workloads and can test different Hadoop ecosystem tools. In order to be able to mention which system and benchmarking test are appropriate for E-care, Section 12.8 will make system comparisons as found in the reviewed literature.

12.8 Benchmark comparison

There are many benchmark big data systems in the market. Some of them are developed directly in Apache with the purpose of examining their own systems: MapReduce, Hive, Pig, Spark, etc. Others are developed for external companies and are implemented in the Apache systems, namely AMPLab, BigBench, BigDataBench, and TPC.

Each benchmark has its own advantages. In their homepages, they display their competitive features over other alternatives. In the available literature, some systems are described and analyzed. Others try to demonstrate why a particular benchmark is the best option. It must be considered that there is not a correct answer or a benchmarking that covers all the features of all the systems. Every system is different; some need batch information, SQL analytics, graph processing, stream processing, or a combination of those.

For a system like E-care which seeks to migrate from a traditional system to a big data system, the most important thing at the beginning is to find a platform that helps the program to have the best performance and can handle all the information. For the moment, E-care's plan is to use batch and stream processing. The other processing schemes will be taken into account for the future of the application. In addition, E-care needs to have benchmarking options with an extensive set of workloads.

Even if there are studies talking about the benchmarking and workloads systems in Hadoop ecosystem [17,80–83], the most popular and/or complete programs are MapReduce, Spark, and Flink. MapReduce is the most studied in the literature [84,85]. It is the oldest and the native batch processing benchmark of Hadoop. It is also compatible with other Hadoop's frameworks with multiple workloads. Spark, the successor of MapReduce with streaming processing, focuses on the speed of the batch processes in data memory. Flink can also handle stream and batch processes. It is still a young system, and even though it has a lot of advantages, there are not many studies regarding its limitations.

The thesis of Liu [86] makes a comparison using HiBench between the results of the workloads of MapReduce and Spark (PageRank, WordCount, Sort, TeraSort,

K-means, and Naïve Bayes). They put Spark with an outstanding performance on machine learning workloads: K-means and Naïve Bayes [20,87]. Other workloads have also better results than MapReduce. The problem mentioned with Spark in this and other investigations [87] is its restricted memory. If the input size is big and the system does not have a lot of memory, the result is that MapReduce will be faster. MapReduce tends to be fast with the largest data sets; also disk space is not a resource problem, unlike Spark.

An interesting comparison between Spark and Flink is shown in Marcus' paper [88], which is focused on comparing their frameworks. The study uses batch workloads (Word, Count, Grep, and TeraSort) and iterative workloads (K-Means, PageRank, and Connected Components). The identified parameters are the following: task parallelism, network behavior during the shuffle phase, memory, and data serialization. For each run, they measure the time needed to finish the execution (excluding the time to start and stop the cluster).

The results of their experiment were the following:

- For the aggregation component, Flink seems to be more efficient than Spark.
- For complex workflows with multiple filter layers, Spark seems to be more efficient in the control over RDDs than Flink which does not have that implementation yet.
- For the execution of the pipeline (TeraSort), Flink is more efficient in resource usage.
- For iteration performance (K-means), both frameworks have similar resource usage when loading the data point and processing the iterations. Flink has a better execution than Spark by 10%.
- For Graph processing (PageRank and Connected Components), the results depend on the size and nodes used. For larger graphs, Spark has better results, and for smaller graphs, Flink has better results.

The above-presented results are important because there are very few works analyzing the frameworks of Spark and Flink. With their experiments, they conclude that Flink does not accumulate many objects in the memory region unlike Spark. The analysis of the pipelined execution is that, in general, Flink is better than Spark but has issues related to the fault of tolerance. Flink can automatically build optimizations unlike Spark and requires less memory configuration.

Even if MapReduce is the best studied system of all, E-care needs a big data system that has a better design in its architecture for streaming processes. MapReduce is a good and less expensive option for batch systems. For batch and stream systems, Spark and Flink are both good options. Flink seems to have a unique framework but lacks research and more workload tests compared to Spark, which is a more constitutive system. For the E-care platform, it is vital to migrate the program to a well-known system, where its strengths and weaknesses are recognized. Similarly to MapReduce, Spark has compatibility with other Apache systems, and this can help E-care to have a better interconnectivity in the future.

12.9 Proposal

With all the data sets extracted from different sensors and the increase of the IoT in the medical field, the only alternative for E-care is to migrate to a big data system in order to make a real integration of medical information, process the data, and improve the patient's quality of life. The goal of E-care is to make a better decision support system using an existing ontology. The system must be able to help to move from patients' generic information to personalized data in real time, with the intention to have a learning process by looking for similar patterns in each patient. Big data algorithms can handle and process this large, different, and changing information on its system.

For E-care, Apache Spark is the closest option to satisfy its needs. It has a good performance in batch and streaming applications (lambda architecture), and the studies show Spark with an outstanding performance on machine learning. It has a large library for machine learning and iteration performance. Even if Spark has low latency process, its other qualities compensate it. Knowing the characteristics of Spark will help to accomplish the best algorithms for the E-care system at the time of migration and for the data mining analysis that will be needed to improve the ontology. It will benefit the E-care's personal staff making the data easy to use and the system resilient for any error.

HiBench and SparkBench have an interesting and complete set of workloads that can be used for stressing E-care and predict the performance of the system. Both can perform the first benchmarking part, which consists in stressing the system and discovering E-care flaws points and resilience capacity. Machine learning and data mining are the central keys for E-care goals, and both systems have very complete workloads to run in Spark when E-care migrates.

For HiBench, the workloads that will be used are from the category of Microbenchmarks (except for Enhanced DFSIO), Streaming Benchmarks, and Machine Learning. In the case of SparkBench, the workloads that will be used are principally from the Streaming Workloads and Machine Learning Workloads categories. The workloads exhibit different characteristics, stress different system bottlenecks, and enable a comparison for Spark system. They cover CPU, memory, scheduling, and I/O workloads. For streaming data, Spark will be integrated with Kafka, which connects and streams different systems from beginning to end.

The workloads algorithms from machine learning are used for classification, clustering, prediction, and a decision support. Spark system will support group creation considering the patients' characteristics and their future predictions. Some of them are the following:

- **Classification:** E-care already knew, from the previous ontology, the patients' characteristics (antecedents, clinical history, chronic diseases, etc.). In this case, it is easier to place their new patients and learn from previous information. The benchmark techniques used for classification are SVM, The Bayesian Classification, Decision Tree, etc.

- **Clustering:** In this case, even if E-care uses the existing ontology, it will learn new information from patients who can make a new group arrangement. An example of clustering consists of predicting if a patient with certain characteristics will have a heart attack two months later or will develop a sinus arrhythmia without a previous examination. The benchmark techniques used for clustering are K-means and Matrix Factorization.

After the migration to Spark, E-care's first tests will be for stressing the system. This is to check the capacity of handling a bigger amount of information (e.g. new patients with new data entries), different types of data (e.g. tests with different measurements and comments from the patient), and the capacity to stream the data swiftly. The second group of tests will focus on machine learning benchmarks.

12.10 Conclusion

There is limited information available in the literature about the complex process of implementing big data in healthcare systems such as E-care. There is also little evidence related to benchmarking tests to prove the strengths and weaknesses of E-care. These changes aiming at maintaining the medical field in the forefront of progress and big data, especially Hadoop ecosystems, must be given the opportunity to be accomplished. In this way, the patient's quality of life will be improved and the availability of knowledge about medicines will increase.

In the current technological era, it is vital that telemedicine has an orderly, simple and understandable data management. A good distant-monitoring system makes it possible to reach people from remote locations and improves their well-being while generating cost-saving alternatives for the health system. This will also give health staff and researchers the opportunity to analyze patients' data and improve the ontology of chronic diseases mentioned at the beginning of the chapter. E-care believes that the best way to have the information ready for analysis and the architecture that allows it is through big data tools with a constant improvement of benchmarking tests. Benchmark tests are the tools that make a system work in its best capacity, for a remote system in the medical field. This is the key for life improvement for patients with chronic diseases.

References

[1] E-care. *E-care* [online]. Mulhouse: NEWEL Informatique SARL; 2014. Available from http://www.projet-e-care.fr/ [Accessed 11 August 2017].

[2] American Heart Association. *Classes of Heart Failure* [online]. Boston: American Heart Association; 2017. Available from http://www.heart. org/HEARTORG/Conditions/HeartFailure/AboutHeartFailure/Classes-of-He art-Failure_UCM_306328_Article.jsp#.WRwYrXWGObk [Accessed 11 August 2017].

[3] Andrès E., Talha S., Hajjam M., Hajjam J., Ervé S., Hajjam A. "E-care project: A promising E-platform for optimizing management of chronic heart failure

and other chronic diseases." *Heart Res Open J.* 2015; 2(1): 39–45. doi:10. 17140/HROJ-2-107.

[4] Ministère de l'Enseignement supérieur, de la Recherche et de l'Innovation. *Investissements d'avenir* [online]. 2017. Available from http://www. enseignementsup-recherche.gouv.fr/pid24578/investissements-d-avenir.html [Accessed 11 August 2017].

[5] Andrès E., Talha S., Hajjam M., Hajjam J., Ervé S., Hajjam A. "Telemedicine to monitor elderly patients with chronic diseases, with a special focus on patients with chronic heart failure." *Journal of Gerontology & Geriatric Research.* 2016; 5(3): 1–5. doi:10.4172/2167-7182.1000311.

[6] Andrès E., Talha S., Ahmed B.A., *et al.* "Monitoring patients with chronic heart failure using a telemedicine platform: Contribution of the E-care and INCADO projects." *International Archives of Nursing and Health Care.* 2015; 1(2): 1–5.

[7] Ahmed Benyahia A., Moukadem A., Dieterlen A., Hajjam A., Talha S., Andres E. "Adding ontologies based on PCG analysis in E-care project." *International Journal of Engineering and Innovative Technology (IJEIT).* 2013; 3: 1–7.

[8] Ahmed Benyahia A., Hajjam A., Hilaire V., Hajjam M. "E-care: Ontological architecture for telemonitoring and alerts detection." *Proceedings of the 24th International Conference on Tools with Artificial Intelligence*; Athens, Greece, November 2012. IEEE Computer Society; 2012. pp. 13–17.

[9] Akopian D., Chronopoulos, A.T. "A privacy protection for an mHealth messaging system." *Proceedings of SPIE – The International Society for Optical Engineering,* March 2015. 2015.

[10] Zhang K., Yang K., Liang X., Su Z., Shen X., Luo H.H. "Security and privacy for mobile healthcare networks: From a quality of protection perspective." *IEEE Wireless Communications.* 2015; 22(4): 104–12.

[11] Al-Janabi S., Al-Shourbaji I., Shojafar M., Shamshirband S. "Survey of main challenges (security and privacy) in wireless body area networks for healthcare applications." *Egyptian Informatics Journal.* 2017; 18(2): 113–22.

[12] Al Ameen M., Liu J., Kwak K. "Security and privacy issues in wireless sensor networks for healthcare applications." *Journal of Medical Systems.* 2012; 36(1): 93–101.

[13] ASIP Santé (France). PGSSI-S : Politique générale de sécurité des systèmes d'information de santé Authentication of healthcare actors. 2 vols. Paris, 2014.

[14] Health Information Privacy. *Health Information Privacy* [online]. Available from https://www.hhs.gov/sites/default/files/ocr/privacy/hipaa/ understanding/consumers/privacy-security-electronic-records.pdf [Accessed 11 January 2018].

[15] Raghunathan B. *The complete Book of Data Anonymization: From Planning to Implementation*. Boca Raton (Fla.): CRC Press; 2013.

[16] Ivanov T., Zicari R.V., Izberovic S., Tolle K. Goethe Universitat, Big Data Lab. *Performance Evaluation of Virtualized Hadoop Clusters*. Technical report No 2014-1.

[17]   White Paper. "Extract, transform, and load big data with Apache Hadoop." 2010.

[18]   Mukherjee A., Datta J., Jorapur R., Singhvi R., Haloi S., Akram W. "Shared disk big data analytics with Apache Hadoop." *Proceedings of the 19th International Conference.* Pune, India, December 2012. IEEE; 2013. pp. 1–6. doi: 10.1109/HiPC.2012.6507520.

[19]   M. Marjani, Nasaruddin F., Gani A., *et al.* "Big IoT data analytics: Architecture, opportunities, and open research challenges." *Journal of IEEE Access.* 2017; 5: 5247–61.doi: 10.1109/ACCESS.2017.2689040.

[20]   Aydin G., Hallac I.R., Karakus B. "Architecture and implementation of a scalable sensor data storage and analysis system using cloud computing and big data technologies." *Journal of Sensors.* 2015: 11: 1–11. doi:10.1155/2015/834217.

[21]   Rouse M., Martinek L., Stedman C. *Big Data Analytics* [online]. Newton: TechTarget; 2013. Available from http://searchbusinessanalytics. techtarget.com/definition/big-data-analytics [Accessed 11 August 2017].

[22]   Zicari R.V., Rosselli M., Ivanov T., *et al.* "*Big Data Optimization: Recent Developments and Challenges.*" Cham: Springer International Publishing. 2016. pp. 17–47.

[23]   Huang, S., Huang, J., Liu, Y., Dai, J. "HiBench: A representative and comprehensive Hadoop benchmark suite." Intel Asia-Pacific Research and Development Ltd., Shanghai. 2012.

[24]   Gartner. *What is Big Data?* [online]. Available from https://www.gartner.com/ it-glossary/big-data [Accessed 11 August 2017].

[25]   Han R., Lu X., Xu J. "Big data benchmarks, performance optimization, and emerging hardware." Salt Lake City, UT: Springer International Publishing; 2014. On Big Data Benchmarking. pp. 3–18.

[26]   Luo J., Wu M., Gopukumar D., Zhao Y. "Big data application in biomedical research and health care: A literature review." *Biomedical Informatics Insights.* 2015; 2016(8) 1–10. doi: 10.4137/BIII.S31559.

[27]   Rabl T., Ghazal A., Hu M., *et al.* "BigBench specification V0. 1." *In Specifying Big Data Benchmarks.* 2014. Berlin, Heidelberg: Springer; 2014. pp. 164–201.

[28]   Apache Hadoop. *Welcome to Apache Hadoop* [online]. Apache Software Foundation; 2017. Available from http://hadoop.apache.org/ [Accessed 11 August 2017].

[29]   McKnight W., Dolezal J. "Hadoop integration benchmark." *MCG Global Services.* 2015.

[30]   GitHub. *The Hadoop Ecosystem Table* [online]. San Francisco: GitHubInc. Available from https://hadoopecosystemtable.github.io/ [Accessed 11 August 2017].

[31]   Apache Hadoop. *MapReduce Tutorial* [online]. Apache Software Foundation; 2017. Available from https://hadoop.apache.org/docs/r2.8.0/hadoop-mapreduce-client/hadoop-mapreduce-client-core/MapReduceTutorial.html [Accessed 11 August 2017].

[32] Apache Spark. *Apache Spark* [online]. Apache Software Foundation; 2017. Available from https://spark.apache.org/ [Accessed 11 August 2017].

[33] Li M., Tan J., Wang Y., Zhang L., Salapura V. "SparkBench: A spark benchmarking suite characterizing large-scale in-memory data analytics." *Cluster Computing*. 2017; 20(3): 2575–2589.

[34] Apache HBase. *Welcome to Apache HBase* [online]. Apache Software Foundation; 2017. Available from https://hbase.apache.org/ [Accessed 11 August 2017].

[35] Apache Hadoop. *Welcome to Apache Pig!* [online]. Apache Software Foundation; 2017. Available from https://pig.apache.org/ [Accessed 11 August 2017].

[36] Hive. *Apache Hive TM* [online]. Apache Software Foundation; 2014. Available from https://hive.apache.org/ [Accessed 11 August 2017].

[37] Apache Storm. *Why Use Storm* [online]. 2017. Storm. Available from https://storm.apache.org/ [Accessed 11 August 2017].

[38] Apache Flink. *Flink* [online]. Apache Software Foundation; 2017. Available from http://flink.apache.org/ [Accessed 11 August 2017].

[39] Kalantari A., Kamsin A., Shamshirband S., Gani A., Alinejad-Rokny H., Chronopoulos A.T. "Computational intelligence approaches for classification of medical data: State-of-the-art, future challenges and research directions." *Neurocomputing*. 2018; 276: 2–22.

[40] Nithya B., Ilango V. "Predictive analytics in health care using machine learning tools and techniques." *2017 International Conference on Intelligent Computing and Control Systems (ICICCS)*. 2017.

[41] Dai W., Brisimi T.S., Adams W.G., Mela T., Saligrama V., Paschalidis I.C. "Prediction of hospitalization due to heart diseases by supervised learning methods." *International Journal of Medical Informatics*. 2015; 84(3): 189–97.

[42] Liang Z., Zhang G., Huang J.X., Hu Q.V. "Deep learning for healthcare decision making with EMRs." *2014 IEEE International Conference on Bioinformatics and Biomedicine (BIBM)*. 2014.

[43] Boonchieng E., Duangchaemkarn K. "Digital disease detection: Application of machine learning in community health informatics." *2016 13th International Joint Conference on Computer Science and Software Engineering (JCSSE)*. 2016.

[44] Asri H., Mousannif H., Moatassime H.A. "Real-time miscarriage prediction with SPARK." *Procedia Computer Science*. 2017; 113: 423–8.

[45] Harnie D., Vapirev A.E., Wegner J.K., *et al*. "Scaling machine learning for target prediction in drug discovery using Apache Spark." *2015 15th IEEE/ACM International Symposium on Cluster, Cloud and Grid Computing*. 2015.

[46] Dong M., Huang X., Bi S., *et al*. "The elderly health monitoring platform based on Spark." *2015 IEEE International Conference on Cyber Technology in Automation, Control, and Intelligent Systems (CYBER)*. 2015.

[47] Center for Machine Learning and Intelligent Systems. *UCI Machine Learning Repository* [online]. Irvine: Center for Machine Learning and Intelligent Systems; 2017. Available from http://archive.ics.uci.edu/ml/index.php [Accessed 28 January 2018].

[48]   Joy R., Sherly K.K. "Parallel frequent itemset mining with spark RDD framework for disease prediction." *2016 International Conference on Circuit, Power and Computing Technologies (ICCPCT)*. 2016.

[49]   Nair L.R., Shetty S.D., Shetty S.D. "Applying spark based machine learning model on streaming big data for health status prediction." *Computers & Electrical Engineering*. 2018; 65: 393–399.

[50]   Chen J., Li K., Rong H., Bilal K., Yang N., Li K. "A disease diagnosis and treatment recommendation system based on big data mining and cloud computing." *Information Sciences*. 2018; 435: 124–49.

[51]   Spendolini M. *The Benchmarking Book*. New York: Amacom; 1992.

[52]   TPC. *TPC* [online]. 2017. Available from http://www.tpc.org [Accessed 11 August 2017].

[53]   Shanley K. *History and Overview of the TPC* [online]. TPC; 1998. Available from http://www.tpc.org/information/about/history.asp [Accessed 11 August 2017].

[54]   Floratou A., Özcan F., Schiefer B. "Benchmarking SQL-on-Hadoop systems: TPC or not TPC?." *In Workshop on Big Data Benchmarks*; Postdam, Germany, August 2014. Cham: Springer; 2014. pp. 63–72.

[55]   TPC. *TPCx-HS – Version 2* [online]. TPC; 2017. Available from http://www.tpc.org/tpcx-hs/default.asp [Accessed 11 August 2017].

[56]   Business Wire. *Launches TPCx-HS Version 2 – Augmenting Its Arsenal of Big Data Benchmarks – and Introduces Pricing Specification for Cloud Deployments* [online]. San Francisco: Business Wire; 2017. Available from http://www.businesswire.com/news/home/20170522006356/en/Transaction-Processing-Performance-Council-TPC-Launches-TPCx-HS [Accessed 11 August 2017].

[57]   Ivanov T., Izberovic S. "Evaluating Hadoop clusters with TPCx-HS." *arXiv preprint arXiv*:1509.03486. 2015.

[58]   Obaidat M.S., Boudriga N.A. *Fundamentals of Performance Evaluation of Computer and Telecommunication Systems*. Hoboken, NJ: Wiley; 2010.

[59]   Xiong W., Yu Z., Bei Z., et al. "A characterization of big data benchmarks." *Proceedings of Big Data, 2013 IEEE International Conference*; Silicon Valley, USA, October 2013. IEEE; 2013. pp. 118–125.

[60]   Akioka S. "Benchmarking big data applications: A review." *Proceedings of the 8th International Conference on Future Computational Technologies and Applications*; Rome, Italy, March, 2016. Future Computing; 2016. pp. 59–64.

[61]   Quan J., Shi Y., Zhao M., Yang W. "The implications from benchmarking three big data systems." *Proceedings of the IEEE International Conference on Big Data*; Silicon Valley, CA, 2013. IEEE. pp. 31–38. doi: 10.1109/BigData.2013.6691706.

[62]   Apache Pig. *PigMix* [online]. 2013. Available from https://cwiki.apache.org/confluence/display/PIG/PigMix [Accessed 11 August 2017].

[63]   Apache Hadoop. *GridMix* [online]. Apache Software Foundation; 2013. Available from https://hadoop.apache.org/docs/r1.2.1/gridmix.html [Accessed 11 August 2017].

[64] Nutch. *Apache Nutch New* [online]. Apache Software Foundation; 2017. Available from http://nutch.apache.org/ [Accessed 11 August 2017].

[65] Gowda B.D., Ravi N. *BigBench: Toward an Industry-Standard Benchmark for Big Data Analytics* [online]. Cloudera; 2014. Available from https://blog.cloudera.com/blog/2014v/11/bigbench-toward-an-industry-standard-benchmark-for-big-data-analytics/ [Accessed 11 August 2017].

[66] BigDataBench. *BigDataBench* [online]. Available from http://prof.ict.ac.cn/#Benchmarks [Accessed 11 August 2017].

[67] GitHub. *BigFrame* [online]. San Francisco: GitHubInc.; 2014. Available from https://github.com/bigframeteam/BigFrame [Accessed 11 August 2017].

[68] GitHub. *HiBench Suite* [online]. San Francisco: GitHubInc. Available from https://github.com/intel-hadoop/HiBench [Accessed 11 August 2017].

[69] GitHub. *Benchmark Suite for Apache Spark* [online]. San Francisco: GitHubInc.; 2015. Available from https://github.com/SparkTC/spark-bench [Accessed 11 August 2017].

[70] Chen Y., Alspaugh S., Ganapathi A., Griffith R., Katz R. *Statistical Workload Injector for MapReduce (SWIM)* [online]. San Francisco: GitHubInc; 2013. Available from https://github.com/SWIMProjectUCB/SWIM/wiki [Accessed 11 August 2017].

[71] Big Data Benchmark. *Big Data Benchmark* [online]. AmpLab; 2014. Available from https://amplab.cs.berkeley.edu/benchmark/ [Accessed 11 August 2017].

[72] Amazon. *Amazon Redshift* [online]. Amazon; 2017. Available from https://aws.amazon.com/es/redshift/ [Accessed 11 August 2017].

[73] Xin R. *Shark, Spark SQL, Hive on Spark, and the Future of SQL on Apache Spark* [online]. Databricks; 2014. Available from https://databricks.com/blog/2014/07/01/shark-spark-sql-hive-on-spark-and-the-future-of-sql-on-spark.html [Accessed 11 August 2017].

[74] Kornacker M, Erickson K. *Cloudera Impala: Real-Time Queries in Apache Hadoop, For Real* [online]. Cloudera; 2012. Available from http://blog.cloudera.com/blog/2012/10/cloudera-impala-real-time-queries-in-apache-hadoop-for-real/ [Accessed 11 August 2017].

[75] Shanklin C. *Announcing Stinger Phase 3 Technical Preview* [online]. Hortonworks; 2014. Available from https://es.hortonworks.com/blog/announcing-stinger-phase-3-technical-preview/ [Accessed 11 August 2017].

[76] TPC. *TPC-DS* [online]. TPC; 2017. Available from http://www.tpc.org/tpcds/ [Accessed 11 August 2017].

[77] Wang L., Zhan J., Luo C., *et al.* "BigDataBench: A big data benchmark suite from Internet services." *Proceedings of the High Performance Computer Architecture (HPCA), 2014 IEEE 20th International Symposium;* February 2014. IEEE; 2014. pp. 488–499.

[78] Ivanov T., Rabl T., Poess M., *et al.* "Big data benchmark compendium" In *Performance Evaluation and Benchmarking: Traditional to Big Data to Internet of Things.* Kohala, HI: Springer. 2015. pp.135–155. DOI: 10.1007/978-3-319-31409-9_9.

[79]   Apache Kafka. *Apache Kafka* [online]. Kafka. Apache Software Foundation; 2016. Available from https://kafka.apache.org/ [Accessed 11 August 2017].

[80]   Chen Y., Ganapathi A., Griffith R., Katz R. "The case for evaluating MapReduce performance using workload suites." In *Modeling, Analysis & Simulation of Computer and Telecommunication Systems (MASCOTS), 2011 IEEE 19th International Symposium;* Singapore, Republic of Singapore, July 2011.pp. 390–399.

[81]   Pääkkönen P., Pakkala D. "Reference architecture and classification of technologies, products and services for big data systems." *Big Data Research.* 2015; 2(4): 166–86.

[82]   Starostenkov V., Grigorchuk K. "Hadoop Distributions evaluating Cloudera, Hortonworks, and MapR in Micro-benchmarks and real-world applications." *Altoros*; 2013.

[83]   Ouaknine K., Carey M., Kirkpatrick S. "The PigMix benchmark on Pig, MapReduce, and HPCC Systems." *Proceedings of the BigData Congress 2015 IEEE International Congress;* June 2015. IEEE. pp. 643–648.

[84]   Buell J. "A benchmarking case study of virtualized Hadoop performance on VMware vSphere 5." *VMware, Inc.*; 2011.

[85]   Huang S., Huang J., Dai J., Xie T., Huang B. "The HiBench benchmark suite: Characterization of the MapReduce-based data analysis." *Proceedings of the Data Engineering Workshops (ICDEW); 2010 IEEE 26th International Conference;* March 2010. IEEE. pp. 41–51.

[86]   Liu L. "Performance comparison by running benchmarks on Hadoop, Spark, and HAMR" [dissertation]. University of Delaware; 2015.

[87]   Samadi Y., Zbakh M., Tadonki C. "Comparative study between Hadoop and Spark based on HiBench benchmarks." *Proceedings of the Cloud Computing Technologies and Applications (CloudTech), 2016 2nd International Conference*; May 2016. IEEE. pp. 267–275.

[88]   Marcu O.C., Costan A., Antoniu G., Pérez-Hernández M.S. "Spark versus Flink: Understanding performance in big data analytics frameworks." *Proceedings from the Cluster Computing (CLUSTER), 2016 IEEE International Conference;* September 2016. IEEE. pp. 433–442.

[89]   Xiong W., Yu Z., Bei Z., *et al.* "A characterization of big data benchmarks." *Proceedings of Big Data, 2013 IEEE International Conference;* Silicon Valley, USA, October 2013. IEEE; 2013. pp 118–125.

Chapter 13

Extracting and understanding user sentiments for big data analytics in big business brands

Jaiteg Singh[1], Rupali Gill[2], and Gaurav Goyal[2]

Consumer behavior has become the niche of the market for every user from a manufacturer to a customer. People are fairly good at expressing what they want, what they like, or even how much they will pay for an item. But they are not very good at accessing where that value comes from. Behavior is triggered from sentiments generated in response to an external stimulus. Sentiments and emotions are the subjects of study of sentiment analysis and opinion mining, and this field of study coincides with rapid growth of social media on the web, e.g. social networks, blogs and Twitter, and for the first time, we have huge volume (big data) of data in digital form with us to analyze. Developing algorithms for computers to recognize emotional expression is a widely studied area, and the study of big data analytics and neuromarketing techniques acts as the most powerful tool to develop these algorithms for better understanding of consumer preferences, purchase behavior and decision patterns. The research aims to extract/read user behavior/sentiment to predict future preferences and to plan the business branding policies.

The major objective of this chapter is to perform data analytics of the sample data using Hadoop framework based on crucial metrics related to consumer behavior: (1) customer acquisition cost; (2) customer retention cost; (3) lifetime value; (4) customer satisfaction and happiness; and (5) average purchase amount and behavior. The understanding of these metrics helps in extraction of customer buying trends leading to match the specific customer personas, hence meeting business strategies. The chapter provides a study of user sentiment using neuromarketing techniques and providing data analytics on the user-recorded sentiments based on consumer behavior metrics. The chapter provides an understanding of (1) user sentiments, (2) consumer behavior and neuromarketing process and (3) big data analytics.

13.1 Introduction

Markets today are controlled by products and services premeditated for the general consumer. According to business dictionary, consumer markets fall into four main

[1]Department of Computer Applications, Chitkara University Institute of Engineering and Technology, Chitkara University, Punjab, India
[2]Department of Computer Science and Engineering, Chitkara University Institute of Engineering and Technology, Chitkara University, Punjab, India

categories: consumer products, FMCG products, sale and retail products, and shipping products. To make a market successful, brand loyalty has become a major concern for the industries to manage the perspective popularity of products and services. Brand loyalty is directly related to consumer satisfaction. Consumer plays a major role in examining whether the product/service provided by the company matches the consumer expectation. Marketers and big business brand owners are provided with a key metric by the consumers to deal with and develop better business strategies.

Markets today do have already changed from buyer market to seller market. Consumer research plays a major role to dig deeper to dredge more consumer insights for a way to sustain growth and ride higher with competitors. Most appropriate way is to understand consumer behavior. Consumer behavior is based on understanding of other people's behavior, habits, motivation to "do the right thing," self-expectations, and loss-averse need to feel involved and effective to make a change.

13.2   Consumer behavior for understanding consumer sentiments

Consumer behavior is classified as making decisions and actions that influence the purchase behavior of a consumer. The marketers analyze product based on consumer decision which is based on emotions and reasoning. Consumer behavior helps in prediction of past and future purchase decisions and patterns.

Sentiment analysis of consumer behavior is required in making decisions in the following areas:

* Effective packaging
* Advertisement efficiency
* Revealing hidden responses
* Brand promotion
* Prototype testing
* Website layout
* Programming promotions
* Product experience and product development.

Sentiment analysis performs analysis of images and videos based on three techniques:

* Machine learning: It involves data replacing experts and creating models.
* Pattern recognition: It entails splitting images into sections and requires human analysis.
* Deep learning: It uses several layers to identify images using visual maps.

13.3   User sentiments

Sentiment analysis is based on understanding of the feelings, attitude, opinion and emotions expressed through written expression, facial expression and other body gestures.

User sentiments are widely used for gathering public opinion for various products, brands, movies, political reviews, etc. Sentiment analysis widely used to extract insights from user opinions is being adopted by big business organizations across the world.

13.4   What is consumer sentiment?

Consumer sentiment is a measurement based on collected statistics and cost-effective sign of the general economic status as determined by consumer expression and sentiment. Consumer sentiment takes into account an individual's feelings toward his or her own current financial health, the health of the economy in the short term and the prospects for longer-term economic growth.

Sentiment analysis for extraction of the user sentiment is based on user understanding of user facial expression, eye gestures, walking traits and inner senses. Analysis based on visual content is easy to understand and explainable to the user. Visual content through image/video is considered to be the most effective way to express opinions and user experiences. Sentiment analysis of visual content can help in better understanding of user emotions.

13.4.1   Why sentiment analysis is required?

Sentiment analysis of images is required in making decisions in the understanding consumer behavior that is used to predict the decision in case of product pricing and promotion.

The decision is based on ten principles of psychology:

- Leading: Decisions based on preconceived expectations and prejudices of what an experience will be, not what it is.
- Frequency illusion: Do not always consider all elements of an experience, but focus on certain noticeable factors of it.
- Social proof: Influenced by social factors that may or may not be directly related to context question
- Distraction effect: Do not know about the things that influence us; just subconsciously perceive get influenced by eye-catching offers.
- Loss Aversion: Emotional twinges affect "in the moment" of decision-making and hence behavior.
- Scarcity: Prone to be cautious of anything that threatens the well-being and scarcity.
- Anchoring: What is expected from an experience at a deep level. People perceive what they like at the first level
- Grouping factor: The memory of an event is not faultless, but is subject to manipulation.
- Word for word effect: Follow the herd, and get influenced with what people say and bored with the same old.
- Reciprocity: Influenced by the public dealings and gift offers.

13.4.2   Need for neuromarketing based on psychology principles

- Human brain processes the data subconsciously, where there is no conscious awareness.
- Subconscious dispensation is emotional. Emotional means dominion of the unintentional or intentional.
- Subconscious dispensation has significant effect on consumer attitude, behavior and emotions.
- Subconscious dispensation leads to a wide variety of decisions.
- Consumers cannot draw any inference from these decisions at subconscious level. So there becomes a need to understand consumer behavior and apply neurological processes to draw inferences from it.

These neuromarketing lessons lead to the study of consumer behavior.

13.4.3   How sentiment analysis can be correlated to consumer behavior?

Sentiments play a large part in purchase and sale of a brand. Understanding of consumer behavior focuses on cognitive and affective response articulated by the viewers to become conscious of intended viewers responds to business, products and brands. Integrating sentiment marketing with consumer behavior focuses on the human brain's responses on the positivity–negativity values, so as to build up an advertising/marketing approach that takes up the user data from business planning and promotion.

This method makes a multilayered process which requires tasks like extraction and pooling of images/videos, understanding the emotions and applying clustering concepts to images/videos.

Sentiment from a video/image to understand the consumer behavior can be detected following neuromarketing tools.

Sentiment analysis of image/video uses neuromarketing techniques to detect human expressions. The expressions can be classified into two types—positive and negative—which can be listed into seven emotional states as anger, dislike, disgust, sadness, joy, fear and surprise as shown in Figure 13.1.

Sentiment analysis of these emotions for an image/video sample is done through webcam for analyzing the emotional responses toward the stimuli and can be performed best using neuromarketing techniques. Neuromarketing tools are used to uncover hidden structures in the mind. The motivation behind using tools is to determine marketing issues, especially with "four Ps" of marketing—Product, Price, Place and Promotion. Neuromarketing provides substantial insight into marketing science and business strategies by discovering decision-making from a consumer behavior.

13.5   The concept of neuromarketing

The concept of neuromarketing was developed at Harvard University in 1990 by psychologists. A nonprofit "Commercial Alert" organization in US claims that brain scanning exists to conquer the mind for marketable growth. The study of consumer

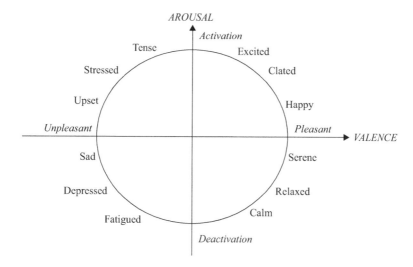

Figure 13.1   Emotion states based on valence and arousal

neuroscience is a most often used concept in modern medical equipment and technologies attempting to provide competence in opposition to conventional set of business methods. The traditional marketing strategy, based on product's inherent properties and tangible features or benefits, is now shifting to branding the product through subconscious brain activities before being bought by the customer. For marketers, it is becoming important to make the product fit into customer's memory, rather than being placed on a shelf.

According to business to consumer (B2C) study [1], 73% of respondents' mobile searches are based on location-based advertising to understand consumer attention.

It's a noteworthy fact that India is the seventh largest nation in size, second most populated country and the seventh largest economy of the world. Neuromarketing may still be talked less in India or not so evidently, globally it is a well-established marketing strategy for many big companies with huge advertising and promotional spends. Arguably, Neuromarketing is becoming a serious research area in application of cognitive science to understand consumer decision-making. The involvement of neuro-scientist varies from user preference over brands and the need of the product. The study is totally based on the understanding the subconscious brain cells to recall and movement of eyes toward a video for an advertisement. Neuromarketing research study can be applied understanding the right mix of product, price, place and promotion by applying neuro-imaging techniques.

Neuromarketing researches are not 100% successful, but they offer great benefit over traditional marketing strategies. Neuromarketing judicially handled through subconscious readings can provide positive and useful impact on understanding and improving hidden market behaviors.

Neuromarketing is market research activity that uses the brain activities to understand and analyze human sentiment to provide insights into marketing activities. (https://www.newneuromarketing.com/what-is-neuromarketing)

13.5.1 Neuromarketing techniques

Neuromarketing techniques can be categorized into five major categories (see Figure 13.2): Neuro-metrics, Facial action coding, Implicit response testing, Eye-tracking and Bio-metrics [2].

Table 13.1 indicates most of the marketing research using functional magnetic resonance imaging (fMRI), electroencephalogram (EEG), facial coding and biometric sensors for understanding basic consumer behavior traits like memory encoding,

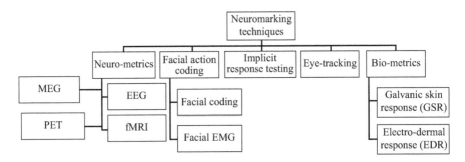

Figure 13.2   Neuromarketing techniques

Table 13.1   Consumer behavior traits measured by neuromarketing techniques [3]

Technique	Memory encoding	Sensory Perception	Valence of emotion	Craving	Trust	Brand loyalty	Brand preference	Brand recall	Attention	Excitement	Engagement/Boredom	Cognition	Recognition	Approach/withdrawal	Visual fixation search	Eye movement patterns	Spatial resolution	Pupil dilution	Non-conscious reactions	Emotion	Social communication	Facial muscles	Action units	Skin conductance
fMRI	Y	Y	Y	Y	Y	Y	Y	Y																
PET		Y	Y																					
EEG			Y						Y	Y	Y	Y	Y	Y										
MEG	Y	Y							Y															
EYE TRACKING									Y	Y					Y	Y	Y	Y						
FACIAL CODING																			Y	Y		Y	Y	
FACIAL EMG			Y							Y										Y				
GSR		Y	Y		Y				Y	Y	Y									Y	Y			Y
EDR			Y						Y	Y	Y									Y	Y			Y

sensory perception, trust, brand loyalty, attention, cognition and emotion detections. The studies also indicated that fMRI and EEG detect most of the basic emotional states but marketing companies nowadays prefer EEG over fMRI to study the consumer behavior due to high equipment cost of fMRI tools. Eye-tracking captures human attention by detection gaze point over various eye positions which are recorded by facial coding or facial EMG using a webcam. The biometric sensors like galvanic skin response (GSR) and electro-dermal response (EDR) detect the loyalty and valence of an emotion. Tables 13.1 and 13.2 indicate the analysis to carry out an effective study that indicates the use of EEG with eye-tracking, facial analyzer and GSR which is preferred these days to understand the consumer behavior.

13.5.2 How it works?

The neuromarketing framework, see Figure 13.3, involves the collection of neuro-metric data so that knowledge base can be driven out of it. The neural response of the volunteers is to be taken with for a given marketing stimulus. For this step, response would be taken by using GSR, eye-tracking, facial expression analyzer and electroencephalogram responses.

- The GSR sensor (Sweating) allows the measurement of the electrical conductance of the skin. It works as an indicator of physio-psychological arousal.

Table 13.2   Parameters tested by neuromarketing techniques [3]

Technique	When to use													
	Testing new products	Testing new campaigns	Testing and developing advertisements	Identifying key movements of an advertisement or video material	Packaging design and prices	Repositioning a brand and predicting choices	Identifying needs	Sensory testing	Celebrity endorsements	Testing website design and usability	Testing in-store experience	Testing tag lines	Testing brand recall	Testing how consumers filters information
fMRI	Y	Y	Y	Y	Y	Y	Y	Y	Y					
PET	Y		Y		Y									
EEG		Y	Y	Y						Y	Y	Y		
MEG														
EYE TRACKING														Y
FACIAL CODING			Y	Y										
FACIAL EMG				Y									Y	Y
GSR								Y						
EDR								Y						

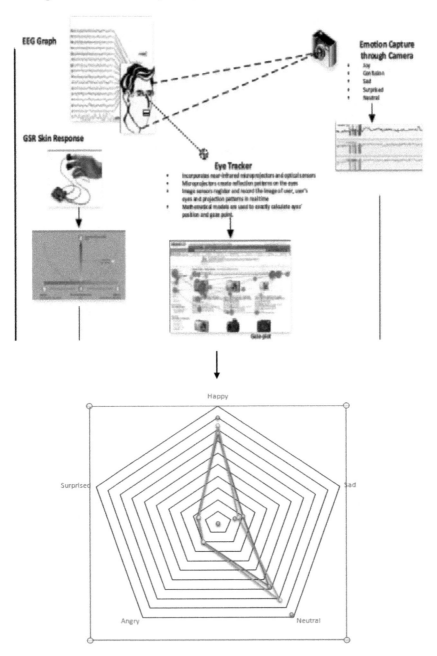

Figure 13.3   Neuromarketing framework

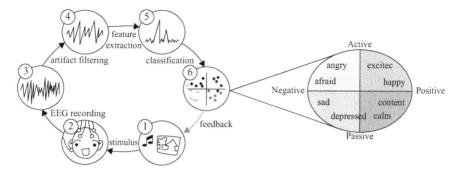

Figure 13.4   Interpretation of EEG signals into classes

- Eye-tracking data can be collected using either a remote or head-mounted "eye-tracker" connected to a computer or it can be hand-coded as well. The most common is to analyze the eye movement of one or more volunteers across an interface such as a computer screen. Each eye data collected through gaze points are converted into pixel coordinates to indicate the eye movement in various screen locations. The detected points from eye are used to analyze the features like attention, pupil dilution and expansion, eye moves, when a particular feature captures attention, how quickly the eye moves, what content is ignored and virtually any other gaze-related question. High accuracy series of facial images (video) would be recorded and fed into a computer for decoding facial expression(s) using a high-resolution webcam.
- EEG-based brain–computer interfaces consist of very typical components, each of which performs its own critical function. Figure 13.4 shows the process cycle to record and interpret EEG data. First a stimulus and test protocol is defined. During testing, the test subject will be exposed to the stimuli according to the test protocol. The resulting voltage changes in the brain are then recorded through an electroencephalogram, from which noise and artifacts are to be removed. The resulting data will be analyzed and relevant features (like power spectra) will be computed. Based on a test set from these features, a classifier will be trained, and the rest of the data will be classified using this classifier. This step provides an interpretation of the original raw brain signals.

The EEG uses receiver operating characteristic (ROC) graph for visualizing, organizing and selecting classifiers based on their performance. The classification is considered by taking only two classes. Formally, each instance I is mapped to one element of the set $\{p,n\}$ of positive and negative class labels. A classification model (or classifier) is a mapping from instances to predicted classes. To distinguish between the actual class and the predicted class, we use the labels $\{Y, N\}$ for the class predictions produced by a model. Given a classifier and an instance, there are four possible outcomes. If the instance is positive and it is classified as positive, it is counted as a true positive; if it is classified as negative, it is counted as a false negative. If the instance is negative and it is classified as negative, it is counted as

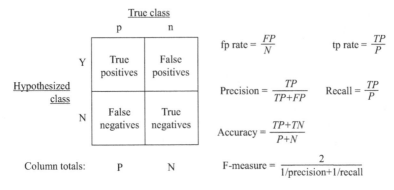

Figure 13.5   Confusion matrix and common performance metrics calculated from it

a true negative; if it is classified as positive, it is counted as a false positive. Given a classifier and a set of instances (the test set), a two-by-two confusion matrix (also called a contingency table) can be constructed representing the dispositions of the set of instances. This matrix forms the basis for many common metrics.

Figure 13.5 shows a confusion matrix and equations of several common metrics that can be calculated from it. The numbers along the major diagonal represent the correct decisions made, and the numbers of this diagonal represent the errors—the confusion—between the various classes. The true positive rate1 (also called hit rate and recall) of a classifier is estimated as follows:

$$tp\ rate \approx \frac{Positives\ correctly\ classified}{Total\ positives}$$

The false positive rate (also called false alarm rate) of the classifier is

$$fp\ rate \approx \frac{Negatives\ incorrectly\ classified}{Total\ negatives}$$

Additional terms associated with ROC curves are the following:

$$sensitivity = recall$$

$$specificity = \frac{True\ negatives}{False\ positives + True\ negatives}$$

$$= 1 - fp\ rate$$

Positive predictive value = precision

Algorithm for multiclass classification of various emotions captured using camera:

1.   Load training data for all emotions (happy, sad, neutral, surprised and angry) that will be used for classification (see Table 13.3).
     * *Training data will be cropped images of dimensions 50 × 30 of eyes and mouth of each emotion for a variety of persons.*

Table 13.3   Size of training data used to detect emotions

Emotion	Cropped object	No. of samples
Happy	Eyes	200
Sad	Eyes	200
Surprised	Eyes	200
Angry	Eyes	200
Neutral	Eyes	200
Happy	Mouth	200
Sad	Mouth	200
Surprised	Mouth	200
Angry	Mouth	200
Neutral	Mouth	200

Training data:
- *Create different csv files containing the names of files for training data for each emotion* (see Figure 13.6).
- *Read each csv file to fetch the names of training data files.*

Code:
with open('smiles2.csv', 'rb') **as** csvfile: → **opens csv file**
    for `rec` **in** csv.reader(csvfile, delimiter='|'):→ **reads each filename into a list "smilefiles"**
        smilefiles += `rec`

```
sadfiles = []
with open('sad.csv', 'rb') as csvfile:
    for rec in csv.reader(csvfile, delimiter='|'):
        sadfiles += rec

surprisefiles = []
with open('surprised.csv', 'rb') as csvfile:
    for rec in csv.reader(csvfile, delimiter='|'):
        surprisefiles += rec

angryfiles = []
with open('angry_mouth.csv', 'rb') as csvfile:
    for rec in csv.reader(csvfile, delimiter='|'):
        angryfiles += rec

neutralfiles = []
with open('neutral2.csv', 'rb') as csvfile:
    for rec in csv.reader(csvfile):
        neutralfiles += rec
```

- Read each training data file and vectorize it, i.e. convert the 2d matrix of 50×30 into oned array of 1 row and 1500 (50×30) columns.

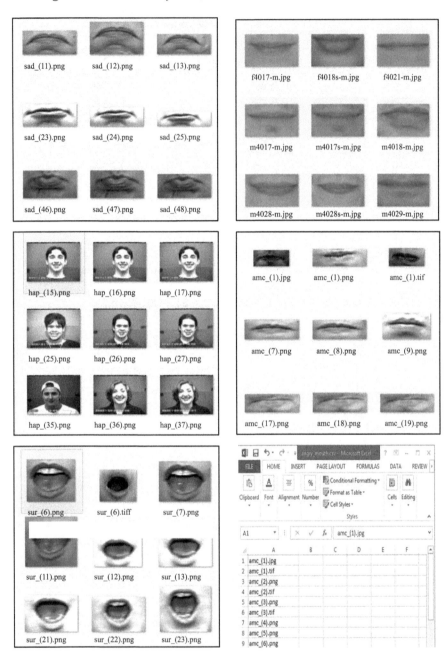

Figure 13.6   Sample training data and created csv file containing names of files within training set

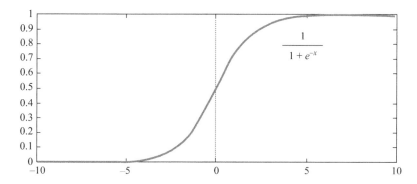

Figure 13.7   Sigmoid of the dot product of the weights

Code:
```
oned_array = im_array.reshape(1, size[0] * size[1])
```
2. Train the training set—Apply logistic regression on the training data to label the data.
    i.   Select random weights using np.random.normal with mean = 0 and standard deviation = 1.
    ii. Update the weights using gradient descent until convergence.
         *   *Calculate hypothesis (y_n), i.e. predict the probability using sigmoid function either 0 or 1 of a training image to be in one of the classes of emotions.*

             Code:
```
y_n = self.evaluate(phi[n],case)
def evaluate(self,phi_n,case):

r=sig (np.dot(self.weights[case], phi_n.T))→Calculate the
sigmoid of the dot product of the weights(assumed slope of
the different features) and feature space (see Figure 13.7).

def sig(x):
return 1.0 / (1.0 + np.exp(-x)) → returns 0 or 1
```
         *   *Compute a gradient of error function, i.e. grad_E = (Hypothesis − Original value) * features.*

             Code:
```
grad_E += (y_n - labels[case][n]) * phi[n]
```
             Update randomly selected weights using gradient descent or error function and a learning rate.

             Code:
```
self.weights[case] = w_prev - (learn_rate * np.array(grad_E))
```
         *   *Stop updating the weights when the absolute difference is less than 0.0001.* This shows that the gradient descent has converged.

Figure 13.8 Captured data image

Mouth: 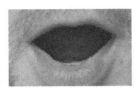 Eyes: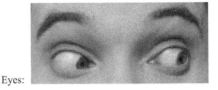

Figure 13.9 Haar cascaded output

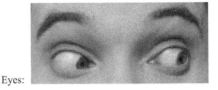

Figure 13.10 Output showing identified emotion

Code:
```
if abs(x) < 0.0001:
    converged = True
```

3. Capture image to be classified using high-resolution camera (see Figure 13.8).
4. Crop eyes and mouth using Haar-cascading (see Figure 13.9).
5. Using One versus All algorithms for multiclass classification, predict the class of the test data (cropped mouth and eye image); see Figure 13.10.

13.6 Big data analytics

Big data is defined in terms of 4 V's—Volume, Velocity, Variety and Variability. Big data is the next context in marketing which leads to big opportunities. In the current digital age, for marketing organizations, to grow big data is the new big opportunity.

Big data analytics is beneficial in solving business dealings and provides important business results. To come up with maximum return on investment from the investment, the new big thing comes up with various challenges as posed by marketing leaders:

- big data analytics roadmap to achieve marketing objectives;
- business outcomes to leverage big data around customers;
- development of services and capabilities to leverage big data for competitive advantage;
- technology preferences to enable big data analytics platform; and
- development of appropriate skills and resources to get onto the big data platform.

13.6.1   Why big data for understanding of consumer behavior?

Bid data $\neq$ Big opportunity $\neq$ Big marketing
Big data does not directly mean bigger opportunity and hence better marketing. But by combining big data with consumer behavior strategies, big business brands can have an insight on three key areas:

- consumer commitment;
- consumer retention and reliability; and
- marketing optimization/performance.

The three keys areas are major focus for understanding consumer behavior. A rewarding cooperation for a better consumer understanding is suggested by applying data mining techniques to neuromarketing data. In the current age, both big data applications and neuromarketing tools mainly focuses on understanding of consumer behavior. Both of emerging fields require collection and analysis of large amounts of data, and extract potentially useful information for supporting management decision-making for better consumer commitment, reliability and retention. Hence, the need of big business brands is to store and receive large amount of data from various sources and apply inventive neuromarketing techniques such as facial coding and implicit action response measures to derive user sentiment for understanding of consumer behavior.

An efficient method of extraction is required to extract large amount of rich, unstructured and dissimilar data from limitless and heterogeneous sources, to detect patterns and derive sentiments from the data. Robust data mining tools, such as machine learning techniques and neural network analytics, are required to practice all the retrieved data and uncover hidden knowledge patterns. That is, to provide better understanding of consumer behavior for effective marketing strategies, the integration of big data and neuromarketing techniques is required. This can be done by applying data mining techniques to big data and recorded sentiments.

The extraction and understanding of user sentiments is three-layered process with big data as the innermost layer, sentiment analysis as the middle layer and neuromarketing techniques as the outer layer as shown in figure [4, 5]:

The model is named as three-layered architecture for neuro-sentiment mining with big data analytics (see Figure 13.11):

- collection of massively large amount of data—big data analytics;

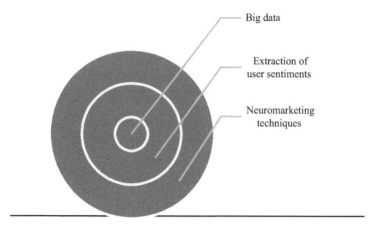

Figure 13.11   Three-layered architecture for neuro-sentiment mining with big data analytics

- collection of user sentiments—sentiment analysis; and
- analysis of user sentiments—neuromarketing techniques.

13.6.2   Big data analytics—next big thing

The "next big thing" providing valuable insights about consumer behavior to the marketers is the combination of "big data" and "neuromarketing." Effective decision-making in the marketing industry requires generation, collection and analysis of data, which the abovementioned technologies can provide by extracting potential useful information. The pace at which data is being generated in today's time has led to the deprecation of structure-based database management systems and has bought big data analytics into the picture. Storing or collection of data is not difficult, but analyzing it for specific patterns is. The managerial implications of big data analytics like affective computing, social media network, smart home and e-Health systems can be used in day-to-day business practices, and to realize the abovementioned managerial implications, an emotion-aware big data framework is the need of the hour.

Understanding consumer behavior is the key requirement of the marketing industry and proceeding with this requirement is a major task. Multiple consumers have multiple perceptions about a single product and it gives rich understanding of product. These perceptions are heavily required for the good understanding of product value. Feedback forms and questionnaires are a thing of the past for analyzing consumer behavior. With the emergence of social media platforms, the consumers are posting their feedbacks on them in textual and non-textual format (videos). The volume and variety of data being generated generates a bottleneck for the marketers. This is the new era of computer and technology which has begun; in old day we used traditional systems to store the data, and then we moved to the computerized databases like dbase, FoxPro, DBMS and RDBMS. But now the data are increasing day by day;

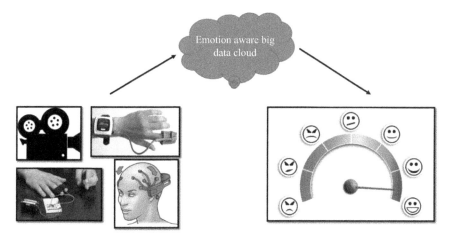

Figure 13.12   Emotion detection with neurotechniques for big data cloud

in 2013 IDC estimated the digital data about 4.5 zettabytes and it is estimated that in 2020 we have around 46 zettabytes of digital data, i.e. around 10 times of 2013 estimated value. There are plenty of sources that can generate huge amount of data every day. Facebook, New York Stock Exchange, Internet Archive stores, Tweeter, Snapchat, etc., are the major sources of digital data.

Not only the volume and variety but to analyze such huge amounts of data for effective understanding of consumer behavior requires the use of specialized hardware such as EEG, GSR and Oximeter. Figure 13.12 shows the various specialized hardware devices under neurometrics techniques that collect a variety of data from potential customers and transfer the same to emotion-aware big data cloud where the data will be filtered and analyzed for specific patterns using predefined business rules. Based on the interpretation, emotions experienced by the consumer will be detected in detail. The challenges regarding users' sentiments or emotions should be taken into consideration in order to create an enhanced mobile user experience.

Consumer behavior can be analyzed by effectively predicting the sentiment of a potential consumer toward a particular product and there is no existing framework that can effectively predict sentiments shown by a human using a big data processing framework and provide instant user feedback to marketers. The answer to the big data problem is Hadoop, which is a new era of databases which is growing rapidly.

13.6.3   HADOOP

Hadoop is an open-source software framework developed by Apache Software Foundation. Hadoop uses clusters to divide the data into smallest units. By using clusters, we can divide the large data sets and provide scalability, reliability and distributed computing. In Apache Hadoop framework, cluster can act as a node and if a node fails at application layer then it provides high availability of the service again (Figure 13.13). Involving Hadoop cluster on more than a single machine is imperative to

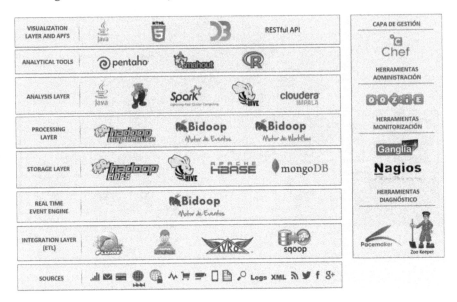

Figure 13.13   Layered architecture of Hadoop

understand what clusters and grids mean, although both can work similar but there is difference in both terms. Hadoop framework can be operated from single server node or from thousands of computers where each computer is responsible for locally processing data and storage. Hadoop takes slightly different approach to store data in parallelism. Parallelism is achieved by a special file system used by Hadoop, i.e. HDFS (Hadoop Distributed File System).

13.6.3.1   What is a cluster?

A cluster is a collection of computers (nodes) that can have an identical hardware configuration and can be connected to each other via LAN (local area network). The result of all the active nodes are collected and then combined to solve problems that require high processing availability of the system with very less computational time. In Hadoop1 by default size of cluster is 64 Mb and in Hadoop2 by default size of cluster is 128 Mb.

Hadoop HDFS can perform five functions that are further divided into two long-run daemons (daemon is a background process):

1.   Master daemon (primary)
2.   Slave daemon (secondary).

Master daemon consists of

1.   NameNode
2.   Standby NameNode
3.   Job Tracker.

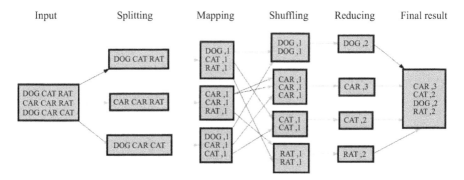

Figure 13.14   Example showing the working of MapReduce

Slave daemon consists of

1. DataNode
2. Task Tracker.

13.6.4   Master/Slave architecture of Hadoop

The primary function of Master daemon is to perform NameNode function, Job Tracker function and Standby NameNode function. Client provides data to NameNode, and it is the responsibility of NameNode to assign task to every single node in a cluster. NameNode takes the data from client and processes the data. If NameNode is a master service then its corresponding slave service is performed by DataNode and if Job Tracker is a master service then its corresponding slave services should be Task Tracker.

13.6.5   What is MapReduce?

MapReduce is a programming model mainly used to implement and process large data sets. MapReduce takes a big task and divides that task into distinct tasks that can be processed on different data nodes in parallel. MapReduce is a combination of map and reduce, map is the first task and reduce is the second; i.e. first map will work and the output of map function is provided to reduce function and then reduce will perform the rest job. The function of map is to process the key/value pair by using two functions shuffle and sort. After shuffling and sorting, all mappers provide the output files to reducer and it is responsibility of reducer to merge the intermediate values to intermediate keys. At the end, single group is created for each unique key (see Figure 13.14).

13.7   Conclusion

This chapter provides the concept of video image-based sentiments extraction using neuromarketing techniques. The chapter introduced the concept of big data analytics which should be merged with neuromarketing techniques for better understanding of user sentiments. In Sections 13.2 and 13.3, we explained the importance of user sentiment and provided the introduction to consumer behavior for understanding of user sentiment. Consumer behavior is the key point for the understanding of user buying and selling behaviors as explained in Section 11.4. The buying and selling behavior can be better understood by applying neuromarketing techniques. Section 13.5 explains neuromarketing framework to extract the user sentiment from a video image by applying neuro-metric techniques like GSR sensors, EEG signals and facial coding analyzer. Facial coding was analyzed using webcam and eye movement recorded using eye-trackers. Section 13.6 detailed the role of big data analytics in understanding user sentiment. Further, it provided an introduction of various big data analytics techniques for understanding user sentiments.

References

[1] http://www.business2community.com/marketing/8-biggest-marketing-trends-watch-2017-01771962#9iQRiJ0h5gr4VpuH.97 (accessed in March 2017).
[2] http://neurostrata.com/neuromarketing-consumer-neuroscience-frequently-asked-questions (2015) (accessed in March 2017).
[3] Bercea, D. (2013). Anatomy of methodologies for measuring consumer behavior in neuromarketing research. *lcbr-online.com*.
[4] Poria, S. (2016). Fusing audio, visual and textual clues for sentiment analysis from multimodal content. Neurocomputing, 174, 50–59.
[5] Stoicescu, C. (2016). Big data, the perfect instrument to study today's consumer behavior. Database Systems Journal, 6(3), 28–42.

Bibliography

[1] Balsdon, T., & Clifford, W.G.C. (2017). A bias-minimising measure of the influence of head orientation on perceived gaze direction. Scientific Reports, 7(article number 41685), 1–10. DOI: 10.1038/srep41685.
[2] Touchette, B., & Lee, S.E. (2017). Measuring neural responses to apparel product attractiveness: an application of frontal asymmetry theory. Clothing and Textiles Research Journal, 35(1), 3–15.
[3] Nyoni, T., & Bonga, W.G. (2017). Neuromarketing: no brain, no gain! Journal of Economics and Finance (DRJ-JEF), 2(2), 17–29.
[4] $22 Million Neuromarketing Technologies Market: Global Report 2015–2020-Research and Markets. 2016, http://www.businesswire.com/news/home/20160711005489/en/22-Million-Neuromarketing-Technologies-Market-Global-Report (accessed in March 2017).
[5] Klincekova, S. (2016). Neuromarketing—research and prediction of the future. International Journal of Management Science and Business Administration, 2(2), 54–57.

[6]   Granero, A.C. (2016). A comparison of physiological signal analysis techniques and classifiers for automatic emotional evaluation of audiovisual contents. Frontiers in Computational Neuroscience, 10. Available from: https://www.frontiersin.org/articles/10.3389/fncom.2016.00074/full.

[7]   López-Gil, J.-M. (2016). Method for improving EEG based emotion recognition by combining it with synchronized biometric and eye-tracking technologies in a non-invasive and low cost way. Frontiers in Computational Neuroscience, 10. Available from: https://www.frontiersin.org/articles/10.3389/fncom.2016.00085/full.

[8]   Salehan, M., & Dan J.K. (2016). Predicting the performance of online consumer reviews: a sentiment mining approach to big data analytics. Decision Support Systems, 81, 30–40.

[9]   Hilderbrand, M.L. (2016). Neuromarketing: an essential tool in the future of advertising and brand development. Doctoral dissertation, The University of Texas at Austin.

[10] Glaenzer, E. (2016). Are the brain and the mind one? Neuromarketing and how consumers make decisions. digitalcommons.colby.edu (accessed in March 2017).

[11] Varshney, N.K. (2016). Exploring neuromarketing dynamics. International Journal of Advance technology in Engineering and Science, 4(1), 97–100.

[12] Taggart, R.W., Dressler, M., Kumar, P., Khan, S., & Coppola, J.F. (2016). Determining emotions via facial expression analysis' software. Proceedings of Student-Faculty Research Day, CSIS, Pace University C2-1–C2-8. https://imotions.com/publications/determining-emotions-via-facial-expression-analysis-software/ (accessed in March 2017).

[13] Trimble, E., Wang, Y., & Kennon, R. (2016). Analysis of consumer behavior by fusing EEG and eye-tracking data. WIT Transactions on Engineering Sciences, 113, 389–395.

[14] Hakala, J., Kätsyri, J., Takala, T., & Häkkinen, J. (2016). Perception of stereoscopic direct gaze: the effects of interaxial distance and emotional facial expressions. Journal of Vision, 16(9):5, 1–15, doi: 10.1167/16.9.5.

[15] Pantelis, C.P., & Kennedy, P.D. (2016). Prior expectations about where other people are likely to direct their attention systematically influence gaze perception. Journal of Vision, 16(3):7, 1–12.

[16] Blum, B.E. (2016). Consumer neuroscience: a multi-disciplinary approach to marketing leveraging advances in neuroscience, Psychology and Economics. Senior Theses, Claremont Colleges Digital Library.

[17] Schilbach, L. (2015). Eye to eye, face to face and brain to brain: novel approaches to study the behavioral dynamics and neural mechanisms of social interactions. Current Opinion in Behavioral Sciences, 3, 130–135. DOI:10.1016/ j.cobeha.2015.03.006.

[18] Dimpfel, W. (2015). Neuromarketing: neurocode-tracking in combination with eye-tracking for quantitative objective assessment of TV commercials." Journal of Behavioral and Brain Science, 5(4),137–147.

[19] Horská, E., Margianti, S. E., Bercik, J., & Gálová, J (2015). Consumer neuroscience solutions: towards innovations, marketing effectiveness and customer driven strategies. (2015): 18–21. DOI: 10.17626/dBEM.ICoM.P00. 2015.p004.

[20] Gîlcă, G., & Bîzdoacă, N.G. (2015). Detecting human emotions with an adaptive neuro-fuzzy inference system. 6th International Conference Computational Mechanics and Virtual Engineering, COMEC 2015, pp. 285–290.

[21] Kumar, H., & Singh, P. (2015). Neuromarketing: an emerging tool of market research, International Journal of Engineering and Management Research, 5(6), 530–535.

[22] Agarwal, S., & Dutta, T. (2015). Neuromarketing and consumer neuroscience: current understanding and the way forward. Decision, 42(4), 457–462.

[23] dos Santos, R.D.O.J., de Oliveira, J.H.C., Rocha, J.B., & Giraldi, J.D.M.E. (2015). Eye tracking in neuromarketing: a research agenda for marketing studies. International Journal of Psychological Studies, 7(1), 32.

[24] Olteanu, M.D.B. (2015). Neuroethics and responsibility in conducting neuromarketing research. Neuroethics, 8(2), 191–202.

[25] Solnais, C., Sánchez-Fernández, J., & Ibáñez-Zapata, J.Á. (2015). Neuromarketing: the future of market research or a passing trend? Proceedings of the 2015 International Marketing Trends Conference, pp. 1–12.

[26] Jaskula, B., Pancerz, K., & Szkola, J. (2015). Toward synchronization of EEG and eye-tracking data using an expert system. In CS&P, pp. 196–198.

[27] Roth, V.A. (2014). The potential of neuromarketing as a marketing tool. Bachelor's thesis, University of Twente.

[28] Šola, M.H. (2014). Neuromarketing—science and practice. FIP—Journal of Finance and Law, 1, 25–34.

[29] Sharma, N., Koc, M., & Kishor, J. (2014). Neuromarketing—a step ahead of traditional marketing tools, In Proceedings of 3rd International Conference on Management Innovations (ICMI-2014).

[30] Medhat, W., Ahmed H., & Hoda K. (2014). Sentiment analysis algorithms and applications: a survey. Ain Shams Engineering Journal, 5(4), 1093–1113.

[31] Chaturvedi, A., & Tripathi, A. (2014). Emotion recognition using fuzzy rule-based system. International Journal of Computer Applications 93(11), 25–28.

[32] Kottier, W.G. (2014) The added value of neuromarketing tools in the area of marketing research. http://essay.utwente.nl/66222/ (accessed in March 2017).

[33] Dervojeda, K., Verzijl, D., Nagtegaal, F., *et al*. (2014). Customer experience-neuro-marketing innovations. Innovative Business Models for Competitiveness European Union, Business Innovation Observatory Contract No 190/PP/ENT/CIP/12/C/N03C01, February 2014.

[34] Agarwal, S., & Xavier, M.J. (2014). Consumers in Emerging Economies. The Wiley Blackwell Encyclopedia of Consumption and Consumer Studies. DOI: 10.1002/9781118989463.wbeccs258.

[35] Barbu, Alina (2013). Eight contemporary trends in the market research industry. Management & Marketing, 8(3), 429–450.

[36]   Russom, P. (2013). Managing Big Data http://www.pentaho.com/sites/default/files/uploads/resources/tdwi_best_practices_report-managing_big_data.pdf (accessed in March 2017).

[37]   https://www.informs.org/ORMS-Today/Public-Articles/October-Volume-40-Number-5/Big-data-analytics-in-marketing (accessed in September 2017).

[38]   https://www.forbes.com/sites/louiscolumbus/2016/05/09/ten-ways-big-data-is-revolutionizing-marketing-and-sales/2/#2ac5f33c25cd (accessed in April 2017).

[39]   https://www.sas.com/en_us/insights/big-data/big-data-marketing.html (accessed in March 2017).

[40]   https://inews.co.uk/essentials/news/business/neuroscience-big-data-combining-reinvent-advertising/ (accessed in September 2017).

[41]   Shih, J.J., Krusienski, D.J., & Wolpaw, J.R. (2012). Brain-computer interfaces in medicine. Mayo Clinic Proceedings, 87(3), 268–279.

Chapter 14

A recommendation system for allocating video resources in multiple partitions

Kostas Kolomvatsos[1,2], Maria G. Koziri[2], and Thanasis Loukopoulos[3]

A recommendation system or recommender aims to deliver meaningful recommendations for items or services to any interested party (e.g., users and applications). Recommenders provide their results on top of the collected data related either to the items' and users' description or ratings defined by users. Recommenders can be adopted in the domain of large-scale data management with significant advantages. Due to huge volumes of data, many techniques consider the separation of data into a number of partitions. Analytics are delivered on top of these data partitions and, accordingly, are aggregated to form the final response into the incoming queries. Data separation techniques can be incorporated to allocate the data into the appropriate partitions, thus, to improve the efficiency in the delivery of analytics. In this chapter, we propose a recommendation system responsible for allocating the data to the most appropriate partition according to their current contents. Our approach facilitates the provision of the analytics for each data partition by collecting "similar" data into the same partition. The aim is to support statistical insights into every partition to efficiently define query execution plans. We adopt a decision-making scheme combined with a naïve Bayesian classifier for deriving the appropriate partition. We focus on the management of streams of video files. The proposed recommender derives the appropriate partition for each incoming video file based on a set of characteristics. We evaluate our scheme through a set of simulations that reveal its strengths and weaknesses.

14.1 Introduction

The current form of Web and the Internet of things makes available to end users a huge infrastructure where numerous devices produce and consume data. Among these

[1] Department of Informatics and Telecommunications, University of Athens, Greece
[2] Department of Computer Science, University of Thessaly, Greece
[3] Department of Computer Science and Biomedical Informatics, University of Thessaly, Greece

data are video files that could be produced and uploaded by end users or enterprises. Personal videos, videos retrieved by security cameras, movies, etc., are common examples. Videos produced are characterized by heterogeneity making difficult the definition of queries for searching on the top of numerous files. In addition, due to huge volumes of data, videos are stored to a set of separate partitions to facilitate their parallel management. Hence, queries should be defined into a number of partitions, e.g., for finding a video file of interest. Analytics on top of the provided files are significant to support intelligent applications. However, the separate storage of videos without adopting a specific technique could increase the heterogeneity of the data present in a partition. For instance, a partition may contain video files that belong to different categories; thus, a querying mechanism should visit multiple locations to derive a list of relevant videos provided to end users or applications. Such an approach requires time and resources before it is in a position to provide the final response.

In the aforementioned setting, there is the need for keeping the relevance/ similarity of the video files in each partition at high levels, thus, to reduce the need for visiting multiple partitions when responding to a query. In addition, the storage of similar files in the same partition increases the statistical "compactness" that positively affects the performance of the query-answering process. In this work, our aim is to keep the statistical "compactness" of each partition to high levels. The better the information we have for the data, the better choices we make for executing the incoming queries. Specific query plans are adopted for the execution of each query. Such plans are defined before the execution thus, we need the statistical information for the underlying data to build efficient plans. Statistics reduce the amount of data that are to be processed during the optimization of a query execution plan.[1] Research efforts so far target to the implementation of data separation algorithms applied after the reception and storage of data. In this chapter, we focus on a streaming environment where video files are reported at high rates limiting the time available for deciding their allocation. The immediate storage and the separation of data afterwards require time and resources due to the huge volumes of data. To alleviate this problem, we propose a scheme that recommends the most appropriate partition for storing the current video file just after receiving it from the stream responding in real time. In general, recommenders produce suggestions, i.e., a list of items, to a user based on her preferences [1]. It is also based on information related to (a) the user preferences, (b) the description of each item, and (c) the preferences of other users. Our scheme differs from these "typical" recommendation systems in the sense that only video files' descriptions are available with no knowledge on the preferences of users/applications realized in the form of queries.

The proposed framework consists of two parts: (a) a *preselection process* based on a decision-making technique (i.e., analytic hierarchy process—AHP); (b) a *classification part* for the final allocation of each video file on the top of the results derived by the preselection process of the proposed recommender. The preselection process

---

[1] https://www.red-gate.com/simple-talk/sql/performance/queries-damned-queries-and-statistics/#third

aims to select the partitions that closely match to the incoming video files based on a set of predefined evaluation criteria. Accordingly, the results of the preselection process are processed by the classification scheme. The preselection process is based on nominal characteristics of the video files while the classification scheme is applied on numeric data to secure the statistical "compactness" of each partition. We aim to maximize the similarity that our scheme enjoys when assigning a video file into a partition. The similarity is affected by the relevance of the current video with the other files stored into a specific partition. We adopt the known AHP and a naïve Bayesian classifier for deriving the solution to our problem. AHP acts on the top of a set of alternative options among which the best decision is to be made. It is important to notice that, since some of the criteria could be contrasting, it is not true that the best option is the one which optimizes each single criterion, rather the one which achieves the most suitable trade-off among the different criteria. Bayes theorem is adopted to derive the most appropriate partition after we select the subset that satisfies our needs according to the AHP execution. The advantage is that our scheme does not require any modeling of the area under consideration while being efficient in practice.

The rest of the chapter is structured as follows. Section 14.2 presents the related work while Section 14.3 provides the description of our problem. In Section 14.4, we provide a discussion on the proposed solution. In Section 14.5, we reveal the strengths of the proposed scheme through an experimental evaluation. Finally, in Section 14.6, we conclude our chapter by giving our future research plans.

14.2 Related work

Large-scale data refer in continuous growing of data that are received and stored in various locations. The management of huge volumes of data requires powerful mechanisms and complex algorithms that will set up the basis for deriving intelligent analytics. In the respective literature, large-scale data are characterized by [2]: (a) large volumes of data generated by numerous resources (e.g., smartphones, applications, social networks, and sensors), i.e., volume; (b) data generated in high speed; thus, they should be immediately (pre-)processed especially when applications require responses in real time, i.e., velocity; (c) data generated by heterogeneous sources, i.e., variety. Such data should be efficiently analyzed to support intelligent applications. However, this is a very difficult task due to that they may contain ambiguous or abnormal information [3]. Therefore, a number of open issues should be handled before the technology is in a mature level. One can find multiple frameworks for the analysis of data like in [4–10]. A comparison between multiple models can be found in [3].

Video files are significant for many applications domains. For instance, video analytics are adopted in machine vision or decision engines. Video is the appropriate format for supporting applications requiring the management of multiple images. They can provide real-time insights on the behavior of entities with great potential for building intelligent applications (e.g., security applications and monitoring activities). Some frameworks adopted for the video management are presented in [11] and [12], while a survey in the field is presented in [13]. The majority of the efforts in the field deal with the analysis of the video files instead of studying the location where files could be stored to efficiently support search queries. For instance, multiple research efforts provide analyses and propose models for supporting security applications. The main focus of these efforts is on the analytics provided by the video contents and not on the efficient searching of the video files just before they are subject of processing.

Additional research efforts can be found for data separation. These efforts are originated in the cloud domain and the majority aim to handle security issues. Data separation provides the basis for splitting the data into partitions/pieces where each partition refers into the same organism. One of the most known approaches is clustering. In [14], the authors present a clustering algorithm for large-scale databases called DBSCAN. DBSCAN is a density-based clustering algorithm applied into large spatial databases. Extensions of DBSCAN are OPTICS [15], ST-DBSCAN [16], and MR-DBSCAN [17]. As DBSCAN exhibits limited efficiency for high dimensions, researchers propose the DENCLUE algorithm [18]. Cloud computing solutions involve mechanisms for separating the data to increase the security levels. In [19], the authors present a framework for a secure data storage strategy in cloud. The proposed model splits data into a number of partitions while ensuring the security level. In [20], an algorithm for separating the data belonging to different organizations is proposed. The discussed solution provides security, reliability, confidentiality, and availability of the data. The authors describe, among others, major issues in data separation and a method through which data are separated. In [21], the authors present a metadata and real data separation model for cloud storage named MeSe. The proposed framework keeps metadata and real data separated aiming to provide integrated cloud storage service with two parts of separate servers.

Recommender systems are widely studied in the past. A variety of algorithms and techniques are adopted to provide efficient results. In general, recommenders could be identified to *content-based* [22] and *collaborative filtering* [23]. Content-based approaches require ratings from users in contrast to collaborative filtering models that cannot derive an efficient result without the ratings of the community of users. Content-based models depend on the performance of the content analysis methodology they utilize. The performance of the matching process between items descriptions with users' profiles is a very significant issue. Some widely adopted techniques in content-based recommenders are keyword-based recommendations [24–27], semantic models [28–32], and probabilistic methods [33–36]. In collaborative filtering approaches, the provided results are based on the similar tastes of users and their combination. New items are handled easier than in other models as the recommendation is based on their descriptions even if ratings are not yet present. Collaborative filtering methods are separated in [23]: (i) user-based, (ii) item-based, (iii) model-based, and (iv) fusion-based approaches. In the user-based approaches [37], a similarity matrix is utilized to store the ratings of each user for every item. The item-based methods [38–40] adopt pairwise item similarities which are more reliable than user similarities, thus, resulting in high quality of the result. The model-based methods [41–43] exploit the sparsity of data in the similarity matrix.

AHP is also adopted in recommenders especially for the support of decision-making. In [44], the authors discuss a decision support system that is responsible to provide salary recommendations. The system adopts the multi-attribute decision theory while being evaluated with the adoption of synthetic data. In [45], the proposed system deals with TV program recommendations. The proposed method adopts AHP for predicting group genre preference and, finally, selecting recommended TV programs. The accuracy of the framework is enhanced by the adoption of parameter learning from users' historical data. Finally, in [46], the authors describe a method to handle the cold start problem based on the AHP. The proposed method calculates the weight between product attributes and creates a candidate product set. Accordingly, it conducts the final recommendation from the candidate set.

All the aforementioned data separation algorithms focus on the "post-processing" of data to result the required partitions. The difference with our work is that our model "pre-processes" the data as they arrive through streams. Our aim is to limit the time and the required computational resources for "post-processing" by providing the appropriate partitions where each data piece (i.e., a video file) should be allocated. In addition, the aforementioned recommenders require the existence of users' ratings for a set of items. In our scenario, the "items" are the data partitions where the incoming files will be stored. We want to limit the storage requirements; thus, historical "ratings" (the "similarity" between files) for each partition are not taken into consideration. We adopt a model that results the appropriate partition in real time. The aim is to find the partition that resembles to the incoming files, however, taking into consideration multiple parameters (i.e., video files characteristics) at the same time.

14.3   Problem description

The envisioned setting consists of a number of partitions where video files will be allocated. Without loss of generality, we consider $|P_A|$ partitions, i.e., $P_A = \{p_1, p_2, \ldots, p_{|P_A|}\}$. Each partition has an upper threshold for storage. This is because we aim to have an environment where the execution time for queries cannot exceed an upper time limit. For instance, if we restrict the size of each partition, we can also positively affect the time required for getting a response from this partition. When the predefined upper size is violated, a new partition is defined in the same location.

Each partition is characterized by a set of attributes that are common with the incoming files, i.e., $C = \{c_1, c_2, \ldots, c_{|C|}\}$. For instance, attributes could be the type of files, the format, the number of image channels, etc. Attributes in each partition are realized in the form of counters, averages, or the number of the files. Such kind of information is available to a Video Files Processing Engine (VFPE). VFPE is responsible to receive video files from streams and, accordingly, based on the proposed recommender to decide the partition where the files should be stored. Files are reported in streams at high rates; thus, the adopted decision-making model should provide solutions in real time. The incoming files should be "matched" against the contents of the partitions to secure the consistency of the stored data. However, the "matching" process is not based only on a single attribute but on the entire set C. For instance, files of the same format should be allocated, if possible, in the same partitions to secure the efficient responses in relevant queries. Our mechanism pays attention on the entire set of the attributes and tries to facilitate the retrieval of documents when queries request for resources. Hence, according to the characteristics of the incoming video files, the VFPE should allocate them to the most appropriate partition.

The characteristics of the files could be separated in two categories: (a) characteristics that take nominal values; (b) characteristics that take numeric values. This means that the set C could be separated in two subsets, i.e., $C = C^M \cup C^N$, where C^M is the subset of nominal attributes and C^N is the subset of numeric attributes. Ordinal values could be easily considered as nominal values. As we discern two main categories for characteristics, we provide a mechanism that builds on the top of these categories. The AHP is adopted to "manage" the nominal characteristics and, afterwards, the numeric data are managed by the classification process. The proposed recommender builds on the top of video files attributes and the attributes of each partition as depicted by the set of files already present there. The recommender, after receiving an incoming file, executes the preselection process (i.e., the AHP—the first part of the proposed approach) and derives a (sub)set of the appropriate partitions, i.e., $SP = \{p'_1, p'_2, \ldots, p'_{|SP|}\}$, $SP \subseteq P_A$. Accordingly, the classification process is applied on the set SP and derives the final recommended partitions, i.e., the set $FL = \{p''_1, p''_2, \ldots\}$. If no partitions are present in the FL or the process does not derive results at a predefined time interval, a partition is randomly selected from SP. The classification process is based on the statistical data of the files present in a partition and derives the probability that a file belongs there. Actually, the classification process tries to find the partition that maximizes the aforementioned probability. The aim is to maximize the similarity between the incoming file and the most appropriate partitions through the maximization of the statistical "compactness." From the final list, the partition exhibiting the highest similarity score is finally selected to host the incoming file.

14.4 The proposed approach

In Figure 14.1, we present the architecture of our scheme. At the bottom layer, a set of streams deliver video files to be allocated in the available partitions placed at the upper layer. Each video file is processed by the proposed parts of our system in a sequential manner. The preselection process identifies the partitions that are closely matching to the file according to a set of predefined criteria. These criteria are evaluated in a hierarchy of importance for the specific scenario. For instance, the format of the file plays an important role as files with the same format could be placed in the same partitions to facilitate relevant queries. The important is that the allocation of a file into a partition should be based not only on a single characteristic (like the format) but also on the entire set of the characteristics. Hence, the first part of our framework deals with multiple criteria and derives a list of candidate partitions (i.e., the set SP). Accordingly, the list of candidates is fed into the Naïve Bayesian classifier applied on the numeric characteristics of the incoming files. The classification process tries to keep the statistical "compactness" of the partitions at high levels while delivering

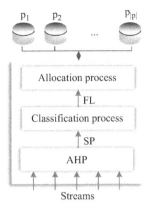

Figure 14.1   The proposed recommender

the final list (i.e., the set *FL*). Finally, the allocation process starts from the partition located in the first place of the *FL* and concludes the partition where each file should be allocated.

The selection of the appropriate partitions involves strategic decision-making to identify the partitions that maximize the similarity of the incoming video files. AHP [47,48] offers a method for decomposing the allocation problem into a hierarchy of subproblems. Each subproblem can be easily evaluated and, thus, solved. A numerical scale is adopted to support the ranking of each alternative, i.e., the allocation of the file in a specific partition. AHP allows users to assess the relative weight of multiple criteria or multiple options against given criteria in an intuitive manner. In case quantitative ratings are not available, policymakers or assessors can still recognize whether one criterion is more important than another. The basic process to carry out the AHP consists of the following steps:

1. The first step is to decompose the problem into a hierarchy or goal, criteria, sub-criteria, and alternatives. The decision problem is separated into its constituent parts. The resulted structure comprises a goal or focus at the topmost level and criteria (and sub-criteria) at the intermediate levels, while the lowest level contains the options.
2. For each pair of criteria, the decision-maker rates the relative "priority" of every criterion against the others. An assignment of a weight between 1 (equal importance) and 9 (extreme importance) to the more important criterion is included in this step.
3. A square matrix is generated for the pair comparisons. The elements in the diagonal are set to 1. When in the place (i, j) of the matrix, it is a value over 1 means that the ith criterion is better than the jth criterion. The opposite stands when the cell (i, j) contains a value lower than 1.

Table 14.1   Example of pairwise comparisons

	Format	Type	Color model		Format	Type	Color model
Format	1/1	5/2	2/1		1/1	5/2	2/1
Type		1/1	4/3	$\Rightarrow$	2/5	1/1	4/3
Color model			1/1		1/2	3/4	1/1

4. We calculate the principal eigenvalue and the normalized eigenvector of the aforementioned matrix to get a relative importance of the criteria under consideration.
5. In a final step, each element's score is combined with the criterion weights to produce an overall score for each option.

As mentioned, in our framework, we consider two types of attributes, i.e., C^M, and C^N. In the first part of our scheme (the preselection process), we take into consideration the attributes that take nominal values, i.e., the set C^M. For C^M, we provide the ranking of each c_i^M, $i = 1, 2 =, \ldots, |C^M|$ and create the $|C^M|X|C^M|$ matrix. Table 14.1 presents an example matrix. In this matrix, we denote that the format of a file is two times more important than the color model and so on.

Based on the aforementioned matrix, we can calculate the "significance" s_j for the jth partition. The parameters s_j shows the similarity between the incoming file and a specific partition according to the adopted strategy as realized through the AHP. s_j is calculated as follows:

$$s_j = \sum w_i \frac{A_{ij}}{\sum A_{ij}}, \begin{cases} 1 \leq i \leq |C^M| \\ 1 \leq j \leq |P| \end{cases} \tag{14.1}$$

where w_i is the weight of ith characteristic derived by AHP and A_{ij} is the frequency of the specific ith characteristic in the jth partition (e.g., format, color model, and type) that matches with the corresponding video file characteristic. If no characteristics are observed in the partition, then the weight is defined equal to 1. The list SP consists of the $|SP|$ partitions with the highest significance as calculated by (14.1).

The second part of the proposed scheme involves the final selection of the partition where the file will be allocated. For this, we adopt a naïve Bayesian classification model [49]. We have to select a single partition from the $|SP|$ available based on the "similarity" of the numeric characteristics with the contents of each partition. The tuple $[c_i^N]$, $i = 1, 2 =, \ldots, |C^N|$ will be the basis for calculating the probability that the video file belongs to each partition. Our scheme tries to predict if the tuple is derived by each partition based on statistics for the numeric characteristics. Based on this rationale, we try to maximize the probability $P(p_i'|C^N)$, $\forall i$. According to the Bayes theorem, we have

$$P(p_i'|C^N) = \frac{P(C^N|p_i')P(p_i')}{P(C^N)} \tag{14.2}$$

Probabilities $P(C^N)$ and $P(p_i')$ can be easily evaluated. $P(C^N)$ is constant for the available partitions and $P(p_i')$ can be evaluated by the adoption of the uniform distribution, i.e., $P(p_i') = \frac{1}{|P_A|}$. Hence, we have to focus on the maximization of $P(C^N|p_i')$. The following equation holds true:

$$P(C^N|p_i') = \prod_{k=1}^{|C^N|} P(c_i^N|p_i') \tag{14.3}$$

Each probability $P(c_i^N|p_i')$ can be calculated through the adoption of statistical measures. In this work, we adopt the Gaussian distribution for depicting the probability that the video file belongs to each partition. The probability is calculated as follows:

$$P\left(c_i^N|p_i'\right) = \frac{1}{\sqrt{2\pi}\,\sigma_i} e^{-\frac{\left(c_i^N - \mu_i\right)^2}{2\sigma^2}} \tag{14.4}$$

The final probability for a partition is multiplied by the similarity of each partition as defined in the first part of our scheme, i.e., (14.1).

14.5 Experimental evaluation

As mentioned, for defining efficient query execution plans, we should have insights on the statistical information of the data in each partition. The proposed model tries to maintain the statistical "compactness" of the data to set up the basis for the definition of efficient execution plans. Increased computational costs will be paid when the query execution optimizer should visit the entire set of data and multiple partitions to derive the necessary statistical information. In this section, we report on the realization and the evaluation of our scheme as a mechanism to support the statistical "compactness" of the partitions.

For characterizing video files and calculating the statistical data, we adopt the following characteristics:

- $C^M = \{\text{Format, Type, Color\_Model}\}$
- $C^N = \{\text{Size, Image\_Channels, Audio\_Channels}\}$

These characteristics can be easily expanded to cover more "aspects" of video files according to the adopted strategy. In our evaluation setup, based to the Saaty's scale, the format of the files is moderately important rather than the type and very strongly important rather than the color model while the type is strongly important rather than the color model. In addition, for numeric characteristics, we assume specific upper values.

We report on the statistical "compactness" of each partition after the management of a high number of files. Initially, for a warm-up period, we insert ten random files in each partition. Afterwards, we simulate the management of 10,000 files with random characteristics. For nominal characteristics, we get a random value in the set of the most frequent values as observed in the relevant literature. For instance, for the format of the files, we adopt famous formats like mpg, avi, mov, asf, flv, and mp4. For numeric

Table 14.2　Statistics for contents of partitions for $|SP| = 2$

		Partitions									
		0	**1**	**2**	**3**	**4**	**5**	**6**	**7**	**8**	**9**
Total files		184	1,670	1,505	405	27	161	1,135	2,262	124	2,627
Format	mpg	0	0	2	0	1	1	1	988	117	452
	avi	1	12	1,497	191	1	1	1	0	1	0
	mov	3	3	1	0	2	151	6	1,011	1	548
	asf	178	3	3	2	1	2	1	0	1	1,500
	flv	1	4	1	211	3	5	1,123	262	2	124
	mp4	1	1,648	1	1	19	1	3	1	2	3
Type	Video	67	582	520	134	13	48	359	1,069	33	498
	Movie	75	561	490	142	8	52	366	1,193	33	497
	Security	42	527	495	129	6	61	410	0	58	1,632
Color	RGB	47	429	397	104	7	35	0	734	32	753
model	CMYK	41	390	376	99	6	52	368	529	29	607
	HSV	52	436	380	98	6	33	379	534	29	640
	HSL	44	415	352	104	8	41	388	465	34	627

characteristics, we get a random value in a specific interval. For instance, the size is randomly selected in the interval [1,100] while image and audio channels are selected in the interval [1,5].

We provide results for $|SP| \in \{2,7\}$. Recall that $|SP|$ defines the number of partitions selected in the first part of the proposed process (preselection) that will be fed into the Bayesian classifier. In Table 14.2, we present our results for nominal characteristics in when $|SP| = 2$. We observe that the majority of files with the same characteristics are allocated in a limited number of partitions (two or three). This observation is more intense in the case of the file format as the format is adopted to be the most significant characteristic in the AHP model. Adopting this strategy, we force the AHP to assign higher similarity to partitions that contain files in the same format as the incoming video file. Video files are concentrated around the most significant nominal characteristic. For instance, mpg files are allocated in the last three partitions, avi files are mainly allocated in partitions 2 and 3 and so on. The concentration of files with similar characteristics in limited number of partitions assists not only in the increment of the statistical "compactness" but also in the allocation of queries when we consider a query processor in front of each partition.

In Figures 14.2–14.4, we provide the statistics for the numeric characteristics (i.e., size, image, and audio channels). We adopt a boxplot for each characteristic where, among others, the mean (with a line) and the median (with the black circle) are depicted. We observe that the mean and the median are at the same levels indicating symmetric data. In addition, the majority of partitions exhibit similar statistics. This stands for all the adopted characteristics. If we combine these results with the outcomes presented in Table 14.2, we conclude that the proposed allocation process

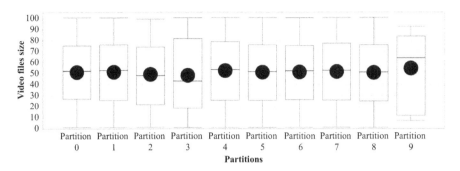

Figure 14.2   Boxplot for video files size (|SP| = 2)

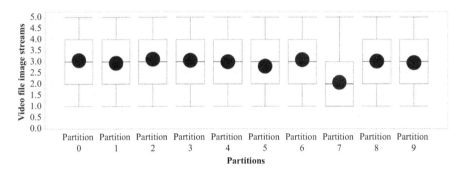

Figure 14.3   Boxplot for video files image streams (|SP| = 2)

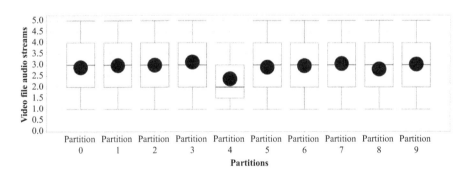

Figure 14.4   Boxplot for video files audio streams (|SP| = 2)

delivers similar files in the partitions maintaining the statistical "compactness" at high levels.

In Table 14.3, we provide our results for nominal characteristics when $|SP| = 7$. We observe similar behavior as in the scenario where $|SP| = 2$. The AHP leads to the allocation of files with similar format to a limited number of partitions (two or three).

Table 14.3 Statistics for contents of partitions for $|SP| = 7$

		Partitions									
		0	**1**	**2**	**3**	**4**	**5**	**6**	**7**	**8**	**9**
Total files		753	6,631	439	23	10	10	11	10	91	2,122
Format	mpg	191	0	108	6	1	1	1	1	26	1,357
	avi	191	1,077	22	0	2	2	1	1	18	356
	mov	0	1,317	88	4	1	1	3	1	0	314
	asf	1	1,533	45	5	1	2	2	2	27	52
	flv	195	1,376	94	8	3	1	2	3	1	42
	mp4	175	1,328	82	0	2	3	2	2	19	1
Type	Video	258	2,302	141	4	5	6	2	3	26	632
	Movie	268	2,114	133	8	1	1	7	4	29	832
	Security	227	2,215	165	11	4	3	2	3	36	658
Color	RGB	181	1,626	167	7	0	2	2	1	25	520
model	CMYK	173	1,686	0	5	3	3	3	2	24	609
	HSV	214	1,733	160	5	4	2	2	5	22	475
	HSL	185	1,586	112	6	3	3	4	2	20	518

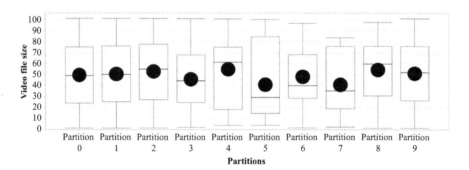

Figure 14.5 Boxplot for video files size ($|SP| = 7$)

The difference with the scenario where $|SP| = 2$ is that the observation stands also for the remaining nominal characteristics and not only for the most significant characteristic (i.e., the format). In general, the majority of files are allocated in a limited number of partitions. The high number of the selected partitions in the preselection process of our scheme leads to a high "compactness" of the partitions related to the nominal characteristics. However, even if it is positive for the creation of query execution plans and queries allocation, such an approach will lead to increased storage requirements in the partitions where the majority of files are assigned to.

In Figures 14.5–14.7, we present our results for numeric characteristics when $|SP| = 7$. We observe a different behavior of the proposed model compared to the scenario where $|SP| = 2$. Statistics are characterized by fluctuations depicted the variations of the files' characteristics stored in each partition. However, statistics

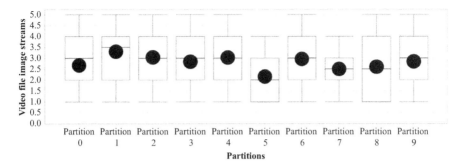

Figure 14.6 Boxplot for video files image streams ($|SP| = 7$)

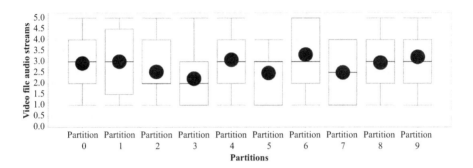

Figure 14.7 Boxplot for video files audio streams size ($|SP| = 7$)

related to the partitions where the majority of files are allocated are characterized by limited fluctuations. In partitions 0, 1, and 9, the mean and the median are very close indicating symmetric data.

We report on the number of video files (V) allocated in each partition. In this set of experiments, we get $|SP|$ as the 60% of $|P_A|$ and experiment with $|P_A| \in \{10, 50, 100, 500, 1,000\}$. We aim to simulate scenarios with a limited number of partitions as well as scenarios where the number of the available partitions is very high. Table 14.4 presents our results. We observe that, as natural, V is reduced as $|P_A|$ increases. A high number of partitions lead to a few video files allocated in each of them. In our model, the $|SP|$ does not affect the performance concerning the pre-processing phase.

An additional set of experiments is devoted to the evaluation of the time (T) required for concluding an allocation of a video file. Actually, we get the average time as recorded for each allocation. Table 14.5 presents our results, i.e., the necessary milliseconds (ms) for each allocation. We observe that the proposed scheme is very efficient as it requires, at most, 2 ms for each allocation. This means that our model could be practically adopted in real applications without limiting the performance of

Table 14.4   The average number of the allocated
files in each partition

$|P_A|$	V
10	920.00
50	209.52
100	109.90
500	29.77
1,000	19.99

Table 14.5   The average time for concluding
allocations

$|P_A|$	T (ms)
10	0.208
50	0.269
100	0.300
500	0.685
1,000	2.034

the system. It should be noted that the discussed results concern both steps of the decision process.

14.6   Conclusions and future work

Recommendation systems have widely been adopted for proposing items to users or applications. This technology could be also adopted for providing the appropriate data partitions where video files arriving through streams could be allocated. In this work, we propose a recommendation system responsible to provide the partition where each file will be assigned to. The decision is based on the characteristics of files that could take nominal or numeric values. Our model tries to handle both types of characteristics and takes them into consideration when deciding the final allocation. The aim is to increase the statistical "compactness" of each partition, thus, to efficiently support the creation of query execution plans and their allocation to specific processors. The proposed scheme consists of two parts: the first realizes a decision-making mechanism and incorporates the desired strategy related to the management of nominal characteristics; the second builds on the top of the results derived by the first part and delivers the final decision, i.e., the partition where the file will be allocated. The first part of the proposed scheme adopts the AHP algorithm and the second is based on a naïve Bayesian classifier. Our experimental results focus on the statistical "compactness" of each partition and show that similar files are allocated in the same partitions. This is more intense when the number of the selected partitions in the first part of the proposed model is high.

Future research plans involve the implementation of a classification scheme that will derive decisions on the top of the entire set of characteristics no matter their type. An automated, dynamic classification process should provide efficient recommendations in real time as the video files arrive in high rates. In this scenario, the training process is significant for the performance of the system while an adaptive approach for the classification scheme should be also incorporated.

References

[1] Burke, R., "Hybrid recommender systems: survey and experiments," User Modeling and User-Adapted Interaction, 12(4), 2002, pp. 331–370.

[2] Furht, B., Villanustre, F., "Introduction to big data," In: Big Data Technologies Application, Springer International Publishing, Cham, 2016, pp. 3–11.

[3] Tsai, C.-W., Lai, C.-F., Chao, H.-C., Vasilakos, A., "Big data analytics: a survey," Journal of Big Data, 2(21), 2015, DOI 10.1186/s40537-015-0030-3.

[4] Apache Mahout, Available: http://mahout.apache.org/.

[5] Cheng, Y., Qin, C., Rusu, F., "GLADE: big data analytics made easy," In: Proceedings of the ACM SIGMOD International Conference on Management of Data, ACM, New York, 2012, pp. 697–700.

[6] Curtin, R.R., Cline, J.R., Slagle, N.P., *et al.*, "MLPACK: a scalable C++ machine learning library," J Mach Learn Res., 14, 2013, pp. 801–805.

[7] Demchenko, Y., de Laat, C., Membrey, P., "Defining architecture components of the big data ecosystem," In: Proceedings of the International Conference on Collaboration Technologies and Systems, IEEE, New York, 2014, pp. 104–112.

[8] Essa, Y.M., Attiya, G., El-Sayed, A., "Mobile agent based new framework for improving big data analysis," In: Proceedings of the International Conference on Cloud Computing and Big Data, IEEE, New York, 2013, pp. 381–386.

[9] Rusu, F., Dobra, A., "GLADE: a scalable framework for efficient analytics," In: Proceedings of LADIS Workshop held in conjunction with VLDB, ACM, New York, 2012, pp. 1–6.

[10] Wonner, J., Grosjean, J., Capobianco, A., Bechmann, D., "Starfish: a selection technique for dense virtual environments," In: Proceedings of the ACM Symposium on Virtual Reality Software and Technology, ACM, New York, 2012, pp. 101–104.

[11] Chandramohan, V., Christensen, K., "A first look at wired sensor networks for video surveillance systems," In: Proceedings of the 27th Annual IEEE Conference on Local Computer Networks (LCN '02), IEEE, New York, November 2002, pp. 728–729.

[12] Karim, A., Shati, N.M., "A survey of intelligent surveillance systems," International Journal of Emerging Trends and Technology in Computer Science, 6(2), 2017, pp. 15–20.

[13]   Liu, H., Chen, S., Kubota, N., "Intelligent Video systems and analytics: a survey," IEEE Transactions on Industrial Informatics, 9(3), 2013, 1222–1233.

[14]   Ester, M., Kriegel, H.-P., Sander, J., Xu, X., "A density-based algorithm for discovering clusters in large spatial databases with noise," In: Proceedings of the Proceedings of the Second International Conference on Knowledge Discovery and Data Mining, vol. 96, AAAI Press, Menlo Park, CA, 1996, pp. 226–231.

[15]   Ankerst, M., Breunig, M.M., Kriegel, H.-P., Sander, J., "Optics: ordering points to identify the clustering structure," In: Proceedings of the ACM Sigmod Record, vol. 28, ACM, 1999, pp. 49–60.

[16]   Birant, D., Kut, A., "ST-DBSCAN: an algorithm for clustering spatial–temporal data," Data & Knowledge Engineering, 60(1), 2007, pp. 208–221.

[17]   He, Y., Tan, H., Luo, W., *et al.*, "MR-DBSCAN: an efficient parallel density-based clustering algorithm using MapReduce," In: Proceedings of the 17th IEEE International Conference on Parallel and Distributed Systems (ICPADS), IEEE, New York, 2011, pp. 473–480.

[18]   Hinneburg, A., Kcim, D.A., "An efficient approach to clustering in large multi-timedia databases with noise," In: Proceedings of the Fourth International Conference on Knowledge Discovery and Data Mining, vol. 98, AAAI Press, Menlo Park, CA, 1998, pp. 58–65.

[19]   Chen, D., He, Y., "A study on secure data storage strategy in cloud computing," Journal of Convergence Information Technology, 5(7), 2010, pp. 175–179.

[20]   Kaur, K., Vashisht, S., "Data separation issues in cloud computing," International Journal for Advance Research in Engineering and Technology, 1, 2013, pp. 26–29.

[21]   Wang, L., Liu, S., Chen, D., Chen, Y., Li, S., Liu, L., "A secured metadata and data separation model for cloud storage," In: Proceedings of the IEEE International Conference on Signal Processing, Communication and Computing, KunMing, China, 2013.

[22]   Lops, P., de Gemmis, M., Semeraro, G., "Content-based recommender systems: state of the art and trends," In: Recommender Systems Handbook, F. Ricci, L. Rokach, B. Shapira, P. Kantor, eds., Springer Verlag, Berlin, 2011, pp. 73–105.

[23]   Khabbaz, M., Lakshmanan, L.V.S., "TopRecs: Top-k algorithms for item-based collaborative filtering," Proc. of EDBT, Sweden, 2011.

[24]   Asnicar, F., Tasso, C., "ifWeb: a prototype of user model-based intelligent agent for documentation filtering and navigation in the World Wide Web," In: Proceedings of the 1st Int. Workshop on Adaptive Systems and User Modeling on the World Wide Web, 1997, pp. 3–12.

[25]   Chen, L., Sycara, K., "WebMate: a personal agent for browsing and searching," In: Proceedings of the 2nd International Conference on Autonomous Agents, ACM, New York, 1998, pp. 9–13.

[26]   Mladenic, D., "Machine learning used by personal WebWatcher," In: Proc. of ACAI-99 Workshop on Machine Learning and Intelligent Agents, 1999.

[27] Moukas, A., "Amalthaea information discovery and filtering using a multiagent evolving ecosystem," Applied Artificial Intelligence, 11(5), 1997, pp. 437–457.

[28] Basile, P., de Gemmis, M., Gentile, A., Iaquinta, L., Lops, P., "The JUMP project: domain ontologies and linguistic knowledge at work," In: Proc. of the 4th Italian Semantic Web Applications and Perspectives – SWAP 2007, 2007.

[29] De Gemmis, M., Lops, P., Semeraro, G., "A content-collaborative recommender that exploits WordNet-based user profiles for neighborhood formation. User modeling and user-adapted interaction," Journal of Personalization Research, 17(3), 2007, pp. 217–255

[30] Eirinaki, M., Vazirgiannis, M., Varlamis, I., "SEWeP: using site semantics and a taxonomy to enhance the web personalization process," In: Proc. of the 9th ACM SIGKDD, ACM, New York, 2003, pp. 99–108.

[31] Magnini, B., Strapparava, C., "Improving user modelling with content-based techniques," In: Proc. of the 8th International Conference of User Modeling, Springer Verlag, Berlin, 2001, pp. 74–83.

[32] Middleton, S.E., Shadbolt, N.R., De Roure, D.C., "Ontological user profiling in recommender systems," ACM Transactions on Information Systems, 22(1), 2004, pp. 54–88.

[33] Billsus, D., Pazzani, M.J., "A hybrid user model for news story classification," In: Proc. of the 7th International Conference on User Modeling, 1999.

[34] Billsus, D., Pazzani, M.J., "User modeling for adaptive news access," User Modeling and User-Adapted Interaction, 10(2-3), 2000, pp. 147–180.

[35] Mooney, R.J., Roy, L., "Content-based book recommending using learning for text categorization," In: Proc. of the 5th ACM Conference on Digital Libraries, ACM, New York, 2000, pp. 195–204.

[36] Pazzani, M., Billsus, D., "Learning and revising user profiles: the identification of interesting web sites," Machine Learning, 27(3), 1997, pp. 313–331.

[37] Herlocker, J.L., Konstan, J.A., Borchers, A., Riedl, J., "An algorithmic framework for performing collaborative filtering," In: SIGIR, 1999.

[38] Deshpande, M., Karypis, G., "Item-based top-N recommendation algorithms," ACM TOIS, 22(1), 2004, pp. 143–177.

[39] Sarvar, B., Karypis, G., Konstan, J., Riedl, J., "Item-based collaborative filtering recommendation algorithms," WWW 2001, pp. 285–295.

[40] Wang, J., de Vries, A.P., Reinders, M.J.T., "Unifying user-based and item-based collaborative filtering approaches by similarity fusion," In: SIGIR, 2006.

[41] Canny, J., "Collaborative filtering with privacy via factor analysis," In: SIGIR, 2002.

[42] Das, A., Datar, M., Garg, A. "Google news personalization: Scalable online collaborative filtering," WWW 2007, pp. 271–280.

[43] Jin, R., Si, L., Zhai, C., "A study of mixture models for collaborative filtering," Journal of Information Retrieval, 2006, 9(3), pp. 357–382.

[44] Troutt, M.D., Tadisina, S.K., "The analytic hierarchy process as a model base for a merit salary recommendation system," Mathematical and Computer Modelling, 16(5), 1992, pp. 99–105.

[45] Quan, J.C., Cho, S.B., "A hybrid recommender system based on AHP that awares contexts with Bayesian networks for smart TV," In: Proceedings of the International Conference on Hybrid Artificial Intelligence Systems, Salamanca, Spain, 2014.

[46] Nguyen, H.D., Lo, W.T., Sheu, R.K., "An AHP-based recommendation system for exclusive or specialty stores," In: Proceedings of the 2011 International Conference on Cyber-Enabled Distributed Computing and Knowledge Discovery, Beijing, China, 2011.

[47] Dagdeviren, M., Yüksel, I. "Developing a fuzzy analytic hierarchy process (AHP) model for behavior-based safety management," Information Sciences, 178(6), 2008, pp. 1717–1733.

[48] Saaty, T.L., "How to make a decision: the analytic hierarchy process," European Journal of Operational Research, 48, 1990, pp. 9–26.

[49] Becker, B., Kohavi, R., Sommerfield, D., "Visualizing the simple Bayesian classifier," In: Information Visualization in Data Mining and Knowledge Discovery, U. Fayyad, G. Grinstein, and A. Wierse, eds., Morgan Kaufmann Publishers, San Francisco, 2001, pp. 237–249.

Chapter 15

A mood-sensitive recommendation system in social sensing

Dong Wang[1]

This chapter reviews a mood-sensitive (MS) recommendation system in social sensing. This work is motivated by the need to provide reliable information recommendation to users in social sensing. The key idea of social sensing is to use humans as sensors to observe and report events in the physical world. We define the measurements from human sensors as claims. A key challenge in social sensing is *truth discovery* where the goal is to identify truthful claims from the false ones and estimate the reliability of data sources with minimum prior knowledge on both sources and their claims. While current solutions have made progress on addressing this challenge, an important limitation exists: the *mood sensitivity* of human sensors has not been fully explored. Therefore, the true claims identified by existing schemes can be biased and lead to useless or even misleading recommendations. In this chapter, we present an MS recommendation system that incorporates the mood sensitivity feature into the truth discovery solution. The reviewed recommendation system estimates (i) the correctness and mood neutrality of claims and (ii) the reliability and mood sensitivity of sources. We compare our model with existing truth discovery solutions using four real-world datasets collected from online social media. The results show the reviewed recommendation system outperformed the baselines by finding more correct and mood neutral claims.

It is a critical challenge in building reliable recommendation systems in social sensing that effectively recommend trustworthy and credible information for decision-making.

15.1 Introduction

This chapter reviews a principle-based mood-sensitive (MS) recommendation system to address the truth-discovery problem in social sensing [1,2]. Social sensing becomes an emerging research area where the humans are used as sensors to their observations about physical environment [3]. Social sensing is driven by the rapid integration of digital sensors with mobile and IoT devices [4], increasing network connectivity [5]

---

[1] Department of Computer Science and Engineering, University of Notre Dame, United States

and open information sharing platforms (e.g., Twitter, Facebook) [6]. For example, people may report the damage and outage in a city on Twitter when disasters happen. Citizens may report geotagged photos to document the potholes on city streets or litter locations in a park [7,8]. We define these human-sensed measurements as claims. A key challenge in social sensing is *truth discovery* where the goal is to identify truthful claims from the false ones and estimate the reliability of data sources with minimum prior knowledge on both sources and their claims [9].

One real-world example of the truth discovery problem in social sensing is Hurricane Sandy (Nov. 2012). In the aftermath of the hurricane, people were posting the gas availability of different stations on Twitter when they tried to find places to fuel their cars. A reliable information recommendation system could accurately identify the gas stations that are most likely to have gas from the large amount of noisy and emotionally biased tweets. However, the data sources in social sensing are not necessarily reliable, and we often do not have sufficient prior knowledge about the source reliability [10]. Furthermore, sources may generate completely mood-biased claims in relation to the disastrous event to attract public attention or show their personal opinions [11,12].

There exist a few important challenges in addressing MS truth discovery problem. First, the data sources and their reliability are often *unknown* a priori in a social-sensing application due to the open data contribution paradigm and unvetted nature of data sources [13]. Second, identifying MS claims from the neutral ones is a nontrivial problem since human sensors are often good at mingling their emotions with the reported observations [14]. The ignorance of MS aspect of the truth discovery problem can lead to biased and uncertain results that can significantly affect the decision-making process [15,16].

This chapter reviews a principled approach to solve the *MS truth discovery* problem by addressing the above challenges. In particular, the reviewed approach develops a multidimensional expectation maximization (EM) scheme known as MS-EM. The scheme solves the problem by jointly estimating (i) correctness and mood neutrality of claims and (ii) reliability and mood sensitivity of sources without knowing either of them a priori. In the evaluation, we reviewed the performance comparison between the MS-EM and several state-of-the-art mood-ignorant truth discovery solutions through real-world case studies using data from online social media. The case studies include Brussels bombing, Oregon shooting, Baltimore riots and Paris attacks, which occurred in 2015 and 2016. The reviewed MS truth discovery scheme is important because it directly contributes to building reliable recommendation systems in social sensing that explicitly considers the unique complexity of human sensors (e.g., mood sensitiveness).

15.2   Related work

Unknown source reliability has been studied in data mining and machine-learning communities, and a set of models on fact finding have been developed to address this problem [17]. *Hubs and Authorities* [18] developed an intuitive fact-finding algorithm that estimates the reliability of a source based on the credibility of claims made by the source. Similarly, it estimates the credibility of a claim based on the estimated reliability of sources that make the claim. Yin *et al.* proposed *TruthFinder*, an enhanced fact-finding framework, that replaces the linear assumption between source reliability and claim credibility used in Hubs and Authorities with a probabilistic model [19]. Qi *et al.* further improved the above fact-finding frameworks by explicitly considering the dependency between the data sources and studied how such dependency would affect the estimation on the source reliability [20]. Inspired by the insights from the fact-finding literature, MS-EM scheme builds a principled framework that jointly estimates the source reliability and claim credibility by explicitly considering the moody nature of human sensors and factor that developed into a solution.

Truth discovery is a critical problem in social sensing that receives a great amount of attention recently [21]. Several principled based solutions have been developed to address this problem. For example, Wang *et al.* proposed a maximum likelihood estimation (MLE) framework that models both the source reliability and claim credibility as unknown parameters of the model [10]. It developed an iterative algorithm to estimate the parameters in a way that is most consistent with the observed sensing data from the participants in social sensing. The follow up studies further quantified the confidence of the MLE estimation [22,23], considered the dependency between human sensors [24,25] and the dependency between claims [26,27], handled streaming data [28], addressed conflicting claims [29] and hardness of the claims [30], and studied the uncertain data provenance issue [31]. More recently, a set of new truth discovery models has been developed to consider the scalability [32], data sparsity [33,34], sensor selection [35,36], resource allocation [37], heterogeneous data [38] and the physical world constraints [39,40]. However, the mood sensitiveness aspect of the truth discovery problem has not been fully explored by the current literature; the MS-EM scheme reviewed in this chapter is one of the pioneering work along this direction.

Finally, MS-EM is an initial effort that belongs to a new type of reliable information recommendation systems [41]. In recommendation systems, EM-based approaches have been widely adopted in both content-based analysis [42] and collaborative filtering [43]. For example, Wang *et al.* proposed an online recommendation system that suggests scientific articles using EM-based collaborative filter technique [43]. Pomerantz *et al.* developed a movie recommendation system that explicitly considers the context information using EM-based content analysis [42]. In contrast, the MS-EM solves a different recommendation problem where the goal is to recommend high-quality information from a massive set of noisy and moody sensing report from human sensors. Furthermore, a reasonable training dataset is often assumed in traditional recommendation system. However, we often do not have such training dataset in social-sensing applications, which often leads to unsupervised or semi-supervised learning approaches.

15.3   Problem formulation and terminology definition

We first review the formulation of the MS truth discovery problem. In particular, the problem is formulated as a constraint multidimensional MLE problem. For example, consider a social-sensing application that consists of a set of M sources (Users) $S = (S_1, S_2, \ldots, S_M)$ and a set of N claims $C = C_1, C_2, \ldots, C_N$ reported by the users. In the MS truth-discovery problem, two important dimensions of a claim are explicitly considered: (i) mood sensitivity: it indicates if a claim is of MS or not and (ii) correctness: it indicates if a claim is true or not. We define some notations: S_u represents the uth source and C_k represents the kth claim. $C_k = O$ and $C_k = \overline{O}$ represent that C_k is MS or not, respectively. $C_k = T$ and $C_k = F$ represent the claim to be true or not, respectively. We further define the following terms to be used in our model.

- SM, a *source-mood matrix* that represents if a source indicates a claim to be MS or not. In SM, $S_uM_k = 1$ when source S_u indicates C_k to be MS and $S_uM_k = -1$ when source S_u indicates C_k to be mood neutral and $S_uM_k = 0$ if S_u does not make C_k at all.
- SC is defined as a *source-claim matrix* that represents if a source reports a claim to be true. In SC, $S_uC_k = 1$ if source S_u reports claim C_k to be true and $S_uC_k = 0$ otherwise.

In social sensing, not all claims are truthful and mood neutral. In MS-EM, we define the *mood sensitivity* of S_u as M_u:

$$
\begin{aligned}
M_u &= \Pr(C_k = O | S_uM_k = 1) \\
R_u &= \Pr(C_k = T | S_uC_k = 1)
\end{aligned}
\tag{15.1}
$$

A set of additional probabilities that are related with M_u and R_u are defined as below using the notations we defined.

$$
\begin{aligned}
V_{u,O}^T &= \Pr(S_uM_k = 1 | C_k = O) \\
V_{u,O}^F &= \Pr(S_uM_k = -1 | C_k = O) \\
V_{u,\overline{O}}^T &= \Pr(S_uM_k = 1 | C_k = \overline{O}) \\
V_{u,\overline{O}}^F &= \Pr(S_uM_k = -1 | C_k = \overline{O})
\end{aligned}
\tag{15.2}
$$

$$
\begin{aligned}
I_u &= \Pr(S_uC_k = 1 | C_k = T) \\
J_u &= \Pr(S_uC_k = 1 | C_k = F)
\end{aligned}
\tag{15.3}
$$

To capture the fact that sources may make different numbers of claims; we further define the likelihood that S_u reports a claim to be MS and mood neutral as $mp_{u,O}$ (i.e., $mp_{u,O} = \Pr(S_uM_k = 1)$) and $mp_{u,\overline{O}}$ (i.e., $mp_{u,\overline{O}} = \Pr(S_uM_k = -1)$), respectively. Additionally, we define the likelihood that source S_u reports a claim to be true by sp_u

(i.e., $sp_u = \Pr(S_u C_k = 1)$). We further denote $h_O = \Pr(C_k = O)$ and $d = \Pr(C_k = T)$. We can derive the relationship between the above items as below.

$$V_{u,O}^T = \frac{M_u \times mp_{u,O}}{h_O}, \quad V_{u,O}^F = \frac{(1 - M_u) \times mp_{u,O}}{h_O}$$

$$V_{u,\overline{O}}^T = \frac{(1 - M_u) \times mp_{u,\overline{O}}}{1 - h_O}, \quad V_{u,\overline{O}}^F = \frac{M_u \times mp_{u,\overline{O}}}{1 - h_O}$$

$$I_u = \frac{R_u \times sp_u}{d}, \quad J_u = \frac{(1 - R_u) \times sp_u}{(1 - d)} \tag{15.4}$$

Finally, Υ represents hidden truth on the mood neutrality of claims and Z represents the hidden truth on the correctness of claims. In particular, $r_k = 1$ in Υ when claim C_k is MS and $r_k = 0$ otherwise. $z_k = 1$ in Z when C_k is true and $z_k = 0$ when C_k is false. The MS truth discovery problem can be formulated as follows:

$$\forall k, 1 \le k \le N : \Pr(C_k = O | SM, SC)$$
$$\forall k, 1 \le k \le N : \Pr(C_k = T | SM, SC)$$
$$\forall u, 1 \le u \le M : \Pr(C_k = O | S_u M_k = 1)$$
$$\forall u, 1 \le u \le M : \Pr(C_k = T | S_u C_k = 1) \tag{15.5}$$

15.4 Mood sensitive truth discovery

In this section, we review the solution of the MS-EM solution to address the MS truth-discovery problem. We first derive the likelihood function $L = (\Theta_{ms}; X, \Upsilon)$ for MS-EM as follows:

$$L(\Theta_{ms}; X, \Upsilon) = \Pr(X, \Upsilon | \Theta_{ms})$$
$$= \prod_{k \in C} \Pr(r_k | X_k, \Theta_{ms}) \times \prod_{u \in S} \Psi_{k,u} \times \Pr(r_k) \tag{15.6}$$

where $\Theta_{ms} = (V_{1,O}^T, \ldots, V_{M,O}^T; V_{1,O}^F, \ldots, V_{M,O}^F; V_{1,\overline{O}}^T, \ldots, V_{M,\overline{O}}^T; V_{1,\overline{O}}^F, \ldots, V_{M,\overline{O}}^F; h_O)$ represents the model parameters. $\Psi_{k,u}$ and $\Pr(r_k)$ are defined in Table 15.1. Other notations are defined in the previous section. The model structure is illustrated in Figure 15.1.

Following the EM steps, the E-step of the MS-EM scheme is derived as follows:

$$Q(\Theta_{ms} | \Theta_{ms}^{(n)}) = V_{\Upsilon | X, \Theta_{ms}^{(n)}}[\log L(\Theta_{ms}; X, \Upsilon)]$$
$$= \sum_{k \in C} \Upsilon(n, k) \times \sum_{u \in S} (\log \Psi_{k,u} + \log \Pr(r_k)) \tag{15.7}$$

where $\Upsilon(n, k)$ is defined in Table 15.1.

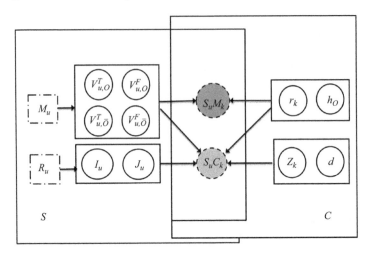

Figure 15.1   MS-EM model

Table 15.1   MS-EM notations

$\Psi_{k,u}$	$\Pr(r_k)$	$\Upsilon(n,k)$	**Constrains**
$V_{u,O}^T$	h_O	$\Upsilon^O(n,k)$	$S_uM_k^O = 1, S_uM_k^{\overline{O}} = 0, r_k = 1$
$V_{u,O}^F$	h_O	$\Upsilon^O(n,k)$	$S_uM_k^O = 0, S_uM_k^{\overline{O}} = 1, r_k = 1$
$V_{u,\overline{O}}^T$	$h_{\overline{O}}$	$1 - \Upsilon^O(n,k)$	$S_uM_k^O = 1, S_uM_k^{\overline{O}} = 0, r_k = 0$
$V_{u,\overline{O}}^F$	$h_{\overline{O}}$	$1 - \Upsilon^O(n,k)$	$S_uM_k^O = 0, S_uM_k^{\overline{O}} = 1, r_k = 0$
$1 - V_{u,O}^T - V_{u,O}^F$	h_O	$\Upsilon^O(n,k)$	$S_uM_k^O = 0, S_uM_k^{\overline{O}} = 0, r_k = 1$
$1 - V_{u,\overline{O}}^T - V_{u,\overline{O}}^F$	$h_{\overline{O}}$	$1 - \Upsilon^O(n,k)$	$S_uM_k^O = 0, S_uM_k^{\overline{O}} = 0, r_k = 0$

$\Upsilon^O(n,k)$ can be further expressed as

$$\Upsilon^O(n,k) = \frac{\Pr(r_k = O; X_k, \Theta_{ms}^{(n)})}{\Pr(X_k, \Theta_{ms}^{(n)})}$$

$$= \frac{L^O(n,k) \times h_O}{L^O(n,k) \times h_O + L^{\overline{O}}(n,k) \times h_{\overline{O}}} \tag{15.8}$$

where $L^O(n,k), L^{\overline{O}}(n,k)$ are defined as

$$L^O(n,k) = \Pr(X_k, \Theta_{ms}^{(n)} | r_k = O)$$

$$= \prod_{u=1}^{M} (V_{u,O}^T)^{S_uM_k^O} \times (V_{u,O}^F)^{S_uM_k^{\overline{O}}}$$

$$\times (1 - V_{u,O}^T - V_{u,O}^F)^{1 - S_uM_k^O - S_uM_k^{\overline{O}}}$$

Table 15.2   Optimal solutions of MS-EM

Notation	Solution	Notation	Solution
$(V_{u,O}^T)^*$	$(\sum_{k \in SF_u^O} \Upsilon^O(n,k)/\sum_{k=1}^N \Upsilon^O(n,k))$	$(V_{u,O}^F)^*$	$(\sum_{k \in SF_u^{\overline{O}}} \Upsilon^O(n,k)/\sum_{k=1}^N \Upsilon^O(n,k))$
$(V_{u,\overline{O}}^T)^*$	$(\sum_{k \in SF_u^O} \Upsilon^{\overline{O}}(n,k)/\sum_{k=1}^N \Upsilon^{\overline{O}}(n,k))$	$(V_{u,\overline{O}}^F)^*$	$(\sum_{k \in SF_u^{\overline{O}}} \Upsilon^{\overline{O}}(n,k)/\sum_{k=1}^N \Upsilon^{\overline{O}}(n,k))$
h_O^*	$(\sum_{k=1}^N \Upsilon^O(n,k)/N)$	$h_{\overline{O}}^*$	$(\sum_{k=1}^N \Upsilon^{\overline{O}}(n,k)/N)$

$$L^{\overline{O}}(n,k) = \Pr(X_k, \Theta_{ms}^{(n)}|r_k = \overline{O})$$

$$= \prod_{u=1}^M (V_{u,\overline{O}}^T)^{S_u M_k^O} \times (V_{u,\overline{O}}^F)^{S_u M_k^{\overline{O}}}$$

$$\times (1 - V_{u,\overline{O}}^T - V_{u,\overline{O}}^F)^{1 - S_u M_k^O - S_u M_k^{\overline{O}}} \tag{15.9}$$

In the M-step, we set derivatives $(\partial Q/\partial V_{u,O}^T) = 0$, $(\partial Q/\partial V_{u,O}^F) = 0$, $(\partial Q/\partial V_{u,\overline{O}}^T) = 0$, $(\partial Q/\partial V_{u,\overline{O}}^F) = 0$, $(\partial Q/\partial h_O) = 0$, $(\partial Q/\partial h_{\overline{O}}) = 0$. The results are shown in Table 15.2 where SF_u^O is the set of claims that S_u reports to be MS and $SF_u^{\overline{O}}$ is the set of claims that S_u reports to be mood neutral.

15.5   Evaluation

In this section, we review the evaluation of the MS-EM scheme through several real-world case studies using data from Twitter. The evaluation results show that MS-EM can successfully identify both neutral and correct claims and outperformed the state-of-the-art baselines.

15.5.1   Datasets and preprocessing

15.5.1.1   Information about datasets

Social sensing is an emerging area in networked sensing community where the humans are used as sensors to collect observations about the physical environment. The human-reported measurements in social sensing are known to be noisy, moody and unstructured [3]. We collected four real-world datasets from Twitter for our evaluation: (i) Brussels Bombing (Mar. 22, 2016); (ii) Paris Terrorists Attack (Nov. 13, 2015); (iii) Oregon College Shooting (Oct. 1, 2015); and (iv) Baltimore Riots (Apr. 14, 2015). We summarize the information of the four datasets in Table 15.3.

15.5.1.2   Preprocessing steps

We preprocess the raw datasets to generate the meta-data that MS-EM scheme needs to perform the MS truth discovery problem.

Clustering: The goal of clustering step is to generate the "claims" in the application by grouping tweets that have similar content into the same cluster. In particular,

Table 15.3   Data traces statistics

Data trace	Brussels bombing	Paris attack	Oregon shooting	Baltimore riots
Start date	Mar. 22, 2016	Nov. 13, 2015	Oct. 1, 2015	Apr. 14, 2015
Time duration	7 days	11 days	6 days	17 days
Location	Brussels, Belgium	Paris, France	Umpqua, Oregon	Baltimore, Maryland
Search keywords	Brussels, Attacks, Explosions	Paris, Attacks, ISIS	Oregon, Shooting, Umpqua	Baltimore, Riots
# of Tweets	986,560	873,760	210,028	952,442
# of users Tweeted	466,398	496,753	122,069	425,552

we use the Jaccard distance metric to compute the "distance" between any pair of tweets and choose the K-means clustering algorithm to generate the claims. The Jaccard distance measures the distance (i.e., similarity) between two tweets by checking the words that appear in both tweets [44].

Source-mood matrix and source-claim matrix generation: The *SM* matrix is generated as follows: if S_u reports C_k using a moody word, $S_u M_k = 1$. Similarly, if S_u reports claim C_k without using any moody words, $S_u M_k = -1$. Otherwise, $S_u M_k = 0$. A list of moody words are pre-collected from Twitter for this task [45]. The *SC* matrix is generated as follows: if S_u reports C_k, $S_u C_k = 1$. Otherwise, $S_u C_k = 0$.

15.5.2   Performance evaluation of MS-EM

We reviewed the performance of the MS-EM scheme in comparison with a few existing truth discovery solutions that do not explicitly explore the MS aspects of the reported claims.

15.5.2.1   Evaluation on mood neutral identification

We first study the performance of the MS-EM scheme in terms of identifying the mood neutral claims. A few baselines are used for performance comparison: *Voting*: it correlates the neutrality of a claim with the number of times it is reported by different sources. *Mood classifier*: it is a bag-of-word-based approach where a claim is considered as neutral if it does not contain the moody word in the pre-collected corpus. *Sums* [18]: it is a modified fact-finding algorithm where the credibility of a claim is replaced by the neutrality of the claim. *TruthFinder* [19]: it is a modified version of the original TruthFinder scheme by replacing the claim correctness with claim neutrality.

We manually graded the claims to decide its mood sensitiveness. We collected the ground truth labels of all claims using the following rubric:

- MS claims: Claims that clearly reflect the user's emotions (e.g., anger, sadness, excitement, disappointment).
- Mood neutral claims: Claims that do not contain any of the user's emotions.

We report the results of the MS-EM scheme on the Brussels bombing dataset in Table 15.4. We can observe that *MS-EM* performs best (shown as bold numbers in

Table 15.4   Performance results

Algorithm	Precision	Recall	F1-measure	Accuracy	Precision	Recall	F1-measure	Accuracy
	Brussels bombing				Baltimore riots			
MS-EM	**0.72**	**0.79**	**0.74**	**0.71**	**0.79**	**0.74**	**0.75**	**0.77**
Mood-classifier	0.64	0.62	0.63	0.61	0.69	0.62	0.66	0.67
TruthFinder	0.64	0.57	0.53	0.54	0.65	0.59	0.57	0.53
Sums	0.6	0.66	0.61	0.58	0.66	0.6	0.62	0.64
Voting	0.54	0.59	0.57	0.54	0.63	0.58	0.56	0.5
	Oregon shooting				Paris attacks			
MS-EM	**0.72**	**0.74**	**0.73**	**0.72**	**0.72**	**0.69**	**0.68**	**0.69**
Mood-classifier	0.63	0.62	0.64	0.65	0.63	0.6	0.59	0.59
TruthFinder	0.6	0.59	0.57	0.54	0.6	0.58	0.56	0.52
Sums	0.63	0.58	0.56	0.55	0.59	0.55	0.54	0.52
Voting	0.57	0.64	0.61	0.54	0.56	0.59	0.57	0.6

the table) compared to all other baselines. For example, *MS-EM* outperforms the best performed baseline by 11% and 10% on F1-measure and accuracy, respectively. Such performance gain is achieved by explicitly modeling the MS aspect of the claims in the truth-discovery problem and derive a principled solution to address the problem. The results on Baltimore Riots, Oregon Shooting and Paris Attacks are similar and MS-EM continues to outperform other baselines.

15.5.2.2   Mood-sensitive truth-discovery evaluation

We further review the evaluation results of the MS-EM in terms of solving the MS truth-discovery problem. We added one more baseline *Regular EM* [10], which also uses an MLE-based framework to solve the truth discovery problem. The only difference is it completely ignores the mood-sensitiveness aspect of the claims in its solution.

We define a new concept of *valuable* claim to represent the claims that are both correct and mood neutral. The valuable calms are the describable outputs of the reliable information recommendation system since they represent the credible and factual information, which will be critical to facilitate decision-making. We collected the ground truth of valuable claims using the following rubric:

* Valuable claims: Claims that are statements that are both neutral and credible (e.g., can be cross validated by the mainstream news media).
* Unconfirmed claims: Claims that do not meet the above definition of valuable claims.

We report the evaluation results of MS-EM scheme on Brussels bombing dataset in Figure 15.2. We observe that the *MS-EM* is the best performed scheme over different evaluation metrics. Specifically, the largest performance gains achieved

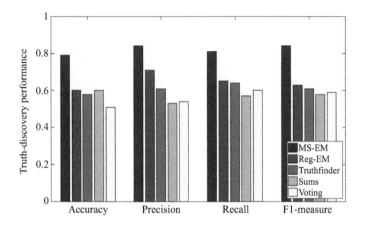

Figure 15.2   Truth discovery results on Brussels bombing dataset

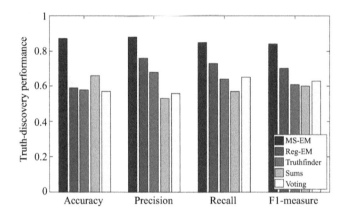

Figure 15.3   Truth discovery results on Baltimore riots dataset

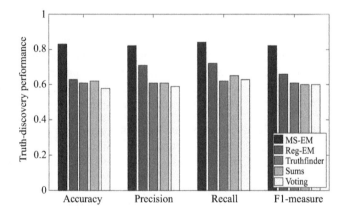

Figure 15.4   Truth discovery results on Oregon shooting dataset

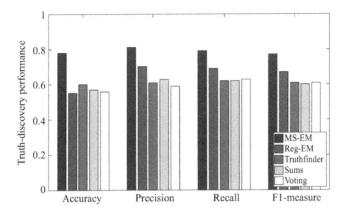

Figure 15.5   Truth discovery results on Paris attack dataset

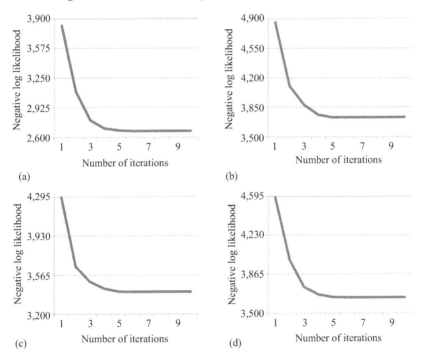

Figure 15.6   Convergence rate of MS-EM: (a) Brussels bombing dataset,
(b) Baltimore riots dataset, (c) Oregon shooting dataset, (d) Paris
attack dataset

by *MS-EM* are 13%, 16%, 20% and 19% on precision, recall, F1-measure and accuracy, respectively. The results on Baltimore riots, Oregon shooting and Paris attacks
datasets are presented in Figures 15.3, 15.4 and 15.5, respectively. MS-EM continues
to outperform other baselines. The MS-EM achieves the above performance gains

by exploiting the both mood-sensitiveness and correctness aspects of claims under a rigorous analytical framework.

The convergence results of the MS-EM scheme are shown in Figure 15.6. MS-EM scheme converges quickly on all four datasets we experiment with.

15.6   Conclusion

This chapter reviews a reliable information recommendation system in social sensing applications. The reviewed system takes a principled approach to solve an MS truth-discovery problem where both mood-sensitiveness and reliability of data sources are unknown to the application a priori. The proposed solution (i.e., MS-EM) has been evaluated extensively on four real-world social-sensing datasets collected from Twitter during disaster and emergence events. The evaluation results showed that the MS-EM scheme outperform the current truth discovery solutions in terms of identifying more valuable claims. The reviewed system lays out an important analytical foundation to build principled reliable information recommendation system that can identify both credible and mood neutral claims from a large set of noisy and biased human-sensing measurement in social-sensing applications.

Acknowledgments

This research is supported in part by the National Science Foundation under Grant No. CBET-1637251, CNS-1566465 and IIS-1447795 and Army Research Office under Grant W911NF-17-1-0409. The views and conclusions contained in this document are those of the authors and should not be interpreted as representing the official policies, either expressed or implied, of the Army Research Office or the US government. The US government is authorized to reproduce and distribute reprints for government purposes notwithstanding any copyright notation here on.

References

[1]   Jermaine Marshall and Dong Wang. Mood-sensitive truth discovery for reliable recommendation systems in social sensing. In *Proceedings of the 10th ACM Conference on Recommender Systems*, pages 167–174. ACM, 2016.

[2]   Dong Wang. Data reliability challenge of cyber-physical systems. In *Cyber-Physical Systems*, pages 91–101. Elsevier, 2017.

[3]   Charu C Aggarwal and Tarek Abdelzaher. Social sensing. In *Managing and Mining Sensor Data*, pages 237–297. Springer, 2013.

[4]   Jianwei Wang, Dong Wang, Yuping Zhao, and Timo Korhonen. Fast anti-collision algorithms in RFID systems. In *Mobile Ubiquitous Computing, Systems, Services and Technologies, 2007. UBICOMM'07. International Conference on*, pages 75–80. IEEE, 2007.

[5]   Jianwei Wang, Yuping Zhao, and Dong Wang. A novel fast anti-collision algorithm for RFID systems. In *Wireless Communications, Networking and Mobile Computing, 2007. WiCom 2007. International Conference on*, pages 2044–2047. IEEE, 2007.

[6]   Dong Wang, Tarek Abdelzaher, and Lance Kaplan. *Social Sensing: Building Reliable Systems on Unreliable Data*. Morgan Kaufmann, 2015.

[7]   Daniel Yue Zhang, Dong Wang, Hao Zheng, Xin Mu, Qi Li, and Yang Zhang. Large-scale point-of-interest category prediction using natural language processing models. In *2017 IEEE International Conference on Big Data (IEEE BigData 2017)*. IEEE, 2017.

[8]   Dong Wang, Kun Qiu, and Li-cun Wang. Design of DBA algorithm in EPON upstream channel in support of SLA. *Journal of China Institute of Communications*, 26(6):87, 2005.

[9]   Dong Wang, Tarek Abdelzaher, and Lance Kaplan. Surrogate mobile sensing. *IEEE Communications Magazine*, 52(8):36–41, 2014.

[10] Dong Wang, Lance Kaplan, Hieu Le, and Tarek Abdelzaher. On truth discovery in social sensing: A maximum likelihood estimation approach. In *The 11th ACM/IEEE Conference on Information Processing in Sensor Networks (IPSN 12)*, April 2012.

[11] Hsia-Ching Chang. A new perspective on twitter hashtag use: diffusion of innovation theory. *Proceedings of the American Society for Information Science and Technology*, 47(1):1–4, 2010.

[12] Dong Wang, Hossein Ahmadi, Tarek Abdelzaher, Harsha Chenji, Radu Stoleru, and Charu C Aggarwal. Optimizing quality-of-information in cost-sensitive sensor data fusion. In *Distributed Computing in Sensor Systems and Workshops (DCOSS), 2011 International Conference on*, pages 1–8. IEEE, 2011.

[13] Chao Huang, Dong Wang, Shenglong Zhu, and Daniel Yue Zhang. Towards unsupervised home location inference from online social media. In *Big Data (Big Data), 2016 IEEE International Conference on*, pages 676–685. IEEE, 2016.

[14] Jermaine Marshall and Dong Wang. Towards emotional-aware truth discovery in social sensing applications. In *Smart Computing (SMARTCOMP), 2016 IEEE International Conference on*, pages 1–8. IEEE, 2016.

[15] Aditya Mogadala and Vasudeva Varma. Twitter user behavior understanding with mood transition prediction. In *Proceedings of the Workshop on Data-Driven User Behavioral Modelling and Mining from Social Media*, 2012.

[16] Dong Wang. Big data and information distillation in social sensing. *In Big Data: Storage, Sharing, and Security*, CRC Press, page 121, 2016.

[17] Manish Gupta and Jiawei Han. Heterogeneous network-based trust analysis: a survey. *ACM SIGKDD Explorations Newsletter*, 13(1):54–71, 2011.

[18] Jon M. Kleinberg. Authoritative sources in a hyperlinked environment. *Journal of the ACM*, 46(5):604–632, 1999.

[19] Xiaoxin Yin, Jiawei Han, and Philip S Yu. Truth discovery with multiple conflicting information providers on the web. *IEEE Transactions on Knowledge and Data Engineering*, 20:796–808, 2008.

[20] Guo-Jun Qi, Charu C Aggarwal, Jiawei Han, and Thomas Huang. Mining collective intelligence in diverse groups. In *Proceedings of the 22nd International Conference on World Wide Web*, pages 1041–1052. International World Wide Web Conferences Steering Committee, 2013.

[21] Dong Wang, Boleslaw K Szymanski, Tarek Abdelzaher, Heng Ji, and Lance Kaplan. The age of social sensing. *arXiv preprint arXiv:1801.09116*, 2018.

[22] Dong Wang, Lance Kaplan, Tarek Abdelzaher, and Charu C Aggarwal. On credibility tradeoffs in assured social sensing. *IEEE Journal On Selected Areas in Communication (JSAC)*, 31(6):1026–1037, 2013.

[23] Dong Wang, Lance Kaplan, Tarek Abdelzaher, and Charu C Aggarwal. On scalability and robustness limitations of real and asymptotic confidence bounds in social sensing. In *The 9th Annual IEEE Communications Society Conference on Sensor, Mesh and Ad Hoc Communications and Networks (SECON 12)*, June 2012.

[24] Dong Wang, Md Tanvir Amin, Shen Li, *et al.* Using humans as sensors: An estimation-theoretic perspective. In *Proceedings of the 13th International Symposium on Information Processing in Sensor Networks*, pages 35–46. IEEE Press, 2014.

[25] Chao Huang and Dong Wang. Topic-aware social sensing with arbitrary source dependency graphs. In *The 15th ACM/IEEE Conference on Information Processing in Sensor Networks (IPSN 16)*. ACM/IEEE, 2016.

[26] Dong Wang, Tarek Abdelzaher, Lance Kaplan, Raghu Ganti, Shaohan Hu, and Hengchang Liu. Exploitation of physical constraints for reliable social sensing. In *The IEEE 34th Real-Time Systems Symposium (RTSS'13)*, 2013.

[27] Dong Wang, Tarek Abdelzaher, Lance Kaplan, Raghu Ganti, Shaohan Hu, and Hengchang Liu. Reliable social sensing with physical constraints: analytic bounds and performance evaluation. *Real-Time Systems*, 51(6):724–762, 2015.

[28] Dong Wang, Tarek Abdelzaher, Lance Kaplan, and Charu C Aggarwal. Recursive fact-finding: A streaming approach to truth estimation in crowdsourcing applications. In *The 33rd International Conference on Distributed Computing Systems (ICDCS'13)*, July 2013.

[29] Dong Wang, Lance Kaplan, and Tarek Abdelzaher. Maximum likelihood analysis of conflicting observations in social sensing. *ACM Transactions on Sensor Networks (ToSN)*, 10(2), 2014, Article 30.

[30] Jermaine Marshall, Munira Syed, and Dong Wang. Hardness-aware truth discovery in social sensing applications. In *Distributed Computing in Sensor Systems (DCOSS), 2016 International Conference on*, pages 143–152. IEEE, 2016.

[31] Dong Wang, Md Tanvir Al Amin, Tarek Abdelzaher, *et al.* Provenance-assisted classification in social networks. *IEEE Journal of Selected Topics in Signal Processing (J-STSP)*, 8(40):624–637, 2014.

[32] Daniel Yue Zhang, Chao Zheng, Dong Wang, *et al.* Towards scalable and dynamic social sensing using a distributed computing framework. In

Distributed Computing Systems (ICDCS), 2017 IEEE 37th International Conference on, pages 966–976. IEEE, 2017.

[33]   Daniel Yue Zhang, Rungang Han, Dong Wang, and Chao Huang. On robust truth discovery in sparse social media sensing. In *Big Data (Big Data), 2016 IEEE International Conference on*, pages 1076–1081. IEEE, 2016.

[34]   Daniel Yue Zhang, Dong Wang, Yang Zhang, Nathan Vance, and Steven Mike. On scalable and robust truth discovery in big data social media sensing applications. *IEEE Transaction on Big Data*, 2018.

[35]   Dong Wang, Nathan Vance, and Chao Huang. Who to select: Identifying critical sources in social sensing. *Knowledge-Based Systems*, 145:98–108, 2018.

[36]   Chao Huang and Dong Wang. Critical source selection in social sensing applications. In *Distributed Computing in Sensor Systems (DCOSS), 2017 International Conference on to Appear*, 2017.

[37]   Daniel Yue Zhang, Yue Ma, Yang Zhang, Suwen Lin, X. Sharon Hu, and Dong Wang. A real-time and non-cooperative task allocation framework for social sensing applications in edge computing systems. In *In 24th IEEE Real-Time and Embedded Technology and Applications Symposium (RTAS 2018)*. IEEE, 2018.

[38]   Prasanna Giridhar, Md Tanvir Amin, Tarek Abdelzaher, *et al.* ClariSense+: An enhanced traffic anomaly explanation service using social network feeds. *Pervasive and Mobile Computing*, 33:140–155, 2016.

[39]   Daniel Yue Zhang, Dong Wang, and Yang Zhang. Constraint-aware dynamic truth discovery in big data social media sensing. In *2017 IEEE International Conference on Big Data (IEEE BigData 2017)*. IEEE, 2017.

[40]   Jermaine Marshall, Arturo Argueta, and Dong Wang. A neural network approach for truth discovery in social sensing. In *2017 IEEE 14th International Conference on Mobile Ad Hoc and Sensor Systems (MASS)*, pages 343–347. IEEE, 2017.

[41]   Dietmar Jannach, Markus Zanker, Alexander Felfernig, and Gerhard Friedrich. *Recommender Systems: An Introduction*. Cambridge University Press, 2010.

[42]   Daniel Pomerantz and Gregory Dudek. Context dependent movie recommendations using a hierarchical Bayesian model. In *Advances in Artificial Intelligence*, pages 98–109. Berlin, Heidelberg: Springer, 2009.

[43]   Chong Wang and David M Blei. Collaborative topic modeling for recommending scientific articles. In *Proceedings of the 17th ACM SIGKDD International Conference on Knowledge Discovery and Data Mining*, pages 448–456. ACM, 2011.

[44]   Kevin Dela Rosa, Rushin Shah, Bo Lin, Anatole Gershman, and Robert Frederking. Topical clustering of tweets. In *Proceedings of the ACM SIGIR: SWSM*, 2011.

[45]   Panagiotis Gayo-Avello, Eni Takis Metaxas, Markus Mustafaraj, *et al.* Predicting information credibility in time-sensitive social media. *Internet Research*, 23(5):560–588, 2013.

Chapter 16

The paradox of opinion leadership and recommendation culture in Chinese online movie reviews

Jie Yang[1] and Brian Yecies[2]

In this empirical study of online leadership, analysis for movie recommendations on Douban, one of the biggest interest-oriented online Chinese-language social networking systems of its kind, we address the identification of the characteristics of key opinion leaders using a big data processing framework. As an illustrative case study, we focus on a niche subset of popular audience content on Douban: approximately a half million short comments regarding the top 94 most popular South Korean films produced between 2003 and 2012. Raw data samples, including film details, review comments, and user profiles, are harvested via one asynchronous scraping crawler, and then their heterogeneous features are manipulated accordingly. Finally, a parallel association rule-mining (ARM) algorithm is employed for revealing leadership patterns. The proposed framework explains how to extract high-level features that can then be used to gauge the effectiveness of these so-called key leaders and their ability to generate word-of-mouth (WOM) awareness and interest surrounding their recommendations. In turn, researchers can edge closer to determining the kind of charismatic 'soft power' appeal of leading reviewers and reviews that are facilitating among follower networks new opportunities to evaluate a film and ultimately to decide to view it.

16.1 Introduction

With the increasing global popularity of social media, and its expanding role in the commercialisation of China's digital platforms and applications, it has become imperative for scholars and industry stakeholders to develop new understandings of audiences and online opinion leadership. Investigating this aspect of Internet WOM

[1]SMART Infrastructure Facility, Faculty of Engineering and Information Sciences, University of Wollongong, Australia
[2]Communication and Media Studies, School of the Arts, English and Media, University of Wollongong, Australia

recommendation culture and the agents who help drive it is essential for improving communication about digital media content, which is rapidly transforming Chinese society. At the same time, it is encouraging deeper engagement and a higher level of recommendation activity for both content producers and user communities. Key opinion leaders, that is, individuals that demonstrate expertise in the field and to whom others look for informed WOM viewpoints on movies and a range of other popular topics, play a crucial role in improving communication and encouraging group members to have greater level of information exchange. Yet, ironically, identifying such pivotal active social media users who voice leading WOM opinions continues to pose new challenges for industry players, such as Hollywood and Chinese media companies, which rely on big data to guide current promotional campaigns and to shape future productions around changing audience tastes.

Presently, from what the authors have learned by regularly interviewing a number of active film industry representatives in China, some of the chief problems facing this arena include a lack of access to relevant big data, ways of categorising data, and strategies for identifying key opinion leaders.[1,2] In spite of the growing interest in opinion leadership and WOM analysis in general, there has been little research into these three problem areas, and how one might overcome their limitations. Thus, there is an increasing need to develop alternative frameworks for conducting opinion leadership analysis. Our aim is to develop an efficient and practical technique for investigating online opinion leadership based on massive user-generated content (hereafter UGC). The main contribution of this proposed work can be summarised as follows:

- An efficient analytical framework is implemented for investigating large volumes of online user-generated data (i.e. collection, distribution, storage, and process) using the cloud-computing platform.
- A comprehensive analysis is executed to construct high-level features using original film metadata, textual reviews, and user profiles. In addition, we also manage to facilitate quantification of the constructed features;
- We further apply our framework to explore opinion-leader characteristics. A parallel rule-mining algorithm is introduced to discover patterns within 'leader' and 'non-leader' groups. These functionalities hold significant meaning for improving user experience, and for advising both film producers and distributors.

The preliminary research can be found in our previous study [1]. However, the current chapter builds upon this former work by introducing additional user-activity features and conducting different experiments. Furthermore, in experiments of the performance validation through an analysis of features among movie metadata, textual

[1]The authors thank industry leaders Niel Xie (Base FX, Beijing), Christopher He (Twilightstar Entertainment, Beijing), Even Yang (Douban Film Operations), Charles Wang (Beijing Film Academy), Liao Zhuodi (T2Cloud, Beijing), Fay Wang and Marja Zhang (Perfect World Pictures, Beijing), and Wang Ting and Nicole Li (U17, Beijing) for sharing their insights on this evolving topic.
[2]This research was supported by the Australian Research Council Discovery Project (DP170102176), titled Digital China: From Cultural Presence to Innovative Nation.

content from review comments, and user profiles, the results show the flexibility and applicability of the proposed framework for extracting important information from complex social media data. It is hoped that the specific findings provided in this study can be used to inform strategies not only for promoting opinion leadership but also for customising recommendation cultures and practices among specific markets, regions, and target audiences that are rapidly increasing in China and beyond.

The remainder of this chapter is organised as follows. The following section briefly sets the scholarly background of opinion leadership within recommendation culture and other related studies. A survey of the relevant literature in Section 16.2 reveals that previous investigators have devised a number of approaches regarding leadership analysis and recommendation systems. Next, the implemented framework is introduced in Section 16.3. We first provide the general architecture and then elaborate its three major modules, i.e. data collection, feature builder, and rule-mining functionality. In Section 16.4, we evaluate the performance of the implemented framework by discovering leadership patterns using real-word social media data. We also quantitatively characterise the significance of the proposed features with regard to opinion leadership. Finally, the article concludes by suggesting further prospects for the proposed work in Section 16.5.

16.2 Related work on online leadership and recommendation

This section offers a brief review on the study background related to the 'rise of China', as well as existing work on online leadership and recommendation systems. First, we discuss the general nature of China's changing media landscape. Second, we address leadership identification gleaned from users' comments and their profiles. We then investigate recommendation approaches associated with user preference.

16.2.1 The rise of China

For many people, China is associated with an authoritarian regime, propaganda, corruption, mass production, pollution, and the manufacture of fake goods [2]. While China's economy is undoubtedly powerful, it is more bad than good news when it comes to its international reputation. Writing a decade ago, Ramo asserted, 'China's image of herself and other nations' views of her are out of alignment' [3]. Since then, China's image has undergone some refashioning, its global strategy taking a new form, concomitant with a powerful push into global markets via the production of legacy media. Both developments have contributed to the transformation of China's international image. For many Chinese people the 'going out' of this varied type of media culture is a means to tell China's story through its own words, rather than through the foreign lenses of the BBC or Hollywood. Notwithstanding, the domestic and diasporic expansion of social media WOM platforms such as Douban, considered as 'essential reading for any serious movie fan in China' [4], has accentuated China's leadership contributions to the global media playing field – especially now that translation websites and applications are making Chinese-language content more accessible than ever before.

In a survey of scholarship, Sun observes that Chinese scholars regard the media and communication sectors, including social media platforms, as 'the backbone of China's going global effort' [5]. Some commentators noted in Sun's survey suggest that China's media is successfully challenging international giants. There is no doubt, for instance, that Dalian Wanda's acquisition in 2014 of the AMC Entertainment cinema chain (in the US), and in 2015 Hoyts (Australia), as well as the purchase of Hollywood's Legendary Pictures in 2016 have provided it with Hollywood clout as well as new global outlets for Chinese content. More recently, Douban has followed in some of Wanda's, as well as Baidu, Alibaba and Tencent's footsteps by expanding into the media production arena with Douban Time, a fee-based web series in which experts and stars, serving as 'change agents', discuss and recommend content, such as poetry, novels, music, and films to audiences. Clearly, 'opinion leadership' and the WOM clout that they are generating among followers is become the driving force behind the continued expansion and commercialisation of the legacy and social mediasphere in China.

16.2.2   Opinion leadership

The general concept of opinion leadership and personal WOM influence has a long history spanning across multiple fields, such as the humanities, management and marketing, and computer science. Suffice it to say that early theories of opinion leadership were popularised by Lazarsfeld *et al.* in their study on the decision-making processes of voters in the USA during the 1940 presidential election [6]. Through this study, as well as subsequent studies, such as Katz and Lazarsfeld [7], it was discovered that mass media messages were mediated by a number of so-called opinion leaders that stood out for their increased familiarity with related mass media content and a concentrated dose of group discussion. In short, such key opinion leaders provided a critical link between specific information and ideas generated by the media and circulating among the wider population in the public sphere. Today, it has become conventional, for example when theorising how social influence in addition to mass media coverage, for such agents to play a determinant role in the diffusion and adoption of new ideas, products, and innovations [8,9].

Here, depending on the level of trust among social media followers, user-generated reviews – or what is generally known as e-WOM – enable users to judge the quality and rating of particular media or products. However, at face value, the rating system used by Chinese film fans, at least on the Douban site, seems less efficacious as a measure of audience approval than ratings used on English-language sites by western film fans – for example on IMDb or Metacritic. Chinese users on Douban – that is, members of a 'collectivist society' – have been observed showing increased alignment with their fellow netizens in terms of film ratings. In other words, they value group harmony over the expression of individual opinions that are extremely different from the group. As a result, we may ask what are some of the other ways of measuring or gauging audience opinions of a film? And, how is it possible to employ a new framework to conduct this analytical process?

As a concept, WOM is considered by industry professionals and theorists alike as a powerful communication tool and social-networking channel for spreading awareness of a product or service in both offline and online worlds. WOM appears most effective when knowledgeable consumers stand out by actively creating and/or distributing information about or recommendations of products and services to other consumers. This process creates an ostensible sense of grassroots legitimacy because the message appears to be initiated by a member of one's own peer or interest group rather than by the manufacturer of the product or service. Via online platforms and mobile applications such as Douban, social media networks have radically changed the ways in which information is shared and spread beyond traditional offline WOM, that is, face-to-face conversations. This tool has also given rise to the creation of new opinion leaders that generate a kind of power to motivate the decisions and actions of their followers who actively seek and accept recommendations online. Today, e-WOM appears to be a critical factor in a film's commercial success.

With this background in mind, the value of using data quarried from Douban to achieve a better quantitative and qualitative understanding of Chinese audience tastes becomes apparent. Yet, the technical process of identifying online leaders in this domain is more complex and non-linear than it may appear. Therefore, a variety of sophisticated algorithms is required to extract subjective information from UGC and categorise particular reviewers either as a 'leader' or a 'non-leader'. To express this matter in mathematical terms, let $x = \{x_1, x_2, \ldots, x_n\}$ be a vector representing n high-level features extracted from UGC (such as textual reviews and user profiles), and $y \in \{leader, non - leader\}$ be the class label. Leadership identification aims to train a classifier that extracts the decision rule subject to the following constraint:

$$y = f(x) + e, \tag{16.1}$$

where $f(\cdot)$ is an unknown decision function to be estimated by the classifier and e is the corresponding error. Essentially, UGC features (x_i, $i \in [1, n]$) and classification function ($f(\cdot)$) play the largest and most critical role in accurately determining the leadership of a given user. Here we review a number of existing technical studies on which our study builds.

Some studies linked to the search for online leadership trends have been developed by using available information from user networks. The basic idea is to represent users as nodes within a large network topology and then compute their leader score before ranking nodes with higher scores as opinion leaders. In [10], an improved PageRank algorithm is presented while employed features include reviewers' liveness, degree of attention, and reviewers' awareness; another reviewer-network-based method has been introduced in [11], in which the network topology is defined using directional links between fans and their leaders, and a modified PageRank algorithm is applied. Another type of leadership identification algorithm is based on textual content to distinguish leaders from their followers. In [12], for example, authors harvest quantitative review contents and ratings, etc. Then the polarity of the original posts is calculated, followed by a consensus-based approach to classify influential reviewers.

More recently, some alternative hybrid algorithms have been proposed. In [13], the authors propose an opinion-leader identification approach in cloud environments. Leadership is measured by the availability, reliability, data integrity, identification, and capability presented in different cloud environments. They further apply three topological measures, including input-degree, output-degree, and trust to evaluate a leadership value.

Zhao *et al*. have introduced an improved bounded confidence model to simulate the opinion dynamics [14]. The traditional-bounded confidence model is an agent-based method, where each agent is associated with a continuous value that represents a certain opinion level. The interaction among agents occurs only if they have a similar opinion value, which is referred to as the bounded confidence level. Then to better simulate the opinion evolution, two additional extensions are made on the traditional-bounded confidence model by dividing agents into conflict opinion groups and taking the environment uncertainty into account.

A supernetwork-based algorithm is presented in [15] to discover opinion leadership patterns, which combine both network topology and textual content. The method first defines four networks, including node superdegree, superedge degree, superedge–superedge distance, and superedge overlap. These four-layer supernetworks are further associated with information, psychology, viewpoint to a paralleled position with opinion leaders. Then the supernetwork theory is applied to describe and express the interaction and effect between networks and eventually identify opinion leadership. While each of these above-mentioned studies has their own merits, the processes required to generate results and findings remain overly complex and with limitations in their applicability to industry stakeholders.

16.2.3   Recommendation system

Recommendation systems aim to suggest new items such as films, products and services to audiences based on their established preferences and historical search activities. There is a long history of studies on developing personal recommendation technology that date back to the 1990s. In academia, one of the earliest recommendation systems is called MovieLens developed by the GroupLens initiative at University of Minnesota in the United States. The system was designed to collect individual ratings from a series of favourite films and then predict what each member might be interested in watching. As a practical application, industry stakeholders attempt to make full use of this type of recommendation technology in order to promote their products among targeted relevant groups, such as Amazon [16].

Most existing recommendation systems fall into two categories: content-based (CB) and collaborative filtering (CF) methods. On the one hand, the CB recommendation system considers an item's metadata. For instance, in terms of a film recommendation, the metadata could be film genre, actor, director, and basic descriptions [17–19]. That is to say, the correlation between multiple items is utilised as the key criteria for recommendations. Let the list $\mathcal{M} = \{m_i | \forall m_i \in \mathcal{M}\}$ be the favourite item list for the ith user. Let the *content*($\cdot$) function represent item metadata, i.e. a set of predefined attributes or features characterising selected items. Accordingly, CB methods estimate a user's (u_i) preference for other items m_j ($m_j \notin \mathcal{M}$) based on their similarity with $\mathcal{M}$:

$$sim\{\mathcal{M}, m_j\} = \sum sim\left(content(m_i), content(m_j)\right), \tag{16.2}$$

where $sim\{*\}$ denotes a predefined function to measure the similarity between $\mathscr{M}$ and m_j.

By contrast, the CF method makes recommendations based on a group of users outside the sample group that share similar preferences. Given a user list $\mathscr{U} = \{u_i | \forall u_i \in \mathscr{U}\}$, for any one target user u_i, CF methods generate a sorted user list $\widehat{\mathscr{U}}$, which satisfies the following conditions:

- $\widehat{\mathscr{U}} \subset \mathscr{U}$, and $u_i \notin \widehat{\mathscr{U}}$;
- $sim\{u_j, u_i\} \geq sim\{u_k, u_i\}$, subject that $\forall u_j, u_k \in \widehat{\mathscr{U}}$ and $j < k$.

Again, the variable $sim\{u_j, u_i\}$ represents the similarity between user u_j and u_i. By finding the most similar user(s) to u_i, the recommendation is made by aggregating the historical watching information from $\widehat{\mathscr{U}}$. Examples of the CF-based recommendation system include [20–22].

More recently, several hybrid algorithms have been proposed to improve the accuracy of recommendations. For instance, in [23], both CF and CB-based recommenders are employed in parallel. A K-nearest-neighbourhood algorithm is implemented to estimate similarity. Meanwhile, clustering algorithms are also combined with the CF method to combine similar items before making a recommendation [24]. Li *et al.* further suggest using a fuzzy K-means algorithm to cluster items with similar profiles [25]. These hybrid algorithms demonstrate their superiority over traditional recommendation systems by addressing problems such as data sparsity and cold start.

16.2.4 Leadership for recommendations among social networks

Now we address the intersections between opinion leadership and recommendation. The basic recommendation system is a two-way communication platform that enables the circulation of opinions. Typically, recommenders express and share opinions with their peers, while readers contribute feedback with regard to the received opinion with their own experience.

Further, an online or mobile recommendation system provides a convenient channel for opinion leaders to influence their followers because of the e-WOM power that they possess. This reflects a natural social process as people are mostly likely to follow recommendations from a perceived leader. In practice, for example, a review written by a well-known celebrity or highly recognised leader from a digital platform, such as YouTube, can result in better product sales and/or generate increased attention among the user network. Therefore, discovering leadership patterns can assist with discovering what kinds of opinions people will follow or adopt, so as to improve the performance of the recommendation service.

16.3 Methodology

In this section, we introduce the leadership analytical framework used to analyse massive quantities of UGC. To store and process the large data collected from social network applications, a platform with a high storage capacity and computing power is essential. As a result, the proposed analytical framework is built using some

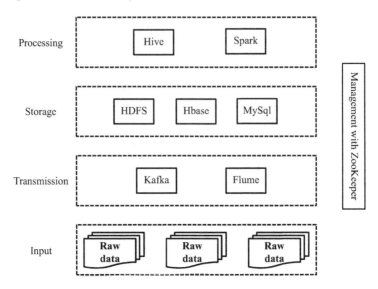

Figure 16.1   Architecture of the implemented big-data processing platform for leadership analysis

cutting-edge software for the reliable, scalable, and distributed-computing purpose. The system architecture is shown in Figure 16.1.

As observed, raw data samples are imported to this platform through a transmission module, which provides real-time and stable transmission using Kafka [26] and Flume [27]. More precisely, collected data records will first reach the Kafka component that is employed to process and save individual samples into one or more message queues according to a predefined format or user's operation. Furthermore, Kafka is also utilised for performing a data-distribution task so that data from message queues can be (re)consumed by other components as many times as required. Kafka also provides a fault-tolerant way to store streams of records in this message queue. Without Kafka, however, raw data samples can only be consumed by one simultaneous process (such as writing or reading), and the data flow with high-throughput, low-latency is not guaranteed. Next, Flume is employed to move data from Kafka to other components in the storage module. In other words, Kafka is employed as a Flume source, and Flume helps to move large amounts of streaming data efficiently to different destinations via its sinks. Due to the distributed Flume capability, the data can flow smoothly from Kafka to various storage components.

In the storage module, due to the diversity of the data format, three storage mechanisms are employed, i.e. Hadoop Distributed File System (HDFS) [28], HBase [29], and MySql [30]. MySql performs well for a small amount of data, while HDFS is used to store and distribute much more samples. The reliability of HDFS enhances the big data processing capability, and the storage space under HDFS can be extended easily by adding hard disks or new machines. Compared to the structured data in relational database management system (RDBMS) and HDFS, non SQL (NoSQL) is employed to store semi-structured records with a good scalability and fault-tolerance capability. In our study, the RDBMS is used to store the 'movie' metadata as the number of films is relatively smaller than that of the comments. The massive 'review' data is then saved using HDFS given its huge volume, and 'User' profile and behaviour (such as their watching lists) data is saved into HBase due to the semi-structured data format.

Next, we use Hive [31] and Spark [32] to process the massive data. Hive is a big data extraction, transformation and load tool; Spark is an open source environment for fast data analytic, which provides a scalable platform for in-memory computing, thereby achieving advanced performance over other approaches. In addition, to monitor the whole platform, we also have developed a management module using ZooKeeper [33] to maintain configuration information, naming, and to provide distributed synchronisation and group services.

Based on this implemented big-data processing platform, we introduce the leadership analytical framework, consisting of an asynchronous scraping crawler (harvesting film details, online reviews, and user profiles), a feature builder (removing data noise and extracting high-level features from raw data), and rule-mining functionality (discovering opinion leadership patterns). More details are given below.

16.3.1   Data collection

The proposed work focuses narrowly on a subset of popular Korean films and their influence on Douban, one of the biggest interest-oriented Chinese social networking site (SNS) of its kind. This social media networking digital platform currently attracts approximately nearly 400 million unique visitors and over 1 billion unique page views per year. The result is the generation of vast quantities of self-interested reviewer records, including online reviews and users' profiles.

To explore this rapidly changing arena, we selected a total of 94 Korean films released between 2003 and 2012. This subset includes the top ten performing films in each year according to Korean box office statistics, which are publically available on the Korean Film Council online database [34]. Whilst these films were conspicuously popular among Korean fans, the case is not necessarily the same for Chinese fans, and thus this particular dataset offers a relatively unbiased opportunity to investigate the nature of their reception in user comments on Douban. The open nature of the Korean and Chinese-Douban dataset and its potential for reuse makes it possible for independent observers and readers to replicate and build upon the results discussed below.

Accordingly, an asynchronous scraping crawler has been developed with certain functionalities, such as multiple-thread collection, to access the Douban data via the public application programming interface. This implemented crawler consists of one global controller and multiple workers, which are configured separately in different computer nodes. Among them, the controller is used to manage the entire collection task and split it into sub-jobs, while workers execute harvesting sub-jobs concurrently. Additional details on this implementation can be found in [1]. To this end, three categories of Douban content are collected and extracted, including movie

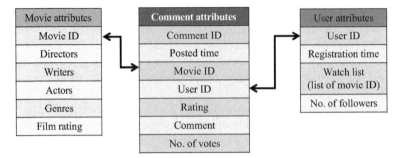

Figure 16.2   Data structure and relationships between Douban contents – films, reviews and users

Table 16.1   Summary for generated features representing raw attributes

Category	Generated features
Film	Genres, movie rating
Review	Actor, director, writer, story, emotion, review rating, length, posted time, leadership label
User	Activity, membership duration, centrality

details, textual comments, and user profiles. Raw attributes are then illustrated in Figure 16.2.

16.3.2   Feature builder

A high-level feature can be regarded as a user-defined hierarchical representation of these initial raw attributes. In accordance with the record category, related feature lists are generated to cover the same aspects: film details, review comments, and user profiles, and the outcome of this feature builder is summarised in Table 16.1 . These features are generated as they are typically found in English-language comments on most OSNs. Among these, the 'Genres' feature can be directly extracted from raw attributes, whereas others require high-level aggregation and quantification process. More details about extracting and quantifying features, including movie rating, actor, director, writer, story, emotion, review rating, activity, membership duration, can be found in our previous study [1]. Next we will elaborate newly introduced features such as length, posted time, leadership label, and centrality.

   Length is a simple but efficient measurement for evaluating review content, which is counted as the total number of written words from a review. In addition, the posted time feature is used to discover the exact time when a review has been made. Centrality is the feature for estimating the potential influence exerted by a given reviewer within his/her entire social network. In this study, the centrality is calculated as the number of followers a reviewer has, which is also known as the connection ratio of one given reviewer compared to all others within the entire user network.

Therefore, let $l_{i,j}$ represent the length from the jth reviewer's review to the ith film, and l_i be the number of words from the longest review for the ith film; the length feature $L_{i,j}$ can be calculated as follows:

$$L_{i,j} = \frac{l_{i,j}}{l_i}. \tag{16.3}$$

Furthermore, let $d_{i,j}$ be the posted time of the review made by the jth reviewer to the ith film, d_i represent the time when the first review appears, T_{now} be the constant for the current date, and the function $date(*)$ for the number of days between two given dates, we have posted time as

$$T_{i,j} = \frac{date(d_{i,j}, T_{now})}{date(d_i, T_{now})}. \tag{16.4}$$

As for the centrality (C_j) feature, let K be the total number of collected users, and k_j the number of followers for the given jth reviewer. To this end, we have centrality estimated as follows:

$$C_j = \frac{k_j}{K}. \tag{16.5}$$

At last, we mark different reviewers with a 'Leadership Label' to separate opinion leaders from others, which is done by determining leading reviews. The basic assumption here is that a leading review will be prone to receiving a higher number of votes than other reviews. Accordingly, the reviewers with the larger number of votes can be identified as the key opinion leaders. To split so-called leaders and non-leaders, we first rank all reviews based on the number of votes that they receive. Then we further select reviews that have received more votes than a predefined threshold. The selected reviews are regarded as the leading reviews, and accordingly, their authors become key opinion leaders, whereas the rest of the users are taken as non-leaders. Note that there is usually a host of opinion leaders for a single film. Conversely, a single reviewer can also become a leader for numerous movies.

In summary, a total of 14 features are produced using the feature builder, and raw data samples are represented accordingly and categorised to cover online contents from the Douban site, including film details, review content, and user profile. Then the mapping algorithm for feature quantification from [1] is introduced to discretise continuous features. Finally, Table 16.2 shows the final outcome for generated features and relevant value ranges.

16.3.3 Rule-mining functionality

In the final stage of the proposed framework, we implement an ARM algorithm to discover the leadership pattern due to its efficiency. In general, ARM has been widely used to search for correlation or dependence among the item set. In our case, the entire item set consists of two parts: one independent set and one dependent item. More precisely, the independent item set includes extracted features from textual reviews and user profiles, and the dependent item is the label of opinion leader. The process of discovering such leadership patterns now is equivalent to finding the relationship

Table 16.2   Extracted high-level features and relevant quantification outcomes for Douban contents

Features	Quantification outcomes
Genres	剧情 (drama), 喜剧 (comedy), 动作 (action), 惊悚 (Thriller), 爱情 (love), 犯罪 (crime), 历史 (history), 悬疑 (Mystery)
Movie rating	High, medium, low
Actor, director, writer, story	Mentioned at least once, none
Emotion	Positive, neutral, negative
Review rating	High, medium, low
Length	Long, medium, short
Posted time	Early, medium, late
Leadership label	Leader, non-leader
Activity	High, medium, low
Membership duration	Long, medium, short
Centrality	High, medium high, medium low, low

between the independent item set and dependent item. Thus, the ARM approach is introduced herein. In addition, we consider to facilitate ARM parallelisation using the FP-Growth strategy from the Spark platform [32].

The advantages of the parallel-ARM are two-fold. First, the proposed method has less constraints on the item set, either independent sets or the dependent item. By contrast, other approaches, such as linear or nonlinear multiple regression, require a linear relationship between the dependent and independent items. Second, the proposed algorithm is cost-effective because it is faster than traditional ARM methods. For instance, one traditional way is to utilise a 'bottom-up' strategy to compute all candidate frequent-item sets, requiring researchers to scan the entire dataset repeatedly. This typically leads to the combinatorial explosion problem if the input data size increases. By contrast, the implemented parallel ARM method aims to find all frequent item sets without generating and testing all candidates, thereby reducing the computational time and storage cost. Overall, we adopt this parallel-ARM algorithm to discriminate a reviewer's leadership traits.

Furthermore, ARM might result in thousands of rules, some of which are more significant than others. There are some common critical measurements determining the significance of rules, including support and confidence degree. Support degree indicates to what extent both the antecedent(s) and consequence(s) occur simultaneously in the dataset. Confidence degree indicates to what extent the consequence(s) occurs following the antecedent(s). We will adopt these three measurements later in our experiment to evaluate the significance of a rule and a feature.

16.3.4   Methodology outline

In summary, the proposed leadership analytical framework is shown in Figure 16.3, consisting of a scraping crawler for harvesting streaming data, a feature builder to

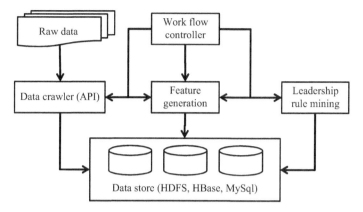

Figure 16.3   Proposed framework of mining opinion leadership for user recommendation

extract high-level features, and association-rule-based analysis. The outcome of the proposed framework will offer better insights into the characteristics from review opinion leaders, which can be tailored to provide better recommendation service for audiences.

16.4   Leadership and recommendation analytics

This section presents experimental results following the application of the proposed framework for leadership analysis. We first present the experimental setup and data sets in Section 16.4.1. And then we provide a detailed overview of the correlation between independent features and leadership in Section 16.4.2. Finally, the performance of the rule-mining algorithm is evaluated in Section 16.4.3.

16.4.1   Experimental setup

Our cloud-computing platform is built upon a virtual computer cluster infrastructure. In our work, two Dell servers with Intel Xeon (R) E5-2609 2.4 GHz cores and 32 GB memory are employed. A virtual cluster of eight nodes is then deployed accordingly. For each node, two virtual CPU and 6 GB of memory are allocated. In addition, one node is set up as the master machine for data collection module, Hadoop and Spark, while the rest is used as the slaver node or worker. In addition, for the Hadoop platform, the 1.2.X version is installed. Accordingly, we take Spark 1.5.X as the running version and the standalone model is adapted to cope with the Hadoop framework. Other details about the system environment configuration are shown in Table 16.3.

Table 16.4 shows the summary statistics for the data harvested from Douban for 94 Korean films until April 2015. During this period, a total of 451,145 comments are collected from 190,665 distinct users. Each film received, on average, around 4,799 comments. In addition, from all collected comments, 35,397 were made without

Table 16.3   System environment configuration

Service	Details
Kafka	3 nodes with 4 cores and 4 GB memories
Flume	3 nodes with 4 cores and 4 GB memories
MySQL	8 cores and 32 GB memories
HBase	3 nodes with 4 cores and 16 GB memories
ZooKeeper	6 nodes with 4 cores and 4 GB memories
Hadoop/Spark	1 NameNode (master) and 6 DataNodes (workers)

Table 16.4   Descriptive statistics relating to film data collected

Variable	Mean	Standard deviation	Total
Number of comments	4,799	1,127	451,145
Rating	3.68	1.15	1.664×10^6
Number of users	2,028	915	190,665

allocating a rating. These statistics resulted in an average film rating of 3.68 (with a range of 1–5) for all films, suggesting they are in fact popular films in their own right among some of Douban's film literati.

Next, the leading reviews for each of the selected films are determined based on the number of received votes per comment. More precisely, a threshold parameter λ is introduced by which reviews receiving votes above this threshold are considered as the leading ones. To discover an optimised value for λ, we first look at the statistics for received votes. As shown in Table 16.5, the majority of comments has no votes, while only 2.4% of them received more than one vote. To this end, we set $\lambda = 1$ to learn about any potential motivations for people to vote for one particular comment. Consequently, there are a total of 10,828 leading reviews against 440,317 non-leading reviews, and 7,075 distinct reviewers have accordingly been selected as the opinion leaders.

16.4.2   Feature statistics

In this section, we will provide a comprehensive understanding of individual features. More precisely, a calculation is performed to highlight the comparison between leaders and non-leaders in terms of the review content each has posted, and users' profile. We try to provide answers to questions like 'Is there any significant difference in terms of users' profile between different reviewer groups?', 'What is the unique characteristic of textual content from leaders compared to non-leaders?', 'Do leaders have a different membership duration than non-leaders' and 'Will leaders post their review at same time as others?', etc.

*Table 16.5   Descriptive distribution relating to
the number of received votes*

Value of votes	Number
= 0	440,317
(0, 1]	7,996
(1, 10]	1,597
(10, 100]	936
(100, 1,000]	286
(1,000, 7,730]	13

*Table 16.6   Comparison of the feature statistics from textual review between
leaders and non-leaders*

Leader	Actor	Director	Writer	Story
Mentioned at least once (%)	23.38	4.67	3.25	20.87
None (%)	76.62	95.33	96.75	79.13

Non-leader	Actor	Director	Writer	Story
Mentioned at least once (%)	15.73	2.24	2.59	15.24
None (%)	84.27	97.76	97.41	84.76

	Emotion			Review rating		
	Positive	Neutral	Negative	High	Medium	Low
Leader (%)	85.23	4.67	10.10	47.94	10.01	42.05
Non-leader (%)	85.03	4.01	10.96	48.03	14	37.97

	Length			Posted time		
	Long	Medium	Short	Early	Medium	Late
Leader (%)	52.34	28.20	19.46	58.49	25.55	15.97
Non-leader (%)	36.78	31.99	21.23	33.41	33.30	33.29

To begin with, we first look at the features from a textual review. In total, eight features, including actor, director, writer, story, emotion, review rating, length, and posted time, are compared between leading and non-leading commentators, and the average results from these two groups are shown in Table 16.6.

In terms of features like actor, director, writer, story, we mainly focus on whether reviewers mentioned relevant people from films when they posted their comments. Overall, fewer reviewers mentioned film-related people from both leader and

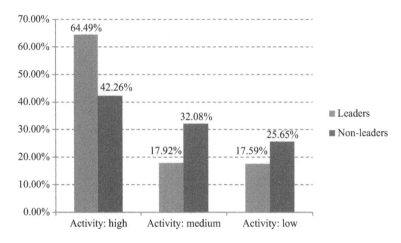

Figure 16.4   Responses from both the leading and non-leading reviews in terms of readers and reviewers

non-leader groups. For instance, the comparison of average percentage between mentioned and non-mentioned is 13.04%, 86.96%, respectively, from the leader group. However, for those who indeed mentioned film-related people, they are likely to write more about actor and story rather than the director or the writer. In particular, leaders seem to mention more about actor and story compared to non-leaders, as the percentage of mentioning film-related people is at least 5% higher.

Not surprisingly, on the other hand, the majority of reviewers show the positive emotion. Besides, more reviewers offered a higher rating from both the leader and non-leader group. This again shows the popularity of selected films among Douban's film literati.

One of the major differences between the two groups under investigation derives from the length and posted time features. As observed from Table 16.6, leaders are prone to write much longer reviews than non-leaders, indicating the review length seems to play a significant role while promoting the leadership. In other words, by writing longer comments, reviewers have a higher probability to become the opinion leaders.

Similarly, leaders also posted their comments much earlier than their peers. For instance, more than half of leading reviews appear in the early stage after the film release, compared to a mere 33.41% non-leading reviews. Generally speaking, this suggests that review leaders posted their comments before a film's popularity begins to fade away so as to catch other readers' attention.

Building upon the above features regarding textual reviews, next is a discussion about the features derived from reviewers' profile, including their activity, membership duration, and centrality. Among them, the activity feature is computed from users' previous comment lists. The more comments a user made to Korean films, the higher activity level he/she has. Figure 16.4 shows the quantified measurement of user activities between leaders and non-leaders. In particular, the blue colour represents

Table 16.7 Comparison of membership duration between leaders and non-leaders

	Membership duration		
	Long	**Medium**	**Short**
Leader (%)	16.40	63.19	20.41
Non-leader (%)	10.18	63.18	26.64

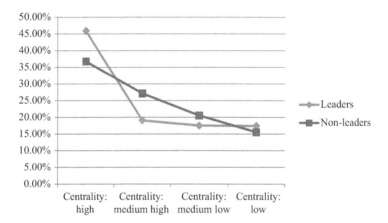

Figure 16.5 Comparison of centrality (reviewer's influence) from both leaders and non-leaders

the activities (measured using the number of comments made to Korean films) from leaders while the red represents non-leaders. Not surprisingly, on average, leaders achieve a higher activity than those of non-leaders. This demonstrates that leading reviewers spend more time or give more attention to post Korean-film comments.

The membership duration feature is used to measure the period of time elapsed since a user's registration. Obviously, the earlier the date of registration with Douban, the longer the time-span. The analysis of membership duration belonging to reviewers in the leading and non-leading groups is shown in Table 16.7. Both leaders and non-leaders have a similar distribution in terms of their membership duration. For example, a majority of reviewers has a medium membership background. This suggests that the individual membership is not a dominant feature enabling a reviewer to become an opinion leader. When readers vote for a review, they would not depend on whether the comment's author has an earlier registration date.

Finally, the centrality feature is considered to measure a reviewer's influence around his/her social network. The results (shown in Figure 16.5) indicate that the leader group attracts a larger number of follower than the non-leader group. For instance, the average of followers from leader groups is 196.7, which is more than

25.3 of non-leaders from all selected films. Therefore, the leader groups have a stronger centrality than their peers.

In the sections above, we have analysed each single features from either textual review or a user's profile. Overall, by summarising the statistics of individual features with regard to leader and non-leader groups, it is clear that a commentator needs to grow a larger follower network, write a long comment, and also post their comments as early as possible.

16.4.3   Discovering leadership patterns

Hereafter, we apply the parallel-ARM algorithm to discover leadership patterns using all of the proposed features. The purpose of applying the ARM method on the extracted features is to identify where potentially significant relationships may exist.

To do this, leadership was chosen as a threshold to investigate patterns within different groups. Accordingly, two datasets are created: dataset 1 includes only leaders while dataset 2 includes data from all non-leaders. In this way, we are able to discover important patterns within the same opinion group, while also making the relevant comparison between different reviewer groups.

To run the parallel-ARM algorithm, we further decide the minimum support threshold (μ). A smaller value for μ is more prone to generating more rules than a larger value for μ. To analyse the impact of the minimum support threshold, we then consider to use different values for μ – i.e. μ was set at 10%, 20%, 30%, 40%, and 50%, respectively, while minimum confidence c was maintained at 50%. As a result, only rules that satisfied the predefined μ and c were selected. Again, our parallel-ARM algorithm is implemented based on Spark [32] so that data can be processed and cached in the machine memory.

Table 16.8 shows the running outcome in terms of the number of generated rules, frequent itemset, and execution time with two different datasets. As observed, with a decrease in the minimum support threshold, more rules (as well as frequent itemsets) are generated. For instance, the proposed ARM algorithm produced 198 and 25,942 rules for $\mu = 50\%$ and 10% using only leader data, respectively.

In addition, the reported execution time reflects the entire mining process including loading data, execution of rules mining algorithm, and generation of the rule results. The proposed parallel mining algorithm performs stably as there is a linear (not exponential) growth in terms of execution time with the decreasing μ, indicating its flexibility and suitability for massive-data mining.

For generated association rules, we are more interested in rules with high lift, which is a measurement to investigate the interest value of rules [35]. Herein we summarise some critical rules from two datasets, while the minimum support threshold, confidence, and lift values are set at 40%, 50%, and 100%, respectively. Furthermore, to better understand those rules, we employ a graphical representation to visualise and interpret the results. There are two main advantages to representing generated rules in the directed graph form: (1) the directed graph provides an efficient way to visualise hundreds of thousands of rules, which can be difficult or impossible using conventional techniques; and (2) it enables the analysis of interactions among different

Table 16.8   *Performance of parallel-ARM algorithm in terms of number of generated rules and execution time as a function of μ*

D1 (only leaders)	$\mu = 50\%$	$\mu = 40\%$	$\mu = 30\%$	$\mu = 20\%$	$\mu = 10\%$
Number of generated rules	198	661	2,275	8,221	25,942
Number of frequent itemset	101	243	611	1,875	10,109
Execution time (seconds)	14.88	23.32	17.32	34.73	40.42
D2 (only non-leaders)	$\mu = 50\%$	$\mu = 40\%$	$\mu = 30\%$	$\mu = 20\%$	$\mu = 10\%$
Number of generated rules	446	941	1,786	5,287	21,750
Number of frequent itemset	139	243	527	1,793	9,449
Execution time	20.67	21.11	27.31	56.75	58.05

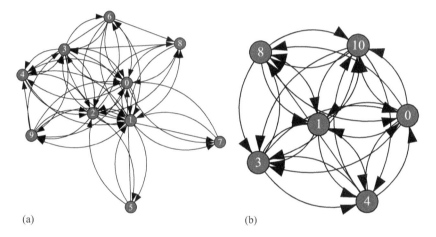

(a)   (b)

Figure 16.6   *Comparison between rules identified from the leader and non-leader group, while the minimum support threshold μ, confidence c, and lift values were set at 40%, 50%, and 100%, respectively: (a) leader rules and (b) non-leader rules*

factors, that is, it provides an intuitive way to understand influence or relationships among individual factors.

As a result, rules generated from two datasets are converted to two directed graphs, in which each feature from the antecedent and consequent set (of a rule) is converted as a single node in the graph. A directed connection is made between two feature nodes if these features exist in the same rule. For instance, a typical rule takes the form $A \longrightarrow C$, where A and C represent the antecedent and consequent set of the rule, respectively. We then add a directed edge (in the form of an arrow) from the node A to C, which implies that the feature A has a high probability of being associated with C. Figure 16.6 presents visualisations of important rules identified from leader

Table 16.9   Mapping between node index and actual feature

Index	Actual feature	Index	Actual feature
0	Emotion = positive	1	Director = none
2	**Leader**	3	Actor = none
4	Story = none	5	Centrality = high
6	Activity = high	7	Length = long
8	Membership = medium	9	Posted = early
10	**Non-leader**		

and non-leader groups, and the mapping between the node index from visualisations and the actual feature is shown in Table 16.9.

Visualisations of these rules reveal unique and interesting patterns between leader and non-leader groups, and a few observations can be made. First, there is a notable absence of significant rules that relate to features, such as movie rating and review rating. This may be because the specific cohort under investigation at this time pays less attention to a commercial film's production context.

Second, features like '(0) emotion = positive', '(1) director = none', '(3) actor = none', '(4) story = none', and '(8) membership = medium' appear within both leader and non-leader groups, indicating those features play less of a role while differentiating opinion leaders with non-leaders. On the other hand, features such as a high user centrality, elevating activity, and early posting of longer comments (node index: 5, 6, 7, 9) help to promote the leadership. Therefore, they are found in Figure 16.6(a) instead of (b). This finding is consistent with the feature statistics analysis in Section 16.4.2.

16.4.4   Discussion

In the sections above, a parallel rule-mining algorithm is applied quantitatively to characterise the relationship of individual features with regard to the leading and non-leading groups. The results show that the adapted features are capable of effectively differentiating leaders from other non-leading commentators.

As our findings highlight, among features investigated, opinion leaders follow a number of distinctive behaviour patterns, compared to non-opinion leaders. For instance, they generally post early and longer comments and also actively post reviews on a range of South Korean films. As a result, they are likely to hold a larger number of followers (high centrality).

Still, both opinion leaders and non-opinion leaders are paradoxically similar in terms of their membership duration. For instance, both opinion leaders and non-leaders turn out to be members registered for about 12 months. Thus, they are likely to generate a similar amounts of WOM awareness of and interest in the same films.

16.5   Conclusion

An important part of information gathering has always been to discover how people behave. With the growing availability and popularity of opinion-rich resources, new opportunities and challenges arise – especially in China where the traditional and digital media landscapes are rapidly transforming. People now can, and will, actively use information communication technologies to seek out and share opinions and recommendations with others via online and mobile platforms and applications. The eruption of various activities in the social mediasphere, particularly involving digital media, has thus attracted great interest and new development.

Our focus in this chapter is on methods that seek to address new challenges raised by discovering key opinion leadership behaviour patterns for one of the most popular Chinese social media platforms. A big data analytic framework is proposed by implementing the Hadoop-based cloud-computing platform, which is used as the fundamental tool for storing and processing massive data sets. Accordingly, raw data samples are collected, processed, and categorised to cover details such as film meta-data, textual content, and user profiles. In addition, a parallel rule-mining algorithm is employed to discover leadership patterns.

An exploratory simulation of results demonstrates the flexibility and applicability of the proposed work on identifying key opinion leaders based on their complex online behaviour. This process can further help in maximising users' satisfaction towards the recommendation service, while assisting in the promotion of other digital media content.

References

[1]   Yang J, Yecies B. Mining Chinese social media UGC: a big-data framework for analyzing Douban movie reviews. Journal of Big Data. 2016;3(1):1–23.

[2]   Yang F. Faked in China: Nation Branding, Counterfeit Culture, and Globalization. Bloomington, IN: Indiana University Press; 2016.

[3]   Ramo JC. Brand China. In: London: Foreign Policy Centre; 2007.

[4]   Frater P. Chinese Movie Portal Douban. In: Mulls Overseas IPO (Report); 2017.

[5]   Sun W. Slow boat from China: public discourses about the going out policy. International Journal of Cultural Policy. 2015;21(4):400–418.

[6]   Lazarsfeld PF, Berelson BR, Gaudet H. The people's choice: How the voter makes up his mind in a presidential campaign. In: New York, NY: Duell, Sloan & Pierce; 1948.

[7]   Katz E, Lazarsfeld PF. Personal Influence. In: Glencoe, IL: The Free Press; 1955.

[8]   Broekhuizen TLJ, Delre SA, Torres A. Simulating the cinema market: how cross-cultural differences in social influence explain box office distributions. Journal of Product Innovation Management. 2011;28:204–217.

[9]   Shen XL, Zhang K, Zhao SJ. Herd behavior in consumers' adoption of online reviews. Journal of the Association for Information Science and Technology. 2016;67:2754–2765.

[10]   Li H, Huang S, Sun G. An opinion leader perceptual model based on PageRank algorithm. In: International Conference on Behavioral, Economic and Socio-cultural Computing (BESC); 2015. p. 150–155.

[11]   Lu L, Zhang YC, Yeung CH, *et al.* Leaders in social networks, the delicious case. Pattern Analysis and Applications. 2011;6(6):1–9.

[12]   Wang MH, Lei CL. Modelling polarity of articles and identifying influential authors through social movements. In: IEEE International Conference on Systems, Man, and Cybernetics; 2015. p. 1664–1669.

[13]   Chiregi M, Navimipour NJ. A new method for trust and reputation evaluation in the cloud environments using the recommendations of opinion leaders' entities and removing the effect of troll entities. Computers in Human Behavior. 2016;60:280–292.

[14]   Zhao Y, Zhang L, Tang M, *et al.* Bounded confidence opinion dynamics with opinion leaders and environmental noises. Computers & Operations Research. 2016;74:205–213.

[15]   Ma N, Liu Y. SuperedgeRank algorithm and its application in identifying opinion leader of online public opinion supernetwork. Expert Systems with Applications. 2014;41(4):1357–1368.

[16]   Mangalindan JP. Amazon's recommendation secret. 2012. Available from: http://fortune.com/ 2012/07/30/amazons-recommendation-secret/.

[17]   Kawase R, Nunes BP, Siehndel P. Content-based movie recommendation within learning contexts. In: International Conference on Advanced Learning Technologies (ICALT); 2013. p. 171–173.

[18]   Nessel J, Cimpa B. The MovieOracle – content based movie recommendations. In: International Conference on Web Intelligence and Intelligent Agent Technology (WI-IAT). vol. 3; 2011. p. 361–364.

[19]   Dumitras A, Haskell BG. Content-based movie coding – an overview. In: IEEE Workshop on Multimedia Signal Processing; 2002. p. 89–92.

[20]   Chang A, Liao JF, Chang PC, *et al.* Application of artificial immune systems combines collaborative filtering in movie recommendation system. In: International Conference on Computer Supported Cooperative Work in Design (CSCWD); 2014. p. 277–282.

[21]   Barrio JB, Rubio XA. Geolocated movie recommendations based on expert collaborative filtering. In: Proceedings of the Fourth ACM Conference on Recommender Systems. New York, NY, USA; 2010. p. 347–348.

[22]   Singh V, Mukherjee M, Mehta G. Combining collaborative filtering and sentiment classification for improved movie recommendations. In: Multi-disciplinary Trends in Artificial Intelligence. vol. 7080 of Lecture Notes in Computer Science; 2011. p. 38–50.

[23]   Amolochitis E, Christou IT, Tan ZH. Implementing a commercial-strength parallel hybrid movie recommendation engine. IEEE Intelligent Systems. 2014;29(2):92–96.

[24]   Wang Z, Yu X, Feng N, *et al.* An improved collaborative movie recommendation system using computational intelligence. Journal of Visual Languages & Computing. 2014;25(6):667–675.

[25]   Li Q, Kim BM. Clustering approach for hybrid recommender system. In: Proceedings of IEEE/WIC International Conference on Web Intelligence; 2003. p. 33–38.

[26]   Kafka. Available from: http://kafka.apache.org/ Accessed 12 December 2018.

[27]   Flume. Available from: http://flume.apache.org Accessed 12 December 2018.

[28]   HDFS. Available from: http://hadoop.apache.org Accessed 12 December 2018.

[29]   Hbase. Available from: http://hbase.apache.org Accessed 12 December 2018.

[30]   MySql. Available from: http://www.mysql.com Accessed 12 December 2018.

[31]   Hive. Available from: https://hive.apache.org/ Accessed 12 December 2018.

[32]   Spark. Available from: https://spark.apache.org/ Accessed 12 December 2018.

[33]   ZooKeeper. Available from: https://zookeeper.apache.org/. Accessed 12 December 2018.

[34]   Korean Film Council. Available from: https://www.koreanfilm.or.kr/eng/films/index/filmsList.jsp.

[35]   Brin S, Motwani R, Jeffrey D. Dynamic itemset counting and implication rules for market basket data. In: Proceedings of the ACM SIGMOD International Conference on Management of Data; 1997. p. 265–276.

Chapter 17

Real-time optimal route recommendations using MapReduce

Majid Khalilian[1], Lida Farajpour[1], and Maryam Fathi Ahmadsaraei[1]

17.1   Introduction

Nowadays, we observe the global consumer confusion phenomenon. The growth in the amount of information supplied the world with various forms of products and services, making it grueling to decide which product to buy or which service to choose. To avoid complication related to the decision-making process, Recommendation System are introduced to suggest a ranked list of items which most meet special user's requirements [1]. One of the useful types of Recommendation Systems is Route Recommendation System (RRS). The Route Recommendation apps provide a variety of services for their users. Some of these services are beating the traffic, finding the new and ideal route that depends on roads condition, aiding disabled people to find their destination independently, guiding strangers such as tourists in an unfamiliar area, leading pedestrian in emergency, etc.

In this chapter, we will present an overview of RRSs and their details. After presenting the basic concepts, we can classify them based on services which they provide. Besides, we are going to discuss about the input data and answer the question "Why it is big?" Our aim is to provide you with a layered architecture of RRSs which can deal with such big data and also be able to serve optimal real-time recommendation. In order to achieve our purpose, the big data technologies mapped to each layer are introduced. Moreover, we will set up a brief discussion about MapReduce paradigm and its strengths as one of the techniques to make parallel computation possible.

17.2   An overview of RRSs

In this section, we introduce RRS as a kind of Recommendation System. First we define Recommendation Systems then take a look at the kinds of applications in which these systems are practically helpful.

---

[1]Department of Computer Engineering, Karaj Branch, Islamic Azad University, Iran

17.2.1   Recommendation Systems

Recommendation Systems can be considered as a subclass of information filtering system. Reference [2] is a fully functional software system which provides users with special interesting information. It tries to decrease the amount of information which particular user is drowning in by just retrieving a piece of information that was recognized interesting from similar users' points of view [3].

Generally, a Recommendation System tries to forecast a user rate or preference of an item by considering his/her profile and comparing it to some reference attributes. The question is, What are these comparing attributes achieved from? To answer the question, two approaches should be introduced: the collaborative filtering approach and the content-based filtering approach.

Collaborative filtering approaches use a model to predict the list of items (or rank the items) which is probable that a specific user is interested in. This model is driven from the user's former behavior. In fact, the items which were purchased or chosen by user and/or also the rates that he/she gave to the items are considered as the user behavior.

Content-based filtering approaches are able to suggest extra items by using some distinct and separate attributes of an item and find the items which have similar characteristics.

Since both approaches have some advantages and disadvantages, the combination of them is often applied in a Recommendation System [3].

17.2.2   Route Recommendation Systems

Compared with the modern lifestyle with the old one, people are more mobile. We are eager to travel and take a trip to new places and go for sightseeing in strange ones and even go for a coffee to some new coffee bars. However, it is not always easy to find our way in strange places or choose the best route among others in order to satisfy our personal preferences. Thanks to the RRS, we have been provided with guide in new places [4].

As mentioned before, the RRS is one of the kinds of Recommendation Systems and extensively applied location-based services recently. This system is playing a leading role in reducing traffic and making a big difference to our state of driving. Given a pair of user-specified origin and destination, a route recommendation service aims to provide users with the routes of the best travelling experience according to given criteria [5]. Just specify the points of beginning and destination and get all the information you required by one click [6].

You may think there is no difference which one to use since they all perform only one main function—helping users to find the shortest and fastest way to their destination. It seems all RRSs are the same since their main function, directing user to his/her destination through the fastest or shortest route, are exactly like each other. However, it is not entirely correct if you consider the details which are provided by them to help users more [4].

While generally both time and distance are the most important parameters for those types of systems, the mechanisms which they apply are not identical in detail [5].

Nowadays, those routing services are routinely used, which affect many aspects of our lives. Therefore, a question comes into our mind, Are the suggested routes the best route for people at all times?

Some studies discovered that experienced drivers would rather not follow the route chosen by Recommendation Systems [5,7]. Popular routes differ enormously from suggested ones because there are other parameters besides time and distance which affect drivers' choice. Traffic lights' count, weather information, speed limitation, and road condition are some of the parameters. To consider the variety of the preference factors at the same time, some previous studies suggest using usual and favorite routes obtained from historical paths as recommended route, while others take the emerging idea of crowdsourcing that clearly leverages human knowledge [5,6].

The second group believes that the first approach has noticeable disadvantages such as adequate volume of historical trajectories is not always available in order to obtain reliable route recommendation. CrowdPlanner is one of the examples of a system which is an innovative crowd-based RRS that asks some people to assess candidate routes which are recommended by various sources and methods, and specify the best route by considering the feedbacks of these people [8].

17.2.3 Classification of RRSs

Users have different tastes and requirements which cannot meet in one route recommendation app. The varieties of apps are developed to provide specific group of people such as taxi drivers, disabled person, and passengers with specialized navigation services they demand. We classify them based on their services to some categories as below:

17.2.3.1 RRS for individual drivers

Thanks to the fast development of Global Positioning System (GPS) technologies and a few navigation service providers (such as Google Map, Bing Map, and TomTom), nowadays people are able to go around the world and also strange areas more easily than before, by just following the recommended routes.

People who drive to their destination may consider some parameters such as distance, the number of speed bumps, the number of traffic lights, fuel consumption, and weather prediction to choose their path. Each of the existing RRSs has its own specifications and attempts to outperform its competitors in meeting their users' demands and requirements.

Google Maps, Waze, Maps.Me, Sygic GPS Navigation, and Navigon are five examples of this type of apps which will be briefly discussed in the following.

Google Maps: The app was exclusively created by Google. Some of its strengths are the following:

- its user-friendly and intuitive interface
- to be applied simply
- being precise
- giving users possible driving options in detail
- providing users with information about traffic dynamics and it is multifunctional

- being useful not even for drivers but also for pedestrian
- free to download.

    Its weakness is

- not to gather the most recent data on abnormal conditions such as damages caused by bad weather or a road under construction [4].

    Waze: With Waze, users know about what is going on along the road. Some of its strengths are the following:

- It warns about police, dangers, traffic, your speed, etc., during your drive.
- It suggests immediate routing changes in order to eschew heavy traffic.
- It provides you with estimated time to arrive, based on live traffic data.
- It directs you to the cheapest gas station around you.
- It offers you different kinds of voices of director who guides you while you drive.
- It's free to download.

    Its weakness is

- its ability that depends on drivers' activity [4,9].

    Maps.Me: It is appropriate and free navigation app. Some of its strengths are the following:

- It provides user with offline navigation without any charge.
- It is used by not only drivers but also pedestrian and cyclists.
- It provides users with points of interest such as ATM machines, petrol stations, and subway.

    Its weakness is the following:

- It is not able to present real-time information during offline mode [4,10].

    Sygic GPS Navigation: It effectively merges online real-time tracking with the possibility to download maps for the offline usage as well. Some of its strengths are the following:

- It's a precise navigation system.
- It provides you with data about lane traffic.
- It finds the cheapest gas station around you.
- It shows you parking spots.
- It determines speed limits.

    Its weakness is

- achieving full features of the app, you have to pay for them [4].

    Navigon: This app merges the best industry practices in its navigation system. It has a nearly large number of users in spite of its high price. Some of its strengths are the following:

- It provides users with complete interface and a lot of different helpful features.

- It is quite accurate.
- It is able to work in offline mode.

  Its weakness is that

- the download of full app is not free of charge [4].

17.2.3.2 RRS for pedestrians

Fast is just one option. You might look for the path that is not only the shortest one but also the safest or will burn the most calories. Some people may prefer emotionally pleasant route rather than the short one. Some RRSs have been developed recently; some of them are introduced in the following.

In [11], a system presented computes a globally optimal pedestrian route assignment that keeps people flow safe while proposing efficient routes to all pedestrians.

Lujack and Ossowski in [12] have explained that due to environmental unsafe conditions, under panic, people may exhibit herding and stampeding behaviors. To achieve efficient and safe pedestrian transit, these behaviors should be prevented. Their approach to this issue is based on finding critical network areas where personally adaptable real-time smart space guidance will facilitate a coordinated people flow while reducing irrational behaviors. It is known that pedestrians tend to evacuate together if they are familiar with one another. Thus, they apply individual and collective rationality in pedestrian route optimization depending on the characteristics of each pedestrian and, therefore, minimize the triggers for panic-induced irrational behaviors.

Lujack and Ossowski in [13] first analyze quantity and distribution of various kinds of landmarks in a given zone. They partition the given zone into some small regions. After determining regions, they classify them into two categories: quiet regions and bustling regions. Finally, they create bustling or quiet route from a start point to a destination. Experiment results show that it efficiently obtains both bustling routes and quiet routes in urban and rural zone.

Pedestrian Pal is an android-based app that provides its users with route recommendation according to their requirements and preferences. Although it is probable that the recommended routes are not the fast one, it meets the users' requirements and preferences since it considers collected user ratings, aesthetic interests, and users' inputted parameters in order to recommend the route. The goal of this project was to develop a mobile device's application that uses Google Maps in order to find routes in a strange city and then try to recommend beautiful, safe, and user-targeted one to its user. Despite the project just developed for Missoula, a city in the US state of Montana, it is possible to expand its scope [14].

In reference [15], they treat pedestrian evacuation in emergency scenarios of networked smart areas. Personal safety may be endangered because of natural disasters (e.g., hurricanes, tornadoes, and earthquakes) and/or actions of deliberate foes. The intensity of emergency evacuation throughout evacuation may increase leading to partial or complete blockage in some routes. Therefore, (re)routing those people based on updated real-time structure safety conditions is absolutely necessary.

They have proposed a multi-agent based architecture for dynamic route safety optimization in large smart area evacuation. The goal of this system is to ensure that the smart space network becomes evacuated securely while appropriately responding to sudden happenings in the network safety.

17.2.3.3 RRS for riding bicycle

Cycling has obtained more enthusiasts than few years ago as a result of increasing in a number of health-conscious and eco-friendly individuals. MapMyRide, Cycle Meter, Strava, RiderLog, Runtastic, MotiFit, Ride Report, Ride Star, iBiker, Bike Computer, and Ryde are some examples of apps that you can use while cycling. In addition to bike share services and enhanced paths for riding, there are several distinctive apps to guide you through planning your biking route and navigate simply. Some of them have other features along with providing their users with the best route. These features include calculating users' duration, distance, space, and calories burned that eliminate the need for other apps in order to track their cycling fitness. Others focus on individuals using cycling as transport [16]. We will discuss about four famous apps among others in the following.

MapMyRide provides a lot of features which you may require during mapping out your bike route. You are able to not only choose a route among more than 120 million bike routes but also create yours. The site also has online training tools for competitive bikers, nutrition tracking calculators, and the capability to share your routes with friends. The design of app is very clean and it is very simple to use and you can specify your personal motivation and objectives on it in order to observe and control your progress with ease [16].

BikeMap has 900,000 worldwide biking routes. It enables you to explore the routes around you or other situations you are going to visit. In addition, BikeMap updates in real time to make you aware of your exact location and share it with your friends. You can download it without any charge and easily set up it on your iOS, Android, and Windows Phone [16].

Possibly the most all-encompassing biking app out there, **BikeBrain** is a big win for habitual bikers searching anything from GPS mapping and in-app picture uploads to sport cyclers looking for heart rate monitoring and training mode features. In addition, the app doesn't require a reminder that you will want to keep your previous biking routes on hand: it automatically archives details of your rides and optimizes battery life so pulling up those routes won't deplete your battery [16].

Bike Hub is another biking app since efficiency is one of the most important features nowadays; it could have been named the modern world biking app. It recommends you a fastest safe biking route including both road and cycle paths from beginning point to your destination. The app uses voice directions to alert you to upcoming turns or a sudden shortcut Voice direction is another its feature to warn cyclist about imminent turns or an abrupt shortcut [16].

17.2.3.4 RRS for disabled people

As full citizens, people with disabilities have same rights and are entitled to dignity, identical treatment, living without dependency, and full participation in society.

A clear acknowledgement of the requirements of an impaired citizen demonstrates the level of integration within the society. There are two major aspects which have effect on the mobility of an individual in an area: the locomotion capability and the ability to perceive distinct elements from each other in the area. The locomotion ability is intended as the possibility to physically move. On the other hand, the perception ability influences the real possibility to arrive at the intended destination, through the knowledge of reference points and obstacles along the path. People affected by specific pathologies or disabilities, with a reduced ability to move or to perceive the environment, suffer from low autonomy in mobility. As a matter of fact, people with reduced mobility move almost only in limited environments, typically near their home. Regarding to blind people, moving through routes which are strange and also not safe can jeopardize their safety. In addition to this, we should consider that any technology allotted to diminish obstacles and cause life to get better has to take into account the social and emotional aspects that come out with everyday use, because the adaption of a device specially designed to help the disabled can sometimes cause the refusal, as it highlights even more the "diversity" feeling.

Everyday a person with disabilities has to control all the action that he is able to complete in autonomy, because sometimes even a small act, e.g., going out for a walk, hides insurmountable obstacles [17].

Using recent technologies make it possible for people with physical disabilities to travel more safely and comfortably. The following is a brief introduction of such apps:

HEARE: Disabled people can make their own 3d audio route here and instantly use it in this app. They can guide people to their office, home, or wherever they want, or select one of the routes made by their selected partners. Even blind people can use it [18].

TripTripHurray: It is a free travel platform for people with particular requirements and lets him/her fast search for accommodation, public transport, places of interest, shops, restaurants, and services. It is efficaciously a customized trip recommender. It demonstrates related options both locally and worldwide [19].

WheelyApp: This app aims to help New Yorkers navigate the subway [20].

LoroDux: It helps in pedestrian routing for mobile devices for the blind [21].

Rollstuhlfahrer-Routing: It's a German project for wheelchair routing [21].

17.2.3.5   RRSs for taxi drivers to pick up passengers

A 2006 study reported that taxis spend 35%–60% of their time cruising along the roads looking for passengers. The diminution of taxis' cruising distances and, consequently, energy consumption cause an urgent challenge [22].

There are some mobile Recommendation Systems that offer taxi drivers possibly fruitful driving routes in a city. This system takes as input data in the form of GPS traces of the routes that taxi drivers took while working, which include location (latitude and longitude), time stamps, and operational status (with or without passengers). It then recommends a list of pickup points along a route that will lead to optimal occupancy times and profits. This kind of system is clearly location-dependent [3].

Smartaxi is an app for taxi drivers. It tries to collect and store the location data of taxis in a city. The data are stored and processed to be sent back to taxi drivers through the Internet, showing them a heat map with colors that indicate the best areas in their city to find customers. After processing those stored data, it provides taxi drivers with a heat map with colors in order to show the best local places to find passengers. Having a smartphone or tablet connected to the Internet is the only necessity that a taxi driver should have to use this useful app. First of all, it needs information shared by taxi drivers: the moment a client enters a taxi, the driver has to open the application on his phone or tablet and tap on the Start button. When the customer arrives at his destination, the driver taps on the Finish button. With this simple gesture, the drivers generate information about where a client was picked up and what was his destination. The idea of this app is very simple. It requires that drivers share the information about the points they pick up customers and the destination by just tap on the Start button of the app when a customer enters their taxi and tap on the Finish button when arrive at the destination. Smartaxi processes the information by using an artificial intelligence system to predict which areas have most demands for taxis. Providing the taxi drivers with the heat map helps them to find the best area at that special time at first glance.

Pick-Up Sign is another example of this kind of app. It is especially designed for taxi drivers, chauffeurs, and other professionals who need to pick up people from airports, railway stations, etc. [23].

17.2.3.6   RRS for passengers

The passengers who prefer to use public transport system such as bus and are informed about the arrival, the departure, and also the location of bus or other public transportation are the next users of RRSs.

With rising urban population, there is a growing demand an efficient public transport system to make cities environmentally sustainable and economically competitive.

Reference [24] classifies the studies which have done on personalizing transport services into three groups:

- The first group focuses on developing an adaptive interface by using commuter context and historical data.
- The second group is developing algorithms in order to recommend routes based on commuter interests.
- The third group passively determines commuter preferences by considering information which is stored in Automated Fare Collection cards.

The authors of [24] believe most of them personalize commuter experience based on their convenience demands. They offer the "best" path among the possible paths recommended by multiple transit modes and their interconnections.

Finding this personal "best" path for a commuter needs to realize his/her perception of convenience by considering the parameters which are identified by the application and also it should be done in real time due to the dynamic nature of the transit network [24].

In [24], MetroCognition, an Android participatory sensing application, fully-functional personalized RRS is developed. Providing exact and appropriate information such as schedules of transit for commuters, on-demand navigation support, and real-time traffic updates are some of the services which are offered by this app [24].

ROSE (ROuting SErvice) is another application for mobile phones. It proposes events and locations to the users and directs them to those via public transportation. It provides its users with recommending events and navigating them by live public transport system. It reacts in real time to delays in the public transport system and calculates alternative routes when necessary. If it is essential, it will calculate alternative routes in order to react to real-time events and delays [25].

17.2.3.7   More gentle RRSs for senior citizens

Over the last 50 years, the number of elderly people has increased dramatically, nearly triple that of the past. The same trend has happened in Canada, USA, Japan, and the other developed countries. They will become more than triple again for the next few decades. The number of elderly drivers will correspondingly grow globally and therefore particular and targeted care for this part of drivers should be considered.

Driving is very significant and necessary for maintaining elderly individuals' mobility and living without dependency, making it easy for them to take part in their common social activities and carry out practical routine requirements. However, researchers state that they are not able to judge speed and distance precisely and multi-tasking is much harder to them than other drivers. They often have an accident where fast deciding and rapid reactions are needed such as at an intersection. Some apps are developed in order to help them in this section of their lives.

In-vehicle navigation systems (IVNS) are common applications using feedback and support. They use a Geographic Information System (GIS), which combines a map and a database, and a satellite navigation system such as GPS.

IVNS have the potential to maintain elderly drivers' mobility and therefore preserve their independence and enhance quality of life. For instance, they can provide distance information to determine the location of imminent maneuvers to create opportunity and more time for elderly drivers in order to properly prepare for them. They also make elderly drivers be able to travel unfamiliar places where they often feel disinclined to travel. Another problem that they may face with is being lost in a familiar area due to dementia. IVNS helps elderly drivers in the early stages of dementia to return to their home [26].

17.2.3.8   RRS for sailing

The ship routing agency issues initial route recommendations and advice before sailing in order to eliminate or decline the effects of bad weather or sea conditions. It suggests track changes while underway (diversions), and weather advisories to warn the commanding officer or master about approaching adverse weather and sea conditions which cannot be effectively evaded by a diversion. The initial route recommendation is based on a survey of weather and sea prediction between the starting point and the destination. It considers the type of vessel, hull type, speed capability, safety considerations, cargo, and loading conditions. The vessel's progress is regularly observed, and if bad weather and sea conditions are predicted along the vessel's current track, a recommendation for a diversion or weather advisory is transmitted.

Therefore, maximizing both speed and safety are the results of the actions of ship routing agency that include offering an initial route and monitoring the vessels along their track to avoid or decrease the affection of adverse weather and sea conditions [27].

Three conditions are required in order to gain the best result of weather routing:

- The passage should be almost long, about 1,500 miles or more.
- The area should be unrestricted; thus, there exist a number of routes which can be selected.
- Weather is a parameter which defines the best route [27].

17.3 The requirements for RRS

The Recommendation System uses data mining methods and prediction algorithms to forecast the interest of its users on information, product, and services [3]. The principal methods and algorithms within the data mining process used to Recommendation System are categorized into three phases according to the reference [28]:

- Phase 1 (pre-processing): Data cleaning, filtering, or transformation are the steps of this phase.
- Phase 2 (data analysis): It is the main phase since the algorithms of this phase (especially Machine Learning classifiers and clustering methods) are applied to find items to recommend.
- Phase 3 (interpretation of results): The data, acquired during the second phase, are applied to deliver business value [1].

In this section, we introduce RRS as a kind of Recommendation System. First, we discuss about the data as a raw material of RRS then continue with the layered architecture of this type of apps. Finally we are going to answer the question of what items and techniques can be applied.

17.3.1 Data requirements

Although data collection was expensive and hard process a few years ago, thanks to the recent technologies such as public transport smart card records, passive positioning counts for car navigation systems and bike share program records, it is easy and cheap nowadays [29].

Apps are able to gain information about location and enable their users to view, store, and share travel routes. The data can be collected, analyzed, and visualized to yield insights into the time and location individuals are navigating through the built environment, providing an opportunity to enhance our comprehension of urban movements. Data produced by the users are becoming more important with the ubiquity of smartphones, the diversity of embedded sensors in these devices, and the increased usage of mobile phone apps for day-to-day activities in the society [29].

Data mostly used in RRSs are the following:

- Personal information of users, e.g., gender and age.
- Location tags
- Geo-coordinates
- Data generated by sensor networks about the urban traffic situation, etc.
- Traffic status which some apps such as Millennium and TrafficSense produced by using smartphones that users have with themselves all the time as traffic probes
- Weather forecasting
- Data that come from blogs, freely available community-contributed pictures, videos, posts in social networks, user's reviews, and log messages from servers containing the navigation and any relevant actions of users [14,30].

The sources of data used for learning and the recommending can be categorized into three classes:

- GPS trajectory data
- Travelogues (blogs)
- Geo tagged pictures.

Geo-tagged and timestamps pictures will create the typical pathways which individuals move along [31].

For achieving the data from geo-tagged photos, it needs some steps to be done. First is to gather pictures from websites like Facebook, Instagram, or Flickr, where members share and tag their pictures. Then recognize the place where pictures are taken. In the next step, the specifications of individuals present in pictures are discovered. Gender, age, race, and travel season are the example of the specifications. After discovering them, group types such as family, friends, couple, and solo are forecasted from discovered individuals' specifications. Routings are produced from those specifications by sorting out pictures of users in accordance with captured date and time [31].

17.3.2 Big or small Data?

Data is nothing new. We have been creating data for centuries. What has changed is the amount of data we produce [32].

Each app generates huge volume of data despite their differences. The explosion of data has produced an unheard amount of data and several new apps to use this amount, leading to a novel reality which is called big data [1].

Contemporary datasets are described by their volume (large size of the data), their velocity (data are created fast and continuously), and variety (data are of multiple types and acquired from various sources). These are known as the 3 Vs of big data, and have been updated in the literature to 5 Vs, through the addition of veracity and value. While the first 3 Vs (volume, velocity, and variety) focused on the issues related to the origin and characteristics of big data, the additional two (veracity and value) highlight issues associated to the use and application of the data to related purposes [29].

The data evolution is indeed creating new opportunities that are changing whole ecosystems. New business models are appearing that did not exist before and are only made possible through data. But more data alone does not mean more business models or more insights. More data means more pain. It means more issues in handling the data and finding what you really want. We need to make binary decisions, yes or no; therefore, what we want is small data, not big data. We want information. Thus should we then dismiss all of those big data discussions? No, not at all. Some things only work because we have big data. However, the important part is to reduce these data so you are looking at the right metric [32].

Big data has created three different kinds of data-driven products:

- Data used to benchmark
- Data used for recommendation and filter systems
- Data used for predictions.

A Recommendation System proposes a few data points out of this volume of data. The section of "people you may know" on LinkedIn for instance suggests only a few members out of a database of 300,000,000 members [33].

It is apparent that both archived and real-time data used in Recommendation Systems could potentially be remarkable big [30]. These systems face the challenge of finding right data through this huge volume of data. In addition, transmuting such large and complex datasets into forms that are usable for urban research and planning, however, entails several challenges including device inaccuracies, human inconsistency, sampling bias, and privacy issues.

Although GPS-tracked data by smartphones is one of the most useful in terms of the application models, these kinds of data lead to challenges with respect to precision and volume. GPS is known to generate error and location imprecision for various reasons. Automating the process of decreasing or eliminating errors from GPS-tracked data is not a simple task, especially with high amounts of data produced by smartphone apps. In spite of many analytic tools that have been developed, handling high amounts of data changing in time stays problematic [29].

In reference [29], they compared smartphone application samples (self-selected sample) to traditional travel surveys (statistically defined sample) for seven cities in the USA. They found that smartphones tended to undersample females, older adults, and lower-income populations, and to oversample some minority ethnicity populations [29]. Moreover online photos are noisy [34].

17.3.3 Real-time issue

RRS's objective is guiding users to their destinations considering individually optimal routes while optimizing global people flow based on the infrastructure real-time conditions. It is the other challenging issue that should be considered in RRS Architecture. As the response must take place in real time, all the computational complexity is better to be done in the offline mode and distributed. We will focus more on it in the proposed architecture in the following.

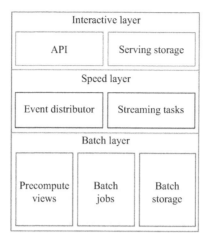

Figure 17.1   The layered architecture of Recommendation System [1]

17.3.4   An architecture

Although each company's Recommendation System has its exclusive architecture with different implementations, they are sharing identical issues. Hence, providing a software architecture which can be simply comprehended, implemented, and extended, if essential, would assist any companies to develop their own efficient Recommendation System, contributing to maintaining and expanding their business [1].

The architecture in [1] is able to handle a high amount of data, answer user interactions, and deliver real-time recommendations. This architecture is modular, admitting of applying different technologies and platforms on each component, consequently making it easy to use the technology that has the best implementation to solve the problem in spite of e-commerce size.

One of the key points of the architecture is how to combine and manage online and offline computation in a seamless manner. Therefore, the architecture is categorized into three principal layers. Each layer has its responsibility, with components to perform various roles. It has been observable in Figure 17.1 that the each component can have one or more technologies, letting the architecture to be extended according to the complexity of the problem. Three main layers have included some components.

- **First layer:** Interactive layer is responsible for receiving, interpreting, and forwarding e-commerce requests. It has API (Application Programming Interface) and Serving Store module.
  - API: It is the interface between the e-commerce and the Recommendation System. All the requests are made in this module which has high availability as its main requirement.
  - Serving Storage: It stores all the recommendations processed by Streaming Tasks and Batch Jobs modules.

- **Second layer:** Speed layer processes real-time recommendation. Consequently, it does not perform machine learning training algorithms, but it applies the trained models and pre-processed data to perform the recommendation. It has Event Distributor and Streaming Tasks modules.
  - Event Distributor: It is a service that can decide whether the request should be handled by speed or batch layers, forwarding the message to the correct recipient.
  - Streaming tasks: It processes a task in real time. Processing the recommendation trained using templates and pre-processed data by batch layer is the main task of this module.
- **Third layer:** Batch layer is the next one that its tasks are performed with a long response time. It has the precomputed views, Batch Jobs, and Batch Storage Modules.
  - Precomputed views: It provides data to be consumed by the speed layer. Among these data, there are trained machine learning models and the prepared information used for recommendation. The storage is optimized for reading and searching.
  - Batch bobs: It processes request on tasks like machine learning training algorithms and calculates product similarity and pre-processing data (products and users). The result is stored in Precomputed views module.
  - Batch storage: It stores the recovered raw data of e-commerce (user, product, and tracking). Storage is optimized for writing.

Big data technologies have been developed to handle massive data sets and provide scalability for data analysis. In addition, almost all these technologies are open source and can be used for a low cost. Figure 17.2 has shown the implementation of the proposed architecture which investigates the performance of some big data technologies in each layer. The technology mapped to the architecture proposed:

- API: Java EE (Servlets or frameworks such as Spring and Playframework), Spray (http://spray.io/), NodeJS, and .NET.
- Serving store: Redis and MongoDB.
- Event distributor: Apache Kafka and RabbitMQ.
- Streaming tasks and batch jobs: Apache Hadoop (YARN/HDFS), Apache Mahout, Apache Spark, and Apache Hive.
- Batch storage and precompute views: Apache Cassandra and Apache HBase.
- Possible programming languages: Java, Scala, Python, R, and C#.

The technologies of streaming tasks, batch jobs, batch storage and precompute views are the Recommendation System architecture key points. The Apache Hadoop is open source technology reported by many authors as the main piece of a big data environment that can be used in these modules. Apache Hadoop was developed by the Yahoo Company; the principal goal of its developer was to provide a fault-tolerant and highly available scalable parallel computing environment. Hadoop enables the distributed processing of large data sets across clusters of computers using easy

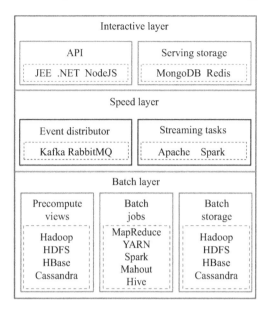

Figure 17.2 Applying some technologies of big data in layers of the architecture [1]

programming models. It is designed to scale up from single servers to thousands of machines, each of them offering local computation and storage.

Apache Hadoop is divided into four modules:

- Hadoop Common: Bundle of utilities and programs that support the other modules.
- Hadoop Distributed File System (HDFS): Distributed File System for data storage.
- Hadoop YARN: Platform that manages cluster resources and performs processing tasks.
- Hadoop MapReduce: It implements the MapReduce paradigm parallel programming proposed by Google which more details about it will be provided further.

There are many projects which have been developed around the Hadoop and others are still being developed. This induces Hadoop to consider as a perfect ecosystem which is used for data processing and storage:

- Apache Hive enables queries through a similar SQL (Structured Query Language) to the HDFS.
- Apache HBase produces a database structure NoSQL (not only SQL) using HDFS as storage, facilitating reading and writing in real time.
- Apache Mahout, a scalable machine learning API and data mining, has algorithms implemented in the **MapReduce** paradigm developed to run at YARN.

All of these are big data technologies and also open source and scalable. Redis database was designed to store all the recommendations processed by Spark and Mahout. The reason is to make certain that when the API requested it, the response would be in real time.

In the proposed architecture, Hadoop can be used for the recommendation processing by the machine learning algorithm implementations using MapReduce paradigm (Apache Mahout) and other paradigms (Apache Spark) executed in YARN. In addition, the architecture enables the development of specific jobs using Java and R, since both are compatible and are able to be run on a Hadoop cluster (Java is the native Hadoop language).

Apache Kafka and RabbitMQ technologies stand out as a distributed messaging system based on the publish–subscribe model capable of playing as an event distributor.

The NoSQL databases MongoDB and Redis can store the recommendation in serving store. These technologies are emphasized since they can read and write quickly. The API can be developed with any technology, language, or platform that meets the HTTP requests. The JavaEE and .NET technologies stand out as the most used while Spray and NodeJS stands out for its performance.

The languages listed can be used to develop jobs inside Hadoop (Java), Mahout (Java), Spark (Scala, Java, R) and implement statistical functions and machine learning (R, Python).

In spite of meeting the requirements proposed, each of the items of Recommendation System can be changed to others without affecting on the other layers of the architecture, reinforcing the modularity importance.

17.3.4.1   MapReduce

Generating high-quality recommendations has become a challenge recently. Traditional Recommendation Systems are not able to fetch and examine the huge data. Undeniably, increasing in the amount of data involved in the recommendation process causes some scalability and effectiveness problems. Researchers try to parallelize data mining algorithms in order to accelerate the mining of the ever-increasing sized databases.

While the parallelization may enhance the mining performance, it also raises several issues for solution containing load balancing, jobs assignment and monitoring, data partition and distribution, parameters passing between nodes, etc. These issues have encouraged the research of novel technologies. A distributed framework was considered based on the known quality and ease of the MapReduce project [34,35].

MapReduce brings its users several advantages containing easily performing parallel computation, simply distributing data to the processors and effortlessly load balancing between them, and effortlessly providing an interface that is not depending on the backend technology [36].

When the user program calls the MapReduce function, the following order of actions happens (the numbered labels in Figure 17.3 match to the numbers in the list below): The MapReduce library in the user program first divides the input files into M pieces of typically 16 megabytes to 64 megabytes (MB) per piece (identified in

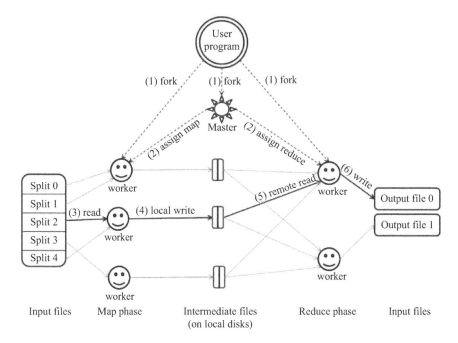

Figure 17.3   Execution overview [3]

an optional parameter by the user). It then starts up many copies of the program on a cluster of machines. One of the copies must be the master and others are workers assigned work by the master. There are M map tasks and R reduce tasks to assign. The master picks vacant workers and assigns each one a map task or a reduce task. A map worker reads the contents of the corresponding input split. It parses key/value pairs out of the input data and transfers each pair to the user-defined Map function. The intermediate key/value pairs produced by the Map function are buffered in memory. Periodically, the buffered pairs are written to local disk, partitioned into R regions by the partitioning function [3].

The locations of these buffered pairs on the local disk are passed back to the master in order to be able to forwarding these locations to the reduce workers. When a reduce worker is informed about these locations by the master, it reads the buffered data from the local disks of the map workers by remote procedure calls. When a reduce worker has read all intermediate data, it sorts it by the intermediate keys so that all occurrences of the same key are grouped together. The sorting is required since typically many distinct keys map to the same reduce task. If the intermediate data is larger than the size of memory, an external sort is applied. The reduce worker iterates over the sorted intermediate data, and for each unique intermediate key encountered, it transfers the key and the corresponding set of intermediate values to the user's Reduce function. The output of the Reduce function is added to a final output file for this reduce partition. After all map tasks and reduce tasks have been finished, the master wakes up the user program. At this point, the MapReduce call in the user program returns back to the user code. After finishing it successfully, the output of the MapReduce execution is available in the R output files (one per reduce task, with file names as specified by the user). Typically, users do not require to combine these R output files into one file—they often pass these files as input to another MapReduce call, or use them from another distributed app that is able to deal with input that is partitioned into multiple files [3].

17.3.5   The categories of requirements from another perspective

Reference [14] looks at the RRSs from another perspective. It provides a list of the requirements for its system as follows:

- Project requirements:
  The mobile devices range in screen sizes from device to device, and user interfaces can change significantly on different displays. To avoid major discrepancies and possible problems (buttons that show only half on a screen or are absent entirely), they carefully designed the interface with cross-platform flexibility in mind.
- Functional requirements:
  The user will be able to
  - Create a profile with name and password
  - Rate routes based on the overall appeal
  - Rate sections of routes
  - Create new routes and sections
  - Choose whether to use global, group, and/or personal data and ratings
  - Request a quick suggestion for a route based on location in an urban setting and distance of routes
  - Hide/show overlays
  - Login to the system and Logout of the application
  - Select a route from a list.
- Data requirements:
  - Geo-coordinates
  - Personal information (users)
  - Location tags (strings describing locations—street names or specifics about setting).
- Usability requirements:
  - The user should be able to receive a route recommendation (drawn on map with overlain information) within one minute of starting the task.
  - The user should be able to rate a route or a section of route under 30 seconds.
  - All colors of the interface (menus, buttons, and overlays) will remain consistent throughout the application.
  - The buttons and menus of the interface should be sensible—with icons and choices that are not confusing or misleading.
  - The system will be intuitive and has an easy and brief learning curve. (Depending on the user's ability, learning the basic functionality of the system should not take longer than 15 minutes.)

– User documentation will offer helpful insights, with photographs and walkthroughs, for using the application.
– Any error messages will offer clear problems and solutions.

17.4 Summary

This chapter highlighted the benefits of RRSs in daily life. These types of Recommendation Systems use some sources of data to provide user with optimal route recommendation based on his/her query. There are lots of apps in this field which give different types of services to people who have plans to go to destination on foot, by taxi, using public transport system, or by driving his/her car.

The chapter has showed that developing RRSs is a fairly challenging process due to several reasons, such as the data are extremely big and the response must produce in real time. Cloud infrastructure is able to elastically manage such huge amount of data and successfully providing almost unlimited computing by using MapReduce paradigm and storage resources to hosted apps, to perform analysis for both long-term decision-making and near real-time query.

References

[1] A.V. Prando and S.Solange, "Modular Architecture for Recommender Systems Applied in a Brazilian e-Commerce," *Journal of Software,* vol. 11, no. 9, pp. 912–923, 2016.
[2] U. Tochukwu Livinus, R. Chelouah and H. Senoussi, "Recommender System in Big Data Environment," *IJCSI International Journal of Computer Science Issues,* vol. 13, no. 5, pp. 1–9, 2016.
[3] A. Johnson and R. Divya, "A Survey On Efficient Service Recommendation on Large Data Clusters," *IJCSET,* vol. 6, no. 2, pp. 78–81, 2016.
[4] "techgenyz," 10 June 2017. [Online]. Available: https://www.techgenyz.com/apps/5-best-navigation-apps-android/ [Accessed 10 June 2017].
[5] B. Zheng, H. Su and X. Zhou, "Landmark-Based Route Recommendation with Crowd," *Data Science and Engineering,* vol. 1, no. 2, pp. 86–100, 2016.
[6] V. Ceikute and C.S. Jense, "Routing Service Quality—Local Driver Behavior Versus Routing Services," in MDM '13 Proceedings of the 2013 IEEE 14th International Conference on Mobile Data Management, vol. 1, pp. 97–106. IEEE Computer Society Washington, DC, USA, 2013.
[7] J. Dai, B. Yang and C. Guo, "Personalized Route Recommendation Using," in *ICDE Conference*, Seoul, 2015.
[8] H. Su, K. Zheng, J. Huang, H. Jeung, L. Chen and X. Zhou, "CrowdPlanner: A Crowd-Based Route Recommendation System," in *Data Engineering (ICDE)*, Chicago, 2014.
[9] "Google Play," Google, 2017. [Online]. Available: https://play.google.com/store/apps/details?id=com.waze&hl=en [Accessed 15 June 2017].

[10]   "Digital Geography," 22 June 2015. [Online]. Available: http://www.digital-geography.com/pros-cons-using-smartphone-gps-tool/. [Accessed 13 July 2017].

[11]   M. Lujak and S. Ossowski, "Intelligent People Flow Coordination in Smart Spaces," in *Multi-Agent Systems and Agreement Technologies*, Athens, 2015.

[12]   M. Lujak and S. Ossowski, "On Avoiding Panic by Pedestrian Route Recommendation in Smart Spaces," in *International Black Sea Conference on Communications and Networking*, Varna, 2016.

[13]   S. Bao, T. Nitta, D. Shindou, M. Yanagisawa and N. Togawa, "A Landmark-Based Route Recommendation Method for Pedestrian Walking Strategies," in *IEEE 4th Global Conference on Consumer Electronics (GCCE)*, Osaka, 2015.

[14]   B.H. Bahls, "Pedestrian Pal: A Route Recommendation System for the Android Mobile Phone," Theses, Dissertations, Professional Papers, Montana, 2011.

[15]   M. Lujaka, S. Giordanib and S.I. Ossowsk, "An Architecture for Safe Evacuation Route Recommendation in Smart Spaces," in *ATT@ IJCAI*, 2016.

[16]   E. Hartwig, "mashable," 11 September 2013. [Online]. Available: http://mashable.com/2013/09/11/bike-route-apps/#_TGLwSAUsPqH. [Accessed 3 July 2017].

[17]   R. Muscinelli, F. Neccia and G. Graglia, *Satellite Navigation Supporting Disabled People: The NADIA Project Demonstration Phase assessment.* [Performance]. Italian Agency Space.

[18]   "heare," Stichting Accessibility. [Online]. Available: http://www.heareapp.com/usage.php. [Accessed 7 September 2017].

[19]   C. Aimes, "disability horizons," 5 September 2016. [Online]. Available: http://disabilityhorizons.com/2016/09/top-10-apps-disabled-people/. [Accessed 9 July 2017].

[20]   L. Poon, "City Lab," 29 June 2016. [Online]. Available: https://www.citylab.com/life/2016/06/how-apps-help-people-with-disabilities-navigate-the-city/489128/. [Accessed 8 September 2017].

[21]   "Wiki," 26 August 2017. [Online]. Available: http://wiki.openstreetmap.org/wiki/Routing. [Accessed 14 July 2017].

[22]   W. Yang, X. Wang and J. Luo, "Recommending Profitable Taxi Travel Routes Based on Big Taxi Trajectory Data," in *Advances in Knowledge Discovery and Data Mining. PAKDD*, Ho Chi Minh City, 2015.

[23]   "itunes," Apple, [Online]. Available: https://itunes.apple.com/us/app/pick-up-sign/id567997800?mt=8. [Accessed 7 September 2017].

[24]   G. Bajaj, R. Agarwal, G. Bouloukakis and P. Singh, "Towards Building Real-Time, Convenient Route Recommendation System for Public," in *IEEE International Smart Cities Conference*, Trento, 2016.

[25]   "Recommendation of Personalized Routes with," in *Intelligent Interactive Assistance and Mobile Multimedia Computing. Communications in Computer and Information Science*, Springer, Berlin, Heidelberg, 2009, pp. 97–107.

[26]   A. Weihong Guo, J.F. Brake, S.J. Edwards, P.T. Blythe and R.G. Fairchild, "The Application of In-Vehicle Systems for Elderly Drivers," *European Transport Research Review,* vol. 2, no. 3, p. 165–174, 2010.

[27] N. Bowditch, "Weather Routing," in *The American Practical Navigator: An Epitome of Navigation*, Maryland, National Imagery and Mapping Agency, 2002, pp. 545–557.

[28] X. Amatriain, "Mining large Streams of User Data for Personalized Recommendations," *ACM SIGKDD Explorations Newsletter,* vol. 14, no. 2, pp. 37–48, 2013.

[29] S.Z. Leao, S.N. Lieske, L. Conrow, J. Doig, V. Mann and C.J. Pettit, "Building a National-Longitudinal Geospatial Bicycling Data Collection from Crowdsourcing," *Urban Science,* vol. 1, no. 3, pp. 23–39, 2017.

[30] W.Q. Wang, X. Zhang, J. Zhang and H.B. Lim, "Smart Traffic Cloud: An Infrastructure for Traffic Applications," in *IEEE 18th International Conference on Parallel and Distributed Systems*, Singapore, 2012.

[31] V. Subramaniyaswamy, V. Vijayakumar and R. Logesh, "Intelligent Travel Recommendation System by Mining Attributes from Community Contributed Photos," in *2nd International Symposium on Big Data and Cloud Computing (ISBCC'15)*, Chennai, 2015.

[32] L. Finger, "LinkedIn," 18 June 2014. [Online]. Available: https://www.linkedin.com/pulse/20140618141134-6074593-rule-the-world-with-small-data. [Accessed 1 September 2017].

[33] L. Finger, "forbes," 2 September 2014. [Online]. Available: https://www.forbes.com/sites/lutzfinger/2014/09/02/recommendation-engines-the-reason-why-we-love-big-data/#73f6dcd11077. [Accessed 29 July 2017].

[34] Z. Farzanyar and N. Cercone, "Trip Pattern Mining Using Large Scale Geo-tagged Photos," in *International Conference on Computer and Information Science and Technology*, Ottawa, 2015.

[35] K.R. Shrote and A.V. Deorankar, "Hotel Recommendation System Using Hadoop and MapReduce for Big Data," *International Journal of Computer Science and Information Technology & Security (IJCSITS),* vol. 6, no. 2, pp. 18–31, 2016.

[36] W. Zhao and H. T. Zhang, "E-Commerce Recommendation System based on MapReduce," *Computer Modelling & New Technologies*, vol. 18, no. 12, pp. 264–269, 2014.

Chapter 18

Investigation of relationships between high-level user contexts and mobile application usage

Takahiro Hara[1] and Jun Osawa[1]

Along with the widely spreading of smartphones, users leverage various functions of the smartphones in their everyday life. To reveal the behavior of smartphone users, many existing works collect low-level contexts such as location and movement status of users from sensors (e.g., GPS, acceleration sensor) to predict the users' situations when they use smartphones. However, it seems that not only low-level contexts but also high-level contexts (e.g., how busy, how good in health, working/day off, and with whom the user is) have significant impact on smartphone users' behavior. In our previous work, we developed a log-collection system to collect high-level contexts by questioning users directly. In this system, to collect a large amount of logs from general smartphone users from whom we have adopted a game-based approach. So far, we have collected approximately 0.7 millions of logs from about 400 users.

In this chapter, we investigate relationships between high-level user contexts and application usage by analyzing a large amount of application usage logs collected through this system. Specifically, we report our experiments which have conducted association rule mining on the collected logs and show some findings.

Our study described in this chapter will be a guideline on how to collect big data on user's high-level contexts, and how to apply them for important context-aware applications such as application recommendation.

18.1 Introduction

Recently, smartphones equipped with highly functional operating systems, such as iOS, Android OS, and Windows Phone OS, are widely spreading. Applications for these operating systems are explosively increasing because everyone who has software-developing kit can develop applications and release them on application markets. Therefore, various kinds of applications are available on markets, for example, social network service (SNS), web browser, news, game, map, camera. Users can choose and install ones in their own smartphone freely; thus, functions of smartphones are much more various than feature phones.

[1] Department of Multimedia Engineering, Osaka University, Japan

It is changing the mobile user's lifestyle to have highly functional device every time and everywhere. Users leverage various functions according to their context. For example, a user who is on a trip may use a map application to check sightseeing spots while a user who goes out with some of his/her friends may use a restaurant search application to have a dinner with them at a good restaurant. In order to improve or invent services for smartphones, it has recently been gathering considerable attentions to understand smartphone user's behavior.

Almost all existing works that aim to reveal user's behavior deal with low-level contexts (e.g., GPS data, acceleration data) to know how the user uses mobile applications. To recognize the semantics of the sensor data, low-level contexts should be converted to high-level contexts by adapting some preprocessing or analysis. For example, if a user records the same GPS location at daytime on every weekday, that location is predicted to be work place. However, such prediction often fails when the volume of data is not enough or high-level contexts of interest do not often occur (i.e., rare contexts). Furthermore, some high-level contexts (e.g., the person who is with the user, the user's current activity, feeling good or bad) are almost impossible to predict from the sensors equipped on current smartphones.

In this study, we aim at investigating relationships between application usage and high-level context. For this purpose, in our previous work [1], we have implemented a log-collection system, which requires a user to input information about high-level contexts and monitors the user's application usage at the same time. In this way, we have collected high-level contexts by questioning users directly. The advantage of our approach is that it can deal with any contexts that the user can recognize, including the user's subjective feelings. Therefore, the data we have collected can describe the user's situation more directly and concretely. In order to reduce user's burden of inputting information and collect a large number of logs (i.e., context information and application usage logs) from ordinary people, we have adopted a game-based approach for this system. Concretely, we have implemented the system as a monster breeding game. To encourage a user to provide information about his/her contexts, a monster gets some experience points and grows up when the user inputs his/her information. We have released this system since October 2012. Until March 2017, we have collected approximately 0.7 millions of application usage logs from about 400 users.

In this chapter, we report our experiments which have conducted association rule mining on the collected logs and show some findings. The main contributions of this chapter are as follows:

- We have collected a large volume of log data that contain the information on application usage and high-level contexts.
- We have observed concrete application usage patterns of smartphone users.
- We have found that combinations of multiple contexts bring different impact on applications from each single context.

The rest of this chapter is organized as follows. In Section 18.2, we review related work. In Section 18.3, we describe our log-collection system. In Section 18.4, we observe the logs collected by our system. In Section 18.5, we investigate relationships between application usage and high-level contexts. In Section 18.6, we provide some discussion on this study. Finally, in Section 18.7, we conclude this chapter.

18.2   Related work

18.2.1   Investigation of mobile user's behavior

Mobile devices are used anytime and anywhere in various situations, and it is known that information requirements are different on each situation. To improve or invent services of mobile devices, it is necessary to know how the users use their mobile devices.

For this reason, a number of researches focus on the investigation of mobile users' behavior [2–6]. Kamvar *et al.* [4] investigated a large volume of Google search history data obtained from mobile devices. Bina *et al.* [3] conducted a questionnaire-based survey on usage of mobile services. Both of the researches suggest that the usage of mobile device differs if the usage scene (i.e., situation) differs. The difference between these two works is how to collect data for investigation. The former collected usage logs of mobile search. This approach can collect a large volume of data and, thus, can observe a general trend of users' behavior accurately. However, it is difficult to know concrete user's situations because the data are merely histories of the service usage. On the other hand, questionnaire-based survey is not suitable for collecting a large volume of data because it takes a high cost to gather many examinees. Meanwhile, this approach can know concrete users' situations such as when, where, and why a user used his/her device, i.e., high-level contexts.

In recent years, smartphones which are equipped with highly functional operating systems have been widely spreading. Functions of smartphones are much more various than feature phones because many developers are providing enormous number of applications. Thus, investigating users' activities and information requirements through mobile devices (smartphones) have been much more attention and become getting more important. Xu *et al.* [7] investigated the smartphone usage by observing the network traffics of smartphone's applications. Karlson *et al.* [8] conducted a diary study using screen shots of the examinees' smartphones. However, both studies have the same problems as described above, i.e., the former cannot know high-level contexts, and the latter cannot collect a large volume of data.

18.2.2   Collecting application usage logs

A difference between smartphone and feature phone is that smartphones are highly functional enough to install a program to monitor application usage. Many of recent works collected application usage logs. Girardello *et al.* [9] and Davidsson *et al.* [10] collect application installation logs, while Yan *et al.* [11] and Costa-Montenegro *et al.* [12] collected application usage logs. These four works applied the collected application usage history to a recommendation system of smartphone applications. Sun *et al.* [13] developed a dynamic application launcher which predicts applications to be used next based on the application usage history. However, these works did not take user context into account. Since both applications of smartphones and their usage situations are significantly diverse, recommendation or prediction of applications should take user context into account.

18.2.3   Collecting context information

Another difference between smartphone and feature phone is that smartphones are equipped with various sensors and other devices such as GPS, acceleration sensor, Bluetooth. Using such sensors and devices, a situation when a smartphone is used can be predicted. For example, using GPS data, it can be predicted where the user is. Using acceleration data, the user's physical state (walking, pausing, etc.) can be predicted. Falaki *et al.* [14] and Do *et al.* [15] used special smartphones where a logging system is installed to collect logs of application usage and sensor readings, and collected the logs from the examinees to investigate the usage patterns.

To reveal natural (not biased) behavior of smartphone users, it is more desirable to investigate users' behavior on devices which the users regularly use. Böhme *et al.* [16] have released a log-collection system to an application market and collected a large amount of application usage logs with sensor data from general smartphone users.

Since raw sensor data represent low-level contexts, they need to be converted to high-level contexts, whose semantics is intuitively understandable. To convert low-level contexts to high level ones, some preprocessing or analysis is needed. However, such processing often fails if the volume of sensor data is not enough or high-level contexts of interest rarely occur. In addition, it is almost impossible to predict detail situations and subjective feelings of the user. Therefore, for example, in order to collect information about people around the user, the user's current activity, and whether the user feels good or bad, it is needed to apply some questionnaire-based method, i.e., directly ask the user.

In our study, we aim to collect a large volume of high-level contexts and application-usage logs. For this aim, we have adopted a questionnaire-based approach and implemented an application log-collection system. In our system, users are periodically asked to answer questions about contexts. Here, in order to solve the problem of questionnaire-based approach and collect a large volume of logs from ordinary smartphone users, we have adopted a game-based approach [17]; we have implemented the system as a game application and released it to an application market.

18.3   Log-collection system

In this section, we describe the log-collection system that we have developed [1]. This system requires a user to input information about his/her contexts and monitors his/her application usage as a background process.

18.3.1   Initialization of the system

When the system starts for the first time, it shows the user a simple explanation of data to be collected, its purpose, and some tutorials. Next, the system requires a user to input some of his/her profile such as gender, age, and living region (individual cannot be identified only by them) in order to know who the user is roughly. After these steps, the log-collection procedure starts. In this way, a user can understand the aim of the system in advance, i.e., users have agreed to provide data.

18.3.2   Questions about contexts

The system collects log data by requiring a user to answer questions about his/her high-level contexts directly. We set five questions that are expected to have some impact on application usage. A user can always update his/her answer to each question. However, it is difficult or burdensome for a user to always keep on updating his/her own information. For this reason, we set a valid time for each question, and when the valid time expires, the system notices it and requires the user to update the information about the corresponding context. Specifically, we set the following questions:

1.   *Today* (valid time: a day):
     asks the main activity of today, e.g., work, holiday, school, business trip, travel.
2.   *Subjective feeling* (valid time: 4 h):
     asks the degree of subjective feelings, and consists of four questions: (i) *health*, (ii) *tiredness*, (iii) *mind*, and (iv) *busyness*, e.g., fine, bad, (for "health")
3.   *Place* (valid time: 3 h):
     asks the user's current place, e.g., home, work, trip, restaurant.
4.   *Companion* (valid time: 2 h)
     asks about the user's accompany person(s) and consists of the following two questions.
     i.   *Number of people*
          asks the number of accompany people (option: 0, 1, 2, 3, 4, 5 and over)
     ii. *Category of people*
          asks the category of the accompany people, e.g., friend, family, lover, boss. The user needs not to answer this question if the user choose 0 for the question regarding the number of people.
5.   *Activity* (valid time: 2 h)
     asks the user's current activity, e.g., work, rest, meal, read.

A user answers each question by selecting an option from the option list provided by the system. Here, a user can add a new option to the option list if there is no appropriate option in the list. In order to reduce user's burden, options which are frequently selected by the user appear in the upper part of the list. Figure 18.1(a) shows an example of a question about high-level context provided to a user.

All answers of a user (which represent the information on high-level contexts) are stored on the user's mobile device with the time information (time stamp).

18.3.3   Collection of application usage logs

This system monitors and records the usage of applications which are installed in the user's device. Android OS can recognize applications which run at the forefront.

(a)   (b)

*Figure 18.1   Examples of user interface: (a) question about context and
(b) breeding a monster*

Table 18.1   Examples of collected logs

Time	App	Place	Companion	Activity	...
12.00	Twitter	School	Friend	Meal	...
12.15	Line	School	Friend, senior	Meal	...
12.25	Browser	School	Friend, senior	Rest	...
13.30	Facebook	School	(Alone)	Rest	...

Thus, we have implemented a resident program which records the application ID and start time of forefront applications (i.e., applications used by the user).

In this study, we aim to investigate relationships between application usage and high-level contexts. To this end, we do not collect any personal information which has high privacy such as name and phone number, and any detail information inside the used applications such as historical data of phone calls and web browsing.

By combining the information on high-level contexts obtained through questions and that on application usage by time, our system creates application usage logs. Table 18.1 shows some examples of logs collected in our study. The collected logs are stored in a database on the user's device and periodically sent to the server of our system.

18.3.4 Game-based approach

It is obvious that a simple log-collection system that just requires a user to input his/her context information does not work well because it is burdensome for user to often answer to the questions without any incentives. To solve this problem and collect a large volume of context information from ordinary users, it is needed to give some incentives to the users. For such requirements, recently, game-based approach has been attracting much attention [17]. In this study, we have implemented our log-collection system as a game application. In this game, a user can breed monsters which we designed, and the monsters say various things as they grow up. Figure 18.1(b) shows an example of an interface of our system where a monster speaks. Specifically, we the functions stated in the following subsections have been implemented.

18.3.4.1 Experience point

To keep a user's motivation high, a return of the user's burden should be paid immediately. So, we have adopted a concept of experience point, and regarded inputting context information as feeding a monster. More specifically, when a user inputs the information about his/her contexts, a monster which he/she is breeding eats the information, and the user gets some experience points. On the top of the main interface of the game (Figure 18.1(b)), a user can check the progress bar that indicates how many experience points the user has got so far.

18.3.4.2 Evolution

In order to motivate a user, it is also effective to sometimes give a bulk return to the user when his/her accomplishment reaches to some degree. For this aim, we have adopted a concept of evolution. Specifically, when the accomplished experience points reach to some degree, a monster which the user is breeding evolves to a different species; changes its appearance and characteristics (i.e., what it says).

As mentioned above, in our implemented log-collection system, users can enjoy a monster-breeding game, while contributing to the log collection. We have released this system on Google Play, which is an application market for Android OS [18] since October 2012.

18.4 Collected logs

Through our implemented system, we have collected approximately 0.7 millions of application usage logs from about 400 distinct users from October 2012 to January 2017. In these logs, we distinguished individual users by ID number of a smartphone device. Due to this, some users might be duplicated if they have more than one device or replace their own device. In the following, we present the results of our preliminary data analytics on about 0.5 millions logs collected from October 2012 to January 2014 from 203 users. The ratio of male to female of users was approximately 7:3. The age range was broad; the lowest was teenage, and the highest was fifties, while most of the users were teens or twenties. The majority of users live in Osaka, Japan.

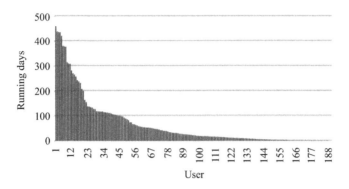

Figure 18.2   Persistence of log-collection system

Figure 18.2 shows the persistence rate of the system, which is represented by running days of the system after its installation. The horizontal axis is sorted by running days. As shown in this figure, some users continued to use the system for very long time while some others uninstalled the system within a day. About half of the users continued to use the system more than 2 weeks which shows the effectiveness of a game-based approach as an incentive.

18.4.1   High-level contexts

By observing the collected logs, we have examined how many different types of answers we got for each question. We got 97 types of answers to the question for today, 144 types for place, 55 types for companion, and 182 types for activity. As shown, the types of answers were quite diverse. One reason for this is that some users added too specific options to the option list. For example, in the answers for place, we found a certain person's house and a certain station. Another reason is that it sometimes happened that some users added different options (expressions) for a same thing or added slightly different options (e.g., "move," "moving," "moving by car/train").

Figures 18.3–18.7, respectively, show the selection frequencies of options for each of the questions. In these figures, we only show options which were selected by at least four users. Overall, we can confirm that the frequently selected options are related to the users' daily routine (e.g., "school" for today, "home" for place, "family," and "friend" for companion) while options which were not frequently selected include unusual contexts such as "travel," "business trip," "leisure," and "sightseeing."

In this way, we have grasped the overview of contexts. Since we allowed users to add new options by free words, the types of answers were quite diverse. From the different selection frequencies by time, we have found some tendency based on the daily routine of ordinary users.

18.4.2   Application usage frequency

We chose ten representative applications for this observation. Table 18.2 shows the applications for this observation and the total usage count (during the whole

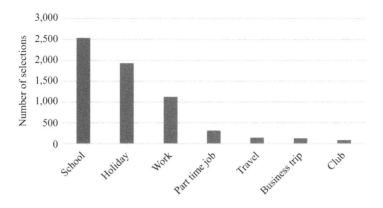

Figure 18.3 Selection frequencies for today

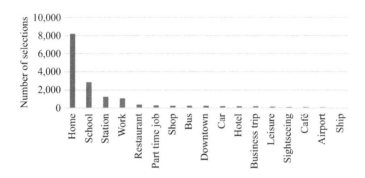

Figure 18.4 Selection frequencies for place

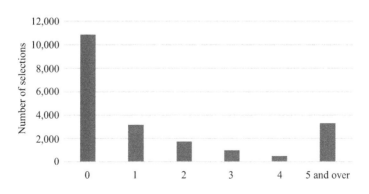

Figure 18.5 Selection frequencies for companion number

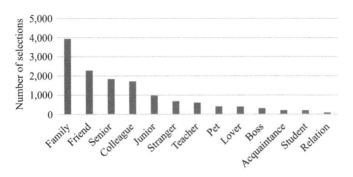

Figure 18.6   Selection frequencies for companion category

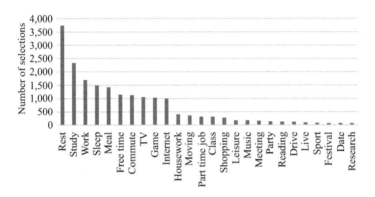

Figure 18.7   Selection frequencies for activity

Table 18.2   Applications and usage count

Application name	Usage count
LINE	94,592
Twitter	62,377
Browser	48,644
Facebook	17,333
Gmail	11,279
Phone	7,519
Camera	6,741
Puzzle & Dragons	6,375
YouTube	3,717
Map	2,249

experiment period). As for the usage count, Line, Twitter, and Browser were used especially frequently. This implies that many users regularly use only a few applications in daily life. A similar fact has been reported by MMD institute [19] in 2012;

Table 18.3   Applications categories

Category	Meaning	Examples
Browser	General browsing applications	Chrome, Firebox, Dolphin Browser
SNS	General SNS applications	Facebook, Twitter, Google+, mixi
Communication	Communication applications, e.g., voice, E-mail, instant messenger	LINE, Phone, Gmail, Hangouts
Business	Practical applications, e.g., scheduling and memo	Calendar, Evernote, Adobe Reader
Information	Web applications for information and entertainment	Transfer information, 2chmate, weather
Game	Game applications	Puzzle & Dragons, LINE POP
Multimedia	Image, video, and music applications	YouTube, gallery, QuickPic, niconico
Camera	Camera applications	Camera, LINE camera
Map	Map applications	Google Maps, Foursquare

according to a questionnaire survey, 50 per cent of smartphone users regularly use at most five applications.

18.4.3   Tendency of application usage by time

In this subsection, we present the temporal tendency of application usage frequency. Here, we discuss based not on individual applications but on categories of applications, which are shown in Table 18.3.

Figures 18.8–18.11 show the change of usage frequency of each application (category) by time. Here, the vertical axis denotes the application usage frequency, i.e., usage count of each application normalized by the total usage count of all applications. Figure 18.8 shows the general tendency of change of usage frequency for all applications. From this result, the frequency is low from 2 AM to 5 AM. After 6 AM, it increases gradually, having a local maximum point at 12 PM. As shown in Figure 18.9, communication, SNS, and browser have a similar tendency.

From Figure 18.10, information, business, and game were frequently used especially at 12 PM. This is mainly because business and information applications are strongly needed during free time. From Figure 18.11, camera and map were often used during daytime, and their frequencies decrease while that of multimedia increasing after 10 PM. This tendency clearly represents general users' daily life, i.e., users often try to find a way using a map application and take a photograph using a camera when they are away from home during daytime, while they often view multimedia contents after going back to their home.

In this way, we have grasped the tendency of application usage. In particular, we have found that only a few applications (communication, SNS, and browser) were regularly used. We have also found some tendencies regarding the change of application-usage frequency, which represents the features of applications.

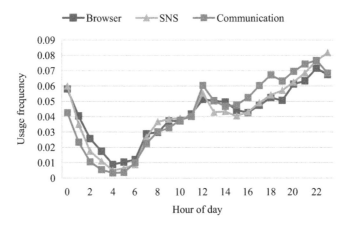

Figure 18.8   Usage frequency of all applications by time

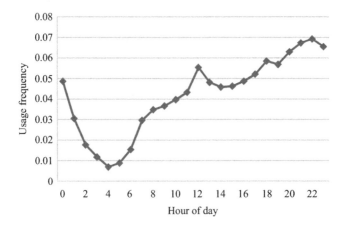

Figure 18.9   Usage frequency of each application by time I

18.5   Relationships between applications and contexts

Next, we have examined combinations of contexts and applications to know in what situation users use applications. For this aim, we applied association rule mining [20] to application usage logs we collected, aiming to find patterns of application usage that frequently occur, which represent ordinary smartphone users' behavior. In addition, we also have focused on finding some interesting patterns which do not frequently occur, because they might represent unexpected application usage, which have some important meanings.

Association rule mining is often used for marketing purposes to find some characteristic combinations of products which are often bought together. The expression of combinations is a form of rule such as $\{A\} \Rightarrow \{B\}$; A is called the condition part,

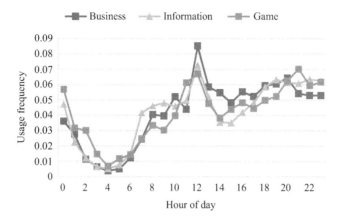

Figure 18.10   Usage frequency of each application by time II

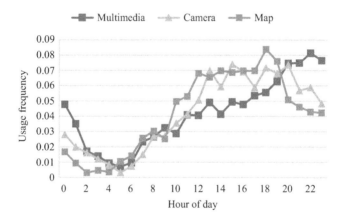

Figure 18.11   Usage frequency of each application by time III

and *B* is called the conclusion part. The rule means that *B* happens under condition of *A*. In case of applying association rule mining to a purchase history, a rule is expressed like {beer, sausage} ⇒ {diaper}; generally, the condition part consists of several items and the conclusion part consists of single item.

Each rule has some indicators that are given to evaluate the rule: *support*, *confidence*, and *lift*. These are defined as follows:

$$support(\{A\} \Rightarrow \{B\}) = \frac{N(A \cap B)}{M} \tag{18.1}$$

$$confidence(\{A\} \Rightarrow \{B\}) = \frac{support(\{A\} \Rightarrow \{B\})}{support(A)} \tag{18.2}$$

$$lift(\{A\} \Rightarrow \{B\}) = \frac{confidence(\{A\} \Rightarrow \{B\})}{support(B)} \tag{18.3}$$

where $N(X)$ represents the total number of logs which include X, and M represents the total number of all logs. *support* is defined as the joint probability of A and B (if the argument is not a rule but just X, *support*(X) just indicates the probability of X). *confidence* is defined as the conditional probability of B under the condition of A. *lift* is defined as the scaling factor that indicates what times the probability of occurrence of B increases under the condition of A compared with the probability under no condition. Generally, it is said that the rule having high *confidence* is valuable because its relation between A and B is strong. However, *confidence* is sometimes high if B is a phenomenon that happens very frequently regardless of condition. In that case, *lift* is useful to find valuable rules. Therefore, it is important to evaluate these three indicators depending on characteristics of data.

In this study, we used the log data we collected; a set of high-level contexts and applications. Before applying the rule extraction, we filtered the log data to use only options of contexts which were selected by at least four users and types of applications shown in Table 18.2. As a result, the number of logs for the rule extraction was 61,267. When applying the rule extraction, we set the following thresholds:

$$support \geq 6.0 \times 10^{-5} \tag{18.4}$$

$$confidence \geq 0.001 \tag{18.5}$$

In order to observe the usage patterns of applications which do not occur frequently, we set these low thresholds. Here, the minimum *support* ensures that logs corresponding to an extracted rule appear at least four times. The condition part of a rule is a set of options for questions about contexts. The conclusion part consists of single application which is used in the situation described in condition part. As a result, we have extracted approximately 1.5 millions of rules.

18.5.1 Characteristic rules

We have firstly observed rules which have high indicators (i.e., support, confidence, and lift). Through this observation, we have found some characteristic and concrete usage patterns of smartphones.

18.5.1.1 Most frequent situations

Rules which have high *support* value describe frequent situations of corresponding application usage. Table 18.4 shows some example rules having high *support* value. From this table, most applications seem to be mainly used while working alone. Gmail and Facebook are used at school. Camera is used in a business trip, and game is used in bed. From this, it can be said that situations in which applications are frequently used are same for most applications, with some exception.

18.5.1.2 Specific usage

Rules which have high *confidence* value describe specific usage of corresponding application. On the other hand, if the total frequency of corresponding application usage is low, the *lift* value tends to be high. More specifically, if the *lift* value is high, the corresponding application is specifically used in that situation. Table 18.5 shows

Table 18.4   Example rules having high support

Condition part	Conclusion part	Support	Confidence	Lift
Activity = work, companion# = 0, place = work, today = work	LINE	0.0168	0.379	1.253
Companion# = 5 and over, companion = senior, place = school, today = school	Gmail	0.00346	0.121	2.255
Activity = work, companion# = 0, place = work, today = work	Phone	0.00142	0.0321	0.989
Activity = work, companion# = 0, place = work, today = work	Browser	0.0116	0.262	1.210
Activity = work, companion# = 0, place = work, today = work	Twitter	0.108	0.244	1.082
Companion# = 5 and over, companion = senior, place = school, today = school	Facebook	0.00307	0.108	1.063
Activity = work, companion# = 0, place = work, today = work	YouTube	0.00121	0.0273	1.826
Companion# = 5 and over, companion = colleague, companion = student, today = business trip	Camera	0.000539	0.210	10.196
Activity = work, companion# = 0, place = work, today = work	Map	0.000473	0.107	1.394
Activity = sleep, companion# = 0, place = home, today = holiday	Puzzle & Dragons	0.00101	0.124	4.978

some example rules having high *confidence* and *lift*. As for LINE and Gmail, the representative situation is having a meal with superiors. In such a situation, while it is not favorable for users to focus on their smartphones, LINE and Gmail are often used probably because the users received some message. Twitter seems to be used while having a meal on travel, Facebook seems to be used while having a meal with family and friend, and Camera seems to be used while dating with a lover. A common point of them is an extraordinary situation. These applications might be used to record the experience or share it with someone. As for Map, the *lift* value is very high. This indicates that the usage probability of Map increases significantly while driving with friends. Thus, it can be said that Map is specialized in such a situation.

18.5.2   Effect of single context

Second, we have investigated how retain the intended meaning, and correct if necessary. single context affects application usage. For this aim, we extracted rules that have the following format:

$$\{C_x\} \Rightarrow \{App_x\} \tag{18.6}$$

where C_x is a single context and App_x is an application. In this case, the *lift* value of the rule indicates how the usage probability of App_x changes by C_x. For example, the lift value of $\{place = home\} \Rightarrow \{app = YouTube\}$ is 1.40; it means that the context

Table 18.5   Example rules having high confidence and lift

Condition part	Conclusion part	Support	Confidence	Lift
Activity = meal, companion# = 2, companion = senior, place = restaurant	LINE	0.000294	0.947	3.131
Activity = meal, companion# = 5 and over, companion = senior, companion = boss, today = work	Gmail	0.0000653	0.800	14.848
Activity = shopping, companion = friend, place = shopping, today = school	Phone	0.000163	0.385	11.847
Activity = moving, companion# = 5 and over, companion = stranger, place = train, today = work	Browser	0.000604	0.841	3.893
Activity = meal, companion = friend, companion = junior, today = travel	Twitter	0.000114	0.875	3.878
Companion# = 5 and over, companion = family, companion = friend, place = restaurant	Facebook	0.0000816	0.714	7.047
Activity = sleep, companion# = 3, companion = pet, companion = family, today = holiday	YouTube	0.0000979	0.429	28.665
Activity = date, companion# = 1, companion = lover, today = holiday	Camera	0.0000816	0.132	6.383
Activity = drive, companion# = 3, companion = friend, place = car	Map	0.0000653	0.571	74.489
Activity = study, companion = friend, companion = colleague, today = school	Puzzle & Dragons	0.000225	0.279	11.211

Table 18.6   Lift value of each place

Place	YouTube	Camera	Map	PAD
Home	1.40	0.54	0.45	1.56
School	0.36	0.75	0.49	1.50
Downtown	0.35	1.77	2.21	0.50
Restaurant	0.82	2.35	1.10	0.40
Sightseeing	0.00	5.27	2.57	0.89
Station	0.52	0.98	1.58	0.31
Airport	4.67	2.46	0.00	4.34

(home) increases the usage probability of YouTube by 1.40 times. In other words, "home" brings a positive impact on "YouTube."

As a result of observing rules from the above view, we have found that some pairs of single context and application have clear relationships. Tables 18.6 and 18.7 show some example rules (PAD is abbreviation of Puzzle & Dragons). From Table 18.6, YouTube, Camera, Map, and PAD seem to be notably influenced by place. YouTube and PAD tend to be used at home, while Camera and Map tend to be used when

Table 18.7   Lift value of each state of mind

Mind	Phone	Browser	Camera	PAD
Positive	1.02	0.94	1.09	0.98
Negative	0.75	1.13	0.54	1.48

going out. In particular, the more the place is extraordinary, the more Camera is used frequently. At an airport, YouTube and PAD are used probably during a long waiting time. From Table 18.7, we have found some relationships between subjective feelings and application usage; phone, browser, camera, and PAD seem to be notably influenced by state of mind. Phone and camera seem not to be used when the user is feeling down; on the other hand, Browser and PAD seem to be used in such a situation.

18.5.3   Effect of combination of contexts

Third, we have investigated the effect of combination of contexts. We have found that some combinations of multiple contexts bring different impact on applications from each single context. For example, the *lift* values of the following rules

$$\{companion = friend\} \Rightarrow \{app = Twitter\} \tag{18.7}$$

$$\{activity = free\ time\} \Rightarrow \{app = Twitter\} \tag{18.8}$$

are 1.29 and 1.33. They both have positive impact on Twitter. However, when the two contexts are combined,

$$\left\{ \begin{array}{l} companion = friend \\ activity = free\ time \end{array} \right\} \Rightarrow \{app = Twitter\}, \tag{18.9}$$

its *lift* value is 0.77; it turns to have negative impact. If the activity is "study" or "shopping," the combination with *companion = friend* remains to have positive impact. This might be because users want to post to SNS when they do some common activity with their friends.

To investigate how many such cases occurred, we defined *mutuallift* as follows:

$$\begin{aligned} mutuallift(\{C_a, C_b\} &\Rightarrow \{App_x\}) \\ &= \frac{lift(\{C_a, C_b\} \Rightarrow \{App_x\})}{lift(\{C_a\} \Rightarrow \{App_x\}) \cdot lift(\{C_b\} \Rightarrow \{App_x\})}. \end{aligned} \tag{18.10}$$

This measure indicates the impact of combination of two contexts, C_a and C_b. If it is greater than 1, the combination of C_a and C_b has positive impact on application App_x. Otherwise, if it is less than 1, the combination of C_a and C_b has negative impact. We calculated *mutuallift* of 10,843 rules which have the form of $\{C_a, C_b\} \Rightarrow \{App_x\}$. Then we classified them into three groups: rules having value less than 0.9 (negative), between 0.9 and 1.1 (neutral), and greater than 1.1 (positive). The result is shown in Table 18.8: 3,180 rules belong to "negative," 3,238 rules belong to "neutral," and

*Table 18.8   Classification of the value
mutuallift*

mutuallift < 0.9	3,180
0.9 ≤ *mutuallift* ≤ 1.1	3,238
mutuallift > 1.1	4,425

4,425 rules belong to "positive." Within the first group, 76 rules meet the following conditions:

$$lift(\{C_a\} \Rightarrow \{App_x\}) > 1.1, \quad (18.11)$$

$$lift(\{C_b\} \Rightarrow \{App_x\}) > 1.1, \quad (18.12)$$

$$lift(\{C_a, C_b\} \Rightarrow \{App_x\}) < 0.9, \quad (18.13)$$

i.e., combination of two contexts having positive impact turns to negative impact. Within the third group, 173 rules meet the following conditions:

$$lift(\{C_a\} \Rightarrow \{App_x\}) < 0.9, \quad (18.14)$$

$$lift(\{C_b\} \Rightarrow \{App_x\}) < 0.9, \quad (18.15)$$

$$lift(\{C_a, C_b\} \Rightarrow \{App_x\}) > 1.1, \quad (18.16)$$

i.e., combination of two contexts having negative impact turns to positive impact. From the above, it can be said that combination of contexts also has impact on application usage as well as individual single contexts.

18.6   Discussion

18.6.1   Impacts of collecting high-level contexts

We have collected various and concrete answers to questions about high-level contexts. High-level contexts have a significant potential to describe user's situation in detail and intuitively.

As mentioned, because we allowed users to add free word answers, there are many answers which have a little different expression but represent the same thing (e.g., "move" and "moving"). To solve this problem, some improvement should be done on our system.

We have also found that some applications are affected by subjective feelings. In existing studies, relationships between such contexts and application usage have not been fully revealed. Therefore, our approach in this study is an effective way to reveal such relationships.

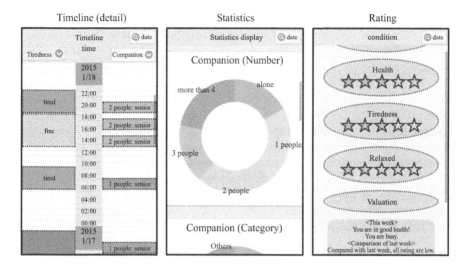

Figure 18.12   Lifelog functions

18.6.2   Possible applications of high-level contexts

High-level contexts can be used for various purposes (not only for analysis in this study), such as user profiling and application recommendation. Here, when applying high-level contexts to such purposes, some findings obtained in this study might be useful in designing a concrete methodology, e.g., (i) high-level contexts have significant impacts on application usage and (ii) a combination of multiple contexts has different impact from each single context. Currently, based on our findings, we have been developing a system to predict an application which a user will use next. Some recent studies applied machine-learning techniques on big data such as deep neural networks (DNNs) to predict or recognize users' situations and activities [21–23]. We have also applied a DNN to our system because a big advantage of our study is that we have collected a large amount of high-level context data.

In addition, the history of high-level contexts can be regarded as lifelogs and, thus, can be used for health care. We have developed a lifelog service on our monster-breeding game, which provides three functions, (i) *timeline* (showing two types of user's contexts which the user selects in timeline), (ii) *statistics* (showing statistics of user's contexts), and (iii) *rating* (showing the total evaluation of user's condition with some comments from a game character), as shown in Figure 18.12, and released it as a new version of our game application. This lifelog mechanism may have a side effect to retain users in our system, i.e., they continue to use our system because this lifelog mechanism is useful for them.

18.7   Conclusion

In this study, we have investigated the relationships between mobile application usage and high-level contexts. In order to collect data regarding high-level context and application usage, we have developed a log-collection system which asks users to answer questions about contexts. Furthermore, to collect a large amount of logs from general smartphone users for a long term, we have adopted the game-based approach in the system.

We have conducted association rule mining on the collected logs. With the extracted association rules, we have found (i) characteristic and concrete usage patterns of smartphones, (ii) some pairs of single context and application have clear relationships, and (iii) some combinations of multiple contexts bring different impact on applications from each single context. Our findings are expected to contribute to further understanding of behavior of smartphone users.

In this work, the users of our system were skewed in terms of age and region. It is preferable to gather more users from difficult background. As part of our future work, in order to get users more broadly, we plan to adopt some other approaches to motivate users to use our system.

References

[1]   Hara T. 'Fusion of heterogeneous mobile data, Challenges and solutions' in Migliardi M., Merlo A., Al-HajBaddar S. (ed.). *Adaptive Mobile Computing: Advances in Processing Mobile Data Sets*. Amsterdam, Netherlands: Elsevier, 2017, Chapter 3, pp. 47–63.

[2]   Church K., Banovic N., Ferreira D., Lyons K. 'Understanding the challenges of mobile phone usage data'. *Proceedings of the 17th International Conference on Human Computer Interaction with Mobile Devices and Services*; Copenhagen, Denmark, 2015, pp. 504–514.

[3]   Bina M., Giaglis G. 'Exploring early usage patterns of mobile data services'. *Proceedings of International Conference on Mobile Business*; Sydney, Australia, 2005, pp. 363–369.

[4]   Kamvar M., Baluja S. 'A large scale study of wireless search behavior: Google mobile search'. *Proceedings of the 24th International Conference on Human Factors in Computing Systems*; Montreal, Canada, 2006, pp. 701–709.

[5]   Welke P., Markowetz A., Blaszkiewicz K., Markowetz A. 'Differentiating smartphone users by app usage'. *Proceedings of the 2016 ACM International Joint Conference on Pervasive and Ubiquitous Computing*; Heidelberg, Germany, 2016, pp. 519–523.

[6]   Zhao S., Ramos J., Tao J., *et al.* 'Discovering different kinds of smartphone users through their application usage behaviors'. *Proceedings of the 2016 ACM International Joint Conference on Pervasive and Ubiquitous Computing*; Heidelberg, Germany, 2016, pp. 498–509.

[7]   Xu Q., Mao Z.M., Arbor A., *et al.* 'Identifying diverse usage behaviors of smartphone apps'. *Proceedings of the 2011 Internet Measurement Conference*; Berlin, Germany, 2011, pp. 329–344.

[8]   Karlson A.K., Iqbal S.T., Meyers B., Ramos G., Lee K., Tang J.C. 'Mobile taskflow in context: A screenshot study of smartphone usage'. *Proceedings of the 28th International Conference on Human Factors in Computing Systems*; Atlanta, GA, USA, 2010, pp. 2009–2018.

[9]   Girardello A., Michahelles F. 'AppAware: Which mobile applications are hot?'. *Proceedings of the 12th International Conference on Human-Computer Interaction with Mobile Devices and Services*; Lisbon, Portugal, 2010, pp. 431–434.

[10] Davidsson C., Moritz S. 'Utilizing implicit feedback and context to recommend mobile applications from first use'. *Proceedings of Workshop on Context-awareness in Retrieval and Recommendation*; Palo Alto, CA, USA, 2011, pp. 19–22.

[11] Yan B., Chen G. 'AppJoy: Personalized mobile application discovery'. *Proceedings of the 9th International Conference on Mobile Systems, Applications, and Services*; Washington, DC, USA, 2011, pp. 113–126.

[12] Costa-Montenegro E., Barragáns-Martínez A.B., Rey-López M. 'Which app? A recommender system of applications in markets: Implementation of the service for monitoring users' interaction'. *Expert Systems with Applications*, 2012;**39**(10):9367–9375.

[13] Sun C., Zheng J., Yao H., Wang Y., Hsu D.F. 'AppRush: Using dynamic shortcuts to facilitate application launching on mobile devices'. *Procedia Computer Science*, 2013;**19**:445–452.

[14] Falaki H., Mahajan R., Kandula S., Lymberopoulos D., Govindan R., Estrin D. 'Diversity in smartphone usage'. *Proceedings of the 8th Annual International Conference on Mobile Systems, Applications, and Services*; San Francisco, CA, USA, 2010, pp. 179–194.

[15] Do T., Blom J., Gatica-Perez D. 'Smartphone usage in the wild: A large-scale analysis of applications and context'. *Proceedings of the 13th International Conference on Multimodal Interaction*; Alicante, Spain, 2011.

[16] Böhme M., Hecht B., Schöning J., Krüger A., Bauer G. 'Falling asleep with angry birds, Facebook and Kindle – A large scale study on mobile application usage'. *Proceedings of the 13th International Conference on Human Computer Interaction with Mobile Devices and Services*; Stockholm, Sweden, 2011, pp. 47–56.

[17] Deterding S., Dixon D., Khaled R., Nacke L. 'From game design elements to gamefulness: Defining gamification'. *Proceedings of the 15th International Academic MindTrek Conference: Envisioning Future Media Environments*; Tampere, Finland, 2011, pp. 9–15.

[18] *Google Play*. https://play.google.com/.

[19] *MMD Labo Inc*. http://mmdlabo.ne.jp/.

[20] Agrawal R., Srikant R. 'Fast algorithms for mining association rules in large databases'. *Proceedings of the 20th International Conference on Very Large Data Bases*; Santiago de Chile, Chile, 1994, pp. 487–499.

[21] Vu T.H., Wang J.C. 'Transportation mode detection on mobile devices using recurrent nets'. *Proceedings of the 2016 ACM on Multimedia Conference*; Amsterdam, Netherlands, 2016, pp. 392–396.

[22]   Yu F., Liu Q., Wu S., Wang L., Tan T. 'A dynamic recurrent model for next basket recommendation'. *Proceedings of the 39th International ACM SIGIR conference on Research and Development in Information Retrieval*; Pisa, Italy, 2016, pp. 729–732.

[23]   Zhang Y., Dai H., Xu C., *et al.* 'Sequential click prediction for sponsored search with recurrent neural networks'. *Proceedings of the 28th AAAI Conference on Artificial Intelligence*; Quebec City, Canada, 2014, pp. 1369–1375.

Chapter 19

Machine learning and stock recommendation

Chulwoo Han[1] and Zhaodong He[1]

In this chapter, we develop a neural network (NN) model for stock classification using input features derived from widely known momentum factors and apply it to two problems; long–short strategy construction and stock recommendation. Empirical findings suggest that our model can create a long–short portfolio generating a significant profit and high Sharpe ratio (SR). It is also effective in making buy/hold/sell recommendation, although the evidence is less strong. Our model seems to be more powerful for cross-sectional prediction while having a limited ability for time-series prediction. We also find that economic performance of a model can be very different from its statistical performance. This signifies the importance of choosing an objective function that reflects economic performance and evaluating models from both statistical and economic perspectives.

19.1 Introduction

Recently, there has been a resurgence of interest in machine learning, in large part due to its spectacular successes in image classification, natural language processing, and various time-series problems [1–3]. Underlying this progress is the development of a feature-learning framework known as deep learning [4], whose basic structure is best described as a multilayer NN, and whose success can be attributed to a combination of increased computational power, availability of large datasets, and more sophisticated algorithms [5–9].

With its successful applications in various areas, finance industry's interest in machine learning has exploded over the last few years, and the related literature is proliferating [10–20]. However, the majority of the literature focuses on methodology, lacks financial context, and remains in the domain of computer science being disregarded by finance community.

This chapter demonstrates two case studies that apply machine learning to stock market prediction and evaluates the results with an emphasis on economic significance. By helping the computer science community understand the importance of a

[1]Finance Department, Durham University, United Kingdom

financial perspective and showing the finance community the potential of machine learning as a new toolkit, we hope to contribute to narrowing the gap and enhancing communication between the two.

Following Han and He [21], our study addresses two classification problems in the stock market and distinguish itself from most of the existing studies that are concerned about return prediction. With the various classification algorithms machine learning offers, we feel that machine learning is particularly well suited to stock classification problems.

The first case study applies machine learning to long–short portfolio construction, which has an important role in empirical asset pricing. A typical method to test the existence of anomaly is to classify stocks into quantiles according to a new anomaly measure and examine the profitability of the long–short portfolio that buys the stocks in the first quantile and sells the stocks in the last quantile. Long–short portfolio strategy is also one of the most popular market-neutral strategy adopted by hedge funds. We develop a machine-learning-based momentum long–short strategy and evaluate it using the data taken from the US stock market. Among the hundreds of factors that are known to have return predictability, we focus on momentum factors as recent studies have found that they are persistent while most other factors are no longer effective [22,23]. We show that our strategy outperforms conventional momentum strategies and produces statistically and economically significant returns.

The second case study employs machine learning for stock recommendation. Stock recommendations (buy/hold/sell) announced by analysts are an important guideline for individual investors. Analysts assess the value of a firm using various accounting ratios and industry outlook and compare it against its current stock price to make a recommendation. These recommendations are, however, often biased and turn out to be a poor predictor of future stock price movement. We examine whether the role of analysts can be replaced by a machine and find that a machine-learning-based stock recommendation system can successfully categorize stocks into buy, hold, and sell.

These case studies suggest that machine learning can help classify stocks by jointly examining many features and extracting hidden information in them. This capability cannot be offered by conventional linear approaches. With the rich set of firm characteristics that are available today, machine learning is expected to help us get the most of their informational content and play an essential role in the asset pricing literature.

The remainder of the chapter is organized as follows. Section 19.2 describes momentum strategies and their profitability, with a brief review of related literature. Section 19.3 develops the machine-learning-based momentum strategy adopted in our research. Detailed feature engineering process and training and testing procedure including sample data construction and portfolio formation are provided in this section. Section 19.4 demonstrates empirical results and evaluates our strategy against conventional momentum strategies. Section 19.5 is devoted to the construction and evaluation of a stock recommendation system. Concluding remarks with suggestions for the future research are given in Section 19.6.

19.2   Momentum and stock-return predictability

19.2.1   Momentum effects

While the efficient market hypothesis is still the dominant theory of market, many empirical studies show that financial markets are to some extent predictable [24–27]. Past price movements, in particular, have been widely used to imply future price movements. De Bondt and Thaler [28] find a long-term reversal of stock returns by formulating portfolios with holding periods of 3–5 years. They show that previously underperformed stocks gained higher profits after a long holding period than those with past superior performance and construct a contrarian strategy that buys past losers and sells short-past winners. Jegadeesh [29] and Lehmann [30] document short-term reversal of stock returns. They argue the abnormal return of the contrarian strategy comes from short-term price movement and the lack of liquidity in the market.

Jegadeesh and Titman (JT) [31] utilize return continuation and develop a momentum strategy that buys high-performance stocks (past winners) and sells poor-performance stocks (past losers), where past performance is defined by the past J-month return (price momentum factor). Using the US stock market data over the sample period from 1965 to 1989, they show that the momentum strategy can realize significant abnormal returns, e.g. a momentum strategy portfolio based on 6-month momentum with 6-month holding period realizes an average excess return of 12.01% per year.

Moskowitz and Grinblatt [32] show that the momentum strategy can be generalized to industries. They find that the stocks belonging to the past winning industry continue to outperform the stocks in the past losing industry. Interestingly, abnormal profits disappear when the momentum portfolio is constructed within the same industry. Lewellen [33] extends the idea of Moskowitz and Grinblatt and shows that the momentum effect can also be found among the size and book-to-market portfolios and is as strong as that of industry portfolios.

Lee and Swaminathan [34] argue that trading volume is closely related to the price momentum factor in terms of both magnitude and persistence. After sorting all firms first by price momentum and then by trading volume, they form a long–short portfolio by buying high price momentum, low trading volume stocks and selling low-price momentum, high trading volume stocks, and demonstrate that this strategy exhibits better performance than the original JT momentum strategy.

Another interesting momentum strategy is based on the 52-week high (WH) (52WH) momentum factor proposed by George and Hwang [35]. The 52WH momentum factor is defined as the current stock price divided by the highest price during the previous 52 weeks. The authors argue that the long–short portfolio based on the 52WH momentum factor yields promising abnormal profits with no short-term reversal within 12 months.

The glamour of momentum is that its effect is not only discovered in the US equity market but also found in global stock markets [36], currencies [37], bonds [38], and even in residential real estate markets [39]. In some cases, the momentum strategy maintains its predictability for years. Israel and Moskowitz [40] show that the price momentum strategy is robust from 1926 to date. Geczy and Samonov [41] conduct backtesting from 1801 to 2012 in the US equity market and find the momentum profit is robust over the extended period. Momentum remains to be one of the most persistent anomalies that cannot be fully explained by other factors.

The momentum strategy, of course, does not always guarantee superior performance. In 2009, after the global financial crisis, the momentum strategy crashed when the loser portfolio dramatically outperformed the winner portfolio. According to Daniel and Moskowitz [42], if an investor had held a momentum long–short portfolio from March to May 2009, she would have suffered a great loss as the winner portfolio gained only 8% while the loser portfolio made a profit of 163%. To avoid the risk involved in the momentum strategy, they propose a hedge method to adjust the portfolio dynamically by scaling volatilities. Barroso and Santa-Clara [43] also present a hedge method to eliminate momentum risks, where they argue systematic risks have the most influence on the momentum strategy.

19.2.2 .Jegadeesh–Titman (JT) momentum strategy

Momentum strategies are built on the belief that firms performing well in the past would remain in a good state in the future. In the JT momentum strategy, past performance is measured by the previous J-month return. The momentum portfolio is then constructed by classifying stocks into quantiles based on their past performance and buying the stocks in the first quantile (past winners) and selling the stocks in the last quantile (past losers). More specifically, suppose we want to build a momentum strategy based on the previous J-month return and K-month holding period. The strategy can be carried out following the procedure below.

1. At the beginning of month t, compute the J-month cumulative return over the period from $t - J$ to $t - 2$:

$$R_i^J = \prod_{j=t-J}^{t-2} (r_i^j + 1) - 1 \tag{19.1}$$

   where r_i^j denotes the monthly return of stock i in month j. For example, R_i^{12} is the 11-month cumulative return over the period from $t - 12$ to $t - 2$. The 1-month gap between portfolio formation and factor calculation is to avoid the short-term reversal documented by Jegadeesh [29] and Lehmann [30]. $J = 6, 12$ are typically used.

2. Sort the stocks in descending order according to R_i^J and split them into quantiles so that each quantile has the same number of stocks. This study uses deciles.

3. Construct a long–short portfolio by buying the stocks in the first quantile and selling the stocks in the last quantile. Stocks in each lag are equally weighted.

4. This portfolio is held for K months.

5. Repeat the above steps every month. At month t, the entire portfolio is an equally weighted portfolio consisting of K long–short portfolios constructed during months $t - K + 1$ and t.

19.2.3 52-Week high (52WH) momentum strategy

The 52WH momentum strategy is constructed in the same way as the JT momentum strategy except for the measure of past performance. In the 52WH strategy, stocks are ranked according to the following measure:

$$H_i^{52} = \frac{P_i^{t-2}}{\text{maximum price during } \{t - 12, \dots, t - 2\}} \tag{19.2}$$

where P_i^t is the price of stock i at the end of month t and the denominator denotes the highest daily price of the stock during the previous 52 weeks ahead of t with 1 month gap.

19.3 Machine-learning-based momentum strategy

Machine learning offers several multiclass classification algorithms and is therefore suitable for a long–short portfolio construction problem where stocks need to be classified into quantiles. As stocks are classified and labelled according to their future returns, this problem becomes a supervised learning problem. One advantage of machine learning is that it allows us to classify stocks jointly using the information from several features. We build an NN momentum strategy and compare it with the JT and 52WH momentum strategies as well as a random forest momentum strategy.

19.3.1 Feature engineering

As mentioned earlier, our aim is to utilize momentum factors as the input for a machine-learning-based long–short strategy and examine whether we can obtain a superior performance compared to the traditional momentum strategies. Therefore, we restrict the input features only to momentum factors and other variables derived from them. The input features we use in our model are listed in Table 19.1 and their definitions are described below. These features are mostly borrowed from Han and He [21].

We first consider the JT and 52WH momentum factors and their variants. More specifically, we use J-month price momentum factors (JT_i^J) with $J = 2, 3, 6, 9, 12$ and W-WH momentum factors (WH_i^W) with $W = 26, 52$. We also include lagged momentum factors, $JT_i^J(L)$ and $WH_i^W(L)$, i.e., the momentum factors calculated L periods ahead. For example, $JT_i^6(2)$ is the 6-month JT momentum factor calculated 2 months ahead. L in the WH momentum factors is in weeks.

The next features capture time-series characteristics such as seasonality, trend, and pulse. The difference of a (lagged) momentum factor is defined as the difference between L- and $L + 1$-lagged momentum factors, i.e. $dJT_i^J(L) = T_i^J(L) - JT_i^J(L + 1)$ and $dWH_i^J(L) = WH_i^J(L) - WH_i^J(L + 1)$. The absolute difference of a momentum factor is the absolute value of the difference.

Table 19.1   Input features of the deep neural network

Momentum factors

JT_i^J	$J \in \{2, 3, 6, 9, 12\}$
WH_i^W	$W \in \{26, 52\}$

L-period lagged momentum factors

$JT_i^J(L)$	$J \in \{2, 3, 6, 9, 12\}, L \in \{1, 2, \ldots, 10\}$ and $L + J \leq 12$
$WH_i^W(L)$	$W \in \{26, 52\}, L \in \{13, 26\}$ and $L + W \leq 52$

Difference of (lagged) momentum factors and their absolute values

$dJT_i^J(L) = JT_i^J(L) - JT_i^J(L+1), \quad |dJT_i^J(L)|$

$dWH_i^W(L) = WH_i^W(L) - WH_i^W(L+1), \quad |dWH_i^W(L)|$

Standardized momentum factor ranks

$rankJT_i^J$	$J \subset \{2, 3, 6, 9, 12\}$
$rankWH_i^W$	$W \in \{26, 52\}$

Market and relative momentum factors

$$\overline{JT}^J = \frac{1}{N} \sum_{i=1}^{N} JT_i^J, \qquad\qquad rJT_i^J = JT_i^J - \overline{JT}^J$$

$$\overline{WH}^W = \frac{1}{N} \sum_{i=1}^{N} WH_i^W, \qquad\qquad rWH_i^W = WH_i^W - \overline{WH}^W$$

The rest of the features capture cross-sectional variation. We add the ranks of the stocks based on each momentum factor. Following Wright [44], we use the standardized rank defined as

$$std\_rank_i = \left(rank_i - \frac{N+1}{2} \right) \Big/ \sqrt{\frac{(N-1)(N+1)}{12}}, \tag{19.3}$$

where $rank_i$ is the rank of stock i among all available stocks (with total number N) based on a selected momentum factor. For example, the stock with the highest 12-month momentum factor JT_i^{12} is ranked 1, and the stock with the lowest factor value is ranked N, and these values are standardized using (19.3). Every momentum factor has its corresponding standardized rank, and they are denoted by $rankJT_i^J$ for the JT_i^J momentum factors and by $rankWH_i^W$ for the WH_i^W momentum factors.

We finally include overall market momentum factors and individual stock momentum factors relative to the market. The market momentum factors, $\overline{JT}^J$ and $\overline{WH}^W$, are defined as the mean of the individual momentum factors at a given month, and the relative momentum factors, rJT_i^J and rWH_i^W, are defined as the difference of the individual momentum factors from the market momentum factors.

Put together, there are total 109 features for each stock. These features are standardized so that the mean and the standard deviation of each feature become 0 and 1. It should be noted that when the features are standardized in the test set, the mean and standard deviation from the training set are used. This is because the test set values are unknown until the last month of the test set, and using these values incurs a look-ahead bias.

19.3.2 Labelling

Stocks are labelled based on their future performance. If the holding period is K months, stocks are ranked according to their K-month cumulative return in descending order and classified into deciles so that each decile has the same number of stocks. In our empirical study, 1-month cumulative return ($K = 1$) is used.

19.3.3 Training and testing

19.3.3.1 Data sample

We use the US equity market data available from the Center for Research in Security Prices (CRSP). All stocks with common shares (share code 10 or 11) listed on NYSE, Amex, or Nasdaq (exchange code 1, 2, or 3) are included. The daily and monthly data required for factor construction are collected during the sample period from 1964-12-01 to 2014-11-30.

To ensure the stocks are traded and available at the time of portfolio construction, the following conditions are applied when choosing stocks.[1] To be included in a portfolio for month t, a stock must have a price for the end of month $t - 13$ and a good return for $t - 2$. In addition, any missing returns from $t - 12$ to $t - 2$ must be -99.0, CRSP's code for missing price. Each included stock also must have market equity at the end of month $t - 1$.

Stocks can be delisted during the holding period after they are included in a portfolio, in which case calculation of the holding period return requires caution. While excluding these stocks from the sample can be an easy solution, it can cause a bias when backtesting [45]. If a stock is delisted during the holding period, the delisted return with dividend from the CRSP delist file is used whenever available. If a delisted stock has no recorded delisted return in CRSP, it is assumed to be -30% following Beaver *et al.* [46].

19.3.3.2 Learning the model

We use the first 10 years of the sample data (1964-12-01 to 1974-11-30) as the training set and the rest as the test set. A more realistic approach in practice is to train the machine repeatedly using a rolling window. For example, we can train the machine using the sample from 1964–12 to 1974–11 to make a prediction and form a portfolio in 1974–12, train the machine again using the sample from 1965–01 to 1974–12 to form a portfolio in 1975–01, and so on. However, as our objective is to

---

[1]These conditions are adopted from the K. French website: http://mba.tuck.dartmouth.edu/pages/faculty/ken.french/Data_Library/det_10_port_form_pr_12_2.html.

Table 19.2 List of hyperparameters

Neural network[a]	Candidates	Selected value
Number of hidden layers	$\{1, 2, 3, 4, 5, 6, 7, 8, 9, 10\}$	1
Number of neurons	$\{2, 4, 8, 12, 16, 24, 48, 96, 128\}$	12
Activation function	$\{\text{ReLU, Sigmoid, Tanh}\}$	Sigmoid
Optimization	$\{\text{SGD, Adam, RMSprop}\}$	Adam
Dropout rate	$\{0, 0.1, 0.2, 0.3, 0.4, 0.5\}$	0
L1 regularization	$\{0, 0.01, 0.1, 0.2\}$	0

Random forest[b]	Candidates	Selected value
Number of estimators	$\{30, 60, 100, 150, 200\}$	100
Max depth	$\{30, 60, 100, 150\}$	60
Min samples split	$\{0.05, 0.1, 0.2\}$	0.05
Max leaf nodes	$\{30, 50, 100, 150\}$	150
Min samples leaf	$\{0.01, 0.05, 0.1\}$	0.01

[a]For the details of the parameters, refer to the Keras document at https://keras.io/.
[b]For the details of the parameters, refer to the scikit-learn library at https://scikit-learn.org/.

demonstrate how machine learning can help stock market prediction and the rolling window approach is computationally demanding, we train the machine only once and hold the parameters fixed throughout the test period.

We choose a fully connected multilayer NN as our primary machine-learning algorithm and random forest for comparison. As our problem is a multi-classification problem, the softmax function is chosen for the output layer activation and the cross-entropy function as the cost function. The hyperparameters listed in Table 19.2 are tuned using the last 2 years of the training set. We use the last 2 years rather than a random validation set or a cross-validation method to consider any potential autocorrelation in stock returns.

The NN models are implemented using Keras with Tensorflow backend in Python 3.6. The scikit-learn library is employed for random forest models. The models are trained on a desktop with CPU i7-7700HQ at 2.81 GHz and NVIDIA Geforce 1050Ti GPU.

19.3.4 Portfolio formation

Once the models are trained, stocks are classified into deciles at each month throughout the test period, and a long–short portfolio is formed by buying the stocks in the first decile and selling the stocks in the last. Unlike the JT and 52WH momentum strategies, where the number of stocks is guaranteed to be equal across deciles, the number of stocks in each decile predicted by a machine-learning model will be different. This can cause a problem if the number of stocks varies considerably across deciles, which is indeed the case. To ensure that the stocks are evenly distributed, following two redistribution methods are adopted. Let N, N_{Dk}, P_i^{Dk}, $k = 1, \ldots, 10$, respectively, denote the total number of available stocks in a given month, the predicted number of stocks in the kth decile (Dk), and the probability of stock i being in Dk, given by the softmax function.

Redistribution method a

1. If $N_{D1} \geq 0.1N$, choose $0.1N$ stocks from D1 with the highest P_i^{D1}. Use the rest of the stocks in D1 to fill D2.
2. If $N_{D1} < 0.1N$, use the stocks in D2 to fill D1, starting from the stocks with the highest P_i^{D2}.
3. Apply the same principle moving down the deciles until D5 is filled.
4. Repeat the above steps starting from D10 and moving backwards until the rest deciles are filled.

Redistribution method b

1. Sort the stocks by $P_i^{D1}, \ldots, P_i^{D10}$.
2. For D1, choose the top 10% of all stocks in terms of P_i^{D1}.
3. Apply the same rule for $D2, \ldots, D10$.

The second method can allocate some stocks to multiple classes and others to none. However, it should not cause any serious problem as our strategy only uses the stocks in D1 and D10.

19.4   Empirical results

In this section, we evaluate the performance of our model against benchmark models. NNa, NNb, random forest (RF), JT, and 52WH, respectively, refer to the NN momentum strategy with the two redistribution methods, random forest, JT, and 52WH momentum strategies.

19.4.1   Classification accuracy

Tables 19.3–19.6 report the classification performance of the models. Based on the per-class performance measures, the NN model appears to have predictability for the extreme deciles (1 and 10): it has a high precision for the tenth decile, in particular. However, it should be noted that the recall value of the tenth decile is also very high, which implies that NN tends to classify stocks into the tenth decile. In contrast, NN shows weak predictability for the in-between classes where precision is only marginally higher than 10%, the precision of random prediction. Nevertheless, the overall accuracy (13.98% in the training set and 14.55% in the test set) indicates that our model has some degree of predictability. It is interesting to note that NN performs as well in the test set as in the training set: the overall accuracy and the average precision and recall values are indeed higher in the test set. This is possible because the test set has a different distribution from the training set. While it is ideal to choose a training set that is representative of the test set, this is often not an option

Table 19.3   Classification performance: NN

Decile	Precision	Recall	F1	Support	Predicted
(a) Training set					
1	14.02	21.32	16.92	27,923	42,459
2	12.40	3.71	5.71	27,923	8,345
3	11.55	1.21	2.20	27,923	2,936
4	13.15	17.09	14.86	27,923	36,272
5	14.47	5.19	7.64	27,923	10,006
6	12.75	9.26	10.73	27,923	20,272
7	11.90	19.94	14.91	27,923	46,779
8	11.11	2.84	4.53	27,923	7,146
9	11.19	10.92	11.06	28,043	27,364
10	17.32	47.71	25.41	28,395	78,243
All	12.99	13.98	11.42	279,822	279,822
Accuracy	13.98				
(b) Test set					
1	12.63	19.19	15.23	235,298	357,597
2	11.93	3.64	5.57	235,298	71,696
3	12.05	1.26	2.29	235,298	24,698
4	13.65	14.43	14.03	235,298	248,828
5	16.30	7.80	10.55	235,298	112,648
6	13.08	8.24	10.11	235,298	148,137
7	12.12	18.14	14.53	235,298	352,271
8	11.12	2.30	3.82	235,298	48,759
9	10.81	9.71	10.23	235,778	211,733
10	18.39	60.43	28.20	237,031	778,826
All	13.21	14.55	11.47	2,355,193	2,355,193
Accuracy	14.55				

in financial applications where the training set needs to be drawn strictly from the past and the test set from the future to prevent a look-ahead bias.

The overall performance of RF is comparable to that of NN. It has a slightly higher overall accuracy but lower average F1 score. Focusing on the extreme deciles, RF tends to predict fewer stocks to be in the first decile and more stocks in the last one and produces a lower F1 score for the first decile and a similar score for the last decile, compared with NN. Although RF appears to perform comparably to NN, it performs much poorer economically as will be shown later.

JT and 52WH both underperform NN. JT outperforms 52WH in all aspects and exhibits reasonable predictability for extreme deciles. Meanwhile, 52WH performs hardly better than random prediction and is especially poor in selecting the stocks in the first decile. Classification performance reflects economic performance to an extent, but they often disagree with each other, as illustrated in the next section.

Table 19.4   Classification performance: RF

Decile	Precision	Recall	F1	Support	Predicted
(a) Training set					
1	13.83	12.99	13.40	27,923	26,212
2	12.12	5.57	7.63	27,923	12,819
3	13.19	0.57	1.10	27,923	1,213
4	13.06	13.95	13.49	27,923	29,831
5	13.52	28.32	18.30	27,923	58,496
6	12.67	11.32	11.96	27,923	24,940
7	11.27	1.67	2.91	27,923	4,136
8	12.04	2.67	4.37	27,923	6,194
9	11.27	4.55	6.48	28,043	11,316
10	16.15	59.52	25.40	28,395	104,665
All	12.92	14.18	10.53	279,822	279,822
Accuracy	14.18				
(b) Test set					
1	11.47	13.35	12.34	235,298	273,892
2	11.33	5.77	7.64	235,298	119,731
3	12.56	0.71	1.34	235,298	13,212
4	12.64	10.84	11.67	235,298	201,759
5	14.75	29.78	19.73	235,298	474,981
6	12.23	8.08	9.73	235,298	155,516
7	11.24	1.34	2.39	235,298	28,002
8	11.14	1.76	3.05	235,298	37,262
9	10.87	3.33	5.10	235,778	72,263
10	17.45	72.03	28.09	237,031	978,575
All	12.57	14.74	10.12	2,355,193	2,355,193
Accuracy	14.74				

19.4.2   Portfolio performance

Good classification performance does not necessarily lead to a good economic performance of the long–short portfolio as the portfolio return is affected not only by the returns of true positives but also by those of false positives, whose true class can be either close or far from the class at hand.

Table 19.7 reports the mean returns of the decile portfolios in excess of the risk-free rate. All classifiers classify the stocks reasonably well as evidenced by the decreasing mean returns along the deciles. NNa and JT perform superior with respect to the mean return of the long–short portfolio in both training and test sets. RF does not perform well in the training set but performs comparably to NNa and JT in the test set. 52WH, as opposed to the superior performance documented in the original paper [35], performs poorly in both datasets. Despite not relying on any statistical method, JT yields a remarkably high mean return. However, as evidenced by the

Table 19.5   Classification performance: JT

Decile	Precision	Recall	F1	Support	Predicted
(a) Training set					
1	13.55	13.55	13.55	27,923	27,923
2	10.86	10.86	10.86	27,923	27,923
3	11.02	11.02	11.02	27,923	27,923
4	11.20	11.20	11.20	27,923	27,923
5	11.13	11.13	11.13	27,923	27,923
6	11.16	11.16	11.16	27,923	27,923
7	10.73	10.73	10.73	27,923	27,923
8	10.86	10.86	10.86	27,923	27,923
9	11.76	11.76	11.76	28,043	28,043
10	18.62	18.62	18.62	28,395	28,395
All	12.10	12.10	12.10	279,822	279,822
Accuracy	12.10				
(b) Test set					
1	13.68	13.68	13.68	235,298	235,298
2	11.03	11.03	11.03	235,298	235,298
3	11.36	11.36	11.36	235,298	235,298
4	12.18	12.18	12.18	235,298	235,298
5	12.40	12.40	12.40	235,298	235,298
6	11.62	11.62	11.62	235,298	235,298
7	10.84	10.84	10.84	235,298	235,298
8	10.61	10.61	10.61	235,298	235,298
9	12.32	12.32	12.32	235,778	235,778
10	24.60	24.60	24.60	237,031	237,031
All	13.07	13.07	13.07	2,355,193	2,355,193
Accuracy	13.07				

t-statistics, it is NNa and NNb that has the most significant return. The returns of RF and JT, while significant, have lower t-statistics in the test set compared to NNa and NNb, and the return of 52WH is marginally significant in the training set and becomes insignificant in the test set.

Table 19.8 examines the economic significance of the long–short portfolio returns obtained from different models. When risk is taken into account, the advantage of the NN-based models becomes manifest. Although JT has the highest mean return, it is also characterized by high volatility and produces a small SR; 0.3 in the training set and 0.11 in the test set. In contrast, NNb has a remarkably low volatility and, despite its low return level, achieves impressive SRs in both datasets; 0.62 and 0.25, respectively. NNa also achieves a comparably high SR in both datasets; 0.70 and 0.21, respectively. The high risk-adjusted returns of NNa and NNb are evident in Figure 19.1, where their cumulative returns grow distinctively smoothly compared to the other models.

Table 19.6   Classification performance: 52WH

Decile	Precision	Recall	F1	Support	Predicted
(a) Training set					
1	8.58	8.58	8.58	27,923	27,923
2	10.67	10.67	10.67	27,923	27,923
3	11.38	11.38	11.38	27,923	27,923
4	11.12	11.12	11.12	27,923	27,923
5	10.21	10.21	10.21	27,923	27,923
6	10.31	10.31	10.31	27,923	27,923
7	10.07	10.07	10.07	27,923	27,923
8	10.35	10.35	10.35	27,923	27,923
9	11.90	11.90	11.90	28,043	28,043
10	18.23	18.23	18.23	28,395	28,395
All	11.29	11.29	11.29	279,822	279,822
Accuracy	11.29				
(b) Test set					
1	7.16	7.16	7.16	235,298	235,298
2	9.94	9.94	9.94	235,298	235,298
3	11.52	11.52	11.52	235,298	235,298
4	11.67	11.67	11.67	235,298	235,298
5	10.84	10.84	10.84	235,298	235,298
6	9.84	9.84	9.84	235,298	235,298
7	9.64	9.64	9.64	235,298	235,298
8	10.26	10.26	10.26	235,298	235,298
9	12.34	12.34	12.34	235,778	235,778
10	24.39	24.39	24.39	237,031	237,031
All	11.77	11.77	11.77	2,355,193	2,355,193
Accuracy	11.76				

NNb, in particular, shows a remarkably stable growth of profit throughout the entire sample period that includes the momentum crash (2009.03-2009.05), where all other strategies suffer a huge loss. NNa also performs robustly during the momentum crash compared to other models.

To see whether the returns of the long–short portfolios can be explained by risk factors, we regress the returns using three-factor models, capital asset pricing model (CAPM) and Fama-French three-factor model [47], and Carhart four-factor model [48] and present the abnormal returns (α) and their t-statistics in Table 19.8. The abnormal returns from the CAPM and Fama-French three-factor model are comparable to the mean returns and mostly significant across all portfolios. This implies that these models have little explanatory power for the profits of the strategies. When the Carhart four-factor model is employed, abnormal returns of some strategies become no longer significant: the abnormal returns of RF, JT, and 52WH are

Table 19.7   Mean excess returns of decile portfolios

Decile	NNa	NNb	RF	JT	52WH
(a) Training set					
1	1.29	0.40	0.88	0.93	0.37
2	1.32	1.52	0.52	0.60	0.21
3	0.64	0.52	0.29	0.34	0.23
4	0.43	0.18	0.00	0.15	0.23
5	0.08	−0.03	0.00	0.03	0.19
6	−0.47	−0.09	−0.21	−0.08	0.11
7	−0.61	−0.33	−0.36	−0.09	−0.04
8	−0.91	−0.89	−0.14	−0.39	−0.05
9	−0.91	−0.89	−0.14	−0.38	−0.33
10	−0.75	−0.43	−0.46	−0.91	−0.70
1–10	2.04	0.83	1.34	1.84	1.07
t-Stat	7.64	6.71	2.59	3.25	1.94
(b) Test set					
1	1.46	1.25	1.53	1.50	1.19
2	1.33	1.49	1.27	1.36	1.23
3	1.23	1.11	1.04	1.24	1.19
4	1.02	1.02	0.99	1.15	1.14
5	0.97	0.96	0.96	1.00	1.09
6	0.89	0.90	0.98	0.90	1.02
7	0.82	0.78	0.94	0.88	0.86
8	0.82	0.73	0.90	0.74	0.69
9	0.82	0.73	0.90	0.61	0.69
10	0.68	0.70	0.74	0.65	0.93
1–10	0.78	0.55	0.79	0.85	0.26
t-Stat	4.69	5.39	2.13	2.36	0.64

considerably smaller than their mean returns in the training set and become insignificant in the test set. This is somewhat expected as the fourth factor of the Carhart model is the price momentum factor. To our surprise, however, the abnormal returns of NNa and NNb are not smaller than their mean returns and remain strongly significant. This implies that the NN models, even though their input features are based on momentum factors, successfully draw hidden information that is not revealed by plain momentum strategies. The information ratio (IR) also strongly supports the NN models.

19.5   Machine-learning-based stock recommendation

In the previous sections, stocks are classified into quantiles, and a long–short portfolio is formed by buying past winners and selling past losers. In this strategy, only the cross-sectional difference is important: as long as the past winners continue to

Table 19.8   Performance of long–short portfolios

	NNa	NNb	RF	JT	52WH	Market
(a) Training set						
r	2.04	0.83	1.34	1.84	1.07	−0.25
t-Stat	7.64	6.71	2.59	3.25	1.94	−0.60
σ	2.91	1.36	5.66	6.18	6.02	4.50
SR	0.70	0.62	0.24	0.30	0.18	−0.06
CAPM α	2.03	0.85	1.25	1.79	0.94	
t-Stat	7.58	7.02	2.50	3.18	1.85	
IR	0.70	0.65	0.23	0.29	0.17	
FF α	2.22	0.89	1.65	2.13	1.32	
t-Stat	9.86	7.29	4.16	4.06	3.43	
IR	0.93	0.69	0.39	0.38	0.32	
Carhart α	2.01	0.84	0.77	0.81	0.40	
t-Stat	9.01	6.67	2.78	2.75	1.67	
IR	0.89	0.66	0.27	0.27	0.16	
(b) Test set						
r	0.78	0.55	0.79	0.85	0.26	0.68
t-Stat	4.69	5.39	2.13	2.36	0.64	3.30
σ	3.65	2.23	8.16	7.88	8.98	4.49
SR	0.21	0.25	0.10	0.11	0.03	0.15
CAPM α	0.85	0.49	1.10	0.97	0.77	
t-Stat	5.07	4.83	2.99	2.68	2.00	
IR	0.24	0.22	0.14	0.12	0.09	
FF α	0.91	0.54	1.19	1.16	0.85	
t-Stat	5.72	5.28	3.28	3.18	2.27	
IR	0.27	0.25	0.15	0.15	0.11	
Carhart α	0.78	0.59	0.18	−0.06	−0.18	
t-Stat	4.92	5.70	0.64	−0.25	−0.62	
IR	0.24	0.27	0.03	−0.01	−0.03	

outperform the past losers, the overall market performance does not matter. On the other hand, stock recommendation (buy, hold, or sell) issued by analysts is concerned about the absolute performance of individual stocks. Buy recommendation implies the price of the stock is expected to rise, whereas sell implies it is expected to fall. Hold means the price is expected to remain around the current value.

While analysts incorporate various information, e.g. accounting ratios and industry prospects, into their forecast, their predictability is known to be rather limited. In this section, we examine whether machine learning can effectively classify stocks into the three recommendation categories using only the momentum-related features. This will reveal the time-series predictability of our model, unlike the long–short strategy where only the cross-sectional difference matters.

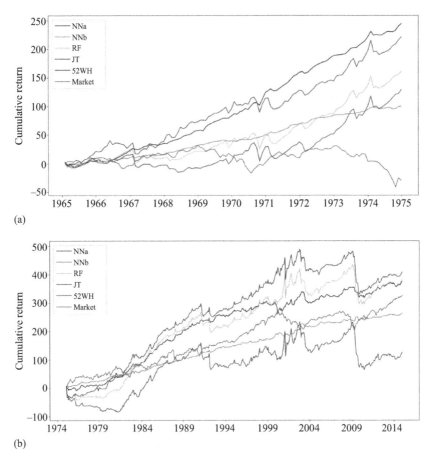

Figure 19.1 Cumulative returns of long–short portfolios: (a) training set and (b) test set

19.5.1 Design of the model

As before, we choose an NN with the same features defined in Table 19.1 as our model. At month t, all available stocks are labelled as buy, hold, or sell using the following criteria:

$$\text{Buy, if } r_i^t > m + \tau;$$
$$\text{Sell, if } r_i^t < m - \tau; \tag{19.4}$$
$$\text{Hold, otherwise.}$$

Considering that the monthly market volatility is about 4.5%, we set $\tau = 4\%$. For the value of m, we test two values, $m = 0\%$ and $m = 1\%$.[2] An alternative method would be to set different thresholds for different stocks using their characteristics. For instance, the mean and standard deviation of each stock returns could be employed to determine m and τ for the stock. One difficulty, however, is that the thresholds of the stocks that are not included in the training set cannot be determined until the stocks accumulate a sufficient return history to compute mean and standard deviation. Therefore, we apply the common thresholds as defined above to all stocks.

19.5.2 Empirical results

Table 19.9 reports the performance of our model. In the training set, we obtain the overall accuracy of 46.52% when $m = 0$ and 46.61% when $m = 1$. These values are significantly higher than the accuracy of random classification, 33.3%. Accuracy drops in the test set, but the values are still above 40% for both cases. The per-class precision and recall values indicate that the predictability of the model is comparable across all classes but slightly worse for the buy class and better for the sell class, especially when $m = 1$. The value of m does not appear to make a noticeable difference in the results.

In terms of economic significance, the stocks in the buy class have a higher mean return than those in hold, which subsequently have a higher mean return than those in sell. Furthermore, the return of the buy-minus-sell $(B - S)$ portfolio is significantly greater than 0 in both training and test sets. These indicate that the mean return of the buy stocks is significantly higher than that of the sell stocks, and our model can classify stocks as intended.

However, the predictability of our model appears to be rather weak when the returns are compared to the thresholds. The mean return of the buy stocks are significantly lower than the threshold; 0.4% (training set) and 1.11% (test set) vs. 4% when $m = 0$, whereas that of the sell stocks are significantly higher than the threshold; −0.13% (training set) and 0.79% (test set) vs. −4% when $m = 0$. In addition, although the model works fairly on average, Figures 19.2 and 19.3 reveal a reversal of returns between hold and sell for an extended period. Interestingly, the buy and sell stocks are volatile and highly correlated with each other, whereas the hold stocks are less volatile and show a very different behaviour. The return of the $B - S$ portfolio cannot be explained by any of the factor models as evidenced by the significant abnormal returns.

The lower mean return of the $B - S$ portfolio compared to the long–short portfolio in the previous section can be to some extent attributed to its smaller number of classes: the previous long–short portfolio consists of the stocks in the two extreme deciles, whereas the $B - S$ portfolio consists of the stocks in the two extremely terciles. Overall, the empirical results suggest that our NN-based stock recommendation system can distinguish good stocks from bad ones.

---

[2]We could use the mean return of the market, but it is negative during the training sample period.

Table 19.9   Stock recommendation performance

	(a) Training set							
	m = 0				**m = 1**			
	Buy	**Hold**	**Sell**	**B − S**	**Buy**	**Hold**	**Sell**	**B − S**
$r - r_f$	0.40	0.07	−0.13	0.53	0.53	0.30	−0.02	0.55
t-Stat	0.57	0.19	−0.18	2.41	1.05	1.57	0.34	3.78
σ	7.74	4.00	7.62	2.41	8.06	3.78	7.17	2.31
SR	0.05	0.02	−0.02	0.22	0.07	0.08	0.00	0.24
CAPM α	0.77	0.27	0.20	0.57	0.91	0.48	0.30	0.61
t-Stat	2.17	1.78	0.47	2.68	2.32	3.05	0.81	3.12
IR	0.20	0.16	0.04	0.25	0.22	0.28	0.07	0.29
FF3 α	0.38	0.04	−0.32	0.70	0.49	0.26	−0.17	0.65
t-Stat	2.31	0.49	−2.01	3.51	2.55	2.48	−1.52	3.30
IR	0.22	0.04	−0.19	0.33	0.24	0.24	−0.15	0.31
Cahart α	0.21	0.00	−0.30	0.51	0.31	0.22	−0.16	0.48
t-Stat	1.29	−0.02	−1.85	2.60	1.65	2.05	−1.43	2.42
IR	0.13	0.00	−0.18	0.26	0.16	0.20	−0.14	0.24
Precision	41.39	48.00	49.75		39.06	46.67	49.95	
Recall	44.28	40.75	53.65		31.44	40.73	61.58	
F1-score	42.79	44.08	51.62		34.84	43.50	55.16	
Accuracy	46.52				46.61			

	(b) Test set							
$r - r_f$	1.11	0.89	0.79	0.31	1.09	0.92	0.85	0.24
t-Stat	3.72	5.56	2.45	3.33	4.08	7.52	3.68	4.75
σ	6.51	3.51	7.11	2.06	7.19	3.41	6.53	2.26
SR	0.17	0.25	0.11	0.15	0.15	0.27	0.13	0.11
CAPM α	0.29	0.45	−0.05	0.35	0.23	0.49	0.05	0.18
t-Stat	1.74	5.10	−0.27	3.68	1.14	5.76	0.28	1.77
IR	0.08	0.24	−0.01	0.17	0.05	0.26	0.01	0.08
FF3 α	0.08	0.25	−0.35	0.43	0.02	0.31	−0.23	0.25
t-Stat	0.80	3.71	−2.56	4.57	0.12	4.54	−2.11	2.47
IR	0.04	0.17	−0.12	0.22	0.01	0.22	−0.10	0.12
Carhart α	0.18	0.20	−0.11	0.29	0.21	0.25	−0.05	0.26
t-Stat	1.83	2.93	−0.84	3.23	1.63	3.67	−0.49	2.56
IR	0.09	0.14	−0.04	0.16	0.08	0.18	−0.02	0.12
Precision	36.64	47.72	38.10		34.87	48.01	40.13	
Recall	34.07	41.94	45.79		24.28	41.79	55.74	
F1-score	35.31	44.64	41.59		28.63	44.68	46.66	
Accuracy	40.45				41.23			

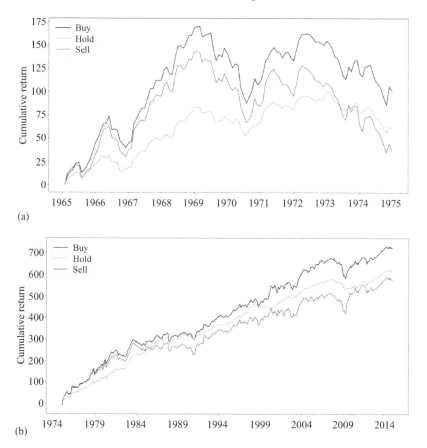

Figure 19.2   Cumulative returns of buy/hold/sell portfolios: m = 0. (a) Training set and (b) test set

19.6   Conclusion

In this chapter, we develop an NN model for stock classification that uses input features primarily derived from momentum factors. We apply the model to two important stock prediction problems, long–short strategy construction and stock recommendation, and evaluate it from both statistical and economic perspectives.

When applied to long–short strategy construction, our model generates a significant profit and outperforms conventional momentum strategies as well as a random forest model. In spite of using only momentum-based features, the long–short portfolio from our model behaves distinctively from other momentum-based portfolios and is characterized by remarkably low volatility. This suggests that our model exploits hidden information in the input features. This claim is further supported by the highly significant abnormal return from the Carhart four-factor model.

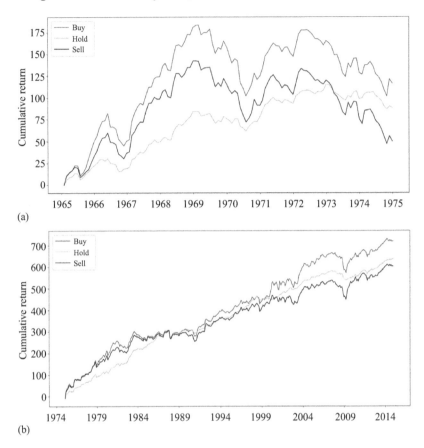

Figure 19.3   Cumulative returns of buy/hold/sell portfolios: m = 1. (a) Training set and (b) test set

Empirical findings from the second case study suggest that our model can distinguish good stocks from bad ones. However, the evidence is not as convincing as in the first case. Our model appears to be better suited to cross-sectional prediction while having a limited ability for time-series prediction.

Good classification performance does not always reflect good economic performance. Our NN model and the random forest model show a similar classification performance, but our model generates a substantially higher SR. This throws two important implications: (1) it is critical to define an objective function for machine learning that is well aligned with economic performance; (2) models should be evaluated not only from a statistical perspective but also from an economic perspective.

This study does not elaborate on feature selection. A sensitivity analysis can help identify input features important for cross-sectional prediction and those for time-series prediction and provides a further insight to discover new features that can enhance the performance.

References

[1] Hinton GE, Salakhutdinov RR. Reducing the dimensionality of data with neural networks. Science. 2006;313(5786):504–507.

[2] Lee H, Pham P, Largman Y, *et al.* Unsupervised feature learning for audio classification using convolutional deep belief networks. In: Advances in neural information processing systems; 2009. p. 1096–1104.

[3] Cireşan D, Meier U, Masci J, *et al.* Multi-column deep neural network for traffic sign classification. Neural Networks. 2012;32:333–338.

[4] LeCun Y, Bengio Y, Hinton G. Deep learning. Nature. 2015;521(7553): 436–444.

[5] Hinton GE, Osindero S, Teh YW. A fast learning algorithm for deep belief nets. Neural Computation. 2006;18(7):1527–1554.

[6] Bengio Y, Lamblin P, Popovici D, *et al.* Greedy layer-wise training of deep networks. Advances in Neural Information Processing Systems. 2007;19:153.

[7] Salakhutdinov R, Hinton GE. Deep Boltzmann machines. In: AISTATS. vol. 1; 2009. p. 3.

[8] Deng L, Yu D. Deep learning. Signal Processing. 2014;7:3–4.

[9] Srivastava N, Hinton GE, Krizhevsky A, *et al.* Dropout: A simple way to prevent neural networks from overfitting. Journal of Machine Learning Research. 2014;15(1):1929–1958.

[10] Armano G, Marchesi M, Murru A. A hybrid genetic-neural architecture for stock indexes forecasting. Information Sciences. 2005;170(1):3–33.

[11] Zhu X, Wang H, Xu L, *et al.* Predicting stock index increments by neural networks: The role of trading volume under different horizons. Expert Systems with Applications. 2008;34(4):3043–3054.

[12] Atsalakis GS, Valavanis KP. Surveying stock market forecasting techniques– Part II: Soft computing methods. Expert Systems with Applications. 2009;36(3):5932–5941.

[13] Tsai CF, Hsiao YC. Combining multiple feature selection methods for stock prediction: Union, intersection, and multi-intersection approaches. Decision Support Systems. 2010;50(1):258–269.

[14] Guresen E, Kayakutlu G, Daim TU. Using artificial neural network models in stock market index prediction. Expert Systems with Applications. 2011;38(8):10389–10397.

[15] Khashei M, Bijari M. A novel hybridization of artificial neural networks and ARIMA models for time series forecasting. Applied Soft Computing. 2011;11(2):2664–2675.

[16] Yeh CY, Huang CW, Lee SJ. A multiple-kernel support vector regression approach for stock market price forecasting. Expert Systems with Applications. 2011;38(3):2177–2186.

[17]   Kazem A, Sharifi E, Hussain FK, *et al.* Support vector regression with chaos-based firefly algorithm for stock market price forecasting. Applied Soft Computing. 2013;13(2):947–958.

[18]   Ticknor JL. A Bayesian regularized artificial neural network for stock market forecasting. Expert Systems with Applications. 2013;40(14):5501–5506.

[19]   Adebiyi AA, Adewumi AO, Ayo CK. Comparison of ARIMA and artificial neural networks models for stock price prediction. Journal of Applied Mathematics. 2014;2014: 1–7.

[20]   Chong E, Han C, Park FC. Deep learning networks for stock market analysis and prediction: Methodology, data representations, and case studies. Expert Systems with Applications. 2017;83:187–205.

[21]   Han C, He Z. Machine Learning Momentum Strategy and Stock Recommendation. Working Paper. 2018.

[22]   McLean RD, Pontiff J. Does academic research destroy stock return predictability?. The Journal of Finance. 2016;71(1):5–32.

[23]   Messmer M. Deep Learning and the Cross-Section of Expected Returns. 2017.

[24]   Ferreira MA, Santa-Clara P. Forecasting stock market returns: The sum of the parts is more than the whole. Journal of Financial Economics. 2011;100(3):514–537.

[25]   Kim JH, Shamsuddin A, Lim KP. Stock return predictability and the adaptive markets hypothesis: Evidence from century-long US data. Journal of Empirical Finance. 2011;18(5):868–879.

[26]   Bollerslev T, Marrone J, Xu L, *et al.* Stock return predictability and variance risk premia: Statistical inference and international evidence. Journal of Financial and Quantitative Analysis. 2014;49(03):633–661.

[27]   Phan DHB, Sharma SS, Narayan PK. Stock return forecasting: Some new evidence. International Review of Financial Analysis. 2015;40:38–51.

[28]   De Bondt WF, Thaler R. Does the stock market overreact?. The Journal of Finance. 1985;40(3):793–805.

[29]   Jegadeesh N. Evidence of predictable behavior of security returns. The Journal of Finance. 1990;45(3):881–898.

[30]   Lehmann BN. Fads, martingales, and market efficiency. The Quarterly Journal of Economics. 1990;105(1):1–28.

[31]   Jegadeesh N, Titman S. Returns to buying winners and selling losers: Implications for stock market efficiency. The Journal of Finance. 1993;48(1):65–91.

[32]   Moskowitz TJ, Grinblatt M. Do industries explain momentum?. The Journal of Finance. 1999;54(4):1249–1290.

[33]   Lewellen J. Momentum and autocorrelation in stock returns. The Review of Financial Studies. 2002;15(2):533–564.

[34]   Lee C, Swaminathan B. Price momentum and trading volume. The Journal of Finance. 2000;55(5):2017–2069.

[35]   George TJ, Hwang CY. The 52-week high and momentum investing. The Journal of Finance. 2004;59(5):2145–2176.

[36]   Rouwenhorst KG. International momentum strategies. The Journal of Finance. 1998;53(1):267–284.

[37] Okunev J, White D. Do momentum-based strategies still work in foreign currency markets?. Journal of Financial and Quantitative Analysis. 2003;38(2): 425–447.

[38] Gebhardt WR, Hvidkjaer S, Swaminathan B. Stock and bond market interaction: Does momentum spill over?. Journal of Financial Economics. 2005;75(3):651–690.

[39] Beracha E, Skiba H. Momentum in residential real estate. The Journal of Real Estate Finance and Economics. 2011;43(3):299–320.

[40] Israel R, Moskowitz TJ. The role of shorting, firm size, and time on market anomalies. Journal of Financial Economics. 2013;108(2):275–301.

[41] Geczy CC, Samonov M. Two centuries of price-return momentum. Financial Analysts Journal. 2016;72(5):32–56.

[42] Daniel K, Moskowitz TJ. Momentum crashes. Journal of Financial Economics. 2016;122(2):221–247.

[43] Barroso P, Santa-Clara P. Momentum has its moments. Journal of Financial Economics. 2015;116(1):111–120.

[44] Wright JH. Alternative variance-ratio tests using ranks and signs. Journal of Business & Economic Statistics. 2000;18(1):1–9.

[45] Shumway T. The delisting bias in CRSP data. The Journal of Finance. 1997;52(1):327–340.

[46] Beaver W, McNichols M, Price R. Delisting returns and their effect on accounting-based market anomalies. Journal of Accounting and Economics. 2007;43(2–3):341–368.

[47] Fama EF, French KR. Common risk factors in the returns on stocks and bonds. Journal of Financial Economics. 1993;33(1):3–56.

[48] Carhart MM. On persistence in mutual fund performance. The Journal of Finance. 1997;52(1):57–82.

Chapter 20

The role of smartphone in recommender systems: opportunities and challenges

*Peifeng Yin**

The popularity of smartphones in people's daily life brings new opportunities as well as challenges in recommender system. New opportunities include new available context data, e.g., user interaction time (usually from native mobile app) and geo-location data (from equipped GPS sensors). These metainformation provides different ways of inferring user preference, which ultimately improves the recommendation performance. For instance, with record of tap-in and tap-out timestamp, the dwell time can be estimated. It thus provides an opportunity to address the "silent viewing" issue by inferring people's implicit rating, which will benefit conventional recommender systems that suffer from rating-sparsity. At the meantime, new challenges are mainly in two-fold. First, such side information is not included in conventional recommendation model, and thus it is not easy for integration. Also, recommendation services via smartphones is itself a scenario different from traditional PC-based one, which leads to "pitfalls" where existing techniques may fail. Particularly, we focus on two representative recommendation scenarios in smartphones, i.e., app and point-of-interest (POI) recommendation. For the former one, conventional model may recommend apps that users would never download due to the ignorance of potential conflict between candidate apps and installed ones. To recommend POI, failure of modeling physical location may lead to candidates that are too far away. In this chapter, we reveal these issues and describe corresponding solutions.

20.1 Introduction

The past decades have seen the popularity of smartphones. As survey shows, online time spent on desktops and laptops decrease year by year, while the mobile internet usage grows rapidly.[1] Such growth of mobile usage leads to the popup of planted and new services, e.g., mobile news, geo-located messages, location-based social

*Center for Social Data Analytics, IBM Almaden Research Center, San Jose, United States
[1]http://www.businessinsider.com/people-now-spend-more-internet-time-on-mobile-than-desktops-or-laptops-2016-4

networks (LBSNs) and mobile app stores. With appearance of these new scenarios, requirement of recommendation also arises. For instance, on mobile news, recommending new articles to people is needed to increase the user engagement in the news feed service. Also, the mobile app recommender system frees the burden of searching desired apps among tons of candidates in the store. Finally in LBSN, recommendation of new POIs not only help people explore the physical environment but also enhance the social interactions among friends in the real world.

Recommendation on smartphone is different from conventional recommender scenarios in three-fold. First, besides explicit rating, the record of user behaviors such as tap-in, tap-out enriches the side information for preference modeling. Second, in app recommendation, installed apps may have conflict with candidate ones. In this case, recommending apps similar to installed ones may fail since user may refuse to replace existing ones. Third, in POI recommendation, vising a location recurs cost that cannot be neglected. Therefore, the success of recommended POI depends not only the user preference but also the physic distance. In the rest of the section, we discuss each one in details.

The task of recommendation is modeled as the prediction of missing rating. Imagine a big matrix, where each row represents a user while each column represents an item. The element value of this matrix is the rating of the corresponding user to that particular item. The recommendation thus aims to find those items that have not been rated by the user but would get high value. In summary, the essence of conventional recommendation is to infer user preference according to his/her historical ratings. For users who do not have many ratings, the effectiveness of interest inference would be discounted. Similarly, to recommend an item, its historical ratings are also important to infer its quality. And if the rating data is sparse, recommendation performance would be affected. This is an issue known as *cold-start* problem.

To address the cold-start problem, many works proposed methods to rely on other information besides rating history, e.g., user profile similarity [1,2], item profile similarity [3,4] and social recommendation [5,6]. Work [7] provides a different angle. Based on an analysis on records of a mobile joke-reading app, the authors found that there are a large number of users who do not give rating while actively using the app to read jokes. This scenario is denoted as *silent viewing behavior*. The existence of silent users reveals such a concern that even as time passes, the rating history will not increase, and thus the cold-start problem is not limited to new users.

Although people may incline not to give explicit ratings, they do spend some time on viewing the item. And the time spent is a useful indicator of his/her altitude. To give an example, consider a customer walking into a shop to buy a handbag. For a handbag of style A, the customer simply gave a glance and walked away. For style B, she spent quite a few minutes, picking it up and carefully checking its details of variant angles. In the end, the customer may buy neither one. But a wise salesman would recommend more candidate handbags whose styles are closer to B rather than A. The smartphone in this scenario facilitates the use of dwell time. Internet usage via smartphones usually happens in the native mobile apps, where recording of people behavior is much more convenient than that via either desktop or laptop. Logs of user actions, such as tap-in and tap-out, together with time-stamps can be easily transformed to dwell time. With this data and sparse explicit ratings, researchers are able to develop models interpreting such implicit feedback. Such extra information finally would help improve the recommendation effectiveness. In Section 20.2, we describe one of these trials.

The popularity of smart phone comes together with the popularity of app stores, where developers publish their developed apps for people to download and use. A statistic report from 2107 indicates that there are about 28 and 22 million apps in Google play and Apple app store, respectively.[2] And the total number of annual app downloads is estimated to be 352.9 billion by 2021.[3] Such large volume generates the need of app recommendation service. Compared to conventional recommendation, app recommendation may rely on the smart phone to collect extra information to improve accuracy. For example, the app usage data could be analyzed to identify useful patterns [8]. Also, this usage data could be further used to adjust the explicit ratings that are shown in the app store [9,10]. Finally, the GPS data may also be exploited as contextual information to help recommend geographical-sensitive apps [11].

Conventional recommendation task aims at recommending candidate items that are predicted to be highly correlated to target user's interest, based on his/her historical ratings. Take the movie recommendation as an example. If the recommender system observed that the user gave high ratings to movies *Star War*, *Guardians of Galaxy*, it would recommend *Spider Man*, *Star Trek*, etc., as they are similar (e.g., all of them belong to the genre of science fiction). This rationale may fail when it comes to recommend mobile apps in app store. Consider the following scenario. Suppose a user installs a weather forecast app in her smartphone and gives a high rating. A content-based recommender system may keep recommending apps of similar functions, i.e., weather forecast in this case. It is highly likely that the user would not install the recommended app since she has already owned the one that works pretty well. On the other hand, with the same scenario, if the app is not weather forecast, but some game, the result would be different.

The above example reveals that the history may not always help but block the future recommendation. In the context of the app recommendation, it means the installment of one app may affect users' future adoption of similar apps [12]. One intuition is that for *one-shot consumption* item such as movies and books, people would usually accept similar items. For *continuous consumption* item such as weather forecast, calculate and phone flashlight, apps of similar functions may not be rejected. However, an analysis reveals that some users did install multiple apps of similar functions [12]. Therefore, in app recommendation, the major challenge is when the user would accept/reject recommended similar apps. We cover details of the solution in Section 20.3

One notable feature of smart phone is its equipment of GPS sensor, which can record the current geographical location. This technology leads to the popularity of diversified LBSN services. In LBSN, people can choose to publish the visited

[2] https://www.statista.com/statistics/276623/number-of-apps-available-in-leading-app-stores/
[3] https://www.statista.com/statistics/271644/worldwide-free-and-paid-mobile-app-store-downloads/

location, also known as POI and share it with his/her online friends. It provides a new way of social interaction. On the other hand, the POI recommendation service is needed to help people explore their nearby environment and facilitate location-based marketing. For conventional recommendation, accessing the recommended item is out of the scope since recommended items, e.g., movies, books and mobile apps, usually brings tiny, if not negligible, cost. For POI recommendation, however, people need to be physically visiting the location in the real world. This is a quite different accessing pattern as the cost can no longer be ignored. Particularly, there are three main factors, i.e., (i) geographical, (ii) social and (iii) temporal.

Geographical factor considers the distance between target user's current location and the recommended POI. In [13], it is found that the check-in pattern satisfies a power-law distribution. That means, the probability of check-in a location exponentially decreases as the distance increases. To put it another way, in reality, people usually do not go far away to visit a location. For conventional recommender system that solely focuses on user preference, it may recommend a New York Chinese restaurant to a Chinese food lover located in San Francisco. This case is definitely insensible.

Social factors consider the influence of social friends on a user to check-in a location. For online recommendation, the item accessing is mainly determined by individual interest. For offline POI check-in, on the other hand, the purpose is not to satisfy personal interest. Sometimes, people visit a location for meeting their friends and may check-in POI that does not match their preference. In POI recommendation, such social influence needs to be considered. Particularly, consider a scenario of recommending a location for group meeting, where individual interests are too diversified to unify, social influence is especially important. In Section 20.4.2, we pick two representative works [14,15] to describe methods of integrating this factor.

The final factor relates to temporal patterns of people's daily life. A few works [16–19] have reported significant temporal patterns, particularly hours of the day, in people's daily location check-in behavior. For example, a person may go to work at 9:00 AM and visit restaurant for lunch and dinner at 12:00 PM and 6:00 PM, respectively. On a weekday evening, he may check-in Gym for workout while going to theatre or bars on weekend night. Considering this pattern, a recommender system may avoid recommending POIs that conflict with it, e.g., recommending bars on weekday or dinner restaurant in the morning. Particular, the temporal pattern can be summarized as two properties, namely, *nonuniformness* and *consecutiveness* [20,21]. The former one captures people's preference to particular locations at specific hours, while the latter one indicates the sequential preference consistency over short time. In Section 20.4.3, we describe details of modeling these two properties and integrating temporal pattern into recommendation.

The rest of this chapter is organized as follows. In Section 20.2, we describe details of modeling user dwell time and show how the inferred "pseudo rating" helps conventional recommendation techniques. In Section 20.3, we introduce models of contest between installed mobile apps and candidates. In Section 20.4, we cover the geographical, social and temporal influence in POI recommendation. Finally we conclude this chapter in Section 20.5.

20.2 Silence is also evidence: interpret dwell time

In [7], an analysis was conducted on 108,743 users' behaviors on a mobile app for joke sharing and it revealed that 95.93% of people never gave a rating. This is a bad news for rating-based recommendation techniques. The issue is thus how to exploit these active viewer's silent patterns to facilitate recommendation.

20.2.1 Modeling the silence behavior

While there is no way to ask the silent users why they do not rate after viewing the item, we may get some insight from psychologic work. In [22], an experiment was conducted to simulate people's process of decision-making. Particularly in the experiment, participants were asked to make a series of two alternative-forced choices, and their spent time was measured. Researchers argue that the time lag between being offered a question and giving an answer represents the process of evidence collection, or exactly *information accumulation*. People would not make a choice until collected evidence (information) accesses some threshold.

Similarly, we may assume the existence of a rating threshold for each person, and the silence behavior suggests the item's quality is lower than her/his threshold. A further analysis demonstrates the potential existence of such action bar. In [7], authors collected all accessed items for each user and grouped them to two categories: positive vote and neutral. The former one means the user gives positive rate to the item after viewing it while the latter one suggests the user kept silent. Then for each category, the average number of total positive votes is calculated. As comparison, it is shown that items of the first category on average have a higher number of total positive votes, suggesting its better quality than that of the other category. This observation reflected that silence is due to the item's quality lower than action bar.

Formally, let b and q denote the action bound of a person and the quality of an item, respectively. The probability that the person would give a positive vote after viewing the item is modeled as a random variable generated by the beta process.

$$\texttt{Beta}(p; b, q) = \frac{\Gamma(q + b)}{\Gamma(q)\Gamma(b)} p^{q-1}(1 - p)^{b-1} \tag{20.1}$$

where $\Gamma(x) = (x - 1)!$ refers to a gamma function. We can see the insight of (20.1) by computing the expected value of silence probability as below.

$$P(v = 0|b, q) = 1 - P(v = 1|b, q) = 1 - \int_0^1 p \cdot \texttt{Beta}(p; q, b) = \frac{b}{q + b} \tag{20.2}$$

where v is a binary variable indicating whether the user votes ($v = 1$) or not ($v = 0$). As can be seen in (20.2), the silence behavior is determined by two factors: item quality and personal action bound. Specifically, the expected probability is correlated with the proportion of action bound b in the sum of action bound b and the quality q. The higher the proportion is, the higher the probability of keeping silence. It captures our earlier assumption that if the user's voting threshold is high, she/he is likely to keep silent unless viewing an excellent item. In the experiment, the action bound b is a personalized parameter that needs to be learned from the data while the item quality q can be approximated by the total number of positive vote it has received.

20.2.2 Modeling the dwell time

With the model of silence behavior with the beta process, we may think about people's dwell time with regard to diversified scenarios. Particularly, given a quality q and action bound b, we categorize different combinations in the following three cases:

- $q \gg b$. The quality largely exceeds the bound and the user would definitely give a vote. In reality, it means the item is far beyond one's expectation, and a person may view it multiple times before switching to others, leading to an extra long dwell time.
- $q \approx b$. The item's quality is approximate to one's action bound, suggesting its falling within one's expectation. A person may view the item but hesitate whether to vote or not. This is a rather ambiguous area and the voing/silence is purely random. And the length of the dwell time would be as expected.
- $q \ll b$. The item is far lower than threshold. The user would not like it and may even quit before finishing viewing this item. This behavior therefore results in an extremely short dwell time.

The three scenarios give a rough concept of how the dwell time could be interpreted to a person's attitude. However, the challenge lies in the mathematical quantification of dwell time in terms of "extra long," "as expected" and "extremely short," as described above.

Normally, we can categorize factors impacting the dwell time into two types: common and personal. The first one represents the expected time required viewing the item. It largely depends on the item format, e.g., picture, texts, video, audio. The second factor captures the person's factor due to the difference between the item's quality and the user's expectation (i.e., action bound in our case). Formally, we may use the following equation to model dwell time t:

$$t = \alpha + \beta + \xi \tag{20.3}$$

where α and β are the common factor and the personal factor, respectively, and ξ is a random noise. For textual data, the common factor is correlated to the length of the item and the average reading speed. Formally, let l and r represent the length and reading speed, we may model the common factor as $\log(l/r)$. For personal factor, we use the difference of quality and action bound to model, i.e., $\gamma \cdot (q - b)$. In general, this form captures the three scenarios mentioned above. When quality is beyond expectation, $q - b$ adds extra dwell time to common one and when quality is smaller than action bound, the $q - b$ is a negative value and thus reduces the dwell time. Particularly, the variable γ is a positive parameter adjusting the contribution of quality-bound difference into the dwell time. Semantically, it represents a person's sensitivity. For instance, big value of γ means the person is really "picky," spending extremely long time on items of good quality and little time on low ones. If α is small, the impact of quality difference is tiny on the dwell time, suggesting the user is quite tolerant to low-quality items. Finally the random noise ξ may be modeled as a Gaussian white noise. In summary, the dwell time distribution can be written as below.

$$P(t|l, q, b, r, \gamma) = \mathcal{N}(\log t; \mu(r, l, \gamma, q, b), \sigma^2) = \frac{1}{\sqrt{2\pi\sigma^2}} \cdot e^{-((\log t - \mu)/2\sigma^2)}$$

$$\text{where } \mu(r, l, \gamma, q, b) = \log(l/r) + \gamma \cdot (q - b) \tag{20.4}$$

Note that the random noise ξ is modeled as the Gaussian distribution with variance σ^2 and thus does not appear in the probability density function. Also, the time is used in logarithmic form. This setting comes from the data analysis that the distribution of dwell time satisfies a log-normal distribution [7]. It is worth noting that the choice of distribution is rather data-driven and may depend on the specific task. In this work, the time of reading jokes fits the log-normal while the viewing of web pages fits better on Weibull distribution [23].

20.2.3 Model inference and application

In earlier sections we assume each user has a single personalized action bound. One issue is a single value may be insufficient. In reality, people could have different action bounds to different items. One factor may be the category. For instance, a movie reviewer may be highly picky (high action bound) for action genre, while rather tolerant (low action bound) for animation. The study of such correlation is out of this chapter's scope. With no extra information, we may assume there is a set of global action bounds shared by all people and each person differs from others by the probability distribution over these bounds. This idea comes from latent topic model, where all documents share the same latent topics and have individual topic-distribution vector.

In summary, each user has personalized distribution vector of action bound π_i, dwell time variance σ_i, reading speed r_i, quality sensitivity γ_i. And all users share a set of K action bounds $\langle b_1, \ldots, b_K \rangle$. Given the data of items quality q_j, length l_j, dwell time t_{ij} and voting behavior v_{ij}, the log-likelihood function can be represented as follows:

$$\mathcal{L}(\Theta) = \sum_{i,j,k} \tau_{ij}^k (\log P(v_{ij}|q_j, b_k) + \log P(t_{ij}|l_j, q_j, b_k, r_i, \gamma_i) + \log \pi_{ik})$$

$$+ \sum_i \lambda_i \left(\sum_k \pi_{ik} - 1 \right) \tag{20.5}$$

where Θ denotes all parameters and τ_{ij}^k is a binary variable denoting whether the ith person used kth action bound when viewing and rating jth item.

$$\tau_{ij}^k = \begin{cases} 1 & \text{if } b_k \text{ is used} \\ 0 & \text{otherwise} \end{cases} \tag{20.6}$$

The probability of voting behavior $P(v_{ij}|q_j, b_k)$ can be computed using (20.2), and the probability of dwell time $P(t_{ij}|l_j, q_j, b_k, r_i, \gamma_i)$ can be referred to (20.4).

The final term is a constraint that the sum of each person's distribution vector should be equal to 1, and the λ_i is a Lagrange multiplier that can be solved during training. With learned parameters, we can now apply the model to interpret silence behavior and facilitate recommendation. Particularly, there are three steps:

Step I
Firstly, given a user's dwell time on a particular item, we estimate the action bound that is most likely used. Formally, given an item's quality q and length l, the estimation of action bound b^* based on ith user's dwell time t is shown as below.

$$b^* = b_{k^*} \text{ where } k^* = \arg\max_k P(t|l, q, b_k, r_i, \gamma_i) \cdot \pi_{ik} \tag{20.7}$$

Step II
Next, the expected rating is then computed, referred to as *pseudo vote*. With an estimated action bound, we can map the user's dwell time to a most likely rate, computed by the expected value of voting, as shown in the following equation:

$$E(v|q, b^*) = 1 \cdot \frac{q}{q + b^*} + 0 \cdot \frac{b^*}{q + b^*} = \frac{q}{q + b^*} \tag{20.8}$$

Step III
Finally, all inferred pseudo votes and real votes are combined together and exploit existing rating-based recommendation techniques to model user preference and make recommendation.

20.3   App recommendation: contest between temptation and satisfaction

As mentioned in Introduction, the app recommendation is different from common recommendation scenario due to potential contest between installed apps and candidates. Ignorance of such factor may result in failure in recommendation. In this section, we give a deep review and analysis about how conventional recommender system may fail and propose solution to address such issue.

20.3.1   Failure of recommendation

App recommendation can be modeled as conventional task where the install/download of an app is treated as a positive rating and the task is to recommend candidate ones the target user may likely install based on the download history. Now we demonstrate scenarios where recommendation fails. Particularly, we focus on three wide-used methods, i.e., user-based collaborative filtering (UCF), item-based collaborative filtering (ICF) and content-based recommendation (CBR).

The key idea of UCF is to find users who have accessed the same items. This set of users is thought to have similar interests. Then when one of them has given a high rating on a new item, it can thus be recommended to other similar users. Consider the scenario in Figure 20.1(a), where user 1 and 2 have installed a large number of

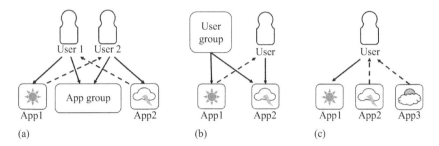

Figure 20.1 Three scenarios of recommendation failure. The solid arrow represents the downloading behavior and the dashed one indicates recommendation: (a) UCF, (b) ICF and (c) CBR

the same apps. Now they, respectively, install app I and app II. Based on the UCF algorithm, app 1 would be recommended to user 2 while app 2 to user 1. Suppose the two apps are of the similar function, e.g., weather forecast, and work pretty well. Then neither of the users would install the recommended apps as there is no motivation to switch.

Similar to UCF, ICF measures similarity of two items based on the set of people who have accessed both. If a user who has not viewed either one gave high rating to one of them, then the other one would be recommended. Consider a scenario where a large number of people who download app 1 also download app 2 in near future. The recommender system would thus recognize app 1 and app 2 are similar items, as shown in Figure 20.1(b). Now a user who does not install either one has downloaded app 2, the system would recommend app 1 based on ICF algorithm. This recommended item may be rejected. The fact that people who have app 1 switch to app 2 suggests the latter one has a better quality. Therefore, if the user has already downloaded the better one, there is no reason to switch to the other app.

Finally, the rationale of CBF is to recommend similar items based on target user's rating history. To differ from ICF, CBF usually measures similarity of two items based on their content, e.g., textual description, tags and categories. Figure 20.1(c) shows an example where the target user receives a list recommended weather forecast apps after downloading one. Again recommendation would fail for the same reason as in first example (Figure 20.1(a)), the user has no motivation to install multiple apps serving the same functionality.

20.3.2 Modeling the contest—actual-tempting model

The above examples demonstrate the potential failure of existing recommender systems. The reason lies in the ignorance of contest between existing apps and the candidate ones. When a user views a candidate app, the final decision of installment depends on his/her estimation that whether this app would bring better user satisfaction compared to similar one(s) he/she is using.

To model such contest, we define two concepts, i.e., *actual value* and *tempting value*. The former one represents a user's rating of an app's quality after installing and using it, while the latter one stands for the user's estimation of the candidate app's quality when viewing it in the list. Given two apps, one of which is installed one and the other is a candidate with similar functionality. The process of decision-making is the contest between the first app's actual value and the second one's tempting value. Formally, let a_i represents ith app's actual value and t_j the jth candidate app's tempting value, the contest result can be modeled by a Bernoulli process where the parameter p_{ij} is generated by a beta process with (a_i, t_j).

$$P(v_{i,j}|a_i, t_j) = \int_0^1 P(v_{ij}|p_{ij})P(p_{ij}|a_i, t_j)dp_{ij} \qquad (20.9)$$

The $v_{ij} \in \{-1, 1\}$ is a binary variable denoting the contest result, where -1 means the user does not download the app$_j$ (candidate loses the contest), while 1 means the install of app$_j$ (candidate wins the contest with existing app$_i$). With no loss of generality, the Bernoulli process of $P(v_{ij}|p_{ij})$ can be written in the following form:

$$P(v_{ij}|p_{ij}) = \begin{cases} p_{ij} & \text{if } v_{ij} = 1 \\ 1 - p_{ij} & \text{otherwise} \end{cases} = v_{ij} \cdot p_{ij} + \frac{1 - v_{ij}}{2} \qquad (20.10)$$

With (20.10), the probability of contest $P(v_{ij}|a_i, t_j)$ can be rewritten as

$$P(v_{ij}|a_i, t_j) = v_{ij} \int_0^1 p_{ij} \mathrm{Be}(p_{ij}; a_i, t_j)dp_{ij} + \frac{1 - v_{ij}}{2} = \frac{t_j}{t_j + a_i} \cdot v_{ij} + \frac{1 - v_{ij}}{2}$$

$$= \begin{cases} \frac{t_j}{a_i + t_j} & \text{if } v_{ij} = 1 \\ \frac{a_i}{a_i + t_j} & \text{otherwise} \end{cases} \qquad (20.11)$$

As shown in the (20.11), the probability of download $v_{ij} = 1$ is associated with the proportional tempting value over actual value. The larger the tempting value is, the higher the probability would be. This equation is the core model for contest. We name it as *actual-tempting model*.

Now we extend the two-app contest to a general case. Suppose the user is viewing a candidate app$_j$ and she has already installed n apps of similar functions. Formally, let $w_{ij} \in [0, 1]$ denote the function similarity between the ith installed app and the target one. That means, $w_{ij} = 0$ suggests the two apps are totally different while $w_{ij} = 1$ indicates the two apps are exactly the same. The similarity thus represents the probability that the installed app would be used to compare with the candidate when the user is making decision. Let $S_{u,j}$ denote the set of installed apps by user u when she is viewing the app$_j$, we can compute the contest probability as

$$P(v_{ij}|A_{u,j}, t_j) = \prod_{i \in S_{u,j}} \left(P(v_{ij}|a_i, t_j)\right)^\tau_{u,i,j} \qquad (20.12)$$

where the $\tau_{u,i,j} \in \{0, 1\}$ is binary variable indicating whether the user selects app$_i$ for comparison when viewing app$_j$. Specifically we constrain that the probability is proportional to the function similarity, i.e., $P(\tau_{u,i,j}) \propto w_{ij}$.

Given the observed user-app interaction (view/download) data **D**, the log-likelihood can be computed as

$$\log P(\mathbf{D}|\mathbf{A}, \mathbf{T}) = \sum_{u,j} \mathbf{I}_{u,j} \sum_{i \in S_{u,j}} \tau_{u,i,j} \log P(v_{i,j}|a_i, t_j) \tag{20.13}$$

where the $\mathbf{I}_{u,j}$ is an indicator variable showing whether the user u has interacted with app$_j$ in the data.

One can see that the log-likelihood objective function cannot be directly solved due to the unknown variable $\tau_{u,i,j}$. To address this issue, we can obtain parameters by maximizing the expected log-likelihood, as shown in the following equation:

$$\mathbf{E}\left(\log P(\mathbf{D}|\mathbf{A}, \mathbf{T})\right) = \sum_{u,j} \mathbf{I}_{u,j} \sum_{i \in S_{u,j}} \mathbf{E}(\tau_{u,i,j}) \log P(v_{ij}|a_i, t_j)$$

$$\propto \sum_{u,j} \mathbf{I}_{u,j} \sum_{i \in S_{u,j}} w_{i,j} \log P(v_{ij}|a_i, t_j) \tag{20.14}$$

So far we have assumed there exists a similarity w_{ij} for each pair of apps since our focus is to model the contest. In practice, there are multiple ways to implement such function. For example, a straightforward way is to use CBR to compute the content similarity based on textual description, tag, category, etc. A more advanced method would use latent topic models, e.g., PLSA [24], LDA [25], to compute the similarity on latent space.

20.3.3 Insights of the model

Although aiming at recommending apps, the trained actual-tempting model defined in (20.11) can provide insights of apps' characteristics such as quality, download volume and category. This "side-product" indirectly demonstrate the effectiveness of the model. By design, the actual value represents the satisfaction of the app brought to users after it is downloaded and used. On the other hand, the tempting value is the user's expectation of the satisfaction that the app will bring. In other words, actual value reflects the user's rating of the app while the tempting value suggests the capability of attracting people. The analysis conducted by [12] demonstrates that there is a linear correlation between actual value and the app's average rating on app store. Also, it shows that larger tempting value also has higher probability of app install.

Another interesting observation comes from the average difference between actual value and tempting value for each app category. Table 20.1 lists app categories

Table 20.1 Example categories of actual-tempting value difference

Actual > Tempting	Actual < Tempting	Actual ≈ Tempting
Photo and video	Reference	Medical
Music	Travel	Education
Social network	–	Books

whose actual value is (i) larger than, (ii) close to, or (iii) smaller than their tempting value. For the first category, the actual value is usually larger than tempting value. This suggests existing apps would block future install of similar apps. Representative examples are photo and video, music and social network. The first one is usually tools to beautify photos or produce short videos, and the second one is usually online music players. Users are unlikely to switch other tools of similar functions if the current one works well. Also, the social network leads to "user engagement." That means once user is active in one type of social network, she is unwilling to switch to a different one with no social friends.

For categories whose actual value are close to tempting value, people usually can accurately estimate its function and clearly know what it provides match their expectations. The examples are reference and education. Apps falling in these categories generally provide guidance or instructions.

Finally, if actual value is smaller than tempting value, people would continuously download similar apps. Examples are education and books, whose apps are usually one or multiple e-books or e-training classes. Once people complete one, they are very likely to continue reading/learning similar ones. This category matches the conventional recommended items and existing recommendation techniques (UCF, ICF, CBR) are supposed to work well.

20.4 POI recommendation: geographical, social and temporal

The goal of POI recommendation in LBSN is to recommend a proper location to check-in at proper time. Besides user interest as common recommender system, there are three additional factors to be considered. First, different from online recommendation where the cost of item access is negligible, POI recommendation needs to consider the cost of physical check-in, i.e., the time and energy of travel from current point to a target one. This factor can be simplified as distance. In [13], the factor is named as *Geographical influence*. Second, the platform of this recommender system is a social network, where people have online social friends. Therefore, people's behavior may be affected by their friends. In context of LBSN, one example is to find a good place for hanging out. This factor is named as *social influence*. Finally, time is an important factor as people's daily life shows a regular pattern. Integrating this factor, *temporal influence*, would definitely improve the acceptance rate of recommendation.

20.4.1 Geographical influence

In general, most of, if not all, humans reside in a limited area for daily activity. Here such limited area could be as small as a town or as big as a city. In data analysis, this phenomenon demonstrates two mobility tendencies: (i) people tend to visit nearby locations compared to distant ones, (ii) if one location is visited by a person, its nearby locations would also be visited by the same person in the near future. In [13], analysis on two LBSN data sets revealed that the check-in behavior satisfies a power-law distribution.

Formally, let y denote the check-in probability and x represent the distance between the target user's current location and a candidate one, the power-law distribution correlates the two variables in the following form:

$$y = a \times x^b \tag{20.15}$$

where a and b are distribution parameters.

We can transform the (20.15) to a linear form by applying logarithmic to both sides:

$$\log y = w_0 + w_1 \log x \tag{20.16}$$

where $w_0 = \log a$ and $w_1 = \log b$.

Equation (20.16) is known as log–log form. In data analysis, the plot forms a straight line if two variables satisfying a power-law distribution are drawn in log–log format. Generally, the dependent variable (i.e., probability y) decreases exponentially as the independent variable (i.e., the distance x) grows.

Given a data set of historical check-in records, we can sample a pair of POIs that are checked-in by the same user and then compute its distance. Among all sampled pairs, the empirical probability can be approximated by the proportion of location pairs whose distance falls in the corresponding distance bin. To learn the power-law distribution parameters, we can minimize the following objective function:

$$\mathcal{L}(w_0, w_1) = \frac{1}{2} \sum_{n=1}^{N} \left(w_0 + w_1 \cdot x_n - t_n \right)^2 + \frac{\lambda}{2} w_1^2 \tag{20.17}$$

where N is the sample size, x_n represents the logarithmic distance of sampled location pairs and t_n is the corresponding empirical check-in probability. Finally, the λ is the regularization term penalizing large parameter values.

With learned parameters, we can apply naive Bayesian framework to recommend POI purely based on geographical influence. For ith target user and her visited locations $\mathbf{L}_i$, we can compute the probability that the user has visited these locations via the product of power-law probability considering all POIs' pair-wise distance.

$$P(\mathbf{L}_i) = \prod_{l_m, l_n \in \mathbf{L}_i \wedge l_m \neq l_n} P(\mathrm{d}(l_m, l_n)) = \prod_{l_m, l_n \in \mathbf{L}_i \wedge l_m \neq l_n} (w_0 + w_1 \cdot \log \mathrm{d}(l_m, l_n)) \tag{20.18}$$

where the function $\mathrm{d}(l_m, l_n)$ calculates the distance between two POIs.

For a particular POI candidate l_j, its ranking score with regarding to the target user's visited locations $\mathbf{L}_i$ can be measured by the likelihood of this user checking-in the location, computed as follows:

$$P(l_i | \mathbf{L}_i) = \frac{P(l_i \cup \mathbf{L}_i)}{P(\mathbf{L}_i)} = \frac{P(\mathbf{L}_i) \prod_{l_m \in \mathbf{L}_i} P(\mathrm{d}(l_j, l_m))}{P(\mathbf{L}_i)} = \prod_{l_m \in \mathbf{L}_i} P(\mathrm{d}(l_j, l_m)) \tag{20.19}$$

Recommendation can be obtained by computing the ranking score as (20.19) for each candidate and returning those with top-k highest scores.

20.4.2 *Social influence*

The popularity of online social network facilitates the social recommendation. The rationale behind is that online social friends share similar interests [5,26,27], and thus items accessed by one's online friend can be recommended to the target user. In [28], on the other hand, it is found that online social friends do not share many offline POIs in LBSN compared to online platform. However, social influence is also an important factor in POI recommendation due to two reasons. First, there is a small portion of online friends who also hang out together offline. Second, social influence needs to be considered when recommending a location for group meeting.

To model social influence, one issue is to find the small portion of friends who actually share offline POIs with the target user. Formally, let $\mathbf{f}_i \in R^m$ denote the check-in vector of user u_i, where m is the total number of locations and the value of each element of $\mathbf{f}_i$ is equal to the number of check-in times in the corresponding locations. Given two users' location check-in vector, cosine similarity function can be applied to measure their offline similarity.

$$\text{sim}(u_i, u_j) = \frac{\mathbf{f}_i \cdot \mathbf{f}_j}{|\mathbf{f}_i|_2 \times |\mathbf{f}_j|_2} \tag{20.20}$$

where $|\cdot|$ denotes the two norms of a vector.

For a target user u_i, the social influence of a candidate location l can be modeled as the weighted sum of the probability that her social friend would check-in this location.

$$P_s(l|u_i) = \sum_{u_j \in N_i} \text{sim}(u_i, u_j) P(l|\mathbf{L}_j) \tag{20.21}$$

where the N_i is a set of user u_i's social friends and $\mathbf{L}_j$ is the set of visited POIs by user u_j. The $P(l|\mathbf{L}_j)$ can use any form of recommendation model (e.g., ICF, CBR) or the geographical influence as defined in (20.19). Particularly in [15], Pitman-Yor process [29,30] is used to model the continuously check-in behavior.

Noting that the similarity function can measure check-in behaviors of any user pairs, one may argue to extend the (20.21) from target user's social friends N_i to all other users in the data set. Theoretically this is a valid and most accurate solution. However, it faces the issue of low efficiency given the large number of user base. Furthermore, statistical test has shown that on average, users with social link has a significantly higher common check-ins than two random strangers [15]. Narrowing down to one's social friends is thus a practical solution.

The above method introduces a heuristic way of modeling social influence. Alternatively, we may model it as a parameter that can be learned from the data. Particularly, the social influence does not mean online friends share common interest. It means a user adopts a suggestion from friends, which may or may not reflect her own interest [14]. This interpretation is meaningful in context of LBSN since people may visit a place in purpose of meeting their friends rather than enjoying the place themselves.

Figure 20.2 shows the general process of how social influence impacts decision-making when a target user goes to visit some offline POI. Essentially, the POI visiting

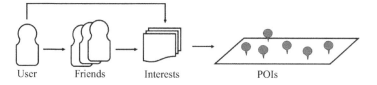

Figure 20.2   Social influence on POI check-in

is determined by user interests, which may come from either the user herself or one of her online friends. In one case, the user herself would determine which location to visit based on her own interest. In another case, one of her friends may be selected and thus that friend's interest would be activated to choose locations. In this case, the location check-in behavior may be quite different from the user's. Therefore, modeling of social influence is transformed to find the mathematical probability that the user may select a particular friend when visiting some location.

Formally, let u and i, respectively, denote a user and POI; the probability of user u visiting POI i can be represented as follows:

$$P(i|u) = \frac{P(u,i)}{P(u)} \propto P(u,i) = \sum_{f \in N_u \cup \{u\}} \sum_z P(u,f,z,i)$$

$$\propto \sum_{f \in N_u \cup \{u\}} \sum_z P(f|u)P(z|f)P(i|z) \tag{20.22}$$

where N_u is the set of user u's social friends and f is the person selected to determine check-in behavior. As can be seen, it is either one of friends or the target user u. The variable z is a latent interest that has preference distribution over all locations.

There are three terms consisting the model in (20.22). The $P(f|u)$ is the social influence of friend f over target user u. Note that we play a trick viewing the user herself as one of her "pseudo" friend. The semantic of self-social influence demonstrates how independent the user is when conducting offline activities. The second term $P(z|f)$ measures a person's distribution over latent interests, which can be viewed as the learning of user preferences. Finally, the $P(i|z)$ is the process of location clustering, where similar locations would be "clustered" together. It is worth noting that here the "cluster" means similar locations would have close appearance probability on the same latent interest z.

Given a data set of user check-in records D, the learning is to maximize the log-likelihood of the data.

$$\mathcal{L}(\theta) = \sum_{(u,i) \in D} \log P(u,i|\theta)$$

$$= \sum_{(u,i) \in D} \sum_{f \in N_u \cup \{u\}} \sum_z \left(\log P(f|u) + \log P(z|f) + \log P(i|z) \right) \tag{20.23}$$

where θ is a summary of all model parameters.

20.4.3 *Temporal influence*

There are many regular patterns in people's daily life. It improves the success rate of recommendation when such temporal pattern is integrated. In this subsection, we introduce the method that extends the most widely used matrix factorization (MF) to time-sensitive one. This method was originally developed in [21].

MF [31] is a very popular recommendation framework and has been demonstrated to be highly effective in the Netflix Competition. Formally, let R denote the rating matrix where each row represents a user, each column stands for an item and the element value is the rating given by the user to the corresponding item. In POI recommendation, the item is location and the element value is the number of check-ins. The MF model assumes there exists k latent factors and each user and item can be represented as a k-dimension feature vector. The rating is modeled as the multiplication of these two vectors. Formally, let r_{ij} denote the frequency that user u_i visits location l_j. The learning of these latent feature vectors is to minimize the following loss function:

$$\mathcal{L}(U,L) = \sum_{i,j} y_{i,j}(u_i \cdot l_j - r_{ij})^2 + \alpha \sum_i ||u_i||_F^2 + \beta \sum_j ||l_j||_F^2 \qquad (20.24)$$

where $y_{ij} \in \{0, 1\}$ is an indicator variable denoting whether user u_i has visited location l_j in the data set. The U, L are set of all users and locations and α, β are nonnegative regularizer weight to avoid over-fit. Finally, the $|| \cdot ||_F^2$ denotes the Frobenius norm of a vector.

In [21], temporal influence are summarized into two patterns, i.e., *nonuniformness* and *consecutiveness*. The first one suggests a user has different check-in behaviors at different time, while the second one indicates such difference is proportional to the time interval. In the following, we extend the basic MF framework to integrate these two patterns.

The nonuniformness indicates a user should have time-sensitive latent feature vectors. To model this property, we assume there exists discrete time frames $\{1, 2, \ldots, T\}$. Here, the unit of time is quite flexible and largely depends on the application. For example, if the goal is to model daily temporal pattern, the time frame can represent the hour. Moreover, if the temporal pattern is weekday/weekend, the time frame can represent a single day. Under such discrete time frames, each user now has T feature vectors, represented as $u_{i,t}$, where $t \in \{1, 2, \ldots, T\}$. The objective function can thus be rewritten as follows:

$$\mathcal{L}_T(U,L) = \sum_{i,j,t} y_{i,j,t}(u_{i,t} \cdot l_j - r_{ij,t})^2 + \alpha \sum_{i,t} ||u_{i,t}||_F^2 + \beta \sum_j ||l_j||_F^2 \qquad (20.25)$$

where $y_{i,j,t}$ indicates whether user u_i has visited POI l_j at time t, and $r_{ij,t}$ represents the number of visits at time t. Note that the location feature vector l_j is still time-insensitive as the temporal pattern is only associated with human behaviors.

The consecutiveness suggests the user's preference do not change much when the time interval is small. This is reasonable due to small variations of people's daily life. For example, a person may check-in a restaurant for dinner in the evening from

6:00 PM to 7:00 PM. The particular check-in time point is quite random during some range since humans are not as accurate as machines. There are always unknown random factors impacting the check-in time. On the other hand, it is rare that the user would have dinner before 5:00 PM or after 9:00 PM. As a result, the user feature vector at 6:00 PM would be close to 7:00 PM.

Furthermore, different people have different concepts of time. Some people are really strict and tightly stick to schedule while others may be quite flexible, and thus the time span of similar check-in behaviors is relatively longer. In modeling, this scenario is transformed to such a mathematic problem that how much weight we need to add to constrain the similarity of two user feature vectors at consecutive time. To address this issue, we define a temporal coefficient $\varphi_i(t, t-1)$ to measure user u_i's deviations on schedule.

$$\varphi_i(t, t-1) = \frac{r_{i,:,t} \cdot r_{i,:,t-1}}{\sqrt{||r_{i,:,t}||_F^2 \times ||r_{i,:,t-1}||_F^2}} \tag{20.26}$$

As shown in (20.26), the metric is the cosine similarity of check-in vectors at two consecutive time. Here, the $r_{i,:,t}$ denotes the row of user u_i's check-in data at time t. One can see that if a person has similar check-in behaviors between consecutive time frames, the coefficient would be close to 1. Otherwise, the value would be close to 0. Note that since the element value are all nonnegative, this metric is thus always no smaller than 0. Also, when $t = 1$, we treat the "0" time frame as the same as T. This is because the circulating timing mechanism. For instance, if the time frame is hour, $t = T = 24$ means the beginning of the next day and thus is the neighbor of $t = 1$. If the time frame is day, $t = T = 7$ means Sunday, and thus the next neighboring day is Monday ($t = 1$).

With defined temporal coefficient, we add it as a penalty to difference between user feature vectors at consecutive time frame, as shown below.

$$\mathcal{L}_t^\varphi = \sum_{i,j,t} y_{i,j,t}(u_{i,t} \cdot l_j - r_{ij,t})^2 + \alpha \sum_{i,t} ||u_{i,t}||_F^2 + \beta \sum_j ||l_j||_F^2$$
$$+ \lambda \sum_{i,t} \varphi_i(t, t-1)||u_{i,:,t} - u_{i,:,t-1}||_F^2 \tag{20.27}$$

where λ is another nonnegative balance weight controlling global degree of constraint for consecutiveness

In this section, we focus on modeling single influence while do not discuss methods of merging them. The combination of different factors into an integrated recommendation framework is quite complex and may depend on data. With no domain knowledge, the linear fusion is usually the first choice due to its simplicity, generality and robustness.

Besides single POI recommendation, one continuous research extends to recommend a series of POIs, which becomes a new topic known as *travel routes, or itinerary* recommendation. Emphasizing more on tourism, travel route recommendation involves different impacting factors. First, the geographical influence considers not only the distance between the user and the POI, but also distances between consequential venues. In [32], Rakesh *et al.* proposed SSTREC model to infer user's

POI vising behavior pattern and the route was generated by sequentially picking next POI that can be visited within a given time window. Second, instead of individual temporal pattern, itinerary recommendation considers the global temporal pattern, i.e., *travel season* [33] for target tour regions. Finally, besides geographical, social and temporal influence, the quality of scene-viewing becomes an important factor. Kurashima *et al.* [34] addressed this issue by making use of high-quality geo-tagged pictures in photo-sharing websites. Specifically, they clustered pictures with mean-shift procedure [35] to identify landmarks of good scene-view. Most recently, Wang *et al.* [36] exploited convolutionary neural net, or exactly, the VGG16 model [37] to directly extract features from pictures shared in LBSN and used them as input of proposed probabilistic model. They demonstrated that the integration of visual contents enhanced the POI recommendation performance.

20.5　Conclusion

In this chapter, we discussed new opportunities and challenges brought by smart phones to recommender system. Specifically, we covered three recommendation scenarios, i.e., common recommendation, app recommendation and POI recommendation. For first one, the convenience of dwell time recording in native smart phone provides opportunity to alleviate the rating sparsity problem. We then introduce methods to model and interpret the dwell time to pseudo user rating. For app recommendation, we illustrate examples where conventional UCF, ICF and CBR techniques may fail due to the existence of contest between installed apps and candidates. Moreover we introduce probabilistic model that can learn such contest from the temporal sequence of user-app interactions. Finally, we introduce the model of geographical, social and temporal influence in POI recommendation on LBSN.

Thanks to the increasing power and diversified apps, smartphones are able to provide more and more context information. For instance, the continuous sampling of GPS data results in a user mobility trajectory, which the user can choose to share with others in trajectory social network. This new format of data brings new challenges in recommendation, i.e., how to extract meaningful features for recommendation or other purpose. Readers can refer to some preliminary trials [38–40]. Another context data comes from the built-in sensors of smartphones, producing novel context-aware recommendation [41–43]. In the future, more functionalities will emerge in smartphones, as new recommendation scenarios and challenges.

References

[1]　Ahn HJ. A new similarity measure for collaborative filtering to alleviate the new user cold-starting problem. Information Sciences. 2008;178(1):37–51.

[2]　Bobadilla J, Ortega F, Hernando A, *et al.* A collaborative filtering approach to mitigate the new user cold start problem. Knowledge-Based Systems. 2012;26:225–238.

[3] Melville P, Mooney RJ, Nagarajan R. Content-boosted collaborative filtering for improved recommendations. In: Aaai/iaai. vol. 23; 2002. p. 187–192.

[4] Schein AI, Popescul A, Ungar LH, *et al.* Methods and metrics for cold-start recommendations. In: Proceedings of the 25th annual international ACM SIGIR conference on research and development in information retrieval. ACM; 2002. p. 253–260.

[5] Ma H, Yang H, Lyu MR, *et al.* SoRec: social recommendation using probabilistic matrix factorization. In: Proceedings of the 17th ACM conference on Information and knowledge management. ACM; 2008. p. 931–940.

[6] Ma H, King I, Lyu MR. Learning to recommend with social trust ensemble. In: Proceedings of the 32nd international ACM SIGIR conference on research and development in information retrieval. ACM; 2009. p. 203–210.

[7] Yin P, Luo P, Lee WC, *et al.* Silence is also evidence: interpreting dwell time for recommendation from psychological perspective. In: Proceedings of the 19th ACM SIGKDD international conference on knowledge discovery and data mining. ACM; 2013. p. 989–997.

[8] Xu Q, Erman J, Gerber A, *et al.* Identifying diverse usage behaviors of smartphone apps. In: Proceedings of the 2011 ACM SIGCOMM conference on Internet measurement conference. ACM; 2011. p. 329–344.

[9] Yan B, Chen G. AppJoy: personalized mobile application discovery. In: Proceedings of the 9th international conference on mobile systems, applications, and services. ACM; 2011. p. 113–126.

[10] Costa-Montenegro E, Barragáns-Martínez AB, Rey-López M. Which App? A recommender system of applications in markets: implementation of the service for monitoring users' interaction. Expert Systems with Applications. 2012;39(10):9367–9375.

[11] Davidsson C, Moritz S. Utilizing implicit feedback and context to recommend mobile applications from first use. In: Proceedings of the 2011 workshop on context-awareness in retrieval and recommendation. ACM; 2011. p. 19–22.

[12] Yin P, Luo P, Lee WC, *et al.* App recommendation: a contest between satisfaction and temptation. In: Proceedings of the sixth ACM international conference on web search and data mining. ACM; 2013. p. 395–404.

[13] Ye M, Yin P, Lee WC, *et al.* Exploiting geographical influence for collaborative point-of-interest recommendation. In: Proceedings of the 34th international ACM SIGIR conference on research and development in information retrieval. ACM; 2011. p. 325–334.

[14] Ye M, Liu X, Lee WC. Exploring social influence for recommendation: a generative model approach. In: Proceedings of the 35th international ACM SIGIR conference on research and development in information retrieval. ACM; 2012. p. 671–680.

[15] Gao H, Tang J, Liu H. Exploring social-historical ties on location-based social networks. In: ICWSM; 2012.

[16] Ye M, Janowicz K, Mülligann C, *et al.* What you are is when you are: the temporal dimension of feature types in location-based social networks.

In: Proceedings of the 19th ACM SIGSPATIAL international conference on advances in geographic information systems. ACM; 2011. p. 102–111.

[17]   Cheng Z, Caverlee J, Lee K, *et al.* Exploring millions of footprints in location sharing services. In: ICWSM. vol. 2011;2011. p. 81–88.

[18]   Ye M, Shou D, Lee WC, *et al.* On the semantic annotation of places in location-based social networks. In: Proceedings of the 17th ACM SIGKDD international conference on knowledge discovery and data mining. ACM; 2011. p. 520–528.

[19]   Malmi E, Do TMT, Gatica-Perez D. Checking in or checked in: comparing large-scale manual and automatic location disclosure patterns. In: Proceedings of the 11th international conference on mobile and ubiquitous multimedia. ACM; 2012. p. 26.

[20]   Gao H, Tang J, Liu H. Mobile location prediction in spatio-temporal context. In: Nokia mobile data challenge workshop. vol. 41; 2012. p. 1–4.

[21]   Gao H, Tang J, Hu X, *et al.* Exploring temporal effects for location recommendation on location-based social networks. In: Proceedings of the 7th ACM conference on recommender systems. ACM; 2013. p. 93–100.

[22]   Ratcliff R, McKoon G. The diffusion decision model: theory and data for two-choice decision tasks. Neural Computation. 2008;20(4):873–922.

[23]   Liu C, White RW, Dumais S. Understanding web browsing behaviors through Weibull analysis of dwell time. In: Proceedings of the 33rd international ACM SIGIR conference on research and development in information retrieval. ACM; 2010. p. 379–386.

[24]   Hofmann T. Probabilistic latent semantic analysis. In: Proceedings of the fifteenth conference on uncertainty in artificial intelligence. Morgan Kaufmann Publishers Inc.; 1999. p. 289–296.

[25]   Blei DM, Ng AY, Jordan MI. Latent Dirichlet allocation. Journal of machine Learning Research. 2003;3:993–1022.

[26]   Singla P, Richardson M. Yes, there is a correlation:-from social networks to personal behavior on the web. In: Proceedings of the 17th international conference on World Wide Web. ACM; 2008. p. 655–664.

[27]   La Fond T, Neville J. Randomization tests for distinguishing social influence and homophily effects. In: Proceedings of the 19th international conference on World Wide Web. ACM; 2010. p. 601–610.

[28]   Ye M, Yin P, Lee WC. Location recommendation for location-based social networks. In: Proceedings of the 18th SIGSPATIAL international conference on advances in geographic information systems. ACM; 2010. p. 458–461.

[29]   Pitman J, Yor M. The two-parameter Poisson-Dirichlet distribution derived from a stable subordinator. The Annals of Probability. 1997;433:855–900.

[30]   Pitman J. Combinatorial Stochastic Processes: Ecole d'Eté de Probabilités de Saint-Flour XXXII-2002. Berlin, Heidelberg: Springer; 2006.

[31]   Koren Y, Bell R, Volinsky C. Matrix factorization techniques for recommender systems. Computer. 2009;42(8):42–49.

[32]   Rakesh V, Jadhav N, Kotov A, *et al.* Probabilistic social sequential model for tour recommendation. In: Proceedings of the tenth ACM international conference on web search and data mining. ACM; 2017. p. 631–640.

[33]   Liu Q, Ge Y, Li Z, *et al.* Personalized travel package recommendation. In: Data mining (ICDM), 2011 IEEE 11th international conference on. IEEE; 2011. p. 407–416.

[34]   Kurashima T, Iwata T, Irie G, *et al.* Travel route recommendation using geotags in photo sharing sites. In: Proceedings of the 19th ACM international conference on information and knowledge management. ACM; 2010. p. 579–588.

[35]   Crandall DJ, Backstrom L, Huttenlocher D, *et al.* Mapping the world's photos. In: Proceedings of the 18th international conference on World Wide Web. ACM; 2009. p. 761–770.

[36]   Wang S, Wang Y, Tang J, *et al.* What your images reveal: exploiting visual contents for point-of-interest recommendation. In: Proceedings of the 26th international conference on World Wide Web. International World Wide Web Conferences Steering Committee; 2017. p. 391–400.

[37]   Simonyan K, Zisserman A. Very deep convolutional networks for large-scale image recognition. https://www.oreilly.com/library/view/deep-learning-with/ 9781787128422/df5b07fb-3906-43ce-aefd-c9814ebfc135.xhtml. (Accessed on 5-March-2019).

[38]   Yin P, Ye M, Lee WC, *et al.* Mining GPS data for trajectory recommendation. In: Pacific-Asia conference on knowledge discovery and data mining. Springer; 2014. p. 50–61.

[39]   Tang L, Yang X, Kan Z, *et al.* Lane-level road information mining from vehicle GPS trajectories based on Naïve Bayesian Classification. ISPRS International Journal of Geo-Information. 2015;4(4):2660–2680.

[40]   Huang TH, Nikulin V, Chen LB. Detection of abnormalities in driving style based on moving object trajectories without labels. In: Advanced applied informatics (IIAI-AAI), 2016 5th IIAI international congress on. IEEE; 2016. p. 675–680.

[41]   Otebolaku AM, Andrade MT. Recognizing high-level contexts from smartphone built-in sensors for mobile media content recommendation. In: Mobile data management (MDM), 2013 IEEE 14th international conference on. vol. 2. IEEE; 2013. p. 142–147.

[42]   He Y, Li Y. Physical activity recognition utilizing the built-in kinematic sensors of a smartphone. International Journal of Distributed Sensor Networks. 2013;9(4):481580.

[43]   Chen CC, Huang TC, Park JJ, *et al.* Real-time smartphone sensing and recommendations towards context-awareness shopping. Multimedia Systems. 2015;21(1):61–72.

Chapter 21

Graph-based recommendations: from data representation to feature extraction and application

Amit Tiroshi[1], Tsvi Kuflik[2], Shlomo Berkovsky[3], and Mohamed Ali (Dali) Kaafar[4]

Modeling users for the purpose of identifying their preferences and then personalizing services on the basis of these models is a complex task, primarily due to the need to take into consideration various explicit and implicit signals, missing or uncertain information, contextual aspects, and more. In this study, a novel generic approach for uncovering latent preference patterns from user data is proposed and evaluated. The approach relies on representing the data using graphs, and then systematically extracting graph-based features and using them to enrich the original user models. The extracted features encapsulate complex relationships between users, items, and metadata. The enhanced user models can then serve as an input to any recommendation algorithm. The proposed approach is domain-independent (demonstrated on data from movies, music, and business systems) and is evaluated using several state-of-the-art machine-learning methods, on different recommendation tasks, and using different evaluation metrics. Overall, the results show an unanimous improvement in the recommendation accuracy across tasks and domains.

21.1 Introduction

Recommender systems aim at helping users find relevant items among a large variety of possibilities, based on their preferences [1]. In many cases, these personal preferences are inferred from patterns that emerge from data about the users' past interactions with the system and with other users, as well as additional personal characteristics available from different sources. These patterns are typically user-specific and are based on the metadata of both the users and items, as well as on the interpretation of the observed user interactions [2,3]. Eliciting user preferences

[1]Atlassian Inc., Australia
[2]Department of Information Systems, University of Haifa, Israel
[3]Australian Institute of Health Innovation, Macquarie University, Australia
[4]Department of Computing, Macquarie University, Australia

is a challenging task because of issues such as changes in user preferences, contextual dependencies, privacy constraints, and practical data collection difficulties [4,5]. Moreover, the collected data may be incomplete, outdated, imprecise, or even completely inapplicable to the recommendation task at hand. In order to address these issues, modern recommender systems attempt to capture as much data as possible and elicit from this data the desired preferences.

Regardless of the technique exploited by a recommender system, it is inherently bound by the available user data and the features extracted/elicited from it. One major question that arises in this context is *how to engineer*[1] *meaningful features from often noisy user data?* Features may be manually engineered by domain experts. This approach is considered expensive and non-scalable because of the deep domain knowledge that is necessary, the creativity required to conceive new features, and the time needed to populate and evaluate the contribution of the features. A notable example of this challenge is provided by the Netflix Prize winning team, in their recap: "while major breakthroughs in the competition were achieved by uncovering new features underlying the data, those became rare and very hard to get" [6].

An alternative to manual feature engineering is automatic feature engineering, which is a major area of research in machine learning [7–9]. So far, automatic feature engineering has mainly focused on either algebraic combinations of existing features, e.g., summation or averaging of existing features [10] or elicitation of latent features [11,12]. The algebraic approaches for automatic feature engineering manage to produce large quantities of features; however, the relationships between the engineered features and the underlying patterns in the data are often not interpretable [13]. Similarly, the latent feature techniques do not provide sufficient insight regarding the meaning of the features [14].

In this work, a novel framework is proposed that uses graph-based representation properties to generate additional features from recommender systems data. The proposed framework is underpinned by the idea of examining the data from the graph theory-based perspective, which represents entities and their relationships as a graph and allows the extraction of a suite of new features computed using established graph-based techniques. The extracted features encapsulate information about the relationships between entities in the graph and lead to new patterns uncovered in the data. In most cases, they are also interpretable, for example, a node's degree represents the importance of the node in the graph, while the path length between two nodes communicates their relatedness.

The proposed framework offers several benefits for automatic feature extraction. Given a new dataset, it is usually impossible to determine a-priori which graph representations will yield the most informative set of features for the recommendation generation. Thus, the proposed framework provides a systematic method for generating and assessing various graph representations, their contribution to the newly extracted features, and, in turn, to the accuracy of the generated recommendations. Additionally, since the number of nodes and relationship types in each graph representation is different, an exhaustive method of distilling the possible graph metrics from each representation is proposed.

---

[1]Feature engineering is also referred to in the literature as feature extraction, generation, and discovery.

Two large-scale case studies are conducted to gather extensive empirical evidence and demonstrate how graph features supplement existing feature sets, improve the accuracy of the recommendations, and perform adequately as stand-alone out-of-the-box features. The case studies answer the following questions:

- How does the use of graph features affect the performance of rating predictions and recommendation generation in different domains and tasks?
- How are the recommendations affected by the subgraphs and their representations used to generate the graph features?

Multiple datasets, machine-learning mechanisms, and evaluation metrics are used across the case studies, in order to demonstrate the effectiveness of the approach. Overall, the results show that graph-based representation and feature extraction allow for the generation of more accurate recommendations. A comparison across various graph schemes is conducted, and the justification for systematic feature extraction is established. Hence, this work concludes the line of research presented in [15–17] and provides a complete picture that validates the applicability of the graph-based feature generation approach to recommender systems.

The rest of the chapter is structured as follows. Next, the necessary background is provided, and the related work is described. Then, the graph representation and graph-based feature extraction process is formalized, and its advantages and disadvantages are discussed. Two case studies demonstrating the contribution of the graph-based features to the recommendation process are then presented. Through these, the overall performance of the framework, as well as the performance of certain graph representations and feature subsets, is evaluated. Finally, the implications of the findings are discussed, together with the suggested future work.

21.2   Background and related work

Graphs have been exploited in recommender system for many tasks, mainly due to their ability to represent many entities of different types and their relationships in a simple data structure that offers a broad variety of metrics and reasoning techniques. In this section, we provide a general background on the use of graphs in recommender systems, followed by specific aspects of graph representation in recommender systems and feature engineering.

21.2.1   Graph-based recommender systems

Since social networks were identified as a major source for freely available personal information, graphs and networks data structures have been used as tools for user modeling, especially since they combine different entities and links into one simple structure capturing the links between the entities. This section aims at giving the readers an idea about how graph techniques are used in graph-based user modeling and recommender systems. Given the vast amount of prior work, this is only a brief presentation of recent studies and not an in-depth survey.

What was clearly noticeable was that most of the graph-based representations were defined for a specific problem, in specific domains, and in many cases they applied variants of random walk as the only graph feature used for recommendations. Pham *et al.* [18] suggested to use a simple graph representation for recommending groups to users, tags to groups, and events to users, using a general graph-based model called HeteRS, while considering the recommendation problem as a query-dependent node proximity problem. Wu *et al.* [19] suggested the use of a heterogeneous graph for representing contextual aspects in addition to items and users, and used random walk for context-aware recommendation. Lee *et al.* [20] used an enhanced version of personalized PageRank algorithm to recommend items to target users and proposed to reduce the size of the graph by clustering nodes and edges. Shams and Haratizadeh [21] also applied personalized PageRank over the user/item graph augmented with pairwise ranking for items recommendation.

In addition to the wide use of random-walk-based algorithms, there is a variety of task-specific representations and metrics. It is interesting to note that even for a specific task, a variety of approaches was suggested. For instance, Ostuni *et al.* [22] suggested to use tags and sound description represented as a knowledge graph, from which similarity of nodes was extracted using a specific metric they defined. In contrast, Mao *et al.* [23] suggested using graph representation for music tracks recommendations, where they represented by graphs the relative preferences of users, e.g., pair-wise preference of tracks. They used the graph as a representation for user preferences for tracks and calculated the probability of a user liking a track based on the probability that s/he likes the in-linked tracks.

Some works suggested to use graph representations as an alternative to the classical collaborative and hybrid recommenders. Moradi *et al.* [24] used clustering of graph representation of users and items for generating a model for item- and user-based collaborative filtering. Bae *et al.* [25] used graphs for representing co-occurrence of mobile apps, as logged from users mobile devices, and the similarity of user graphs was used for finding a neighborhood and generation recommendations. Cordobés *et al.* [26] also addressed the app-recommendation problem and explored the potential of graph representation for several variants of recommendation strategies for recommending apps. Park *et al.* [27] proposed a graph representation for linking items based on their similarity, where users were linked to items they rated, such that items most similar to the items rated by the users could be recommended. Lee and Lee [28] suggested an approach for graph-based representation of the user–item matrix, where links among items represent positive ratings, and use entropy to find the items to recommend to users, thus introducing serendipity into the recommendation process.

A highly relevant line of work focuses on enriching recommender systems dataset with information extracted from graph representation of the data [29]. The authors suggested to enrich a dataset of research papers with what the so-called metapath data links extracted from citations network. They added this information to the existing set of features, then applied classical matrix factorization, and showed an improvement to the results using only the original data. Our framework can be considered as a generalized variant of [29], where a specific set of metrics was extracted from the graph representation of the data and matrix factorization was applied for recommendation generation. The studies presented in this work used a variety of metrics, datasets, and recommendation methods.

Additional applications of graphs for recommendations include cultural heritage, tourism, social networks, and more. Chianese and Piccialli [30] used graphs for representing context evolution in cultural heritage: node-modeled states and transitions between the nodes were based on observation of user behavior. Shen *et al.* [31] used graphs for representing tourist attractions and their similarity, where different graphs could represent content-based, collaborative, and social relationships. Godoy and Corbellini [32] reviewed the use of folksonomies, which can be naturally seen as user–item–tag graphs, in recommender systems. Graph-based approaches in user modeling and recommender systems have become popular, and there exists a number of tools for analysis of large graphs. We refer interested readers to [33] and [34] for encompassing reviews of the area.

21.2.1.1   Similarity measurement using graphs and their application

Previous research on graph-based recommender systems focused on measuring the similarity of two entities in the data (user–item, user–user, or item–item) and associated this with a score or rating [35]. Graph-based similarity measurement is based on metrics extracted from a graph-based representation [36]. Two key approaches for measuring similarity using graphs are based on paths and random walks.

In the path-based similarity, the distance between graph nodes can be measured using the *shortest path* and/or the total *number of paths*. The definition of the shortest path may include a combination of the number of edges connecting the two nodes and the weights of these edges. Shortest path can be computed for a user node and an item node, in order to quantify the extent to which the user prefers the item. The "number of paths" approach works similarly, by calculating the number of paths between the two nodes as a proxy for their relatedness (the more paths, the more related they are). However, this approach is more computationally intensive.

Random walks can be used to compute similarity by estimating the probability of one node being reached from another node, given the available graph paths. The more probable it is that the target node can be reached from the source node, the higher is the relatedness of the two nodes. Random walks can be either unweighted (equal probability of edges) or weighted (edges having different probabilities based on their label, e.g., rating) [36].

Examples of recommendation studies in which the approaches detailed above were applied can be found in [37–39]. Li and Chen [37] reduced the recommendation problem to a link prediction problem. That is, the problem of finding whether a user would like an item was cast as a problem of finding whether a link exists between the user and item in the graph. A similarity measure between user and item nodes was computed using random walks. Items were then ranked based on their similarity scores, such that top scoring items were recommended to users. Using classification accuracy metrics, this approach was shown to be superior to other non-graph based similarity ranking methods.

A similar walking distance metric was used in [38], complemented by graph structure metrics such as the number of sub trees. These metrics were used for the purpose of link prediction and property value prediction in RDF semantic graphs, using a learning technique based on an support vector machine (SVM). Experimental results showed that the graph features varied in their performance based on the graph structure on which they operated, for example, full versus partial subtrees. It was also noted that the newly defined features were not dataset-specific, but could be applied to any RDF graph. The graph structures in the context of RDF are less applicable to those used in the approach proposed in this work, because the recommendation dataset graphs do not follow a hierarchical model of RDFs.

Finally, Konstas *et al.* [39] developed a graph-based approach for generating recommendations in social datasets like Last.fm. The work focused on optimizing a random walk with restarts algorithm. The reported results show an improvement in recommendations using the random walk approach, compared to the baseline collaborative filtering. In the presented work, random walks on a graph, although with static parameters, are represented by the PageRank score feature. The above studies are also extended here by generalizing the adoption of graph metrics beyond random walks and their use for similarity measurements, not bound to any specific graph structure.

21.2.1.2   Representing social data and trust using graphs

Other studies involving graph approaches in recommender systems primarily addressed the context of representing social, semantic, and trust data. In some studies, only the graph representation was used as the means to query the data, e.g., neighboring nodes and the weights of edges connecting to them [40,41], while others utilize both the graph representation and graph-based reasoning methods [42,43].

A survey of connection-centric approaches in recommender systems [44] exemplifies how the data of an email network [45] and of a co-occurrence in web documents [46] can be represented in graphs. The graph representation of the email interactions between users defines each user as a node and edges connect users, who corresponded via email. In the case of web documents, people are again represented as nodes and edges, connecting people who are mentioned in the same document. When these graphs are established, they can be used to answer recommendation-related queries. In the email graph, a query regarding the closeness of users can be answered using a similarity or distance metric, such as those mentioned in the previous section. In the web co-occurrence graph, a query regarding people sharing interests can be answered by counting their common neighbors.

Other graph representation variants are hypergraphs [47]. They differ from graphs by allowing an edge, denoted by a hyperedge, to connect with multiple nodes. Hypergraphs have been proposed in the context of recommendation generation, for the purpose of representing complex associations, such as social tagging [48–50], where a tag is attached to an item by a user. If the tag, user, and item are represented by nodes, at least two edges are required to represent the association between the three entities. This association can be represented by a hyperedge connecting the three nodes. In these studies, similarity metrics are composed based on this structure and used for the recommendation generation. Results presented in [48] show that the similarity metrics from hypergraphs lead to better recommendations.

Prior works focusing on the means of incorporating trust between users for the sake of improving the recommendations were surveyed in [51]. For example, Ma *et al.* [40] proposed a graph representation encapsulating trust between users.

The representation modeled users as the graph nodes, and the trust relationships between them were reflected by the weights on the edges. Data extracted from the graph, e.g., who trusts whom and to what extent, was used in the recommendation process, and it was shown to improve the generated recommendations. However, the graph was used only to represent the data and propagate the trust scores.

Another usage of graphs for recommendation purposes is in the case of geospatial recommendations. Quercia *et al.* used graphs to find the shortest path between geographical locations, while also maximizing the enjoyment of the path for the user [43]. Locations were represented as nodes and connected to each other based on geographical proximity. Nodes were also ranked based on how pleasant (beautiful, quiet, happy) the locations were. Finally, a route that optimizes the shortness and pleasantness was computed based on a graph method and recommended to the user. In this work, both graph-based representation and graph-theory methods are used for recommendation generation.

21.2.2 *Feature engineering for recommendations*

As mentioned at the beginning of the section, another group of related works covers automatic feature engineering. According to Guyon *et al.*, *"feature extraction addresses the problem of finding the most compact and informative set of features, to improve the efficiency or data storage and processing"* [7]. Basic features are a result of quantitative and qualitative measurements, while new features can be engineered by combining these or finding new means to generate additional measurements. In the big data era, the possibilities of engineering additional features, as well as their potential importance, have risen dramatically.

Feature engineering can be performed either manually or automatically. In the manual method, domain experts analyze the task for which the features are required, e.g., online movie recommendation versus customer churn prediction, and conceive features that may potentially inform the task. The engineering process involves aggregating and combining features already present in the data, in order to form new, more informative features. This approach, however, does not scale well because of the need for a human expert, the time it takes to compose features, and the sheer number of possibilities for the new features [52]. Conversely, automatic feature extraction, the process of algorithmically extracting new features from a dataset, does scale up well.

A basic approach for engineering new features from the existing ones is to combine them using arithmetic functions. In one study that evaluated this approach, arithmetic functions, such as min, max, average, and others, were used [10]. The study also presented a specific language for defining features, where the features were described by a set of inputs, their types, construction blocks, and the produced output. A framework for generating a feature space using the feature language as input was evaluated. The evaluation showed that the framework outperformed legacy feature generation algorithms in terms of accuracy. The main difference between the framework presented at [10] and its predecessors was that the framework was generic and applicable to multiple tasks and machine-learning approaches.

Additional automatic feature-engineering methods that are domain-specific were surveyed in [8,9] for image recognition and in [53] for text classification purposes. An example of a feature engineering method for image recognition is quantifying the amount of skin color in an image in order to classify whether it contains a human face or not [54], whereas for text classification a bag-of-words can be generated for every document and used to describe it.

A different suite of methods for eliciting new features, which is also applicable to recommender systems, is latent features computation. Methods such as SVD [11] and PCA [12] can be used to compute new features and support the generation of recommendations by decomposing the available data into components and matching composing factors, i.e., the latent features. When the data is decomposed and there exists a set of latent features that can recompose it with a certain error rate, missing features and ratings can be estimated [35]. Although it has been shown that this approach successfully improves the accuracy of the recommendations [55], it is limited in the interpretability of the latent features found [14].

Unlike previous works, the current work defines an automatic feature-engineering process based on graph-based representation of a recommender system data. The details of this process are provided in the following section.

21.3 Graph-based data modeling for recommendation systems

In this section, an approach for enhancing recommendations based on representing the data as a graph is presented. This representation allows a set of graph algorithms to be applied and a set of graph-related metrics, which offer a new perspective on the data and allow the extraction of new features, to be deduced. Following a brief overview of the approach, the structure of recommender system datasets is formalized (Section 21.3.1). Then a detailed description of porting data from a classical tabular representation to a graph-based representation is given (Section 21.3.2). An elaboration of methods for generating multiple graph representations follows (Section 21.3.2.2), and finally the process of exhaustively distilling graph features from these representations is outlined (Section 21.3.3).[2]

The input to the process (illustrated in Figure 21.1) is a tabular recommender system dataset and the output is a set of graph-based features capturing the relationships between the dataset entities from the graph perspective. The first step deals with the generation of a complete graph representation of the data: the tabular data is converted into a representation where the dataset entities are nodes, connected based on their co-occurrence in the data. Next, a set of partial representations is derived from the complete graph: first the basic representation containing only user and item nodes and then additional alternative representations, each with a unique combination of relationships filtered from the complete graph. The partial representations are passed to the next step, where the extraction of the graph features is performed. Finally, the newly generated graph-based features are used to supplement the original features

---

[2]An open source package implementing the approach is released at http://amitti.github.io/GraphRecSys/.

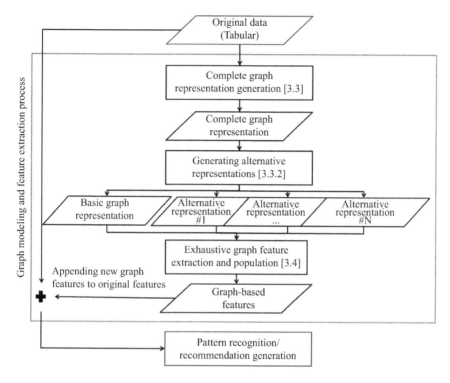

Figure 21.1 Graph modeling and feature extraction flow chart

available in the dataset, and this extended data is fed into the recommender system for the generation of predictions or recommendations. In the following subsections, the above steps of the feature extraction process are elaborated.

21.3.1 The structure of a recommender system dataset

In [4,56], classical recommendation approaches are categorized into several groups: collaborative filtering, content-based filtering, knowledge-based, community-based, and hybrid approaches. We first consider the representation of the data used by these approaches, which can be converted into a tabular form as follows:

- In *collaborative filtering*, the data is represented as a matrix of user feedback on items (matrix dimensions are users×items), where both the users and the items are denoted by their identifiers, and the content of the matrix reflects the user feedback for the items, e.g., numeric ratings or binary consumption logs.
- In *content-based filtering*, the items are modeled using a set of features, e.g., terms or domain features. Here, the matrix dimensions include the identifiers of the users, as well as the identifiers of the content features, and the values represent the preferences of the users for the features. The model also contains a second matrix with item identifiers and the same content features. The values in this matrix represent the weights of the features in each item.

- Two variants of *knowledge-based recommenders*—case-based and constraint-based—break the items into weighted features, e.g., the price of a product and the importance of the price for the user. This model can be represented by two matrices, one contains the items' weighted features and the second contains the users' ranking of the features' importance. In the items matrix, each column represents a feature, each row represents an item, and the values are the strength, or how representative the feature is of the item. Similarly, in the users' matrix, each column represents a feature, each row represents a user, and the values represent the importance of the feature for the given user.

- *Community-based recommenders* combine information regarding users' social relations with their ratings. Therefore, ratings of a socially close user are weighted heavier than of others. The items' rating information can be represented in a matrix identically to the one described in the collaborative filtering approach. The weights of social relations between users can be represented by a second matrix, where the rows and columns represent users and the values quantify the degree of the relationship between them.

- Finally, *hybrid approaches* combine some of the above stand-alone recommendation models and, therefore, can be represented using the matrix representation.

The datasets used by the above approaches, which we denote by D, contain two key types of entities. The first refers to the entity for which the recommendations are generated, i.e., the user; it is referred to as the *source* entity and denoted by D_S. The second refers to the entity that is being recommended, e.g., item, content, product, service, or even another user. This entity is referred to as the *target* entity and denoted by D_T. This notation follows the primary goal of a recommender system: to recommend a target item to the source of the recommendation request. Additional data available in the datasets typically represents the features of the source and/or the target entity, or the relationships between the two. The feature set is denoted by D_F.

For example, in a movie recommendation dataset, D_S refers to the system users and D_T to the recommendable movies. Any available features describing either the users or the movies are denoted by D_F. User features can be the user's age, gender, and location, while movie features can be genre, director, language, and length. A practical assumption is made that in a tabular recommender dataset, all the features associated with an entity are stored in the same table as the entity itself. That is, the gender of a user is stored in the user table rather than in the movie table. A formal representation of the entities and their features in the above example is $D = \{D_S, D_T, D_F\}$, where $D_S = user_{id}$, $D_T = movie_{id}$, and the features D_F are split into $D_F = \{D_{FS}, D_{FT}\}$ as follows: $D_{FS} = \{f_{s1} = age, f_{s2} = gender, f_{s3} = location\}$ and $D_{FT} = \{f_{t1} = genre, f_{t2} = director, f_{t3} = language, f_{t3} = length\}$.

It should be noted that the source and target entities can have common features [57]. For example, in the case of a restaurant recommendation task, the source entity (user) and target entity (business) can both have the "location" feature. The role of the source/target entities and features can also change according to the recommendation task at hand. In the restaurant recommendation example, when the task is to recommend restaurants to users, the users are the source entity, the restaurants are the target entity, and location is a feature of both. However, if the task was to recommend a location, e.g., tourist destinations, for a user to visit based on the restaurants in that location, then the source entity would still be the users, the target entity would be the locations, and the restaurants would be the features of the locations.

An important aspect that needs to be considered is the relationship between the entities, e.g., the fact that a user watched, rated, tagged, or favored a movie. Relationships can be established not only between a source and a target entity, but also between two source/target entities. Examples of relationships between two users are the directional followee–follower relationship or the nondirectional friendship. Relationships between two movies can be established because they are directed by the same director, are in the same language, and so forth. Relationships between entities are defined using the tuple $(source \in D_S, \{features\} \in D_F, target \in D_T)$. For example, user rating for a movie is defined by $rel_{rating} = (user, value, movie)$ and friendship between two users is defined by $rel_{friend} = (user, \{\varnothing\}, user)$.[3] The set of all possible relationships in a dataset is denoted by $D_R = \{rel_i\}$, such as in the movies example $D_R = \{rel_1 = rating, rel_2 = friendship\}$.

Given the above formalization of entities, features, and relationships, a recommendation task implies the prediction of a relationship between entities. For example, the task of a movie recommender can be considered as the prediction of the rel_{rating} relationship. This relationship can be numeric (star rating) or binary (interested or not interested), but the recommendations delivered to the users are guided by the predicted values of rel_{rating}. If, on the contrary, the system is a social recommender that recommends online friends, then the relationship in question is rel_{friend} and its task is to recommend a set of candidate friends.

In addition to the original data that is available to the recommender, more features can be generated and distilled, thus enriching the dataset. For example, two popular features frequently computed in rating-based recommendation datasets are the average rating of a user and the average rating for an item. These features are associated with the users and items, stored in the relevant tables, and they are used to refine, e.g., normalize, the predicted ratings and improve the quality of the recommendations [58]. The question addressed in this work is whether the availability of additional, supposedly more complex, features that encompass more information and stem from graph representation of the data can contribute to the accuracy of the predictions and the quality of the recommendations. In the following subsections, the details of extracting and populating features are provided.

21.3.2   *Transforming tabular into graph-based representation*

21.3.2.1   Basic graph representation for recommender systems data

When moving from the tabular to the graph-based representation of a recommender system data, three key graph design considerations are as follows:

1.   Should the graph encompass all the available data? What parts of the dataset are important and need to be represented by the graph?

---

[3]Additional friendship features, such as duration or strength, can also be included.

2.   Which entities from the selected data should be represented by graph vertices and which entities by graph edges?
3.   How should the edges be defined? Should they be directed or undirected? Should they be labeled? What should the labels be?

Regarding the first question, it is probable that the decision regarding the data to be represented in the graph is data-dependent. For some domains, datasets, and recommendation tasks, certain parts of the data may be more informative than others. Since the space of possible graph-based data representations is too large for determining a-priori the most suitable scheme, a possible alternative is to start with a graph model based on the entire data, and then to systematically extract all subgraph representations and their features. This leads to automatic coverage of the entire search space, inherently uncovering the representations that produce the most effective features. Then, the most informative feature set can be selected.

To answer the second and third questions, an intuitive modeling approach is used. Namely, the graph model considers all the source, target, and feature entities as vertices, while their links and relationships between features (including user feedback on items) are the edges. If the information about the relationship is binary, e.g., the item is viewed or not, the edges are not labeled. Otherwise, the edges' labels communicate the information about the relationship, e.g., rating or type of association. In most cases, the edges are not directed, as information about a feature connected to an entity or about an entity connected to a feature is equivalent. Although this work does not consider directed edges, the proposed approach can be extended to support this (outlined in Section 21.6.2).

Based on the above abstraction of recommender systems datasets, the following basic graph representation emerges. User and item entities are represented by the graph vertices, and edges connect a user and an item vertex when an association between the two is available. This association can be explicit (ratings or likes) or implicit (content or user view). This graph is called a bipartite graph [59], because it can be split into two partitions consisting of the source and target entity vertices, i.e., the users and items, respectively (Figure 21.2(a)).

The basic representation can be extended by adding additional features as new graph vertices and linking them to the existing vertices. For example, if user's locations are provided, each location can be represented by a vertex and the users associated with the locations are linked to their vertices. A similar situation may occur in the target partition of the graph, e.g., the target entity of movies and a variety of their content features: genre, actors, keywords, and more (Figure 21.2(b)). Adding the feature vertices still preserves the bipartite nature of the graph, but the partition with the added features gets virtually split into two groups of vertices: the entities themselves and their features.

The situation changes, however, when adding information within the source or target partitions, e.g., user-to-user social links or item-to-item domain links. This information introduces new links *within* the partitions, which break the bipartite structure (Figure 21.2(c)). Additional information that may break the bipartite structure is the common features shared between the source and target partitions. For example,

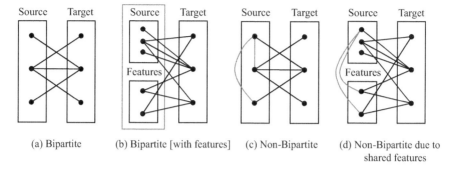

Figure 21.2   *Examples of two types of graph schemes representing a recommender*
system dataset: bipartite ((a) and (b)) and non-bipartite ((c) and (d)).
In (b), the grey block confines the multipart bipartite graph
component. In (c) and (d), the grey edges break the bipartite structure

in the movie domain, the items may be linked to their genres, while the users may
also express their preferences toward the genres. Thus, links to the genre vertices are
established from both the user and item partitions (Figure 21.2(d)), and the graph is
no longer bipartite. Note that each of the four schemes shown in Figure 21.2 generates
different sets of features and the values of the features also vary.

Following is an outline[4] of a high-level approach for generating the *complete
graph*, which includes all the data and relationships of a recommender dataset. The
algorithm scans all the tables in the dataset, and for each column that is not a source
entity column, target entity column, or feedback column, it generates a graph node for
every unique value appearing in the column. Thus, every unique $user_{id}$ and $movie_{id}$
is assigned to a graph vertex, as well as every actor, director, movie genre, keyword,
and so forth. Non-categorical features, e.g., movie budget, can be discretized using
binning, e.g., under $10M, $10M-$20M, $20M-$30M, or based on the observed
distribution, e.g., four equal-sized quarters, each containing 25% of the data. Upon
discretizing the values in the columns and creating the nodes, all the nodes matching
the values that appear in the same row are connected by edges to the source and target
nodes of the same row, if available. The result is a graph that contains all the values of
the features as the graph nodes, which are connected to the source and target entities
based on their co-occurrence in the data.

21.3.2.2   Multiple subgraph representations

Despite being included in a dataset, not all the features are necessarily informative and
contribute to the accuracy of the recommendations. Certain features may be noisy or
bear little information, thus hindering the recommendation process. For example, if a
feature is sparsely populated, its values are identical across users, or it is populated only

---

[4]The pseudo codes omit several technical details that can be found in the accompanying library.

across a certain subset of users, then this feature is unlikely to help the recommender and may not be included in the graph representation. However, it is hard to assess the contribution of the features in advance with a high degree of certainty. This leads to the idea of automatically deriving multiple subgraph representations from the complete graph and extracting the graph features for each subgraph first, and selecting the most informative ones in a later stage. Specifically, all the possible subgraphs are exhaustively generated and their features are extracted. Each subgraph represents a combination of features influenced by the entities and relationships included in the graph. The process is detailed in Algorithm 1.

Algorithm 1: Generate subgraphs and extract features

---

   input : *CompleteGraph* - complete graph representation of the dataset
            PredEdge - edge type of the relationship being predicted
   output: *ExtractedGraphFeatures* - set of features extracted from sub-graph
            representations

1 *GraphEdgeTypeCombinations* ← `GenerateEdgeCombinations`({*EdgeTypes*},
   PredEdge)
2 *ExtractedGraphFeatures* ← ∅

3 **foreach** *EdgeCombination* ∈ *GraphEdgeTypeCombinations* **do**
4   │ *SubGraph* ← `RemoveEdgesFromGraph`(*CompleteGraph, EdgeCombination*)
5   │ *SubGraphFeatures* ← `ExtractGraphFeatures`(*SubGraph, PredEdge*)
6   │ *ExtractedGraphFeatures* ← (*ExtractedGraphFeatures* ∪ *SubGraphFeatures*)
7 **end**

8 return *ExtractedGraphFeatures*

The input to the algorithm is the complete graph representation *CompleteGraph*, which was discussed at the end of Section 21.3.2.1, and the edge *PredEdge* representing the relationship rel_i being predicted. The function `Generate EdgeCombinations` invoked in line 1 returns all the possible combinations of different types of graph edges. Note that this function receives also the type of the predicted edges *PredEdge*. This is done in order to preserve the *PredEdge* edges in all the subgraphs. Namely, this type of edges will not be included in the combinations that are removed from the complete graph and, therefore, will be present in all the subgraphs.

Upon generating all the possible edge type combinations, the set is iterated over and the function `RemoveEdgesFromGraph` is invoked to create a subgraph *SubGraph* by removing the combination *EdgeCombination* from *CompleteGraph* (line 4). Then, the function `ExtractGraphFeatures` is invoked to extract from *SubGraph* the set of possible graph features referred to as *SubGraphFeatures* (line 5, to be elaborated in Section 21.3.3) and append *SubGraphFeatures* to the set of features *ExtractedGraphFeatures* (line 6). Finally, in line 8, the algorithm returns

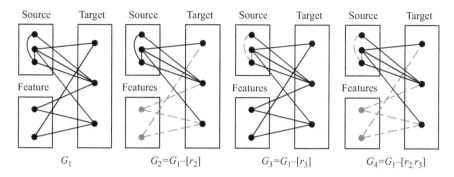

Figure 21.3   Four subgraph schemes generated from the complete schema based on the relationship permutations. Dashed lines represent links removed from the graph

ExtractedGraphFeatures—the set of all the possible graph features from all the possible subgraphs.

The execution of Algorithm 1 is illustrated by an example in Figure 21.3. Consider a graph $G = (V, E)$, where $V = \{V_S \cup V_T \cup V_F\}$ is the set of vertices of the source entities $V_S = \{V_{S1}, \ldots, V_{Sm}\}$, target entities $V_T = \{V_{T1}, \ldots, V_{Tn}\}$, and domain feature values $V_F = \{V_{F1}, \ldots, V_{Sk}\}$. In addition, $E = \{rel_1, rel_2, rel_3\}$ is the set of graph edges, reflecting three relationship types: rel_1 is the source-target relationship being predicted; rel_2 is the relationship between the target entities and domain features; and rel_3 is the relationship between the source vertices. In graph terminology, the recommendation task is to predict the label (or the existence) of an edge $rel_1(i, j)$ between a source vertex V_{Si} and a target vertex V_{Tj}.

For this graph, the set *GraphEdgeCombinations* created by `GenerateEdge Combinations` includes *GraphEdgeCombinations*$=\{\{\varnothing\}, \{rel_2\}, \{rel_3\}, \{rel_2, rel_3\}\}$. These are the combinations of edges that are removed from the graph while creating subgraphs, whereas the predicted relationship rel_1 is preserved in all the subgraphs. Removing these combinations of edges, function `RemoveEdgesFromGraph` generates four variants of *SubGraph* shown in Figure 21.3: $G_1 \leftarrow CompleteGraph - \{\varnothing\}$, $G_2 \leftarrow CompleteGraph - \{rel_2\}$, $G_3 \leftarrow CompleteGraph - \{rel_3\}$, and $G_4 \leftarrow CompleteGraph - \{rel_2, rel_3\}$. Note that G_1 is the complete graph, whereas other subgraphs have either rel_2 or rel_3, or both removed. For each *SubGraph*, function `ExtractGraphFeatures` is invoked to extract the respective feature set *SubGraphFeatures* and all the extracted feature sets are appended to *ExtractedGraphFeatures*.

21.3.3   Distilling graph features

The function `ExtractGraphFeatures` in line 5 of Algorithm 1 received a subgraph derived from the complete representation and was invoked to extract a set of graph-based features. Moreover, this function was invoked for all the possible

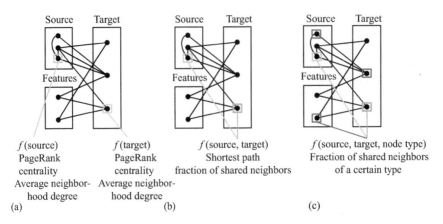

Figure 21.4   Key graph-based feature generator families and their instances: (a) single node generators, (b) dual node generators (c) multiple node generators

subgraphs, to ensure that all the possible graph features are extracted. The graph-based features are extracted using a number of functions, each calculating a different graph metric. These functions, referred as *generators*, are divided into several, families according to the number of graph vertices they process.

The main steps of `ExtractGraphFeatures` are detailed in Algorithm 2, which uses three types of generators:

- `1-VertexGenerators` are applied to a single vertex, either the source or the target entity, and compute features of this vertex, e.g., PageRank (Figure 21.4(a)).
- `2-VertexGenerators` are applied to a pair of vertices, the source and the target entities, and compute graph-based relationships between the two, e.g., the shortest path (Figure 21.4(b)).
- `N-VertexGenerators` are applied to $N > 2$ vertices, two of which are the source and target entities and the rest are not, e.g., "number of vertices common neighbors of the source and target vertices" (Figure 21.4(c)).

Section 21.3.3.1 lists the functions from each generator family that were used. Note that these are executed iteratively, in order to generate all the possible graph features. By no means this list of functions is exhaustive; it exemplifies a number of popular functions that were used, but more functions can be conceived and added.

At the initial stage of Algorithm 2, edges belonging to the predicted relationship are copied to the *SubGraphPredictedEdges* set (line 2). For each *Edge* in this set, the generators are invoked as follows. The `1-VertexGenerators` functions are invoked in lines 5 and 6, respectively, on the *SourceEntity* and *TargetEntity* vertices of *Edge*. Applying these functions to other vertices is unlikely to produce features that can contribute to the prediction of the desired relationship, while leading to significant computational overheads. Hence, `1-VertexGenerators` are

---

Algorithm 2: Extract graph features from a subgraph

---

    input : *SubGraph* - sub-graph derived from the complete graph representation
              PredEdge - edge type of the relationship being predicted
    output: *ExtractedSubGraphFeatures* - set of features extracted from *SubGraph*

1   *ExtractedSubGraphFeatures* ← ∅
2   *SubGraphPredictedEdges* ← ExtractPredictedEdges(*SubGraph*,*PredEdge*)

3   **foreach** *(SourceEntity,TargetEntity) of Edge* ∈ *SubGraphPredictedEdges* **do**
4   **foreach** 1-Function *in* 1-VertexGenerators **do**
5   *SourceFeatures* ← 1-Function(*SourceEntity*)
6   *TargetFeatures* ← 1-Function(*TargetEntity*)
7   *ExtractedSubGraphFeatures* ← (*ExtractedSubGraphFeatures* ∪ *SourceFeatures*
          ∪ *TargetFeatures*)
8   **end**

9   **foreach** 2-Function *in* 2-VertexGenerators **do**
10   *SourceTargetFeatures* ← 2-Function(*SourceEntity*,*TargetEntity*)
11   *ExtractedSubGraphFeatures* ← (*ExtractedSubGraphFeatures* ∪
         SourceTargetFeatures)
12   **end**

13   *MultipleEntityCombinations* ←
      ExtractEntityCombinations({*VertexTypes*})

14   **foreach** *EntityCombination* ∈ *MultipleEntityCombinations* **do**
15   *N* ← |*EntityCombination*|
16   **foreach** N-Function *in* N-VertexGenerators **do**
17   *MultipleEntityFeatures* ← N-Function(*SourceEntity*, *TargetEntity*,
         EntityCombination)
18   *ExtractedSubGraphFeatures* ← (*ExtractedSubGraphFeatures* ∪
         MultipleEntityFeatures)
19   **end**
20   **end**
21   return *ExtractedSubGraphFeatures*
22 **end**

---

restricted to these two vertices only. The 2-VertexGenerators are applied in line 10 to the pairs of vertices *SourceEntity* and *TargetEntity*. Then, the ExtractEntityCombinations function is invoked in line 13, in order to create a set of all the possible entity combinations of vertices, *MultipleEntityCombinations*. These combinations necessarily involve *SourceEntity* and *TargetEntity*, and in addition any other type of graph vertices. For each combination *EntityCombination* of size *N* (line 15), the relevant N-VertexGenerators generators are invoked in line 17. Features extracted by 1-VertexGenerators, 2-VertexGenerators, and N-VertexGenerators are all appended to *ExtractedSubGraphFeatures*.

Note that the value of N determines the `N-VertexGenerators` functions that are invoked and the relationships they uncover. Again, two of the N vertices are necessarily *SourceEntity* and *TargetEntity*, whereas the third vertex can be of any other entity linked to either of them. For instance, for $N = 3$ in the movie recommendation task and entities of user, item, and location, the relationship can be "the number of cinema locations that the user has visited and where the movie is screened." The generator considers the user and movie vertices, and then scans all the location vertices and identifies those, with edges connected to both. More complex relationships with a higher value of N can be considered. As such, the `N-VertexGenerators` extract a number of features that surpasses by far the set of features that can be engineered manually.

21.3.3.1 Distilled graph features

The set of metrics selected for implementation in this work and used for the evaluation of the approach is now given in detail. The metrics are those that are commonly implemented in widely used graph analysis libraries—NetworkX [60], igraph [61], and Gephi [62]—and used in social network analysis and measurement works [63,64]. It is important to stress that this set of metrics is only a portion of those that could be used and serves only as an example. The space of all graph metrics is large, as can be seen in [65–67], and, thus, could not be exhaustively evaluated within the scope of this work.

The set of `1-VertexGenerators` functions were implemented and used for evaluation are degree centrality [68], average neighbor degree [69], PageRank score [70], clustering coefficient [71], and node redundancy [71]. These metrics are referred to as the *basic* graph features.

- *Degree centrality* [68] (or, simply, node degree) quantifies the importance of a vertex through the number of other vertices to which it is connected. Hence, in the bipartite graph, the degree centrality of a user vertex S_i is the activity of i, i.e., the number of items with which S_i is associated, and, vice versa, for an item vertex T_j it is the popularity of j, i.e., the number of users who are associated with T_j. In a graph that includes metadata, the number of metadata vertices associated with either the user or the item vertex are added to the degree centrality score. The degree of centrality of a vertex v is denoted by $Deg(v)$.

- *Average neighbor degree* [69] measures the average degree of vertices to which a vertex is connected. In the bipartite graph, this metric conveys for S_i—the average popularity of items with which S_i is associated, and for T_j—the average activity of users who are associated with T_j. Formally, if $N(v)$ denotes the set of neighbors of a vertex v, then the average neighbor degree is

$$AvgNghDeg(v) = \frac{1}{|N(v)|} \sum_{u \in N(v)} Deg(v) \tag{21.1}$$

In a graph with metadata, the average neighbor degree of a user/item vertex also incorporates the popularity of the metadata features with which it is associated.

- *PageRank* [70] is a widely used recursive metric that quantifies the importance of graph vertices. For a user vertex S_i, the PageRank score is computed through PageRank scores of a set of item vertices $\{T_j\}$ with which S_i is associated and vice versa. Thus, the PageRank score of a user vertex S_i can be expressed as

$$PageRank(S_i) = \sum_{T_j \in N(S_i)} \frac{PageRank(T_j)}{Deg(T_j)}, \qquad (21.2)$$

i.e., the PageRank score of S_i depends on the PageRanks of each item vertex T_j connected to S_i, divided by the degree of T_j. In a graph with metadata, the PageRank scores of user/item vertices are also affected by the PageRank of the metadata vertices to which they are connected.

- *Clustering coefficient* [71] measures the density of the immediate subgraph of a vertex as the ratio between the observed and possible number of cliques of which the vertex may be a part. Since cliques of a size greater than two are impossible in the bipartite graph, *ClustCoef* measures the density of shared neighbors with respect to the total number of neighbors of the vertex:

$$ClustCoef(v) = \frac{\sum_{u \in N(N(v))} (|N(v) \cap N(u)|/|N(v) \cup N(u)|)}{|N(N(v))|} \qquad (21.3)$$

- *Node redundancy* [71] is applicable only to bipartite graphs and shows the fraction of pairs of neighbors of a vertex that is linked to the same other vertices. This metric quantifies for user vertex S_a—the portion of pairs of items with which a is associated that are also both associated with another user b. Likewise, for item vertex T_x, it quantifies the portion of pairs of users associated with x and also both associated with another item y. If the vertex is removed from the graph, node redundancy reflects the fraction of its neighbors that will still be connected to each other through other vertices.

Next, multiple-vertex generator functions are detailed. Specifically, the following functions from the `2-VertexGenerators` and `N-VertexGenerators` families were implemented:

- *Shortest path* [72]. Unlike the above feature generators that operate on a single vertex, shortest path receives a pair of graph vertices: a source entity and a target entity. It evaluates the distance, i.e., the lowest number of edges, between the two vertices. The distance communicates the proximity of the vertices in the graph, as is a proxy for their similarity or relatedness. A short distance indicates high relatedness, e.g., more items shared between users or more features for items, while a longer distance indicates low relatedness.
- *Shared neighbors of type X*. This is one of the `N-VertexGenerators` functions, which receives three parameters: source entity vertex, target entity vertex, and entity type X. It returns the fraction of neighbors shared between the source and target vertices that are of the desired type X. The fraction is computed relatively to the union of the source vertex neighbors with the target vertex neighbors. Note that this feature cannot be populated for graphs that do not have a sufficient variety of entities connected to the source and target vertices.

- *Complex relationships across entities.* Apart from the abovementioned generators, system designers may define other `N-VertexGenerators` functions, which could extract valuable features. For example, it may be beneficial for a movie recommender to extract the portion of users, who watched movies from genres g_1, g_2 directed by person p, and released between years t_1 and t_2. It is clear that it is impossible to exhaustively list all the combinations of such features: this is domain- and application-dependent. Hence, the task of defining these complex generators is left open-ended and invites system designers to use the provided library and develop their own feature generators.

To recap, each of the above `1-VertexGenerators` and `2-Vertex Generators` is applied to every source and target vertex and generates features associated with the vertex or a pair of vertices. In addition, `N-VertexGenerators` is applied to the source and target vertices and all the possible combinations of other entity types. Recall that this is done for every subgraph extracted from the complete graph and the complexity of the feature generation task becomes clear.

21.4   Experimental setting and datasets

It is important to highlight that the product of the presented approach is graph-based features that help to generate recommendations using existing recommendation methods. These features can either be used as stand-alone features, i.e., the only source of information for the recommendation generation, or be combined with other features. Hence, the baseline for comparison in the evaluation part is the performance of common recommendation methods when applied **without the newly generated features**.

To present solid empirical evidence, the contribution of the graph feature extraction to the accuracy of the recommendations was evaluated using three machine-learning methods: random forest [73], gradient boosting [74], and SVM [75]. Both random forest and gradient boosting are popular ensemble methods that have been shown to be accurate and won recommendation [6] and general prediction [76] competitions. The methods are also implemented in widely used machine-learning libraries [77,78] and were shown to perform well in prior recommender systems works [79–81].

In the next section, two case studies showing the contribution of graph-based features are presented. These case studies demonstrate the value of the proposed graph-based approach applied to a range of recommendation tasks and domains. Case study I evaluates the performance of the graph-based approach, evaluating its contribution in different domains and tasks. Case study II focuses on the impact of representing data using different graph schemes on the recommendations.

21.4.1   Dataset I—Last.fm

The first dataset is of users' relevance feedback provided for music performers via the Last.fm online service, which was obtained in [82]. The dataset consists of 1,892 users and 17,632 artists whom the users tagged and/or listened to. More than 95% of users in the dataset have 50 artists listed in their profiles as a result of the method used to collect the data. There are 11,946 unique tags in the dataset, which were assigned by users to artists 186,479 times. Each user assigned on average 98.56 tags, 18.93 of which are distinct. Each artist was assigned 14.89 tags on average, of which 8.76 are distinct. The dataset also contains social information regarding 12,717 bidirectional friendship links established between Last.fm users, based on common music interests or real life friendship.

We briefly characterize the dataset. Initially, we consider the distribution of the number of friends per user. The average number of user-to-user edges is low, where the vast majority of users have less than ten friends and about half of the users have less than four friends. Intuitively, a friendship edge between two users can be an indicator of similar tastes, and as such, friendship-based features are expected to affect the recommendations. Then, we consider the distributions of the number of listens per artist, user, and in total. It can be observed that the overall and per artist distribution are highly similar. The user-based distribution resembles the same behavior but drops faster. This aligns with the intuition that the number of users who listen to hundreds of artists is smaller than the number of artists who are listened by hundreds of users [83].

There are four relationships in the Last.fm dataset: *[user, listens, artist]*, *[user, uses, tag]*, *[tag, used, artist]*, and *[user, friend, user]*. The task defined for this dataset was to predict the artists to whom the users will listen the most, i.e., the predicted relationship was *[user, listens, artist]*. This task requires first predicting the number of times each user will listen to each artist, then ranking the artists, and choosing the top K artists. Based on the subgraph generation process detailed in Algorithm 1 and the relationship being predicted, the data can be represented via eight graph schemes in general. Four graph schemas that incorporate the source and target entities were evaluated:

- Bipartite graph that includes users and artists only, denoted as the baseline (BL).
- Non-bipartite graph that includes users, social links, and artists (BL+F).
- Non-bipartite graph that includes users, artists, and tags assigned by users to artists (BL+T).
- Graph that includes all the entities and relationships: users, tags, artists, and social links (BL+T+F).

The four graphs are illustrated in Figure 21.5. For each of the graphs, two sets of features were generated: basic features as well as a set of extended features associated with the auxiliary data being included. The generated features are used as the input for a Gradient Boosting Decision Tree regressor [74], trained to predict the number of listens for a given user–artist pair.

A five-fold cross-validation was performed. Users with fewer than five ratings were pruned, to ensure that every user has at least one rating in the test set and four in the training set. For each training fold, a graph was created for each graph model shown in Figure 21.5. For each user, in the test set, a candidate set of artists was created by selecting artists out of the set of the artists listened to by the user and complementing these by randomly selected artists. For example, a candidate set of

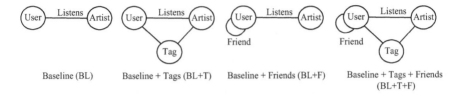

Figure 21.5   Graph representations for dataset I (Last.fm)

100 artists included 10 artists listened to by the user and 90 random artists. Three different candidate sizes were evaluated: 50, 100, and 150.

Then, a regressor was used to predict the number of listens for each artist in the candidate set, rank the set, and compute precision at 10 ($P@10$) as the performance metric [84]. If candidate set CS consists of the artists selected from a user's artist set denoted by UA and the randomly selected artists set RA, then $P@10$ is computed by $P@10 = (UA \cap top\_10\_artists(UA \cup RA))/10$, where $top\_K\_artists$ is the list of top-K artists in CS ranked according to the predicted number of listens. Finally, an average of the $P@10$ scores across all the users in the test set is computed. In order to evaluate the significance in the performance of the various graph schemes feature sets, a two-sided t-test was applied on the results.

21.4.2   Dataset II—Yelp (from RecSys-2013)

The second dataset is of users' relevance feedback given for businesses, such as restaurants, shops, and services. The dataset was released by Yelp for the RecSys-2013 Challenge [85]. For the analysis, users with less than five reviews were filtered out, which resulted in 9,464 users providing 171,003 reviews and the corresponding ratings for 11,197 businesses. The average number of reviews per user is 18.07 and the average number of reviews per business is 15.27. A key observation regarding this dataset is the distribution of ratings, which were almost all positive (more than 60% of ratings were at least 4 stars on a 5-star scale), and the low variance of ratings across businesses and users. This phenomenon is common in star rating datasets, where users tend to review fewer items that they did not like.

We discuss the basic statistics of users and businesses in the Yelp dataset. Initially, we consider the distribution of the number of reviews and ratings per user. A long tail distribution of the number of businesses a user reviewed can be observed, with more than 75% of the users providing less than 10 reviews. Then, we consider the distribution of the number of reviews a business received. Only 24% of businesses attract more than 10 reviews, while only a few businesses (less than 2%) have more than 100 reviews. Despite the high number of categories in the data, the average number of categories with which a business is associated is only 2.68. Every business is also associated with a single location.

The task defined for this dataset is the one originally defined for the RecSys-2013 challenge, i.e., to predict the ratings a user will assign to businesses. Two graph models were implemented and evaluated based on this dataset: a *bipartite* model with

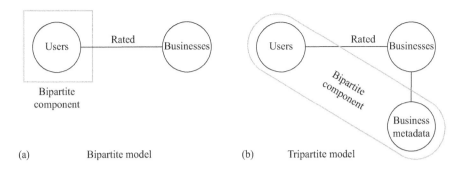

(a)   Bipartite model   (b)   Tripartite model

Figure 21.6   Graph representations for dataset II (Yelp – RecSys-2013 Challenge)

sets of vertices U and B representing users and businesses and a *tripartite*[5] model with sets of vertices U, B, and M representing users, businesses, and metadata items, respectively. The high-level graph representation models are illustrated in Figure 21.6, while the detailed presentation of the subgraphs will be given in Section 21.4.3, in which the follow-up dataset is presented.

The features generated for this dataset were aggregated into three groups:

* *Basic* features that include only the unique identifiers of users $\{u_i\} \in U$ and businesses $\{b_j\} \in B$.
* *Manual* features that include the number of reviews by u_i, average rating of u_i, number of reviews for b_j, number of categories $|\{m\}|$ with which b_j is associated, average number of businesses in $\{m\}$, average rating of businesses in $\{m\}$, the main category[6] of b_j, average degree of businesses associated with the main category of b_j, average degree of businesses in $\{m\}$, and the location of b_j.
* *Graph* features that include the degree centrality, average neighbor degree, PageRank score, clustering coefficient, and node redundancy. These features were generated for both user nodes u_i and business nodes b_j, whereas an additional shortest path feature was computed for the pairs of (u_i, b_j).

In this case, a Random Forest regression model [73] was applied for the generation of the predictions of users' ratings for businesses. At the classification stage, the test data items were run through all the trees in the trained forest. The value of the predicted rating was computed as a linear combination of the scores of the terminal nodes reached when traversing the trees. It should be noted that the ensemble of trees in Random Forest and the selection of the best performing feature in each node inherently eliminate the need for feature selection. Since every node uses a single top performing feature for decision-making, the most predictive features are naturally

---

[5]The use of "tripartite" is somewhat misleading, as the "bipartite graph with metadata nodes" notation would be more appropriate. For the sake of brevity, the bipartite and tripartite terminologies are used.
[6]Each business in the Yelp dataset is associated with multiple categories, some having an internal hierarchy. The main category is the most frequent root category a business was associated with.

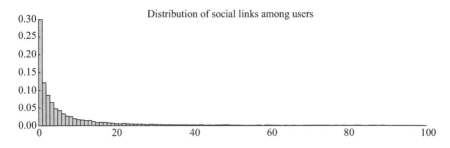

Figure 21.7   Yelp II dataset characteristics—distribution of social links

selected in many nodes and the ensemble of multiple trees virtually replaces the feature selection process.

A five-fold cross-validation was performed. For each fold, the predictive model was trained using both the original features encapsulated in the dataset and the new graph features. The basic and manual groups of features were populated directly from the reviews, whereas the graph features were populated from the bipartite and tripartite graph representations and augmented the former groups of features. Predictive accuracy of various combinations of features was measured using the widely used RMSE metric [84], computed as $RMSE = \sqrt{(\sum_n (\hat{y}_t - y_t)^2/n)}$, where n is the number of predictions, $\hat{y}_t$ are the predicted values, and y_t are the actual user ratings. A two-sided t-test was applied to validate the statistical significance of the results.

21.4.3   Dataset III—Yelp II (with social links)

The third dataset is an extension to the previous dataset released by Yelp. The new data contains more users, businesses and reviews, and, more importantly, new information regarding users' social links. The distribution of the social links among users is illustrated in Figure 21.7. It can be seen that the social links follow a long tail distribution, where most users have a small number of links: 29% with no links, 57% with less than 20 links, and only a few users with more than 20 links. The social links break the bipartite structure of the first Yelp dataset, which influences the generated graph features.

The task here is identical to that of the first Yelp dataset, i.e., predicting users' ratings for businesses. Eight graph models were generated and evaluated based on this dataset. The models are illustrated in Figure 21.8 and, depending on the availability of the user-to-user friendship edges, categorized as bipartite or non-bipartite. The complete graph is shown in the top-left schema. In the following three schemes, one type of edges is missing: either social links, user names, or categories. In the next three, two types of edges are missing: social and categories, social and names, and names and categories. Finally, in the bottom-right graph all three are missing.

The generated features presented in Section 21.3.3.1 are referred to in the evaluation of this dataset as the *basic* features. These features are aggregated into groups, based on the graph scheme from which they were extracted. For example, all the

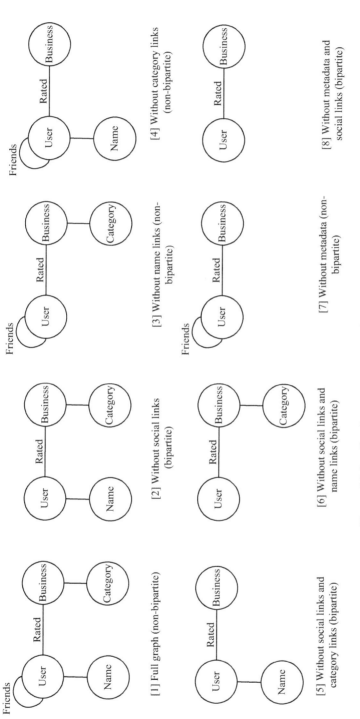

Figure 21.8   Graph representations for dataset III (Yelp II)

features extracted from the graph named "without category links" in Figure 21.8 were grouped into a combination having the same name. Another evaluated combination includes the union of all the features generated from all the graph schemes, and this is named "all graph features." Finally, the union of "all graph features" with the "basic features" is referred to as "all features."

A five-fold cross-validation was performed. For each fold, the predictive models were trained using graph features extracted from each of the above feature sets. The evaluation used different methods (random forests, gradient boosting, and SVM) to evaluate how the choice of method impacts the results. Predictive accuracy of various feature combinations was measured using the RMSE metric [84], and a two-sided *t*-test was applied to validate statistical significance.

21.4.4   Dataset IV—Movielens

Movielens [86] is a classical recommender system's dataset studied in numerous prior works. In this work, it is used to show that the graph-based approach is as effective on legacy datasets as on more recent datasets including social data. The 1M Ratings Movielens dataset consists of 1,000,209 ratings assigned by 6,040 users for 3,883 movies, on a discrete scale of 1–5 stars. Each user in the dataset rated at least 20 movies. The distribution of ratings across users and movies is illustrated in Figures 21.9(a) and (b), respectively. The dataset contains metadata of both users and movies. The user metadata includes the gender, occupation, zip code area, and age group, while the movie metadata contains the genre(s) of the movies.

The task defined for this dataset was to predict user ratings for movies. Based on the above description of the dataset, 32 graph schemes were generated and evaluated (see Figure 21.10). The schemes are categorized based on the number of relationships removed from the complete graph. As can be seen, there are four categories: schemes with a single node type removed, containing five subgraphs, schemes with two node types removed containing ten subgraphs, schemes with three node types removed containing ten more subgraphs, and finally, schemes with four node types removed containing five graphs. The minimal graph scheme is the one from which all the entities and relationships were removed, except for the source and target entities and the predicted "rating" relationships.

Five-fold cross-validation was performed. For each fold, the predictive models were trained using graph features extracted from each of the above graph schemes. The evaluations used the random forest and gradient boosting approaches, in order to evaluate how the choice of the learning method impacts the results. The predictive accuracy of various combinations of the above feature sets was measured again using the RMSE and MAE predictive accuracy metrics [84], and a two-sided *t*-test was applied to validate statistical significance.

21.4.5   Summary of the datasets, features, and metrics

Table 21.1 summarizes this section and presents the experimental datasets, number of source and target entities, various subgraph schemes investigated, number of extracted feature sets, groups of features, and evaluation metrics exploited. The

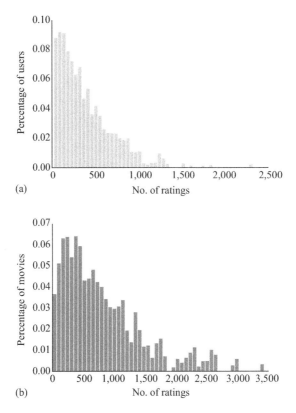

Figure 21.9 Movielens dataset characteristics: (a) distribution of ratings across users and (b) distribution of ratings across movies

datasets contain large numbers of users and items and cover a broad range of data types, application domains, and recommendation tasks. The datasets also contain both legacy and recently collected datasets, such that the evaluation presented in the following section offers solid empirical validity.

21.5 Results and analysis

21.5.1 Case study I: overall contribution of the graph-based approach

This case study answers the broad question: *How does the use of graph features affect the performance of rating predictions and recommendation generation in different domains and tasks?* Each of the above datasets was represented by graphs, and graph-based features were extracted from the graphs using the approach detailed in Section 21.3. For each dataset, a matching recommendation task was defined as

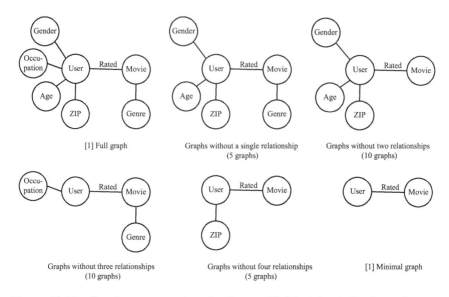

[1] Full graph

Graphs without a single relationship
(5 graphs)

Graphs without two relationships
(10 graphs)

Graphs without three relationships
(10 graphs)

Graphs without four relationships
(5 graphs)

[1] Minimal graph

Figure 21.10   Graph representations for dataset IV (Movielens). Each graph is an example of the subgraphs in the group

follows: for the Last.fm dataset, the task was to predict the artists to which users will listen; for the two Yelp datasets, the task was to predict user ratings for business; and, for the Movielens dataset, to predict user ratings for movies. The tasks were performed and evaluated under three conditions:

- Prediction with versus without the newly extracted graph features.
- Prediction with user-related versus item-related graph features.
- Prediction using features of a bipartite graph versus extended graph schemes.

The evaluations were conducted using the N-fold cross-validation [87], with $N = 5$. For each fold, the complete graph representation was generated based on the entities from both the training and test sets, except for the relationships being predicted in the test set. A two-sided t-test was conducted with the null hypothesis of having identical expected values across the compared prediction sets. The tests assumed that the ratings using feature sets A and B were taken from the same population. The threshold used for a statistically significant difference was $p = 0.05$.

21.5.1.1   Dataset I—Last.fm results

Four graph schemes were generated for the Last.fm dataset, as per the structure in Table 21.2. For each graph scheme, the set of *basic* graph features listed in Section 21.3.3.1 was extracted and populated. The basic features encapsulate only the user-artist listening data and denoted by $\hat{F}$. In addition, when the social and tagging data is available, namely, in the BL+T, BL+F, BL+T+F schemes, the set of *extended* features can be extracted. These features are denoted by F, e.g., F_{BL+T} denotes the set of extended features extracted from the graph with the tagging data. Note that for the

Table 21.1 Summary of datasets characteristics

Dataset	Source and target entities	Graph schemes	Graphs	Feature sets	Extracted features	Learning method	Metric
Last.fm	1,892 (users) 17,632 (artists)	Bipartite + non-bipartite (w/ social links, w/ tags, w/ social links + tags)	4	7	Basic graph features, extended graph features	Gradient Boosting	P@K
Yelp	9,464 (users) 11,197 (businesses)	Bipartite + Bipartite with metadata	2	13	Basic graph features, manually engineered	Random Forest	RMSE
Yelp II	13,366 (users) 14,853 (businesses)	Bipartite + Non-bipartite (w/ social links), with and without metadata	8	13	Basic graph features	Random forest, gradient boosting, support vector machine	RMSE
Movielens	6,040 (users) 3,883 (movies)	Bipartite + Bipartite with metadata	32	36	Basic graph features	Random forest, gradient boosting	RMSE, MAE

Table 21.2 Precision of feature combinations using the four graphs—Last.fm dataset

Feature set	Precision@10
Baseline	0.336
Baseline + Tags	0.548
Baseline + Friends	0.555
Baseline + Tags + Friends	0.571

BL schema in Figure 21.5, having neither social nor tagging data, the basic and extended feature sets are identical, i.e., $F_{BL} = \hat{F}_{BL}$.

The average $P@10$ results obtained for the extended feature sets extracted from the four schemes are summarized in Table 21.2. The baseline for comparison in this case is the performance of the graph features extracted from the bipartite scheme F_{BL}, which scored $P@10 = 0.336$. A notable improvement, between 63% and 70%, was observed when the extended feature sets were extracted. For instance, F_{BL+F}, scored $P@10 = 0.555$, which is an improvement of more than 65%. A combination of the extended features using the graph that includes both social tags and friendships, F_{BL+T+F} is the best performing feature. This scored the highest $P@10 = 0.571$ and improved the baseline $P@10$ by as much as almost 70%.

In order to evaluate the significance of the results, a paired t-test was performed with each group of features, using the $P@10$ values obtained for each of the four graphs. The results show that among the extended feature sets, all the differences were significant, $p < 0.05$. Thus, the inclusion of auxiliary tagging and friendship data improved the accuracy of the predictions, while their combination led to the most accurate predictions. More importantly, the extraction of graph-based features was shown to consistently and significantly boost the performance of the recommender, in comparison to the variant not using the extracted features.

21.5.1.2 Dataset II—Yelp results

Improvements due to the use of the graph-based approach were also evident in experiments using the second dataset (Yelp). As per the description in Section 21.4.2, basic (user and business identifiers), manual (number of reviews, average rating, business category, and location), and graph-based features were extracted and populated. The latter were broken down into the bipartite and tripartite features. In this dataset, the performance of the basic features related to the user-to-business associations was the baseline. Table 21.3 presents the full results for all the feature combinations.

The largest improvement in the RMSE of business ratings prediction was an 8.82% decrease obtained for the combination of graph features with basic and manually engineered ones (row 1). The similarity of the RMSE scores obtained by the various combinations is explained primarily by the low variance of user ratings in the dataset. Since most ratings are similar, they are highly predictable using simple methods and there is only a limited space for improvement. A combination containing

Table 21.3 RMSE of selected feature combinations—Yelp dataset (baseline combination in light gray

	Features combination	Features	RMSE	Improvement (%)
1	All_Features	Basic∪Manual∪Graph	1.0766	8.82
2	AllExcept_Tripartite	Basic∪Manual∪Bipartite	1.0775	8.75
3	AllExcept_Basic	Manual∪Graph	1.0822	8.35
4	Manual_and_Bipartite	Manual∪Bipartite	1.0850	8.11
5	AllExcept_Bipartite	Basic∪Manual∪Tripartite	1.0896	7.72
6	Manual_and_tripartite	Manual∪Tripartite	1.1073	6.22
7	AllExcept_Manual	Basic∪Graph	1.1095	6.04
8	All_Graph	Bipartite∪Tripartite	1.1148	5.59
9	AllExcept_Graph	Basic∪Manual	1.1175	5.36
10	Bipartite		1.1188	5.25
11	Tripartite		1.1326	4.09
12	Basic		1.1809	N/A
13	Manual		1.1853	−0.37

only the graph features (row 5) outperformed the baseline performance by 5.59%. On the contrary, the use of manual features (row 13) slightly deteriorated the accuracy of the predictions. This demonstrates the full benefit of the graph-based approach: extracting the graph features took less time than crafting the manual ones, and the graph features also outperformed the manual ones.

An examination of the differences in the accuracy of the results obtained when combining various groups of features revealed a number of findings. An analysis of the performance of each group of features shows that the bipartite and tripartite features performed noticeably better than the basic and manual feature sets (rows 10 and 11 versus rows 12 and 13). A combination of graph features (row 8) still outperforms slightly, although significantly, the combination of the basic and manually engineered features (row 9). To analyze the impact of the feature groups, each group was excluded from the overall set of features and the change with respect to the All_Features combination (row 1) was measured. When the graph features were excluded (row 9), the predictions were less accurate than when the basic (row 3) or manual features (row 7) were excluded. This indicates that the graph features provide the most valuable information, not covered by the basic and manual features.

21.5.1.3 Dataset III—Yelp II (with social links) results

The results of the evaluation using the extended Yelp II dataset that includes social links between users are in line with the results of the original Yelp dataset. Table 21.4 lists the results of this evaluation for a selected set of feature combinations: basic user and business features, feature of the complete graph, features of all the subgraphs, and the union of all the available features.

The results show that the combinations including graph features generally outperform the basic feature sets. The best performing combination of graph-based features

Table 21.4   RMSE of selected feature combinations—Yelp II dataset (baseline combination in light gray

	Features subset	**RMSE**	**Improvement (%)**
1	All features	1.1416	1.73
2	All graph features	1.1417	1.73
3	Complete graph	1.1450	1.45
4	Business features	1.1465	1.32
5	User features	1.1580	0.33
6	Basic features	1.1619	N/A

only, using all the features from all the subgraph schemes (row 2, RMSE = 1.1417), achieves a 1.73% improvement over the baselines. When adding the basic features to all the graph-based features, a slightly lower RMSE = 1.1416 (row 1) is obtained. Another noticeable difference is between the business-related features, which achieve RMSE=1.1465 and the user-related features, which achieve RMSE=1.158 (rows 4 and 5, respectively). This intuitively indicates that the predicted ratings assigned to the businesses being predicted are more informative than the ratings of the target user. Again, the achieved improvements are generally modest, primarily due to the low variance of ratings in the Yelp II dataset.

The performance differences between the evaluated combinations are mostly significant, $p < 0.01$, except for two pairs of feature sets. The difference between business-related features and complete graph features is borderline, with $p = 0.07$. Also the difference between "all features" and "all graph features" is expectedly insignificant. This shows that the most important contribution to the predictive accuracy comes from the graph features, while the addition of the basic features improves the prediction only a little.

21.5.1.4   Dataset IV—Movielens results

Finally, the experimentation with the Movielens dataset reaffirms the contribution of graph-based feature extraction to the recommendation generation. The task in this dataset was to predict movie ratings, whereas the predictions were evaluated using the MAE and RMSE predictive accuracy metrics. Table 21.5 summarizes the performance of a selected group of features. The basic user–item pairs are compared here with the user and item features used individually, all the extracted graph-based features, and the union of all of them, denoted by "all features" (row 1).

The already discussed superiority of item features over user features (row 3 versus row 5) can be clearly seen again. In this case, the former improve the accuracy of the predictions by 3%–5%, while the latter only deteriorate it. The extraction of the graph-based features (row 2) also leads to an improvement of 3.36% and 5.53% relative to the baseline, using the RMSE and MAE metrics, respectively. When combined with other features, the graph features achieve the best result, which

Table 21.5   Performance of selected features combinations—Movielens dataset (baseline combination in light gray, rows are sorted by RMSE)

	Features subset	RMSE	Improvement	MAE	Improvement (%)
1	All features	1.0272	4.20%	0.8303	6.06
2	All graph features	1.0362	3.36%	0.8349	5.53
3	Movie features	1.0400	3.01%	0.8380	5.18
4	Basic features	1.0722	N/A	0.8838	N/A
5	User features	1.0895	−1.61%	0.8967	−1.46

Table 21.6   Summary of experiments and results for case study I

	Dataset	Metric	Method	Results		
				Baseline	Graph features	Improvement (%)
1	Yelp I	RMSE	Random forest	1.1809	1.1148	5.59
2	Yelp II	RMSE	Random forest	1.1619	1.1417	1.74
3	Yelp II	RMSE	Gradient boosting	1.2480	1.1715	6.13
4	Yelp II	RMSE	SVM	1.1818	1.1783	0.30
5	Movielens	RMSE	Random forest	1.1667	1.0268	11.90
6	Movielens	RMSE	Gradient boosting	1.0722	1.0362	3.36
7	Movielens	MAE	Random forest	0.9144	0.8157	10.79
8	Movielens	MAE	Gradient boosting	0.8838	0.8349	5.53

is RMSE = 1.0272, or a 4.20% improvement over the baseline. Those performance differences were statistically evaluated and found significant.

21.5.1.5   Performance across learning methods, datasets, and metrics

This case investigated the impact of the graph-based features' effect on the accuracy of the recommendations. Although all the evaluations reported so far show that using the graph-based features improves the accuracy of the recommendations, the results cannot be fully corroborated yet, as the conducted experiments use different learning methods, datasets, and evaluation metrics (see Table 21.1). To confidently address the research question, the design of the evaluation has overlaps in these factors, so that the contribution of the graph features can be singled out.

The analysis below aims to establish whether the observed improvements should be attributed to the information contributed by the graph features or to the differences in the experimental settings, i.e., learning method, dataset, and metric. The results of all the experiments are summarized in Table 21.6. In all the cases, the performance of the baseline approaches not using the graph features, which were highlighted in light gray in all the tables, is compared to the performance of all the graph-based features, i.e., row 8 in Table 21.3, row 2 in Table 21.4, and row 2 in Table 21.5.

Included are the results of experiments using the Yelp, Yelp II, and Movielens datasets, which were discussed in Sections 21.5.1.2, 21.5.1.3, and 21.5.1.4. That said, results in rows 3, 4, 5, and 7 of Table 21.6 are presented here for the first time. This is due to the fact that previously reported Yelp experiments (both datasets) used random forest as their learning method, while the Movielens experiments used graduate boosting. Here, new Yelp II results with gradient boosting and SVM, and new Movielens results with random forest are also presented. Experiments using the Last.fm dataset are excluded from the analysis, since they use classification accuracy metrics and differ both in the dataset and evaluation metric.

In order to demonstrate that the improvement is not due to the selected dataset, the metric and learning method were fixed, while the approaches using different datasets were compared. Two evaluations sets are applicable to this scenario: (1) random forest predictions evaluated with the RMSE metric, using the Yelp, Yelp II, and Movielens datasets (rows 1, 2, and 5), and (2) gradient boosting predictions also evaluated with RMSE, but using the Yelp II and Movielens datasets (rows 3 and 6). The results of these experiments show an improvement of 1.74%–11.90%, which allows to eliminate the selected dataset as a possible reason for improvement.

To demonstrate that the improvement is also not due to the selected machine-learning method, the dataset and metric were fixed, while the approaches using different learning methods were compared. Three evaluation sets are applicable to this scenario: (1) RMSE of business predictions using the Yelp II dataset, where the learning methods are random forest, gradient boosting, and SVM (rows 2, 3, and 4), (2) RMSE of movie rating predictions using the Movielens dataset, where the methods are random forest and gradient boosting (rows 5 and 6), and (3) MAE of movie rating predictions using the Movielens dataset, where the methods are random forest and gradient boosting (rows 7 and 8). The results of these experiments show an improvement across all experiments, ranging from 0.30% to 6.13% for the Yelp II dataset, and from 3.36% to 11.90% for the Movielens dataset. The low variance of ratings in the Yelp datasets, which was discussed earlier, is the main reason for the low improvement observed. This is particularly noticeable with the SVM method, which struggles to linearly separate businesses with moderate ratings. Thus, the learning method cannot be the reason for the accuracy improvement.

Finally, to demonstrate that the improvement is not due to the selected evaluation metric, the dataset and method were fixed, while the performance of approaches using different metrics was compared. Two evaluation sets are applicable to this scenario: (1) random forest movie rating predictions using the Movielens dataset, evaluated using RMSE and MAE (rows 5 and 7), and (2) gradient boosting movie rating predictions also using the Movielens dataset, and also evaluated using the RMSE and MAE metrics (rows 6 and 8). The results of these experiments show a clear improvement across, ranging from 3.36% to 11.90%, allowing to eliminate the selected evaluation metric as a possible reason for improvement.

Summing up this causal analysis, all three hypotheses that the improved performance is driven by the differences in the experimental settings (dataset, learning method, and evaluation metric) were rejected. Thus, it can be concluded that the reason for the observed improvement lies in the inclusion of graph-based features, contributing new information to the recommendation process.

21.5.2 Case study II: different graph schemes and their impact on recommendations

As mentioned in the Section 21.3, various subgraphs and graph schemes can be generated for each dataset. The feature extraction process will, thus, yield a number of graph schemes, corresponding feature sets, and even the values of the same graph features. This leads to the second research question: *How are the recommendations affected by the subgraph and its representation used to generate the graph features?* In order to answer this question, another set of experiments was conducted.

In these experiments, the accuracy of recommendations when using various graph schemes was evaluated using four datasets: Last.fm, both Yelp datasets, and Movielens. The recommendation tasks were identical to the previous experiments, i.e., to predict listened artists in the Last.fm dataset, user ratings for businesses in the two Yelp datasets and user ratings for movies in the Movielens dataset. An N-fold cross-validation methodology similar to the one reported in Section 21.5.1 was followed. Also, two-sided t-test statistical significance testing was carried out.

21.5.2.1 Dataset I—Last.fm results

The evaluations using the Last.fm dataset focused on the influence of the social elements, i.e., friendship links and tags, on the obtained recommendation accuracy. In this dataset, the results of recommendations based on the bipartite user–artist graph representation (BL in Figure 21.5) were compared with those of three non-bipartite schemes, BL $+$ T, BL $+$ F, and BL $+$ T $+$ F, including, respectively, the tags assigned by the users to the artists, social friendship links between the users, and tags and friendship links alike. As mentioned in Section 21.5.1.1, two sets of graph features were extracted for each schema: a set of basic features $\hat{F}$ and a set of extended features F. Although the basic feature set $\hat{F}$ is shared across all the schemes, their values may change due to the presence of additional graph nodes. The extended feature set F is composed of the basic features along with new features that were extracted from the social links and tags available in each schema.

Table 21.7 shows the obtained $P@10$ scores averaged over all the users in the test set, when using both the basic and extended feature sets. First, it can clearly be observed that the inclusion of the social auxiliary data of either the assigned tags or friendships links substantially improves $P@10$. When both the tags and friendship links are included in the BL $+$ T $+$ F model, the highest average $P@10$ is observed. Both in the basic and the extended feature sets, the BL+T and BL+F models obtain comparable $P@10$ scores, showing the effect of the inclusion of auxiliary data in the graph schemes. However, as noted in Section 21.4.1, the tag data includes more than 186K tag assignments, whereas the friendship data consists of only 12K user-to-user links. Since the obtained precision scores are comparable, a single friendship link is more influential than a single artist tag and yields a greater improvement in

Table 21.7   Precision of feature combinations using the four graphs—Last.fm
dataset

Feature set	Basic $P@10$	Extended $P@10$
Baseline	0.336	N/A
Baseline + Tags	0.548	0.498
Baseline + Friends	0.555	0.497
Baseline + Tags + Friends	0.571	0.444

the recommendation accuracy. Looking at the significance tests conducted within the basic and extended feature sets, significant differences, $p < 0.05$, were observed between all the pairs of extended features and all the pairs of basic features except for the $\hat{F}_{BL+T}$ and $\hat{F}_{BL+F}$ pair.

When comparing the performance of the extended graph features to the performance of the corresponding basic features (basic versus extended columns in Table 21.7) it can be seen that the extended sets consistently outperformed the basic sets across all the four graph schemes, and the difference within the pairs was statistically significant, $p < 0.05$. In the BL + T scheme, the extended graph features from improved on the basic features extracted from it by 10%, $P@10 = 0.548$ versus $P@10 = 0.498$, while in the BL + F scheme, the improvement was by 11.6%, $P@10 = 0.555$ versus $P@10 = 0.497$. The largest improvement was noted in the BL + T + F scheme, where the extended graph features outperformed the basic features by as much as 28.6%, $P@10 = 0.571$ versus $P@10 = 0.444$. Surprisingly, the basic feature set, $\hat{F}_{BL+T+F}$, was found achieve a lower $P@10$ than $\hat{F}_{BL+T}$ and $\hat{F}_{BL+F}$. A possible explanation for this can be that including both types of social data but not extracting and populating the extended features leads to redundancy in the graph and degrades the performance of the recommender.

21.5.2.2   Dataset II—Yelp results

For the Yelp dataset and the task of business rating prediction, two graph schemes were compared: a pure bipartite graph that contained only the users and businesses, and a tripartite graph that, on top of user and business nodes, also contained metadata nodes describing the businesses. The two-graph schemes are illustrated in Figure 21.6. The reason these were the only graph schemes created is that sparse features having a small number of unique features, were filtered from the dataset. These features would have resulted in most nodes of a group, e.g., users, being connected to a single node, which would render it meaningless. For example, adding three "gender" nodes, male, female, and unspecified, would have resulted in all users being connected to either one of the three, essentially creating three large clusters in the graph.

The complete set of graph features was generated for both the bipartite and tripartite representations. The results in Table 21.8 show the RMSE scores obtained for these feature sets, as extracted from Table 21.3 (original row numbers are preserved).

Table 21.8   Yelp results: RMSE of the bipartite versus the tripartite feature sets

	Features combination	Features	RMSE	Improvement (%)
8	All_Graph	Bipartite∪Tripartite	1.1148	5.59
10	Bipartite		1.1188	5.25
11	Tripartite		1.1326	4.09
12	Basic		1.1809	N/A

Table 21.9   Yelp II results: RMSE of various subgraph feature sets

	Features subset	RMSE	Improvement (%)
2	All graph features	1.1417	1.73
7	Without name links	1.1450	1.45
3	Complete graph	1.1450	1.45
8	Without social links	1.1463	1.33
9	Without social and name links	1.1465	1.32
10	Without category links	1.1508	0.95
11	Without metadata	1.1508	0.94
12	Without social and category links	1.1519	0.85
13	Without metadata and social links	1.1523	0.82
6	Basic features	1.1619	N/A

The experiments showed that the bipartite schema, not including the metadata nodes, performed slightly but significantly better than the tripartite schema with metadata, RMSE = 1.1188 versus RMSE = 1.1326. The relative improvement with respect to the baseline recommendations was 1.16% higher. This difference in the performance of the schemas led to their unified feature set, which is the All_Graph, to outperform the two feature sets individually.

21.5.2.3   Dataset III—Yelp II (with social links) results

The richer information provided by the Yelp II datasets allowed for the creation of a larger set of subgraphs. These are illustrated in Figure 21.8, where various combinations of entities are removed from the complete graph. Thus, in addition to the complete graph, seven subgraph representations can be created and the performance of the feature sets extracted from these can be compared. The results of this experiment are presented in Table 21.9. The complete graph and the seven subgraphs are compared to the basic feature set and the union of all the graph features, which were, respectively, the baseline and best performing combination in Table 21.4. The numbering of rows already presented in Table 21.4 is preserved (rows 2, 3, and 6), while the rows of all the subgraphs from Figure 21.8 are numbered 7–13.

21.5.2.4　Dataset IV—Movielens results

The Movielens dataset offered an even richer information about users and items and allowed for the extraction of 32 subgraph schemes. Only a small sample of these is illustrated in Figure 21.10. The MAE and RMSE scores obtained for the 32 subgraphs are listed in Table 21.10. The subgraphs are compared to the basic feature set and the union of all the graph features, which were presented in Table 21.5 (rows 2 and 4).

Table 21.10　Performance of selected features combinations—Movielens dataset (baseline combination in light gray, rows are sorted by RMSE)

	Features set	RMSE	Improvement (%)	MAE	Improvement (%)
2	All graph features	1.0362	3.36	0.8349	5.53
6	graph w/[Age, Gender, Genre, Zip]	1.0369	3.29	0.8353	5.48
7	graph w/[Age, Gender, Occupation, Zip]	1.0373	3.25	0.8357	5.44
8	graph w/[Gender, Genre, Occupation, Zip]	1.0384	3.16	0.8365	5.35
9	graph w/[Genre, Occupation]	1.0410	2.91	0.8391	5.06
10	graph w/[Age, Genre, Zip]	1.0411	2.90	0.8386	5.12
11	graph w/[Genre, Occupation, Zip]	1.0411	2.90	0.8385	5.12
12	graph w/[Age, Genre, Occupation]	1.0412	2.90	0.8390	5.07
13	graph w/[Age, Gender, Genre]	1.0412	2.89	0.8392	5.05
14	graph w/[Age, Gender, Genre, Occupation]	1.0413	2.89	0.8390	5.07
15	graph w/[Age, Genre, Occupation, Zip]	1.0413	2.89	0.8388	5.10
16	graph w/[Genre]	1.0413	2.89	0.8393	5.04
17	graph w/[Gender, Genre, Occupation]	1.0413	2.88	0.8392	5.04
18	graph w/[Age, Genre]	1.0414	2.88	0.8395	5.02
19	graph w/[Age, Gender, Genre, Occupation, Zip]	1.0414	2.88	0.8390	5.08
20	graph w/[Genre, Zip]	1.0415	2.87	0.8388	5.09
21	graph w/[Gender, Genre]	1.0416	2.86	0.8396	5.00
22	graph w/[Gender, Genre, Zip]	1.0416	2.85	0.8391	5.06
23	graph w/[Age]	1.0425	2.77	0.8413	4.81
24	graph w/[Zip]	1.0426	2.77	0.8407	4.88
25	graph w/[Age, Zip]	1.0426	2.76	0.8409	4.86
26	graph w/[Age, Occupation]	1.0426	2.76	0.8412	4.82
27	graph w/[Age, Gender]	1.0427	2.76	0.8413	4.81
28	graph w/[Age, Gender, Zip]	1.0427	2.75	0.8408	4.87
29	graph w/[Age, Occupation, Zip]	1.0427	2.75	0.8408	4.86
30	graph w/[Occupation, Zip]	1.0427	2.75	0.8410	4.84
31	graph w/[Occupation]	1.0428	2.75	0.8414	4.80
32	graph w/[Gender, Occupation, Zip]	1.0428	2.74	0.8409	4.85
33	graph w/[Gender, Zip]	1.0431	2.72	0.8411	4.83
34	graph w/[Gender]	1.0431	2.71	0.8418	4.75
35	graph w/[Gender, Occupation]	1.0432	2.70	0.8417	4.77
36	graph w/[Age, Gender, Occupation]	1.0433	2.70	0.8417	4.77
4	Basic features	1.0722	N/A	0.8838	N/A

The rows corresponding to the various subgraph representations are numbered 6–36. For the sake of clarity, the subgraphs are denoted by the entity types *included* rather than excluded. For example, "graph w/[Age, Genre, Zip]" denotes the subgraph with the "Age," "Genre," and "Zip" entities, which is identical to the complete graph with the "Occupation" and "Gender" entities excluded.

As can be seen, the "genre" relationship in Movielens subgraphs plays a similar role to the "category" relationship in Yelp. Subgraphs containing this relationship (rows 6–22) outperformed those, where it was excluded (rows 23–36). A common link between the "category" relationship in Yelp II and the "genre" relationship in MovieLens is that they both divide the item space—be it businesses or movies—into connected groups, which affects values of the item features. In agreement with previous results, the feature set that unifies all the graph features from all the subgraph schemes ("all graph features," row 2) achieves the highest accuracy and outperforms any other feature set. Again, this is attributed to the broad coverage of the proposed feature extraction mechanism, which produces and aggregates promising feature combinations.

21.5.2.5 Summary

The purpose of this analysis was to analyze the differences driven by the subgraphs that are used for the feature extraction. To recap the results obtained using the four datasets, the following was established:

- Features extracted from different graph schemes performed differently, not following a certain pattern tied to the entities or relationships included in the subgraph. This means that it was not possible to conclude which relationships lead to better results if included in the graph. We posit that this is dataset-specific and may be affected by additional factors, such as density of a specific feature, distribution of its values, domain-specific considerations, and so forth. This finding comes through in the "category" and "genre" relationships in the Yelp II and Movielens datasets, but not in the Yelp I dataset. Notably, the social links had a major contribution in the Last.fm dataset, but not in the Yelp II dataset, possibly due to the sparsity of the latter.
- Features extracted from the complete graph representations, i.e., those containing all the relationships and entities in the dataset, were not necessarily the best performing feature sets. A negative example can be seen in the basic features of the BL+F+T schema in Table 21.7 that are dominated by the basic feature of BL+F and BL+T alike. Having said that, the feature set that aggregated (i.e., unified) all the graph features from all the subgraph schemes performed the best in the other three scenarios in which it was evaluated: Yelp, Yelp II, and Movielens. We consider this to be a strong argument in favor of using the proposed approach, as its exhaustive nature allows to cover a range of features and determine the most informative ones, as well as their best combination.

The differences across the obtained results do not allow to generalize and determine a priori the best performing subgraph and feature set. Due to this, the suggested approach of generating subgraphs, populating features from each of them, and then aggregating the features in the feature sets is more likely to uncover the best performing feature combination. We believe that future research may unveil rating patterns or characteristics of datasets, which may predict the contribution of certain subgraph, data entities, or even types of features.

21.6   Discussion and conclusions

21.6.1   *Discussion*

This work demonstrated the effectiveness of the graph-based approach for improving recommendations. It has been shown that precision and accuracy gains can be achieved by representing tabular data by graphs and extracting new features from them. This contrasts and complements prior approaches that improved recommendations by enhancing the recommendation techniques themselves. Also established are the benefits of the graph-based approach across recommendation domains, tasks, and metrics. These findings show that the graph representation exploits indirect latent links in the data, which lead to an improved recommendation accuracy. Finally, the approach is generic and can be applied to many recommender system datasets.

The process is automatic and can be run end-to-end without human intervention, unlike manual feature extraction methods, which are often time-consuming and require domain expertise. Using the proposed approach, rich features, based on intricate relationships between various data entities and subgraph scheme variations, can be systematically extracted from a dataset. This allows for a better coverage of the features space with a considerable lower effort, as discussed in Section 21.3. Next, we discuss some limitations of our work.

21.6.1.1   Overfitting

Regarding concerns referring to possible overfitting due to the newly generated features, as long as the volume of available data greatly exceeds the number of extracted features, there is little risk that the features will be the cause of overfitting. The high diversity of unique data characteristics can hardly be captured in full by a smaller subset of features. Recommender system datasets tend to be in the medium to large scale (tens of thousands to millions of data points), while the number of features generated by the current approach is still in the scale of tens to hundreds.

Additionally, machine-learning methods such as random forests have internal mechanisms for feature selection and can filter out features that overfit. They do so by training on a sample of the dataset and evaluating the performance of the features on the rest of the data. A feature that performs well on the sample but underperforms on the test data is ranked low. In the evaluations, cross-validation was used with at least $N = 5$ folds, showing that the models and features on which they are built are generalizable. Moreover, it was shown that in cases of sparse data, which require a higher degree of generalization, the graph features still outperformed other features.

21.6.1.2 Scalability

A possible disadvantage of the proposed approach is that some graph-based computations, e.g., PageRank, are iterative and may take a long time to converge. In the age of big data, recommender system datasets are getting larger and so is their graph representation, which may lead to a computational issue. A general approach for handling this in a deployed system would be to extract the graph-based features offline and use the precomputed values for real-time predictions. This may resolve the problem under the reasonable assumption that the values do not change substantially. Another means to overcome the computational latency is through using a graph feature computation library, e.g., Okapi, which can use distributed tools in order extract the graph features.

Another factor that adds to the computational complexity of the approach is the exhaustive search for new features. It should be noted that the complexity of the process of generating every possible subgraph and populating the matching feature combinations is exponential. The number of relationships in current recommendation datasets (as surveyed in Section 21.3.1) is still manageable and can be accommodated by the proposed approach. However in the future, with additional data sources being integrated for recommendation purposes, this might become unsustainable and will require a long-term solution. Two possible approaches for handling this issue are parallelization, e.g., each subgraph being processed by a different machine, and heuristics for pruning less-relevant subgraph representations.

21.6.1.3 Initial transition to the graph model

Another possible disadvantage of graph-based features is the possible need for human intervention when generating the initial complete graph. Non-categorical feature values, e.g., income or price, may generate a large number of vertices, which would lead to a low connectivity of the graph, since not many users or items would share the exact value of the feature. This would lead to a very sparse graph and will need to be addressed by a manual intervention by a domain expert, who can determine how the non-categorical values can be grouped and categorized, e.g., by creating appropriate income or price buckets. A naive solution for this might be to attempt to auto-categorize such features based on the observed distribution of their values, e.g., first quarter and second quarter. This may, however, mask the differences between fine-grained groups and cause information loss.

Also to be acknowledged in this context is the historic human contribution that was required in order to conceive the graph methods exploited in this work for the generation of the various basic graph features: shortest path, degree, PageRank, etc. Indeed, these methods took a considerable amount of time and effort to evolve; however, they are reusable for generations and the overheads related to their development have been shared across many subsequent applications, while manually engineered features would usually not be highly reusable. Overall, when weighting the ease, quantity, and the possible contribution of the graph-based features to the accuracy of the generated recommendations against the abovementioned disadvantages, it can be concluded that it is worth to generate and populate such features, when designing a recommendation engine.

21.6.2 Conclusions and future work

In this work, a new approach for improving recommendations was presented and evaluated. Unlike many previous works, which focused on addressing the recommendation problem by making improvements to the recommendation algorithms, the presented approach does so by suggesting a different way of looking at the dataset used for recommendation. It proposed representing the datasets using graphs and then to extract and populate new features from those graphs, all in a systematic fashion, and feed the new features into existing recommendation algorithms. New features and relationships that were not visible in the original tabular form can be thus uncovered. In this manner, applying this approach may compliment classical recommendation approaches and further enhance them.

The methodology, implementation, and analysis of the approach were described in detail and the approach was evaluated from two main perspectives: the overall contribution to recommendations and the impact of various graph representations. The evaluation encompassed a number of datasets, recommendation tasks, and evaluation metrics. Furthermore, the datasets belonged to four application domains (movies, music, businesses, and personal interests) that in part included metadata and in part included social links. The recommendation tasks varied from binary link predictions to star rating predictions. A number of state-of-the-art classifiers and regressors were used for the generation of the predictions. All in all, the presented evaluations examined the impact of the graph representations and showed that the approach had a profound effect on the accuracy of the recommendations.

The graph-based representation and features were shown to lead to the generation of more accurate recommendations. The variations in performance across various graph schemes and the justification for systematically extracting them, due to that, was established. The approach presented was implemented in a library and is being provided as open-source software for the community to use and build on-top. Given such a library, the cost of generating additional features that can improve recommendations becomes substantially lower, in terms of computation time and effort. It can be adopted as a natural first resort, when given a dataset and recommendation task, or as a complementary aid to enhance the standard manual feature engineering.

The conducted evaluations demonstrated the potential of the proposed approach in improving the recommendations by exploiting the benefits of links between entities and characteristics of entities extracted from the graph representations. Therefore, this work lays the foundations for further exploring how graph-based features can enhance recommender systems and automatic feature engineering in the more general context. Several variables were investigated in this work but many more require additional attention. The following paragraphs identify several directions of exploration, which were identified as possible research directions in future works.

- Temporal aspects. Given a dataset that includes dated actions that are not sparse, the time aspect can be used to build a different type of graphs. Each graph will represent a snapshot in time and will either contain or exclude a link between vertices based on whether it was available in the dataset at that time. A combination of two temporally adjacent graphs will reflect the evolution of the data over that period of time. The main question in this setting is how such temporal graphs will affect the values of features extracted from them and how a recommender systems that use these features will perform in their respective recommendation tasks.

- Weighted and labeled graphs. Several features in a dataset can be used to populate the edge labels when constructing the graph-based representation. The labels, once set, can be taken into consideration in some graph features being extracted. One example would be to calculate a weighted PageRank score that will have jumps from a vertex to its neighbors based on a skewed probability correlated with the weight on the edge linking to the neighbor. This could lead to further improvement in the recommendations; however, this requires fine-tuning of initial weights on edges that do not naturally have them, e.g., social relationship edges in the Last.fm dataset.
- Directed graphs. Similarly, in cases where the direction of the edges can be important, the process can be extended to include this aspect by generating additional graph representations, with various combinations of the edge directions. For example, in one variant, edges will be directed from the source vertex to the target vertex, in another, in the opposite direction, and in a third one there will be no direction. This will guarantee coverage in terms of expressing the direction of the edges, and the performance of the features in the various scenarios can be evaluated.

The effects of these modifications on the scalability of the approach can be handled using the previously suggested methods, either by scaling the computations (e.g., computing the features of each subgraph in a separate process), or using distributed graph computation libraries, or identifying heuristics for pruning the feature and subgraph space.

References

[1] Adomavicius, G., Tuzhilin, A.: Toward the next generation of recommender systems: A survey of the state-of-the-art and possible extensions. IEEE Transactions on Knowledge and Data Engineering, **17**(6), 734–749 (2005).

[2] Kobsa, A.: Generic user modeling systems. User Modeling and User-Adapted Interaction **11**(1–2), 49–63 (2001).

[3] Zukerman, I., Albrecht, D.W.: Predictive statistical models for user modeling. User Modeling and User-Adapted Interaction **11**(1–2), 5–18 (2001).

[4] Ricci, F., Rokach, L., Shapira, B.: Introduction to Recommender Systems Handbook. Boston, MA: Springer (2011).

[5] Berkovsky, S., Kuflik, T., Ricci, F.: The impact of data obfuscation on the accuracy of collaborative filtering. Expert Systems with Applications **39**(5), 5033–5042 (2012).

[6] Koren, Y.: The BellKor solution to the Netflix Grand Prize. Netflix Prize Documentation, vol. 81, pp. 1–10 (2009).

[7]   Guyon, I., Gunn, S., Nikravesh, M., Zadeh, L.: Feature extraction. Foundations and Applications (2006).

[8]   Nixon, M.: Feature Extraction & Image Processing. London: Academic Press (2008).

[9]   Due Trier, Ø., Jain, A.K., Taxt, T.: Feature extraction methods for character recognition-a survey. Pattern Recognition **29**(4), 641–662 (1996).

[10] Markovitch, S., Rosenstein, D.: Feature generation using general constructor functions. Machine Learning **49**(1), 59–98 (2002).

[11] Klema, V., Laub, A.J.: The singular value decomposition: Its computation and some applications. IEEE Transactions on Automatic Control **25**(2), 164–176 (1980).

[12] Wold, S., Esbensen, K., Geladi, P.: Principal component analysis. Chemometrics and Intelligent Laboratory Systems **2**(1), 37–52 (1987).

[13] Kotsiantis, S., Kanellopoulos, D., Pintelas, P.: Data preprocessing for supervised leaning. International Journal of Computer Science **1**(2), 111–117 (2006).

[14] Koren, Y., Bell, R., Volinsky, C.: Matrix factorization techniques for recommender systems. Computer **42**(8), 30–37 (2009).

[15] Tiroshi, A., Berkovsky, S., Kaafar, M.A., Chen, T., Kuflik, T.: Cross social networks interests predictions based on graph features. In: ACM Conference on Recommender Systems, RecSys'13, pp. 319–322 (2013).

[16] Tiroshi, A., Berkovsky, S., Kaafar, M.A., Vallet, D., Chen, T., Kuflik, T.: Improving business rating predictions using graph based features. In: International Conference on Intelligent User Interfaces, pp. 17–26. ACM (2014).

[17] Tiroshi, A., Berkovsky, S., Kaafar, M.A., Vallet, D., Kuflik, T.: Graph-based recommendations: Make the most out of social data. In: User Modeling, Adaptation, and Personalization, pp. 447–458. Aalborg: Springer (2014).

[18] Pham, T.N., Li, X., Cong, G., Zhang, Z.: A general graph-based model for recommendation in event-based social networks. In: International Conference on Data Engineering, ICDE, pp. 567–578 (2015).

[19] Wu, H., Yue, K., Liu, X., Pei, Y., Li, B.: Context-aware recommendation via graph-based contextual modeling and postfiltering. International Journal of Distributed Sensor Networks **2015**, 16:16–16:16 (2015).

[20] Lee, S., Park, S., Kahng, M., Lee, S.: Pathrank: Ranking nodes on a heterogeneous graph for flexible hybrid recommender systems. Expert Systems with Applications **40**(2), 684–697 (2013).

[21] Shams, B., Haratizadeh, S.: Graph-based collaborative ranking. Clinical Orthopaedics and Related Research **67**, 59–70 (2017). **abs/1604.03147**.

[22] Ostuni, V.C., Noia, T.D., Sciascio, E.D., Oramas, S., Serra, X.: A semantic hybrid approach for sound recommendation. In: International Conference on World Wide Web, pp. 85–86 (2015).

[23] Mao, K., Chen, G., Hu, Y., Zhang, L.: Music recommendation using graph based quality model. Signal Processing **120**, 806–813 (2016).

[24] Moradi, P., Ahmadian, S., Akhlaghian, F.: An effective trust-based recommendation method using a novel graph clustering algorithm. Physica A: Statistical Mechanics and its Applications **436**, 462–481 (2015).

[25] Bae, D., Han, K., Park, J., Yi, M.Y.: Apptrends: A graph-based mobile app recommendation system using usage history. In: International Conference on Big Data and Smart Computing, BIGCOMP, pp. 210–216 (2015).

[26] Cordobés, H., Chiroque, L.F., Anta, A.F., *et al.*: Empirical comparison of graph-based recommendation engines for an apps ecosystem. International Journal of Interactive Multimedia and Artificial Intelligence **3**(2), 33–39 (2015).

[27] Park, Y., Park, S., Jung, W., Lee, S.: Reversed CF: A fast collaborative filtering algorithm using a k-nearest neighbor graph. Expert Systems with Applications **42**(8), 4022–4028 (2015).

[28] Lee, K., Lee, K.: Escaping your comfort zone: A graph-based recommender system for finding novel recommendations among relevant items. Expert Systems with Applications **42**(10), 4851–4858 (2015).

[29] Vahedian, F., Burke, R.D., Mobasher, B.: Meta-path selection for extended multi-relational matrix factorization. In: Proceedings of the Florida Artificial Intelligence Research Society Conference, FLAIRS, pp. 566–571 (2016).

[30] Chianese, A., Piccialli, F.: A smart system to manage the context evolution in the cultural heritage domain. Computers & Electrical Engineering **55**, 27–38 (2016).

[31] Shen, J., Deng, C., Gao, X.: Attraction recommendation: Towards personalized tourism via collective intelligence. Neurocomputing **173**, 789–798 (2016).

[32] Godoy, D., Corbellini, A.: Folksonomy-based recommender systems: A state-of-the-art review. International Journal of Intelligent Systems **31**(4), 314–346 (2016).

[33] Batarfi, O., Shawi, R.E., Fayoumi, A.G., *et al.*: Large scale graph processing systems: Survey and an experimental evaluation. Cluster Computing **18**(3), 1189–1213 (2015).

[34] Zoidi, O., Fotiadou, E., Nikolaidis, N., Pitas, I.: Graph-based label propagation in digital media: A review. ACM Computing Surveys **47**(3), 48 (2015).

[35] Amatriain, X., Jaimes, A., Oliver, N., Pujol, J.M.: Data mining methods for recommender systems. In: Recommender Systems Handbook, pp. 39–71. Boston, MA: Springer (2011).

[36] Desrosiers, C., Karypis, G.: A comprehensive survey of neighborhood-based recommendation methods. In: Recommender Systems Handbook, pp. 107–144. Boston, MA: Springer (2011).

[37] Li, X., Chen, H.: Recommendation as link prediction: a graph kernel-based machine learning approach. In: Proceedings of the 9th ACM/IEEE-CS Joint Conference on Digital Libraries, pp. 213–216. ACM (2009).

[38] Lösch, U., Bloehdorn, S., Rettinger, A.: Graph kernels for RDF data. In: The Semantic Web: Research and Applications, pp. 134–148. Springer (2012).

[39] Konstas, I., Stathopoulos, V., Jose, J.M.: On social networks and collaborative recommendation. In: SIGIR, pp. 195–202 (2009).

[40] Ma, H., King, I., Lyu, M.R.: Learning to recommend with social trust ensemble. In: Proceedings of the 32nd International ACM SIGIR Conference on Research and Development in Information Retrieval, pp. 203–210 (2009).

[41] Said, A., Berkovsky, S., De Luca, E.W., Hermanns, J.: Challenge on context-aware movie recommendation: Camra2011. In: Proceedings of the Fifth ACM Conference on Recommender Systems, pp. 385–386. ACM (2011).

[42] Massa, P., Avesani, P.: Trust-aware recommender systems. In: Proceedings of the 2007 Conference on Recommender Systems, pp. 17–24 (2007).

[43] Quercia, D., Schifanella, R., Aiello, L.M.: The shortest path to happiness: Recommending beautiful, quiet, and happy routes in the city. In: Proceedings of the ACM Conference on Hypertext and Social Media, pp. 116–125 (2014).

[44] Perugini, S., Gonçalves, M.A., Fox, E.A.: Recommender systems research: A connection-centric survey. Journal of Intelligent Information Systems **23**(2), 107–143 (2004).

[45] Schwartz, M.F., Wood, D.: Discovering shared interests using graph analysis. Communications of the ACM **36**(8), 78–89 (1993).

[46] Kautz, H., Selman, B., Shah, M.: Referral web: Combining social networks and collaborative filtering. Communications of the ACM **40**(3), 63–65 (1997).

[47] Berge, C., Minieka, E.: Graphs and Hypergraphs, vol. 7. North-Holland Publishing Company, Amsterdam (1973).

[48] Jäschke, R., Marinho, L., Hotho, A., Schmidt-Thieme, L., Stumme, G.: Tag recommendations in folksonomies. In: Knowledge Discovery in Databases: PKDD 2007, pp. 506–514. Springer (2007).

[49] Bu, J., Tan, S., Chen, C., *et al.*: Music recommendation by unified hypergraph: combining social media information and music content. In: Proceedings of the International Conference on Multimedia, pp. 391–400. ACM (2010).

[50] Tan, S., Bu, J., Chen, C., He, X.: Using rich social media information for music recommendation via hypergraph model. In: Social Media Modeling and Computing, pp. 213–237. New York: Springer (2011).

[51] O'Donovan, J., Smyth, B.: Trust in recommender systems. In: International Conference on Intelligent User Interfaces, pp. 167–174 (2005).

[52] Domingos, P.: A few useful things to know about machine learning. Communications of the ACM **55**(10), 78–87 (2012).

[53] Scott, S., Matwin, S.: Feature engineering for text classification. In: ICML, vol. 99, pp. 379–388 (1999).

[54] Garcia, C., Tziritas, G.: Face detection using quantized skin color regions merging and wavelet packet analysis. IEEE Transactions on Multimedia **1**(3), 264–277 (1999).

[55] Bennett, J., Lanning, S.: The Netflix Prize. In: Proceedings of KDD Cup and Workshop, vol. 2007, p. 35 (2007).

[56] Burke, R.: Hybrid web recommender systems. In: The Adaptive Web, pp. 377–408. Berlin, Heidelberg: Springer (2007).

[57] Berkovsky, S., Kuflik, T., Ricci, F.: Mediation of user models for enhanced personalization in recommender systems. User Modeling and User-Adapted Interaction **18**(3), 245–286 (2008).

[58] Schafer, J.B., Konstan, J., Riedl, J.: Recommender systems in e-commerce. In: ACM Conference on Electronic Commerce, pp. 158–166 (1999).

[59] West, D.B.: Introduction to Graph Theory, vol. 2. Prentice Hall, Upper Saddle River, NJ (2001).

[60] Hagberg, A., Swart, P., Schult, D.: Exploring network structure, dynamics, and function using NetworkX. Tech. Rep., LANL (2008).

[61] Csardi, G., Nepusz, T.: The igraph software package for complex network research. InterJournal Complex Systems **1695**(5), 1–9 (2006).

[62] Bastian, M., Heymann, S., Jacomy, M., *et al.*: Gephi: An open source software for exploring and manipulating networks. In: ICWSM, vol. 8, pp. 361–362 (2009).

[63] Wilson, C., Boe, B., Sala, A., Puttaswamy, K.P., Zhao, B.Y.: User interactions in social networks and their implications. In: Proceedings of the 4th ACM European Conference on Computer Systems, pp. 205–218. ACM (2009).

[64] Lewis, K., Kaufman, J., Gonzalez, M., Wimmer, A., Christakis, N.: Tastes, ties, and time: A new social network dataset using Facebook.com. Social Networks **30**(4), 330–342 (2008).

[65] Costa, L.d.F., Rodrigues, F.A., Travieso, G., Villas Boas, P.R.: Characterization of complex networks: A survey of measurements. Advances in Physics **56**(1), 167–242 (2007).

[66] Wasserman, S.: Social network analysis: Methods and applications, vol. 8. Cambridge: Cambridge University Press (1994).

[67] Coffman, T., Greenblatt, S., Marcus, S.: Graph-based technologies for intelligence analysis. Communications of the ACM **47**(3), 45–47 (2004).

[68] Borgatti, S.P., Halgin, D.S.: Analyzing affiliation networks. The Sage Handbook of Social Network Analysis (2011).

[69] Barrat, A., Barthelemy, M., Pastor-Satorras, R., Vespignani, A.: The architecture of complex weighted networks. Proceedings of the National Academy of Sciences of the United States of America **101**(11), 3747–3752 (2004).

[70] Page, L., Brin, S., Motwani, R., Winograd, T.: The Pagerank Citation Ranking: Bringing Order to the Web. TR 1999-66, Stanford InfoLab (1999).

[71] Latapy, M., Magnien, C., Vecchio, N.D.: Basic notions for the analysis of large two-mode networks. Social Networks **30**(1), 31–48 (2008).

[72] Floyd, R.W.: Algorithm 97: Shortest path. Communications of the ACM **5**(6), 345 (1962).

[73] Breiman, L.: Random forests. Machine Learning **45**(1), 5–32 (2001).

[74] Friedman, J.H.: Greedy function approximation: A gradient boosting machine. Annals of Statistics **29**, 1189–1232 (2000).

[75] Gunn, S.R.: Support vector machines for classification and regression. ISIS Technical Report, vol. 14 (1998).

[76] Yu, H.F., Lo, H.Y., Hsieh, H.P., *et al.*: Feature engineering and classifier ensemble for KDD cup 2010. In: KDD Cup (2010).

[77] Pedregosa, F., Varoquaux, G., Gramfort, A., *et al.*: Scikit-learn: Machine learning in python. The Journal of Machine Learning Research **12**, 2825–2830 (2011).

[78]   Hall, M., Frank, E., Holmes, G., Pfahringer, B., Reutemann, P., Witten, I.H.: The WEKA data mining software: an update. ACM SIGKDD Explorations Newsletter 11(1), 10–18 (2009).

[79]   Jahrer, M., Töscher, A., Legenstein, R.: Combining predictions for accurate recommender systems. In: SIGKDD International Conference on Knowledge Discovery and Data Mining, pp. 693–702 (2010).

[80]   Bellogín, A., Cantador, I., Díez, F., Castells, P., Chavarriaga, E.: An empirical comparison of social, collaborative filtering, and hybrid recommenders. ACM Transactions on Intelligent Systems and Technology 4(1), 14 (2013).

[81]   Töscher, A., Jahrer, M., Bell, R.M.: The BigChaos solution to the Netflix Grand Prize. Netflix Prize Documentation 1, 1–52 (2009).

[82]   Cantador, I., Brusilovsky, P., Kuflik, T.: Second workshop on information heterogeneity and fusion in recommender systems. In: RecSys (2011).

[83]   Haupt, J.: Last.fm: People-powered online radio. Music Reference Services Quarterly 12(1–2), 23–24 (2009).

[84]   Shani, G., Gunawardana, A.: Evaluating recommendation systems. In: Recommender Systems Handbook, pp. 257–297. Boston, MA: Springer (2011).

[85]   Blomo, J., Ester, M., Field, M.: RecSys challenge 2013. In: Proceedings of the ACM Conference on Recommender Systems, pp. 489–490. ACM (2013).

[86]   Lam, S., Herlocker, J.: Movielens 1m Dataset (2012).

[87]   Kohavi, R.: A study of cross-validation and bootstrap for accuracy estimation and model selection. International Joint Conference on Artificial Intelligence 14(2), 1137–1145 (1995).

Chapter 22

AmritaDGA: a comprehensive data set for domain generation algorithms (DGAs) based domain name detection systems and application of deep learning

R. Vinayakumar[1], K.P. Soman[1], Prabaharan Poornachandran[2], Mamoun Alazab[3], and Sabu M. Thampi[4]

In recent days, botnet plays an important role in malware distribution. This has been used as a primary approach for the proliferation of the malicious activities via the internet by attackers. To evade blacklisting, recent botnets make use of domain flux or internet protocol (IP) flux. This work focuses on domain flux. Domain flux uses domain generation algorithms (DGAs) to generate a list of domain names based on a seed and these domain names contacts command and control (C&C) server till it gets access permission to the system. This work presents the fully labeled domain name data set entitled as AmritaDGA which can be used for doing research in the field of detecting domain names which are generated using DGAs. We evaluate the efficacy of deep learning architectures with Keras embedding as domain name representation method on AmritaDGA. AmritaDGA is composed of two data sets. The first data set is collected from the publicly available sources. The second data set is collected from an internal real-time network. The performance of the trained model on public data set is evaluated on unseen samples of a public data set and private corpora. Deep learning architectures performed well in most of the cases of test experiments. The baseline system has been made publicly available and the data set is distributed for Detecting Malicious Domain names (DMD 2018) shared task.[1]

22.1 Introduction

In initial days, the malicious authors embed the malware with the fixed domain name or the internet protocol (IP) address to reach out to the command and control (C&C) server, to get benefits, by conducting the malicious activities.

[1]Center for Computational Engineering and Networking (CEN), Amrita School of Engineering, Amrita Vishwa Vidyapeetham, India
[2]Center for Cybersecurity Systems and Networks, Amrita School of Engineering, Amrita Vishwa Vidyapeetham, India
[3]College of Engineering, IT & Environment, Charles Darwin University, NT 0810, Australia.
[4]Indian Institute of Information Technology and Management-Kerala, India
[1]http://nlp.amrita.edu/DMD2018/

In initial days, the malicious authors embed the malware with the domain name or the fixed IP address to reach out to the C&C server, to get benefits, by conducting. This can be easily detected using blacklisting method [1]. To evade blacklisting, malicious authors use domain flux and IP flux methods. Domain generation algorithms (DGAs) is a domain flux technique which facilitates to generate a large number of malicious domain names based on a seed, and a subset of malicious domain names is used constantly to get access to C&C server [2]. A seed is a number which helps to reverse engineer the particular malware. According to DGArchive[2], to date, more than 72 different DGAs are known, and the number is expected to further increase [3] as DGAs significantly improve botnets resistance to take down. The domain names which are not present receive nonexistent (NX)-Domain response message which means the corresponding domain name or IP address does not exist [4]. The amount of domains generated per day varies between 1 and 10,000 depending on the DGA [3]. Due to these reasons, detecting malicious domain names (DMD) and categorizing them into their family is considered as one of the significant tasks.

Earlier most commonly used methods for detecting malicious domain names are based on blacklisting. These methods are robust for detecting the malicious domain names which already exist in the dictionary. It completely fails to detect new malicious domain names. This approach contained two types, one is public and other is vendor-provided blacklist. The performance of vendor provided blacklist was good in comparison to the public blacklist. The detailed analysis of blacklisting was done by [1]. Blacklisting relies on domain experts as they reverse engineer the new malware and generate a signature to them. Pleiades was the first automated system which facilitated detecting DGA-based domains without reverse engineering the bot [2]. The detailed analysis of DGA detection methods was done by [5]. Most commonly used methods for DGA detection are based on machine learning with various feature engineering techniques [6–9]. Largely used feature engineering technique is n-gram text representation. In recent days, the application of deep learning architectures have performed well in comparison to the conventional machine learning algorithms in various tasks which are related to natural language processing (NLP), computer vision and speech processing [10]. This has been applied to DGA detection and categorization [9]. Most of the methods have used Keras embedding as their DGA representation method. This facilitates to learn the syntactic and semantic similarity among the characters in a domain name. The Keras embedding matrix is passed into several deep learning layers such as a convolutional neural network (CNN), recurrent neural network (RNN), long short-term memory (LSTM) and CNN-LSTM. In most of the cases, the deep learning architectures performed well. Moreover, deep learning-based method is more effective in an adversarial environment in comparison to the conventional machine learning. In this work, the application of deep learning with Keras embedding is applied toward DGA detection and categorization. The major contributions of the current research work are as follows:

1. This work proposes cyber threat situational awareness framework. It is a robust, distributed and scalable framework that can collect and process trillions of events

---

[2]https://dgarchive.caad.fkie.fraunhofer.de/

data generated from domain name system (DNS) queries by the Ethernet LAN connected hosts.

2. This work creates AmritaDGA, a comprehensive data set for DGAs.
3. The performance of various deep learning architectures is evaluated for AmritaDGA. The source code and the data set are publicly available for further research.
4. AmritaDGA has been used in DMD 2018 shared task. The overall summary of each submitted system details is discussed in detail.

The rest of the sections are organized as follows. Section 22.2 includes related work of deep learning-based DGA detection and categorization. Summary of submitted systems of DMD 2018 is given in Section 22.3. Section 22.4 provides background information about DNS protocol. Section 22.5 contains information on domain fluxing. Section 22.6 provides details of the scalable framework. Section 22.7 contains information of real-time DNS data collection inside an Ethernet LAN. The description of the data set is provided in Section 22.8. Section 22.9 provides background details of deep learning architectures. Section 22.10 discusses the details of AmritaDGANet. The experiments, results and observations for AmritaDGA are placed in Section 22.11. At last, conclusion and future work are placed in Section 22.12.

22.2   Related methods toward deep learning-based DGA detection and categorization

In order to classify DGA and Non-DGA domains, five highly efficient deep learning-based models including AlexNet, VGGNet, SqueezeNet, Inception and ResNet is proposed [11]. Unlike the conventional models which make use of hand crated features, the process of feature extraction from the raw input is automated by utilizing pretrained deep learning models and adopting transfer learning. The model achieved the best evaluation result of 99.86% true positive rates (TPRs) with a 0.011 false positive rate (FPR). The model also achieved better inference speed, performance accuracy and scalability compared to the already existing models. Modern botnets are based on DGAs which builds a resilient communication between bots and C&C servers. The basic aim is to avoid blacklisting and evade the intrusion prevention system. A thorough investigation of methods like Hidden Markov Model, C4.5 decision tree, extreme learning machine, LSTM, support vector machine (SVM), recurrent SVM, CNN-LSTM, bidirectional LSTM is done in which recurrent SVM and bidirectional LSTM achieved highest detection rate on both binary and multiclass classification problem. In [12], a comparative study of five different deep learning architectures for DGA detection problem is put forward. All the models had character level embedding and belonged to either RNN, CNN or hybrid deep learning architectures. The chosen models were able to detect 97%–98% of malicious domain names against an FPR of 0.001. On evaluation and training, the results confirmed that these CNN and RNN-based architectures displayed similar accuracy, adding to the favor of simpler architectures which requires comparatively shorter training and also faces less overfitting problems. In [13], a scalable distributed framework using Apache spark for the analysis of the huge volume of DNS logs in Ethernet local area network (LAN) and to trace the attack patterns in order to prevent further attacks is introduced. For the detection of malicious domain names, both conventional machine learning classifiers and deep learning models such as RNN and LSTM were employed and the results were evaluated. Deep learning-based approaches achieved results better since they are capable of figuring out the correct features implicitly. In [14], a relevant machine learning approach for DGA detection using RNN network is introduced. The model achieved a high precision on a huge data set and was able to automatically detect 93% of malware-generated domain names for an FPR of 1:100. The fact that the model does not require any handcrafted feature and can be easily retrained to detect new malware contributes to its relevance. And also, the model works using the raw domain names and does not require any additional contextual information. In [15], a DGA classifier using LSTM is developed. The model obtained high accuracy for multiclass classification giving the ability to attribute a DGA generated domain to a specific malware family. The LSTM-based technique is easy to implement and it also outperformed all the state-of-the-art models by attaining a 90% detection rate with a 1:10,000 FPR. In [16], leveraged the embedding concepts from NLP into cybersecurity uses cases to propose a new in-house model christened S.P.O.O.F Net, which is a combination of CNN and LSTM Networks when incorporated. On evaluation, S.P.O.O.F Net achieved an accuracy of 98.3% for DGA detection and 99% for malicious URL detection and hence outperformed current state-of-the-art techniques. S.P.O.O.F Net does not suffer from the drawbacks of conventional threat-detection strategies like the need of domain expert for training database maintenance, blacklisting and sinkholing. Since deep learning architectures can obtain optimal feature representations themselves, they are regarded as having a black box view which makes them less vulnerable to malicious adversaries. In [17], a deep learning-based-method to classify huge amount of real traffic data into DGA and non-DGA is proposed. Since the model can deal with the massive amount of real data, it ensures better performance also. The methodology involves simple filtering steps to attain more representative DNS traffic samples, automatic feature extraction as well as online learning to adapt to new DGA domain patterns. This deep learning model resulted to be better DGA detector in comparison to conventional methods. Along with this evaluation, it was also discovered that our model was tuned and set in such a way that it can get a low FPR such as 0.01%. Detection and classification of the pseudorandom domain names without relying on the feature engineering or any other linguistic, contextual or semantics and statistical information is evaluated by adopting deep learning approaches. The family of the RNN and its hybrid network (formed using CNN) has significantly performed well in comparison to the methods of handcrafted features and bigrams in both binary and multiclass classification settings.

For deep learning approaches in DGA-generated domain name analysis and its classification, [18] stays as a standard framework to comprehend their viability. To address the cybersecurity attacks and malicious activities in the digital world, numerous security solutions have been proposed. The reasons which lead to inefficiency in attack detection on the devices are (1) the absence of computational power for detecting attacks, (2) the absence of interfaces that could possibly show a compromise on these devices and (3) the absence of the capacity to cooperate with the framework to execute diagnostic tools. A study has been carried out in cyber threat situational awareness on cybersecurity events and a framework with high scalability is created which is the first of its kind to employ deep learning techniques for dealing with extensive scale information handled in real time. This is the main structure that works over several Internet service providers, this works as the main structure which acts as a single unified system providing cyber threat situational awareness at an internet service provider (ISP) level [19].

22.3   Summary of submitted systems of DMD 2018 shared task

In recent years, a lot of research is being carried out in DMD using various techniques such as domain name based, network traffic based and the combination of these methods. Malware domains generated by domain generation algorithms (DGA) are highly dynamic in nature. The conventional approach of blacklisting the malicious domains is a time-consuming approach and is not effective, as the DGA randomly generate the domain names for the malware. For real-time applications, malware detection is to be performed on the fly, and hence sophisticated techniques are in demand to address this issue. Even though various machine learning techniques are employed for this purpose, the performance of such algorithms depends on how good the features are designed. The data set for all the related works mentioned here is provided by the shared task on DMD 2018.

Researcher's analyzed the possibility of detection of malicious domain names using deep neural network based models. In a study, Bidirectional LSTM network has been developed and trained on the DMD 2018 data set [20]. Two tasks were given. The first task was to identify the malicious domain name, and the second task was to identify the class of domain name. In this study, the researchers were able to produce an accuracy of 98.9% in task 1 and 69.7% in task 2. Another study compares the performance of various machine learning-based approaches such as featureful (Random Forest (RF)) and featureless (Deep Neural Network)-based classifiers for DGA detection, trained with various sources of publicly available and DMD 2018 provided data [21]. For the binary classification task of determining whether a domain name is benign or malicious, researchers obtained the best results with a deep learning approach where the features are learned automatically from the data during the training process. For the multiclass classification task of determining which malware family a DGA domain name belongs to, they obtained the best results with a one versus rest RF model trained on 28 features extracted from the domain names. Real-time prediction of malicious domains generated using the domain generation algorithms (DGAs) is a demanding as well as difficult tasks in cybersecurity where deep learning architectures are able to achieve promising results. A study uses LSTM architecture for prediction of the malicious domains that are generated using the DGAs [22]. For the binary class classification, the LSTM model gave 98.7% and 71.3% accuracy and for the multi-class classification 68.3% and 67.0% accuracy on two different data sets. Two diversified data sets were used to analyze the robustness of the LSTM architecture. Researchers were able to achieve an overall second position in the shared task of DMD 2018. Researchers built a system based on a deep learning architecture using character embeddings and bidirectional LSTM [23]. In task 1, an accuracy of 98.1% and 71.4% was achieved for the testing collected publicly and via real-time system, respectively. The results for the multiclass task produced 65.5% and 67.1% in respective testing sets. Another study uses a transfer learning technique by combining the best performing CNN with the machine learning algorithms such as Naive Bayes classifier for detection and classification of DGA-generated domains [24]. Researchers conducted baseline experiments with CNN alone by varying the number of convolution layers and optimizers. Using the data set released by DMD 2018 shared task for both binary classification and multiclass classification scenario, this study using methods such as CNN with NB for binary classification has been awarded the first rank in this DMD 2018 shared task. Reference [25] shows a string of characters given as input from the domain name and classifying them as either benign or malicious domain name using deep learning architectures such as LSTM and bidirectional LSTM. Using this method, researchers have observed that this model for binary classification performed better than multiclass classification. From this study, it can be inferred that the true negative metric is better than true positive. The performance of this study can be further improved by employing character to vector representation algorithm. A study uses the DNN along with 3-gram representation to transform the domain names into numeric representation [26]. Deep neural networks have a certain level of complexity since it uses sophisticated mathematical modeling to process data. The network parameters and network 3-g representation are used to transform the domain names into a numeric representation. The network parameters and network structures for DNN are selected by hyper-parameter selection method. All experiments are run until 100 times with learning rate inside the range 0.01–0.5. In this study, the researchers have obtained an accuracy of 97.6% and 78.2% in binary class classification task and an accuracy of 60.1% and 53.1% in the multi-classification task.

22.4   Domain name system (DNS)

Internet the crucial part of the current global communication scenario and infrastructure since it connects billions of nodes facilitating communication. The most important protocol that the Internet uses, also known as the core domain, is the domain name system (DNS). Figure 22.1 illustrates the hierarchical level in a DNS. Since the Internet addresses comprise a long sequence of a number, they become difficult for people to memorize. This is where the DNS protocol comes to play. It provides human-readable IP names that correspond to this Internet addresses.

   Usually, the access to the Internet is through the use of a web browser such that the domain name is typed in the address bar of the browser and the end user can exchange information and transactions through the web pages and portals. There are two different types of classification available for the DNS server: non-recursive/ iterative servers and recursive servers. Iterative DNS servers are those in which queries returns an answer without querying other DNS server, even if they cannot provide a definitive answer. Therefore, it acts as the State of Authority. Unlike non-recursive servers, recursive servers respond to the client request from the DNS server that is

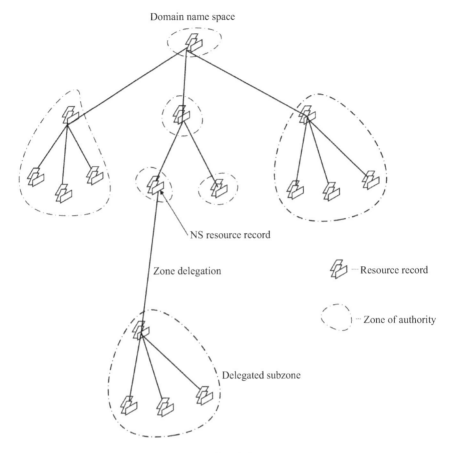

Domain name space

NS resource record

Zone delegation

Resource record

Zone of authority

Delegated subzone

Figure 22.1   Hierarchical domain name system

set to query subsequent DNS server until a definitive answer is returned as shown in Figure 22.2. Figure 22.3 shows an example for recursive DNS servers. Some of the popular cyberattack that compromises the computer security is the distributed denial of service (DDoS) attacks, DNS cache poisoning, unauthorized use of resources, root name server performance degradation, etc. Among malware, botnets are highly advanced malware which when infecting a system or a host can be automated to do various malicious works such as stealing personal and sensitive data, keystroke logging, sending malware, participation in C&C-based DDoS attacks. Other than these attacks, it can affect local systems with various malware such as Adware's, Spyware and Click fraud. Click fraud feeds on the pay-per-click online advertising scheme by automating fraud computer program which will click an advertisement without the knowledge of the end user with an intent to make financial gain illegitimately. One of the malicious activities performed by botnets is Fast flux. There are two types of fast flux, they are domain flux and IP flux. This work is mainly studies domain flux.

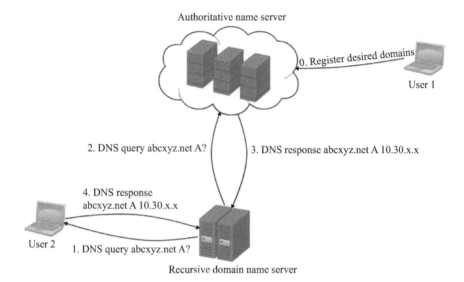

Figure 22.2   *Working flow of a legitimate DNS query*

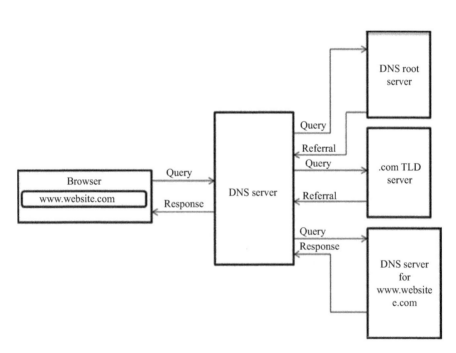

Figure 22.3   *Recursive DNS query*

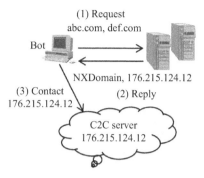

Figure 22.4   Discover process of DGA based botnet

22.5   Domain fluxing

Domain fluxing is a technique in which domain names linked with the IP address of C&C servers are frequently changed to keep the botnets in operation. To carry out this operation, bot master makes use of domain generation algorithm (DGA) to generate domain names on a large scale which can bypass blacklisting and heuristics methods for DMD. There are different types of DGAs such as Conflicker, Torpig, Kraken, Murofet. Kwyjibo is harder to detect since its uses advanced DGA which generates domain names that are very similar to English dictionary words. In the process of domain fluxing, randomly generated domain names are used by botnets to communicate with their C&C server. Botnets try to connect with these C&C servers using hit and trial method. As a result, the majority of trials create domain queries for which there exists no record or IP address. Such queries are known as NX-domain response queries which are illustrated in Figure 22.4.

22.6   Scalable framework

To meet the requirements such as collecting and processing the data in real time, a highly scalable framework has been developed to handle several billions of data events per minute which are produced by DNS. In this framework, the data is collected in a distributed manner using DNS sensors. The configuration details of the framework cannot be revealed due to the confidential nature of the research. Each system has configuration of (32 GB RAM, 2 TB hard disk, Intel(R) Xeon(R) CPU E3-1220 v3 @ 3.10 GHz) running over 1 Gbps Ethernet network. Apache Spark [27] cluster set up is developed on top of Apache Hadoop [28].

22.7   Real-time DNS data collection in an Ethernet LAN

To capture the DNS event traffic, four different classifications are (1) using hub, (2) port mirroring, (3) bridge mode, (4) ARP spoof and (5) remote packet capture. Port mirroring is used in our experimental setup.

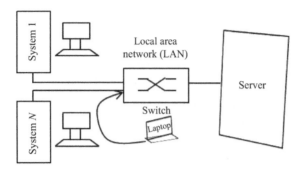

Figure 22.5   Port mirroring

Figure 22.5 shows the process of port mirroring in which the user can duplicate the traffic and mirror it to a port when they want to. A protocol analyzer can be used to receive the mirrored data. With the use of a protocol analyzer on the port, the administrator can analyze the switch performance. Depending on manufacturers, port mirroring is known by different names such as switched port analyzer is the name for port mirroring by CISCO.

At first, the port mirroring is configured by means of assigning a port from which we copy all packets and assign every other port to which one's packet might be dispatched. At the point when packets are received for quite a while, in some cases, packets are exchanged to some different ports. This issue is comprehended with the use of a protocol analyzer on the receiver's port. Every single section of the mirrored data is being monitored by the protocol analyzer one by one. Such a protocol analyzer is known as the packet sniffer. Intrusion detection systems (IDS) and other analyzing tools are installed using port mirroring. Network traffic is sent to network analyzer tools by port mirroring. Screen events such as IDS, network anomaly detection, monitoring and forecasting network trends are analyzed with the help of network analyzer tools.

Using default mode, the network traffic of every connected host is not available in our experimental LAN. Network adapters ensure that the packets ought to be received by the predetermined receiver. With the assistance of Ethernet LAN, the issue is solved where it can acknowledge packets in spite of the fact that those are not routed to them. In this approach, the network adapter grants permission to receive every packet which is streaming inside the network. We experimented with the hub-based network so as to receive all the network traffic within the LAN. To achieve this, we switched the network adapter to the promiscuous mode which gave an added advantage as there is no compelling reason for not using network analyzers on various ports. The hub transmits the received packets to every single other port. In this way, connecting with any of the port and the network traffic is observed.

We have a switch-based LAN in our experimental setup which transmits packets to just a single port and keeps records of all connected host-media access control (MAC) addresses and the related port address. This recognizes connected hosts with the predetermined port. At the point when a switch gets a packet, it scans for the MAC

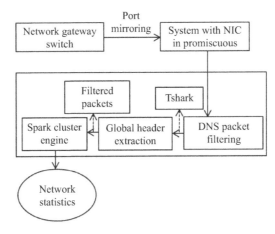

Figure 22.6   DNS packets collection

address in the record and picks the correct port to forward the packet. This enables the adapter to acknowledge only those packets which are routed to corresponding host. It limits the network load without limiting its bandwidth. As shown in Figure 22.6, we have connected with a particular switch port and utilized the promiscuous mode. A LAN cable is connected from the port mirroring enabled port on the switch which is connected to a computer with its network interface card (NIC) in promiscuous mode. This enables the NIC to gather every packet from the network.

The storage of DNS logs is in unstructured text format. To stay away from memory issues every day, the gathered DNS information is compacted and changed to slave nodes in a distributed computing platform. The extracted DNS log contains much data and looks more mind boggling. In any case, we apply to preprocessing for extracting the time, date, IP and domain field information. With a specific end goal to keep the required data for some time later, the preprocessed DNS logs are independently stored in Apache Cassandra [29] database, appeared in Figure 22.7. An example DNS log is illustrated using Figure 22.8.

22.8   Description of data set

AmritaDGA data was collected from both the public and private sources. It contains a very large number of domain names, categorized into two categories. One is just classifying domain names as either benign or malicious and another one is categorizing malicious domain names to their corresponding DGA malware family. To make a comprehensive data set addressing ongoing challenges that exist in DMD, the domain names are collected from both the public sources and private real-time DNS events. To meet the zero-day malware detection, the significance of the time-split strategy was used in the data-collection process. The malicious domain names for the first data set were collected using the publicly available DGAs [30], OSINT DGA feeds [31] and

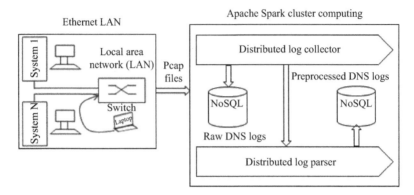

Figure 22.7   DNS data processing

```
19:35:04.167395 IP censerver.local.27062 > 172.17.9.2.domain: 30578+ [b2&3=0x182] A?
www.mail.bel.co.in. (36)E..@..@.@.p...h...
.i..5.,c.wr...........www.mail.bel.co.in.....19:35:10.491014 IP censerver.local.65203 >
172.17.9.2.domain: 43048+ A? a.sitemeter.com. (33)E..=..@.@.p...h...   .....5.)t-.
(...........a   sitemeter.com.....19:35:10.491507 IP censerver.local.40442 >
172.17.9.2.domain: 42818+ A? www.google-analytics.com. (42)E..F..@.@.p...h...
....5.2>..B...........www.google-analytics.com.....19:35:11.387909 IP
censerver.local.61213 > 172.17.9.2.domain: 58471+ A? www.google.com. (32)
E..<..@.@.p...h...   ....5.(.L.g...........www.google.com.....19:35:11.402801 IP
censerver.local.32595 > 172.17.9.2.domain: 57996+ A? googleads.g.doubleclick.net. (45)
E..I..@.@.p...h...   ..5.5.5.............  googleads.g.doubleclick.net.....
19:35:11.402970 IP censerver.local.36159 > 172.17.9.2.domain: 1089+ A? r.casalemedia.com.
(35)E..?..@.@.p...h...  ..?.5.+*:.A...........r.casalemedia.com.....19:35:11.403070 IP
censerver.local.15131 > 172.17.9.2.domain: 18278+ A? t0.gstatic.com. (32)
E..<..@.@.p...h...   ..;..5.(..Gf...........t0.gstatic.com.....19:35:11.403128 IP
censerver.local.65465 > 172.17.9.2.domain: 17500+ A? t3.gstatic.com. (32)
E..<..@.@.p...h...   ....5.(74D\...........t3.gstatic.com.....19:35:11.403248 IP
censerver.local.49894 > 172.17.9.2.domain: 60342+ A? www.facebook.com. (34)
E..>..@.@.p...h...   ....5."............www.facebook.com.....19:35:11.547008 IP
```

Figure 22.8   DNS log

netlab-360 [32]. The legitimate domain names for the first data set were collected from the Alexa [33] and OpenDNS [34]. There are 20 DGAs that were considered. The second data set is collected privately within a lab using port mirroring approach, as already discussed. The detailed statistics of the data set is shown in Tables 22.1 and 22.2. Training and Testing 1 are collected from a public source and Testing 2 is collected privately. Recently, the data set was used as part of the shared task on DMD 2018[3], a workshop colocated with ICACCI'18[4] and SSCC'18.[5] The data analysis of AmritaDGA features problem statements in the field of conventional machine learning, deep learning and text analysis in cybersecurity. This data set was made publically available to the research community without any costs.[6] It can be used for further research in the field of DMD. The specification details of AmritaDGA and its statistics are summarized in Tables 22.3 and 22.4, respectively.

---

[3] http://nlp.amrita.edu/DMD2018/
[4] http://icacci-conference.org/2018/
[5] http://www.acn-conference.org/sscc2018/
[6] https://github.com/vinayakumarr/DMD2018

Table 22.1   Data statistics for classifying domain name into either benign or DGA

Type	Benign	Malicious	Total
Training	655,683	135,056	790,739
Testing 1	2,349,331	108,076	2,457,407
Testing 2	182	2,740	2,922

Table 22.2   Data statistics for classifying domain name into either benign or DGA and categorizing DGA generated domain named to DGA family

Class	Training	Testing 1	Testing 2
Benign	100,000	120,000	40,000
Banjori	15,000	25,000	10,000
Corebot	15,000	25,000	10,000
Dircrypt	15,000	25,000	300
Dnschanger	15,000	25,000	10,000
Fobber	15,000	25,000	800
Murofet	15,000	16,667	5,000
Necurs	12,777	20,445	6,200
Newgoz	15,000	20,000	3,000
Padcrypt	15,000	20,000	3,000
Proslikefan	15,000	20,000	3,000
Pykspa	15,000	25,000	2,000
Qadars	15,000	25,000	2,300
Qakbot	15,000	25,000	1,000
Ramdo	15,000	25,000	800
Ranbyus	15,000	25,000	500
Simda	15,000	25,000	3,000
Suppobox	15,000	20,000	1,000
Symmi	15,000	25,000	500
Tempedreve	15,000	25,000	100
Tinba	15,000	25,000	700
Total	**397,777**	**587,112**	**103,200**

To understand the characteristics of train and test data sets of DMD 2018, various visualization are provided. Train data set visualization is shown in Figures 22.9–22.13. Test data set 1 visualization is shown in Figures 22.14–22.18. Test data set 2 visualization is shown in Figures 22.19–22.23. The detailed description for visualization used for generating Figures 22.9–22.13 are given below:

1. Box plot grouped by class character length for AmritaDGA train data set: The character length distribution for both the DGA generated domain names and legitimate domain names is plotted using the box plot for comparison. Box plot is

Table 22.3   Specification of AmritaDGA data set

Subject area	Machine learning, deep learning, cybersecurity, natural-language processing, machine intelligence
More specific subject area	Detection of malicious and DGA generated domain name, Character level text classification
How data was acquired	• Public data set (Training and Testing 1): The malicious domain names for the first data set were collected using the publicly available DGAs [30], OSINT DGA feeds [31] and netlab-360 [32]. The legitimate domain names for the first data set were collected from the Alexa [33] and OpenDNS [34] • Private data set (Testing 2): The second data set is collected privately within a lab using port mirroring approach
Data format	Preprocessed domain name is available in text format
Data source location	• Public data set (Training and Testing 1): Publicly available DGAs [30], OSINT DGA feeds [31] and netlab-360 [32]. The legitimate domain names for the first data set were collected from the Alexa [33] and OpenDNS [34] • Private data set (Testing 2): CEN Lab, Amrita Vishwa Vidyapeetham
Data accessibility	The data set is available at [35]. This is publicly available for further research toward research purpose

Table 22.4   Value of the data

- In recent days, attackers use malicious domain names to run attacks over the Internet. Thus, detecting malicious domain names has been considered as a vivid area of research. The AmritaDGA is a resource that can be used to learn the patterns to differentiate the malicious domain and benign domain names and to categorize malicious domain names to their DGA family. This requires the techniques of natural language processing and machine learning. The improvement in detection of malicious domain names of AmritaDGA remains as a research area for the research community.
- The AmritaDGA data set has unique domain names in both the training and testing. Two types of data sets are collected. This is due to show the performance of the machine learning model on the testing data set of public and private sources.
- The meet zero-day malware detection, the data set collection carefully followed the time-related information.
- This is the only potential data set publicly available for research. This data set is used for DMD 2018. This was the second shared task in the cybersecurity domain.

used for depicting and comparing the class data graphically interpreting through the quartiles. Box plot consists of box and whisker. The line on the box represents the median. It gives the dispersion of the data, and distribution of data can be visualized. It infers the dispersion and skewness of the data. Box plot is nonparametric, i.e., it is plotted without requiring the prior knowledge of the underlying statistical distribution of the data set. The statistics for train data set were shown in Figure 22.9. Box plot displays the distribution of the data by dividing it into mainly five quartiles (minimum, Q1, median, Q3, and maximum).

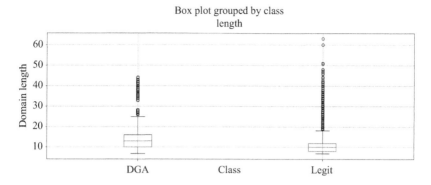

Figure 22.9   Box plot grouped by class length for AmritaDGA train data set

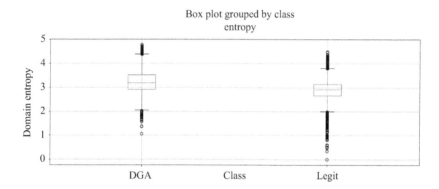

Figure 22.10   Box plot grouped by class entropy for AmritaDGA train data set

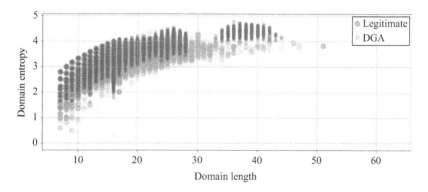

Figure 22.11   DGA domains do tend to have higher entropy than legitimate on average

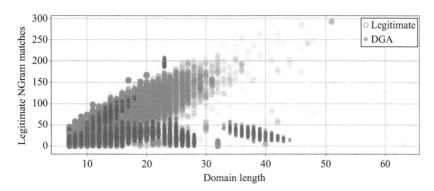

Figure 22.12   Legitimate N-Grams feature can help us differentiate between legitimate and DGA

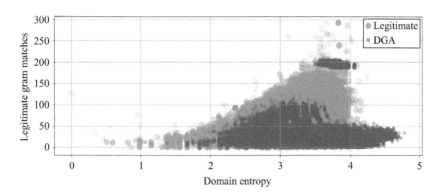

Figure 22.13   Legitimate NGrams feature can help us differentiate between legitimate and DGA

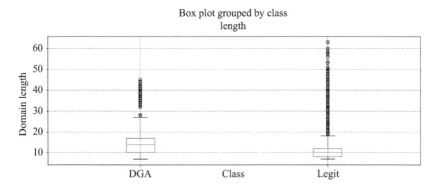

Figure 22.14   Box plot grouped by class length for AmritaDGA test 1 data set

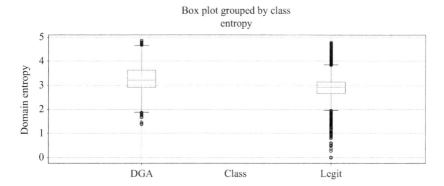

Figure 22.15   Box plot grouped by class entropy for AmritaDGA test 1 data set

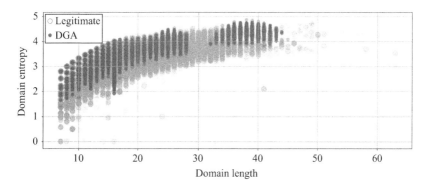

Figure 22.16   DGA domains do tend to have higher entropy than legitimate on average

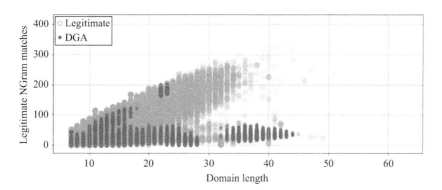

Figure 22.17   Legitimate NGrams feature can help us differentiate between legitimate and DGA

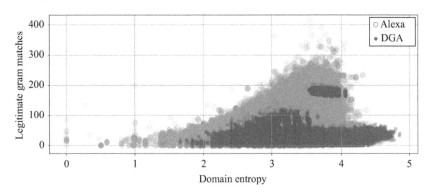

Figure 22.18   *Legitimate NGrams feature can help us differentiate between legitimate and DGA*

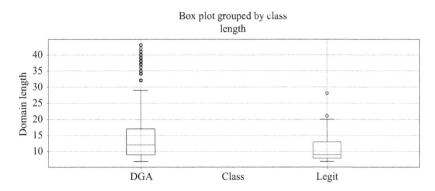

Figure 22.19   *Box plot grouped by class length for AmritaDGA test 1 data set*

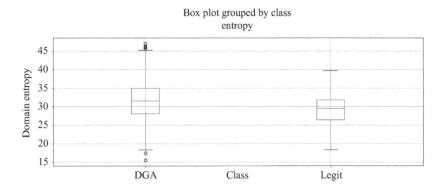

Figure 22.20   *Box plot grouped by class entropy for AmritaDGA test 1 data set*

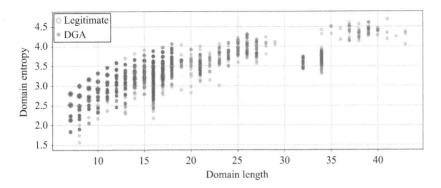

Figure 22.21 DGA domains do tend to have higher entropy than legitimate on average

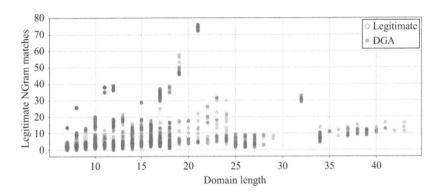

Figure 22.22 Legitimate NGrams feature can help us differentiate between legitimate and DGA

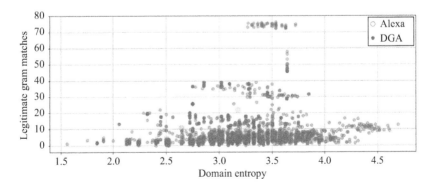

Figure 22.23 Legitimate NGrams feature can help us differentiate between legitimate and DGA

The box is around the 25th and 75th percentiles that captures the middle 50 percent of observations. Median is the center line drawn at the 50th percentile. The legitimate domain has more negative skewness compared to the DGA-generated domains. The data is distributed uniformly along the whisker for the legitimate domains, but for DGA domains, it is concentrated densely at some fixed points.

2. Box plot grouped by class entropy for AmritaDGA train data set: The box plot using the class entropy is shown in Figure 22.10 for train data set. Entropy-based feature selection is frequently used for NLP applications. Entropy attribute indicates the average uncertainty of a single random variable. Entropy is the amount of the uncertainty in a random variable. The entropy for the DGA-generated domains and the legitimate domains can help in distinguishing the respective classes. In DGA botnet detection, it is the information that is produced on the average for each 1-gram of the domain.

3. Figure 22.11 shows the scatter plot that is plotted using the domain name length versus the domain name entropy for train data set. The Figure 22.11 shows that the DGA domains do tend to have higher entropy than legitimate on average. We can clearly distinguish the DGA domains and the legitimate domains because of the differences in the entropy. The DGA domains will have high entropy when compared to the legitimate domains because the DGA generate the domains using a random distribution.

4. Legitimate n-gram feature can help us differentiate between legitimate and DGA: n-gram is the widely used technique for the detection of DGA generated domains. n-gram can be character level and word level but here character level n-gram with length 3, 4 and 5 are used. The minimum document frequency is 0.1% which signifies that n-gram should occur in at least 0.1% of the total domain names. A dictionary of legitimate n-gram is created. n-gram matching is performed for DGA domains and legitimate domains and shown in Figure 22.12. The difference for the DGA domains and legitimate domains is clearly inferred from the figures.

5. Domain name entropy versus legitimate n-gram matches: A dictionary of legitimate n-gram is created and matching is performed. Entropy for all the domain names is calculated. Domain name entropy versus legitimate n-gram matches is shown in Figure 22.13. The domain entropy for DGA generated domains have a higher variance and lower mean when compared to the legitimate domains. This can be used as a feature for detecting the DGA domains.

The above-discussed methodology is used for generating images. Test data set 1 visualization is shown in Figures 22.14–22.18. Test data set 2 visualization is shown in Figures 22.19–22.23. The detailed description for visualization used for generating Figures 22.9–22.13. Interpretability is crucial for the classical machine learning and deep learning architectures because a single wrong decision of domain name can be extremely cause many damages. To identify the reason behind an accurate and as well as wrong decision by both the machine learning and deep learning model, the above discussed visualization methods can be employed. These visualization methods help to understand the characteristics of domain name and most importantly the distribution of domain name samples.

22.9   Deep learning

22.9.1   Recurrent structures

The most commonly used recurrent-based sequence models are RNN, LSTM and gated recurrent unit (GRU). These networks are referred to as recurrent since units in RNN have a self-loop. This loop stores detail of all the previous calculations computed [36]. RNN can generally refer back only to few time steps, and it faces a problem of vanishing gradient, which made to compare the results with the improved versions of it. LSTM [37] and GRU [38] do not face a problem of vanishing gradient in comparison to RNN, and they are efficient in handling long-term dependencies. LSTM has memory block instead of simple units in RNN. This helps to store the previous information, and this information is controlled by gating functions. GRU is a variant of LSTM which has the capability to reduce the computational complexity of the LSTM network. Given an input sequence $X = (x_1, x_2, \ldots, x_T)$, the transition function for RNN is mathematically represented as follows:

$$h = \sigma(w_{xh}x + w_{hh}h + b_h) \tag{22.1}$$

$$o_t = A(w_{oh}h_t + b_o) \tag{22.2}$$

The transition function for LSTM is mathematically represented as follows:

$$i_t = \sigma(w_{xi}x_t + w_{hi}h_{t-1} + w_{mi}m_{t-1} + b_i) \tag{22.3}$$

$$f_t = \sigma(w_{xf}x_t + w_{hf}h_{t-1} + w_{mf}m_{t-1} + b_f) \tag{22.4}$$

$$m_t = f_t \odot m_{t-1} + i_t \odot \tanh(w_{xm}x_t + w_{hm}h_{t-1} + b_m) \tag{22.5}$$

$$o_t = \sigma(w_{xo}x_t + w_{ho}h_{t-1} + w_{mo}m_t + b_o) \tag{22.6}$$

$$h_t = o_t \odot \tanh(m_t). \tag{22.7}$$

The transition function for GRU is mathematically represented as follows:

$$i\_f_t = \sigma(w_{xi\_f}x_t + w_{hi\_f}h_{t-1} + b_{i\_f}) \tag{22.8}$$

$$f_t = \sigma(w_{xf}x_t + w_{hf}h_{t-1} + b_f) \tag{22.9}$$

$$m_t = \tanh(w_{xm}x_t + w_{hm}(f \odot h_{t-1}) + b_m) \tag{22.10}$$

$$h_t = f \odot h_{t-1} + (1 - f) \odot m \tag{22.11}$$

where h denoted hidden state, A is nonlinear activation function, i, f, o and m denotes input gate, forget gate, output gate and memory cell, respectively, i_f is a combination of input and forget gate typically called as update gate.

22.9.2   Convolutional neural network

CNN is the most commonly used method in image processing [32]. This is primarily composed of convolution, pooling and fully connected layer. A convolution layer has a number of filters or kernels which it learns to extract specific types of features from the data. The kernel is a 1D window normally in texts and signals which is slid over the input data performing the convolution operation. Convolutional layer follows the

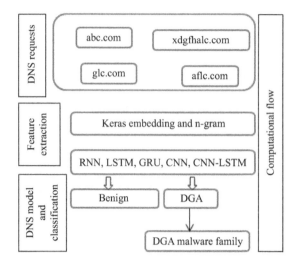

Figure 22.24   AmritaDGANet

pooling layer which contains max-pooling or min-pooling operation. Pooling layer is a downsampling operation and it reduces the CNN layer features. This reduced feature representation is, in turn, passed into one or more fully connected layers for classification. Otherwise, the reduced feature representation is passed into any other recurrent structures to capture the sequence information among the character in the domain name.

22.10   AmritaDGANet

The proposed architecture for detection and classification of DGA-generated domain name is typically called as AmritaDGANet. An overview of a new in-house model christened AmritaDGANet (see Figure 22.24) which is a combination of specialized deep learning architectures like CNN and LSTM. AmritaDGANet is composed of three main important sections. In the input section, it takes domain names, applies to preprocess, created a dictionary and generates embedding vector by following Keras embedding. The embedding vectors are passed into different deep learning architectures such as RNN, LSTM, GRU, CNN and CNN-LSTM to learn optimal feature representation. Deep learning layers follow a fully connected layer for classification. The best performed model is a combination of a CNN and LSTM is employed in AmritaDGANet. All architectures have used learning rate 0.01, the batch size of 64 and *adam* as an optimizer. A dictionary size is 39 and the Keras embedding size is set to 128. To give freedom in learning domain name representation, the Keras embedding size is set to 128. All recurrent structures contain 128 units/memory blocks. Followed by a full connected layer for classification, CNN layer contains 64 filters with filter length 3 and followed by a max-pooling layer with pooling size 2. Max-pooling layer follows two fully connected layers. First, fully connected layer contains 128 units followed by dropout 0.4. Dropout randomly removes the neurons and its connections randomly to avoid overfitting. The second fully connected layer is used for classification. The pooling layer outputs are passed into LSTM to learn the sequence information among characters in the domain name. This layer contains memory blocks of size 70. For binary classification, the fully connected layer contains *sigmoid* activation function and for multi-class classification *softmax* is used. The loss function for *sigmoid* and *softmax* activation function are defined as binary cross entropy and categorical cross entropy. These are mathematically defined as follows.

$$loss\,(pd, ed) = -\frac{1}{N} \sum_{i=1}^{N} [ed_i \log pd_i + (1 - ed_i) \log (1 - pd_i)] \tag{22.12}$$

$$loss\,(pd, ed) = -\sum_{x} pd(x) \log (ed(x)) \tag{22.13}$$

where *ed* is true probability distribution and *pd* is predicted probability distribution. We have used *adam* as an optimizer to minimize the loss of binary cross entropy and categorical cross entropy.

22.11   AmritaDGA data analysis, results and observations

All deep learning architectures are implemented using TensorFlow[7] with Keras[8] as a higher level framework. Machine learning algorithms are implemented using Scikit-learn.[9] All experiments are run on GPU-enabled computers. The parameters of deep learning and machine learning algorithms are set based on following hyperparameter selection method. Initially, all models are trained using the training data set and evaluated its performance on the testing data set. All deep learning architectures are run till 100 epochs during training. The performance of all deep learning architectures in terms of accuracy is shown in Figure 22.25. All deep learning architectures obtained the highest training accuracy within 10 epochs. After 10 epochs, the performance of RNN started to decrease due to overfitting. Once GRU reaches 40 epochs, the performance started to decrease, and after 90 epochs, the GRU has seen the sudden increase in accuracy. But the performance of LSTM, CNN-LSTM and CNN maintained consistent accuracy till 100 epochs. Among all, LSTM performed well. The combination of hybrid pipeline CNN-LSTM performance is good in comparison to CNN. To evaluate the trained model on completely unseen samples, the trained model on public data set is evaluated on the private data set. In all the cases, deep learning architectures performed well in comparison to the machine learning algorithm. Moreover, the performance of CNN-LSTM pipeline is good in comparison to the other deep learning architectures. The detailed results of both binary and multi-class

[7]https://www.tensorflow.org/
[8]https://keras.io/
[9]http://scikit-learn.org/stable/

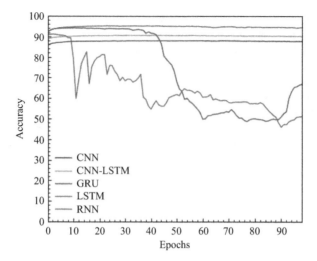

Figure 22.25   Train accuracy over epochs

classification are reported in Table 22.5. In binary class classification, the first row results of each deep learning model are for Testing 1 and second row results of each deep learning model are for Testing 2. In multi-class classification, the first row results of each deep learning model are for data set 2 and second row results of each deep learning model are for data set 1. The receiver-operating characteristic (ROC) curve for Testing data sets 1 and 2 is shown in Figures 22.26 and 22.27. The detailed results in terms of TPR and FPR of each class for Testings 1 and 2 are reported in Tables 22.6 and 22.7, respectively.

AmritaDGA data set is used for the Shared task on DMD 2018 [35]. Totally, 19 teams registered, the baseline system and the data set are shared with the participants [39]. Out of 19, 8 teams submitted models. The detailed results are reported in Tables 22.8–22.11 for binary and multi-class classification, respectively [35].

22.12   Conclusion and future work

This work proposes AmritaDGA which can be used for research in the field of DMD. Additionally, the performances of various deep learning architectures are evaluated on AmritaDGA to detect and categorize malicious domain names to corresponding DGA family. The experiments of deep learning performed well, and the results of most of the deep learning architectures are closer. The performance of these models can be enhanced by following hyperparameter-selection methods. Thus, this has remained as one of the significant direction toward future work. To find the best model and its performance, the DGA data set is used as part of DMD 2018 shared task. We have made both the data set, and the baseline system is available for further research.

Table 22.5   Detailed results of binary and multi-class classification

Model	Accuracy	Precision	Recall	F1-score
Binary classification				
RNN	0.979	0.688	0.944	0.796
	0.767	1.000	0.752	0.858
LSTM	0.988	0.797	0.960	0.871
	0.700	0.999	0.680	0.809
GRU	0.987	0.791	0.946	0.861
	0.718	0.999	0.700	0.823
CNN	0.978	0.673	0.965	0.793
	0.759	0.999	0.744	0.853
CNN-LSTM	0.985	0.772	0.938	0.847
	0.727	0.999	0.709	0.829
Multi-class classification				
RNN	0.662	0.627	0.662	0.609
	0.658	0.636	0.658	0.626
LSTM	0.669	0.695	0.669	0.627
	0.672	0.663	0.672	0.622
GRU	0.665	0.718	0.665	0.637
	0.649	0.655	0.649	0.601
CNN	0.643	0.691	0.643	0.596
	0.604	0.629	0.604	0.568
CNN-LSTM	0.658	0.676	0.658	0.625
	0.599	0.615	0.599	0.556

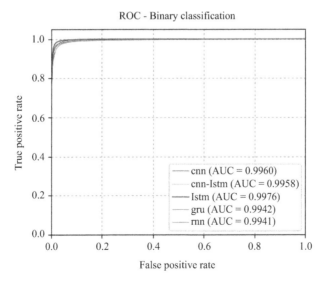

Figure 22.26   ROC curve for Testing 1 data set

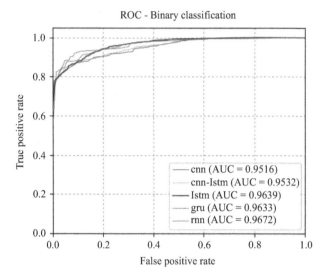

Figure 22.27   ROC curve for Testing 2 data set

Table 22.6   Detailed test results for Testing 1 data set

Classes	LSTM		RNN		GRU		CNN		CNN-LSTM	
	TPR	FPR	TPR	FPR	TPR	FPR	TPR	FPR	TPR	FPR
Benign	0.92	0.06	0.90	0.05	0.89	0.06	0.88	0.05	0.90	0.11
Banjori	0.0	0.00	0.0	0.00	0.0	0.0	0.0	0.00	0.0	0.00
Corebot	1.0	0.00	0.99	0.00	0.99	0.00	0.99	0.00	0.99	0.0
Dircrypt	0.77	0.03	0.71	0.03	0.78	0.04	0.62	0.06	0.48	0.04
Dnschanger	0.99	0.05	0.98	0.05	0.95	0.05	0.91	0.09	0.98	0.06
Fobber	0.0	0.00	0.0	0.00	0.0	0.01	0.0	0.0	0.0	0.01
Murofet	0.0	0.01	0.0	0.07	0.00	0.02	0.01	0.00	0.0	0.00
Necurs	0.86	0.01	0.84	0.00	0.85	0.01	0.76	0.02	0.66	0.01
Newgoz	1.0	0.00	0.99	0.00	1.0	0.00	1.0	0.01	0.99	0.00
Padcrypt	0.99	0.0	0.99	0.0	1.0	0.0	1.0	0.00	1.0	0.0
Proslikefan	0.71	0.02	0.67	0.01	0.71	0.02	0.62	0.01	0.56	0.03
Pykspa	0.84	0.02	0.73	0.03	0.84	0.03	0.65	0.03	0.62	0.02
Qadars	0.12	0.0	0.75	0.00	0.05	0.0	0.43	0.0	0.00	0.0
Qakbot	0.65	0.08	0.43	0.03	0.57	0.07	0.46	0.03	0.37	0.08
Ramdo	1.0	0.0	0.99	0.0	1.0	0.0	0.99	0.00	1.0	0.0
Ranbyus	0.87	0.00	0.85	0.00	0.85	0.00	0.73	0.01	0.78	0.00
Simda	0.01	0.0	0.00	0.00	0.01	0.0	0.08	0.0	0.25	0.00
Suppobox	0.7	0.00	0.74	0.00	0.77	0.00	0.86	0.00	0.42	0.00
Symmi	0.50	0.0	0.18	0.0	0.29	0.0	0.12	0.0	0.21	0.0
Tempedreve	0.14	0.02	0.12	0.01	0.15	0.02	0.19	0.02	0.12	0.02
Tinba	0.92	0.00	0.92	0.00	0.94	0.00	0.29	0.01	0.95	0.00
Accuracy	67.2		65.8		64.9		60.4		59.9	

Table 22.7 Detailed test results for Testing 2 data set

Classes	LSTM		RNN		GRU		CNN		CNN-LSTM	
	TPR	FPR	TPR	FPR	TPR	FPR	TPR	FPR	TPR	FPR
Benign	0.97	0.10	0.95	0.19	0.96	0.06	0.94	0.11	0.97	0.10
Banjori	0.0	0.0	0.0	0.00	0.0	0.0	0.00	0.0	0.0	0.0
Corebot	0.22	0.0	0.22	0.0	0.22	0.0	0.22	0.00	0.22	0.0
Dircrypt	0.77	0.08	0.7	0.05	0.79	0.1	0.6	0.05	0.44	0.07
Dnschanger	0.99	0.01	0.98	0.01	0.96	0.01	0.91	0.07	0.98	0.01
Fobber	0.0	0.00	0.0	0.00	0.0	0.00	0.0	0.00	0.0	0.00
Murofet	0.0	0.0	0.0	0.00	0.01	0.00	0.01	0.00	0.0	0.00
Necurs	0.86	0.02	0.83	0.02	0.85	0.02	0.77	0.02	0.64	0.01
Newgoz	1.0	0.05	0.99	0.00	0.99	0.05	0.99	0.02	0.99	0.05
Padcrypt	0.99	0.0	0.99	0.01	1.0	0.0	1.0	0.00	0.99	0.0
Proslikefan	0.33	0.00	0.33	0.00	0.36	0.00	0.32	0.00	0.62	0.01
Pykspa	0.85	0.02	0.73	0.03	0.83	0.02	0.64	0.03	0.61	0.02
Qadars	0.01	0.0	0.49	0.00	0.04	0.0	0.32	0.0	0.00	0.00
Qakbot	0.64	0.03	0.39	0.03	0.57	0.02	0.43	0.01	0.39	0.05
Ramdo	1.0	0.0	0.99	0.0	1.0	0.0	0.99	0.00	1.0	0.0
Ranbyus	0.86	0.00	0.84	0.00	0.85	0.00	0.73	0.00	0.78	0.00
Simda	0.04	0.00	0.00	0.00	0.09	0.00	0.0	0.0	0.19	0.0
Suppobox	0.83	0.00	0.78	0.00	0.82	0.00	0.89	0.00	0.54	0.00
Symmi	0.97	0.00	0.95	0.00	0.99	0.0	0.71	0.00	0.97	0.00
Tempedreve	0.18	0.02	0.17	0.01	0.17	0.03	0.25	0.01	0.16	0.02
Tinba	0.19	0.00	0.12	0.00	0.34	0.00	0.25	0.00	0.66	0.00
Accuracy	66.9		66.2		64.9		66.5		65.8	

Table 22.8 Results for binary class classification in Testing 1 data set

	Testing 1			
Team	Accuracy	Recall	Precision	F1-score
UWT	0.99	0.828	0.966	0.89
Deep_Dragons	0.987	0.787	0.955	0.86
CHNMLRG	0.988	0.819	0.944	0.88
BENHA	0.963	0.795	0.199	0.32
BharathibSSNCSE	0.615	0.037	0.311	0.07
UniPI	0.981	0.724	0.919	0.81
Josan	0.989	0.822	0.947	0.88
DeepDGANet	0.976	0.658	0.938	0.77

Table 22.9   Results for binary class classification in Testing 2 data set

	Testing 2			
Team	Accuracy	Recall	Precision	F1-score
UWT	0.766	0.999	0.751	0.86
Deep_Dragons	0.987	0.787	0.955	0.86
CHNMLRG	0.787	0.999	0.774	0.87
BENHA	0.564	0.974	0.55	0.7
BharathibSSNCSE	0.562	0.956	0.559	0.71
UniPI	0.714	0.999	0.696	0.82
Josan	0.711	0.999	0.692	0.82
DeepDGANet	0.782	0.997	0.769	0.87

Table 22.10   Results for multi-class classification Testing 1 data set

	Testing 1			
Team	Accuracy	Recall	Precision	F1-score
UWT	0.633	0.633	0.618	0.602
Deep_Dragons	0.987	0.787	0.955	0.86
CHNMLRG	0.648	0.648	0.662	0.6
BENHA	0.272	0.272	0.194	0.168
BharathibSSNCSE	0.18	0.18	0.092	0.102
UniPI	0.655	0.655	0.647	0.615
Josan	0.697	0.697	0.689	0.658
DeepDGANet	0.601	0.601	0.623	0.576

Table 22.11   Results for multi-class classification Testing 2 data set

	Testing 2			
Team	Accuracy	Recall	Precision	F1-score
UWT	0.887	0.887	0.924	0.901
Deep_Dragons	0.67	0.67	0.678	0.622
CHNMLRG	0.674	0.674	0.683	0.648
BENHA	0.429	0.429	0.34	0.272
BharathibSSNCSE	0.335	0.335	0.229	0.223
UniPI	0.671	0.671	0.641	0.619
Josan	0.679	0.679	0.694	0.636
DeepDGANet	0.531	0.531	0.653	0.541

Acknowledgments

This research was supported in part by Paramount Computer Systems and Lakhshya cybersecurity Labs. We are grateful to NVIDIA India, for the GPU hardware support to a research grant. We are also grateful to Computational Engineering and Networking (CEN) department for encouraging the research. Many thanks to all the members of the organizing and technical program committee and advisory committee of DMD 2018 shared task and workshop. Thanks to the participants of DMD 2018.

References

[1]   Kührer M, Rossow C, Holz T. Paint It Black: Evaluating the Effectiveness of Malware Blacklists. Cham, Springer; 2014 September. p. 1–21.

[2]   Antonakakis M, Perdisci R, Nadji Y, *et al.* From Throw-Away Traffic to Bots: Detecting the Rise of DGA-Based Malware. In: USENIX Security Symposium. vol. 12; 2012.

[3]   Plohmann D, Yakdan K, Klatt M, Bader J, Gerhards-Padilla E. A Comprehensive Measurement Study of Domain Generating Malware. USENIX Association; 2016. p. 263–278.

[4]   Abu Rajab M, Zarfoss J, Monrose F, *et al.* A Multifaceted Approach to Understanding the Botnet Phenomenon. In: Proceedings of the 6th ACM SIGCOMM conference on Internet measurement. ACM; 2006. p. 41–52.

[5]   Will C. Botnet Detection with DNS Monitoring. Network. 2014;25.

[6]   Hoang XD, Nguyen QC. Botnet Detection based on Machine Learning Techniques Using DNS Query Data. Future Internet. 2018;10(5):43.

[7]   Yadav S, Reddy AKK, Reddy A, *et al.* Detecting Algorithmically Generated Malicious Domain Names. In: Proceedings of the 10th ACM SIGCOMM Conference on Internet Measurement. ACM; 2010. p. 48–61.

[8]   Wang T, Chen LC. Detecting Algorithmically Generated Domains Using Data Visualization and N-Grams Methods.

[9]   Zhauniarovich Y, Khalil I, Yu T, Dacier M. A Survey on Malicious Domains Detection through DNS Data Analysis. 2018.

[10] LeCun Y, Bengio Y, Hinton G. Deep Learning. Nature. 2015;521(7553):436.

[11] Mac H, Tran D, Tong V, *et al.* DGA Botnet Detection Using Supervised Learning Methods. In: Proceedings of the Eighth International Symposium on Information and Communication Technology. ACM; 2017. p. 211–218.

[12] Yu B, Pan J, Hu J, *et al.* Character Level Based Detection of DGA Domain Names. 2018.

[13] Vinayakumar R, Soman K, Poornachandran P. Detecting Malicious Domain Names Using Deep Learning Approaches at Scale. Journal of Intelligent & Fuzzy Systems. 2018;34(3):1355–1367.

[14] Lison P, Mavroeidis V. Automatic Detection of Malware-Generated Domains with Recurrent Neural Models. arXiv preprint arXiv:170907102. 2017.

[15] Woodbridge J, Anderson HS, Ahuja A, *et al.* Predicting Domain Generation Algorithms with Long Short-term Memory Networks. arXiv preprint arXiv:161100791. 2016.

[16] Vysakh S Mohan, Vinayakumar R, Soman KP, Poornachandran P. SPOOF Net: Syntactic Patterns for Identification of Ominous Online Factors. In: 2018 IEEE Security and Privacy Workshops (SPW). IEEE; 2018 May. p. 258–263.

[17] Yu B, Gray DL, Pan J, *et al.* Inline DGA Detection with Deep Networks. In: 2017 IEEE International Conference on Data Mining Workshops (ICDMW). IEEE; 2017. p. 683–692.

[18] Vinayakumar R, Soman K, Poornachandran P, *et al.* Evaluating Deep Learning Approaches to Characterize and Classify the DGAs at Scale. Journal of Intelligent & Fuzzy Systems. 2018;34(3):1265–1276.

[19] Vinayakumar R, Poornachandran P, Soman K. Scalable Framework for Cyber Threat Situational Awareness Based on Domain Name Systems Data Analysis. In: Big Data in Engineering Applications. Springer; 2018. p. 113–142.

[20] Josan GS, Kaur J. LSTM Network Based Malicious Domain Name Detection: A Shared Task.

[21] Choudhary C, Raaghavi S, Pereira M, Yu B , Nascimento AC, De Cock M. Algorithmically Generated Domain Detection and Malware Family Classification. In: International Symposium on Security in Computing and Communication. 2018.

[22] Amara Dinesh Kumar HT, Soman KP. Real Time Character Level Malicious Domain Name Prediction Using Deep Learning. In: International Symposium on Security in Computing and Communication; 2018.

[23] Giuseppe Attardi DS. UniPI at DMD 2018 Shared Task: Bidirectional LSTM Models for DGA Classification. In: International Symposium on Security in Computing and Communication; 2018.

[24] Rajalakshmi R SRKR Ramraj. Transfer Learning Approach for Identification of Malicious Domain Names. In: International Symposium on Security in Computing and Communication; 2018.

[25] Bharathi B, Bhuvana J. Domain Name Detection and Classification Using Deep Neural Networks. In: International Symposium on Security in Computing and Communication; 2018.

[26] Jyothsna PV, Greeshma P, Shahina KK, *et al.* Detecting DGA Using Deep Neural Networks. In: International Symposium on Security in Computing and Communication; 2018.

[27] Apache Spark. Available at https://spark.apache.org/.

[28] Apache Hadoop. Available at http://hadoop.apache.org/.

[29] Apache Cassandra. Available at http://cassandra.apache.org/.

[30] Domain Generation Algorithms. Available at https://github.com/baderj/domain_generation_algorithms.

[31] OSINT feeds. Available at http://osint.bambenekconsulting.com/feeds/.

[32] DGA. Available at https://data.netlab.360.com/dga/.

[33] Does Alexa Have a List of Its Top-ranked Websites?. Available at https://support.alexa.com.

[34]   OpenDNS Domain List. Available at https://umbrella.cisco.com/.

[35]   Shared Task on Detecting Malicious Domain Names (DMD 2018). Available at http://nlp.amrita.edu/DMD2018/.

[36]   Elman JL. Finding Structure in Time. Cognitive Science. 1990;14(2):179–211.

[37]   Hochreiter S, Schmidhuber J. Long Short-Term Memory. Neural Computation. 1997;9(8):1735–1780.

[38]   Chung J, Gulcehre C, Cho K, *et al.* Empirical Evaluation of Gated Recurrent Neural Networks on Sequence Modeling. arXiv preprint arXiv:14123555. 2014.

[39]   DMD2018. Available at https://github.com/vinayakumarr/DMD2018.

Index

acquisition probability strategies 40
active learning in recommender systems
    38–40
actual-tempting model 393–5
AdaBoost 77, 215
Adware's 461
Alexa 466
Amazon web store 1
American Library Association (ALA)
    174
Amp Lab Benchmark 220
AmritaDGA 455
    AmritaDGANet 476–7
    data analysis, results and
        observations 477–8
    data set, description of 465–74
    deep learning 475
        convolutional neural network
            475–6
        recurrent structures 475
    domain fluxing 463
    domain name system (DNS) 460–2
    future work 478–82
    real-time DNS data collection in an
        Ethernet LAN 463–5
    related methods toward deep
        learning-based DGA detection
        and categorization 457–9
    scalable framework 463
    submitted systems of DMD 2018
        shared task 459–60
analytic hierarchy process (AHP)
    260–3, 265, 268–9
Android OS 343, 345
anonymization 136, 210
Apache Flink 214

Apache Hadoop 212, 251, 330–1,
    463
Apache Hadoop YARN 192
Apache HBase 214, 330–1
Apache Hive 214, 331
Apache Kafka 192, 332
Apache Pig 214
Apache Samza 192
Apache Spark 119, 121, 195, 206, 213,
    215, 217–18, 224, 227, 332,
    457, 463
Apache Storm 190, 202, 214
API (application programming
    interface) 75, 190, 195, 329–30,
    332
application usage logs, collecting
    339–45, 350
app recommendation 387, 392
    actual-tempting model 393–5
    failure of recommendation 392–3
    insights of model 395–6
Artemis 201
article-recommendation module 179
artificial immune recognition system
    (AIRS) 215
artificial immune system (AIS) 215
artificial neural networks (ANNs) 130,
    158
ASIP Santé (Agence des Systèmes
    d'Information Partagés de
    Santé) 209–10
association rule-mining (ARM)
    algorithm 293, 303, 350
audio-representation learning,
    convolutional neural network
    (CNN) for 20

autoencoder 11
  -based collaborative filtering 14–16
  representation learning with 18
average neighbor degree 424

batch processing vs. stream processing
      188–9
Bayesian personalized ranking
      (BPR)–based matrix
      factorization model 18
Bayes theorem 261, 266
benchmarking 206, 217
  and big data 217–18
  comparison 225–6
  in Hadoop and Spark 220
    Amp Lab Benchmark 220
    BigBench 220
    BigDataBench 220
    BigFrame 220
    GridMix 221–2
    HiBench 222–4
    PigMix 224
    SparkBench 224
  types of 219–20
bibliotherapy 173–4
  categories of adolescent stress and
      reading articles 177
  recommending procedure 178
  unifying stress easing and reading
      interests for articles
      recommendation 177
bidirectional LSTM network 457, 459
BigBench 220
big data analytics (BDA) 126, 211–12,
      248–51
  HADOOP 251–2
  MapReduce 253
  Master/Slave architecture of Hadoop
      253
  for smart grids: *see* smart grids, big
      data analytics for
  for understanding of consumer
      behavior 249–50
BigDataBench 220
BigFrame 220

BikeBrain 322
Bike Hub 322
BikeMap 322
bipartite graph 418, 424–5
bipartite model 428–9
botnets 455–7, 461, 463
box plot 467–72, 474
brand loyalty 236
business to consumer (B2C) 239

C4.5 decision tree 457
call detail records (CDRs) 71–3
capital asset pricing model (CAPM)
      373
Carhart four-factor model 373, 379
Cassandra database 135, 195, 214
CDAE projects 15–16
Center for Research in Security Prices
      (CRSP) 367
Chinese online movie reviews: *see*
      paradox of opinion leadership
      and recommendation culture
CIPHER project 107, 109–12
  as decision model 112
  decision support system 112–14
  future works 121–2
  predictive model 113
  technological architecture of 111
  validation 114
    algorithm selection 118–19
    data processing 114–18
    first results 119–21
CISCO 464
Click fraud 461
Cloud architecture 146
Cloud-based application 164–5
cloud computing (CC) model 125, 135,
      262, 305
ClustCoef 425
clustering 228, 252–3
clustering coefficient 425
CNN-LSTM 456–7, 476–7
cold-start problem 35, 386
cold-start solutions for recommendation
      systems 35

active learning in recommender
    systems 38–40
collaborative filtering 37
cross-domain recommender systems
    45–6
personality-based recommender
    systems 43–5
recommendation approaches 36
semantic-based recommender
    systems 40–2
visual features, recommendation
    based on 42–3
collaborative deep learning (CDL) 18
collaborative filtering (CF) 2, 36–7,
    176, 262, 298, 415
autoencoder-based 14–16
collaborative variational autoencoder
    (CVAE) 18
Common Information Model (CIM)
    152
community-based recommenders 416
complex event processing (CEP) 187,
    202
composite VOs (CVOs) 164
computational intelligence (CI)
    techniques 215
computational techniques 215
machine learning techniques in
    medical field 215–16
spark with machine learning
    techniques in medical field
    216–17
Conflicker 463
connection-centric approaches 412
consumer behavior 235
sentiment analysis of 236
for understanding consumer
    sentiments 236
consumer sentiment 237–8
content analyzer 175
content-based (CB) class of RSs 36
content-based (CB) recommendation
    system 298
content-based filtering (CBF) 175–6,
    415

content-based recommendation (CBR)
    392
content-based recommenders 262
context-aware recommender systems
    (CARS) 57, 59
choosing an appropriate evaluation
    metrics 67
diversity measurement in 66
    Shannon's diversity index,
        normalized 67
    Simpson's diversity, normalized
        66
    Tidemann & Hall's diversity index
        (TH) 67
prediction accuracy metrics 60
    average RMSE and average MAE
        61
    mean average error (MAE) 61
    normalized RMSE and normalized
        MAE 61
    root-mean-squared error 60
rank accuracy metrics 63
    normalized distance-based
        performance measure (NDMP)
        63–4
    online evaluation of ranking 65–6
    reference ranking 63
    utility-based ranking 64–5
recommendation accuracy
    measurement in 66
usage prediction
    measurement/classifying
    accuracy metrics 61–3
convolutional neural network (CNN)
    11, 18, 457–8, 460–76
for audio-representation learning 20
for image representation learning
    19–20
representation learning with 18–20
for text representation learning 19
co-occurrence recommendation 176
CPAM (Caisse Primaire d'Assurance
    Maladie) 205
credit card records (CCRs) 71–3

cross-domain recommender systems
45–6
CrowdPlanner 319
Current Web 41
cycling 322

data-driven dynamic energy
management 128–9
data mining tools 129, 249
datasets and preprocessing 283–4
data summarization 133
data visualization 155
DBSCAN 262
"decision model" (DM) module
112–14
decision-tree-based strategies 40
DecissionTree 119
deep belief network (DBN) 216
DeepFM 16
deep learning 361, 457–9, 475–6
deep neural networks (DNNs) 9, 357
autoencoder 11
autoencoder, representation learning
with 18
convolutional neural network (CNN)
11, 18
for audio-representation learning
20
for image representation learning
19–20
for text representation learning 19
deep hybrid models for recommender
systems 24–5
future challenges 27–8
generative adversarial networks
(GANs) 26–7
metric learning 25–6
multilayer perceptron 10
multilayer perceptron, representation
learning with 17–18
neural autoregressive distribution
estimator (NADE) 27
recommender systems, introducing
nonlinearity to 12

autoencoder-based collaborative
filtering 14–16
deep neural generalization of
factorization machine 16
neural matrix factorization 13–14
recurrent neural network (RNN)
11–12
sequence modelling for recommender
systems 21
sequence-aware recommender
systems 23–4
session-based recommendations
21–3
Word2Vec, representation learning
with 20–1
deep semantic similarity model
(DSSM) 17–18
degree centrality 424
demand response (DR) and energy
management program 160
home demand management 161–2
demand side management (DSM)
127–8, 160
demographic class of RSs 36
DENCLUE algorithm 262
Density-Peaked Clustering Analysis
(DPCA) 217
Detecting Malicious Domain names
(DMD) 455–6
dimensionality reduction 11, 18, 133
direct load control (DLC) 128
disabled people, Route
Recommendation Systems for
322–3
Disease Diagnosis and Treatment
Recommendation System
(DDTRS) 217
distributed data mining 134
distributed denial of service (DDoS)
attacks 461
Distributed File System 153
distribution networks (DNs) 163
distribution system state estimation
(DSSE) 164
domain flux 455–7, 461, 463

domain generation algorithms (DGAs) 455–6, 459, 463
  comprehensive data set for: *see* AmritaDGA
domain name system (DNS) 460–2
  packets collection 465
  real-time DNS data collection in an Ethernet LAN 463–5
DStream (Discretized Stream) 199–200
dwell time, modeling 388–91
dynamic Cloud-based DSSE, big data of 165–6
dynamic DSSE, application benefits of 166
dynamic energy management (DEM) 126–7
  data-driven DEM 128–9
  demand side management 128

E-care project 205–6
  architecture 208
  ontology architecture 208
E-care system 227
efficient computing 134–5
efficient processing of extreme size of data 132
  data summarization 133
  dimensionality reduction 133
  distributed data mining 134
  efficient computing 134–5
  MapReduce parallel processing 134
  redundancies, avoidance of 132–3
  testbeds and platforms 135
8- vs. 16-bit architectures 85–6, 95–100, 102
electric vehicles power demand, predictive control for 131–2
electroencephalogram (EEG)-based brain–computer interfaces 243
electronic health record (EHR) 108
electronic medical record (EMR) 216
energy-management systems (EMSs) 128
enterprise data warehouse (EDW) 211
Enterprise Service Bus (ESB) 152

error reduction strategies 39
Ethernet LAN 464
e-WOM 296–7, 299
expectation maximization (EM) scheme 278
eXtended classifier system 130
extreme learning machine (ELM) 215, 457
eye-tracking data 243

factorization machine (FM) 12
  deep neural generalization of 16
false alarm rate 244
false positive rate 62, 244
Fama-French three-factor model 373
fast flux 461
feature engineering for recommendations 413–14
field-programmable gate arrays (FPGAs) 84
52-week high (52WH) momentum strategy 363, 365
Flink 214, 225–6
Flume 300
Fog computing 146, 149, 153–5, 158
fog infrastructure implementation in Smart Grid 146, 150
FourSquare 1–2
fuzzy logic (FSVM) 215

galvanic skin response (GSR) sensor 241
gated recurrent unit (GRU) 475–6
generalized matrix factorization (GMF) 14
General Security Policy of Health Information Systems (PGSSI-S) 210
generative adversarial networks (GANs) 26–7
generators 422
genetic algorithm (GA) 215
Geographic Information System (GIS) 325
Gephi 424

Global Positioning System (GPS)
satellites 164
Global Positioning System (GPS)
technologies 319
global relevance approach 176
Google Maps 319–21
gradient boosting 426, 432, 440
graph-based approach 176, 411–12,
426
graph-based recommendations 407
discussion 446
initial transition to graph model
447–8
overfitting 446
scalability 447
experimental setting and datasets
426
dataset I—Last.fm 426–8
dataset II—Yelp 428–30
dataset III—Yelp II 430–2
dataset IV—Movielens 432
datasets, features, and metrics
432–3
feature engineering for
recommendations 413–14
graph-based recommender systems
409–13
representing social data and trust
412
similarity measurement 411–12
for recommendation systems 414
distilling graph features 421–6
structure of dataset 415–17
transforming tabular into
graph-based representation
417–21
results and analysis 433
different graph schemes and their
impact on recommendations
441
overall contribution of the
graph-based approach 433–4
Graph Benchmark 223
graph representation for recommender
systems data 417–19

Green SG (G-SG) 150–1
GridMix 221–2
GRU4REC model 21–3

Hadoop Distributed File System
(HDFS) 195, 213, 300
Hadoop ecosystem 205–6, 212–14
MapReduce 213
Spark 213–14
Hadoop framework 212–13, 235,
251–2, 305
hardware architecture vs. multicore
approach 100–1
Hbase 195, 214, 300–1
Health Insurance Portability and
Accountability Act (HIPAA)
regulations 209
HEARE 323
HeteRS 410
HiBench 222–4, 227
Hidden Markov Model 129, 457
HiveQL 214
home demand management (HDM)
161–2
hybrid approaches 177
hybrid class of RSs 36
hybrid strategies 40
hypergraphs 412

igraph 424
image representation learning,
convolutional neural network
(CNN) for 19–20
information accumulation 389
Information and Communication
Technology (ICT) 146
Internet of Things (IoT) 147–51, 188
internet protocol (IP) flux 461
Internet WOM 293
intrusion detection systems (IDS) 464
in-vehicle navigation systems (IVNS)
325
item-based collaborative filtering (ICF)
392
item-based NeuRec (I-NeuRec) 14

Java Database Connectivity (JDBC) 195
Jegadeesh–Titman (JT) momentum strategy 364

Kafka 199, 223–4, 300
Keras embedding matrix 455–6, 477
Kernel methods 130
K-likelihood ratio test 215–16
K-means 216–17, 222, 226, 284, 299
K-nearest-neighbourhood algorithm 299
knowledge-based class of RSs 36
knowledge-based recommenders 145, 416
Kraken 463
Kwyjibo 463

Last.fm 426–8, 434–6, 441–2
latent Dirichlet allocation (LDA) 74
leadership and recommendation analytics 305
   discovering leadership patterns 310–12
   discussion 312
   experimental setup 305–6
   feature statistics 306–10
linked data principles 41–2
LinkedIn 192–3
Linked Open Data 42
load classification (LC) 126, 130, 157
location-based social networks (LBSNs) 384–7, 396
log-collection system 342
   collection of application usage logs 343–4
   game-based approach 345
   initialization of 342–3
   questions about contexts 343
long short-term memory (LSTM) 457–60, 475
LoroDux 323

machine learning (ML) 38, 222–3, 227, 446
   in medical field 215–16
   properties 131
machine learning and stock recommendation 361
   empirical results 369
      classification accuracy 369–71
      portfolio performance 371–4
   machine-learning-based momentum strategy 365
      feature engineering 365–7
      labelling 367
      portfolio formation 368–9
      training and testing 367–8
   machine-learning-based stock recommendation 374
      design of model 376–7
      empirical results 377–9
   momentum and stock-return predictability 363
      52-week high (52WH) momentum strategy 365
      Jegadeesh–Titman (JT) momentum strategy 364
      momentum effects 363–4
malware domains 459, 461
MapMyRide 322
MapReduce 213–14, 225, 253
   parallel processing 134
   real-time optimal route recommendations using: *see* Route Recommendation Systems (RRS)
Maps.Me 320
Master/Slave architecture of Hadoop 253
matrix factorization (MF) 12, 400
   collective matrix factorization 77–8
   generalized matrix factorization (GMF) 14
   neural matrix factorization 13–14
   neural network matrix factorization (NNMF) 13

maximum likelihood estimation (MLE) framework 279
mean average error (MAE) 61
 average RMSE and average MAE 61
 normalized RMSE and normalized MAE 61
media access control (MAC) addresses 464–5
MeSe 262
metapath data links 410
metric learning 25–6
MetroCognition 325
microbenchmarks 219, 222
mining urban lifestyles 71
 discovering shopping patterns 74
 dual lifestyles 78–9
 mobility pattern extraction 74
  characterizing mobility patterns 77
  extracting cellular tower location types 75–6
  primary shopping behavior, classification of 77
  regression on average amount spent 77
 predicting shopping behavior 77
  collective matrix factorization 77–8
 prediction 78
 shopping and mobility patterns 72
  adding contextual information to location data 72–3
  multi-perspective lifestyles 73
  prediction of shopping behavior with data sparsity 72
Mise-en-scene features 42
mobile user's behavior, investigation of 341
mobility pattern extraction 74
 baseline methods 77
  primary shopping behavior, classification of 77
  regression on average amount spent 77

extracting cellular tower location types 75–6
 mobility patterns, characterizing 77
MongoDB 332
mood classifier 284
mood neutral identification, evaluation on 284
mood-sensitive (MS) recommendation system in social sensing 277
 evaluation 283
  datasets and preprocessing 283–4
  performance evaluation of MS-EM 284–8
 mood sensitive truth discovery 281–3
 problem formulation and terminology definition 279–81
mood sensitive truth discovery 281–3
 evaluation 285–8
Movielens 298, 432, 438, 440, 444–5
multidimensional expectation maximization (MS-EM) 279, 284–8
multilayer perceptron 10
 representation learning with 17–18
multiple subgraph representations 419–21
Murofet 463
mutuallift 355
MySql 300

NameNode 253
Navigon 320–1
Naïve Bayesian classifier 264
Netflix, Spark at 58, 63, 196
NetworkX 424
neural autoregressive distribution estimator (NADE) 27
neural collaborative filtering (NeuMF) 13–14
neural FM (NFM) 16
neural matrix factorization 13–14
neural network matrix factorization (NNMF) 13

neuromarketing 235, 238–48
  consumer behavior traits measured by
    240
  framework 241–8
  techniques 240–1
node redundancy 425
nonlinearity introduction to
    recommender systems 12
  autoencoder-based collaborative
    filtering 14–16
  deep neural generalization of
    factorization machine 16
  neural matrix factorization 13–14
non SQL (NoSQL) 300
normalized distance-based performance
    measure (NDMP) 63–4
Not Only Structured Query Language
    (NoSQL) databases 153, 332
NWeight 223

one-shot consumption 387
online evaluation of ranking 65–6
online leadership and recommendation
    295
  leadership for recommendations
    among social networks 299
  opinion leadership 296–8
  recommendation system 298–9
  rise of China 295–6
ontologies 207
Open DataBase Connectivity (ODBC)
    connectivity 195
OpenDNS 466
opinion leadership 294–8
OSINT DGA feeds 465
Osmotic computing 146, 150, 155,
    166–7
overfitting 446
OWL (Ontology Web Language) format
    118

packet sniffer 464
PAD (Puzzle & Dragons) 354
PageRank algorithm 223, 297, 410,
    425, 447

paradox of opinion leadership and
    recommendation culture 293
  leadership and recommendation
    analytics 305
    discovering leadership patterns
      310–12
    discussion 312
    experimental setup 305–6
    feature statistics 306–10
  methodology 299–301
    data collection 301–2
    feature builder 302–3
    methodology outline 304–5
    rule-mining functionality 303–4
  online leadership and
    recommendation 295
    leadership for recommendations
      among social networks 299
    opinion leadership 296–8
    recommendation system 298–9
    rise of China 295–6
passengers, Route Recommendation
    Systems for 324
passive learning 38
Pedestrian Pal 321
pedestrians, Route Recommendation
    Systems for 321–2
Peripheral Component Interconnect
    express (PCIe) communication
    86
personality-based recommender
    systems 43–5
phasor measurement unit (PMU)-based
    DSSE, communication
    architectures for 164–5
Pig Latin 214
PigMix 224
plug-in electric vehicles (PEVs) 131–2
point-of-interest (POI) recommendation
    396
  geographical influence 396–7
  social influence 398–9
  temporal influence 400–2

PRADO (Programme
        d'Accompagnement du Retour à
        Domicile) program 205
prediction accuracy metrics 60
    accuracy measurement for rating
        predictions 60
        average RMSE and average MAE
            61
        mean average error (MAE) 61
        normalized RMSE and normalized
            MAE 61
        root-mean-squared error (RMSE)
            60
prediction-based strategies 40
price forecasting 131
primary shopping behavior,
        classification of 77
principal component analysis (PCA)
        87–8
    embedding PCA inference in expert
        sensors 83
        8- vs. 16-bit architectures 95–100
        experimental methodology 93–4
        experimental results 94–101
        hardware architecture vs. multicore
            approach 100–1
        PCA inference IP description
            91–3
        related work 86–7
        system-level architecture 89–91
        workflow description 88–9
pseudo vote 392

Quality of Protection (QoP) 209

random forest 368, 426, 429, 432, 440
random projection (RP) 133
random walks 411–12
rank accuracy metrics 63
    normalized distance-based
        performance measure (NDMP)
        63–4
    online evaluation of ranking 65–6
    reference ranking 63
    utility-based ranking 64–5

real-time data processing 188
real-time load forecasting (RTLF) 158
real-time optimal route
        recommendations using
        MapReduce: *see* Route
        Recommendation Systems
        (RRS)
real-time processors 190
    Samza platform 192–5
    Spark platform 195–200
    Storm platform 190–1
real-time renewable energy forecasting
        (RTREF) 159
real-time solar energy forecasting
        (RTSEF) 159
receiver operating characteristic (ROC)
        graph 243
recommender systems (RSs) 10, 35–6
recurrent neural network (RNN)
        11–12, 24, 457–8, 475–6
recurrent SVM 457
Redis 332
redundancies, avoidance of 132–3
reference ranking 63–4
regression on average amount spent 77
relational database (RD) 211
relational database management system
        (RDBMS) 300–1
remote terminal units (RTUs) 158
renewable energy forecasting 159–60
renewable generation forecasting 131
Resilient Distributed Dataset (RDD)
        213, 216
Resource Description Framework
        (RDF) 42
Rollstuhlfahrer-Routing 323
root-mean-squared error (RMSE)
        59–60, 72, 430, 432
    average RMSE and average MAE 61
    normalized RMSE and normalized
        MAE 61
ROSE (ROuting SErvice) 325
Route Recommendation Systems (RRS)
        317–19
    classification of 319 326

for disabled people 322–3
for individual drivers 319–21
for passengers 324
for pedestrians 321–2
requirements for 326
    architecture 329–32
    big or small data 327–8
    categories of requirements 334–5
    data requirements 326–7
    MapReduce 332–4
    real-time issue 328
for riding bicycle 322
for sailing 325–6
for senior citizens 325
for taxi drivers to pick up passengers
    323–4
R-Score metric 65

S3 195
Sailing
    Route Recommendation Systems for
        325–6
Samza platform 192–5
scalability 447
semantic-based recommender systems
    40–2
senior citizens, RRSs for 325
sentiment analysis of consumer
    behavior 236–7
sequence modelling for recommender
    systems 21
    sequence-aware recommender
        systems 23–4
    session-based recommendations
        21–3
service-oriented architecture (SOA)
    152
session-based recommendations 21–3
Shannon's diversity index 67
Sharpe ratio (SR) 361
short-term load forecasting (STLF)
    130–1, 158
sigmoid 477
silence behavior, modeling 389–90
silent viewing behavior 386

similarity measurement using graphs
    and their application 411–12
Simpsons's diversity index 66
single instruction multiple data (SIMD)
    approach 91
Smartaxi 324
smart grid (SG) 145
    big data in 151–6
    demand response (DR) and energy
        management program 160
        home demand management 161–2
    fog infrastructure implementation in
        150
    Internet of Things (IoT)-supported
        SG 147–51
    load forecasting 158–9
    renewable energy forecasting
        159–60
    security and privacy issues in 135–6
    SG state estimation 162
        dynamic Cloud-based DSSE, big
            data of 165–6
        dynamic DSSE, application
            benefits of 166
        phasor measurement unit
            (PMU)-based DSSE,
            communication architectures for
            164–5
    vision 148
smart grids, big data analytics for 125
    dynamic energy management (DEM)
        127
        data-driven DEM 128–9
        demand side management 128
    efficient processing of extreme size
        of data 132
        avoidance of redundancies 132–3
        data summarization 133
        dimensionality reduction 133
        distributed data mining 134
        efficient computing 134–5
        MapReduce parallel processing
            134
        testbeds and platforms 135

electric vehicles power demand,
  predictive control for 131–2
failure protection 129
load classification 130
price forecasting 131
renewable generation forecasting
  131
security and privacy issues in smart
  grid 135–6
short-term load forecasting 130–1
smartphone in recommender systems
  385
  app recommendation 392
    actual-tempting model 393–5
    failure of recommendation 392–3
    insights of model 395–6
  dwell time, modeling 390 1
  model inference and application
    391–2
  POI recommendation 396
    geographical influence 396–7
    social influence 398–9
    temporal influence 400–2
  silence behavior, modeling 389–90
social data and trust representation,
  using graphs 412–13
social sensing 277
  mood-sensitive (MS)
    recommendation system in: *see*
    mood-sensitive (MS)
    recommendation system in
    social sensing
softmax 21, 368, 477
source-claim matrix (SC) 280, 284
SourceEntity 416, 424
source-mood matrix (SM) 280, 284
Spark 213–14, 225–6
SparkBench 224, 227
Spark platform 195–201
  runtime architecture 198
Spark streaming 196, 199–201
sparse linear method (SLIM) 14
sparse matrix problem 176
S.P.O.O.F Net 458
Spyware 461

Statistical Workload Injector for
  MapReduce (SWIM) 225
stereotyping 175
Storm platform 190–1
Strasbourg CHRU 206
stream event processing (SEP) 187
Streaming Benchmarks 223–4, 227
stream processing 187
  batch processing vs. 188–9
  challenges of 189–90
  in e-health care 201
  for low-latency analytics 188–90
Structured Query Language (SQL)
  135, 223, 331
subgraph representations 419–21
Sums 284
supervisory control and data acquisition
  (SCADA) systems 126, 135,
  158
support vector machine (SVM)
  215–16, 411, 426, 440, 457
Sygic GPS Navigation 319–20
system implementation 179
  framework 179
  system interfaces 179–83

TargetEntity 416, 424
taxi drivers to pick up passengers,
  Route Recommendation
  Systems for 323–4
TensorFlow 477
testbeds and platforms 135
text representation learning,
  convolutional neural network
  (CNN) for 19
Tidemann & Hall's diversity index (TH)
  67
Torpig 463
TPC (Transaction Processing
  Performance Council) 218
TPCx-HS measurements 218
tripartite model 429
TripTripHurray 323
truth discovery 278–9
TruthFinder 284

Uber, Spark at 196
uncertainty reduction strategies 39
user adaptation strategies 39–40
user-based collaborative filtering (UCF)
        392, 410
user-based NeuRec (U-NeuRec) 14
user contexts and mobile application
        usage, investigation of 339
    collected logs 345
        application usage frequency
        346–9
        high-level contexts 346
        tendency of application usage by
        time 349
    collecting application usage logs
        341–2
    collecting context information 342
    impacts of collecting high-level
        contexts 356
    investigation of mobile user's
        behavior 341
    log-collection system 342
        collection of application usage logs
        343–4
        game-based approach 345
        initialization of 342–3
        questions about contexts 343
    possible applications of high-level
        contexts 357
    relationships between applications
        and contexts 350
        characteristic rules 352–3
        effect of combination of contexts
        355–6
        effect of single context 353–5
user-management module 179
user sentiments 236–7, 249
utility-based class of RSs 36
utility-based ranking 64–5

vector space model 41
very short-term load forecasting
        (VSTLF) 158

VGG16 model 402
Video Files Processing Engine (VFPE)
        263–4
video resources in multiple partitions,
        recommendation system for 259
    experimental evaluation 267–72
    future work 272–3
    problem description 263–4
    proposed approach 264–7
    related work 261–3
Virtex-6 FPGA 86
Virtex-7 FPGA 86
virtual objects (VOs) 164
visual Bayesian personalized ranking
        (VBPR) 19
visual features, recommendation based
        on 42–3

Waze 320
Web of Document 41
websearch benchmarks 223
weighted approximate-rank pairwise
        loss (WARP) 26
WheelyApp 323
wide area measurement (WAM) 164
wide-area situational awareness
        (WASA) 156
wireless body area network (WBAN)
        209
wireless sensor networks (WSNs) 159
Word2Vec 20–1
word-of-mouth (WOM) 293–4,
        297

Xerox 206, 218

Yahoo, Spark at 196
Yelp 428–30, 436–7, 442–3
Yelp II 430–2, 437–8, 443
Yet Another Resource Negotiator
        (YARN) 213
YouTube 2, 17, 299, 355

ZooKeeper 301
Zynq-7010 FPSoC 86